EXAM ✓ PREP

CCENT

Jeremy Cioara, David Minutella, Heather Stevenson

que®
CERTIFICATION

800 East 96th Street • Indianapolis, Indiana 46240 USA

CCENT Exam Prep (Exam 640-822)

ISBN-13: 978-0-7897-3716-8
ISBN-10: 0-7897-3716-7

Library of Congress Cataloging-in-Publication Data:

Cioara, Jeremy.

  CCENT exam prep: (exam 640-822)/Jeremy Cioara, David Minutella, Heather Stevenson.

    p. cm.

  ISBN 978-0-7897-3716-8 (pbk. w/cd)

  1. Electronic data processing personnel–Certification. 2. Computer networks–Examinations–Study guides. I. Minutella, David. II. Stevenson, Heather. III. Title.

  QA76.3.C477 2008

  004.6--dc22   2007043315

Printed in the United States on America

First Printing: December 2007

Trademarks

All terms mentioned in this book that are known to be trademarks or service marks have been appropriately capitalized. Que Publishing cannot attest to the accuracy of this information. Use of a term in this book should not be regarded as affecting the validity of any trademark or service mark.

Cisco, Cisco Systems, CCENT, and CCNA are registered trademarks of Cisco Systems, Inc. or its affiliates in the U.S. and certain other countries. All other trademarks mentioned in this book are the property of their respective owners.

Warning and Disclaimer

Every effort has been made to make this book as complete and as accurate as possible, but no warranty or fitness is implied. The information provided is on an "as is" basis. The authors and the publisher shall have neither liability nor responsibility to any person or entity with respect to any loss or damages arising from the information contained in this book or from the use of the CD or programs accompanying it.

Bulk Sales

Que Publishing offers excellent discounts on this book when ordered in quantity for bulk purchases or special sales. For more information, please contact

  U.S. Corporate and Government Sales
  1-800-382-3419
  corpsales@pearsontechgroup.com

For sales outside the U.S., please contact

  International Sales
  international@pearsoned.com

Associate Publisher
David Dusthimer

Executive Editor
Brett Bartow

Senior Development Editor
Christopher Cleveland

Technical Editors
David Camardella

Steve Kalman

Managing Editor
Patrick Kanouse

Project Editor
Mandie Frank

Copy Editor
Gayle Johnson

Indexer
Ken Johnson

Proofreader
Water Crest Publishing

Publishing Coordinator
Vanessa Evans

Designer
Gary Adair

Page Layout
S4 Carlisle Publishing Services

 The Safari® Enabled icon on the cover of your favorite technology book means the book is available through Safari Bookshelf. When you buy this book, you get free access to the online edition for 45 days. Safari Bookshelf is an electronic reference library that lets you easily search thousands of technical books, find code samples, download chapters, and access technical information whenever and wherever you need it.

To gain 45-day Safari Enabled access to this book:

▶ Go to http://www.quepublishing.com/safarienabled.
▶ Complete the brief registration form.
▶ Enter the coupon code T6EH-14ED-9VHE-DEDE-CNHD.

If you have difficulty registering on Safari Bookshelf or accessing the online edition, please email customer-service@safaribooksonline.com.

Contents at a Glance

Cisco ICND1 Exam Objectives   xxv

Introduction   1

CHAPTER 1   Standard Internetworking Models   7

CHAPTER 2   Physical Layer Networking Concepts   51

CHAPTER 3   Data Link Networking Concepts   81

CHAPTER 4   General Network Security   119

CHAPTER 5   IP at the Network Layer   141

CHAPTER 6   Introduction to Cisco Routers and Switches   185

CHAPTER 7   Foundation Cisco IOS Operations   207

CHAPTER 8   Foundation Cisco Configurations   239

CHAPTER 9   Understanding the Cisco SDM   293

CHAPTER 10   Introduction to Routing and Routing Protocols   317

CHAPTER 11   Distance Vector Routing Protocols   355

CHAPTER 12   Enabling Internet Connectivity with NAT   387

CHAPTER 13   Foundation Switching Operations   423

CHAPTER 14   Implementing Switch Security   455

CHAPTER 15   Understanding Wireless Networking   473

CHAPTER 16   Wireless Security and Implementation Considerations   491

CHAPTER 17   Wide Area Network Connections   515

Fast Facts   549

Practice Exam   583

Answers to Practice Exam   601

Appendix   What's on the CD-ROM   611

Glossary   615

Index   643

Table of Contents

Cisco ICND1 Exam Objectives . . . . **xxv**

    Exam Description xxv

    Exam Topics xxv

        Describe the operation of data networks xxv

        Implement a small switched network xxv

        Implement an IP addressing scheme and IP services to
          meet network requirements for a small branch office xxvi

        Implement a small routed network xxvi

        Explain and select the appropriate administrative tasks
          required for a WLAN xxvii

        Identify security threats to a network and describe general
          methods to mitigate those threats xxvii

        Implement and verify WAN links xxvii

Introduction **1**

    How This Book Helps You 1

    Network Hardware and Software Requirements 3

    Advice on Taking the Exam 4

Chapter 1:
Standard Internetworking Models **7**

    Introduction 10

    What Is an Internetwork? 10

    Types of Internetworks 11

        Local Area Network (LAN) 11

        Metropolitan Area Network (MAN) 12

        Wide Area Network (WAN) 12

        Storage Area Network (SAN) 13

        Virtual Private Network (VPN) 14

    Open Systems Interconnection (OSI) Model 14

        Upper Layers 15

        Application Layer 15

        Presentation Layer 17

Session Layer 18

Lower Layers 18

Transport Layer 18

Network Layer 20

Data Link Layer 21

Physical Layer 23

OSI Layered Communications 23

TCP/IP Model 25

Application Layer 26

Transport Layer 27

Internet Layer 31

Network Interface Layer 33

Cisco 3-Layer Hierarchical Model 33

Access Layer 34

Distribution Layer 35

Core Layer 35

Chapter Summary 37

Key Terms 37

Apply Your Knowledge 40

Exercises 40

Review Questions 41

Exam Questions 41

Answers to Review Questions 45

Answers to Exam Questions 47

Suggested Readings and Resources 49

Chapter 2:
Physical Layer Networking Concepts **51**

Introduction 54

Network Topologies 54

The Bus Topology 54

The Ring Topology 55

The Star Topology 56

The Mesh Topology 57

Cabling 58

Coaxial Cable 59

Twisted-Pair Cable 60

Fiber-Optic Cable 63

Wireless 64

Wireless Fidelity (Wi-Fi) 65

Infrared 65

Bluetooth 66

Physical Layer Devices 66

Repeaters 66

Hubs 67

Network Interfaces 67

Chapter Summary 68

Key Terms 68

Apply Your Knowledge 69

Exercises 69

Review Questions 70

Exam Questions 70

Answers to Review Questions 77

Answers to Exam Questions 77

Suggested Readings and Resources 79

Chapter 3:
Data Link Networking Concepts **81**

Introduction 84

Data Link Protocols 84

Token Ring 84

FDDI 86

Ethernet at the Data Link Layer 87

Physical Ethernet Standards 93

Ethernet 93

Fast Ethernet 96

Gigabit Ethernet 97

10-Gigabit Ethernet (10GbE) 99

Long Reach Ethernet 100

Data Link Layer Devices 100

Bridges 101

Switches 104

Duplex 105

Microsegmentation 106

Chapter Summary 107
    Key Terms 107
Apply Your Knowledge 109
    Exercises 109
    Review Questions 110
    Exam Questions 110
    Answers to Review Questions 114
    Answers to Exam Questions 115
    Suggested Readings and Resources 117

Chapter 4:
General Network Security **119**

Introduction 122
Classes of Attack 122
    Access Attacks 123
    Reconnaissance Attacks 125
    Denial of Service (DoS) Attacks 127
Mitigating Network Threats 130
    AAA 130
    Cisco ACLs 130
    Cisco IOS Secure Management Features 131
    Encryption Protocols 132
    Security Appliances and Applications 132
Chapter Summary 134
    Key Terms 134
Apply Your Knowledge 135
    Exercise 135
    Review Questions 136
    Exam Questions 136
    Answers to Review Questions 138
    Answers to Exam Questions 138
    Suggested Readings and Resources 139

Chapter 5:
IP at the Network Layer **141**

Introduction 144
Network Layer Functions 144
IP Addressing and Formats 145

Binary 145
Hexadecimal 150
IP Address Classes 151
Subnet Masks 154
Private (RFC 1918) Addressing 156
Subnetting IP 156
Calculating Hosts in a Subnet 159
Calculating Networks in a Subnet 161
The Increment 162
Determining the Range of Valid IPs 165
Network Layer Devices 167
Routers 167
Layer 3 Switches 170
Chapter Summary 171
Key Terms 171
Apply Your Knowledge 172
Exercises 172
Review Questions 175
Exam Questions 175
Answers to Review Questions 179
Answers to Exam Questions 181
Suggested Readings and Resources 183

Chapter 6:
Introduction to Cisco Routers and Switches **185**
Introduction 188
Interfaces and Modules 188
LAN Interfaces 188
WAN Interfaces 189
Cisco Memory Components 192
ROM 193
Flash 193
RAM 193
NVRAM 193
Cisco Internetworking Operating System 193
Feature Sets 194
IOS Image File Naming 195

Cisco Router Models and Features 196
Cisco Switch Models and Features 197
Chapter Summary 199
    Key Terms 199
Apply Your Knowledge 200
    Exercises 200
    Review Questions 200
    Exam Questions 201
    Answers to Review Questions 203
    Answers to Exam Questions 204
    Suggested Readings and Resources 205

Chapter 7:
Foundation Cisco IOS Operations

Foundation Cisco IOS Operations **207**

Introduction 210
Terminal Options 210
    Console Port 210
    Auxiliary Port 212
    Telnet 212
    HTTP and HTTPS 212
    SSH 213
Router/Switch Startup Procedures 214
    POST 214
    Bootstrap 215
    IOS Loading 215
    Configuration Loading 217
Navigating the IOS 220
    User EXEC 220
    Privileged EXEC 221
    Global Configuration 222
    Context-Sensitive Help 224
    Abbreviations 226
    Shortcut Keys 226
    Common Syntax Errors 227
Chapter Summary 230
    Key Terms 231

Apply Your Knowledge 231

    Exercises 231

    Review Questions 233

    Exam Questions 233

    Answers to Review Questions 235

    Answers to Exam Questions 236

    Suggested Readings and Resources 237

Chapter 8:
Foundation Cisco Configurations **239**

Introduction 242

Global Configuration 242

    Altering the Boot Sequence 242

    Changing the Hostname 244

    Creating a Login Banner 244

    Assigning a Password for Privileged EXEC Mode 245

    Domain Name–Specific Commands 246

    Enabling SSH 247

Line Configurations 248

    Securing Console Access to User EXEC 248

    Securing Auxiliary Access to User EXEC 250

    Securing Telnet and SSH Access to User EXEC 250

Router Interface Configurations 253

    Assigning an IP Address 254

    Enabling the Interface 255

    LAN-Specific Commands 255

    WAN-Specific Commands 256

Saving Configurations 256

Using the show Command to Get Information 258

    Verifying Your Configurations 259

    Viewing Interface Statuses and Statistics 260

    IOS File Version show Commands 264

Troubleshooting Commands 266

Backing Up and Restoring Configurations and
  IOS Using TFTP 269

Neighbor Discovery with CDP 272

Using Telnet for Virtual Terminal Access 276

    Terminal Monitor 277

IOS DHCP 278

Chapter Summary 281

    Key Terms 282

Apply Your Knowledge 284

    Exercises 284

    Review Questions 285

    Exam Questions 286

    Answers to Review Questions 289

    Answers to Exam Questions 290

    Suggested Readings and Resources 291

Chapter 9:
Understanding the Cisco SDM **293**

Introduction 296

Getting Started 296

Global Configurations 298

    Changing the Hostname, Banner, Domain Name,
    and Secret Password 299

    Router Access 303

    DNS 304

    DHCP 305

Router Interface Configurations 308

    Assigning an IP Address 308

    Enabling the Interface 309

    Saving and Verifying Your Configurations 310

Monitoring 310

Chapter Summary 312

    Key Terms 312

Apply Your Knowledge 312

    Exercise 312

    Review Questions 312

    Exam Questions 313

    Answers to Review Questions 315

    Answers to Exam Questions 316

    Suggested Readings and Resources 316

Chapter 10:
Introduction to Routing and Routing Protocols. **317**

Introduction. 320
The Default Gateway. 320
    Verifying and Troubleshooting the Default Gateway. 322
Routing Sources 323
    Administrative Distance. 324
Static Routes 325
    Configuring Static Routes 326
    Floating Static Routes. 327
Default Routes. 328
Configuring Static and Default Routes with SDM 329
Verifying Static and Default Routes. 330
    Dynamic Routing Protocols 331
    Routing Metrics. 332
    Classful and Classless Routing Updates. 333
VLSM. 336
    Interior and Exterior Gateway Routing Protocols. 340
    Distance Vector Routing Protocols 340
    Link-State Routing Protocols 341
    Advanced Distance Vector/Hybrid Routing Protocols 341
The Routing Table Revisited. 342
Routing Redistribution. 343
Chapter Summary. 345
    Key Terms 346
Apply Your Knowledge. 347
    Exercises 347
    Review Questions 348
    Exam Questions. 348
    Answers to Review Questions 351
    Answers to Exam Questions. 351
    Suggested Readings and Resources. 353

Chapter 11:
Distance Vector Routing Protocols **355**

Introduction. 358
    Distance Vector Operations. 358

Routing Loops 360

Routing Loop Mitigation 362

Counting to Infinity 363

Split Horizon 363

Route Poison, Poison Reverse, and Hold-Down Timers 364

Triggered Updates 366

Invalid/Dead Timers 367

RIP 367

RIP Characteristics 367

RIP Configuration 368

Passive Interfaces 371

RIPv2 Characteristics 371

RIPv2 Configuration 372

Configuring RIP with SDM 373

RIP Verification 374

Troubleshooting RIP 375

Chapter Summary 379

Key Terms 380

Apply Your Knowledge 380

Exercises 380

Review Questions 382

Exam Questions 382

Answers to Review Questions 384

Answers to Exam Questions 385

Suggested Readings and Resources 386

Chapter 12:
Enabling Internet Connectivity with NAT **387**

Introduction 390

NAT Concepts 391

Static NAT 392

Dynamic NAT 393

NAT Overload and Port Address Translation 394

NAT Terminology 395

Configuring NAT Using Cisco SDM 397

Configuring NAT Overload 397

Verifying NAT Configuration 410

Troubleshooting NAT 413
Chapter Summary 415
　　Key Terms 415
　　Review Questions 416
Apply Your Knowledge 416
　　Exam Questions 416
　　Answers to Review Questions 419
　　Answers to Exam Questions 419
　　Suggested Reading and Resources 421

Chapter 13:
Foundation Switching Operations **423**
Introduction 426
　　Switching Functionality 426
Frame Transmission Methods 427
　　Store-and-Forward 428
　　Cut-Through 428
　　Fragment-Free 428
Half- and Full-Duplex Connections 429
Switching Design 430
Spanning Tree Protocol 430
　　Root Bridge 431
　　Root Ports 432
　　Designated Ports 434
　　Blocked Ports 435
Port State Transitions 437
Initial Switch Configurations 438
　　Assigning a Management IP Address to a Switch 439
　　Defining a Default Gateway 439
　　IP Assignment Using DHCP 440
　　Configuring Multiple Switch Interfaces 441
　　Verifying Spanning Tree Protocol 442
Troubleshooting Basic Switch Connectivity 442
Chapter Summary 445
　　Key Terms 445
Apply Your Knowledge 446
　　Exercises 446

Review Questions 448

Exam Questions 449

Answers to Review Questions 452

Answers to Exam Questions 452

Suggested Readings and Resources 454

Chapter 14:
Implementing Switch Security **455**

Introduction 458

Securing Physical Access to the Catalyst Switch 458

Securing Terminal Access to the Catalyst Switch 458

To Telnet or Not to Telnet 460

Additional IOS Security Practices 461

Layer 2 Security 461

Port Security 462

"See"DP 464

Chapter Summary 466

Key Terms 466

Apply Your Knowledge 467

Exercises 467

Review Questions 469

Exam Questions 469

Answers to Review Questions 471

Answers to Exam Questions 472

Suggested Readings and Resources 472

Chapter 15:
Understanding Wireless Networking **473**

Introduction 476

The Business Case 476

The Players in the 802.11 Market 477

Entering the Radio Frequency World 478

Understanding Wireless Transmission 478

Unlicensed RF Bands 479

The Key to Successful Wireless: Channel Surfing 480

The 802.11 Standards Family 483

Party Like It's 1999: 802.11a and 802.11b 483

2003 Delivers: 802.11g 483
The Next Generation: 802.11n 484
Chapter Summary 485
Key Terms 485
Apply Your Knowledge 486
Exercise 486
Review Questions 486
Exam Questions 487
Answers to Review Questions 489
Answers to Exam Questions 489
Suggested Readings and Resources 490

Chapter 16:
Wireless Security and Implementation Considerations **491**
Introduction 494
Understanding the Threats 494
War Driving 494
Direct Hacking 495
Employee Ignorance 495
Deploying a Secure Wireless Network 496
Wireless Encryption 496
Wireless Authentication (802.1x) 499
Wireless Intrusion Prevention System (IPS) 500
Wireless Implementation Guidelines 501
Understanding Wireless Topologies 501
Understanding Wireless Data Rates 503
General Wireless Implementation Steps 506
Wireless Troubleshooting 506
Chapter Summary 508
Key Terms 508
Apply Your Knowledge 509
Review Questions 509
Exam Questions 509
Answers to Review Questions 512
Answers to Exam Questions 512
Suggested Readings and Resources 513

Chapter 17:
Wide Area Network Connections **515**

   Introduction 518

   WAN Connection Types 518

      Leased Lines 519

      Circuit-Switched Networks 519

      Packet-Switched Networks 520

      Broadband 520

      Virtual Private Networks (VPNs) 521

      Metropolitan Ethernet (Metro Ethernet) 521

   The WAN Physical Layer 522

   WAN Data Link Encapsulations 523

      Serial Line Internet Protocol (SLIP) 523

      Point-to-Point Protocol (PPP) 524

      Cisco High-Level Data Link Control (HDLC) 524

      X.25 Link Access Procedure, Balanced (LAPB) 524

      Frame Relay 524

      Asynchronous Transfer Mode (ATM) 524

      PPP over Ethernet (PPPoE) and PPP over ATM (PPPoA) 525

   Cisco HDLC 525

   PPP 525

      Sub-Layer 1: ISO HDLC 527

      Sub-Layer 2: Link Control Protocol (LCP) 527

      Sub-Layer 3: Network Control Protocol 532

   Configuring PPP 532

      Authentication 532

      Compression 534

   Verifying PPP 535

      Troubleshooting PPP 537

   Chapter Summary 539

      Key Terms 539

   Apply Your Knowledge 540

      Exercises 540

      Review Questions 543

      Exam Questions 544

      Answers to Review Questions 546

Answers to Exam Questions 546

Suggested Reading and Resources 548

Fast Facts: **549**

OSI Model in Review 550

Application Protocols Supported by the Application Layer 551

Network Domains 554

Cabling, Lines, and Services 554

MAC Addressing 556

Framing and Duplex Types 556

WAN Interfaces 557

Memory Types 557

IOS File Naming Conventions 558

Utilities Using ICMP 558

Network Security 558

Access Attacks 559

Reconnaissance Attacks 559

Denial of Service (DoS) Attacks 559

Mitigating Network Threats 559

IP Addressing 560

Classless Addressing 561

Private Ranges 561

Subnetting 561

IPv6 562

Types of IPv6 Addresses 563

Integrating IPv4 and IPv6 563

Layer 3 Functions 563

IOS Terminal Access Methodologies 564

IOS Boot Processes 564

IOS Navigation 565

Context-Sensitive Help 565

Terminal Editing Keys 565

Syntax Errors 566

Global Configuration Commands 566

Securing the IOS 566

SSH 567

Interface Configuration Commands 568
Switch Commands 568
The Copy Command 568
The Show Command 569
    Interface Status 569
Cisco Discovery Protocol 570
Telnet 570
DHCP 571
Switches 571
    Duplex Connections 572
    Port Security 572
Routing Characteristics 572
    Routing Sources 572
    Static and Default Routes 573
Dynamic Routing Protocols 574
    Routing Metrics 574
    Interior and Exterior Gateway Routing Protocols 574
    Classful and Classless Routing Updates 575
    Routing Protocol Classes 575
    Redistribution 575
Distance Vector Routing Loop Mitigation 576
RIP and RIPv2 576
    RIP Configuration 577
Wireless Networking 577
    Wireless Security and Implementation 578
    Network Address Translation (NAT) 579
    Wide-Area Networks 580

Practice Exam **583**

Answers to Practice Exam **601**

Answers at a Glance 602
Answers with Explanations 603

Appendix:
What's on the CD-ROM **611**

Multiple Test Modes 611

Study Mode 611
Certification Mode 611
Custom Mode 611
Attention to Exam Objectives 612
Installing the CD. 612
Creating a Shortcut to the MeasureUp Practice Tests. 613
Technical Support 614

Glossary **615**

Index **643**

About the Authors

Jeremy Cioara (CCIE, CCVP, CCSP) works in many facets of the Cisco networking realm. As an author, he has written multiple books for Cisco Press and Exam Cram. As an instructor, he teaches at Interface Technical Training (www.interfacett.com) in Phoenix, Arizona. Likewise, Jeremy has recorded many E-Learning titles at CBTNuggets (www.cbtnuggets.com). Finally, Jeremy is the CIO of AdTEC Networks and works as a network consultant focusing on Cisco network and Voice over IP (VoIP) implementations. What's more? Jeremy also runs the Cisco Blog (www.ciscoblog.com) in his "free time." Thankfully, he is married to the Certified Best Wife in the World (CBWW) who helps him manage his time and priorities and prevents him from getting an enormous Cisco logo tattooed across his chest.

Dave Minutella (CCNP, CCDP, INFOSEC, CISSP, CTP, MCSA, MCDST, Security+, Network+, A+) has been working in the IT and telecom industry for over 14 years. He currently serves as Vice President of Educational Services for Training Camp. Before that, he was the lead Cisco instructor, primarily teaching CCNA, CCDA, and CCNP courses. Dave is also the technical author of CSVPN Exam Cram 2 from Que Publishing and is the present Cisco certifications expert for SearchNetworking.com's Ask the Networking Expert panel.

Heather Stevenson (CCNP) has over seven years of experience in the IT industry and is currently a Senior Network Engineer at a global manufacturing company. She has written a number of technical training guides and mentored fellow IT professionals throughout her career. When she is not working, Heather still loves spending time with her network of friends and family.

Dedications

From Jeremy: *I'd like to dedicate this book to my newest daughter, Isabella. She's currently six months old and is staring at me right now from a soft blanket on the floor. By the time she's old enough to read this, this book will probably be outdated as we will all have Ethernet ports implanted in our skull (I'm opting for a wireless connection, myself). Hopefully, if we remember to pull this book off the shelf and read this dedication, I can tell her what amazing joy she has brought me. This tiny, arm flailing, cooing, cheesy-grinning, soft, delicate, playful, yet scandalously sly, giggling little girl has become my addiction. I hope I can always help her know how incredibly special she is to me.*

From Dave: *This book is dedicated to my soon-to-be daughter, Chloe. By the time this book is printed, you will be born and your exquisite mother and I can have longwinded debates about which event was more distressing. I very well may have written books about Cisco technology and whatnot, but as for incredible blessings, it's you who wrote the book.*

From Heather: *I would like to dedicate this book to anyone and everyone who has ever helped me in my pursuit to learn. I have been fortunate enough to have many wonderful teachers in my life. Not just school teachers, but family and friends who have given me their hand along the way.*

Acknowledgments

From Jeremy: My number-one acknowledgment always goes to God who has blessed me in more ways than I even realize. Thank you for granting me the talent to be successful in the realm of Cisco networking. Please allow me to use these talents to accomplish more for Your kingdom than an Ethernet cable ever could. Thanks to my darling wife, Susan. You are my eyes and ears that help me to see what is REALLY going on around me. I love you! And last, but not least: Thank you fish swimming in the big fish tank next to me. You bring me much peace and serenity as I sit here typing these acknowledgments. Especially the big yellow Butterfly fish that swims this way and that. Swish, swish swish. Swish, swish.

From Dave: As always, I would like to put to paper yet again my undying gratitude and love to my wife, Marsha. Your beautiful spirit outshines the sun even on the brightest of days. I also would like to thank my family and family-in-laws for your unwavering support. I especially want to honor my mother-in-law, Pattie, who has touched so many throughout her life. Words cannot fill the sorrow in our hearts, but your memories and spirit give us strength. We will miss you.

From Heather: I would like to send out a huge hug and thank you to my parents and my Dustin. Dustin has been by my side for as long as I have been working in this industry. He even took me to my junior prom many, many years ago. His support is immeasurable. I am so lucky to have amazing people around me to keep me sane. Finally, DYB Bear and Grumpy Nigel also deserve a special hello. Hello!

We Want to Hear from You!

As the reader of this book, *you* are our most important critic and commentator. We value your opinion and want to know what we're doing right, what we could do better, what areas you'd like to see us publish in, and any other words of wisdom you're willing to pass our way.

As an associate publisher for Que Publishing, I welcome your comments. You can email or write me directly to let me know what you did or didn't like about this book—as well as what we can do to make our books better.

Please note that I cannot help you with technical problems related to the topic of this book. We do have a User Services group, however, where I will forward specific technical questions related to the book.

When you write, please be sure to include this book's title and author as well as your name, email address, and phone number. I will carefully review your comments and share them with the author and editors who worked on the book.

Email: feedback@quepublishing.com

Mail: Dave Dusthimer
            Associate Publisher
            Que Publishing
            800 East 96th Street
            Indianapolis, IN 46240 USA

Reader Services

Visit our website and register this book at www.quepublishing.com/register for convenient access to any updates, downloads, or errata that might be available for this book.

Cisco ICND1 Exam Objectives

Interconnecting Cisco Networking Devices Part 1 (ICND1)

Exam Number: 640-822 ICND1

Associated Certifications: CCENT and CCNA

Duration: 90 Minutes (50-60 questions)

Exam Description

The 640-822 Interconnecting Cisco Networking Devices Part 1 (ICND1) is the exam associated with the Cisco Certified Entry Network Technician (CCENT) certification and a tangible first step in achieving the Cisco Certified Network Associate certification. Candidates can prepare for this exam by taking the Interconnecting Cisco Networking Devices Part 1 (ICND1) v1.0 course. This exam tests a candidate's knowledge and skills required to successfully install, operate, and troubleshoot a small branch office network. The exam includes topics on networking fundamentals; connecting to a WAN; basic security and wireless concepts; routing and switching fundamentals; the TCP/IP and OSI models; IP addressing; WAN technologies; operating and configuring IOS devices; configuring RIPv2, static and default routing; implementing NAT and DHCP; and configuring simple networks.

Exam Topics

The following topics are general guidelines for the content likely to be included on the Interconnecting Cisco Networking Devices Part 1 exam. However, other related topics may also appear on any specific delivery of the exam. In order to better reflect the contents of the exam and for clarity purposes, the guidelines below may change at any time without notice.

Describe the operation of data networks

- ► Describe the purpose and functions of various network devices
- ► Select the components required to meet a given network specification
- ► Use the OSI and TCP/IP models and their associated protocols to explain how data flows in a network
- ► Describe common networking applications including web applications
- ► Describe the purpose and basic operation of the protocols in the OSI and TCP models
- ► Describe the impact of applications (Voice Over IP and Video Over IP) on a network
- ► Interpret network diagrams
- ► Determine the path between two hosts across a network
- ► Describe the components required for network and Internet communications
- ► Identify and correct common network problems at layers 1, 2, 3 and 7 using a layered model approach
- ► Differentiate between LAN/WAN operation and features

Implement a small switched network

- ► Select the appropriate media, cables, ports, and connectors to connect switches to other network devices and hosts
- ► Explain the technology and media access control method for Ethernet technologies
- ► Explain network segmentation and basic traffic management concepts
- ► Explain the operation of Cisco switches and basic switching concepts

Continues on Following Page

- ▶ Perform, save, and verify initial switch configuration tasks including remote access management
- ▶ Verify network status and switch operation using basic utilities (including: ping, traceroute, telnet, SSH, arp, ipconfig), SHOW & DEBUG commands
- ▶ Implement and verify basic security for a switch (port security, deactivate ports)
- ▶ Identify, prescribe, and resolve common switched network media issues, configuration issues, auto-negotiation, and switch hardware failures

Implement an IP addressing scheme and IP services to meet network requirements for a small branch office

- ▶ Describe the need and role of addressing in a network
- ▶ Create and apply an addressing scheme to a network
- ▶ Assign and verify valid IP addresses to hosts, servers, and networking devices in a LAN environment
- ▶ Explain the basic uses and operation of NAT in a small network connecting to one ISP
- ▶ Describe and verify DNS operation
- ▶ Describe the operation and benefits of using private and public IP addressing
- ▶ Enable NAT for a small network with a single ISP and connection using SDM and verify operation using CLI and ping
- ▶ Configure, verify, and troubleshoot DHCP and DNS operation on a router.(including: CLI/SDM)
- ▶ Implement static and dynamic addressing services for hosts in a LAN environment
- ▶ Identify and correct IP addressing issues

Implement a small routed network

- ▶ Describe basic routing concepts (including: packet forwarding, router lookup process)
- ▶ Describe the operation of Cisco routers (including: router bootup process, POST, router components)
- ▶ Select the appropriate media, cables, ports, and connectors to connect routers to other network devices and hosts
- ▶ Configure, verify, and troubleshoot RIPv2
- ▶ Access and utilize the router CLI to set basic parameters
- ▶ Connect, configure, and verify operation status of a device interface
- ▶ Verify device configuration and network connectivity using ping, traceroute, telnet, SSH, or other utilities
- ▶ Perform and verify routing configuration tasks for a static or default route given specific routing requirements
- ▶ Manage IOS configuration files (including: save, edit, upgrade, restore)
- ▶ Manage Cisco IOS
- ▶ Implement password and physical security
- ▶ Verify network status and router operation using basic utilities (including: ping, traceroute, telnet, SSH, arp, ipconfig), SHOW & DEBUG commands

Explain and select the appropriate administrative tasks required for a WLAN

- ▶ Describe standards associated with wireless media (including: IEEE WI-FI Alliance, ITU/FCC)
- ▶ Identify and describe the purpose of the components in a small wireless network (including: SSID, BSS, ESS)
- ▶ Identify the basic parameters to configure on a wireless network to ensure that devices connect to the correct access point
- ▶ Compare and contrast wireless security features and capabilities of WPA security (including: open, WEP, WPA-1/2)
- ▶ Identify common issues with implementing wireless networks

Identify security threats to a network and describe general methods to mitigate those threats

- ▶ Explain today's increasing network security threats and the need to implement a comprehensive security policy to mitigate the threats
- ▶ Explain general methods to mitigate common security threats to network devices, hosts, and applications
- ▶ Describe the functions of common security appliances and applications
- ▶ Describe security recommended practices including initial steps to secure network devices

Implement and verify WAN links

- ▶ Describe different methods for connecting to a WAN
- ▶ Configure and verify a basic WAN serial connection

Introduction

The Cisco Certified Entry Networking Technician (CCENT) is a new accreditation offered by Cisco for entry-level network technicians. The ICND1 exam for CCENT certification covers a broad range of networking concepts to prepare candidates for the technologies they are likely to work with in today's network environments.

This book is your one-stop shop. Everything you need to know to pass the exam is in here. You do not have to take a class in addition to buying this book to pass the exam. However, depending on your personal study habits or learning style, you might benefit from buying this book *and* taking a class. Taking a CCENT certification class gives you dedicated study time and precious hands-on experience with live Cisco equipment.

Exam Preps are meticulously crafted to give you the best possible learning experience for the particular characteristics of the technology covered and the actual certification exam. The instructional design implemented in the *Exam Preps* reflects the task- and experience-based nature of Cisco certification exams. The *Exam Preps* provide the factual knowledge base you need for the exams and then take it to the next level, with exercises and exam questions that are required in the ICND1 exam.

The CCENT certification consists of a single exam called Interconnecting Cisco Networking Devices Part 1 (ICND1). Candidates who would like to continue with the Cisco certification path and obtain their CCNA accreditation can then take the ICND2 exam. The *CCENT Exam Prep* prepares you for the ICND1 exam, which covers the foundational Cisco network concepts and configurations.

How This Book Helps You

This book takes you on a self-guided tour of all the areas covered by the CCENT exam and teaches you the specific skills you need to achieve your certification. This book also contains helpful hints, tips, real-world examples, and exercises, as well as references to additional study materials. Specifically, this book is set up to help you in the following ways:

- ▶ **Organization:** This book is organized by individual exam objectives. Every objective you need to know for the CCENT exam is covered in this book. It presents the objectives in an order as close as possible to that listed by Cisco. However, we did not hesitate to reorganize them where needed to make the material as easy as possible for you to learn. We also make the information accessible in the following ways:

  - ▶ The full list of exam units and objectives is included.

- ▶ Each chapter begins with an outline that provides an overview of the material and the pages on which particular topics can be found.

- ▶ The objectives are repeated where the material most directly relevant to them is covered.

▶ **Instructional features:** This book provides multiple ways to learn and reinforce the exam material. Following are some of the helpful methods:

- ▶ **Exam Alerts:** These provide specific exam-related advice. Such tips might address what material is covered (or not covered) on the exam, how it is covered, mnemonic devices, or particular quirks of that exam.

- ▶ **Review Breaks and Summaries:** Crucial information is summarized at various points in the book in lists or tables. Each chapter ends with a summary as well.

- ▶ **Key Terms:** A list of key terms appears at the end of each chapter.

- ▶ **Notes:** Notes contain various kinds of useful or practical information, such as tips on technology or administrative practices, historical background on terms and technologies, or side commentary on industry issues.

- ▶ **Warnings:** When using sophisticated information technology, there is always the potential for mistakes or even catastrophes because of improper application of the technology. Warnings alert you to such potential problems.

- ▶ **In the Field sidebars:** These relatively extensive discussions cover material that might not be directly relevant to the exam but that is useful as reference material or in everyday practice. In the Field sidebars also provide useful background or contextual information necessary for understanding the larger topic under consideration.

- ▶ **Exercises:** Found at the end of the chapters in the "Apply Your Knowledge" section and in the Challenges found throughout chapters, exercises are performance-based opportunities for you to learn and assess your knowledge.

▶ **Extensive practice test options:** This book provides numerous opportunities for you to assess your knowledge and practice for the exam. The practice options include the following:

- ▶ **Exam Questions:** These questions appear in the "Apply Your Knowledge" section. You can use them to help determine what you know and what you need to review or study further. Answers and explanations for these questions are provided in a separate section, titled "Answers to Exam Questions."

- ▶ **Practice Exam:** A practice exam is included in the "Final Review" section of the book.

▶ **Final Review:** This part of the book provides two valuable tools for preparing for the exam:

  ▶ **Fast Facts:** This condensed version of the information contained in the book is useful for last-minute review.

  ▶ **Practice Exam:** A practice test is included. Questions on this practice exam are written in styles similar to those used on the actual exam. Use the practice exam to assess your readiness for the real thing. Use the extensive answer explanations to improve your retention and understanding of the material.

This book includes several other features, such as a "Suggested Readings and Resources" section at the end of each chapter. It directs you to additional information that can aid you in your exam preparation and your real-life work. Also included are a glossary and an appendix describing what is on the CD-ROM.

For more information about the exam or the certification process, refer to the Cisco website at www.cisco.com/certification.

Network Hardware and Software Requirements

As a self-paced study guide, *CCENT Exam Prep* is meant to help you understand concepts that must be refined through hands-on experience. To make the most of your studying, you need to have as much background in and experience with both common operating systems and network environments as possible. The best way to do this is to combine studying with work on actual networks. These networks need not be complex. The concepts involved in configuring a network with only a couple of routers and a switch follow the same principles as those involved in configuring a network that has hundreds of connected systems. This section describes the recommended equipment for a solid practice environment.

To fully practice some of the exam objectives, you need to create a network with two (or more) routers networked together with one (or more) Cisco switches. We recognize that your finances may be limited, so we suggest purchasing routers from the Cisco 800 or 3600 series (primarily the 851W, 3620, and 3640 routers). These can commonly be found for between $100 and $500 through a used-equipment vendor or online auction. A Catalyst 1912 or 1924 switch can typically be found for less than $50. Some of the syntax on the 1900 series switches may be slightly different from Cisco's mainline switches, but most of the commands are similar. Remember that Cisco has strict restrictions about using used or remanufactured equipment in production networks. Although Cisco hardware can be resold, the software that runs it (Cisco IOS software) cannot. Before used or remanufactured equipment can be used in a production environment, Cisco IOS software must be relicensed through Cisco or an authorized reseller. Be sure to verify these regulations before using your lab equipment in a production network.

If you are looking to build a lab environment, the following is a more detailed list of the minimum equipment you need. Keep in mind that this is the minimum equipment that we suggest for the CCENT. If you plan on moving into the CCNA, CCNP, CCVP, or CCSP programs, you may want to look into the more advanced (and expensive) Cisco equipment such as the 2800 routers.

▶ At least one Cisco 851W router, which has four 10/100Mbps Ethernet ports to test configurations such as NAT, one fixed port to simulate WAN connectivity, wireless LAN with a detachable antenna, up to five VPN tunnels, and SDM capabilities.

▶ One additional Cisco router, such as the 2501, with one Ethernet port and two serial ports to create and test WAN connectivity.

▶ A DB-60 DTE to DB-60 DCE cross-over serial cable.

▶ At least one Cisco switch, ideally a 2900XL or 2950; however, a 1900 series switch will also suffice. If you decide to use a 1900 series switch, be sure it is equipped with the Enterprise IOS version, which includes the command-line interface. The Standard IOS for the 1900 allows only a menu-driven configuration.

▶ At least one rollover console cable.

▶ Multiple straight-through and cross-over network cables.

▶ Optionally, adding one or more PCs to the network can add realism and troubleshooting advantages. These PCs can be connected to the switch and act as network clients in your scenarios.

It's easy to get access to the necessary computer hardware and software in a corporate business environment. It can be difficult, however, to allocate enough time within the busy workday to complete a self-study program. Most of your study time will occur after normal working hours, away from the everyday interruptions and pressures of your regular job.

Advice on Taking the Exam

Keep this advice in mind as you study:

▶ **Read all the material:** Cisco has been known to include material that is not expressly specified in the objectives. This book includes additional information that is not reflected in the objectives in an effort to give you the best possible preparation for the examination—and for your real-world experiences to come.

▶ **Complete the exercises in each chapter:** They will help you gain experience in using the specified methodology or approach. Cisco exams require task- and experienced-based knowledge and require you to understand how certain network procedures are accomplished.

▶ **Use the exam questions to assess your knowledge:** Don't just read the chapter content; use the exam questions to find out what you know and what you don't know. If you are struggling, study some more, review, and then reassess your knowledge.

▶ **Review the objectives:** Develop your own questions and examples for each objective listed. If you can develop and answer several questions for each objective, you should not find it difficult to pass the exam.

NOTE

Exam-Taking Advice   Although this book is designed to prepare you to take and pass the Cisco certification exam, there are no guarantees. Read this book, work through the questions and exercises, and when you feel confident, take the practice exam. Your results should tell you whether you are ready for the real thing. Keep in mind that lots of capable, intelligent people fail these exams one or more times. Cisco exams are some of the most difficult in the industry; if you do fail the exam, use it as a tool to help you focus your studies in the areas where you felt weak. As overused as this guidance is, we still need to say it: Don't give up. Every author writing this book has hit his or her own low points in the certification journey. Trust us—after you pass the CCENT exam, the benefits far outweigh the cost.

When taking the actual certification exam, be sure that you answer all the questions before the time limit expires. Do not spend too much time on any one question. If you are unsure about a question, answer it as best you can and move on. This especially applies to simulation-based questions. Partial credit is given on these questions if you have completed the majority of the steps, so don't get hung up on any one simulation objective for an extended time.

Remember that the primary objective is not to pass the exam but to understand the material. When you understand the material, passing the exam should be simple. Knowledge is a pyramid; to build upward, you need a solid foundation. This book and the CCENT certification are designed to ensure that you have that solid foundation.

Good luck!

CHAPTER ONE

Standard Internetworking Models

Objectives

This chapter covers the following Cisco-specific objectives for the "Describe the operation of data networks" section of the 640-822 ICND1 exam:

► **Use the OSI and TCP/IP models and their associated protocols to explain how data flows in a network**

► **Describe common networked applications including web applications**

► **Describe the purpose and basic operation of the protocols in the OSI and TCP models**

► **Determine the path between two hosts across a network**

Outline

Introduction	**10**
What Is an Internetwork?	**10**
Types of Internetworks	**11**
Local Area Network (LAN)	11
Metropolitan Area Network (MAN)	12
Wide Area Network (WAN)	12
Storage Area Network (SAN)	13
Virtual Private Network (VPN)	14
Open Systems Interconnection (OSI) Model	**14**
Upper Layers	15
Application Layer	15
Presentation Layer	17
Session Layer	18
Lower Layers	18
Transport Layer	18
Network Layer	20
Data Link Layer	21
Media Access Control (MAC)	21
Logical Link Control (LLC)	22
Physical Layer	23
OSI Layered Communications	23
TCP/IP Model	**25**
Application Layer	26
Transport Layer	27
TCP	27
UDP	30
Internet Layer	31
IP	31
ICMP	32
ARP, RARP, and Proxy ARP	33
Network Interface Layer	33

Cisco 3-Layer Hierarchical Model	**33**
Access Layer	34
Distribution Layer	35
Core Layer	35
Chapter Summary	**37**
Key Terms	37
Apply Your Knowledge	**40**
Exercises	40
Review Questions	41
Exam Questions	41
Answers to Review Questions	45
Answers to Exam Questions	47
Suggested Readings and Resources	**49**

Study Strategies

▶ Read through the exam objectives at the beginning of the chapter.

▶ Review the characteristics of each internetwork and keep in mind which network would be appropriate based on a given company and its individual requirements.

▶ Identify the names and primary functions of each OSI model layer. Create a mnemonic device to help you remember the seven layers.

▶ Identify the protocols and standards that are used at each layer of the OSI model. Pay close attention to the application protocols used at the Application layer.

▶ Review and memorize associated UDP and TCP port assignments for several well-known protocols.

Introduction

Whether you already work in the computer technology industry, or you are trying to enter the field as a newcomer, it is important in this day and age to back up your resume with a vendor-specific certification. If you search job postings on the Internet, it is commonplace for hiring companies today to require or recommend that an applicant have at least one vendor certification. Other companies ask that their current employees obtain certifications as a way to meet goals for advancement. Regardless of the underlying reason, studying for the CCENT is a smart move.

The CCENT certification was developed by Cisco to test your knowledge of networking at a beginner's level. Cisco wants to identify individuals capable of installing, configuring, and maintaining small-scale networks, which include Local Area Networks (LANs) and Wide Area Networks (WANs).

The purpose of this first chapter is to provide a general overview of the concepts that will ultimately be the foundation for the rest of this book. To start this chapter, the first step is to define the term *internetwork*. It then reviews the general concepts that pertain to LAN and WAN internetworks, as well as the Metropolitan Area Network (MAN), Storage Area Network (SAN), and Virtual Private Network (VPN). Later chapters go into more detail regarding the technologies that are related to both LAN and WAN.

This chapter also gives an in-depth look at the three networking reference models that are likely to be tested on the CCENT exam. These are the Open Systems Interconnection (OSI), Transmission Control Protocol/Internet Protocol (TCP/IP), and Cisco 3-Layer Hierarchical models. Being familiar with these models is fundamental to understanding how networks operate, as well as how various devices and protocols fit into their structure. By using these models, you can design an infrastructure based on a given organization's specific requirements.

What Is an Internetwork?

Simply put, an internetwork is the connection of more than one network. These networks are linked together by an internetworking device to provide communication between the networks. Internetworks may also be referred to as an *internet*. Notice the lowercase *i* at the beginning of the word *internet*—this differentiates it from the Internet. The Internet is considered to be the largest internet in the world. I know the phrase sounds odd, but it is a great example of how thousands of smaller networks are joined together to form one large global internetwork. Another example of an internet would be the connection of individual LANs to form a WAN.

The term *internetworking* signifies the industry, products, and processes that are required to handle the challenges of network interoperability. Such issues can be quite complex because of the existence of multiple vendors and protocols.

Types of Internetworks

There are various types of internetworks discussed in greater detail. I already mentioned LAN and WANs, which are the most common types of internetworks. Other important internetworks include MANs, SANs, and VPNs, which are also reviewed in this section.

Local Area Network (LAN)

Like the name suggests, LANs are limited to a local or small geographical area. An example of a LAN would be a network of individual computers or workstations that are connected in a single department. These users have shared access to resources such as data and network devices. Users on a LAN segment can share a network printer and communicate with one another via email. Also, they are governed by one authoritative administrator.

NOTE

LAN is the smallest network in geographical size.

Given the size constraints, downsides of a LAN network are limited distance that data can travel and a limited number of computers that can be connected. An upside of a LAN is fast data transfer with data speed that can reach up to 10Gbps.

Xerox Corporation worked in collaboration with DEC and Intel to create ethernet, which is the most pervasive LAN architecture used today. Ethernet has evolved and has seen significant improvements in regard to speed and efficiency.

Other significant LAN technologies are Fiber Distributed Data Interface (FDDI) and token ring.

EXAM ALERT

An understanding of LAN technology is required for the CCENT exam. Each ethernet version is discussed in detail in Chapter 3, "Data Link Networking Concepts."

Local area networking uses switches, bridges and/or repeaters, and hubs to interconnect LANs and increase overall size. Routers are used to connect a LAN to a WAN or MAN. Both of these scenarios form an internetwork.

Figure 1.1 provides an example of a LAN. A single switch connects to all the peripheral network devices in this example.

EXAM ALERT

Multiple LANs are interconnected with switches, bridges, or repeaters.
LANs are connected to a MAN or a WAN with a router.

FIGURE 1.1   Example of a LAN.

Metropolitan Area Network (MAN)

A MAN is larger than a LAN but smaller than or equal in size to a WAN. Think of it as the size of a city or college campus network, which can range anywhere from 5 to 50km in diameter. MANs are typically owned and managed by a single entity. This could be an ISP or telecommunications company that sells its services to end-users in that metropolitan area. For all intents and purposes, a MAN has the same characteristics as a WAN with distance constraints.

Wide Area Network (WAN)

WANs cover more than one geographical area. This is ideal for a company that has offices in different cities around the country or even the world. Each office can connect to the other sites in the WAN via a router. Connectivity from router to router is a circuit leased from a telephone or communications company, such as AT&T to name one. The larger the circuit a company needs to transmit data, the more it costs to lease. The company also needs to pay close attention to the performance of its WAN connection because that cost can directly impact its ability to do business. It is important to keep an eye on the amount of traffic that is going over each circuit to ensure that you have sufficient throughput. *Throughput* refers to the amount of data transferred in a specified timeframe.

NOTE

Earlier I mentioned that the Internet is the perfect example of an internetwork. It is also an excellent example of a WAN network where thousands of small networks are joined together to form one large global network.

The following are WAN encapsulations that are reviewed in Chapter 17, "Wide Area Network Connections":

▶ Frame Relay

▶ PPP

▶ HDLC—Cisco standard

Figure 1.2 provides an example of a WAN. In this example, a central router connects two LANs to create the WAN. Each LAN has a switch connected to its local end-user devices.

FIGURE 1.2 Example of a WAN.

Storage Area Network (SAN)

SAN may be referred to as a subnetwork or special purpose network. Its special purpose is to allow users on a larger network to connect various data storage devices with clusters of data servers. Cisco offers this service with its Cisco MDS 9000 Series Multilayer SAN Switches. These switches provide scalable storage solutions for the end user.

Virtual Private Network (VPN)

VPN is a private network that can access public networks remotely. VPN uses encryption and security protocols to retain privacy while it accesses outside resources. When employed on a network, VPN enables an end user to create a virtual tunnel to a remote location. Typically, telecommuters use VPN to log in to their company networks from home.

Open Systems Interconnection (OSI) Model

Objectives:

▶ Use the OSI and TCP/IP models and their associated protocols to explain how data flows in a network

▶ Describe common networked applications including web applications

▶ Describe the purpose and basic operation of the protocols in the OSI and TCP models

By now you understand the concept of an internetwork. Now the OSI model will help you see just how an internetwork operates by using a *layered architecture*.

The International Organization for Standardization (ISO) created the OSI model as the first major attempt to internetwork various vendor-specific networks, the ultimate goal being that these different vendor networks could work together in harmony. This model consists of seven layers. Although it is not widely used today, the terminology is prevalent in the networking community. The OSI model may also be helpful when troubleshooting a network issue.

First of all, it is important to know the name of each layer and its corresponding layer number. This will help you remember where the layers reside in the OSI model. You may also hear the layers referred to by number, so knowing them will also help in that respect. Table 1.1 provides a list of all seven layers.

TABLE 1.1   The Seven Layers of the OSI Model

Layer Number	Layer Name
7	Application
6	Presentation
5	Session
4	Transport
3	Network
2	Data Link
1	Physical

In general, each layer communicates with the adjacent layers on the OSI model and the corresponding layer on another system. For example, the Presentation layer communicates with the Application layer, the Session layer, and also with the Presentation layer of another connected system.

EXAM ALERT

It is crucial that you learn the layers of the OSI model and their respective functions. Also know that the OSI model helps with multi-vendor integration. The functions are reviewed in this chapter. For now, to help you remember the names of the layers and their order, it may be helpful to come up with a mnemonic device. The most commonly used phrase is "All People Seem To Need Data Processing." There are many other phrases out there, some of which are quite crass, but it is ultimately up to you to decide whether this will help.

Upper Layers

Now that you know the layers in order, it is also important to know that the layers may also be referred to as the *upper* and *lower* layers. Primarily, the upper layers of the OSI model define communications between applications that reside on end-user stations. This is generally related to software communication. Table 1.2 provides a list of the layers considered as the upper layers.

TABLE 1.2   The Upper Layers of the OSI Model = Applications

Layer Number	Layer Name
7	Application
6	Presentation
5	Session

Application Layer

Layer 7 provides an interface between a host's communication software and any necessary external applications (such as email, file transfers, and terminal emulation). This layer can also evaluate what resources are necessary to communicate between two devices and determine their availability.

Layer 7 also provides the following functionality:

▶ Synchronization of client/server applications

▶ Error control and data integrity between applications

▶ System-independent processes to a host

Table 1.3 provides a list of the protocols supported by the Application layer.

TABLE 1.3 Application Protocols Supported by the Application Layer

Application Protocols	Function
Telnet	A TCP/IP protocol that provides terminal emulation to a remote host by creating a virtual terminal. Secure CRT is one program that can be installed on a user computer to create telnet sessions. This protocol requires authentication via a username and password.
Hypertext Transfer Protocol (HTTP)	Enables web browsing with the transmission of Hypertext Markup Language (HTML) documents on the Internet.
Secure Hypertext Transfer Protocol (HTTPS)	Enables secure web browsing. A secure connection is indicated when the URL begins with https:// or when there is a lock symbol at the lower-right corner of the web page that is being viewed.
File Transfer Protocol (FTP)	Enables a user to transfer files. Provides access to files and directories. Securely implemented with telnet, which allows remote authentication to an FTP server.
Trivial File Transfer Protocol (TFTP)	A bare-bones version of FTP that does not provide access to directories. With TFTP, you can just send and receive files. Unlike FTP, TFTP is not secure and sends smaller blocks of data.
Domain Name System (DNS)	Resolves hostnames such as www.cisco.com into IP addresses.
Simple Mail Transfer Protocol (SMTP)	Sends electronic mail across the network.
Post Office Protocol 3 (POP3)	Receives electronic mail by accessing an Internet server.
Network File System (NFS)	Enables users with different operating systems (for example, NT and Unix workstations) to share files.
Network News Transfer Protocol (NNTP)	Offers access to Usenet newsgroup postings.
Simple Network Management Protocol (SNMP)	Monitors the network and manages configurations. Collects statistics to analyze network performance and ensure network security.
Network Time Protocol (NTP)	Synchronizes clocks on the Internet to provide accurate local time on the user system.
Dynamic Host Configuration Protocol (DHCP)	Works dynamically to provide an IP address, subnet mask, domain name, and a default gateway for routers. Works with DNS and WINS (used for NetBIOS addressing).

EXAM ALERT

Know the Protocols Be prepared to identify which protocols are used at the Application layer of the OSI model. Also familiarize yourself with the general functions of these protocols.

Presentation Layer

Layer 6 presents data to the Application layer and acts as a data format translator. Format translation is necessary to ensure that the data can be read by applications. Layer 6 also handles the structuring of data and negotiating data transfer syntax to Layer 7. Processes involved include data encryption, decryption, compression, and decompression.

NOTE

The Presentation layer is the only layer that can actually change data.

Layer 6 protocols include the following:

▶ Joint Photographic Experts Group (JPEG)

▶ American Standard Code for Information Interchange (ASCII)

▶ Extended Binary Coded Decimal Interchange Code (EBCDIC)

▶ Tagged Image File Format (TIFF)

▶ Graphic Image File (GIF)

▶ Picture (PICT)

▶ Moving Picture Experts Group (MPEG)

▶ Musical Instrument Digital Interface (MIDI)

▶ QuickTime

▶ Rich Text Format (RTF)

NOTE

Graphic and visual images use PICT, TIFF, and JPEG. Audio and video formatting uses MIDI, MPEG, QuickTime, and RTF.

Session Layer

Layer 5 is primarily concerned with dialog control among devices. This layer determines the beginning, middle, and end of a session or conversation that occurs between applications. In this way, the Session layer acts as an intermediary for those applications. Table 1.4 lists the Session layer protocols and their functionality.

TABLE 1.4   Session Layer Protocols and Their General Functionality

Session Layer Protocol	Function
Network File System (NFS)	Accesses remote resources transparently and represents files and directories as if local to the user system. Developed by SUN and used on Unix workstations.
Structured Query Language (SQL)	Functions as a query language that requests, updates, and manages databases. Developed by IBM and compatible with XML and HTML.
Remote Procedure Call (RPC)	Basis for client/server communications. Calls are created on the client and then carried out on the server.
AppleTalk Session Protocol (ASP)	Also client/server–based communications, but specific to AppleTalk client and server devices.
X Window	Communicates with remote Unix machines and enables the user to operate the device as if attached locally.
Digital Network Architecture Session Control Protocol (DNA SCP)	A proprietary Digital Equipment Corporation Networking (DECnet) protocol, also referred to as a DECnet session.

Lower Layers

The lower layers of the OSI model focus on data transport, which can be achieved via a router, switch, or a physical wire. They are listed in Table 1.5.

TABLE 1.5   The Lower Layers of the OSI Model—Responsible for Data Transport

Layer Number	Layer Name
4	Transport
3	Network
2	Data Link
1	Physical

Transport Layer

Layer 4 is responsible for end-to-end connections and data delivery between two hosts. The ability to segment and reassemble data is a key functionality of this layer. For example, when one system is sending data to another system, that data can be segmented into smaller data blocks and transmitted across the network. The receiving system can then reassemble the segmented data blocks at the Transport layer. Transmissions occur via logical connectivity between the sender and destination. Layer 4 provides transparent data transfer by hiding details of the transmission from the upper layers.

EXAM ALERT

Segmenting and reliable end-to-end data delivery occurs at the Transport layer.

Layer 4 also provides the following functionality:

- ▶ Fault detection

- ▶ Error recovery

- ▶ Establishing, maintaining, and tearing down virtual circuits

The Transport layer can provide reliable networking via acknowledgments, sequencing, and flow control.

- ▶ **Acknowledgments**—Delivered segments are acknowledged to the sender. If they are not acknowledged, the sender will retransmit.

- ▶ **Sequencing**—Data segments are sequenced into their original order when they arrive at the destination.

- ▶ **Flow Control**—Provides buffer controls that prevent packet flooding to the destination host. Buffers store bursts of data for processing when the transmission is complete.

Layer 4 protocols include the following:

- ▶ Transmission Control Protocol (TCP)

- ▶ User Datagram Protocol (UDP)

- ▶ Sequenced Packet Exchange (SPX)—A reliable communications protocol created by Novell NetWare

NOTE

TCP and UDP protocols are important to know for the exam. These are discussed later in this chapter, under the "Transport Layer" section of the TCP/IP model.

Network Layer

Layer 3 is where the best path determination is made for packet delivery across the network. Routed protocols such as IP are used to determine logical addressing, which can identify the destination of a packet or datagram. The most common network device found at the Network layer is a router; however, Layer 3 switches may also be implemented.

A router at the Network layer follows these general steps to ensure proper data transport:

1. The router checks the destination IP address of the incoming packet on the router interface.

2. Packets destined for that router are processed, whereas packets destined for another router must be looked up in the routing table.

3. The router determines an exit interface based on the routing table and sends the packet to the interface for framing and forwarding. If there is no route in the routing table, the packet is dropped by the router.

A routing table on a router contains the following information:

▶ Network Address

▶ Interface—Exit interface used to forward packets

▶ Metric—Distance to reach a remote network

There are two packet types utilized at Layer 3:

▶ **Data Packets**—Transport data across the internetwork and are supported by IP and IPX protocols.

▶ **Route Update Packets**—Send updates to neighbor routers about all networks connected to that internetwork and are supported by routing protocols such as RIP, EIGRP, and OSPF.

Layer 3 routed protocols include the following:

▶ Internet Protocol (IP)

▶ Internet Packet Exchange (IPX)—Part of the IPX/SPX protocol suite created by Novell NetWare

▶ AppleTalk DDP—Datagram delivery protocol used by Apple

EXAM ALERT

For the exam, this book focuses on IP, which is reviewed in Chapter 5, Implementing IP Addressing.

NOTE

Routers and logical addressing (that is, IP addresses) are used at Layer 3. Data at Layer 3 is in the form of packets or a datagram.

Data Link Layer

Layer 2 ensures reliable data transfer from the Network layer to the Physical layer for transmission across the network.

Two domains determine data transport reliability:

▶ **Broadcast Domain**—A group of nodes that can receive each other's broadcast messages and are segmented by routers.

▶ **Collision Domain**—A group of nodes that share the same media and are segmented by switches. A collision occurs if two nodes attempt a simultaneous transmission. *Carrier Sense Multiple Access Collision Detection (CSMA/CD)* is an access method that sends a jam signal to notify the devices that there has been a collision. The devices then halt transmission for a random back-off time.

EXAM ALERT

Routers segment broadcast domains, whereas switches segment collision domains.

Data received from the Network layer is formatted into frames to be transmitted to the Physical layer. Physical addressing or hardware addressing (rather than logical addressing) ensures that data is delivered to the appropriate node on the LAN. This layer is also responsible for error notification (not correction), network topology, and flow control.

This is the only layer of the OSI model that has sublayers. The two sublayers in question define the IEEE Ethernet 802.3 frame, which in turn provides physical addressing and flow control. Also, routed protocol information (IP, IPX, AppleTalk, and so on) is provided to the upper layers.

The IEEE Ethernet 802.3 sublayers are Media Access Control (MAC) and Logical Link Control (LLC), and are described in the following sections.

Media Access Control (MAC)

The MAC address is the hard-coded address on the network interface controller (NIC) of the Physical layer node attached to the network. Although the source address will always be a unicast or single destination address, the destination address can be a unicast, multicast (a determined subset of nodes), or broadcast (all nodes in a broadcast domain) address.

Each MAC address must be unique and follow this format:

▶ It must consist of 48 bits.

▶ It must be displayed by 12 hexadecimal digits (0-9, A-F).

▶ The first 6 hexadecimal digits in the address are a vendor code or organizationally unique identifier (OUI) assigned by the NIC manufacturer.

This is an example of a MAC address: 00:00:07:A9:B2:EB

EXAM ALERT

Know the structure of a MAC address and that the broadcast address value is FFFF FFFF FFFF.

Logical Link Control (LLC)

The LLC sublayer complements the MAC sublayer in the ethernet model; the LLC is responsible for framing, error, and flow control. LLC provides a service access point (SAP) identifier in the frame. The SAP field of the frame consists of one byte that identifies an upper layer protocol (for example, 06 = IP, whereas E0 = IPX). The LLC inserts a destination SAP (DSAP) and a Source SAP (SSAP) in the frame. Figure 1.3 provides an example of an ethernet frame.

FIGURE 1.3 Example of an ethernet frame.

Two devices are used at the Data Link layer:

▶ **Bridges**—Bridges connect two segments in a single network or two networks together. They simply forward data between those segments/networks without performing an analysis or redirection of the data.

▶ **Switches**—At Layer 2, switches are multi-port bridges that utilize Application Specific Integrated Circuit (ASIC) to forward frames. Each port of the switch has a dedicated bandwidth.

EXAM ALERT

Dedicated bandwidth enables the switch port to guarantee the speed assigned to that port. For example, 100Mbps port connections get 100Mbps transmission rates.

Although both devices create a separate collision domain for each connected device, all the devices connected to either are a part of the same broadcast domain. Remember that broadcast domains are segmented at the Network layer by routers.

Switches and bridges identify MAC addresses by scanning for the source MAC address of each frame received.

NOTE

Bridging and switching are discussed in more detail in Chapter 3.

Physical Layer

Layer 1 moves bits between nodes. Electrical, mechanical, procedural, and functional requirements are defined at the Physical layer to assist with the activation, maintenance, and deactivation of physical connectivity between devices.

Other attributes of Layer 1 include the following:

▶ Specification of voltage, wire speed, and pin-out cables

▶ Capability to receive and transmit a data signal

▶ Identification of the interface that is set up between the data terminal equipment (DTE) and the data communication equipment (DCE)

NOTE

Although DTE is the locally attached device, DCE is typically found at the service provider. DTE services can be accessed with either a model or a channel service unit/data service unit (CSU/DSU). For additional information on associated Layer 1 technologies, continue on to Chapter 2, "Physical Layer Networking Concepts."

Devices at the Physical layer include hubs and repeaters. Hubs and repeaters *extend* a network, whereas Layer 2 and Layer 3 devices *segment* a network.

OSI Layered Communications

Now that you have reviewed all seven layers of the OSI model, it is a good time to see how those layers communicate with each other. Each layer passes information to adjacent layers by using Protocol Data Units (PDUs). The PDU includes both the message and the protocol/control information from the forwarding layer. That control information can be in the form of a header or trailer. The process of adding a header or trailer to the PDU at each layer of the OSI is called *encapsulation*.

Each layer has an associated control information name, which is listed in Table 1.6.

TABLE 1.6   OSI Model Layers and Their Control Information Names

OSI Layer	Control Information Name
Application	Data
Presentation	
Session	
Transport	Segment
Network	Packet
Data Link	Frame
Physical	Bit

Based on this chart, you can see how information is encapsulated as it travels down through the various layers. The correct order for data encapsulation is data, segment, packet, frame, and bit.

EXAM ALERT

It is important to know the control information name for the OSI layers and the correct order for data encapsulation.

REVIEW BREAK

Let's take a few minutes to go over the OSI model. Table 1.7 lists the seven layers and significant aspects of each layer.

TABLE 1.7   OSI Model Layers and Their Respective Functionalities

OSI Layer	Important Functions
Application	Provides an interface between a host's communication software and any necessary external applications.
	Evaluates what resources are necessary and the available resources for communication between two devices.
	Synchronizes client/server applications.
	Provides error control and data integrity between applications.
	Provides system-independent processes to a host.

TABLE 1.7 *Continued*

OSI Layer	Important Functions
Presentation	Presents data to the Application layer.
	Acts as a data format translator.
	Handles the structuring of data and negotiating data transfer syntax to Layer 7.
	Processes involved include data encryption, decryption, compression, and decompression.
Session	Handles dialog control among devices.
	Determines the beginning, middle, and end of a session or conversation that occurs between applications (intermediary).
Transport	Manages end-to-end connections and data delivery between two hosts.
	Segments and reassembles data.
	Provides transparent data transfer by hiding details of the transmission from the upper layers.
Network	Determines best path for packet delivery across the network.
	Determines logical addressing, which can identify the destination of a packet or datagram.
	Uses data packets (IP, IPX) and route update packets (RIP, EIGRP, and so on).
	Uses routed protocols IP, IPX, and AppleTalk DDP.
	Devices include routers and Layer 3 switches.
Data Link	Ensures reliable data transfer from the Network layer to the Physical layer.
	Oversees physical or hardware addressing.
	Formats packets into a frame.
	Provides error notification.
	Devices include bridges and Layer 2 switches.
Physical	Moves bits between nodes.
	Assists with the activation, maintenance, and deactivation of physical connectivity between devices.
	Devices include hubs and repeaters.

TCP/IP Model

Objectives:

▶ Use the OSI and TCP/IP models and their associated protocols to explain how data flows in a network

▶ Describe common networked applications including web applications

▶ Describe the purpose and basic operation of the protocols in the OSI and TCP models

▶ Determine the path between two hosts across a network

The TCP/IP model, also known as the Department of Defense (DoD) model, was created by the DoD when they developed the TCP/IP protocol suite. Their goal was to provide reliable networking and data integrity in the event of a disaster. This model is prevalent in the current networking community. Although the OSI model is rarely used (except for the terminology), TCP/IP communications are ingrained in today's networking fabric and are a focal point on the CCENT exam.

NOTE

So far, the Internet has been a great example of an internetwork and a WAN. It's also a great example of the TCP/IP protocol suite at work.

Essentially the TCP/IP model has many similarities to the OSI model. Table 1.8 lists the layers of the OSI model in the left column and the related layers of the TCP/IP model in the right.

TABLE 1.8   Layers of the OSI and TCP/IP Models

OSI Layer	TCP/IP Layer
Application Presentation Session	Application
Transport	Transport
Network	Internet
Data Link	Network Access
Physical	

Application Layer

This layer combines functionalities of the three top layers of the OSI model and may also be called the Process/Application layer. Also, some of the most popular applications (email, file transport, and so on) interface with this layer to communicate with other applications on the network.

If you'll remember, the description of the Application layer of the OSI model included a list of application protocols and their primary functions. (Refer to Table 1.3.) These applications are also relative to the Application layer of the TCP/IP model.

Table 1.9 provides a quick list of the protocols at their respective layers of the TCP/IP model.

TABLE 1.9   Protocols for Each Layer of the TCP/IP Model

TCP/IP Layer	Protocols			
Application	Telnet	HTTP/HTTPS	FTP	TFTP
	DNS	SMTP	POP3	NFS
	NNTP	SNMP	NTP	DHCP

TABLE 1.9 *Continued*

TCP/IP Layer	Protocols			
Transport	TCP		UDP	
Internet	ICMP	ARP	RARP	IP
Network Interface	Ethernet	Fast Ethernet	Token Ring	FDDI

Transport Layer

The Transport layer corresponds with the Transport layer of the OSI model and is also known as the Host-to-Host layer. Not only is this layer responsible for reliable data delivery, but it can also make certain that data arrives in the proper order. You will see two transport layer protocols on the CCENT exam. These protocols are TCP and UDP. The following sections cover each protocol and its related applications.

TCP

TCP is a reliable connection-oriented protocol. TCP uses acknowledgments, sequencing, and flow control to ensure reliability (please refer back to the "Transport Layer" section of the OSI model for definitions of these terms). A TCP segment contains fields for the Sequence, Acknowledgment, and Windowing numbers. These fields help make sure that datagrams arrive undamaged. This is considered to be reliable delivery.

TCP uses Positive Acknowledgment and Retransmission (PAR):

▶ The source device begins a timer when a segment is sent and retransmits if the timer runs out before an acknowledgment is received.

▶ The source device keeps track of segments that are sent and requires an acknowledgment for each segment.

▶ The destination device acknowledges when a segment is received by sending a packet to the source that iterates the next sequence number it is looking for from the source.

Figure 1.4 shows the TCP segment header format.

Source Port	Destination Port
Sequence Number	
Acknowledgement Number	
Miscellaneous Flags	Window (Flow Control)
Checksum	Urgent
Options	

FIGURE 1.4 TCP segment header format.

Flow control via TCP includes *windowing*. Windowing is a method for traffic congestion control where a window is determined by the receiving system to limit the number of data segments (bytes) that can be sent by the source device without an acknowledgment from the recipient. The size of a window determines the number of unacknowledged data segments allowed by the receiving system. Window sizes vary and can change throughout the duration of a connection. Increasing a window size enables more data segments to be transmitted to the recipient before acknowledgment, whereas decreasing the window size allows for fewer data segments to be transmitted before an acknowledgment is sent.

As mentioned at the beginning of this section, TCP is a connection-oriented protocol. When a source device is ready to transmit data, it sets up a Connection-Oriented Communication session with the intended recipient. This is a *call setup* or a *three-way handshake*. When the data is successfully transmitted, a call termination occurs to disconnect the virtual circuit.

The three-way handshake includes the following steps:

1. A "connection agreement" segment is sent to the recipient asking to synchronize systems. This step is associated with the term *SYN packet*.

2. The second and third segments acknowledge the request to connect and determine the rules of engagement. Sequencing synchronization is requested of the receiving device. A two-way connection is established. This step is associated with the term *SYN-ACK packet*.

3. A final segment is sent as an acknowledgment that the rules have been accepted and a connection has been formed. This step is associated with the term *ACK packet*.

For the exam, you may also be asked to identify the applications that use TCP and their respective port numbers. Both TCP and UDP use port numbers. Public applications are assigned port numbers below 256. Numbers 256-1023 are allocated to companies. Numbers above 1023 are dynamically assigned by an application. Access lists can use port numbers to filter traffic. Table 1.10 lists applications that use TCP.

TABLE 1.10   Applications Using TCP

Application	Port Number(s)
FTP	20,21
Telnet	23
SMTP	25
DNS (zone transfers)	53

TABLE 1.10 *Continued*

Application	Port Number(s)
HTTP	80
POP3	110
NNTP	119
HTTPS	443

UDP is the other protocol that is used at the Transport layer of the TCP/IP model.

UDP

UDP is much simpler than TCP because it is a connectionless protocol. UDP headers contain only the source and destination ports, a length field, and a checksum. Because of the lack of a sequence, acknowledgment, and windowing field, UDP cannot guarantee delivery. Because there are no delivery guarantees, UDP is considered unreliable. With this protocol, it is up to the application to provide reliability. Figure 1.5 shows a UDP segment header.

Source Port	Destination Port
Length	Checksum

FIGURE 1.5 The UDP header.

On the plus side, UDP is considerably cheaper to implement and has faster transfer rates. Table 1.11 lists the applications that use UDP.

TABLE 1.11 **Applications Using UDP**

Application	Port Number(s)
DHCP	67,68
DNS (name resolution)	53
TFTP	69
NTP	123
SNMP	161

> **NOTE**
>
> DHCP uses UDP as its transport layer protocol. UDP port number 67 identifies the DHCP server port, while UDP port number 68 identifies the DHCP client port.

EXAM ALERT

Note that DNS is listed for both TCP and UDP because it can be used with both protocols. With TCP, DNS is used for zone transfers and with UDP, it is used for name resolution.

Challenge

As mentioned in the TCP section of this chapter, knowing the applications that use TCP and UDP is important for the CCENT exam. It is also important that you know which port number is assigned to each application. Fill in the blanks that are given in each of the following tables. You may reference Tables 1.10 and 1.11, but I strongly suggest that you keep using these charts until you have this information memorized.

Applications Using TCP

Application	Port Number(s)

Applications Using UDP

Application	Port Number(s)

Internet Layer

The Internet layer corresponds with the Network layer of the OSI model.

The following protocols relate to the logical transmission of packets:

- ▶ IP
- ▶ ICMP
- ▶ ARP, RARP, and Proxy ARP

IP

IP uses logical or virtual addressing to get a packet from a source to its destination. IP addresses are used by routers to make forwarding decisions.

Some key characteristics of IP addresses include the following:

- ▶ Addresses are allocated by the Internet Assigned Numbers Authority (IANA).
- ▶ IPv4 IP addresses are 32 bits, divided into four octets (8 bits each). An example of an IP address in dotted decimal format would be 172.16.122.204.
- ▶ The minimum value (per octet) is 0 and the maximum value is 255.
- ▶ IPv6, which is the future of IP addresses, is 128 bits.

Figure 1.6 shows the data fields that make up an IP datagram.

Version	Length	Service Type	Total Length
Identification		Flags	Fragment Offset
Time to Live	Protocol	Header Checksum	
Source IP Address			
Destination IP Address			
IP Options (optional)		Padding	
Data			

FIGURE 1.6 IP datagram.

NOTE

IP addressing is a topic discussed with additional detail in Chapter 5.

ICMP

Internet Control Messaging Protocol is used by ping and traceroute utilities.

Ping (Packet Internet Groper) enables you to validate that an IP address exists and can accept requests. The following transmissions are used by the Ping utility:

▶ Ping sends an echo request packet to receive the echo response.

▶ Routers send Destination Unreachable messages when they can't reach the destination network and they are forced to drop the packet. The router that drops the packet sends the ICMP DU message.

The following is an example of a successful ping test run from a computer command prompt:

```
C:\Documents and Settings>ping 10.0.0.1

Pinging 10.0.0.1 with 32 bytes of data:

Reply from 10.1.1.1: bytes=32 time<1ms TTL=255
Reply from 10.1.1.1: bytes=32 time<1ms TTL=255
Reply from 10.1.1.1: bytes=32 time<1ms TTL=255
Reply from 10.1.1.1: bytes=32 time<1ms TTL=255

Ping statistics for 10.0.0.1:
    Packets: Sent = 4, Received = 4, Lost = 0 (0% loss),
Approximate round trip times in milli-seconds:
    Minimum = 0ms, Maximum = 0ms, Average = 0ms
```

The following is an example of an unsuccessful ping test run from a computer command prompt:

```
C:\Documents and Settings>ping 10.0.0.2

Pinging 10.0.0.2 with 32 bytes of data:

Request timed out.
Request timed out.
Request timed out.
Request timed out.

Ping statistics for 10.0.0.2:
    Packets: Sent = 4, Received = 0, Lost = 4 (100% loss)
```

EXAM ALERT

Ping is used at the Internet layer of the TCP/IP model and network layer of the OSI model.

Traceroute traces the route or path taken from a client to a remote host. Traceroute also reports the IP addresses of the routers at each next hop on the way to the destination. This is especially useful when you suspect that a router on the route to an unreachable network is responsible for dropping the packet.

> **NOTE**
>
> Extended ping enables you to select a datagram size and a timeout.

ARP, RARP, and Proxy ARP

The Address Resolution Protocol (ARP), Reverse Address Resolution Protocol (RARP), and Proxy Address Resolution Protocol (Proxy ARP) are all protocols used at the TCP/IP model's Internet layer.

ARP maps a known IP address to a MAC address by sending a broadcast ARP. When the destination IP address is on another subnet, the sender broadcasts ARP for the router's ethernet port or default gateway, so the MAC address sent back is that of the router's ethernet port.

RARP maps a known MAC address to an IP address.

Proxy ARP enables a router to respond to an ARP request that has been sent to a remote host. Some Unix machines (especially Solaris) rely on Proxy ARP versus default gateways.

Network Interface Layer

This layer corresponds with the Data Link and Physical layers of the OSI model. As mentioned earlier in the chapter, this layer manages hardware addressing and physical data transfer.

Cisco 3-Layer Hierarchical Model

When I think of the word *hierarchy* outside the realm of networking, I think of the military. Each branch of the military has a list of ranks that is assigned to each soldier. In the Army for example, the ranks range from an enlisted private all the way up to the General of the Army. Each soldier reports to a higher-ranking soldier, and each rank has its own group of functions and responsibilities, much like the layers of the Cisco hierarchical model.

The term *hierarchy* as it pertains to this model is the classification of a group of functions or responsibilities into a logical layer where each layer is subordinate to the layer above it in the hierarchy. This model is most effective when you plan to implement a small- to moderate-sized network.

The following sections start from the bottom and work up through the ranks to the top of the hierarchy. First though, take a look Figure 1.7 for an example of the Cisco hierarchical model in its entirety.

FIGURE 1.7 Cisco hierarchical model.

Access Layer

End users are connected at the Access layer; therefore, this layer may also be referred to as the *desktop* layer. These end users may also be combined to form a workgroup. Virtual LAN (VLAN) workgroups are defined by virtual access lists or filter lists at the Access layer to allow for a continuation of the policies implemented at the Distribution layer. This functionality further controls internetwork resource access granted to each end user or workgroup. Users may access locally available resources at this level or they may be directed to the Distribution layer to access remotely available resources.

Distribution Layer

In the hierarchy, the Distribution layer is the middle man between the access and core layers. You may also hear this layer called the *workgroup* layer. Although the Distribution layer acts as a gathering point for the Access layer devices, it also uses a router or Layer 3 switch whenever necessary to determine how to traverse packets to the core layer.

You achieve traffic control at this layer by using various policies that ultimately provide network management and security.

Primary functions of the Distribution layer include the following:

- ▶ Routing (best path determination)
- ▶ Routing between VLANs
- ▶ Filtering—Access lists provide packet filtering, Quality of Service (QoS), network address translation (NAT), and route filtering
- ▶ Accessing WAN
- ▶ Defining broadcast and multicast domains
- ▶ Translating between different types of media (for example, ethernet and token ring)

EXAM ALERT

Chapter 6, "Introduction to Cisco Routers and Switches," reviews Cisco routers and switches that may be used at the Distribution layer. The 2600 series Cisco routers and 4000 series Cisco switches are included in that chapter.

Core Layer

The Core layer is the foundation or backbone of the network. Much like a building would falter without its foundation, a network would fall apart without the structure provided by the core layer. As mentioned before, the Distribution layer manages access to the core. This enables the core to focus on speed and reliability. The goal is to provide high-speed switching as quickly and efficiently as possible. Any latency or delay can affect everyone on that network. Because speed is of the essence, the policies implemented at the Distribution layer (for example, filtering, access lists, and so on) should not occur at the Core layer.

Redundancy and fault tolerance are also important to the successful design of a core. If a network is set up with full redundancy, any failures should be transparent to the end user, which is the definition of a fault tolerant network.

NOTE

You might see Enterprise servers (server farms) connected to the core. Devices used at the core layer may include the Catalyst 6500 series switch or the 7000 series routers. These devices also are reviewed in Chapter 6.

If you were tasked with the design of a new network, would you select a Layer 2 core or a Layer 3 core? Although the Layer 2 core consists of a switched hierarchical setup, a Layer 3 core consists of a routed hierarchical setup.

The answer depends upon the individual requirements of the company in question. If the primary requirement is speed, perhaps a Layer 2 core is appropriate. If a stated desire is the additional network control that is available with a routed solution, then a Layer 3 core would fit the bill.

EXAM ALERT

Remember that routers segment broadcast domains (Layer 3 core) while switches segment collision domains (Layer 2 core).

Challenge

This chapter discusses three different layered models, including the Cisco 3-Layer Hierarchical model. To enhance your understanding of network communications with a layered architecture, please list each layer of the hierarchical model in the correct order and also list its primary responsibilities.

Layer Name	Layer Responsibilities

Although the hierarchical model is typically mentioned in published reviews for the CCENT examination, Cisco also created the Enterprise Composite Network Model (ECNM) for larger-scale network implementations.

The hierarchical model can assist in the implementation of a small- to moderate-sized network. The composite model goes a step further and provides a guide for creating a larger network. Because Cisco has a group of topics listed as "Planning and Designing," it is important to have a general knowledge of their models for network design.

Chapter Summary

The term *internetworking* signifies the industry, products, and processes that are required to handle the challenges of interconnecting networks. Various internetworks can be used, depending on the user's specific needs. For example, a LAN is a small network that is confined to a local geographical area. A LAN can connect to another LAN via a switch, bridge, or repeater. If a LAN attempts to connect to a MAN or WAN, it needs to interconnect via a router. WANs are much larger in scope. WANs are good for a company that has offices in multiple cities around the country. LAN and WAN technology are discussed in greater detail in later chapters of this book.

This chapter also discusses the importance of layered reference models such as the OSI model, TCP/IP model, and the Cisco 3-Layer Hierarchical model. The OSI model is important to discussions of internetworking because the terminology related to each layer has endured the test of time. Seven layers essentially map out the transmission of data from one end-user system to another. Multiple protocols relate to the interoperation of each layer. Special focus is placed on the Application layer protocols and their primary functions.

The TCP/IP model is implemented in a large portion of the networks that are set up today. The model is a condensed version of the OSI model with four related layers. The two most important protocols discussed in the TCP/IP suite for this first chapter are TCP and UDP. TCP is a connection-oriented protocol that provides for reliable data transport. UDP is a connectionless protocol that is considered unreliable. There are advantages and disadvantages to each protocol. Although TCP is reliable, it also costs more to implement on a network.

Overall, this chapter was designed to provide a general overview of standard internetworks and the layered architecture that was designed to represent network interactions. Now that you have gone over all of the internetworking models that are relevant to the exam, you are ready to move on to Chapter 2 and review the concepts related to networking at the Physical layer.

Key Terms

- ▶ Internetwork
- ▶ LAN
- ▶ MAN
- ▶ WAN
- ▶ SAN
- ▶ VPN
- ▶ OSI model

- ▶ Application layer
- ▶ Telnet
- ▶ HTTP
- ▶ HTTPS
- ▶ FTP
- ▶ TFTP
- ▶ DNS
- ▶ SMTP
- ▶ POP3
- ▶ NFS
- ▶ NNTP
- ▶ SNMP
- ▶ NTP
- ▶ DHCP
- ▶ Presentation layer
- ▶ Session layer
- ▶ NFS
- ▶ SQL
- ▶ RPC
- ▶ ASP
- ▶ X Window
- ▶ DNA SCP
- ▶ Transport layer
- ▶ Segment
- ▶ Acknowledgment
- ▶ Sequencing
- ▶ Flow control
- ▶ Buffers
- ▶ Network layer

- ▶ Packet
- ▶ Datagram
- ▶ Data packets
- ▶ Route update packets
- ▶ Data Link layer
- ▶ Broadcast domain
- ▶ Collision domain
- ▶ CSMA/CD
- ▶ Grame
- ▶ MAC
- ▶ MAC address
- ▶ LLC
- ▶ Ridge
- ▶ Switch
- ▶ Physical layer
- ▶ Hub
- ▶ Repeater
- ▶ Bit
- ▶ DCE
- ▶ DTE
- ▶ CSU/DSU
- ▶ Encapsulation
- ▶ PDU
- ▶ TCP/IP model
- ▶ TCP/IP
- ▶ TCP
- ▶ PAR
- ▶ Windowing
- ▶ UDP

▶ IP

▶ ICMP

▶ ARP

▶ RARP

▶ Proxy ARP

▶ Cisco 3-Layer Hierarchical model

▶ VLAN

▶ Routing

▶ Filtering

▶ Packet filtering

▶ Route filtering

▶ QoS

▶ NAT

Apply Your Knowledge

Exercises

1.1 OSI Layered Model Identification

This has been mentioned throughout the chapter, but it is extremely important for the CCENT exam to know the seven layers of the OSI model and their general functions. If you have not decided on a mnemonic device that you like, you may want to take another look because most people find them to be very helpful with this type of exercise.

Estimated Time: 10 minutes

List the name of the appropriate layer next to the number listed and then identify two primary functions of that layer. Refer to Table 1.7 to check your responses.

1. _____Layer

Functions: _____

2. _____Layer

Functions: _____

3. _____Layer

Functions: _____

4. _____Layer

Functions: _____

5. _____Layer

Functions: _____

6. _____Layer

Functions: _____

7. _____Layer

Functions: _____

Review Questions

1. Briefly list the communication application protocols that are used at the Application layer of the OSI model and what service they provide.

2. Describe how information is passed through the layers of the OSI model.

3. Define Positive Acknowledgments and Retransmission (PAR).

4. Describe the steps involved in a three-way handshake.

5. List the differences between TCP and UDP.

6. List the key functionalities of the Access layer of the Cisco hierarchical model.

7. List the key functionalities of the Distribution layer of the Cisco hierarchical model.

8. List the key functionalities of the Core layer of the Cisco hierarchical model.

Exam Questions

1. What information can DHCP provide to clients? (Choose the three best answers.)

    ○ **A.** Clock information

    ○ **B.** IP information

    ○ **C.** DNS information

    ○ **D.** Gateway information

2. Which of the protocols are used by email? (Choose the two best answers.)

    ○ **A.** POP3

    ○ **B.** SMTP

    ○ **C.** SNMP

    ○ **D.** DHCP

3. What takes place when a collision occurs on an ethernet network? (Choose the three best answers.)

    ○ **A.** Every device stops transmitting for a short time.

    ○ **B.** A jam signal is sent to notify devices of a collision.

    ○ **C.** A collision signal is sent to notify devices of a collision.

    ○ **D.** A random back-off algorithm starts.

4. What is the OUI of the MAC address 01:AB:4D:F2:89:10?

    ○ **A.** 01

    ○ **B.** F2:89:10

    ○ **C.** 01:AB

    ○ **D.** 01:AB:4D

5. A MAC address is… (Choose the two best answers.)

    ○ **A.** A unique hardware address in a broadcast domain

    ○ **B.** A unique IP address in a broadcast domain

    ○ **C.** Provided by the manufacturer of the NIC

    ○ D. Configured manually by the network administrator

6. At what layer of the OSI model do you find MAC addresses?

    ○ **A.** Transport

    ○ **B.** Network

    ○ **C.** Data Link

    ○ **D.** Physical

7. At what layer of the OSI model do you find sequence numbers?

    ○ **A.** Application

    ○ **B.** Presentation

◯   **C.**   Session

◯   **D.**   Transport

8. At what layer of the OSI model do you find IP addresses?

    ◯   **A.**   Transport

    ◯   **B.**   Network

    ◯   **C.**   Data Link

    ◯   **D.**   Physical

9. What kind of PDU is used at the Data Link layer of the OSI model?

    ◯   **A.**   Bit

    ◯   **B.**   Segment

    ◯   **C.**   Packet/Datagram

    ◯   **D.**   Frame

10. What kind of PDU is used at the Network layer of the OSI model?

    ◯   **A.**   Segment

    ◯   **B.**   Packet/Datagram

    ◯   **C.**   Bit

    ◯   **D.**   Frame

11. What kind of PDU is used at the Transport layer of the OSI model?

    ◯   **A.**   Segment

    ◯   **B.**   Data

    ◯   **C.**   Frame

    ◯   **D.**   Bit

12. What is the correct order for data encapsulation?

    ◯   **A.**   Segment, packet, frame, data, bit

    ◯   **B.**   Data, segment, packet, frame, bit

    ◯   **C.**   Bit, frame, packet, segment, data

    ◯   **D.**   Data, packet, segment, frame, bit

13. Routers look at the _____ when making a routing decision.

   ○ **A.** Destination IP address

   ○ **B.** Source IP address

   ○ **C.** Destination MAC address

   ○ **D.** Source MAC address

14. What protocol is assigned to port numbers 20 and 21?

   ○ **A.** DNS

   ○ **B.** Telnet

   ○ **C.** FTP

   ○ **D.** SMTP

15. What protocol is assigned to port number 80?

   ○ **A.** SNMP

   ○ **B.** HTTP

   ○ **C.** POP3

   ○ **D.** DHCP

16. Which of the following are TCP? (Choose the two best answers.)

   ○ **A.** Telnet

   ○ **B.** HTTP

   ○ **C.** TFTP

   ○ **D.** NTP

17. Which of the following are UDP? (Choose the two best answers.)

   ○ **A.** DHCP

   ○ **B.** SMTP

   ○ **C.** SNMP

   ○ **D.** POP3

18. What commands use ICMP? (Choose the two best answers.)

   ○ **A.** Show cdp neighbor

   ○ **B.** traceroute

    ○ **C.** Telnet

    ○ **D.** ping

19. What protocol maps a known MAC address to an IP address?

    ○ **A.** RARP

    ○ **B.** ARP

    ○ **C.** ICMP

    ○ **D.** Proxy ARP

20. What TCP/IP protocol provides terminal emulation to a remote host?

    ○ **A.** HTTP

    ○ **B.** VPN

    ○ **C.** Telnet

    ○ **D.** SNMP

Answers to Review Questions

1. The following is a list of the protocols utilized at the Application layer of the OSI model and the functionality of each protocol.

Telnet—Terminal emulation to a remote host

HTTP—Web-browsing service

HTTPS—Secure web browsing

FTP—File transfer

FTP—Bare-bones file transfer

DNS—Name management

SMTP—Send emails

POP3—Receive emails

NFS—File sharing

NNTP—Usenet newsgroups

SNMP—Network management

NTP—Time management

DHCP—Dynamic host configuration

2. The upper layers (Application, Presentation, and Session) pass data to the Transport layer. The Transport layer encapsulates the data into a segment that is handed down to the Network layer. The Network layer encapsulates the segment into a packet (or datagram) to be handed down to the Data Link layer. The Data Link layer encapsulates the packet (or datagram) into a frame and sends it to the Physical layer. The Physical layer then encapsulates the frame into a bit to be sent over the network.

3. Used by TCP, PAR is the process by which the source device begins a timer when a segment is sent and retransmits if the timer runs out before an acknowledgment is received. The source device keeps track of segments that are sent and requires an acknowledgment for each segment. The destination device acknowledges when a segment is received by sending a packet to the source that iterates the next sequence number for which it is looking from the source.

4. First, a connection agreement segment is sent to the recipient asking to synchronize systems. Second, a second and third segment acknowledge the request to connect and determine the rules of engagement. Sequencing synchronization is requested of the receiving device. A two-way connection is established. Third, a final segment is sent as an acknowledgment that the rules have been accepted and a connection has been formed.

5. The following table lists comparisons of the key characteristics of the TCP and UDP protocols.

TCP	UDP
Uses sequenced data transmissions	Does not use sequenced data transmissions
Reliable protocol	Unreliable protocol
Connection-oriented	Connectionless
Expensive to implement	Inexpensive to implement
Sends acknowledgments	Does not send acknowledgments
Uses windowing flow control	Does not use windowing or flow control

6. The following list includes the key functionalities of the Access layer of the Cisco hierarchical model:

Desktop layer

End-user connectivity

Virtual LAN (VLAN) workgroup definition

Continuation of the policies implemented at the distribution layer by using virtual access lists or filter lists

User access to locally available resources

7. The following list includes the key functionalities of the Distribution layer of the Cisco hierarchical model:

Control layer

Middleman between the access and core layers

Acts as an aggregation point for access layer devices

Determines how and when to traverse packets to the core layer

Policy implementation

Network security

Routing (best path determination)

Routing between VLANs

Filtering

Access lists

Packet filtering

Quality of Service (QoS)

Network address translation (NAT)

Route filtering

WAN access

Defines broadcast and multicast domains

Translates between different types of media (i.e., ethernet and token ring)

8. The following list includes the key functionalities of the Core layer of the Cisco hierarchical model:

Backbone layer

The Distribution layer manages access to the core.

High-speed switching

Reliability

Redundancy

Fault tolerance

Low latency

Enterprise servers (server farms)

Answers to Exam Questions

1. **B, C, D.** DHCP works dynamically to provide IP address, DNS, and default gateway information. Answer A is incorrect because the Network Time Protocol (NTP) provides clock information.

2. **A, B.** POP3 receives email on an Internet server and SMTP sends email across a network. Answer C is incorrect because SNMP is a network management protocol and answer D is incorrect because DHCP is the dynamic host configuration protocol.

3. **A, B, D.** When a collision occurs on an ethernet network a jam signal is sent to notify devices of a collision and a random back-off algorithm starts while every device stops transmitting for a short time. Answer C is incorrect because a jam signal is sent rather than a collision signal.

4. **D.** The OUI of a MAC address is the organizationally unique identifier that is assigned by the manufacturer of the network interface card (NIC). The OUI consists of the first 6 hexadecimal digits. Answer A is incorrect because it only consists of 2 hexadecimal digits. Answer B is incorrect because it is not the first 6 hexadecimal digits of the MAC address 01:AB:4D:F2:89:10. Answer C is incorrect because it only consists of 4 hexadecimal digits.

5. **A, C.** The MAC address is a unique hardware address in the broadcast domain and the manufacturer of the NIC provides MAC addresses. Answer B is incorrect because IP addresses are logical addresses used by the Network layer. Answer D is incorrect because a MAC address is not configured manually by a network administrator.

6. **C.** MAC addresses are found at the Data Link layer of the OSI model. Answers A, B, and D are incorrect because MAC addresses are not found at the Transport, Network, or Physical layer of the OSI model.

7. **D.** The Transport layer uses sequence numbers. Data segments are sequenced into their original order when they arrive at the destination. Answers A, B, and C are incorrect because sequence numbers are not found at the Application, Presentation, or Session layer of the OSI model.

8. **B.** Answer B is correct because IP addresses are found at the Network layer of the OSI model. IP addresses are logical or virtual addresses that are assigned at Layer 3 to identify the destination of a packet or datagram. Answers A, C, and D are incorrect because IP addresses are not found at the Transport, Data Link, or Physical layer of the OSI model.

9. **D.** The Data Link layer uses frame PDUs to encapsulate data. Answers A, B, and C are incorrect because segments are used at the Transport layer, whereas packet/datagrams are used at the Network layer and bits are used by the Physical layer of the OSI model.

10. **B.** The Network layer of the OSI model uses packets/datagrams. Answers A, C, and D are incorrect because the Application, Presentation, and Session layers of the OSI model transmit data.

11. **A.** Segments are used at the Transport layer of the OSI model. Answer B is incorrect because the three upper layers of the OSI model transmit data. Answer C is incorrect because the Data Link layer transmits frames, and answer D is incorrect because the Physical layer transmits bits.

12. **B.** Encapsulation occurs from the Application layer and then is passed down through the lower layers of the OSI model. The PDUs are sent by the Application layer as data and then they are encapsulated with a segment at the Transport layer. At the Network layer, the segment is encapsulated into a packet/datagram that is passed down to the Data Link layer, which encapsulates a frame and hands it off to the Physical layer, which uses bits.

13. **A.** Routers look at the destination IP address to determine where to forward the packet. Answers B, C, and D are incorrect because a router does not examine the source IP address, destination MAC address, or source MAC address to make forwarding decisions.

14. **C.** FTP is assigned to port numbers 20 and 21. Answers A, B, and D are incorrect because Telnet is assigned port number 23, DNS is assigned port number 53, and SMTP is assigned port number 25.

15. **B.** HTTP is assigned port number 80. Answers A, C, and D are incorrect because SNMP is assigned port number 161, POP3 is port number 110, and DHCP is assigned ports 67 and 68.

16. **A, B.** Telnet and HTTP are both protocols that use TCP. Answers C and D are incorrect because TFTP and NTP use UDP.

17. **A, C.** DHCP and SNMP use UDP, whereas answers B and D are incorrect because SMTP and POP3 use TCP.

18. **B, D.** Traceroute and ping are both commands that use ICMP. Traceroute traces the route or path taken from a client to a remote host. Ping enables you to validate that an IP address exists and can accept requests. Answers A and C are incorrect because neither show cdp neighbor nor Telnet use ICMP.

19. **A**. RARP maps MAC addresses to an IP address, whereas answer B is incorrect because ARP maps an IP address to a MAC address. Answer C is incorrect because ICMP sends messages across the network via ping, and traceroute enables a router to respond to an ARP request that has been sent to a remote host. Answer D is also incorrect because some Unix machines (especially Solaris) rely on Proxy ARP rather than default gateways.

20. **C.** Telnet provides for terminal emulation to a remote host. Answers A, B, and D are incorrect because HTTP is a web-browsing application, VPN is a private network that can access public networks remotely, and SNMP is a network management application.

Suggested Readings and Resources

The following are some recommended readings on the subject of standard internetworking models:

1. "Open Systems Interconnection Protocols," http://www.cisco.com/univercd/cc/td/doc/cisintwk/ito_doc/osi_prot.htm.

2. "OSI Model," http://en.wikipedia.org/wiki/OSI_model.

3. "TCP/IP Overview," http://www.cisco.com/univercd/cc/td/doc/cisintwk/ito_doc/osi_prot.htm.

4. "TechEncyclopedia," www.techweb.com/encyclopedia.

CHAPTER TWO

Physical Layer Networking Concepts

Objectives

This chapter covers the following Cisco-specified objectives from the "Describe the operation of data networks" and "Implement a small switched network" sections of the 640-822 ICND1 exam:

▶ **Interpret network diagrams**

▶ **Select the appropriate media, cables, ports, and connectors to connect switches to other network devices and hosts**

▶ **Describe the purpose and functions of various network devices**

Outline

Introduction   54

Network Topologies   54

  The Bus Topology   54
  The Ring Topology   55
  The Star Topology   56
  The Mesh Topology   57

Cabling   58

  Coaxial Cable   59
  Twisted-Pair Cable   60
    Straight-Through Cable   61
    Cross-Over Cable   62
    Rolled Cable   63
  Fiber-Optic Cable   63

Wireless   64

  Wireless Fidelity (Wi-Fi)   65
  Infrared   65
  Bluetooth   66

Physical Layer Devices   66

  Repeaters   66
  Hubs   67
  Network Interfaces   67

Chapter Summary   68

  Key Terms   68

Apply Your Knowledge   69

  Exercises   69
  Review Questions   70
  Exam Questions   70
  Answers to Review Questions   77
  Answers to Exam Questions   77

Suggested Readings and Resources   79

Study Strategies

▶ Identify the four physical network topologies discussed in this chapter.

▶ Know the different types of network cables and the characteristics that differentiate them from one another.

▶ Review the wireless technology standards.

▶ Be able to identify devices that are used at the Physical layer.

Introduction

Chapter 1, "Standard Internetworking Models," went over the layers of the OSI and TCP/IP models. This chapter goes into more detail regarding the Physical layer. Remember that electrical, mechanical, procedural, and functional requirements are defined at this layer. Such requirements provide assistance with the activation, maintenance, and deactivation of physical connectivity between devices.

Concepts covered include the topologies, cabling, and devices that are relevant at the physical level and important to understand when studying for the ICND1 exam. Also, because wireless communications are constantly evolving and are flourishing in today's marketplace, several significant wireless technologies are covered as well.

Network Topologies

Objective:

▶ Interpret network diagrams

Topology can be defined as either the physical or logical layout of a network. Typically, a physical topology is documented with a network diagram, such as a Visio diagram. Diagrams can prove to be extremely helpful when troubleshooting a network issue. Most companies keep a database with copies of their entire network as well as individual site connections. If you work in a sales capacity, diagrams are drawn up to plan out the network setup and to ensure that all bases are covered to meet customer expectations.

Just as you might imagine, a physical topology consists of the cables, workstations, and other peripheral devices that comprise the network. A logical topology refers to how the network actually communicates. This may differ from the physical topology; therefore, this section covers the four most common physical network topologies and what the associated logical network topology is for the physical star network.

The Bus Topology

A *bus network* topology may also be referred to as a *linear bus* topology. This topology is set up so that the network nodes are connected via a single cable (also referred to as a *trunk* or a *backbone*). Electrical signals are sent from one end of the cable to the other. When this occurs, all connected devices receive that electrical signal transmission. Network devices are connected directly to the trunk with a T connector. Both ends of the trunk use a terminator to stop the electrical signal from echoing back down the cable. Figure 2.1 represents a physical bus topology.

Because the bus topology uses a single cable, it is a low-cost option that is easily implemented. The downside to this setup is the lack of redundancy. If the cable breaks, the entire network goes down.

FIGURE 2.1 Example of a physical bus topology.

The Ring Topology

A *ring network* topology is set up so that one device is directly connected to two other devices on the same network. When a device emits a data signal transmission, the transmission is sent in a single direction to the next connected device. The transmission continues to pass along each device successively until it arrives back at the original transmitting device. This method creates a ring or a loop. Figure 2.2 shows an example of a physical ring topology.

FIGURE 2.2 Example of a physical ring topology.

With this topology, a single ring configuration lacks a failover solution. If there is a break anywhere on the ring, it brings down the entire network. This was the same situation with the bus network topology. For this reason, you may also configure a dual ring topology. If there is a failure on one physical ring, the other physical ring passes data transmissions to ensure network operability. Figure 2.3 shows an example of a physical dual ring network topology.

FIGURE 2.3 Example of a physical dual ring topology.

The Star Topology

The *star network* topology is the most commonly implemented network design. With this topology, there is a central device with separate connections to each end node. Each connection uses a separate cable, which adds to the cost of implementation. When hubs are used in a star topology, a logical bus is created. This type of network star is called a hub-and-spoke topology. Figure 2.4 shows an example of a physical star topology.

Figure 2.4 Example of a physical star topology.

Because there are separate connections between end nodes and the central device, this topology enables the network administrator to add or remove end nodes without affecting service to all other nodes on that network. This is also possible with the token ring topology, which enables you to add multistation access units (MAUs) to the network without disrupting service. The same cannot be said for the physical bus network topologies.

The Mesh Topology

The full mesh network topology is set up so that each device is directly connected to every other device on the network. This connection method has built-in redundancy. If one link goes down, the device transmits via another link. Figure 2.5 shows an example of a physical full mesh topology.

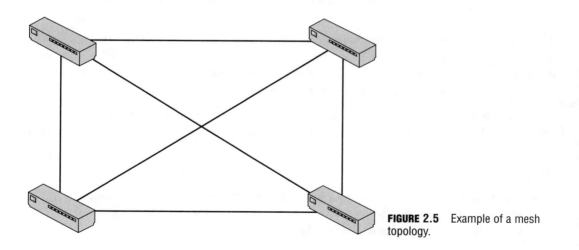

FIGURE 2.5   Example of a mesh topology.

A partial mesh network topology has direct connectivity between some of the network devices, but not all of them, as the full mesh topology does. Figure 2.6 shows an example of a physical partial mesh topology.

Overall, mesh topologies are much more expensive to implement. However, the cost may be acceptable given the reliability of this design.

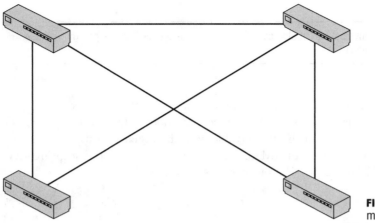

FIGURE 2.6   Example of a partial mesh topology.

Cabling

Objective:

▶ Select the appropriate media, cables, ports, and connectors to connect switches to other network devices and hosts

This section reviews the types of media or cable that are used for LAN connectivity. The primary media types include coaxial, twisted-pair, and fiber-optic cables. Cable media offer physical connectivity to network devices. Cables may consist of metal, glass, or plastic. Copper is the most popular metal cable. Fiber-optic uses glass or plastic cabling.

Before you look at each medium in greater detail, it's a good idea to discuss several important terms related to data transmission that are directly affected by what type of cable media is used on a network.

Review the following terminology:

▶ **Bandwidth**—The total amount of information that can traverse a communications medium, measured in bits per second. Measurement of bandwidth is helpful for network performance analysis. Also, availability is increasing but limited.

EXAM ALERT

For the exam, remember that bandwidth is used to analyze network performance and that although availability is increasing, it is also limited.

▶ **Attenuation**—Occurs over long distances as a signal loses strength.

▶ **Electromagnetic Interference (EMI)**—Interference or noise caused by electromagnetic signals, which can decrease data integrity.

▶ **Crosstalk**—An electrical or magnetic field originating from one communications signal that can affect the signal in a nearby circuit.

   ▶ **Near-end Crosstalk (NEXT)**—Crosstalk measured at the transmitting end of a cable.

   ▶ **Far-end Crosstalk (FEXT)**—Crosstalk measured at the far end of the cable from where the transmission was sent.

EXAM ALERT

Know the terms NEXT and FEXT and what they represent for the ICND1 exam.

Coaxial Cable

Coaxial cables for data consist of a single copper wire surrounded by a plastic insulation cover and a braided copper shield. Primarily, two types of coaxial cables are used in conjunction with Ethernet LAN networks. They are called *thin* and *thick coax*.

Thin coax has the following characteristics:

▶ Also called thinnet

▶ .25 inches in diameter

▶ Maximum cable length = 185 meters

▶ Uses Bayonet Neill Concelman connectors (BNCs)

▶ 10BASE-2 ethernet standard

NOTE

The Institute for Electrical and Electronics Engineers (IEEE) ethernet standards are reviewed in Chapter 3, "Data Link Networking Concepts."

Thick coax has the following characteristics:

▶ Also called thicknet

▶ Maximum cable length = 500 meters

▶ Uses vampire taps (where the tap goes through the shield to touch the copper wire)

▶ Uses attachment unit interface (AUI) adapters

▶ 10BASE-5 ethernet standard

The coaxial cable media is not nearly as popular as twisted pair or fiber optic. It is not as flexible or cost effective as other options. You may see this cable implemented on an older network.

Twisted-Pair Cable

Just as the name indicates, twisted-pair cables twist two wires together to form a pair. This solution helps to reduce interference and attenuation. There are two types of twisted-pair cabling defined by the Telecommunications Information Association (TIA). Those types are unshielded twisted pair (UTP) and shielded twisted pair (STP). UTP is the more common and cost-effective solution. STP has an additional shield, which provides additional reduction of interference and attenuation, but also makes it the more expensive solution. For the exam, UTP is reviewed in greater detail.

UTP key characteristics include the following:

▶ Eight color-coded wires

▶ Four pairs

▶ Uses an RJ-45 connector

▶ Vulnerable to EMI

▶ Maximum, practical length is 100 meters

▶ 10BASE-T, 100BaseT, and 1000BaseT ethernet standards

TIP

When reviewing for the exam, note that UTP is vulnerable to EMI and uses an RJ-45 connector.

EXAM ALERT

Because attenuation causes a signal to lose strength as the length of a cable increases, the maximum, practical length of a UTP cable is 100 meters.

UTP can be broken down into six more categories. You may have heard someone talk about a Cat5 cable. They are referring to a Category 5 UTP cable. Each category has different characteristics:

▶ **Category 1**—Telephone cable that is not used for data transmission.

▶ **Category 2**—Data cable that can handle speeds up to 4Mbps. This is no longer fast enough for networks today.

▶ **Category 3**—Data cable that can handle speeds up to 10Mbps. It is faster than the Cat2 cable, and this was quite popular until network speeds surpassed the 10Mbps threshold.

▶ **Category 4**—Data cable that can handle speeds up to 16Mbps. Meant to be used with token ring.

▶ **Category 5**—Data cable that can handle speeds up to 100Mbps. This is currently the most popular cable selection.

▶ **Category 5e**—Data cable that can handle speeds up to 1Gbps. This is a popular choice for Gigabit Ethernet networks.

▶ **Category 6**—This cable was created to exceed speeds of 1Gbps.

It is also important to know the pinouts for twisted-pair cables. The term *pinout* is used in the electronic industry to describe the purpose of each pin in a connector. When choosing your cable, you need to know which pinout is appropriate to connect the devices on your network. The following sections cover the straight-through and cross-over cables.

Straight-Through Cable

Straight-through cables use four wires and pins 1, 2, 3, and 6. Given those pins, pin 1 is connected on one end of the cable to pin 1 on the opposite end of the cable. Pin 2 at one end is connected to pin 2 on the far end, and so on. Figure 2.7 shows an example of a straight-through cable pinout.

These cables are meant only for interface to interface connections on ethernet networks, so you cannot use them with token ring, ISDN, and so on.

FIGURE 2.7 Example of a straight-through cable pinout.

Use a straight-through cable for the following connection types:

▶ From a PC to a switch or a hub

▶ From a router to a switch or a hub

TIP

For the ICND1 exam, you need to know which devices can be connected with a straight-through cable. Remember that straight-through cables are used to connect unlike device interfaces. Different devices = straight-through cable.

Cross-Over Cable

Cross-over cables also use four wires and pins 1, 2, 3, and 6. The difference is in how the pins are connected at each end. With cross-over cables, pin 1 connects to pin 3 and pin 2 connects to pin 6. Figure 2.8 shows an example of a cross-over cable pinout.

FIGURE 2.8 Example of a cross-over cable pinout.

Use a cross-over cable for the following connection types:

▶ From a switch to another switch

▶ From a router to another router

▶ From a PC to another PC

► From a PC to a router

► From a hub to another hub

► From a hub to a switch

TIP

For the ICND1 exam, you need to know which devices can be connected with a cross-over cable. Remember that for the most part, cross-over cables are used to connect similar device interfaces.

Rolled Cable

Rolled or rollover cables use eight wires and connect from a host to a console serial communications (com) port on a router. You may also hear this cable referred to as a *console cable*. Make sure not to confuse a rollover cable with a cross-over cable for the ICND1 exam.

Challenge

Knowing the type of twisted-pair cable that is used to connect one device to another is an important networking concept. If you use the wrong cable, you will not have a working connection. So in this challenge, I give you various connectivity scenarios, and you must decide whether you should use a straight-through or cross-over cable between the devices.

Connecting a...	Type of Cable
Switch to a switch	
Hub to a switch	
PC to a switch or hub	
PC to a PC	
Hub to a hub	
Router to a router	
PC to a router	
Router to a switch or hub	

Fiber-Optic Cable

Fiber-optic cables use light rather than electric signals to send data transmissions. These optical light signals travel a fiberglass core, and you may hear this technology referred to as *fiber optics* or *optical cabling*.

Two categories of fiber-optic cabling are

▶ *Multimode (MM)*—This is generally used for shorter distances and is ideal for a campus-sized network. MM also has a larger diameter of optical fiber than SM fiber.

▶ *Single-mode (SM)*—This mode is used to span longer distances. SM also allows for a higher data rate than MM and faster data transmission speeds.

Fiber-optic cables may use a subscriber connector (SC), straight tip (ST), or MegaTransfer-Registered Jack (MT-RJ) connector. There are several Layer 2 ethernet protocols that can pass data over fiber-optic cables. Those Layer 2 ethernet standards are 10BASE-FL, 100Base FX, 1000BaseSX, 1000BaseLX, and 1000BaseZX.

All in all, fiber is the best choice for a secure connection over longer distances. Because fiber uses optical light signals for data transmission, it is not as easy to "eavesdrop" on communications as it is with copper cabling using electrical signals. Fiber is not susceptible to EMI and crosstalk, as coaxial and twisted-pair cables are. It also offers the highest maximum speed of the different cable types. You may have already guessed, but fiber is also the most expensive option.

TIP

Fiber-optic cables are not susceptible to EMI.

On the ICND1 exam, you may see the terms *Main Distribution Frame (MDF)* and an *Intermediate Distribution Frame (IDF)*. A distribution frame is a physical rack that allows for the termination and interconnection of cables. This process creates network cross-connects. With that in mind, the MDF provides a point of interconnection between external telecommunications cabling and internal cabling in a facility. The IDF is the point of interconnection for cabling between the MDF and end-user devices.

Wireless

Wireless technology uses radio transmissions rather than data transmissions over copper wire or fiber-optic media. With wireless LANs (WLANs), a physical connection is no longer necessary. Electromagnetic energy, whose existence was proven way back in 1867, passes through the atmosphere in varied wavelengths. Different wavelengths are differentiated by their different names. Spread Spectrum WLANs determine how data traverses the Radio Frequency (RF) media. The most common applications for wireless technology are Wireless Fidelity, Infrared, and Bluetooth technologies. Because of the widespread popularity of wireless technology in business today, an entire section of this book is now devoted to wireless networking.

TIP

Keep in mind that Spread Spectrum WLANs allow for high-speed transmissions over short distances. There are two types of spread spectrum radio: Direct Sequencing Spread Spectrum (DSSS) and Frequency-Hopping Spread Spectrum (FHSS).

Wireless Fidelity (Wi-Fi)

IEEE created the 802.11 designation as the standard for wireless networking. IEEE 802.11 may be further defined by three more specific standards: 802.11a, 802.11b, and 802.11g. The speed, distance, and features of 802.11 specifications are variable. The most common of these specifications is the 802.11b standard, which may also be referred to as Wireless Fidelity (Wi-Fi) or High Rate 802.11. IEEE 802.11b can allow for transmission speeds of up to 1–2Mbps. It also uses a Radio Frequency (RF) of 2.4GHz.

> **TIP**
>
> For the ICND1 exam, remember that the 802.11b standard is also known as Wi-Fi or High Rate 802.11.

802.11 can also be broken down again into the following wireless standards:

- ▶ 802.11a
  - ▶ RF is 5GHz.
  - ▶ Speed up to 54Mbps.
  - ▶ Range of transmission is generally lower than that of 802.11g.
- ▶ 802.11b
  - ▶ RF is 2.4GHz.
  - ▶ Uses different channels to cover subfrequencies in the 2.4Ghz band.
  - ▶ Speed up to 11Mbps.
  - ▶ Range of transmission is generally greater than that of 802.11a and 802.11g.
- ▶ 802.11g
  - ▶ RF is 2.4GHz.
  - ▶ Speed up to 54Mbps.
  - ▶ Range of transmission is generally lower than that of 802.11b.

Based on these summarizations, you can see the similarities and differences of each standard. Please note that only 802.11a uses a different RF. This means that 802.11a is not compatible with either 802.11b or 802.11g.

Infrared

Infrared resides in a region of the electromagnetic spectrum just beyond the red end of our visible spectrum. Infrared wireless technology uses infrared beams to pass data across a network. Your television remote uses infrared technology to send requests to the television set. Speeds can reach a maximum of 16Mbps and signals are used for short-distance communications.

Infrared can eliminate the need for those pesky cables that connect your keyboard or mouse to your PC and cause clutter in your workspace. On the other hand, infrared may be easily refracted or reflected so it should not be used near windows or glass objects.

Bluetooth

Bluetooth technology utilizes a short-range wireless radio connection to enable various devices to interconnect. Such devices include cell phones, PCs, and Personal Digital Assistants (PDAs). The only requirement to establish connectivity is a 10-meter range (approximately 33 feet) between communicating devices. When in range, Bluetooth uses an RF link in the 2.4GHz range that has a 720Kbps per channel capacity to transfer voice or data. The Bluetooth specification also has two power levels defined; a lower power level that covers the shorter personal area within a room, and a higher power level that can cover a medium range like the range within a home.

Physical Layer Devices

Objective:

▶ Describe the purpose and functions of various network devices

The discussion so far of physical layer networking concepts has gone over the physical network topologies, cables, and wireless technology standards. Several network devices also are utilized at the Physical layer. Those include repeaters, hubs, and network interfaces.

Repeaters

Chapter 1, with its discussion of the Physical layer, mentioned that repeaters and hubs extend a network rather than segment a network. In fact, repeaters were introduced to increase or extend the distance between end nodes. A repeater consists of a transmitter and a receiver. When a signal is received by the repeater, it amplifies the signal and then retransmits. This effectively enables the signal to travel over a greater distance.

Please note that repeaters are an outdated technology. A separate device is no longer needed to perform this functionality. Both active hubs and switches can be used in place of a repeater.

Hubs

A *hub* can be defined as a multiple port repeater. A hub consists of 2 to 24 ports and may be called a *workgroup hub*. When data is received, the hub then retransmits that data out on all the other ports. Physical connectivity is achieved via a twisted-pair cable.

There are active and passive hubs. Active hubs have a separate power supply to assist with the gain of a signal before it is forwarded out all connected ports. *Gain* is an electrical term used to identify the ratio of signal output to signal input of a system. A power signal increased by a factor of 10 would indicate a gain of 10. Passive hubs do not regenerate the incoming signal.

Although they are very inexpensive, hubs may not be the best solution if you require a more efficient use of bandwidth and its distribution among ports. Traffic may become congested because of collisions on the network. Traffic is being forwarded out on all ports of a single collision domain. To decrease congestion, the network administrator might consider replacing the hub with a switch.

TIP

Know that a viable solution to decrease network congestion is replacing a hub with a switch. A switch creates a separate collision domain for each network segment, therefore increasing the number of collision domains.

EXAM ALERT

Hubs and repeaters are Layer 1 devices that can be used to increase the size of a single LAN segment.

Network Interfaces

A network interface provides connectivity from an end-user PC or laptop to the public network. Depending on the interface, you might see up to three light-emitting diodes (LEDs) that help to determine the connection's status. The link light LED should light up if you have connectivity. The activity light LED should flicker if there is activity on the line. There may also be a speed light LED that is used to verify the connection speed in a 10/100/1000Mbps network. Blinking lights and colors other than green can indicate error conditions that can be investigated by a technician.

Chapter Summary

Chapter 2 has taken the Physical layer and expanded the discussion to include physical network topologies and various network components. All these concepts are relevant when mapping out the design of a new network. Many of the topics in this chapter also touch upon ethernet technologies, which Chapter 3 continues to discuss, along with devices that are used at the Data Link layer.

Key Terms

- ▶ Physical topology
- ▶ Logical topology
- ▶ Bus topology
- ▶ Ring topology
- ▶ Dual ring topology
- ▶ Star topology
- ▶ Full mesh topology
- ▶ Partial mesh topology
- ▶ Bandwidth
- ▶ Attenuation
- ▶ EMI
- ▶ Crosstalk
- ▶ NEXT
- ▶ FEXT
- ▶ Coaxial cable
- ▶ Twisted-pair cable
- ▶ Unshielded twisted-pair cable
- ▶ Shielded twisted-pair cable
- ▶ Straight-through cable
- ▶ Cross-over cable
- ▶ Fiber-optic cable

- ► Multimode
- ► Single-mode
- ► Wireless fidelity
- ► 802.11
- ► 802.11a
- ► 802.11b
- ► 802.11g
- ► Infrared
- ► Bluetooth
- ► Repeaters
- ► Hubs
- ► Network interface

Apply Your Knowledge

Exercises

2.1 UTP Cable Categories

Each category of UTP cabling has different characteristics. In this exercise, please list the characteristics of each category of UTP cable.

Estimated Time: 10 minutes

UTP Category	Characteristics
Category 1	
Category 2	
Category 3	
Category 4	
Category 5	
Category 6	

Review Questions

1. Draw out a simple physical bus topology.

2. Draw out a simple physical single ring and dual ring topology.

3. Draw out a simple physical star topology.

4. Draw out a simple physical partial mesh and full mesh topology.

5. Describe the pinout of a straight-through cable.

6. Describe the pinout of a cross-over cable.

Exam Questions

1. Which physical network topology is shown in the following diagram?

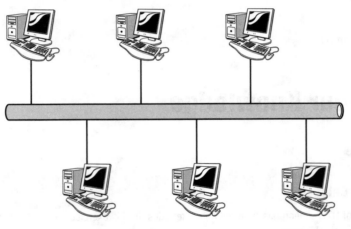

   ○ **A.** Ring

   ○ **B.** Bus

   ○ **C.** Star

   ○ **D.** Mesh

2. Which physical network topology is shown in the following diagram?

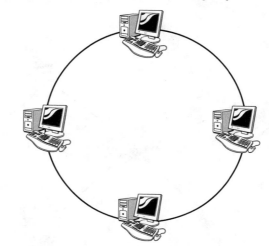

   ○ **A.** Ring

   ○ **B.** Bus

   ○ **C.** Star

   ○ **D.** Mesh

3. Which physical network topology is shown in the following diagram?

   ○ **A.** Single ring

   ○ **B.** Partial mesh

   ○ **C.** Full mesh

   ○ **D.** Dual ring

4. Which physical network topology is shown in the following diagram?

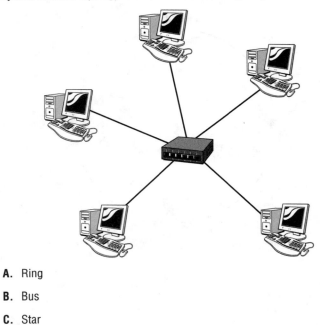

    ○ **A.** Ring

    ○ **B.** Bus

    ○ **C.** Star

    ○ **D.** Mesh

5. Which physical network topology is shown in the following diagram?

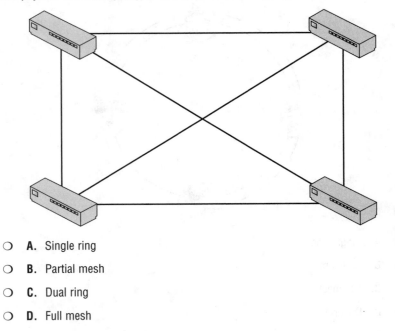

    ○ **A.** Single ring

    ○ **B.** Partial mesh

    ○ **C.** Dual ring

    ○ **D.** Full mesh

6. Which physical network topology is shown in the following diagram?

- ○ **A.** Single ring
- ○ **B.** Partial mesh
- ○ **C.** Dual ring
- ○ **D.** Full mesh

7. Which of the following is not susceptible to EMI?

- ○ **A.** Fiber
- ○ **B.** Thin coaxial cable
- ○ **C.** Category 3 UTP cable
- ○ **D.** Category 5 UTP cable

8. Which connector does a UTP cable use?

- ○ **A.** MT-RJ
- ○ **B.** SC
- ○ **C.** ST
- ○ **D.** RJ-45

9. Because of attenuation, the maximum, practical length of a UTP cable is _____.

- ○ **A.** 10 meters
- ○ **B.** 100 meters
- ○ **C.** 200 meters
- ○ **D.** 500 meters

10. The total flow of information over a certain time period on a communications medium measured in bits per second is called _____.

    ○ **A.** Bandwidth

    ○ **B.** Crosstalk

    ○ **C.** Attenuation

    ○ **D.** Electromagnetic interference

11. Which cable consists of a single copper wire surrounded by a plastic insulation cover and a braided copper shield?

    ○ **A.** Coaxial cable

    ○ **B.** UTP

    ○ **C.** STP

    ○ **D.** Category 5 cable

12. What type of UTP cable would you use to connect a switch to a router?

    ○ **A.** Coaxial cable

    ○ **B.** Straight-through cable

    ○ **C.** Cross-over cable

    ○ **D.** Thin coax

13. What type of UTP cable would you use to connect a PC directly to another PC?

    ○ **A.** Coaxial cable

    ○ **B.** Straight-through cable

    ○ **C.** Cross-over cable

    ○ **D.** Thick coax

14. If you have a network that is connected through a hub and experiencing congestion, which of the following is the best solution to decrease congestion on your network?

    ○ **A.** Install a second hub.

    ○ **B.** Replace the hub with a repeater.

    ○ **C.** Replace the hub with a switch.

    ○ **D.** Replace the hub with a network interface.

15. What is the IEEE standard for wi-fi?

    ○   **A.**   802.1q

    ○   **B.**   802.11b

    ○   **C.**   802.3u

    ○   **D.**   802.3ab

16. Which IEEE wireless standard uses a 5GHz radio frequency and is not compatible with other wireless standards?

    ○   **A.**   802.11

    ○   **B.**   802.11a

    ○   **C.**   802.11b

    ○   **D.**   802.11g

17. Which cable pinout is shown in the following diagram?

    ○   **A.**   Thin coax cable

    ○   **B.**   Thick coax cable

    ○   **C.**   Straight-through cable

    ○   **D.**   Cross-over cable

18. Which cable pinout is shown in the following diagram?

○   **A.** Thin coax cable

○   **B.** Thick coax cable

○   **C.** Straight-through cable

○   **D.** Cross-over cable

19. Which of the following connectors are used by fiber? (Choose the three best answers.)

○   **A.** MT-RJ

○   **B.** SC

○   **C.** ST

○   **D.** RJ-45

20. Which of the following are wireless technologies? (Choose the three best answers.)

○   **A.** Fast Ethernet

○   **B.** Bluetooth

○   **C.** Infrared

○   **D.** Wi-fi

Answers to Review Questions

1. Refer to Figure 2.1 to check your design of a physical bus topology.

2. Refer to Figure 2.2 to check your design of a physical single ring topology and Figure 2.3 to check your design of a physical dual ring topology.

3. Refer to Figure 2.4 to check your design of a physical star topology.

4. Refer to Figure 2.6 to check your design of a physical partial mesh topology and Figure 2.5 to check your design of a physical full mesh topology.

5. Straight-through cables use four wires and pins 1, 2, 3, and 6. Given those pins, pin 1 is connected on one end of the cable to pin 1 on the opposite end of the cable. Pin 2 at one end is connected to pin 2 on the far end. Pin 3 is connected to pin 3 and pin 6 is connected to pin 6.

6. Cross-over cables also use four wires and pins 1, 2, 3, and 6. The difference is in how the pins are connected at each end. With cross-over cables, pin 1 connects to pin 3 and pin 2 connects to pin 6.

Answers to Exam Questions

1. **B.** This diagram represents the physical bus topology or the linear bus topology. This topology uses one cable as the trunk or backbone.

2. **A.** This diagram represents the physical ring topology. Each device is connected to two other devices on the network. Data traverses the network and creates a ring or loop.

3. **D.** This diagram represents the physical dual ring topology. Unlike a single ring topology, this design offers redundancy if either ring breaks.

4. **C.** This diagram represents the physical star topology. It may also be referred to as a hub-and-spoke topology.

5. **D.** This diagram represents the full mesh topology. All the devices on the network are directly connected to every other device on that same network.

6. **B.** This diagram represents the partial mesh topology. Some but not all of the devices are connected to all of the other devices on the network.

7. **A.** Fiber is not susceptible to EMI. Answers B, C, and D are all incorrect because thin coaxial cable, category 3 UTP, and category 5 UTP are all susceptible to EMI.

8. **D.** UTP cables use RJ-45 connectors. Answers A, B, and C are incorrect because fiber uses ST, SC, or MT-RJ connectors.

9. **B.** Because of attenuation, the maximum, practical length of a UTP cable is 100 meters.

10. **A.** The total flow of information over a certain time period on a communications medium measured in bits per second is called bandwidth. Answer B is incorrect because crosstalk is an electrical or

magnetic field that is a result of one communications signal affecting the signal in a nearby circuit. Answer C is incorrect because attenuation occurs over long distances as a signal loses strength. Answer D is incorrect because EMI is the interference caused by electromagnetic signals.

11. **A.** A coaxial cable consists of a single copper wire surrounded by a plastic insulation cover and a braided copper shield. Answer B is incorrect because UTP cables use eight colored wires in four pairs. Answer C is incorrect because STP has an additional layer of shielding. Answer D is incorrect because Category 5 is a UTP cable.

12. **B.** When connecting a switch to a router, you must use a straight-through UTP cable.

13. **C.** When directly connecting two PCs, you can use a cross-over UTP cable.

14. **C.** The best answer here is to replace a hub with a switch. Switches can segment the network. Answers A and B are incorrect because a repeater or an additional hub simply extends the network further. Answer D is incorrect because the network interface connects a PC or laptop to the public network.

15. **B.** The IEEE standard for Wireless Fidelity is 802.11b. Answer A is incorrect because IEEE standard 802.1q defines VLAN. Answer C is incorrect because IEEE standard 802.3u defines Fast Ethernet. Answer D is incorrect because IEEE standard 802.3ab defines Gigabit Ethernet on a Category 5 cable.

16. **B.** 802.11a uses a 5GHz RF. Answer A is incorrect because IEEE standard 802.11 is the basis for the 802.11a, 802.11b, and 802.11g wireless standards. Answers C and D are incorrect because 802.11b and 802.11g use 2.4GHz RF. 802.11a is not compatible with 802.11b and 802.11g.

17. **C.** A straight-through cable uses pins 1, 2, 3, and 6. Given those pins, pin 1 is connected on one end of the cable to pin 1 on the opposite end of the cable. Pin 2 at one end is connected to pin 2 on the far end, and so on. Answers A and B are incorrect because pinouts do not apply to coaxial cable because it is a single copper wire. Answer D is incorrect because cross-over cables also use four wires and pins 1, 2, 3, and 6. The difference is in how the pins are connected at each end. With cross-over cables, pin 1 connects to pin 3 and pin 2 connects to pin 6.

18. **D.** Cross-over cables also use four wires and pins 1, 2, 3, and 6. The difference is in how the pins are connected at each end. With cross-over cables, pin 1 connects to pin 3 and pin 2 connects to pin 6. Answers A and B are incorrect because pinouts do not apply to coaxial cable because it is a single copper wire. Answer C is incorrect because straight-through cable uses pins 1, 2, 3, and 6. Given those pins, pin 1 is connected on one end of the cable to pin 1 on the opposite end of the cable. Pin 2 at one end is connected to pin 2 on the far end, and so on.

19. **A, B, and C.** Fiber uses an MT-RJ, SC, or ST connector. Answer D is incorrect because RJ-45 is used by a UTP cable.

20. **B, C,and D.** Bluetooth, infrared, and wi-fi are all wireless technologies. Answer A is incorrect because Fast Ethernet is an ethernet LAN technology.

Suggested Readings and Resources

The following are some recommended readings on network components and related terminology:

1. Habraken, Joe. *Absolute Beginner's Guide to Networking*, Fourth Edition. Que Publishing, 2003.

2. "Fiber Optic Connector Guide," http://www.commspecial.com/connectorguide.htm.

3. "Network Cabling Help," www.datacottage.com.

CHAPTER THREE

Data Link Networking Concepts

Objectives

This chapter covers the following Cisco-specified objectives from the "Describe the operation of data networks" and "Implement a small switched network" sections of the 640-822 ICND1 exam:

▶ **Describe the purpose and functions of various network devices**

▶ **Select the components required to meet a network specification**

▶ **Use the OSI and TCP/IP models and their associated protocols to explain how data flows in a network**

▶ **Interpret network diagrams**

▶ **Explain the technology and media access control method for Ethernet networks**

Outline

Introduction   84

Data Link Protocols   84

Token Ring   84
FDDI   86
Ethernet at the Data Link Layer   87
   Ethernet Addressing   87
   Ethernet Framing   91

Physical Ethernet Standards   93

Ethernet   93
   10BASE2   94
   10BASE5   94
   10BASE-T   95
   10BASE-FL   95
Fast Ethernet   96
   100BASE-T4   96
   100BASE-TX   96
   100BASE-FX   96
Gigabit Ethernet   97
   1000BASE-T 802.3ab   97
   1000BASE-X 802.3z   98
10-Gigabit Ethernet (10GbE)   99
Long Reach Ethernet   **100**

Data Link Layer Devices   **100**

Bridges   101
Switches   104

Duplex   **105**

Microsegmentation   **106**

Chapter Summary   **107**

Key Terms   107

Apply Your Knowledge   **109**

Exercises   109
Review Questions   110
Exam Questions   110
Answers to Review Questions   114
Answers to Exam Questions   115
Suggested Readings and Resources   117

Study Strategies

▶ Read the objectives at the beginning of the chapter.

▶ Familiarize yourself with token ring and FDDI protocols.

▶ Define the IEEE MAC unicast, broadcast, and multicast addresses.

▶ Review the ethernet family of protocols and be able to identify the characteristics of each protocol.

▶ Name the devices that are used at the Data Link layer and important traits of each device.

▶ Define *duplex*.

▶ Describe microsegmentation.

Introduction

Several data link networking concepts were first introduced in the discussion of the Data Link layer or Layer 2 of the OSI model in Chapter 1, "Standard Internetworking Models." Again, it is important to understand the layered architecture of the OSI model to grasp the fundamentals of how a network operates. Although Chapter 2, "Physical Layer Networking Concepts," went over concepts that define the Physical layer of the OSI model, this chapter goes over concepts that define how a network operates at the Data Link layer specifically.

Important Data Link LAN topics to understand for the ICND1 exam include the protocols, addressing, and devices that are used at Layer 2. Cisco specified several objectives related to LAN technologies, which are prevalent at Layer 1 and Layer 2. Let's begin with three Data Link layer protocols: token ring, FDDI, and ethernet.

> **NOTE**
>
> Remember that the Physical and Data Link layers are combined in the TCP/IP model to form the Network Interface layer.

Data Link Protocols

Objectives:

▶ Explain the technology and media access control method for Ethernet networks

▶ Interpret network diagrams

▶ Use the OSI and TCP/IP models and their associated protocols to explain how data flows in a network

In this section, you will learn about network protocols that can be utilized at the Data Link layer of the OSI model. These protocols include token ring, FDDI, and ethernet. Ethernet Data Link protocols are broken out into addressing and framing standards.

Token Ring

Token ring is a LAN protocol that utilizes a token-passing media access technology in a physical ring or physical star topology, which creates a logical ring topology. This protocol was first developed by IBM but then standardized by IEEE with the 802.5 specification. With token-passing, a three-byte token (or special bit pattern) is inserted in a frame and passed in a single direction from one node to another until it forms a complete loop. The node that has possession of the token is the only one that can send data at any given time on that LAN. Because only one node can send data at a time, collisions are avoided.

Rather than using a hub or switch, Token ring uses a multistation access unit (MAU) to send a token across the network. The MAU has Ring In (RI) and Ring Out (RO) ports. The RO of the first MAU is connected to the RI of the next MAU. This continues until the final MAU, which connects back to the first MAU RI port via its own RO port. As mentioned, a logical ring is created with this setup. Figure 3.1 shows how a token ring network operates with MAUs.

FIGURE 3.1 Token ring network.

A token ring LAN can run at either 4Mbps or 16Mbps. Each device must be configured for the same speed; otherwise, the token-passing does not work at all. Overall, although this protocol provides a collision-free network, it is also more expensive to implement than ethernet. This is a major reason why ethernet is the most popular Data Link layer protocol, making token ring a rather distant second.

Let's recap what you've learned about token ring:

▶ Standardized by the IEEE 802.5 specification

▶ A token-passing media access technology

▶ Set up as a physical ring or physical star topology

▶ Creates a logical ring topology

▶ Speeds are assigned as either 4Mbps or 16Mbps

▶ Utilizes an MSAU rather than a switch or hub

▶ Provides collision-free data transfer

▶ High overhead

FDDI

FDDI is a LAN protocol that utilizes a token-passing media access method on a dual ring topology. This protocol was created by the American National Standards Institute (ANSI) with the ANSI X3T9.5 specification. Data transmission occurs on fiber-optic cables at a rate of 100Mbps. Primarily, FDDI was developed to run data across the network backbone of a larger company. Dual ring is configured for FDDI to provide redundancy and fault-tolerance. Also, because it runs over fiber it is not susceptible to EMI like other media options. Figure 3.2 shows the dual ring topology of an FDDI network.

FIGURE 3.2   FDDI network.

NOTE

Copper Distributed Data Interface (CDDI) is a 100Mbps token-passing protocol that runs over copper wire rather than fiber-optic cable.

FDDI uses a method called *beaconing* to signal when a failure is detected on the network. Beaconing enables a device to send a signal informing the other devices on that LAN that token passing has stopped. The beacon travels around the loop from one device to the next until it reaches the last device in that ring. To troubleshoot, the network administrator can find the beacon at that last device and then check the connection between that device and the next connected device on the FDDI network.

Like token ring, FDDI is costly to implement, which is a disadvantage when designing a small network.

Let's recap what you've learned about FDDI:

- ▶ Developed by ANSI with the ANSI X3T9.5 specification
- ▶ A token-passing media access technology
- ▶ Set up as a dual ring topology

▶ Redundant, fault-tolerant network

▶ Speed is 100Mbps

▶ Runs over fiber-optic cable

▶ Not susceptible to EMI

▶ Provides collision-free data transfer

▶ Fault-detection provided by beaconing

▶ High overhead

Ethernet at the Data Link Layer

Ethernet, ethernet, ethernet . . .

The most popular LAN by a mile, ethernet is a group of protocols and standards that work at either the Physical or Data Link layer of the OSI model. This section covers ethernet technology that is relevant to Layer 2. Ethernet is defined by the IEEE 802.3 specification. As technology advancements occur, IEEE has defined additional classifications of 802.3, which include Fast Ethernet, Gigabit Ethernet, 10-Gigabit Ethernet, and Long Reach Ethernet. The physical implementations of each Ethernet standard are covered in greater detail in a moment, but first I would like to review ethernet addressing and ethernet framing. Ethernet addressing can be achieved with unicast, multicast, or broadcast addresses at the Data Link layer.

Ethernet Addressing

The Data Link layer uses physical or hardware addressing to make sure data is delivered to the appropriate end device in a LAN. Physical addresses or what are commonly referred to as *MAC addresses* are used at Layer 2. Before you go any further, it's a good idea to take a minute to review what you learned in Chapter 1.

The Data Link layer of the OSI model is the only one that has sublayers. Table 3.1 shows the breakout of Layer 2.

TABLE 3.1   Data Link Layer and Sublayers

OSI Model Layer	Sublayer
Data Link Layer	Media Access Control (MAC) IEEE 802.3
	Logical Link Control (LLC) IEEE 802.2

A MAC address is hard-coded (burnt in) on the network interface controller (NIC) of the Physical Layer device attached to the network. Each MAC address must be unique and use the following format:

▶ The address must consist of 48 bits (or 6 bytes).

▶ It must be displayed by 12 hexadecimal digits (0–9, A–F).

▶ The first 6 hexadecimal digits in the address are a vendor code or organizationally unique identifier (OUI) assigned to that NIC manufacturer.

▶ The last 6 hexadecimal digits are assigned by the NIC manufacturer and must be different from any other number assigned by that manufacturer.

An example of a MAC address would be 00:00:07:A9:B2:EB. The OUI in this example is 00:00:07.

EXAM ALERT

MAC Address Structure Know that a MAC address consists of 48 bits and is expressed as 12 hexadecimal digits from either 0–9 or A–F. Also, know that the vendor code or OUI is the first 6 hexadecimal digits of the MAC address.

NOTE

Check out an actual example of a physical address on your own PC. From the Start menu, select Run. Then type in `cmd` to enter the command prompt for your PC. You should see a new window open on the screen where you can type in `ipconfig/all` at the prompt. Among other things, the output includes the physical or MAC address of your PC.

Ethernet LAN addresses can be broken down into two subcategories: individual and group addresses. An individual address is referred to as a *unicast address*. A unicast address identifies the MAC address of an individual LAN or NIC card. The source address on an ethernet frame will always be a unicast address. When a packet from the Network layer is framed for transport and is being forwarded to a single destination, a unicast address is also the destination address on an ethernet frame. Figure 3.3 represents an example of frame forwarding between

UNICAST SOURCE
ADDRESS = 0000.0C12.3456

Bill's PC

UNICAST DESTINATION
ADDRESS = 0000.0712.3456

FIGURE 3.3 Unicast frame transmission.

a unicast source and a unicast destination device. Cisco devices typically use three groups of four hexadecimal digits separated by periods, such as 0000.0C12.3456. Cisco's OUI is 0000.0C.

In the example in Figure 3.3, Bill's computer checks the destination address on the ethernet frame. If the destination address is the MAC on his computer, the frame is processed. If the destination address does not match up, the frame is dropped.

Group Ethernet LAN addresses classify more than one LAN or NIC card. Multicast and broadcast addresses are both classified as group addresses and can be described as follows:

> ▶ **Multicast addresses**—Addresses where a frame can be sent to a group of devices in the same LAN. IEEE ethernet multicast addresses always begin with 0100.5E in hexadecimal format. The last three bytes can be any combination of hexadecimal digits. The IP routed protocol supports multicast addressing with three groups of four hexadecimal digits separated by periods (like Cisco devices), so it appears as 0100.5Exx.xxxx, where the x's can represent any hex digit from 0–9 or A–F. Figure 3.4 shows a frame that is being forwarded from a unicast source to an IP multicast destination address.

FIGURE 3.4 Multicast frame transmission.

In this example, the switch sends a frame from its own unicast address to the multicast address of 0100.5E12.3456. Each device in that LAN segment checks the destination address to see whether it should be processed. Although Bill and Carol's computer will review and process the frame, Dustin's does not care about it and therefore drops the frame.

> ▶ **Broadcast addresses**—Addresses where a frame is sent to all devices in the same LAN segment. Multicast and broadcast addresses are limited to a LAN or network segment.

Broadcast addresses are always the same value, which is FFFF.FFFF.FFFF. Figure 3.5 shows a switch sending a frame to the destination address FFFF.FFFF.FFFF. Because this is the broadcast address value, all the devices in that LAN should process the frame.

FIGURE 3.5 Broadcast frame transmission.

Challenge

You should be able to recognize the difference between a unicast, multicast, and broadcast address for the exam. In this challenge, I give you an address and ask that you identify whether it is a unicast, multicast, or broadcast address.

Unicast, Multicast, and Broadcast Addresses

This Address Is...	Unicast, Multicast, or Broadcast
0100.5C12.3456	
0100.5E11.2345	
FFFF.FFFF.FFFF	
0100.5E12.3456	
0000.0C12.3456	

Ethernet Framing

As you will recall from Chapter 1, data traverses the layers of the OSI model and is encapsulated from layer to layer.

Table 3.2 shows the process of using the OSI model to encapsulate data.

TABLE 3.2 OSI Model Layer and Related Control Information

OSI Layer	Control Information Name
Application Presentation Session	Data
Transport	Segment
Network	Packet
Data Link	Frame
Physical	Bit

EXAM ALERT

The correct order for data encapsulation is data, segment, packet, frame, and bit.

The Data Link layer uses frames to transport data between layers. Framing is the process of interpreting data that is either received or sent out across the network. The 802.2 LLC Data Link sublayer is an extension of 802.3 and is responsible for framing, error-detection, and flow control. Figure 3.6 represents an 802.3 frame.

FIGURE 3.6 802.3 frame.

EXAM ALERT

For the ICND1 exam, review the structure of the 802.3 frame, specifically, the Destination/Source MAC address fields of the data-link header, the DSAP/SSAP fields of the LLC portion of the frame, and the FCS field of the Data and CRC data-link trailer.

The three main parts of an 802.3 frame can be broken down and described as follows:

▶ The Data Link header portion of the frame contains the destination MAC address (6 bytes), source MAC address (6 bytes), and length (2 bytes).

▶ The Logical Link Control portion of the frame contains Destination Service Access Point (DSAP), Source Service Access Point (SSAP), and control information. All three are 1 byte long. The Service Access Point (SAP) identifies an upper-layer protocol such as IP (06) or IPX (E0).

▶ The data and cyclical redundancy check (CRC) portion of the frame is also called the *data-link trailer*. The data field can be anywhere from 43 to 1497 bytes long. The frame check sequence (FCS) field is 4 bytes long. FCS or CRC provides error detection.

Error detection is used to determine whether bit errors happened during frame transmission. The sender and receiver of a frame use the same mathematical formula to analyze the information in the FCS field of the data-link trailer. If the calculations match up, there were no errors on that frame transmission.

EXAM ALERT

The FCS field of a frame is used for error detection.

Challenge

Given the necessity that you know the layout of the 802.3 frame, I will provide you with an outline. Fill out the fields that belong to each portion of the frame.

Data Link Header	Logical Link Control	Data and CRC

Now that you have filled out the fields, provide the full names of the following acronyms that are used in conjunction with the 802.3 frame.

MAC =

LLC =

DSAP =

SSAP =

CRC =

FCS =

I mentioned how the SAP in the 802.3 frame identifies an upper-layer protocol with 1 byte or 2 hexadecimal digits. The IP SAP is 06. Well, it turns out that 1 byte was insufficient for the number of protocols that

(continues)

(continued)

> need to be recognized by an 802.3 frame. To accommodate the influx of protocols, IEEE permitted for an additional header in the 802.3 frame called a *Subnetwork Access Protocol (SNAP)* header.
>
> The SNAP header serves the same purpose as the DSAP field; however, it consists of 2 bytes. For example, 0800 is the hexadecimal format assigned to IP with SNAP. RFC 1700 identifies all the values that are associated with SAP and SNAP.

Physical Ethernet Standards

Objective:

▶ Select the components required to meet a network specification

Have I said that ethernet is the most popular LAN protocol? Ethernet started in the 1970s when Xerox needed a networking system to connect personal computers. Xerox joined forces with Digital Equipment Corp. (DEC) and Intel to develop the protocol, which is why the very first ethernet standards were referred to as DIX Ethernet. This section covers the progression of ethernet standards from the earlier 10Mbps connections to the more recent 10 gigabit ethernet connections.

Each standard has a maximum connection length and speed. Individual ethernet standards also specify which cables and connectors can be used for network connectivity. You will be introduced to each group of standards starting with the 10Mbps ethernet connections, then the 100Mbps Fast Ethernet connections, 1Gbps ethernet, and 10Gbps ethernet connections.

Ethernet

The IEEE 802.3 ethernet standards are covered in the following sections. The following list contains all the ethernet standards that are covered in this chapter, in order:

▶ 10BASE2

▶ 10BASE5

▶ 10BASE-T

▶ 10BASE-FL

▶ 100BASE-T4

▶ 100BASE-TX

▶ 100BASE-FX

▶ 1000BASE-T

- ▶ 1000BASE-TX
- ▶ 1000BASE-CX
- ▶ 1000BASE-SX
- ▶ 1000BASE-LX
- ▶ 10GbE

10BASE2

10BASE2 networks are connected with RG-58 coaxial cables that use Bayonet Neill Concelman (BNC) connectors. There are no other hardware devices such as hubs or switches to connect devices, just the coaxial cables. This creates a physical bus topology. An electrical signal is sent by each device that wants to transmit data on that network. If more than one device sends a signal at the same time, this causes a collision and the signal is lost. To prevent loss of data transmissions, an algorithm called *Carrier Sense Multiple Access Collision Detection (CSMA/CD)* was defined. This algorithm sends a jam signal to notify the devices that there has been a collision. The devices then halt transmission for a random back-off time. CSMA/CD must be activated for 10Base ethernet LANs that are connected with a hub.

EXAM ALERT

For the exam, know the definition of CSMA/CD and its capability to act as an arbitrator for devices in an ethernet LAN.

The name 10BASE2 breaks down as follows:

10—10Mbps data transmission speed

BASE—Represents baseband, the signaling mode where the media can only send one signal per wire at a time

2—Actually refers to 185m or the maximum segment length (where 185 is rounded up to 200 and 2 is a multiple of 100m)

NOTE

So what you can see from the naming scheme is that the first number represents the speed, the word *base* means the baseband signaling mode, and the last helps you determine the type of cable used.

10BASE5

10BASE5 has the same characteristics as 10BASE2, but with a maximum segment length of 500m. The 5 is also a multiple of 100m.

10BASE-T

10BASE-T has a maximum segment length of 100m and has a 10Mbps data transmission speed. 10BASE-T can use Category 3, 4, or 5 unshielded twisted-pair (UTP) or shielded twisted-pair (STP) cables for connectivity. If you recall, UTP is the more common and cost-effective solution. STP has an additional shield that provides additional reduction of interference and attenuation, but it is also the more expensive solution. The following cables can be used with a 10BASE-T connection:

- ▶ **Category 3**—Data cable that can handle speeds up to 10Mbps.

  Although it is faster than the Cat2 cable, this was quite popular until network speeds surpassed the 10Mbps threshold.

- ▶ **Category 4**—Data cable that can handle speeds up to 16Mbps and is meant to be used with token ring LANs.

- ▶ **Category 5**—Data cable that can handle speeds up to 100Mbps and is currently the most popular cable selection.

EXAM ALERT

UTP is vulnerable to electromagnetic interference (EMI) and uses an RJ-45 connector.

10BASE-FL

10BASE-FL also has a 10Mbps data transmission speed, but it runs over fiber-optic cables. This option allows for a maximum segment length up to 2km.

Table 3.3 compares the 802.3 ethernet characteristics, listing the key characteristics of each specification.

TABLE 3.3   Summary of Ethernet 802.3 Characteristics

Standard	Speed	Maximum Distance	Media Type	Connector Used
10BASE2	10Mbps	185m	RG-58 coaxial	BNC
10BASE5	10Mbps	500m	RG-58 coaxial	BNC
10BASE-T	10Mbps	100m	Category 3, 4, or 5 UTP or STP	RJ-45
10BASE-FL	10Mbps	Up to 2km	Fiber-optic	SC or ST

As you can see, the early standards are all limited to 10Mbps. More recent ethernet specifications allow for faster data transmission speeds and are more popular for today's networks.

Fast Ethernet

Fast Ethernet was derived for networks that needed speeds in excess of 10Mbps. The IEEE 802.3u defines standards for 100BASE-T4, 100BASE-TX, and 100BASE-FX. You may also hear them collectively referred to as 100BASE-X. Based on what you learned from the 10Base naming scheme, you would be correct to infer that the 100 represents 100Mbps. Also, all three standards are baseband like the 10Mbps family of protocols.

NOTE

Fast Ethernet is defined in the IEEE 802.3u standard.

100BASE-T4

100BASE-T4 has the same characteristics as 100BASE-TX except that it can use Category 3, 4, or 5 UTP or STP cables.

100BASE-TX

100BASE-TX, like 10BASE-T, uses either UTP or STP. Category 5 UTP cable is used with this implementation. 10BASE-T has a maximum segment length of 100m.

100BASE-FX

100BASE-FX uses either single-mode or multimode fiber-optic cables to connect. Multimode (MM) fiber set for half-duplex can reach a distance of 412m. Single-mode (SM) fiber set for full-duplex can reach a distance of 10,000m. SC or ST connectors can be used. The drawback, as mentioned before with fiber implementations, is the high overhead.

▶ **Multimode (MM) fiber**—This is generally used for shorter distances and is ideal for a campus-sized network. MM also has a larger diameter of optical fiber than SM fiber.

▶ **Single-mode (SM) fiber**—This mode is used to span longer distances. SM also allows for a higher data rate than MM and faster data transmission speeds.

EXAM ALERT

Fiber-optic cable is not susceptible to EMI, Near-end Crosstalk (NEXT), or Far-end Crosstalk (FEXT).

REVIEW BREAK

Table 3.4 compares Fast Ethernet 802.3u standards.

TABLE 3.4 Comparison of Fast Ethernet 802.3u Characteristics

Standard	Speed	Maximum Distance	Media Type	Connector Used
100BASE-T4	100Mbps	100m	Category 3, 4, or 5 UTP or STP	RJ-45
100BASE-TX	100Mbps	100m	Category 5 UTP or STP	RJ-45
100BASE-FX	100Mbps	412m with half-duplex MM fiber 10,000m with full-duplex SM fiber	Fiber-optic	SC or ST

Gigabit Ethernet

Gigabit Ethernet standards all have a data transmission speed of 1000Mbps (1Gbps) and use a baseband signaling mode. Gigabit Ethernet can be broken down into two IEEE standards, 802.3ab or 1000BASE-T and 802.3z or 1000BASE-X.

1000BASE-T 802.3ab

1000BASE-T or 1000BASE-TX is defined by the 802.3ab standard and can reach a maximum total distance per segment of 75m. This standard uses a minimum of Category 5 UTP cable with an RJ-45 connector.

▶ **Category 5e**—Data cable that can handle speeds up to 1Gbps; a popular choice for Gigabit Ethernet networks.

▶ **Category 6**—Cable that was created to exceed speeds of 1Gbps.

Table 3.5 summarizes the primary points of interest that are relevant for the 1000BASE-T standard.

TABLE 3.5 Summary of Gigabit Ethernet 802.3ab Characteristics

Standard	Speed	Maximum Distance	Media Type	Connector Used
1000BASE-T or 1000BASE-TX	1000Mbps or 1Gbps	75m	Category 5 UTP or higher	RJ-45

1000BASE-X 802.3z

1000BASE-X is the collective name for 802.3z standards 1000BASE-CX, 1000BASE-SX, and 1000BASE-LX that have the following characteristics respectively:

▶ **1000BASE-CX**—1000BASE-CX is the unique standard in this family because it uses shielded copper wire cable with a 9-pin shielded connector instead of fiber-optic cable for connectivity. The maximum total distance per segment is a mere 25m.

▶ **1000BASE-SX**—1000BASE-SX transmits short-wavelength laser over fiber-optic cable. Either 50-micron or 62.5-micron (diameter) MM fiber can be used with this option. Lengths may vary depending on the type of MM fiber and duplex chosen for each connection as follows:

  ▶ Half-duplex 62.5-micron MM fiber connections can reach a maximum segment length of 275m.

  ▶ Half-duplex 50-micron MM fiber connections can reach a maximum segment length of 316m.

  ▶ Full-duplex 62.5-micron MM fiber connections can reach a maximum segment length of 275m.

  ▶ Full-duplex 50-micron MM fiber connections can reach a maximum segment length of 550m.

As you can see, the 50-micron MM fiber can offer longer segment distances. The 62.5-micron MM fiber reaches the same maximum segment length of 275m regardless of the duplex.

▶ **1000BASE-LX**—1000BASE-LX transmits long-wavelength laser over fiber-optic cable. Either 50-micron or 62.5-micron (diameter) MM fiber can be used with this option. SM fiber can also be used with 1000BASE-LX, which differentiates this standard from 1000BASE-SX. The same MM fiber length restrictions apply based on the implementation of half- or full-duplex. The following lengths apply when SM fiber is used:

  ▶ Half-duplex SM fiber connections can reach a maximum segment length of 316m.

  ▶ Full-duplex SM fiber connections can reach a maximum segment length of 5000m.

  Using full-duplex SM fiber allows for a huge increase in distance. As you can imagine, this is also the more expensive option.

Table 3.6 compares Fast Ethernet 802.3z standards.

TABLE 3.6   Comparison of Gigabit Ethernet 802.3z Characteristics

Standard	Speed	Maximum Distance	Media Type	Connector Used
1000BASE-CX	1000Mbps or 1Gbps	25m	Shielded copper wire connector	9-pin shielded
1000BASE-SX	1000Mbps or 1Gbps	275m with half or full-duplex 62.5-micron MM fiber 316m with half-duplex 50-micron MM fiber 550m with full-duplex 50-micron MM fiber	MM fiber-optic	SC or ST
1000BASE-LX	1000Mbps or 1Gbps	275m with half- or full-duplex 62.5-micron MM fiber 316m with half-duplex 50-micron MM fiber or SM fiber 550m with full-duplex 50-micron MM fiber 5000m with full-duplex SM fiber	MM or SM fiber-optic	SC or ST

EXAM ALERT

Gigabit Ethernet comprises the 802.3ab and the 802.3z standards.

10-Gigabit Ethernet (10GbE)

You guessed it: 1Gbps just wasn't a fast enough option. Actually, it is just the nature of tech-nology to constantly strive for faster speeds. Yet another new standard was defined by IEEE and labeled 802.3ae. Earlier in this chapter, you saw 10BASE-2, which has data transmission speeds of 10Mbps. 10-Gigabit Ethernet transmits data at 10,000Mbps. That is quite an upgrade! IEEE 802.3ae uses 62.5-micron MM, 50-micron MM, or SM fiber-optic cabling for connectivity and a baseband signaling mode.

> **NOTE**
>
> All of the ethernet standards, regardless of their speed, use the same 802.3 MAC and 802.2 LLC headers and trailers.

Long Reach Ethernet

Cisco Long Reach Ethernet (LRE) was developed to provide broadband service over existing telephone-grade or Category 1, 2, or 3 wiring. Speeds vary between 5–15Mbps and can reach a maximum segment length of up to 5000m. Cisco LRE may be a viable networking solution for a LAN or MAN that already has Category 1/2/3 cabling installed. A hotel could benefit from Cisco LRE to provide high-speed Internet or video conferencing solutions to their clientele.

> **NOTE**
>
> Broadband is a signaling method that supports various frequencies such as audio and video.

Data Link Layer Devices

Objective:

▶ Describe the purpose and functions of various network devices

At the Data Link layer, either a bridge or a Layer 2 switch can be installed to segment a LAN. Hubs and repeaters at the Physical layer only serve to extend a network. With segmentation, switches and bridges create a separate collision domain for each connected node, which effectively reduces the number of collisions that occur on that network.

Remember from Chapter 1 that a collision domain is a group of nodes that shares the same media and are segmented by switches or bridges. A collision occurs if two nodes attempt a simultaneous transmission within the same collision domain. This reinforces the need for an increased number of collision domains. Figure 3.7 demonstrates how a bridge creates two collision domains.

Figure 3.8 provides an example of a situation in which a switch creates separate collision domains.

> **EXAM ALERT**
>
> **Know what a collision domain is and that a bridge and/or switch will segment a network and create an additional collision domain for each segment. Routers not only segment collision domains, but they also segment broadcast domains.**

FIGURE 3.7 Example of a bridged network.

FIGURE 3.8 Example of a switched network.

Bridges

Bridges were created to alleviate several expansion-related network issues. As networks were growing and becoming more complex, hubs and repeaters no longer provided sufficient network resources. Because they do not segment the network, all the devices connected to a hub or repeater had to share the same bandwidth. Also, if one device sent a frame, it could collide with a frame from another device on that LAN. This meant that all devices on that LAN had to take turns sending frames. Again, this is not very efficient as additional devices are added to a network.

Transparent bridges were introduced and helped solve these growing pains. The word *transparent* is used to indicate that the other devices on a network are not aware of its existence.

Bridges use a software application to forward frames.

The following are the primary tasks performed by both bridges and switches:

▶ The source MAC address of every inbound frame is examined to learn its MAC address.

▶ Frames may either be forwarded or filtered depending on the destination MAC address (they can also be flooded if the destination is unknown).

▶ Eliminates loops that are caused by redundant connections by configuring Spanning Tree Protocol (STP).

Learned MAC addresses and their interfaces are stored in a *bridge table* on the bridge or switch. When a new frame arrives on that bridge or switch, the device refers to the bridge table to decide how to forward or filter the frame. If the frame's destination MAC address is on a different segment of that LAN, the device forwards the frame to that segment. If the frame's destination MAC address is on the same segment as the source MAC address, the device filters the frame. That frame reaches its destination without the assistance of a bridge or switch. Figure 3.9 shows a segmented LAN with the MAC addresses of each end user.

As frames are received by the bridge or switch from each end user, it updates its bridge table with their MAC addresses and the interface on which the frame came into the device. Table 3.7 shows the bridge table of this bridge.

FIGURE 3.9 Bridge LAN.

TABLE 3.7 Example Bridge Table for Figure 3.9

MAC Address	Interface
0200.1111.1111	E0
0200.2222.2222	E0

TABLE 3.7 *Continued*

MAC Address	Interface
0200.3333.3333	E1
0200.4444.4444	E1

If the incoming frame destination address is...

► **Unicast**—The bridge checks the bridge table first. If the destination unicast address is not in the bridge table, it forwards the frame to all interfaces except for the interface that originally sent the frame. If the destination unicast address is in the bridge table and on a different interface than the interface that originally sent the frame, it forwards the frame. If the destination unicast address is in the bridge table and on the same interface as the sender, the frame is filtered.

► **Multicast**—The bridge forwards the frame to all interfaces except for the interface that originally sent the frame.

► **Broadcast**—The bridge forwards the frame to all interfaces except for the interface that originally sent the frame.

Challenge

Based on what you just learned about bridge and switch frame filtering or forwarding, take a look at Figure 3.10 and fill out the bridge table for this network that is using a switch for connectivity.

FIGURE 3.10 Switch LAN.

(continues)

Continued

Bridge Table

Address	Interface

Using the same diagram and your new bridge table, I will give you a source and destination address. Please fill out whether the frame will be filtered or forwarded. If it is forwarded, also fill out the outbound interface to which the frame will be sent.

MAC Filtering or Forwarding

Source Address	Destination Address	Filter or Forward	Outbound Interface(s)
0200.1111.1111	0200.2222.2222		
0200.2222.2222	0200.3333.3333		
0200.3333.3333	0200.4444.4444		
0200.2222.2222	FFFF.FFFF.FFFF		
0200.4444.4444	0200.1111.1111		
0200.1111.1111	0100.5E12.3456		

> **EXAM ALERT**
>
> Bridges and switches examine the source MAC address of each inbound frame to learn MAC addresses.

Switches

Layer 2 switches are multi-port bridges; therefore, they have all the same functionality of bridges. There are differences that differentiate a switch from a bridge. For example, switches utilize hardware or Application-Specific Integrated Circuit (ASIC) chips to forward frames rather than software. Also, each port of the switch has a dedicated bandwidth. If the dedicated port on a switch is 10Mbps, the connected LAN segment has a dedicated bandwidth of 10Mbps. This works in the same manner for 100Mbps and 1000Mbps dedicated switch ports. This feature also sets a switch apart from a bridge that has a low port density.

> **EXAM ALERT**
>
> For the test, know that switches are multi-port bridges that use ASIC hardware chips for frame forwarding. Dedicated bandwidth enables the switch port to guarantee the speed assigned to that port. For example, 100Mbps port connections get 100Mbps transmission rates.

A popular ethernet switch port is the 10/100 ethernet port, where you can set the port to pass traffic at 10Mbps or 100Mbps. Chapter 6, "Introduction to Cisco Routers and Switches," goes into more detail regarding specific Cisco devices, including the 2950 series switches.

Challenge

Do you recall the difference between straight-through and crossover cables? Both cables are used with ethernet networks. In Chapter 2, Figure 2.7 and Figure 2.8 demonstrate the differences between straight-through and crossover. Selecting the right cable for your network connections is vital. The following connections are all related specifically to switch connectivity. Please determine whether you should use a straight-through or crossover cable between the devices.

Connecting a...	Type of Cable
Switch to a switch	
Switch to a hub	
Switch to a PC	
Plugged into a dedicated switch port	
Switch to a router	

Duplex

It is important that you understand duplex logic and how it affects traffic on a network. The communication mode of a device may either be half-duplex or full-duplex, depending on the connection type.

Half-duplex allows for one-way communication, which means that a device can only send or receive a data transmission at any given time. This option does not allow for simultaneously sending and receiving data. As part of a shared collision domain, hubs are inherently set up for half-duplex. Bandwidth suffers because a collision detection technology such as the CSMA/CD algorithm must be implemented. Collision detection can chew up 50–60% of the bandwidth on that ethernet LAN.

Full-duplex allows for two-way communication, which means that a device can simultaneously send and receive data transmissions. Full-duplex is available with dedicated switch port connections to a single device. If a switch port connection is configured for full-duplex, the CSMA/CD algorithm must be disabled. An ethernet connection set for full-duplex allows for 100% transmission speeds in both directions. For example, a 100Mbps connection can transmit data simultaneously at 100Mbps in each direction.

With ethernet, if a switch port and NIC offer multiple speed options as well as half- and full-duplex settings, autonegotiation can be configured on both devices. The switch and NIC automatically negotiate the connection speed and duplex so that the settings on both ends match.

You may have heard of a 10/half or 100/full connection before. The term 10/half refers to a 10Mbps half-duplex connection. It is more likely that you will see 100/full, which indicates a 100Mbps full-duplex connection.

NOTE

Autonegotiation may not always be a reliable option. There have been some instances where the switch port goes into error disable mode because of massive errors. Configuring or "hard coding" the port and NIC to the appropriate speed and duplex settings may resolve the issue when the port is reactivated.

EXAM ALERT

Hubs use half-duplex technology. Switches can be set up for full-duplex.

Microsegmentation

Microsegmentation occurs when a switch creates a dedicated path for sending and receiving transmissions with each connected host. Each host then has a separate collision domain and a dedicated bandwidth.

Chapter Summary

Many important functions occur at the Data Link layer of the OSI model. Different technologies can be implemented at Layer 2 to transmit data across the network. Token ring and FDDI networks use token-passing to send frames, whereas ethernet uses the 802.3 frame standard with 802.2 LLC specifications. Ethernet framing and ethernet addressing are both significant topics for the ICND1 exam. Other key ethernet functions include error detection and arbitration. Although the FCS field of the 802.3 frame detects errors on a LAN, the CSMA/CD algorithm arbitrates how data is transmitted on a LAN.

Data Link layer devices include bridges and switches. Switches are really multi-port bridges, so they share the same general functionalities. New networks are most likely to use a Layer 2 switch in place of a bridge. Switches have been improved upon over the years and offer more options for the consumer, such as dedicated bandwidth and full-duplex communications.

Although the Data Link layer uses frames to transmit data, the Network layer uses Internet Protocol or IP addresses to route traffic. Chapter 5 discusses IP addressing and subnetting at length. Both topics are imperative for the ICND1 exam.

Key Terms

- ▶ Token-passing
- ▶ Token ring
- ▶ 802.5
- ▶ MSAU
- ▶ RI
- ▶ RO
- ▶ FDDI
- ▶ ANSI X3T9.5
- ▶ Unicast
- ▶ Multicast
- ▶ Broadcast
- ▶ Frame
- ▶ 802.2
- ▶ MAC
- ▶ LLC

- ▶ SAP

- ▶ DSAP

- ▶ SSAP

- ▶ SNAP

- ▶ 802.3

- ▶ 10BASE-2

- ▶ 10BASE-5

- ▶ 10BASE-T

- ▶ 10BASE-FL

- ▶ 802.3u

- ▶ 100BASE-T4

- ▶ 100BASE-TX

- ▶ 100BASE-FX

- ▶ 802.3ab

- ▶ 1000BASE-T

- ▶ 802.3z

- ▶ 1000BASE-CX

- ▶ 1000BASE-SX

- ▶ 1000BASE-LX

- ▶ 802.3ae

- ▶ 10GbE

- ▶ Baseband

- ▶ Broadband

- ▶ LRE

- ▶ EMI

- ▶ Coaxial cable

- ▶ Unshielded twisted-pair cable

- ▶ Shielded twisted-pair cable

- ▶ Fiber-optic cable

- ▶ Multimode

- ▶ Single-mode

- ▶ Switch

- ▶ ASIC

- ▶ Bridge

- ▶ Transparent bridges

- ▶ Spanning Tree Protocol

- ▶ Duplex

- ▶ Microsegmentation

Apply Your Knowledge
Exercises

3.1 IEEE 802.3 Ethernet Standards

You may be asked to identify the standards associated with IEEE Ethernet on the CCNA exam. In this exercise, I am listing the ethernet specification and want you to complete the table to include the IEEE-defined standard, the associated speed, and the cable or media type used for each specification. You may refer back to Tables 3.4, 3.5, 3.6, and 3.7 to check your answers.

Estimated Time: 10 minutes

IEEE Standard	IEEE Standard #	Maximum Speed	Cable or Media
10BASE-2			
10BASE-5			
10BASE-T			
10BASE-FL			
100BASE-T4			
100BASE-TX			
100BASE-FX			
1000BASE-T or 1000BASE-TX			
1000BASE-CX			
1000BASE-SX			
1000BASE-LX			
10GbE			

Review Questions

1. Define token-passing.

2. List the characteristics of a token ring network.

3. List the characteristics of an FDDI network.

4. Define unicast, multicast, and broadcast.

5. Describe CSMA/CD.

6. What are the primary tasks performed by both bridges and switches?

7. Describe half- and full-duplex.

8. Define microsegmentation.

Exam Questions

1. Which of the following is the IEEE standard for token ring?

   ○ **A.** 802.2

   ○ **B.** 802.3a

   ○ **C.** 802.3u

   ○ **D.** 802.5

2. ANSI X3T9.5 is the specification for which LAN technology?

   ○ **A.** Token ring

   ○ **B.** Fast Ethernet

   ○ **C.** FDDI

   ○ **D.** LLC

3. What Data Link layer technology inserts a three-byte token (or special bit pattern) into a frame and passes it in a single direction from one node to another until it forms a complete loop?

   ○ **A.** Token-passing

   ○ **B.** Unicast

   ○ **C.** Multicast

   ○ **D.** Broadcast

4. Which of the following LAN protocols use token-passing for frame transmission? (Choose the two best answers.)

 ○ **A.** Fast Ethernet

 ○ **B.** Token ring

 ○ **C.** Gigabit Ethernet

 ○ **D.** FDDI

5. This MAC sublayer address type identifies the MAC address of an individual LAN or NIC card.

 ○ **A.** Unicast

 ○ **B.** Multicast

 ○ **C.** Broadcast

 ○ **D.** Token

6. Which of the following addresses is an example of a unicast address? (Choose all that apply.)

 ○ **A.** 0000.0C12.3456

 ○ **B.** 0100.5E12.3456

 ○ **C.** FFFF.FFFF.FFFF

 ○ **D.** 0200.1111.1111

7. This MAC sublayer address type sends a frame to a subset of devices on the LAN.

 ○ **A.** Unicast

 ○ **B.** Multicast

 ○ **C.** Broadcast

 ○ **D.** Token

8. Which of the following addresses is an example of a multicast address?

 ○ **A.** 0000.0C12.3456

 ○ **B.** 0100.5E12.3456

 ○ **C.** FFFF.FFFF.FFFF

 ○ **D.** 0200.1111.1111

9. This MAC sublayer address type sends a frame to all the devices on the LAN.

   ○ **A.** Unicast

   ○ **B.** Multicast

   ○ **C.** Broadcast

   ○ **D.** Token

10. Which of the following addresses is an example of a broadcast address?

    ○ **A.** 0000.0C12.3456

    ○ **B.** 0100.5E12.3456

    ○ **C.** FFFF.FFFF.FFFF

    ○ **D.** 0200.1111.1111

11. The OSI model Data Link layer uses _____ to transport data between layers.

    ○ **A.** Bits

    ○ **B.** Frames

    ○ **C.** Packets

    ○ **D.** Segments

12. Which field of a frame is used for error detection?

    ○ **A.** SAP

    ○ **B.** DSAP

    ○ **C.** SSAP

    ○ **D.** FCS

13. Which IEEE Ethernet standards define Gigabit Ethernet? (Choose all that apply.)

    ○ **A.** 802.3u

    ○ **B.** 802.3ab

    ○ **C.** 802.3z

    ○ **D.** 802.3ae

14. Bridges and switches segment a network and create an additional _____ domain for each segment.

    ○ **A.** Collision

    ○ **B.** Broadcast

○ **C.** Unicast

○ **D.** Multicast

15. Bridges and switches examine the _____ of each inbound frame to learn MAC addresses.

   ○ **A.** Multicast MAC address

   ○ **B.** Broadcast MAC address

   ○ **C.** Source MAC address

   ○ **D.** Destination MAC address

16. Which device uses ASIC hardware chips for frame forwarding?

   ○ **A.** Hub

   ○ **B.** Repeater

   ○ **C.** Bridge

   ○ **D.** Switch

17. With a 10Mbps ethernet LAN, dedicated bandwidth enables a switch port to guarantee what data transmission speed?

   ○ **A.** 10Mbps

   ○ **B.** 100Mbps

   ○ **C.** 1000Mbps

   ○ **D.** 10,000Mbps

18. This Data Link protocol eliminates loops that are caused by redundant connections.

   ○ **A.** CRC

   ○ **B.** FCS

   ○ **C.** CSMA/CD

   ○ **D.** STP

19. This communication mode allows for only one-way data transmissions at any time.

   ○ **A.** 10Mbps

   ○ **B.** 100Mbps

   ○ **C.** Half-duplex

   ○ **D.** Full-duplex

20. This communication mode allows for simultaneous two-way data transmissions.

    ○ **A.** 10Mbps

    ○ **B.** 100Mbps

    ○ **C.** Half-duplex

    ○ **D.** Full-duplex

Answers to Review Questions

1. Token-passing is a Data Link protocol that inserts a three-byte token (or special bit pattern) into a frame and passes it around the network in a single direction from one node to another until it forms a complete loop. The node that has possession of the token is the only one that can send data at any given time on that LAN. Because only one node can send data at a time, collisions are avoided.

2. Standardized by the IEEE 802.5 specification

   A token-passing media access technology

   Set up as a physical ring or physical star topology

   Creates a logical ring topology

   Speeds are assigned as either 4Mbps or 16Mbps

   Utilizes an MSAU rather than a switch or hub

   Provides collision-free data transfer

   High overhead

3. Developed by ANSI with the ANSI X3T9.5 specification

   A token-passing media access technology

   Set up as a dual ring topology

   Redundant, fault-tolerant network

   Speed is 100Mbps

   Runs over fiber-optic cable

   Not susceptible to EMI

   Provides collision-free data transfer

   Fault-detection provided by beaconing

   High overhead

4. A unicast address identifies the MAC address of an individual LAN or NIC card.

   A multicast address forwards a frame to a subset of devices in the same LAN. IEEE ethernet multicast addresses always begin with 0100.5E in hexadecimal format. The last three bytes can be any combination.

   A broadcast address sends a frame to all devices in the same LAN. Broadcast addresses are always the same value, which is FFFF.FFFF.FFFF.

5. CSMA/CD or Carrier Sense Multiple Access Collision Detection is an algorithm that sends a jam signal to notify the devices that there has been a collision. The devices then halt transmission for a random back-off time.

6. The primary tasks performed by both bridges and switches are as follows:

   The source MAC address of every inbound frame is examined to learn its MAC address.

   You can decide whether to forward or filter a frame based on the destination MAC address.

   Eliminate loops that are caused by redundant connections by configuring Spanning Tree Protocol (STP).

7. Half-duplex allows for one-way communication, which means that a device can only send or receive a data transmission at any given time. As a part of a shared collision domain, hubs must use half-duplex.

   Full-duplex allows for two-way communication, which means that a device can simultaneously send and receive data transmissions. Full-duplex is available with dedicated switch port connections to a single device. If a switch port connection is configured for full-duplex, the CSMA/CD algorithm must be disabled. Also, an ethernet connection set for full-duplex allows for 100% transmission speeds in both directions.

8. Microsegmentation occurs when a switch creates a dedicated path for sending and receiving transmissions with each connected host. Each host then has a separate collision domain and a dedicated bandwidth.

Answers to Exam Questions

1. **D.** IEEE 802.5 defines token ring. Answers A, B, and C are incorrect because IEEE 802.2 defines LLC, 802.3a defines ethernet, and 802.3u defines Fast Ethernet.

2. **C.** ANSI X3T9.5 defines FDDI. Answers A, B, and D are incorrect because they are all IEEE standards. IEEE 802.5 defines token ring, 802.3u defines Fast Ethernet, and 802.2 defines LLC.

3. **A.** Token-passing inserts a three-byte token (or special bit pattern) into a frame and passes it in a single direction from one node to another until it forms a complete loop. Answers B, C, and D are all incorrect because unicast, multicast, and broadcast are all types of ethernet addresses.

4. **B, D.** Token ring and FDDI use token-passing to send frames. Answers A and C are incorrect because Fast Ethernet and Gigabit Ethernet both use 802.3 MAC and 802.2 LLC headers and trailers for framing.

5. **A.** Unicast addresses identify the MAC address of an individual LAN or NIC card. Answer B is incorrect because multicast addresses send a frame to a group of devices in the same LAN. Answer C is incorrect because broadcast addresses send a frame to all the devices in the same LAN. Answer D is incorrect because a token is a special bit pattern used with token-passing networks.

6. **A, D.** Both 0000.0C12.3456 and 0200.1111.1111 are unicast addresses. 0000.0C is Cisco's OUI. Answers B and C are incorrect because 0100.5E12.3456 is a multicast address and FFFF.FFFF.FFFF is a broadcast address.

7. **B.** Multicast addresses send a frame to a subset of devices in the same LAN. Answer A is incorrect because unicast addresses identify the MAC address of an individual LAN or NIC card. Answer C is incorrect because broadcast addresses send a frame to all the devices in the same LAN. Answer D is incorrect because a token is a special bit pattern used with token-passing networks.

8. **B.** 0100.5E12.3456 is a multicast address. Multicast addresses always start with 0100.5E. Answers A and D are incorrect because both 0000.0C12.3456 and 0200.1111.1111 are unicast addresses. Answer C is incorrect because FFFF.FFFF.FFFF is a broadcast address.

9. **C.** Broadcast addresses send a frame to all the devices in the same LAN. Answer A is incorrect because unicast addresses identify the MAC address of an individual LAN or NIC card. Answer B is incorrect because multicast addresses send a frame to a subset of devices in the same LAN. Answer D is incorrect because a token is a special bit pattern used with token-passing networks.

10. **C.** Broadcast addresses are always represented as FFFF.FFFF.FFFF. Answers A and D are incorrect because both 0000.0C12.3456 and 0200.1111.1111 are unicast addresses. Answer B is incorrect because 0100.5E12.3456 is a multicast address.

11. **B.** Frames are used by the Data Link layer to transport data between the Network and Physical layer. Framing is the process of interpreting data that is either received or sent out across the network. Answers A, C, and D are incorrect because bits are used at the Physical layer, packets are used at the Network layer, and segments are used at the Transport layer of the OSI model.

12. **D.** The frame check sequence (FCS) field of a frame uses a mathematical formula to determine whether any bit errors occurred during data transmission. Answer A is incorrect because Service Access Point (SAP) identifies the upper-layer protocol such as IP. Answer B is incorrect because DSAP is the destination SAP or destination upper-layer protocol. Answer C is incorrect because SSAP is the source SAP or the source upper-layer protocol.

13. **B, C.** IEEE 802.3ab and 802.3z define Gigabit Ethernet standards. Answers A and D are incorrect because 802.3u defines the Fast Ethernet standard, and 802.3ae defines the 10 Gigabit Ethernet standard.

14. **A.** Collision domains are increased with the addition of bridges or switches on a network. Answer B is incorrect because routers create additional broadcast domains. Answers C and D are incorrect because unicast and multicast are both addresses used by ethernet.

15. **C.** The source MAC address of an incoming frame is examined by a bridge or switch to learn the MAC address for the bridge table. Answers A and B are incorrect because multicast and broadcast addresses can never be the source MAC address. Answer D is incorrect because the destination MAC address is not used by a bridge or switch to create the bridge table.

16. **D.** Switches use ASIC hardware chips for frame forwarding. Answers A and B are incorrect because hubs and repeaters do not forward frames because they are Physical layer or Layer 1 devices. Answer C is incorrect because bridges use software for frame forwarding.

17. **A.** 10Mbps is guaranteed with dedicated bandwidth on a 10Mbps ethernet LAN. Answers B, C, and D are incorrect because other speeds of 100, 1000, and 10,000Mbps are all faster speeds that require a different ethernet LAN standard.

18. **D.** Spanning Tree Protocol (STP) is a Data Link protocol that eliminates loops caused by redundant connections on a LAN. Answers A and B are incorrect because cyclical redundancy check (CRC) and frame check sequence (FCS) both provide error detection. Answer C is incorrect because CSMA/CD is an algorithm that is used for arbitration on an ethernet network.

19. **C.** Half-duplex allows for only one-way data transmissions at any time. Answers A and B are incorrect because 10Mbps and 100Mbps are speed classifications primarily associated with ethernet LANs. Answer D is incorrect because full-duplex allows for two-way data transmissions.

20. **D.** Full-duplex allows for simultaneous two-way data transmissions. Answers A and B are incorrect because 10Mbps and 100Mbps are speed classifications primarily associated with ethernet LANs. Answer C is incorrect because half-duplex allows for only one-way data transmissions at any time.

Suggested Readings and Resources

The following are some recommended readings for LAN networking and related terminology:

1. "TechEncyclopedia," www.techweb.com/encyclopedia.

2. "RFC 1700," www.isi.edu/in-notes/rfc1700.txt.

3. "Layer 1 & 2," www.hojmark.net/layer1-2.html#lan.

4. "Cisco Long-Reach Ethernet," www.cisco.com/warp/public/779/servpro/solutions/long_ethernet/.

5. Barnes, David and Sakandar, Basir. *Cisco LAN Switching Fundamentals.* Cisco Press, 2004.

CHAPTER FOUR

General Network Security

Objectives

This chapter covers the following Cisco-specific objectives for the "Identify security threats to a network and describe general methods to mitigate those threats" section of both the 640-802 CCNA and 640-822 ICND1 exams:

▶ **Describe today's increasing network security threats and explain the need to implement a comprehensive security policy to mitigate the threats**

▶ **Explain general methods to mitigate common security threats to network devices, hosts, and applications**

▶ **Describe the functions of common security appliances and applications**

▶ **Describe security recommended practices including initial steps to secure network devices**

Outline

Introduction   122

Classes of Attack   122

Access Attacks   123
   Password Attacks   123
   Trust Exploitation   124
   Port Redirection   124
   Man-in-the-Middle Attacks   124
Reconnaissance Attacks   125
   Packet Sniffers   125
   Ping Sweeps   125
   Port Scans   126
   Information Queries   126
Denial of Service (DoS) Attacks   127
   Distributed DoS (DDoS)   127
   TCP SYN   128
   Smurf Attack   129

Mitigating Network Threats   130

AAA   130
Cisco ACLs   130

Cisco IOS Secure Management
   Features   131
   SSH   131
   SNMP   131
   Syslog   131
   NTP   132
Encryption Protocols   132
Security Appliances and Applications   132

Chapter Summary   134

Key Terms   134

Apply Your Knowledge   135

Exercise   135
Review Questions   136
Exam Questions   136
Answers to Review Questions   138
Answers to Exam Questions   138
Suggested Readings and Resources   139

Study Strategies

▶ Read the information presented in this chapter, paying special attention to tables, Notes, and Exam Alerts.

▶ Read the objectives at the beginning of the chapter.

▶ Review each class of attack.

▶ Name the specific attacks that comprise each class.

▶ Describe security threat mitigation techniques.

▶ Familiarize yourself with the Cisco devices that assist with general network security.

▶ Complete the Challenges and the Exercises at the end of the chapter.

Introduction

Information technology has evolved and provides countless resources for everyday people to create, maintain, and utilize data. If you have ever seen or read *Spiderman*, you have likely heard the quote "With great power comes great responsibility." Information is power, so it is vitally important to implement safeguards on your LAN and WAN to protect data from hackers. Everyone with a computer is susceptible and should be cautious with important private details such as credit card information. I have worked in the networking department at several types of companies, including a health-care company. Imagine if a hacker were to obtain patient medical records or a list of social security numbers from the human resources database. A company must follow special guidelines to ensure data privacy, which ties directly to network security. To make sure that companies adhere to security guidelines, annual audits are performed on their networks to identify potential weaknesses.

Even though network security has been a hot topic since the advent of computer networking, it is a new set of objectives on the CCENT and CCNA exams. To prepare yourself for the exams, you must know what classes of attack are common today, how to mitigate those attacks, and what features or hardware Cisco offers to assist in protecting your network. This chapter begins with a discussion of prevalent classes of attack.

Classes of Attack

Objective:

▶ Describe today's increasing network security threats and explain the need to implement a comprehensive security policy to mitigate the threats

Any number of motives could inspire an attacker; two motives that we touched on already are financial gain and gathering intelligence. A hacker may also simply enjoy the thrill of successfully breaking into someone's network. There are documented cases of hackers who intentionally attacked government systems simply to prove that it could be done and therefore gain notoriety.

This section discusses three classes of attack that are commonly found in today's network environment:

▶ Access attacks

▶ Reconnaissance attacks

▶ Denial of service (DoS) attacks

Each class has various more-specific subcategories of attack methods that will be covered in greater detail.

> **TIP**
>
> The three common classes of attack are access, reconnaissance, and DoS.

Access Attacks

An access attack is just what it sounds like: an attempt to access another user account or network device through improper means. If proper security measures are not in place, the network may be left vulnerable to intrusion. A network administrator is responsible for ensuring that only authorized users access the network. Unauthorized attacks are attempted via four means, all of which try to bypass some facet of the authentication process: password attacks, trust exploitation, port redirection, and man-in-the-middle attacks.

> **TIP**
>
> The four types of access attacks are password attacks, trust exploitation, port redirection, and man-in-the-middle attacks.

Password Attacks

Nowadays, it seems as if you need a password for everything. I have so many passwords that I find it hard to keep track. Although it might sound like a good idea to keep your passwords simple or to write them down, both practices are highly discouraged. The goal is to make it harder for someone to find or guess your password; therefore, password integrity is necessary. That being said, an attacker might attempt a login with false credentials. It is also important to note that not all attackers are external users. Many recorded instances of attempted and/or successful attacks have come from internal company employees.

There are alternatives to passwords, such as Terminal Access Controller Access Control System (TACACS) or Remote Authentication Dial-In User Service (RADIUS), both of which manage access to network hardware. Passwords are fast becoming as obsolete as rabbit-ear antennas or dialup Internet connections.

Cisco equipment is shipped from the factory with a standard configuration. When the device is turned on, the setup program prompts for a password and leaves all but the enable secret password in plain text. It is the responsibility of the recipient to update the password information before deploying the device on a network. Changing passwords every time an employee leaves the company or in a given time period (every 90 days) would also help protect login credentials.

Trust Exploitation

Trust exploitation can occur in one of two ways:

▶ Reliance on the trust a client has in a server

▶ Reliance on the trust the server has in the client

For example, most companies have a part of their network that lies between the wide-open Internet and the corporate internal network. This in-between part of the network is called the demilitarized zone (DMZ). Servers that communicate from the DMZ and the internal network may have a trust relationship established. The internal devices may be set up to trust information that is received from a DMZ server. An attacker can then compromise the DMZ server and initiate a connection to the internal network. This is an example of phishing. When the trust that the server has in a client is exploited, this is an example of session hijacking.

Port Redirection

Port redirection is a form of trust exploitation in which the untrustworthy source uses a machine with access to the internal network to pass traffic through a port on the firewall or access control list (ACL). The port in question normally denies traffic, but with redirection the attacker can bypass security measures and open a tunnel for communication.

Man-in-the-Middle Attacks

A man-in-the-middle attack happens when a hacker eavesdrops or listens for network traffic and intercepts a data transmission. After the transmission is intercepted, the untrustworthy host can position itself between the two communicating hosts, interpret the data, and steal information from the packets sent. The hacker can also take over the session and reformat the packets to send information to either or both communicating parties. In this situation, it is possible for the hacker to capture credentials, hijack a session, or instigate a DoS attack.

Data sessions are more vulnerable when the packets are left in clear-text format and can be read without additional decryption by the human eye. Proper data encryption, with the use of an encryption protocol, makes the captured data useless.

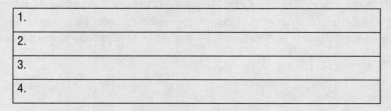

Challenge

In this challenge, write down the four types of access attacks.

1.
2.
3.
4.

Reconnaissance Attacks

When I hear the word reconnaissance, I think of a military reconnaissance mission. The soldier is sent out to gather important information about an area of interest. The same holds true for a reconnaissance attack on a computer network. The hacker surveys a network and collects data for a future attack. Important information that can be compiled during a reconnaissance attack includes the following:

► Ports open on a server

► Ports open on a firewall

► IP addresses on the host network

► Hostnames associated with the IP addresses

As with access attacks, there are four main subcategories or methods for gathering network data:

► Packet sniffers (also known as network monitors)

► Ping sweeps

► Port scans

► Information queries

> **TIP**
>
> The four common tools used for reconnaissance attacks are packet sniffers, ping sweeps, port scans, and information queries.

Packet Sniffers

A packet sniffer may also be called a network analyzer, packet analyzer, or Ethernet sniffer. The packet sniffer may be either a software program or a piece of hardware with software installed in it that captures traffic sent over the network, which is then decoded and analyzed by the sniffer. Network administrators install monitors on dedicated machines or on their workstations when needed. A common software program available today is Wireshark, formerly known as Ethereal.

Ping Sweeps

As you may recall, ping enables you to validate that an IP address exists and can accept requests by sending an echo request and then waiting for an echo reply. A ping sweep tool can send an echo request to numerous host IP addresses at the same time to see which host(s) respond(s) with an echo reply.

> **NOTE**
>
> Refer to Chapter 1, "Standard Internetworking Models," for a review of ping, which uses ICMP.

Port Scans

A port scanner is a software program that surveys a host network for open ports. Because ports are associated with applications, the hacker can use the port and application information to determine a way to attack the network. As mentioned, these programs can be used by a third party to audit a network as well as being used by a hacker for malicious intent.

As mentioned in Chapter 1, it is extremely important that you know the prevalent applications and their matching port numbers. Table 4.1 reviews the applications that use TCP, and Table 4.2 reviews UDP-based applications.

TABLE 4.1   Applications Using TCP

Application	Port Number(s)
FTP	20, 21
Telnet	23
SMTP	25
DNS (zone transfers)	53
HTTP	80
POP3	110
NNTP	119
HTTPS	443

TABLE 4.2   Applications Using UDP

Application	Port Number(s)
DHCP	67, 68
DNS (name resolution)	53
TFTP	69
NTP	123
SNMP	161

Information Queries

Information queries can be sent via the Internet to resolve hostnames from IP addresses or vice versa. One of the most commonly used queries is nslookup. You can use nslookup by opening a Windows or Linux command prompt (CMD) window on your computer and entering `nslookup` followed by the IP address or hostname that you are attempting to resolve.

Here are a couple sample CMD commands:

```
C: nslookup www.cisco.com
C: nslookup 198.133.219.25
```

A multitude of websites offer an nslookup tool.

Challenge

In this challenge, write down the four common tools we discussed for gathering information for a reconnaissance attack.

1.	
2.	
3.	
4.	

Denial of Service (DoS) Attacks

DoS attacks are often implemented by a hacker as a means of denying a service that is normally available to a user or organization. For example, users might be denied access to email as the result of a successful DoS attack. IP spoofing can be used as part of a DoS attack or man-in-the-middle attack and occurs when a valid host IP address is assumed by an attacking system. This provides a way to bypass the trust a machine has in another machine.

Although it has long since been patched, a DoS attack called the ping of death occurred when an ICMP echo request packet larger than 65,535 bytes was sent to a target destination, causing it to overflow, crash, and/or reboot. A current example of a DoS attack is a teardrop, which can cause a system to crash by running the CPU up to 100%. Teardrop sends in thousands of tiny fragments with overlapping offsets.

DoS can also be in the form of a distributed DoS (DDoS) attack, TCP SYN attack, or smurf attack.

Distributed DoS (DDoS)

With distributed DoS, multiple systems are compromised to send a DoS attack to a specific target. The compromised systems are commonly called zombies or slaves. As a result of the attack, the targeted system denies service to valid users. Figure 4.1 illustrates a DDoS attack.

FIGURE 4.1   DDoS attack.

TCP SYN

You may recall from Chapter 1 that a TCP session is established with the use of a three-way handshake, which involves the following steps:

1. A "connection agreement" segment is sent to the recipient, asking to synchronize systems. This step is associated with the bit name SYN.

2. The second and third segments acknowledge the request to connect and determine the rules of engagement. Sequencing synchronization is requested of the receiving device. A two-way connection is established. This step is associated with the bit name SYN-ACK.

3. A final segment is sent as an acknowledgment that the rules have been accepted and a connection has been formed. This step is associated with the bit name ACK.

Figure 4.2 illustrates a proper TCP session.

FIGURE 4.2   TCP session establishment.

In a TCP SYN attack, a SYN request is sent to a device with a spoofed source IP address. The attacking system does not acknowledge the resulting SYN-ACK, which causes the session connection queues to fill up and stop taking new connection requests. TCP intercept can be configured on a router to block a TCP SYN attack. This enables the router to terminate any sessions that have not been established within an allotted time frame.

Smurf Attack

With a smurf attack, multiple broadcast ping requests are sent to a single target from a spoofed IP address. Figure 4.3 illustrates a smurf attack. Adding the no ip directed-broadcast command to a router might help mitigate a potential smurf attack.

FIGURE 4.3   Smurf attack.

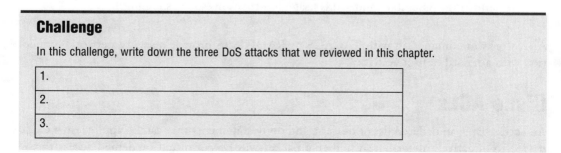

Challenge

In this challenge, write down the three DoS attacks that we reviewed in this chapter.

1.
2.
3.

Mitigating Network Threats

Objectives:

▶ Explain general methods to mitigate common security threats to network devices, hosts, and applications

▶ Describe the functions of common security appliances and applications

▶ Describe security recommended practices including initial steps to secure network devices

By definition, to mitigate is to lessen in force or intensity. Now that you are familiar with the various classes of attack, let's discuss what actions you can take to lessen the impact of an attack on a network. Keep in mind that we already went over some common mitigation techniques, such as password integrity, password encryption, TCP intercept, and `no ip directed-broadcast`. We will continue this chapter with a general overview of additional recommended practices and security measures. Our discussion includes the following mitigation techniques:

▶ Authentication, Authorization, and Accounting (AAA)

▶ Cisco access control lists (ACLs)

▶ Cisco Internetwork Operating System (IOS) secure management features

▶ Encryption protocols

▶ Security appliances and applications

AAA

Commonly called "triple A," AAA is a group of three services that are used to increase network security:

▶ **Authentication:** Identifies a user by login and password.

▶ **Authorization:** Determines what a user is allowed to do.

▶ **Accounting:** Assembles and sends usage information (such as logging).

AAA works in conjunction with TACACS or RADIUS to provide a secure network connection with a record of user activities.

Cisco ACLs

An access list is an ordered list of `permit` and `deny` statements that can be applied on a Cisco device to effectively determine whether a packet will be permitted or denied access to the network. A properly configured access list can help block most of the attack methods described in this chapter:

▶ IP spoofing

▶ TCP SYN attacks

▶ Smurf attacks

▶ ICMP and traceroute

Cisco IOS Secure Management Features

I mentioned earlier that it is the responsibility of the network administrator to configure Cisco equipment with a new password before deployment. You can take this a step further by performing some initial steps to secure Cisco equipment within the IOS. Configuring the following features on your Cisco device helps create a secure network environment:

▶ Secure Shell (SSH)

▶ Simple Network Management Protocol (SNMP)

▶ Syslog

▶ Network Time Protocol (NTP)

SSH

SSH is a data transmission protocol that uses strong authentication and an encrypted tunnel to ensure secure communications between an SSH client and the SSH server. SSH uses TCP port number 22 for connectivity.

SNMP

SNMP is a management protocol that monitors the network and manages configurations by collecting statistics to analyze network performance and ensure network security. It is best to use SNMP version 3, which provides cryptographic authentication and management traffic encryption. SNMP uses UDP port number 161 for connectivity.

Syslog

With syslog, log messages are collected from the Cisco device and are sent to a syslog server to keep record of any network occurrences. For syslog to work properly, NTP must be configured. Each logged message has an associated severity level. Syslog uses UDP port number 514 for connectivity. Table 4.3 lists the severity levels in order, with 0 representing the most critical message.

TABLE 4.3   Syslog Severity Levels

Security Level	Description
0	Emergency
1	Alert
2	Critical
3	Error
4	Warning
5	Notification
6	Informational
7	Debugging

NTP

NTP is a protocol that synchronizes clocks on the local network to provide accurate local time on the user system. As with SNMP version 3, NTP version 3 is preferred because of the ability to provide cryptographic authentication and management traffic encryption. NTP uses UDP port number 123 for connectivity.

Encryption Protocols

Unencrypted data can be easily read by internal or external threats to a network. This is the case when data is left in clear-text format. To help prevent an attack, it is important to encrypt or encode data. Here are three key encryption protocols:

▶ **SSH:** A data transmission protocol that uses strong authentication and an encrypted tunnel to ensure secure communications between an SSH client and the SSH server.

▶ **Internet Protocol Security (IPsec):** Consists of a set of protocols that were developed to secure the transfer of packets above the Network layer (Layer 3) of the OSI model.

▶ **Secure Socket Layer (SSL):** A protocol that provides a secure channel between two devices at the Application layer (Layer 7) of the OSI model. Asymmetric encryption and certificates are used to exchange a session key. Data is encrypted using that key and a block cipher. HTTPS is an example of an SSL secure transaction.

Security Appliances and Applications

The following are security devices used to mitigate security vulnerabilities:

▶ **Firewall:** A firewall can be either software or hardware that is installed to separate a trusted network from a less-trusted network, such as the Internet.

▶ **Intrusion Prevention System (IPS):** IPS is an active device that is inline with the traffic path on a network. An IPS listens promiscuously to all incoming traffic to identify attacks. It works with the firewall to modify rule templates to block traffic from the attacker address(es) while the attack is still in progress.

▶ **Intrusion Detection System (IDS):** IDS is a passive device that may not be inline with the traffic path on a network. An IDS also listens promiscuously to all incoming traffic to record and generate alerts and issue TCP resets if necessary.

REVIEW BREAK

Because so many possible mitigation techniques exist, let's go over them all in a quick review. Table 4.4 lists and describes each method.

TABLE 4.4   Security Mitigation Techniques

Mitigation Method	Description
AAA	A group of three services (authentication, authorization, and accounting) that are used in conjunction with TACACS or RADIUS to provide a secure network connection with a record of user activities.
Cisco ACL	An ordered list of `permit` and `deny` statements that can be applied on a Cisco device to effectively determine whether a packet will be permitted or denied access to the network.
SSH	A data transmission protocol that uses strong authentication and an encrypted tunnel to ensure secure communications between an SSH client and the SSH server. SSH protects otherwise-vulnerable services such as Telnet, news, and mail.
SNMP	A management protocol that monitors the network and manages configurations by collecting statistics to analyze network performance and ensure network security.
Syslog	Log messages are collected from the Cisco device and are sent to a syslog server to keep records of any network occurrences.
NTP	A protocol that synchronizes clocks on the local network to provide accurate local time on the user system.
IPsec	A set of protocols that were developed to secure the transfer of packets at the Network layer (Layer 3) of the OSI model.
SSL	A protocol that provides a secure channel between two devices at the Application layer (Layer 7) of the OSI model.
Firewall	Either software or hardware that is installed to protect a network from outside networks, such as the Internet.
IPS	An active device that is inline with the traffic path on a network. An IPS listens promiscuously to all incoming traffic to identify attacks, which the system can then block.
IDS	A passive device that may not be inline with the traffic path on a network. An IDS also listens promiscuously to all incoming traffic to generate alerts and issue TCP resets if necessary.

Chapter Summary

After reading through this chapter, you should have a general understanding of the types of security threats that are prevalent in our high-tech, information-driven society and various ways to mitigate those threats. A responsible network administrator must be aware of these possible attacks to protect the network from any form of security breach. Cisco offers built-in security management features that can be configured before the equipment is installed on the local network. It is also possible to purchase additional hardware and software to enhance over-all security. The Cisco catalog includes IOS versions of firewall, IPS, IPsec VPN, and SSL VPN. You also have a variety of network security appliances to choose from, depending on the size and needs of your particular company.

Key Terms

- ▶ Access attack
- ▶ Reconnaissance attack
- ▶ Denial of service (DoS) attack
- ▶ Password attack
- ▶ Trust exploitation
- ▶ Port redirection
- ▶ Man-in-the-middle attack
- ▶ Packet sniffer
- ▶ Port scan
- ▶ Ping sweep
- ▶ Information query
- ▶ IP spoofing
- ▶ Ping of death
- ▶ Teardrop attack
- ▶ Distributed DoS attack
- ▶ TCP SYN attack
- ▶ Smurf attack
- ▶ Authentication, Authorization, and Accounting (AAA)
- ▶ Access control list (ACL)

- ▶ Secure Shell (SSH)

- ▶ Simple Network Management Protocol (SNMP)

- ▶ SYSLOG

- ▶ Network Time Protocol (NTP)

- ▶ Internet Protocol Security (IPsec)

- ▶ Secure Socket Layer (SSL)

- ▶ Firewall

- ▶ Intrusion Prevention System (IPS)

- ▶ Intrusion Detection System (IDS)

Apply Your Knowledge

Exercise

4.1 Mitigation Methods

Based on the Cisco-provided exam objectives, you may need to "explain general methods to mitigate common security threats to network devices, hosts, and applications" on the CCNA exam. In this exercise, list the eleven mitigation methods that were covered in this chapter, and write a brief description of each one. You may refer to Table 4.4 to check your answers.

Estimated Time: 20 minutes

1. _____ _____

2. _____ _____

3. _____ _____

4. _____ _____

5. _____ _____

6. _____ _____

7. _____ _____

8. _____ _____

9. _____ _____

10. _____ _____

11. _____ _____

Review Questions

1. Define trust exploitation.

2. Describe a TCP SYN attack.

3. What are the three services that make up AAA?

4. What can a Cisco ACL help mitigate?

5. List the similarities and differences between an IPS and IDS.

Exam Questions

1. What are the three common classes of attack?

   ○ **A.** Access attack

   ○ **B.** DoS attack

   ○ **C.** Smurf attack

   ○ **D.** Reconnaissance attack

2. Which of the following are types of access attacks? (Choose three)

   ○ **A.** Trust exploitation

   ○ **B.** TCP SYN attack

   ○ **C.** Port redirection

   ○ **D.** Man-in-the-middle

3. Which of the following are tools that can be used for a reconnaissance attack? (Choose three)

   ○ **A.** Port redirection

   ○ **B.** Ping sweep

   ○ **C.** Port scan

   ○ **D.** Packet sniffer

4. Which of the following are types of DoS attacks? (Choose three)

   ○ **A.** Smurf attack

   ○ **B.** Packet sniffer

   ○ **C.** DDoS

   ○ **D.** TCP SYN attack

5. What command can be configured on a Cisco device to mitigate smurf attacks?

   ○ **A.** `ip tcp intercept`

   ○ **B.** `ip directed-broadcast`

   ○ **C.** `no ip directed-broadcast`

   ○ **D.** `no ip tcp intercept`

6. When a valid host IP address is assumed by an attacking system, it is called _____.

   ○ **A.** Filtering

   ○ **B.** Ping of death

   ○ **C.** IP spoofing

   ○ **D.** Teardrop attack

7. What do the three A's in AAA stand for?

   ○ **A.** Authentication, authorization, advertising

   ○ **B.** Authorization, accounting, activating

   ○ **C.** Authentication, accounting, activating

   ○ **D.** Authentication, authorization, accounting

8. Which protocol uses TCP port 22?

   ○ **A.** SSL

   ○ **B.** SSH

   ○ **C.** SNMP

   ○ **D.** NTP

9. Which of the following are Cisco IOS secure management features? (Choose three)

   ○ **A.** Syslog

   ○ **B.** SSH

    ○ **C.** AAA

    ○ **D.** SNMP

10. Which protocol provides a secure channel between two devices at the Application layer (Layer 7) of the OSI model?

    ○ **A.** SSL

    ○ **B.** IPsec

    ○ **C.** SNMP

    ○ **D.** NTP

Answers to Review Questions

1. Trust exploitation occurs when a device or group of devices on a shared segment erroneously trusts information that has been provided by an untrustworthy source.

2. In a TCP SYN attack, a SYN request is sent to a device with a spoofed IP address. The attacking system does not acknowledge the resulting SYN-ACK, which causes the session connection queues to fill up and stop taking new connection requests.

3. Authentication identifies a user by login and password. Authorization determines what a user is allowed to do by putting together a list of attributes. Accounting assembles and sends usage information.

4. IP spoofing
   TCP SYN attacks
   Smurf attacks
   ICMP and traceroute

5. Both IPS and IDS listen promiscuously to all incoming traffic. IPS is an active device that is inline with the traffic path. It can identify attacks and block them in the system. IDS is a passive device that may not be inline with the path of traffic. IDS can also generate alerts and send TCP resets when necessary.

Answers to Exam Questions

1. **A, B, D.** The three common classes of attack are access attack, reconnaissance attack, and DoS attack. Answer C is not a class of attack, but rather a type of DoS attack.

2. **A, C, D.** Trust exploitation, port redirection, and man-in-the-middle are all types of access attacks. Answer B is incorrect because a TCP SYN attack is a form of DoS attack.

3. **B, C, D.** Ping sweeps, port scans, and packet sniffers are all tools that can be utilized for a reconnaissance attack. Answer A is incorrect because port redirection is a type of access attack.

4. **A, C, D.** Smurf attacks, DDoS attacks, and TCP SYN attacks are all types of DoS attacks. Answer B is incorrect because a packet sniffer is a tool used for a reconnaissance attack.

5. **C.** The `no ip directed-broadcast` command can be configured on a Cisco device to block smurf attacks. Answers A and D are incorrect because they are related to the TCP SYN attack. Answer B is incorrect because it does not contain the keyword `no`.

6. **C.** When a valid host IP address is assumed by an attacking system, it is called IP spoofing. Answer A is incorrect because filtering is used to filter traffic. Answer B is incorrect because the ping of death is when an ICMP echo request packet that is larger than 65,535 bytes is sent to a target destination, causing it to overflow, crash, and/or reboot. Answer D is incorrect because a teardrop attack happens when the Offset field of the TCP header is changed.

7. **D.** AAA stands for authentication, authorization, and accounting. Answer A is incorrect because advertising is not a service of AAA. Answers B and C are incorrect because activating is not a service of AAA.

8. **B.** SSH uses TCP port 22. Answer A is incorrect because SSL uses TCP port 443. Answer C is incorrect because SNMP uses UDP port 161. Answer D is incorrect because NTP uses UDP port 123.

9. **A, B, D.** Syslog, SSH, and SNMP are all Cisco IOS secure management features. Answer C is incorrect because AAA consists of a group of three services that are used in conjunction with an authentication server and a software service such as TACACS or RADIUS to provide a secure network connection with a record of user activities.

10. **A.** SSL is a protocol that provides a secure channel between two devices at the Application layer (Layer 7) of the OSI model. Answer B is incorrect because IPsec functions at Layer 3 of the OSI model. Answer C is incorrect because SNMP is a management protocol that monitors the network and manages configurations. Answer D is incorrect because NTP is a protocol that synchronizes clocks on the local network to provide accurate local time on the user system.

Suggested Readings and Resources

1. "A Beginner's Guide to Network Security," http://www.cisco.com/warp/public/cc/so/neso/sqso/beggu_pl.pdf.

2. List of Cisco Security products, http://www.cisco.com/en/US/products/hw/vpndevc/index.html.

CHAPTER FIVE

IP at the Network Layer

Objectives

This chapter covers the following Cisco-specific objectives for the "Implement an IP addressing scheme and IP services to meet network requirements for a small branch office" section of the of the 640-822 ICND1 exam:

▶ **Describe the need and role of addressing in a network**

▶ **Describe the operation and benefits of using private and public IP addressing**

Outline

Introduction   **144**

Network Layer Functions   **144**

IP Addressing and Formats   **145**

Binary   145
     Converting Binary to Decimal   146
     Converting Decimal to Binary   148
Hexadecimal   150
     Converting Decimal to Hexadecimal   150
IP Address Classes   151
Subnet Masks   154
Private (RFC 1918) Addressing   156

Subnetting IP   **156**

Calculating Hosts in a Subnet   159
Calculating Networks in a Subnet   161
     Zero Subnet Rule   162
The Increment   162
Determining the Range of Valid IPs   165

Network Layer Devices   **167**

Routers   167
Layer 3 Switches   170

Chapter Summary   **171**

Key Terms   171

Apply Your Knowledge   **172**

Exercises   172
Review Questions   175
Exam Questions   175
Answers to Review Questions   179
Answers to Exam Questions   181
Suggested Readings and Resources   183

Study Strategies

▶ List the characteristics of IPv4.

▶ Make sure you know how to convert binary to decimal.

▶ Make sure you know how to convert decimal to binary.

▶ Make sure you know how to convert decimal to hexadecimal.

▶ Identify IP address classes, including their networks and hosts, and the IP range value of the first octet of each class.

▶ Define subnet masks and the IP subnet mask format.

▶ Describe CIDR notations and how to determine the CIDR notation based on the subnet mask.

▶ Define RFC 1918, NAT, and PAT.

▶ Make sure you know how to calculate hosts and networks in a subnet.

▶ Determine the Network ID, Broadcast IP, and valid IP range of a subnet.

▶ Name the devices that are used at the Network layer and important traits of each device.

Introduction

This chapter elaborates on the fundamental concepts that you learned about the Network layer or Layer 3 of the OSI model in Chapter 1, "Standard Internetworking Models." It reviews the primary functions of the Network layer and then moves right into IP addressing and formats. After you are familiar with address formats and how to convert between them, it reviews subnetting. No matter whether you decide to take the one- or two-test approach to the CCENT certification, you have to know IP address formats and subnetting. They are integral concepts to any Cisco certification. Finally, this chapter discusses network devices that are used at the Network layer, which are routers and Layer 3 switches.

Network Layer Functions

The Network layer of the OSI model serves two primary functions:

- ▶ Determines the best path selection for a packet based on a logical or virtual address on the network (routing)
- ▶ Handles ICMP, ARP, and Proxy ARP requests

First, best path determination is made at the Network layer for packet delivery across the network. Routed protocols such as IP are used to define logical addressing, which can identify the destination of a packet or datagram. Logical addresses used for routing consist of network and host bits. Routers also must determine the path through the internetwork for packet transmission. This is similar to how switches use a MAC address and interface for frame delivery. Routers also use an interface along with the logical or IP address.

Second, the Network layer also handles ICMP, ARP, and Proxy ARP requests on the internetwork. Remember the function of each protocol for the ICND1 exam.

Internet Control Messaging Protocol (ICMP) is used by ping and traceroute utilities. Packet Internet Groper (ping) enables you to validate that an IP address exists and can accept requests.

- ▶ Ping is an echo and the response is an echo response.
- ▶ Routers send Destination Unreachable messages when they can't reach the destination network and they are forced to drop the packet. The router that drops the packet sends the ICMP DU message.

A traceroute traces the route or path taken from a client to a remote host. Traceroute also reports the IP addresses of the routers at each next hop on the way to the destination. This is especially useful when you suspect that a router on the route to an unreachable network is responsible for dropping the packet.

Address Resolution Protocol (ARP) maps a known IP address to a MAC address by sending a broadcast ARP. When the destination IP address is on another subnet, the sender broadcasts

ARP for the router's Ethernet port or default gateway, so the MAC address sent back will be that of the router's Ethernet port.

Reverse ARP (RARP) maps a known MAC address to an IP address.

Proxy ARP enables a router to respond to an ARP request that has been sent to a remote host. Some Unix machines (especially Solaris) rely on Proxy ARP versus default gateways.

IP Addressing and Formats

Objective:

▶ Describe the need and role of addressing in a network

Internet Protocol (IP) uses logical or virtual addressing to get a packet from a source to its destination. At the Network layer, routers use IP addresses to make best path forwarding decisions. Public IP addresses are used for packets destined for the outside world, whereas private addresses can be used if the packet needs to traverse only an internal network. The ICND1 course focuses on IP version 4 (IPv4). The addresses themselves are assigned by the Internet Assigned Numbers Authority (IANA) to individual organizations based on a request for IP address space. Because the total number of IPv4 addresses is not infinite, strict guidelines are placed on IP space requests to ensure that they are justifiable.

IPv4 addresses

▶ Consist of 32 bits.

▶ Are broken into four octets (8 bits each).

▶ Use dotted-decimal format, such as 172.16.122.204.

▶ Have a minimum value (per octet) of 0 and a maximum value of 255.

▶ Have a Network ID of 0.0.0.0.

▶ Have a Broadcast IP of 255.255.255.255.

Another IP version was created in the event that the IP space from IPv4 is exhausted. That version is called IP version 6 (IPv6). IPv6 has emerged in the Cisco professional-level exams and may appear on a future ICND1 exam. For this reason, IPv6 is introduced later in this chapter.

Binary

To understand IP addressing, you must first understand binary. Binary is a computer language that is represented by a bit value of 0 or 1. A 32-bit binary address would resemble

10101010101010101010101010101010. Those 32 bits can be grouped into four octets, or 10101010 10101010 10101010 10101010, for conversion to decimal format. When the bit value is 1, the bit is considered to be on and you can calculate its binary value depending on its placement within the binary octet. When the bit value is 0, the bit is off and has no corresponding binary value. Figure 5.1 displays the binary value and the calculated decimal value of each bit within an octet. Notice that the binary value increases exponentially.

Binary Value	2^7	2^6	2^5	2^4	2^3	2^2	2^1	2^0
Decimal Value	128	64	32	16	8	4	2	1

FIGURE 5.1 A list of binary and decimal conversion values.

Converting Binary to Decimal

By using the value calculated for each bit, you can easily convert to decimal format. Line up the binary octet with the decimal value that was calculated in Figure 5.1. To calculate the total decimal value of each octet, you would add up the binary value of each bit that is on (1) .

The example in Table 5.1 uses binary octet 00000000.

TABLE 5.1   Example #1 of a Binary-to-Decimal Conversion

Bit Value	0	0	0	0	0	0	0	0
Decimal Value	128	64	32	16	8	4	2	1

In this case, all the bit values are off (0), so there is no corresponding decimal value. The IP address octet value is also 0.

Table 5.2 uses binary octet 00010001.

TABLE 5.2   Example #2 of a Binary-to-Decimal Conversion

Bit Value	0	0	0	1	0	0	0	1
Decimal Value	128	64	32	16	8	4	2	1
				16				1

In this example, the fourth and last bit values are 1. Add the decimal values to get the total decimal value of that octet. That is, the total decimal value = 17 (16 + 1).

Table 5.3 uses binary octet 11111111.

TABLE 5.3   Example #3 of a Binary-to-Decimal Conversion

Bit Value	1	1	1	1	1	1	1	1
Decimal Value	128	64	32	16	8	4	2	1
	128	64	32	16	8	4	2	1

In Table 5.3, the total decimal value = 255 (128 + 64 + 32 + 16 + 8 + 4 + 2 + 1).

In this case, all the bit values are on (1), so all the decimal values are added together to calculate the IP address octet. The IP address octet value is 255.

Now, you can convert a 32-bit binary address into a dotted-decimal address. In this example, the binary address is 10101010 01010101 11000011 00111100. Start with the first octet 10110000. Table 5.4 shows the conversion of 10101010 from binary to decimal value.

TABLE 5.4   Binary-to-Decimal Conversion of 10101010

Bit Value	1	0	1	1	0	0	0	0
Decimal Value	**128**	64	**32**	**16**	8	4	2	1
	128		**32**	**16**				

In Table 5.4, the total decimal value = 170 (128 + 32 + 16).

The second octet is 01010101. Table 5.5 shows the conversion of 01010101 from binary to decimal value.

TABLE 5.5   Binary-to-Decimal Conversion of 01010101

Bit Value	0	1	0	1	0	1	0	1
Decimal Value	128	**64**	32	**16**	8	**4**	2	**1**
		64		**16**		**4**		**1**

In Table 5.5, the IP octet value = 85 (64 + 16 + 4 + 1).

The third octet is 11000011. Table 5.6 shows the conversion of 11000011 from binary to decimal value.

TABLE 5.6   Binary-to-Decimal Conversion of 11000011

Bit Value	1	1	0	0	0	0	1	1
Decimal Value	**128**	**64**	32	16	8	4	**2**	**1**
	128	**64**					**2**	**1**

In Table 5.6, the total decimal value = 195 (128 + 64 + 2 + 1)

The fourth and final octet is 00111100. Table 5.7 shows the conversion of 00111100 from binary to decimal value.

TABLE 5.7   Binary-to-Decimal Conversion of 00111100

Bit Value	0	0	1	1	1	1	0	0
Decimal Value	128	64	**32**	**16**	**8**	**4**	2	1
			32	**16**	**8**	**4**		

In Table 5.7, the total decimal value = 60 (32 + 16 + 8 + 4).

Based on these calculations, the IP address in dotted-decimal format is 176.85.195.60.

EXAM ALERT

Whenever the last bit is 1, the decimal value is an odd number. Whenever the last bit is 0, the decimal value is an even number. The ICND1 exam often uses multiple-choice questions, so you may be able to narrow down the possible correct answers quickly with this hint.

Challenge

In this challenge, you are given a bit value for four octets. You need to fill out the corresponding decimal value and then calculate the total decimal value. After you have converted all four octets, you need to fill out the IP address in dotted-decimal format.

Bit Value	1	1	1	0	1	0	1	0
Decimal Value								

Total Decimal Value = _____

Bit Value	0	1	1	0	1	1	0	1
Decimal Value								

Total Decimal Value = _____

Bit Value	0	0	1	0	1	1	0	0
Decimal Value								

Total Decimal Value = _____

Bit Value	1	0	1	0	1	1	1	1
Decimal Value								

Total Decimal Value = _____

The IP Address in dotted-decimal format is _____._____._____._____.

Converting Decimal to Binary

You must also be able to convert an IP address from dotted-decimal format into binary. It helps to work from left to right when converting to binary.

Example IP address = 206.110.28.62

The first octet of 206 can be broken down as follows:

128	64	32	16	8	4	2	1
1	1	0	0	1	1	1	0

The octet value is greater than 128, so the first bit is on. Subtract 128 from 206.

$206 - 128 = 78$

The remainder 78 is greater than 64, so the second bit is also on.

$78 - 64 = 14$

The remainder 14 is less than 32 and 16, so the third and fourth bits are off. However, 14 is greater than 8, so the fifth bit is on.

$14 - 8 = 6$

The remainder 6 is greater than 4, so the sixth bit is on.

$6 - 4 = 2$

The remainder 2 is equal to the seventh bit value, so that bit is also on.

$2 - 2 = 0$

The last bit value is off because the remainder is 0. Remember that it is an even number, so the last bit will always be 0!

Challenge

You've already converted the first octet of 206.110.28.62 into binary. Determine the appropriate bit value for the remaining three octets.

Second octet 110:

128	64	32	16	8	4	2	1
—	—	—	—	—	—	—	—

Third octet 28:

128	64	32	16	8	4	2	1
—	—	—	—	—	—	—	—

Fourth octet 62:

128	64	32	16	8	4	2	1
—	—	—	—	—	—	—	—

Now that all four quartets have been converted, the binary equivalent of 216.110.28.62 is 11001110 _____ _____ _____.

Hexadecimal

Hexadecimal is a numbering system with a base of 16. Numbers 0 through 9 represent the first 10 decimal digits and the next 6 digits are the letters A through F. Each hexadecimal character is equal to four bits. Hexadecimal format was first introduced in Chapter 1, during the discussion of MAC addresses at the Data Link layer. Figure 5.2 shows the decimal values 0 through 15 and their equivalent hexadecimal values.

Decimal Value	0-9	10	11	12	13	14	15
Hexadecimal Value	0-9	A	B	C	D	E	F

FIGURE 5.2 Decimal-to-hexadecimal conversions.

Converting Decimal to Hexadecimal

There are two ways to calculate hexadecimal from decimal format. With the first method, the decimal value should first be converted to binary format.

Decimal value = 141

128	64	32	16	8	4	2	1
1	0	0	0	1	1	0	1

Binary value = 10001101

Now break the binary value into two groups of 4 bits each, which is 1000 and 1101. Then, line up the 4 bits with the last four decimal values that were calculated in Figure 5.1. Again, add up the binary value of each bit that is on (1).

1	0	0	0
8	4	2	1
8				The combined value is 8 so the hexadecimal character = 8

1	1	0	1
8	4	2	1
8	4		1	The combined value is 13 so the hexadecimal character = D

The combined hexadecimal address is 0x8D.

The second method for calculating a hexadecimal address is to divide the decimal number by 16 first. So, 141 divided by 16 equals 8 with a remainder of 13, which matches the results from the binary conversion in the first method.

NOTE

Recall how 8 bits for an octet equals one byte. Well, when you divide an octet into two hexadecimal fields of 4 bits each, each 4-bit field is called a nibble.

Challenge

Here are several decimal values. Calculate the hexadecimal value, using Figure 5.2 as a guideline.

Decimal Value	Hexadecimal Value
210	
193	
245	
161	

IP Address Classes

As you know, IP addresses are 32 bits long, represented by dotted-decimal notation. Each address can be divided into two parts:

▶ Network

▶ Host

The number of network octets and host octets determines the IP address class. Table 5.8 shows the three IP defined network classes.

TABLE 5.8   IPv4 Address Classes

	First Octet	Second Octet	Third Octet	Fourth Octet
Class A	Network	Host	Host	Host
Class B	Network	Network	Host	Host
Class C	Network	Network	Network	Host

TCP/IP defines two additional address classes:

▶ Class D: Used for multicast addresses

▶ Class E: Used for research purposes

Table 5.9 lists the possible values each class network can have in the first octet. With these values, you can easily identify what class network is being referenced on the exam.

TABLE 5.9   Address Class Ranges

Class	First Octet Decimal Range
A	1–126
B	128–191
C	192–223
D	224–239
E	240–255

NOTE

The 127.x.x.x address range is reserved for loopback addresses.

EXAM ALERT

Memorize the decimal range for the first octet of each address class.

The network portion of an address maintains the same value for all the IP addresses that are assigned from a Class A, B, or C network. Remember that one octet is equal to 8 bits or 1 byte. The Class A network portion is 1 byte, and the host portion takes up the remaining 3 bytes. The Class B network portion is 2 bytes, with the remaining 2 bytes making up the host portion. The Class C network portion is 3 bytes, whereas the host portion is 1 byte. It stands to reason that if fewer bytes are devoted to the network portion of an address, fewer networks are possible for that class of network. With that said, the same is true for the host portion of an address. The fewer host bytes, the fewer total hosts that are available for that class of network.

When calculating the total number of Class A, B, or C networks available, you must subtract 2 from the total. This is a Cisco standard implemented for the ICND1 exam. A host address must be unique for each device or interface on a network. For each Class A, B, or C network, there is always a network identifier (ID) and a broadcast IP address. For this reason, you must also subtract two to calculate the total number of valid hosts per network.

A *network ID* is the first IP address in a network. This may also be referred to as a *subnet ID*. Every host bit for the network ID address is turned off (or all 0s). An example of a Class A network ID is 16.0.0.0.

A *broadcast IP* is the last IP address in a network. Every host bit for the broadcast IP address is turned on (or all 1s). An example of a Class A broadcast IP is 16.255.255.255.

EXAM ALERT

Power of 2   When you enter the exam room, it's helpful to write down some things on the paper or white board that is supplied. I would suggest writing down the powers of 2 for quick reference when calculating networks and hosts.

Here's a calculation for the number of networks for each class:

$2^7 - 2 = 126$ total Class A networks

$2^{14} - 2 = 16,382$ total Class B networks

$2^{21} - 2 = 2,097,150$ total Class C networks

> **NOTE**
>
> When calculating the total number of Class A, B, or C networks, the exponent is a multiple of 7.

Now you can calculate the number of hosts per network:

For any Class A network,

Network = 1 byte (8 bits)

Host = 3 bytes (24 bits)

$2^{24} - 2 = 16,777,214$ total hosts per network

For any Class B network,

Network = 2 bytes (16 bits)

Host = 2 bytes (16 bits)

$2^{16} - 2 = 65,534$ total hosts per network

For any Class C network,

Network = 3 bytes (24 bits)

Host = 1 byte (8 bits)

$2^8 - 2 = 254$ total hosts per network

> **NOTE**
>
> When calculating the total number of hosts per network, the exponent is equal to the number of host bits.

Challenge

You will see the terms Class A, B, and C on the ICND1 exam. In this challenge, I would like you to fill in the corresponding values for each network class.

Network Class	First Octet Range (Decimal)	Total Networks	Total Hosts per Network
A			
B			
C			

Subnet Masks

Sub-networks (subnets) enable you to break a large network of IP addresses down into smaller, manageable address ranges. A smaller address range means fewer hosts on a network. Each subnet becomes a separate broadcast domain. All the devices that are in the same broadcast domain receive all broadcasts. Think if it were possible to have all 16,777,214 Class A network hosts sharing a broadcast domain and receiving all broadcasts. That would be a huge amount of traffic. Subnets enable you to break this large network into smaller address ranges. In this case, smaller is better.

A subnet mask is used to identify which part of an IP address is the network portion. Like the IP address itself, a subnet mask consists of 32 bits. The network portion is represented by all 1s.

The default subnet masks for Class A, Class B, and Class C networks are as follows:

- ▶ Class A: 255.0.0.0 (11111111 00000000 00000000 00000000)
- ▶ Class B: 255.255.0.0 (11111111 11111111 00000000 00000000)
- ▶ Class C: 255.255.255.0 (11111111 11111111 11111111 00000000)

Now that you know what an IP address and subnet mask are, there is a mathematical operation called Boolean AND that helps to identify some important aspects of an IP network. With Boolean AND, you can determine the network ID and broadcast IP given an IP address and subnet mask.

Boolean AND works as follows:

- ▶ Determines the binary value of the IP address.
- ▶ Determines the binary value of the subnet mask.
- ▶ Lines up both binary values one on top of the other.
- ▶ If the lined-up bit values in both addresses equal 1, the Boolean bit is also 1.
- ▶ If the lined-up bit values in both addresses do not equal 1, the Boolean bit is 0.

Table 5.10 provides a Boolean example. The decimal IP address value = 124.0.0.0, and the subnet mask = 255.0.0.0.

TABLE 5.10   Boolean AND Example #1

IP Address Binary	01111100	00000000	00000000	00000000
Subnet Mask Binary	11111111	00000000	00000000	00000000
Boolean AND	01111100	**00000000**	**00000000**	**00000000**

The network ID in this example is 124.0.0.0. Using Boolean, you can see that the host bits in the last three octets are 0 bits, which identifies the network ID. I emphasized the last host octet in Table 5.10. If you turn all of those host bits on, you will get the broadcast IP, which in this case is 124.255.255.255.

For the next example (see Table 5.11), the decimal IP address value = 135.252.4.0, and the subnet mask = 255.255.0.0.

Table 5.11   Boolean AND Example #2

IP Address Binary	10000111	11111100	00000100	00000000
Subnet Mask Binary	11111111	11111111	00000000	00000000
Boolean AND	10000111	11111100	**00000000**	**00000000**

The network ID in this example is 135.252.0.0. Using Boolean, you can see that the host bits in the last two octets are 0 bits, which identify the network ID. I emphasized both host octets in the example. If you were to turn all those host bits on, you would get the broadcast IP, which in this case is 135.252.255.255.

Classless Interdomain Routing (CIDR) notation may also be used to identify the subnet mask. The mask is written in slash notation as follows:

▶ Class A: /8

▶ Class B: /16

▶ Class C: /24

EXAM ALERT

The CIDR notation or prefix notation for each network class can be determined by counting the 1s in binary or the number of bits that make up the network portion of the address.

Challenge

In this challenge, please fill in the appropriate default subnet mask and CIDR notation for each network class.

Network Class	Subnet Mask (Decimal)	CIDR Notation
A		
B		
C		

Private (RFC 1918) Addressing

Objective:

Describe the operation and benefits of using private and public addressing

The previously listed Class A, B, and C addresses are all IANA assigned public IP addresses. Although it originally seemed that there was sufficient public IPv4 address space available, resources began being consumed quickly. I mentioned that IPv6 was developed in the event that IPv4 address space became exhausted. Other measures were also implemented to alleviate the shortage of IPv4 public IP address space. These measures include RFC1918, Network Address Translation (NAT), and Port Address Translation (PAT). RFC 1918 defines private IP address space. Private address space can be used for traffic that does not need to leave the internal network. Because this traffic is internal to the network, it does not matter if other organizations are using the same address space. Private IP addresses are not routable on the Internet.

IANA Private Address Space Allocations include the following IP address ranges for Class A, Class B, and Class C networks:

- ▶ Class A: 10.0.0.0–10.255.255.255
- ▶ Class B: 172.16.0.0–172.31.255.255
- ▶ Class C: 192.168.0.0–192.168.255.255

NAT translates one IP address to another. Typically this is done between private and public IP addresses. For example, a private IP address can be translated with NAT to a public IP address for outbound transmission to the Internet. NAT can also translate a public IP address to a private IP address for inbound transmission on the internal network. PAT can translate multiple addresses on an internal network to a single public IP address, which is called one-to-many address translation. PAT is available as NAT overloading on Cisco routers.

Subnetting IP

So far, we have focused on the network classes and key characteristics of each one. As I mentioned, each network class can also be broken down into smaller groups of IP address ranges or subnets, which may also be referred to as variable-length subnet masking (VLSM). *Subnetting* is the process of breaking down those larger IP networks into smaller sub-networks. At first, subnetting IP might seem like a daunting task, but it's not that bad after you get the hang of it. In this section, you need to pull together all the knowledge that you have learned so far about binary, decimal, and subnets.

First, let's get the easy subnetting out of the way.

For an IP address that has a 255.255.0.0 or 255.255.255.0 subnet mask, you can copy the octets that have a subnet mask value of 255 from the original IP address. For the remaining octets, you will put down a 0. Here's an example:

> IP address = 139.42.6.0
>
> Subnet Mask = 255.255.0.0
>
> The Network ID is 139.42.0.0.

To determine the Broadcast IP of this IP address and subnet mask, just replace the 0 octets from the Network ID with 255.

The Broadcast IP is 139.42.255.255.

> **NOTE**
>
> When a subnet mask has a value of 255.255.0.0 or 255.255.255.0, you can copy the original IP octets that match the 255 value subnet octets and then use 0 for any remaining octets to determine your Network ID. The Broadcast IP is the same original IP octets that match the 255 value subnet octets and the number 255 rather than 0 for the remaining octet(s).

To understand more difficult subnetting, you need to break down an IP address into network bits, host bits, and subnet bits. The network bits are determined by the network class. Class A has 8 network bits, Class B has 16 network bits, and Class C has 24 network bits. The network bits value is a constant. The host bits, on the other hand, must share space with the subnet bits. To determine the subnet bits for a network, you need to look at the subnet mask in binary. For example,

> IP address = 176.85.195.60/22
>
> Subnet Mask = 255.255.252.0
>
> Subnet Mask in Binary = 11111111 11111111 11111100 00000000
>
> Network bits = 16
>
> Host bits = 10
>
> Subnet bits = 6

The subnet mask in binary has 22 bits with a value of 1, which means the CIDR notation is /22. Based on the first octet of the IP address, you know that this is a Class B network. Class B networks have 16 network bits. That leaves 16 bits in the address. The bits that have a value of 0 determine the number of host bits. In this case, there are 10 host bits. The rest of the bits are the subnet bits, so there are 6 subnet bits.

Table 5.12 is a conversion table of decimal to binary values that will help you convert addresses more quickly when taking the exam.

TABLE 5.12   Decimal-to-Binary Conversion

Decimal	Binary
0	00000000
128	10000000
192	11000000
224	11100000
240	11110000
248	11111000
252	11111100
254	11111110
255	11111111

You can use the chart to figure out more IP address values:

IP address = 100.15.209.0/23

Subnet Mask = 255.255.254.0

Subnet Mask in Binary = 11111111 11111111 11111110 00000000

Network bits = 8

Host bits = 9

Subnet bits = 15

IP address = 128.216.55.0/24

Subnet Mask = 255.255.255.0

Subnet Mask in Binary = 11111111 11111111 11111111 00000000

Network bits = 16

Host bits = 8

Subnet bits = 8

IP address = 222.110.8.61/28

Subnet Mask = 255.255.255.240

Subnet Mask in Binary = 11111111 11111111 11111111 11110000

Network bits = 24

Host bits = 4

Subnet bits = 4

Challenge

In this challenge, I supply you with the IP address and subnet mask. From there, you need to convert the subnet mask to binary and determine the number of network bits, host bits, and subnet bits for each network.

IP address = 193.216.0.0

Subnet Mask = 255.255.255.248

Subnet Mask in Binary = _____ _____ _____ _____

Network bits = _____

Host bits = _____

Subnet bits = _____

IP address = 130.101.2.0

Subnet Mask = 255.255.255.128

Subnet Mask in Binary = _____ _____ _____ _____

Network bits = _____

Host bits = _____

Subnet bits = _____

Calculating Hosts in a Subnet

To calculate the hosts in a subnet, we can use the formula $2^H - 2$. The exponent H represents the number of host bits in a network. If you use the subnetting examples, you can determine the hosts in each subnet:

IP address = 176.85.195.60/22

Subnet Mask = 255.255.252.0

Network bits = 16

Host bits = 10

Subnet bits = 6

$2^{10} - 2 = 1022$ Hosts

IP address = 100.15.209.0/23

Subnet Mask = 255.255.254.0

Network bits = 8

Host bits = 9

Subnet bits = 15

$2^9 - 2 = 510$ Hosts

IP address = 128.216.55.0/24

Subnet Mask = 255.255.255.0

Network bits = 16

Host bits = 8

Subnet bits = 8

$2^8 - 2 = 254$ Hosts

IP address = 222.110.8.61/28

Subnet Mask = 255.255.255.240

Network bits = 24

Host bits = 4

Subnet bits = 4

$2^4 - 2 = 14$ Hosts

EXAM ALERT

The formula to calculate the number of hosts created is $2^H - 2$. The *H* represents the host bits in a network.

Challenge

In the last challenge, you figured out the network bits, host bits, and subnet bits for two different IP address subnets. In this challenge, please take that information and calculate the number of hosts in each subnet.

IP address = 193.216.10.0

Subnet Mask = 255.255.255.0

Network bits = _____

Host bits = _____

Subnet bits = _____

Hosts = _____

IP address = 130.101.2.0

Subnet Mask = 255.255.255.128

Network bits = _____

Host bits = _____

Subnet bits = _____

Hosts = _____

Calculating Networks in a Subnet

To calculate the networks in a subnet, you can use the formula $2^N - 2$. The exponent N represents the number of subnet bits in a network. You can figure out the number of networks in each subnet with the formula.

IP address = 176.85.195.60/22

Subnet Mask = 255.255.252.0

Network bits = 16

Host bits = 10

Subnet bits = 6

$2^6 - 2 = 62$ Networks

IP address = 100.15.209.0/23

Subnet Mask = 255.255.254.0

Network bits = 8

Host bits = 9

Subnet bits = 15

$2^{15} - 2 = 32,766$ Networks

IP address = 128.216.55.0/24

Subnet Mask = 255.255.255.0

Network bits = 16

Host bits = 8

Subnet bits = 8

$2^8 - 2 = 254$ Networks

IP address = 222.110.8.61/28

Subnet Mask = 255.255.255.240

Network bits = 24

Host bits = 4

Subnet bits = 4

$2^4 - 2 = 14$ Networks

EXAM ALERT

The formula to calculate the number of networks or subnets created is $2^N - 2$. The N represents the subnet bits in a network.

Challenge

In this challenge, please use the subnet bit value that you calculated and determine the number of networks in each subnet.

IP address = 193.216.10.0

Subnet Mask = 255.255.255.0

Network bits = _____

Host bits = _____

Subnet bits = _____

Subnets = _____

IP address = 130.101.2.167

Subnet Mask = 255.255.255.224

Network bits = _____

Host bits = _____

Subnet bits = _____

Subnets = _____

Zero Subnet Rule

Zero subnet may also be referred to as *subnet zero*. The zero subnet is the first subnet in a network and has all binary 0s in the subnet field. For the purpose of taking the ICND1 exam, you should not include the first subnet when calculating the number of networks in a larger subnet. This is one of the two reserved subnet numbers on a network and one of the reasons why you subtract from the total number of networks to get the correct answer for the test. The other network is the broadcast subnet, which has all 1s in the subnet field.

The Increment

We have been working with the IP address subnet 222.110.8.61/28. After you know how many subnets and hosts are in a subnet, you can determine the network ID for that subnet. So far, you know that 222.110.8.61/28 has 14 hosts and 14 subnets. Before subtracting 2 for the valid number of hosts/networks, your calculations were for 16 hosts and 16 networks. This means that a subnet with a 255.255.255.240 mask is part of a larger subnet with a 16-host increment. The variable part of this subnet is the last octet. So you can automatically write down the first three octets as follows:

222.110.8.x (where the x is variable and has a 16-host increment)

Octet values range from 0 to 255. So the first subnet in the larger network is 222.110.8.0. Now you want to add increments of 16 to the last octet, so you get the following networks:

222.110.8.0 (zero subnet—not valid for the ICND1 exam)

222.110.8.16

222.110.8.32

222.110.8.48

222.110.8.64

222.110.8.80

222.110.8.96

222.110.8.112

222.110.8.128

222.110.8.144

222.110.8.160

222.110.8.176

222.110.8.192

222.110.8.208

222.110.8.224

222.110.8.240 (broadcast subnet—not valid for the ICND1 exam)

This is a list of the Network IDs in that Class C network with a subnet of 255.255.255.240. The Network ID is always an even number. There are 16 total subnets. According to the zero subnet and broadcast subnet rule, the first and last subnet cannot be used. The IP address 222.110.8.61 is greater than 48 and less than 64, so the Network ID or subnet number for 222.110.8.61/28 is 222.110.8.48 (which is highlighted in the list of networks). To get the broadcast IP, subtract 1 from the next Network ID in your list. In this example, the broadcast IP is 222.110.8.63.

There is another math shortcut that can be used to identify the Network ID, which then helps you determine the Broadcast IP. Take another look at 222.110.8.61/28.

IP address = 222.110.8.61

Subnet Mask = 255.255.255.240

Look at the first subnet mask octet from the left that is not a value of 255 and subtract it from 256.

256 − 240 = 16

You want to find the closest multiple of 16 that is less than the last octet in the IP address, which equals 61. You are using the last octet because that is the same octet used from the subnet mask.

$16 \times 3 = 48$ and $16 \times 4 = 64$

Based on the calculations, the Network ID increments are as follows:

222.110.8.48

222.110.8.64

So you use 48 because it is less than 61, and 64 is the Network ID of the next subnet. You come up with the same answer as before.

Network ID = 222.110.8.48

Broadcast IP = 222.110.8.63 (one less than the next Network ID of the next subnet)

Here's another example:

IP address = 100.15.209.0

Subnet Mask = 255.255.254.0

The first two octets in the subnet mask equal 255, so you need to use the first octet that is not equal to 255, or in this case the third octet from the left. Now you can subtract 254 from 256.

$256 - 254 = 2$

$2 \times 104 = 208$

$2 \times 105 = 210$

You can see that the valid network ID less than 209 is 208. The next network ID equals 210, so you can fill out the third octet with each value to obtain the following network ID increments:

100.15.208.0

100.15.210.0

For IP address 100.15.209.0 with a subnet mask of 255.255.254.0, you now know the Network ID is 100.15.208.0. The next network is 100.15.210.0, so you want to find the last IP address before that network ID to get the Broadcast IP. Because the value of an octet can range from 0 to 255, the last possible IP before 100.15.210.0 is 100.15.209.255.

Network ID = 100.15.208.0

Broadcast IP = 100.15.209.255

Challenge

Part I:

To help you understand incremental values, make a list of the subnet increments for address 130.101.2.167 with a subnet mask of 255.255.255.224. I will fill in the first and last network ID (neither are valid networks per the ICND1 exam).

130.101.2.0

_____

_____

_____

_____

_____

_____

130.101.2.224

What is the Network ID of 130.101.2.167/27? _____

What is the Broadcast IP of 130.101.2.167/27? _____

Part II:

Given the following IP address and subnet mask, use the shortcut method to determine the Network ID and Broadcast IP.

IP address = 176.85.195.60

Subnet Mask = 255.255.252.0

Determining the Range of Valid IPs

The range of valid IP addresses in a subnet is the first IP address after the Network ID and the last IP address before the Broadcast IP address. If you are given the following IP address and subnet mask, you can determine the range of valid IP addresses:

IP Address = 210.189.16.0

Subnet Mask = 255.255.255.0

First, identify the Network ID, which in this case is 210.189.16.0. Then determine the Broadcast address, which is 210.189.16.255. In this case, the valid IP range is 210.189.16.1 to 210.189.16.254.

Here are some more examples where the Network ID and Broadcast IP have already been determined:

IP address = 100.15.209.0

Subnet Mask = 255.255.254.0

CIDR = /23

Network ID = 100.15.208.0

Broadcast IP = 100.15.209.255

Valid IP range = 100.15.208.1 to 100.15.209.254

IP address = 222.110.8.61

Subnet Mask = 255.255.255.240

CIDR = /28

Network ID = 222.110.8.48

Broadcast IP = 222.110.8.63

Valid IP range = 222.110.8.49 to 222.110.8.62

EXAM ALERT

The valid range of IP addresses always starts with an odd number and ends with an even number.

Challenge

In this challenge, I have supplied the IP address and subnet mask. First, calculate the binary equivalent of the subnet mask. Then determine the CIDR notation. After you have these fields completed, calculate the Network ID and Broadcast IP, using the shortcut provided for subnetting. After you identify the Network ID and Broadcast IP, you can determine the valid IP host range.

IP Address	172.17.8.122
Subnet Mask	255.255.255.224
Binary Subnet Mask	
CIDR Notation	
Network ID	
Broadcast IP	
Valid IP Range	

It is important to understand the general concepts related to IP addressing and subnetting. Figure 5.3 is a chart or quick sheet that will help you check your answers and provide you a guideline for the ICND1 exam. I suggested that you memorize the powers of 2. I also suggest that you memorize this chart and write it down on your scrap paper or white board when you start the exam. I found it to be extremely helpful!

Binary Increment	128	64	32	16	8	4	2	1
Subnet Mask	128	192	224	240	248	252	254	255
CIDR	/17	/18	/19	/20	/21	/22	/23	/24
Hosts-2	32768	16384	8192	4096	2048	1024	512	256
Class B Networks-2	2	4	8	16	32	64	128	256
Class C Networks-2								

128	64	32	16	8	4	2	1
128	192	224	240	248	252	254	255
/25	/26	/27	/28	/29	/30	/31	/32
128	64	32	16	8	4	2	0
512	1024	2048	4096	8192	16384	32768	65536
2	4	8	16	32	64	128	256

FIGURE 5.3 Subnetting quick sheet.

Network Layer Devices

The most common network device found at the Network layer is a router; however, Layer 3 switches may also be implemented to create a WAN.

Both routers and Layer 3 switches can carry out these functions:

- ▶ Suppress broadcasts or multicasts
- ▶ Determine the best path for data transfer (routing)
- ▶ Strip down and add to Data Link layer frames
- ▶ Implement access lists for packet filtering (permit/deny statements)
- ▶ Set up quality of service (QoS) qualifiers to measure network performance

It is important to know that both these devices can be used at the Network layer. However, for the purpose of the ICND1 exam, routers are more widely recognized and, therefore, are referred to when discussing Layer 3 functions.

Routers

Routers join a minimum of two networks together to create an internetwork or WAN. So far, we have discussed devices that are used at the Physical layer (hubs and repeaters) and the Data Link layer (Layer 2 switches and bridges). Layer 2 switches and bridges create a separate collision domain for each segment of the LAN. Routers and Layer 3 switches create a separate broadcast domain for each segment of a WAN. A broadcast domain is a group of nodes that can receive one another's broadcast messages. Figure 5.4 demonstrates how a router creates broadcast domains whereas the connected switches create collision domains.

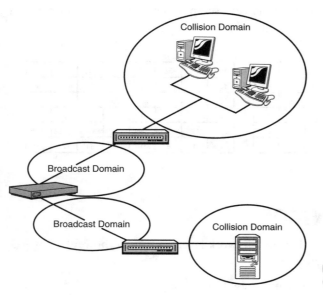

FIGURE 5.4   Broadcast and collision domains.

Figure 5.5 demonstrates a simple LAN with one router and two segments. In this network, any traffic that is generated by Matt's PC has the source MAC and source IP address of that PC. If Matt is sending a frame to the server on the other segment of that WAN, the destination IP address will be that of the server he is trying to reach. Because the server is not on the same segment as Matt, the destination MAC address is that of the router, which is the default gateway. The router takes a look at the frame and at its own routing table. It then decides what interface to use to forward the frame based on the network portion of the IP address. The router attaches its own MAC address as the source MAC address of the frame before sending the frame to the server.

A routing table on a router contains the following information:

▶ Network Address

▶ Interface: Exit interface used to forward packets

▶ Metric: Distance to reach a remote network

EXAM ALERT

For the exam, you should understand how a packet traverses the network and determine the source and destination IP and MAC address as the packet moves from device to device.

FIGURE 5.5 Frame transmission using a router.

Figure 5.6 exemplifies a WAN with two routers. Each router has a separate routing table to make best path decisions.

Routers provide packet switching between networks and can provide packet filtering based on a network address or application layer port level.

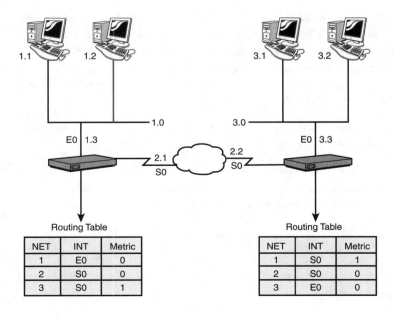

FIGURE 5.6 A WAN with routing tables.

Routing Table

NET	INT	Metric
1	E0	0
2	S0	0
3	S0	1

Routing Table

NET	INT	Metric
1	S0	1
2	S0	0
3	E0	0

EXAM ALERT

Routers provide internetwork communication, packet switching, and packet filtering.

Two packet types are used at Layer 3:

▶ Data packets: Transport data across the internetwork and are supported by routed protocols such as IP and IPX.

▶ Route update packets: Send updates to neighbor routers about all networks connected to that internetwork and are supported by routing protocols such as RIP, EIGRP, and OSPF.

NOTE

Specific Cisco router models are reviewed in Chapter 6, "Introduction to Cisco Routers and Switches."

IP configurations are covered in Chapter 8, "Foundation Cisco Configurations."

Chapter 10, "Introduction to Routing and Routing Protocols," details routing terminology.

Chapter 11, "Distance Vector Routing Protocols," reviews RIP and IGRP routing protocols.

Layer 3 Switches

Layer 3 switches are typically called *multilayer switches*. I already listed the commonalities between routers and Layer 3 switches. There are also a couple of differences worth mentioning. The number one difference between a router and a Layer 3 switch is packet switching throughput. Whereas a router has evolved over the years to process more than one million packets per second (pps), a Layer 3 switch can process millions of pps. That said, Layer 3 switches process more traffic in a shorter time.

Whereas routers use microprocessor-based engines, Layer 3 switches use ASIC hardware to perform packet switching. Layer 2 switches use ASIC hardware to forward frames.

NOTE

The Cisco Catalyst 8500 series switch is an example of a Layer 3 switch. Layer 3 switches are recommended for Campus networks.

Chapter Summary

Take a deep breath. That was a lot to cover! IP addressing and IP subnetting are vital to studying for the ICND1 exam. In fact, they are integral to understanding networking in general. This chapter touched on many of the concepts that are elaborated later in this book. A lot of device configurations are in upcoming chapters. Knowing your IP format and subnet masks is the first big hurdle when working with IP routing protocols such as OSPF and EIGRP. The next chapter introduces Cisco routers and switches as well as other important Cisco network components. You will also be introduced to Cisco IOS Software, which you will need to understand to configure a Cisco device.

Key Terms

- IPv4 (IP version 4)
- Binary
- Network ID
- Broadcast IP
- Subnet
- Subnetting
- Subnet mask
- CIDR (Classless Interdomain Routing)
- Boolean AND
- NAT
- PAT
- Zero subnet rule
- Broadcast subnet
- IPv6
- Link-local address
- Unique/site-local address
- Global address

Apply Your Knowledge

Exercises

5.1 Converting Binary to Decimal

Practice makes perfect! Address conversion is pretty much guaranteed to be on the ICND1 exam. I promise you that it is worth your while to go over these exercises until you have the system down pat. I will give you the bit values for four octets. Convert each octet to decimal and fill in the corresponding dotted-decimal IP address value.

Keep in mind that the bit values for each octet are:

128   64   32   16   8   4   2   1

Estimated Time: 10 minutes

First Octet:

Binary1   1   0   1   1   0   0   0

Decimal_____

Second Octet:

Binary0   1   0   1   1   1   1   1

Decimal_____

Third Octet:

Binary1   0   1   1   1   1   1   1

Decimal_____

Fourth Octet:

Binary1   1   1   0   0   0   0   0

Decimal_____

IP Address = _____. _____. _____. _____

5.2 Converting Decimal to Binary

Conversions go both ways. Now, I will give you the decimal values for four octets. Convert each octet to binary and fill in the corresponding binary address value.

Estimated Time: 10 minutes

First Octet:

Decimal   224

Binary _____

Second Octet:

Decimal   137

Binary _____

Third Octet:

Decimal   15

Binary _____

Fourth Octet:

Decimal   253

Binary _____

Binary Address = _____ _____ _____ _____

5.3 Converting Decimal to Hexadecimal

You may be asked to determine a hexadecimal value given a decimal value. In this challenge, I have given you the decimal value. You need to convert that to binary and then break the binary octet into two 4-bit groups.

Keep in mind that the bit values for each 4-bit group are:

8   4   2   1

Also, Figure 5.2 has the decimal-to-hexadecimal values.

Estimated Time: 10 minutes

Decimal = 105

Binary = ____   ____   ____   ____   ____   ____   ____   ____

First 4 bits of the binary octet:

____ ____ ____   ____   = Decimal _____ Hexadecimal_____

Last 4 bits of the binary octet:

____ ____ ____   ____   = Decimal _____ Hexadecimal_____

The combined hexadecimal value is 0x_____.

5.4 Binary Chart

There are several useful memorization tools for the IP subnetting questions on the ICND1 exam. Fill in the binary equivalent (one octet) for each of the following decimal values.

Estimated Time: 5 minutes

Decimal	Binary
0	
128	
192	
224	
240	
248	
252	
254	
255	

5.5 Identify the Network ID

In this exercise, please use Boolean AND to determine the Network ID, given the IP address 134.141.7.130 and subnet mask 255.255.255.0.

Estimated Time: 5 minutes

IP Address Binary	
Subnet Mask Binary	
Boolean AND	

Network ID = _____ . _____ . _____ . _____

Review Questions

1. Convert binary 00101010 00111111 11011100 11111111 to decimal format.

2. Convert decimal 150.193.6.100 to binary format.

3. What is hexadecimal 0x5F in decimal format?

4. Perform Boolean AND to define the Network ID of IP address 200.62.183.26 255.255.255.0.

5. Given the IP address 32.116.5.0 and subnet mask 255.255.255.0, what is the Network ID?

6. Given the IP address 213.50.201.0 and subnet mask 255.255.255.0, what is the Broadcast IP?

7. What is the valid IP range for 220.9.3.0/24?

8. Define the zero subnet and broadcast subnet rules.

9. Describe the process of routing.

10. List the functions performed by a router or Layer 3 switch.

Exam Questions

1. What is the decimal equivalent of 10010111 00000110 10101100 01110111?

   ○ **A.** 151.6.172.119

   ○ **B.** 151.6.172.120

   ○ **C.** 151.6.172.121

   ○ **D.** 151.6.172.122

2. What is the first octet range for Class B addresses?

   ○ **A.** 1 to 126

   ○ **B.** 128 to 191

   ○ **C.** 192 to 223

   ○ **D.** 224 to 239

3. What is the first octet range for Class C addresses?

   ○ **A.** 1 to 126

   ○ **B.** 128 to 191

   ○ **C.** 192 to 223

   ○ **D.** 224 to 239

4. How many hosts are available with a Class C network?

   ○ **A.** 253

   ○ **B.** 254

   ○ **C.** 255

   ○ **D.** 256

5. What is the network ID for a host with the IP address 124.199.7.18/28?

   ○ **A.** 124.199.7.0

   ○ **B.** 124.199.7.16

   ○ **C.** 124.199.7.32

   ○ **D.** 124.199.7.48

6. You have been assigned a Class C network address. A coworker has requested that you create 10 networks that can support 10 hosts per network. What subnet mask should you use?

   ○ **A.** 255.255.255.0

   ○ **B.** 255.255.255.224

   ○ **C.** 255.255.255.240

   ○ **D.** 255.255.255.248

7. Which of the following are valid host addresses in the 208.62.15.0 network with a 255.255.255.224 subnet mask? (Choose the two best answers.)

   ○ **A.** 208.62.15.0

   ○ **B.** 208.62.15.1

   ○ **C.** 208.62.15.30

   ○ **D.** 208.62.15.32

8. Given the network address 192.131.10.0 and subnet mask 255.255.255.0, what is the total number of networks and the total number of hosts per network?

   ○ **A.** 1 network / 255 hosts

   ○ **B.** 1 network / 254 hosts

   ○ **C.** 2 networks / 62 hosts

   ○ **D.** 6 networks / 30 hosts

9. How many valid host IP addresses are available with a network address of 218.41.99.24 and a subnet mask of 255.255.255.252?

○ **A.** 2

○ **B.** 6

○ **C.** 14

○ **D.** 30

10. If you need at least five subnetworks with a Class C network and you want to have as many hosts as possible on each network, what subnet mask would you use?

○ **A.** 255.255.255.252

○ **B.** 255.255.255.240

○ **C.** 255.255.255.248

○ **D.** 255.255.255.224

11. How many hosts are available with a Class B network?

○ **A.** 254

○ **B.** 64,000

○ **C.** 65,534

○ **D.** 16,777,214

12. What is the Broadcast IP for 196.23.250.32/27?

○ **A.** 196.23.250.32

○ **B.** 196.23.250.33

○ **C.** 196.23.250.63

○ **D.** 196.23.250.64

13. What subnet mask would you use if you had a Class B address and you would like 250 networks?

○ **A.** 255.255.255.0

○ **B.** 255.255.254.0

○ **C.** 255.255.252.0

○ **D.** 255.255.248.0

14. How many subnets can you have with a subnet mask of 255.255.240 on a Class B network?

○ **A.** 6

○ **B.** 14

○ **C.** 16

○ **D.** 30

15. How many hosts are available if you have a Class B network with a subnet mask of 255.255.255.128?

○ **A.** 254

○ **B.** 256

○ **C.** 128

○ **D.** 126

16. Which of the following are considered private addresses per RFC 1918? (Choose the three best answers.)

○ **A.** 1.0.0.0

○ **B.** 10.10.10.20

○ **C.** 172.30.255.10

○ **D.** 192.168.128.128

17. What is the CIDR notation for the 128.250.62.0 network with a subnet mask of 255.255.255.0?

○ **A.** /23

○ **B.** /24

○ **C.** /25

○ **D.** /26

18. Which of the following network classes do not define public IP address space? (Choose the two best answers.)

○ **A.** Class B

○ **B.** Class C

○ **C.** Class D

○ **D.** Class E

19. What is the valid IP host range for 160.254.101.167/27?

- ○ **A.** 160.254.101.128 to 160.254.101.254
- ○ **B.** 160.254.101.129 to 160.254.101.254
- ○ **C.** 160.254.101.160 to 160.254.101.191
- ○ **D.** 160.254.101.161 to 160.254.101.190

20. Given this network diagram, if the Philadelphia router sends a packet to 172.23.0.51, what interface will the Milford router use to forward the packet?

- ○ **A.** E0
- ○ **B.** E1
- ○ **C.** S0
- ○ **D.** S1

Answers to Review Questions

1.

128	64	32	16	8	4	2	1
0	0	1	0	1	0	1	0

32+8+2 = 42

128	64	32	16	8	4	2	1
0	0	1	1	1	1	1	1

32+16+8+4+2+1 = 63

128	64	32	16	8	4	2	1
1	1	0	1	1	1	0	0

128+64+16+8+4 = 220

128	64	32	16	8	4	2	1
1	1	1	1	1	1	1	1

128+64+32+16+8+4+2+1 = 255

The correct answer is 42.63.220.255.

2.

128	64	32	16	8	4	2	1
1	0	0	1	0	1	1	0

128	64	32	16	8	4	2	1
1	1	0	0	0	0	0	1

128	64	32	16	8	4	2	1
0	0	0	0	0	1	1	0

128	64	32	16	8	4	2	1
0	1	1	0	0	1	0	0

The correct answer is 10010110 11000001 00000110 01100100.

3. The first hexadecimal character is 5, which is the same as the decimal value.

8	4	2	1
0	1	0	1

The second hexadecimal character is F, which is 15 in decimal.

8	4	2	1
1	1	1	1

Now you can combine the two 4-bit groups to get 01011111, which converts to 95 in decimal.

4. IP Address Binary = 11001000 00111110 10110111 00011010

Subnet Mask Binary= 11111111 11111111 11111111 00000000

Boolean AND = 11001000 00111110 10110111 **00000000**

The correct answer is 200.62.183.0.

5. This is considered an easy mask. You just write down the original octets with a subnet mask value of 255 and a 0 for each octet with a 0 value in the subnet mask.

The correct answer is 32.116.5.0.

6. Because this has an easy subnet mask, you can copy the first three octets and then replace the last octet with 255.

   The correct answer is 213.50.201.255.

7. This IP address subnet mask is 255.255.255.0, so the network ID is 220.9.3.0. The broadcast IP is 220.9.3.255.

   The correct answer is 220.9.3.1 to 220.9.3.254.

8. Zero subnet may also be referred to as subnet zero. The zero subnet is the first subnet in a network and has all binary 0s in the subnet field. For the purpose of taking the ICND1 exam, you should not include the first subnet when calculating the number of networks in a larger subnet. This is one of the two reserved subnet numbers on a network and one of the reasons why you subtract from the total number of networks to get the correct answer for the test. The other network is the broadcast subnet, which has all 1s in the subnet field.

9. Traffic that is generated by a device has the source MAC and source IP address of that device. If a frame is sent to a server on another segment of a WAN, the destination IP address is that of the server the frame is trying to reach. Because the server is not on the same segment, the destination MAC address is that of the router, which is the default gateway. The router takes a look at the frame and at its own routing table. It then decides what interface to use to forward the frame, based on the network portion of the IP address. The router attaches its own MAC address as the source MAC address of the frame before the frame is sent to the server.

10. Suppress broadcasts or multicasts.

    Determine the best path for data transfer (routing).

    Strip down and add to Data Link layer frames.

    Implement access lists for packet filtering (permit/deny statements).

    Set up quality of service (QoS) qualifiers to measure network performance.

Answers to Exam Questions

1. **A.** The decimal equivalent of 10010111 00000110 10101100 01110111 is 151.6.172.119. Answers B and D can be eliminated right away because both IP addresses end with an even number.

2. **B.** The first octet range for Class B addresses is 128 to 191. Answers A, C, and D are incorrect because the range of 1 to 126 is Class A, 192 to 223 is Class C, and 224 to 239 is reserved for multicast.

3. **C.** Answer C is correct because the first octet range for Class C addresses is 192 to 223. Answers A, B, and D are incorrect because the first octet range for Class A addresses is 1 to 126, for Class B is 128 to 191, and 224 to 239 is reserved for multicast.

4. **B.** There are 254 hosts per Class C network. For any Class C network, there are 24 network bits and 8 host bits: $2^8 - 2 = 254$.

5. **B.** The Network ID of 124.199.7.18/28 is 124.199.7.16. If you write out the subnet mask it is 255.255.255.240. Subtract 240 from 256 and you have 16; 16×1 = 16, which is the first valid increment that can be the network ID. The next network ID is 124.199.7.32.

6. **C.** Subnet mask 255.255.255.240 allows for 14 networks and 14 hosts. Answer A is incorrect because subnet mask 255.255.255.0 allows for only one network with 254 hosts. Answer B is incorrect because subnet mask 255.255.255.224 allows for 6 networks and 30 hosts, and answer D is incorrect because subnet mask 255.255.255.248 allows for 30 networks and 6 hosts.

7. **B, C.** 208.62.15.1 and 208.62.15.30 are valid host addresses in the 208.62.15.0 network with a 255.255.255.224 subnet mask. Answer A is incorrect because 208.62.15.0 is the network ID and therefore is not a valid host address. Answer D is incorrect because 208.62.15.32 is the network ID of the next network and is not valid.

8. **B.** The network address 192.131.10.0 and subnet mask 255.255.255.0 has one network with 254 hosts.

9. **A.** With a network address of 218.41.99.24 and a subnet mask of 255.255.255.252, 2 valid host addresses are available. Answer B is incorrect because subnet mask 255.255.255.248 has 6 available hosts. Answers C and D are incorrect because subnet mask 255.255.255.240 has 14 available hosts, and subnet mask 255.255.255.224 has 30 available hosts.

10. **D.** Subnet mask 255.255.255.224 would allow for 6 networks with 30 available hosts per network. Answer A is incorrect because subnet mask 255.255.255.252 allows for 62 networks but only 2 hosts per network. Answers B and C are incorrect because subnet mask 255.255.255.240 allows for 14 networks with only 14 hosts per network, and subnet mask 255.255.255.248 allows for 30 networks with only 8 hosts per network.

11. **C.** There are 65,534 hosts available for a Class B network. Answers A and D are incorrect because a Class C network has 254 possible hosts, and a Class A has 16,777,214 possible hosts.

12. **C.** The broadcast IP for 196.23.250.32/27 is 196.23.250.63. Answer A is incorrect because 196.23.250.32 is the Network ID of 196.23.250.32/27. Answers B and D are incorrect because 196.23.250.33 is the first valid IP in the /27 network and 196.23.250.64 is the Network ID of the next network.

13. **A.** The only subnet that allows for 250 networks is 255.255.255.0. Subnet mask 255.255.255.0 can create 254 subnets. Answer B is incorrect because subnet mask 255.255.254.0 can create 126 subnets. Answer C is incorrect because subnet mask 255.255.252.0 can create 62 subnets. Answer D is incorrect because subnet mask 255.255.248.0 can create 30 subnets.

14. **B.** You can have 14 subnetworks with a Class B network that has a subnet mask of 255.255.240.0.

15. **D.** Answer D is correct because there are 126 possible hosts for a Class B network with a subnet mask of 255.255.255.128. Answer A is incorrect because a Class B network with a subnet mask of 255.255.255.0 has 254 possible hosts. Answers B and C are incorrect because the Network ID and Broadcast IP addresses were not subtracted from the total number of IPs in each subnet.

16. **B, C, D.** RFC 1918 defines the following private IP address ranges: 10.0.0.0 to 10.255.255.255, 172.16.0.0–172.31.255.255, and 192.168.0.0 to 192.168.255.255. Answer A is incorrect because the address 1.0.0.0 is a Class A public address.

17. **B.** 24 is the correct CIDR notation for the 128.250.62.0 network with a subnet mask of 255.255.255.0. Answer A is incorrect because /23 is the CIDR notation for 255.255.254.0. Answer C is incorrect because /25 is the CIDR notation for 255.255.255.128, and answer D is incorrect because /26 is the CIDR notation for 255.255.255.192.

18. **C, D.** Class D defines multicast address space and Class E defines IP address space reserved for research. Answers A and B are incorrect because Classes B and C are both defined for public use.

19. **D.** The valid host range for 160.254.101.167/27 is 160.254.101.161 to 160.254.101.190. Answers A and B are incorrect because both 160.254.101.128 to 160.254.101.254 and 160.254.101.129 to 160.254.101.254 are part of a 255.255.255.128 subnet. Answer C is incorrect because with the range 160.254.101.160 to 160.254.101.191, the first IP is the Network ID and it is not a valid host IP address.

20. **A.** The Milford router forwards the packet through the E0 interface because the network matches the 172.23.0.0 network. Answer B is incorrect because interface E1 is going to the 172.24.0.0 network, and answer C is incorrect because interface S0 is going to the Philadelphia router via the 172.22.0.0 network. Answer D is incorrect because interface S1 does not exist in this scenario.

Suggested Readings and Resources

The following are some recommended readings on IPv4, private and public IP addressing, subnetting, and routing:

1. "IPv4," http://en.wikipedia.org/wiki/IPv4.

2. "RFC 1918," http://www.faqs.org/rfcs/rfc1918.html.

3. "IP Addressing and Subnetting for New Users," http://www.cisco.com/warp/public/701/3.html.

4. "IP Address Subnetting Tutorial," http://www.ralphb.net/IPSubnet/.

5. "Network Calculators," http://www.subnetmask.info/.

6. Andrew Colton. *Cisco IOS for IP Routing*. Rocket Science Press, Inc., 2002.

CHAPTER SIX

Introduction to Cisco Routers and Switches

Objectives

This chapter covers the following Cisco-specified objectives from the "Describe the operation of data networks" section of the 640-822 ICND1 exam:

▶ **Select the components required to meet a network specification**

▶ **Describe the purpose and functions of various network devices**

Outline

Introduction   **188**

Interfaces and Modules   **188**

LAN Interfaces   188

WAN Interfaces   189

    BRI   189

    Synchronous Serial   190

    Asynchronous Serial   190

    HSSI   190

    T1 Controller Card   190

    Data Communications
      Equipment (DCE)   190

    Data Terminal Equipment (DTE)   191

Cisco Memory Components   **192**

ROM   193

Flash   193

RAM   193

NVRAM   193

Cisco Internetworking Operating
System   **193**

Feature Sets   194

IOS Image File Naming   195

Cisco Router Models and Features   **196**

Cisco Switch Models and Features   **197**

Chapter Summary   **199**

Key Terms   199

Apply Your Knowledge   **200**

Exercises   200

Review Questions   200

Exam Questions   201

Answers to Review Questions   203

Answers to Exam Questions   204

Suggested Readings and Resources   205

Study Strategies

▶ Identify the interfaces and modules used with Cisco devices.

▶ Describe the Cisco memory components ROM, Flash, RAM, and NVRAM.

▶ Familiarize yourself with Cisco Internetworking Operating System (IOS) feature sets.

▶ Review the IOS image file structure.

▶ Identify the Cisco Router models and their features.

▶ Identify the Cisco Switch models and their features.

Introduction

Up to this point, we have discussed general internetworking technologies and devices to provide a background of the material relevant to the ICND1 exam. Now the scope of the discussion widens to include Cisco technology. This chapter reviews internetworking devices (routers and switches) that were developed by Cisco for network implementations. It also discusses the individual hardware components that make up a router and switch, which you must thoroughly understand before the configuration of these devices is explained. This introduction to Cisco technology leads up to Chapter 9, "Understanding the Cisco SDM," and Chapter 7, "Foundation Cisco IOS Operations," where you will delve into hands-on device operations and configurations.

Interfaces and Modules

Objectives:

▶ Select the components required to meet a network specification

▶ Describe the purpose and functions of various network devices

Networks can be connected to Cisco hardware in a variety of ways. Communication lines can be terminated to a Cisco device via hardware interfaces and modules. Interfaces provide a physical point of interaction between two networks. That hardware interface includes the cable, plug, socket, and signal that sync up together to communicate among devices.

Certain Cisco routers are built as fixed-port routers or fixed configuration routers and do not allow for additional network module installations. Cisco also offers modular-port routers. Modular-port routers allow for future system upgrades by mounting network modules in available spaces to accommodate changing network environments. A module is a self-contained component. A Cisco network module has built-in hardware interfaces to add alternate connection options on a network. Because they are modular components, Cisco routers can be upgraded easily and with minimal expense to the company. This chapter reviews the variety of physical connection types on LAN and WAN devices.

LAN Interfaces

Local area network (LAN) interfaces are used to provide a point of interconnection between Cisco switches and other network devices. Cisco provides a wide selection of switches that can be implemented on a LAN and offer end-user connectivity. In Chapter 3, "Data Link Networking Concepts," Layer 2 switches were introduced. The Cisco 2950 series switch family includes various models with different interface options, such as the Cisco 2950-12 and the Cisco 2950-24. The 2950-12 has 12 built-in ethernet ports, whereas the 2950-24 has 24 built-in ethernet ports. Certain models also have Gigabit Ethernet slots.

If Gigabit Ethernet ports are included, the front panel of a 2950 model has 10/100 ethernet ports on the left side of the switch and 2 Gigabit Ethernet slots that accommodate LAN interface modules on the right. The 10/100 ports allow for either a 10Mbps or 100Mbps connection speed. Media connects to an ethernet switch port via an RJ-45 connector. As far as the switch is concerned, each ethernet port is designated as a numbered interface for identification. The top-left port is labeled 1 by the switch. Each interface begins with a 0/#, where the # sign equals the port number on the switch. The top-left port is then named 0/1 on that switch. Given this formula, the bottom-left port is labeled 0/2.

EXAM ALERT

For the ICND1 exam, know how the interfaces are labeled for an ethernet port. This information is necessary for any switch configuration exercises.

The Gigabit Ethernet slots are available for Gigabit Interface Converters (GBICs). A GBIC interface module can be inserted into the Gigabit Ethernet slot to allow for different media connections to that port. The physical media can range from copper to single-mode fiber. A GBIC is also hot swappable, so you can remove and replace it without shutting off power to the switch. This helps to avoid interruption of service to that switch.

The back panel of the 2950 includes power input and the switch's console port. The console port has an RJ-45 connector and is connected to a terminal with a rollover cable for initial switch configuration.

WAN Interfaces

Wide area network (WAN) interfaces are also used to provide a point of interconnection between Cisco routers and other network devices. Types of WAN interfaces include the following:

▶ Basic Rate Interface (BRI)

▶ Synchronous Serial

▶ Asynchronous Serial

▶ High-Speed Serial Interface (HSSI)

▶ T1 Controller Card

BRI

BRI is an Integrated Services Digital Network (ISDN) service that consists of two 64Kbps bearer (B) channels and one 16Kbps data (D) channel. Voice, video, and data traffic can be carried over the B-channels. Signals between telephone company switches use the D-channel.

Cisco offers an 8-port ISDN-BRI with a built-in Network Termination Type 1 (NT-1) Network Module for router installation.

The NT-1 is a telephone company requirement for an ISDN line connection. This network module has a BRI U interface, which means that the NT-1 is built in on the network module and does not require a separate NT-1 device.

Synchronous Serial

A synchronous serial interface synchronizes clocks for the bit stream of both the sending and receiving end of a serial link. This allows for the data rate to be adjusted if necessary to ensure that both ends of a serial link are functioning at the same speed.

Asynchronous Serial

An asynchronous serial interface does the opposite of a synchronous serial interface. It does not synchronize the clocks for the bit stream of the sending and receiving end of a serial link. Cisco offers a 4-port asynchronous/synchronous serial network module.

With the asynchronous/synchronous serial network module, each port can be configured individually as either asynchronous or synchronous, depending on your network setup.

HSSI

High-speed serial interfaces offer up to 52Mbps transmission rates to the WAN from a Cisco router. The higher speed capacity is relevant if the corporate backbone requires high-speed Internet access and VPN connectivity. Cisco offers a 2-port HSSI port adapter.

T1 Controller Card

Also referred to as a *digital signal level 1* (DS1) service, a T1 is a connecting line that offers a 1.544Mbps data transmission speed. A single T1 line consists of 24 digital signal level 0 (DS0) channels that are 64Kbps each and an additional 8Kbps that is reserved for management overhead. A T1 controller card can be installed in a router's T1 slot to communicate with and control the 24 DS0 channels.

Data Communications Equipment (DCE)

Data Communications Equipment (DCE) or Data Circuit-Terminating Equipment (DCE) is the term used to identify a device that connects the Data Terminal Equipment (DTE) to a service provider's communications line. The DCE side of a connection sets the clock speed for a serial connection.

DCE equipment may consist of a:

► Modem

► Channel Service Unit/Data Service Unit (CSU/DSU)

► Basic Rate Interface Network Termination Type 1 (BRI NT-1)

Modems convert a digital signal into an analog signal for transmission over a telephone line. The signal is converted back into a digital format when it reaches the device on the other end of that telephone line.

A Channel Service Unit/Data Service Unit (CSU/DSU) serves as the intermediary between the service provider and the WAN router. In most cases, the CSU/DSU provides the clock speed for the router. A CSU/DSU may be a separate unit or it could be incorporated into a WAN interface card (WIC).

If it is not built in on a Cisco router via a BRI-U (Basic Rate Interface-User) interface, the service provider requires separate BRI NT-1 hardware as a termination point for the communications line. The BRI NT-1 then connects to the Cisco router.

EXAM ALERT

A modem, CSU/DSU, or BRI NT-1 can be used to connect a WAN router at the customer premise to a service provider.

Data Terminal Equipment (DTE)

Data Terminal Equipment is the term used to identify a device at the user end of a network and is connected to the service provider via the DCE device.

DTE equipment may consist of a:

► Router

► PC

► Server

In Figure 6.1, the service provider, whom you will most likely hear called a telco, brings a communication line from its central office (CO) to the customer and terminates its line to the CSU/DSU. The CSU/DSU is then connected to the customer router. The point at which the telco terminates its line to the customer is called a *demarcation point* or *demarc*. Customer-owned equipment, such as the router and typically the CSU/DSU, is referred to as *customer premise equipment (CPE)*.

FIGURE 6.1 An overview of a service provider connection to an end user.

Cabling between the CSU/DSU and router is decided by the type of CSU/DSU that is deployed on that network. If a WIC functions as a CSU/DSU, then the CPE is a telco jack and a Category 5 or Category 6 cable is used with an RJ-45 connector. If a WIC does not function as the CSU/DSU, there are several types of connections possible between a CSU/DSU and the DTE device. With routers, typically a DB-60 connector is used to connect to the router while one of the following connectors is used to connect to the CSU/DSU:

- ▶ EIA/TIA-232

- ▶ EIA/TIA-449

- ▶ EIA/TIA-530

- ▶ V.35

- ▶ X.21

The Electronic Industries Association/Telecommunications Industry Association (EIA/TIA) formed a standards body, which developed the 232, 449, and 530 cables. The V.35 and X.21 cables were developed by the International Telecommunication Union (ITU).

Your best bet is to position the CSU/DSU as close to the router as possible. This requires the shortest amount of cable and therefore ensures maximum speeds.

EXAM ALERT

For the exam, you should know the difference between DCE and DTE equipment. Also, know that the DCE side of a connection must provide the clocking for the serial connection.

Cisco Memory Components

Objectives:

- ▶ Select the components required to meet a network specification

- ▶ Describe the purpose and functions of various network devices

Four memory components are used by Cisco devices. Those components include ROM, Flash, RAM, and NVRAM.

ROM

Read-only memory (ROM) contains the basic code for booting a device and maintaining Power on Self Test (POST), ROM Monitor (ROMmon), bootstrap, and RXBOOT. Because this type of memory is read-only, it cannot be changed by any configuration done at the networking device. ROM is nonvolatile, so data is not lost when the device is powered off.

Flash

Flash is installed on either an electrically erasable, programmable, read-only memory (EEP-ROM) or Personal Computer Memory Card International Association (PCMCIA) card. Flash memory contains the Cisco Internetworking Operating System (IOS) image. The router uses Flash by default to locate the IOS when it is booted. Configuration files may also be stored on a Flash card. Like ROM, Flash is also nonvolatile memory.

RAM

Random-access memory (RAM) is used for short-term storage of a machine's running IOS and running configuration. The IOS is copied from Flash to RAM. This is the only type of system memory that is not permanent. At times, you may hear RAM also referred to as dynamic random-access memory (DRAM). Because this type of memory is volatile, it is lost whenever the machine is shut down.

> **EXAM ALERT**
>
> RAM contains the running IOS, with the exception of Run-From-Flash (RFF) routers. RAM also contains the running configuration or the active configuration that is used after a machine is booted.

NVRAM

Nonvolatile random-access memory (NVRAM) stores the startup configuration. This is the configuration that is loaded when the machine is booted.

Cisco Internetworking Operating System

Cisco IOS software is developed and maintained by Cisco to support a full array of system functions, applications (including Internet applications), and network hardware in a single software package. IOS software is installed on each Cisco router or switch and can accommodate network growth and provide for secure data transfers. The command-line interface (CLI) for routers and switches defines the commands that are used to communicate with the IOS. Future chapters demonstrate the use of CLI commands on both network devices.

> **NOTE**
>
> A Cisco Catalyst switch may use either a Cat OS or Cisco IOS. The major difference with Cat OS is the CLI commands that are used in conjunction with the operating system software.

Cisco releases IOS software using what they call trains. Each release can be further defined by train identifiers. A train identifier determines whether a release is a Technology (T), Enterprise (E), or Service Provider (SP) release. When the IOS version has no train identifier, it is the mainline train. With so many features and applications being offered with each release, a train identifier can further define a specific subset of features. For example, if you have a release named 12.3(1)T, the IOS version number breaks down as follows:

▶ 12.3 refers to the mainline train that will not be added to but will be subject to IOS bug fixes.

▶ (1) represents the release number, which increments with each new release of the mainline train.

▶ T identifies the type of train release where T stands for Technology. This may also be an S (Service Provider) or E (Enterprise) train.

Feature Sets

A feature set is a package of the features that is offered in addition to the basic IOS functions of an IOS software release. You can select more than one feature set per release. Feature sets may be identified as standard, enhanced, or advanced, depending on the services that are supported. To give you an idea of the latest features available with Cisco IOS, current releases offer the following software functionality:

▶ **IP Base**—The base IOS image.

▶ **IP Voice**—Features include Voice over IP (VoIP), and Voice over Frame (VoFR).

▶ **Advanced Security**—Offers advanced protection via firewall, Intrusion Detection System (IDS), Secure Shell (SSH), and IP Security (IPSec).

▶ **SP Services**—Includes service provider services such as IPv6, Netflow SSH, ATM, Voice over ATM (VoATM), and Frame Relay.

▶ **Enterprise Base**—Consists of Enterprise Layer 3 routed protocols, and IBM support.

▶ **Advanced IP Services**—Offers a combination of the Advanced Security and Service Provider Services feature sets.

▶ **Enterprise Services**—Combines the Enterprise Base and Service Provider Services feature sets with full IBM support.

▶ **Advanced Enterprise Services**—Incorporates all the Cisco IOS feature sets.

IOS Image File Naming

The IOS image file represents the name of the system image on a Cisco router or switch. The hardware platform, feature set, compression format, IOS version, and train information are all found in the name of an IOS image file. An IOS image filename can be broken out to identify more specific information about the IOS in use by a device. This is helpful if you are troubleshooting a system issue and need to verify what version is currently in use. Cisco may be aware of an IOS bug, or the version may simply be outdated and an IOS upgrade might be the solution to your trouble. To find the IOS image filename, use the `show version` command from the command prompt.

Given the example filename c2600-ipbase-1.122-1.T.bin (.bin indicates binary format), from left to right, each portion of the filename represents the following:

- ► `c2600`—Hardware platform (Cisco 2600 router)
- ► `ipbase`—Feature set
- ► `1`—File format (compressed re-locatable)
- ► `122`—IOS version number
- ► `1`—Maintenance release number
- ► `T`—Train identifier

EXAM ALERT

Remember the IOS image file structure. If given a filename, you should be able to break down each part of the file and what it represents.

Challenge

Understanding Cisco IOS is necessary for the maintenance and troubleshooting of Cisco routers and switches. I will provide an IOS image filename and would like you to identify the hardware platform, feature set, compression format, IOS version, and train information for that file.

IOS Image filename—c1700-entbase-1.121-1.E.bin

Maintenance Release Number _____

File Format _____

Hardware Platform _____

Train Identifier _____

Feature Set _____

IOS Version Number _____

Cisco Router Models and Features

Objective:

▶ Describe the purpose and functions of various network devices

Cisco offers a wide selection of router models for network implementations. The Cisco family of routers can accommodate networks that range in size and require various network interfaces for WAN connectivity. As mentioned, some router models are fixed port and fixed configuration, whereas others are modular-port routers. To help you prepare for the ICND1 exam, a Cisco 2500 series router model can perform a broad range of the basic routing functions. This router can provide you with sufficient functionality to practice initial router setup and configurations.

The 2500 series hardware can support CSU/DSU, ethernet, token ring, asynchronous or synchronous serial, and ISDN connections. The 2500 series routers coupled with Cisco IOS software can support routed protocols such as IP, Novell IPX, and AppleTalk. They can also support a wide array of routing protocols. Although most of the 2500 family routers are fixed port, the 2524 and 2525 models are both modular-port routers.

In addition to the 2500 series routers, Cisco also offers the following router series:

▶ **800 Series**—Fixed-port and fixed-configuration routers that support Asymmetric Digital Subscriber Line (ADSL), ADSL over ISDN, Single-pair High-Speed DSL (G.SHDSL), Serial, and ethernet to an external cable modem or DSL connections. They can also support a small office or a home office for a telecommuter.

▶ **1600 Series**—Fixed-port routers that support ISDN, asynchronous serial, or synchronous serial connections and can support a small- to moderately-sized business.

▶ **1700 Series**—Modular-port routers that support built-in Fast Ethernet LAN ports and WAN/Voice modular slots, and can support a small- to moderately-sized business.

▶ **1800 Series**—Fixed-port and modular-port routers that build on the 1700 Series router functionality with integrated services such as IPSec VPN, firewall security, inline intrusion prevention (IPS), Network Admission Control (NAC), and URL filtering to small offices.

▶ **2600 Series**—Modular multiservice access routers that support built-in ethernet LAN ports, built-in Fast Ethernet LAN ports, and WAN/voice modular slots. They can support a small to medium office.

▶ **2800 Series**—Integrated service routers that support built-in Fast Ethernet LAN ports, built-in Gigabit Ethernet LAN ports, and WAN/voice modular slots. They can support a small to medium office, its telecommuters, and Wi-Fi connections.

▶ **3600 Series**—Modular multiservice access routers that support data, voice, video, and VPN. They can support a medium to large office or a small Internet Service Provider (ISP).

▶ **3700 Series**—Modular multiservice access routers that support built-in Fast Ethernet LAN ports and WAN/voice modular slots. They can support branch offices.

▶ **3800 Series**—Modular multiservice access routers that support built-in dual Gigabit Ethernet LAN ports and enhanced network module slots. They can support a medium to large business with integrated services.

▶ **7200 Series**—Can be used with an Enterprise Edge or Service Provider Edge environment and support links that range in size from a DS0 (64Kbps) all the way up to an OC12 (655Mbps). They can support Fast Ethernet, Gigabit Ethernet, and Packet over Sonet connections. Chassis slots are open for installation of more than 70 network interfaces.

▶ **7600 Series**—Are likely to be found in a main office of an enterprise business or at a small service provider's point-of-presence (POP) site. Each chassis can support a maximum of 4 slots. Each slot has either a 40Gbps or 720Gbps capacity with advanced optical service modules.

Cisco Switch Models and Features

Objective:

▶ Describe the purpose and functions of various network devices

The Cisco family of switches includes the Catalyst switch models, which as you learned earlier in this chapter might use the Cat OS rather than the IOS. As with Cisco routers, the switch model numbers increase as they are upgraded for enhanced overall operability. Various switches have been developed over the years to accommodate the size and functionality requirements of LANs around the world. You may have a Cisco 1900, 2800, 2900, or 2924 switch to help you study for the Cisco Certified Network Associate. These models should be easy to find and affordable, and they cover all the features necessary for the exam when coupled with Cisco IOS.

In addition to the 1900, 2800, 2900, and 2924 series switches, Cisco also offers the following switch series:

▶ **2950 Series**—Includes a fixed-configuration switch that can support both Fast Ethernet and Gigabit Ethernet connections.

▶ **3500 Series**—Are stackable switches that can employ Cisco Switch Clustering technology and GigaStack GBICs, and support Layer 3 functionality.

▶ **4000 Series**—Can support high-density copper, fiber-based interfaces, Fast Ethernet, Gigabit Ethernet connections, and Layer 3 functionality.

▶ **6500 Series**—Can support Power over Ethernet (PoE) devices, 10/100Mbps ethernet ports, 10/100/1000Mbps ethernet ports, 10Gbps ethernet ports, and Layer 3 functionality.

Cisco switches may also support PoE. PoE enables an end device to receive power over a copper ethernet cable. End devices that might use PoE include wireless access points, IP telephones, video cameras, and card scanners. This technology was originally developed by Cisco and called "inline power." IEEE has since standardized PoE with 802.3af.

Chapter Summary

A general knowledge of Cisco hardware and IOS is integral to your preparation for the ICND1 exam. Chapter 7, "Foundation Cisco IOS Operations," shows you how to correctly navigate through the Cisco IOS. Also, Cisco router and switch configurations are presented throughout the remainder of this book.

Key Terms

- Interface
- Module
- GBIC
- BRI
- Synchronous
- Asynchronous
- HSSI
- T1 controller card
- DS0
- DS1
- T1
- BRI
- ISDN
- NT-1
- HSSI
- DTE
- Modem
- CSU/DSU
- CO
- Demarc
- CPE
- ROM

- ▶ Flash
- ▶ RAM
- ▶ NVRAM
- ▶ IOS
- ▶ Train
- ▶ CLI
- ▶ PoE

Apply Your Knowledge

Exercises

6.1 Cisco Memory Components

You may be asked to identify the memory components that are used on Cisco devices. In this exercise, please list the four types of memory and their respective functions.

Estimated Time: 10 minutes

Memory Component	Memory Component Functionality

Review Questions

1. Describe a GBIC.
2. List the WAN interfaces and their descriptions.
3. Define DCE and DTE.
4. What is the Cisco IOS?
5. Define PoE.

Exam Questions

1. Which WAN interface is an ISDN line that consists of two 64Kbps bearer (B) channels and one 16Kbps data (D) channel?

   ○ **A.** BRI

   ○ **B.** Synchronous serial

   ○ **C.** Asynchronous serial

   ○ **D.** HSSI

2. Which WAN interface synchronizes clocks for the bit stream of both the sending and receiving end of a serial link?

   ○ **A.** BRI

   ○ **B.** Synchronous serial

   ○ **C.** Asynchronous serial

   ○ **D.** HSSI

3. Which WAN interface offers up to 52Mbps transmission rates to the WAN from a Cisco router?

   ○ **A.** BRI

   ○ **B.** Synchronous serial

   ○ **C.** Asynchronous serial

   ○ **D.** HSSI

4. Which of the following devices can be labeled Data Circuit-Terminating Equipment (DCE)? (Choose the three best answers.)

   ○ **A.** Router

   ○ **B.** Modem

   ○ **C.** CSU/DSU

   ○ **D.** BRI NT-1

5. Which of the following devices can be labeled Data Terminal Equipment (DTE)? (Choose the three best answers.)

   ○ **A.** Router

   ○ **B.** Modem

   ○ **C.** PC

   ○ **D.** Server

6. What type of memory contains the basic code for booting a device and maintaining POST, ROMmon, bootstrap, and RXBOOT?

  ○ **A.** ROM

  ○ **B.** Flash

  ○ **C.** RAM

  ○ **D.** NVRAM

7. What type of memory is nonvolatile and contains the Cisco IOS image?

  ○ **A.** ROM

  ○ **B.** Flash

  ○ **C.** RAM

  ○ **D.** NVRAM

8. This type of memory contains the running IOS and the running configuration (active configuration) that is used after a machine is booted.

  ○ **A.** ROM

  ○ **B.** Flash

  ○ **C.** RAM

  ○ **D.** NVRAM

9. This type of memory stores the startup configuration.

  ○ **A.** ROM

  ○ **B.** Flash

  ○ **C.** RAM

  ○ **D.** NVRAM

10. What does the ipbase portion of the Cisco IOS file named c2600-ipbase-1.122-1.T.bin represent?

  ○ **A.** Hardware platform

  ○ **B.** Feature set

  ○ **C.** Train identifier

  ○ **D.** IOS version

Answers to Review Questions

1. A GBIC interface module can be inserted into the Gigabit Ethernet slot to allow for different media connections to that port. The physical media can range from copper to single-mode fiber. A GBIC is also hot swappable, so it can be installed without interrupting service to that switch.

2. Basic Rate Interface (BRI)

    BRI is an ISDN line that consists of two 64Kbps bearer (B) channels and one 16Kbps data (D) channel. Voice, video, and data traffic can be carried over the B-channels. Signals between telephone company switches use the D-channel.

    Synchronous serial

    A synchronous serial interface synchronizes clocks for the bit stream of both the sending and receiving end of a serial link. This enables the data rate to be adjusted if necessary to ensure that both ends of a serial link are functioning at the same speed.

    Asynchronous serial

    An asynchronous serial interface does the opposite of a synchronous serial interface. It does not synchronize the clocks for the bit stream of the sending and receiving end of a serial link.

    High-Speed Serial Interface (HSSI)

    High Speed Serial Interfaces offer up to 52Mbps transmission rates to the WAN from a Cisco router.

    T1 controller card

    A T1 controller card can be installed in a router's T1 slot to communicate with and control the 24 DS0 channels.

3. Data Circuit-Terminating Equipment (DCE) or Data Communications Equipment is the term used to identify a device that connects the Data Terminal Equipment (DTE) to a service provider's communications line. DCE equipment may consist of a modem, CSU/DSU, or BRI NT-1.

    DTE is the term used to identify a device at the user end of a network and is connected to the service provider via the DCE device. DTE equipment may consist of a router, PC, or server.

4. Cisco IOS software is developed and maintained by Cisco to support a full array of system functions, applications (including Internet applications), and network hardware in a single software package. IOS software is installed on each Cisco router or switch and can accommodate network growth and provide for secure data transfers. The command-line interface (CLI) for routers and switches defines the commands that are used to communicate with the IOS.

5. Power over Ethernet (PoE) enables an end device to receive power over a copper ethernet cable. End devices that might use PoE include IP telephones, video cameras, and card scanners. This technology was originally developed by Cisco and called "inline power." IEEE has since standardized PoE with 802.3af.

Answers to Exam Questions

1. **A.** BRI consists of two 64Kbps B channels and one 16Kbps D channel. Answer B is incorrect because synchronous serial synchronizes clocks for the bit stream of both the sending and receiving end of a serial link. Answer C is incorrect because asynchronous serial does not synchronize the clocks for the bit stream of the sending and receiving end of a serial link. Answer D is incorrect because HSSI offers up to 52Mbps transmission rates to the WAN from a Cisco router.

2. **B.** Synchronous serial synchronizes clocks for the bit stream of both the sending and receiving end of a serial link. Answer A is incorrect because BRI consists of two 64Kbps B channels and one 16Kbps D channel. Answer C is incorrect because asynchronous serial does not synchronize the clocks for the bit stream of the sending and receiving end of a serial link. Answer D is incorrect because HSSI offers up to 52Mbps transmission rates to the WAN from a Cisco router.

3. **D.** HSSI offers up to 52Mbps transmission rates to the WAN from a Cisco router. Answer A is incorrect because BRI consists of two 64Kbps B channels and one 16Kbps D channel. Answer B is incorrect because synchronous serial synchronizes clocks for the bit stream of both the sending and receiving end of a serial link. Answer C is incorrect because asynchronous serial does not synchronize the clocks for the bit stream of the sending and receiving end of a serial link.

4. **B, C, D.** Modems, CSU/DSUs, and BRI NT-1s are all Data Circuit-Terminating Equipment. Answer A is incorrect because routers are considered Data Terminal Equipment.

5. **A, C, D.** Answers A, C, and D are correct because routers, PCs, and servers are all Data Terminal Equipment. Answer B is incorrect because modems are Data Circuit-Terminating Equipment.

6. **A.** ROM contains the basic code for booting a device and maintaining POST, ROMmon, bootstrap, and RXBOOT. Answer B is incorrect because Flash memory contains the Cisco IOS image. Answer C is incorrect because RAM is used for short-term storage of a machine's running IOS and running configuration. Answer D is incorrect because NVRAM stores the startup configuration.

7. **B.** Flash memory is nonvolatile and contains the Cisco IOS image. Answer A is incorrect because ROM contains the basic code for booting a device and maintaining POST, ROMmon, bootstrap, and RXBOOT. Answer C is incorrect because RAM is used for short-term storage of a machine's running IOS and running configuration. Answer D is incorrect because NVRAM stores the startup configuration.

8. **C.** RAM contains the running IOS and the running configuration (active configuration) that is used after a machine is booted. Answer A is incorrect because ROM contains the basic code for booting a device and maintaining POST, ROMmon, bootstrap, and RXBOOT. Answer B is incorrect because Flash memory contains the Cisco IOS image. Answer D is incorrect because NVRAM stores the startup configuration.

9. **D.** NVRAM stores the startup configuration. Answer A is incorrect because ROM contains the basic code for booting a device and maintaining POST, ROMmon, bootstrap, and RXBOOT. Answer B is incorrect because Flash memory contains the Cisco IOS image. Answer C is incorrect because RAM is used for short-term storage of a machine's running IOS and running configuration.

10. B. The term *ipbase* refers to the IP Base feature set. Answer A is incorrect because the hardware platform is c2600 or the Cisco 2600 router. Answer C is incorrect because the train identifier is T for Technical. Answer D is incorrect because the IOS version is represented by 122 or version 12.2.

Suggested Readings and Resources

The following are some recommended readings on network components, Cisco devices, and terminology:

1. "Serial Connectivity Network Modules," http://www.cisco.com/en/US/products/hw/routers/ps274/products_data_sheet09186a0 080091b8b.html.

2. "White Paper: Cisco IOS Reference Guide," http://www.cisco.com/warp/public/620/1.html.

3. Boney, James. *Cisco IOS in a Nutshell*, First Edition. O'Reilly, 2001.

4. "Loading and Maintaining System Images," http://www.cisco.com/en/US/products/sw/iosswrel/ps1835/1026071.

5. "Cisco Router Guide," http://www.cisco.com/application/pdf/en/us/guest/products/ps5855/c1031/ cdccont_0900aecd8019dc1f.pdf.

CHAPTER SEVEN

Foundation Cisco IOS Operations

Objectives

This chapter covers the following Cisco-specified objectives for the "Implement a small routed network" section of the 640-822 ICND1 exam:

▶ **Manage Cisco IOS**

▶ **Describe the operation of Cisco routers (including: router bootup process, POST, router components)**

Outline

Introduction   210

Terminal Options   210
  Console Port   210
  Auxiliary Port   212
  Telnet   212
  HTTP and HTTPS   212
  SSH   213

Router/Switch Startup Procedures   214
  POST   214
  Bootstrap   215
  ROMmon   215
  IOS Loading   215
  Configuration Loading   217
    Setup Mode   217
    Password Recovery   218

Navigating the IOS   220
  User EXEC   220
  Privileged EXEC   221

Global Configuration   222
  Interface Configuration   223
  Line Configuration   224
Context-Sensitive Help   224
Abbreviations   226
Shortcut Keys   226
Common Syntax Errors   227

Chapter Summary   230
  Key Terms   231

Apply Your Knowledge   231
  Exercises   231
  Review Questions   233
  Exam Questions   233
  Answers to Review Questions   235
  Answers to Exam Questions   236
  Suggested Readings and Resources   237

Study Strategies

▶ Read the information presented in the chapter, paying special attention to tables, Notes, and Exam Alerts.

▶ This chapter serves as a foundation for all configurations that are to come. It is not enough to just grasp these concepts. You should feel completely comfortable with the navigation of the IOS before tackling advanced configurations in future chapters.

▶ If possible, practice the syntax of every command discussed throughout this chapter (and book) with real or simulated Cisco equipment.

▶ Complete the Challenge Exercises and the Exercises at the end of the chapter. These exercises are designed to give you practical experience using the utilities discussed.

▶ Complete the Exam Questions at the end of the chapter. They are designed to simulate the type of questions you will be asked in the ICND1 exam.

Introduction

Unfortunately, Cisco devices are not yet at the point where they can automatically configure themselves. With that being said, each Cisco device that contains an IOS (internetwork operating system) must have some interface in which you, the expert Cisco administrator, can interact with the operating system to perform any administration, configuration, and troubleshooting services.

This chapter explores the options available for interacting with Cisco IOS using the command-line interface (CLI). In Chapter 9, "Understanding the Cisco SDM," you will see that Cisco has simplified some Cisco device administration by creating a graphical user interface (GUI) in which many configuration and verification command can be performed using a web browser. Granted this is a great tool for many tasks; however, you will inevitably need to access the CLI of Cisco IOS to perform tasks outside of the GUI's capabilities. As a consequence, you will need to understand the command hierarchy of the IOS CLI to accurately navigate your way around to achieve your administrative goal.

This chapter also looks into the multiple boot-up steps that occur when a Cisco router or switch is powered on, and how you can manipulate that startup sequence.

Terminal Options

After starting a router configuration using the Console Port or Auxiliary Port, you can choose from among several options to gain access to Cisco IOS Software. These access methodologies are commonly referred to as EXEC sessions. Assuming that the device model and IOS supports them, certain Cisco devices can support up to five means of gaining an EXEC session to the IOS, which are discussed in the following subsections.

Console Port

Several Cisco devices do not have a default IP address that can be utilized to gain access to the IOS. Therefore, administrators gain initial out-of-band terminal access to Cisco devices via the console port. After an EXEC access is gained, you can configure the device via the CLI of IOS.

NOTE

The term *out-of-band* simply refers to the fact that the console is a management port that is separate from interfaces that are used for networking data transmissions. Conversely, *in-band* management signals traverse over the same networking paths and interfaces as the data stream. This implies that you have IP connectivity to the devices that you are managing.

To connect to a console port, Cisco supplies you with a flat rollover cable. As illustrated in Figure 7.1, the pins in a rollover cable are reverse images of each other when the cable is viewed with both sides of the tabs in the same orientation. Cisco console cables either come with two RJ-45 connectors in which a DB-9 adapter is required for connection to the PC, or come with the DB-9 connector attached to one end of the cable. The 9-pin connector of the console cable connects to your terminal PC's COM port. Keep in mind that this management connection is for initial terminal access only and should not be confused with an actual networking Ethernet cable of any sort.

FIGURE 7.1 Cisco console cable pinouts.

EXAM ALERT

It is imperative to be able to recognize and differentiate between the pin configurations and the usage of a straight-through ethernet cable versus a cross-over ethernet cable versus a rollover console cable.

An ASCII terminal emulation software program must be running on your management PC if it is to interact with the Cisco IOS. There are several different terminal programs available, such as HyperTerminal, TeraTerm, SecureCRT, and others. The terminal setup of the COM port connected to the rollover console cable must be set to the following default console parameters: 9600 baud, 8 data bits, no parity bits, 1 stop bit, and no flow control. After the terminal is set up correctly and you have powered on the Cisco device, you should see the output from your console EXEC session in the terminal window.

Auxiliary Port

Certain Cisco models may contain another out-of-band management port called an auxiliary (AUX) port. This port is very similar to the console port in that it uses a rollover cable and has an RJ-45 connection to the Cisco device. The difference between the auxiliary and the console port is that the auxiliary port has flow control capability, which is useful for analog modem connectivity. By connecting an external modem to this management port, you can dial into the modem remotely and gain an EXEC session without being physically next to the Cisco device.

Telnet

As discussed in Chapter 1, "Standard Internetworking Models," Telnet is an Application layer protocol of the TCP/IP protocol suite that uses TCP port 23 to gain virtual terminal emulation to a device. Telnet is considered in-band management because it is required to have IP connectivity to the Cisco device into which you are trying to Telnet. Most Cisco devices allow at least five Telnet EXEC sessions to be connected for remote terminal access. For the sake of security, there is some configuration involved to allow Telnet access into the Cisco devices. Telnet is discussed in further detail in Chapter 8, "Foundation Cisco Configurations."

HTTP and HTTPS

Similar to Telnet, HTTP and HTTPS are also Application layer protocols of the TCP/IP protocol suite. HTTP uses TCP port 80 to establish a management connection to the Cisco device. HTTPS is a secure version of HTTP over Secure Socket Layer (SSL) and uses TCP port 443. HTTP and HTTPS terminal sessions require IP connectivity to the Cisco device, making it an in-band management communication methodology. The key difference between HTTP/HTTPS and Telnet is that when you use HTTP or HTTPS, you can have a graphical interface to the configuration and administration features of the Cisco IOS.

The HTTP EXEC session is made possible by a HTTP server service that can run if configured on the Cisco device. For security purposes, some Cisco routers do not have this functionality enabled by default. If this functionality is not going to be utilized, it is recommended that you disable this service to avoid any security vulnerabilities.

> **NOTE**
>
> HTTP and HTTPS are utilized in the Security Device Manager (SDM) configuration utility, which will be discussed in greater detail in Chapter 9, "Understanding the Cisco SDM."

SSH

Imagine you have Telntetted into a Cisco device and it is prompting you for a password. If an attacker has the capability to eavesdrop on that Telnet terminal session, he could very well detect the password because the Telnet communications are in clear text.

With SSH (Secure Shell), you are provided a secure terminal EXEC connection through the use of encrypted communications between your terminal client and the Cisco device. Your terminal application must support SSH to connect securely to your Cisco device. Some terminal programs that support SSH are SecureCRT and Putty. In addition, the version and feature set of the Cisco IOS must support SSH. Similar to its brother in-band protocols, SSH also requires initial configurations before gaining access to an EXEC session. Granted, this additional configuration may seem tedious; however, the benefit of having secure remote terminal connections to the Cisco device outweighs the work involved.

REVIEW BREAK

Table 7.1 quickly reviews the five means of gaining EXEC sessions to Cisco Devices.

TABLE 7.1   Cisco EXEC Session Summary

	In-band Versus Out-of-band	Cabling	IP Connectivity Required	Notes
Console	Out-of-band	Rollover	No	Requires physical connectivity.
Auxiliary	Out-of-band	Rollover	No	Requires external modem for remote connectivity.
Telnet	In-band	Network cable	Yes	Can support at least five connections to most Cisco devices.
HTTP/HTTPS	In-band	Network cable	Yes	Must be enabled on Cisco routers. Should be disabled if not utilized.
SSH	In-band	Network cable	Yes	Requires SSH-compliant terminal emulation program and specific Cisco IOS version and feature set.

EXAM ALERT

Successfully initiating a Telnet, HTTP/HTTPS, or SSH session to a Cisco device is an excellent way to test that you have Application layer connectivity to that device.

Router/Switch Startup Procedures

Objective:

▶ Describe the operation of Cisco routers (including: router bootup process, POST, router components)

Now that you have an understanding of how to connect to the Cisco IOS, you can now look at the startup procedures for a Cisco router or switch to determine how the IOS is loaded and running in the first place when you power on those devices. Additionally, these devices would be doing us a huge administrative injustice if they did not load the configurations that you have toiled over in previous EXEC sessions (despite the obvious level of job security). Thus, you also need to look into how a saved configuration is applied after the IOS is loaded. As you will see, each of the memory components that were discussed in Chapter 6, "Introduction to Cisco Routers and Switches," performs a pivotal part in the storing, loading, and running of the IOS and the configuration.

Router and switch startup procedures are extremely similar to a computer's boot-up process. For instance, when you turn on a computer, the computer utilizes ROM (read-only memory) chips to perform a POST (power-on self-test) to check the critical hardware initially for startup. Then it consults the BIOS (basic input/output system) settings to determine the order in which to search the hard drives, floppy drives, or CD drives to locate the operating system. After the operating system is loaded, it applies any custom configurations you have made in the past and utilizes those settings toward its normal operation.

Similarly, when you turn on a Cisco router and a switch, ROM chips perform a POST and then load the IOS process. You can manipulate the location sources of the IOS similar to specifying the boot drive in the BIOS settings on a computer. After the IOS is loaded, your saved configuration is loaded and applied to the device's operating functions. The next sections delve further into the specific processes that are occurring at each stage.

POST

When you first apply power to a Cisco router or switch, a specialized ROM performs a series of tests of the critical hardware components that are pertinent for startup and basic operation such as Flash memory, CPU, and interfaces. It makes sense to utilize ROM chips for this service because they are already hard-coded with their programs and they do not require constant power to keep those programs stored in the memory. If a failure occurs during this stage of the startup process, you may encounter one of several outcomes, ranging from a non-functioning interface all the way to complete device failure. In any case, your equipment should be under warranty or you have an active support contract in place to fix the failing hardware.

Bootstrap

After the hardware passes all its tests (if only the ICND1 was that easy), another ROM seeks out the operating system in accordance to its programming routines. The code that is run in the ROM is commonly referred to as the bootstrap code. If a failure occurs at this stage of the boot-up process, your Cisco device could very likely enter what is known as ROM Monitor or commonly called ROMmon.

ROMmon

In your travels, if you or someone else has ever coined the phrase "hit rock bottom," you have a general idea of what purpose ROMmon serves. The ROM Monitor is a very limited codeset that enables you to perform elementary functions to manually get the router or switch back to a functioning state. You can perform low-level diagnostics and even copy a new IOS file to the Cisco device over the console port or configure TFTP information so the device can download the IOS image off of a TFTP server.

TIP

Keep in mind that your default console speed is 9600bps, and a typical IOS file exceeds 16 megabytes. If you need to re-copy a working IOS to the Cisco device in ROMmon mode over the console, I recommend changing the default console speed in ROMmon to a higher speed or taking a long lunch or dinner break.

ROMmon is also utilized during password recovery on a Cisco router to make it possible to tell the device manually to ignore any saved configurations (including the passwords). It is possible to force your Cisco device to go directly to ROMmon on boot by sending a break sequence in your terminal session in the first 60 seconds of bootup. You can tell you are in ROMmon mode if you are presented with a command prompt that looks like rommon 1 >. Any time you type a command in ROMmon, the number at the prompt increments by one (rommon 2 >, rommon 3 >, and so on).

IOS Loading

Up to this point, the Cisco router or switch has performed only initial diagnostics. With that being said, the IOS itself still has not been located or loaded. The bootstrap's programming has a specific search order in which it typically follows to locate and load the IOS. I say "typically" because you can alter the natural order of things with the router or switch's startup process if you manipulate something called the configuration register.

Located in NVRAM, the configuration register is a 16-bit (4 hexadecimal characters) value that specifies how the router or switch should operate during initialization. For instance, 0x2102 (0x signifies all characters that follow are hexadecimal) is a common configuration register that specifies that the router or switch should boot in its typical fashion. However, if you manipulate certain characters in the configuration register, you can manually modify the startup process to load the IOS from locations other than the default. Specifically, the last hexadecimal character in the configuration register, known as the boot field, is the value that dictates where the bootstrap code can find the IOS. The possible boot field values are as follows:

▶ **0x2100**—When the boot field is a zero, the configuration register instructs the bootstrap to boot directly into ROM and load ROMmon.

▶ **0x2101-0x210F**—When the last field in the configuration register is 1-F, the router or switch boots normally.

TIP

> In older router and switch models, a configuration register of 0x2101 (if the boot field has a value of one), the router or switch would boot a mini IOS located in ROM and commonly referred to as RxBoot. RxBoot looks very similar to the normal IOS; however, it does not provide the majority of the IOS's services. This mini IOS provides just enough functionality to reach a TFTP server and download a working IOS to the Cisco device. You can easily determine you are in RxBoot if the prompt looks like `Router(boot)>` in a router or `Switch(boot)>` in a switch.

Assuming the configuration register is 0x2102 (the default configuration register), the next step for initialization is to have the bootstrap search the configuration located in NVRAM to see whether the Cisco administrator has placed a command telling the router or switch specifically where to boot. The tools to do this are known as `boot system` commands. For example, if you have previously configured your device and put in the `boot system tftp c2600-do3s-mz.123-5.T1 172.16.1.1` command, you have instructed the bootstrap to load the IOS file c2600-do3s-mz.123-5.T1 from a TFTP server located at 172.16.1.1.

NOTE

> Do not confuse this step with loading the configuration. This is just a step in the IOS loading process that enables the bootstrap code to implement any configuration specifications you previously saved that told the device where to boot. The configuration itself is not loaded until after the IOS is located and running.

If the default configuration register is utilized and you have not configured the device with any `boot system` commands, the default action of the bootstrap is to load the first IOS file in Flash memory. After the file is found, it is decompressed and loaded into RAM. At this point, the IOS is successfully loaded and running on your Cisco device.

What would happen if the IOS image were corrupted or missing? As with many functions of Cisco devices, a couple of failsafes are put in place to keep the device in an operating state or a mode in which you can get it back to an operating state. Specifically, if the Cisco router or switch cannot locate a working IOS file, it broadcasts out all interfaces in the hopes that a backup IOS file is stored on a TFTP server on its connected segments. If there isn't a TFTP server or the TFTP server does not contain a valid IOS file, the next failsafe for the IOS is to boot to ROMmon where you can copy the IOS over via the console or TFTP.

Configuration Loading

With the IOS loaded, the router or switch is now able to apply any saved configuration parameters. NVRAM is the first location where the device searches for the configuration. Here, a file called `startup-config` contains all the previous configurations that were present the last time an administrator saved the configuration. As the name states, this is the configuration that is loaded each time the Cisco device starts up. Similar to the IOS, after this configuration file is found, it is loaded into RAM as well. After the configuration is loaded and running at this point, it is conveniently referred to as `running-config`.

EXAM ALERT

The `running-config` is the active configuration running in RAM.

Cisco devices do not ship with a complete startup configuration, which is why you might have to initially configure your Cisco device through some means of out-of-band management such as the console or auxiliary port. So the question begs, what happens when you initially turn on a new Cisco router or switch, or if someone erases the startup configuration?

Many Cisco devices attempt to do an autoinstall by downloading a configuration file from an active TFTP server (similarly to the IOS) when they detect that the `startup-config` is not located in NVRAM. Typically, these files contain enough configuration parameters (such as IP addresses for interfaces) for you to Telnet into the device and configure the remaining parameters. If the Cisco device finds an autoinstall configuration file from a TFTP server, the device loads the file and makes that the `running-config`. On the chance that you were not proactive enough to have an autoinstall configuration on your TFTP server, the router or switch prompts you for something called *Setup Mode*.

EXAM ALERT

It is imperative that you can identify the steps that a switch or router follows during initialization, the memory or device architectures where these steps occur, and the fallback sequences when a failure has occurred in the boot-up sequence.

Setup Mode

With non-CCNA technicians in mind, Cisco created Setup Mode so you can build a working configuration on a device without having to memorize the nuances of the CLI of the IOS. Setup Mode is a friendly interactive dialog in which the IOS asks the administrator questions about common configuration parameters that enable the Cisco device to have basic operations. Illustrated in Figure 7.2, the Setup Mode dialog initially asks you whether you wish to continue with Setup Mode. If you answer "no" to this question, you exit out of Setup Mode and are brought immediately to a CLI EXEC session. In addition, if you want to cancel at any point in the Setup Mode and get to the command prompt, you can use Ctrl+C to terminate the setup dialog. After you complete all questions, Setup Mode displays the parameters that you specified and asks you whether you want to use this configuration. If you answer "yes," the Cisco device saves your configuration and applies the settings to the device's operations.

```
          --- System Configuration Dialog ---

Would you like to enter the initial configuration dialog? [yes/no]: yes

At any point you may enter a question mark '?' for help.
Use ctrl-c to abort configuration dialog at any prompt.
Default settings are in square brackets '[]'.

Basic management setup configures only enough connectivity
for management of the system, extended setup will ask you
to configure each interface on the system

Would you like to enter basic management setup? [yes/no]: yes
Configuring global parameters:

  Enter host name [Router]: CCNA
```

FIGURE 7.2 Setup Mode dialog.

TIP

Throughout the configuration with the IOS, you may encounter several different types of interactive dialogs similar to Setup Mode. To save yourself from unnecessary typing, you can use the default value that is located in the brackets to answer any single-answer question by simply hitting the Enter key. For example, notice in Figure 7.2, the Enter host name prompt contains the word Router in brackets. If you were to press the Enter key at that prompt, this Cisco router would have a host name of Router.

Password Recovery

As the next chapter explains, you can secure access to your Cisco devices in several ways. In times where you inherit a pre-configured device or accidentally forgot or mis-configured a password, you need some loophole in the boot-up process that enables you to regain access to the device. Once again, the configuration register plays a pivotal part in the quest to manipulate the natural order of Cisco device initialization.

The third character in the configuration register enables you to tell the device to ignore any configurations that might be saved in NVRAM. If this field is changed from a 0 to a 4, the device inevitably boots into Setup Mode because the router or switch is fooled that there is no startup configuration. Now, with the configuration register changed to 0x2142, you can reconfigure the Cisco device creating your own unique passwords and save that configuration for future device startups.

CAUTION

Don't Forget the Natural Order   Do not forget when performing password recovery to set your configuration register back to 0x2102. Failing to do so forces your router to constantly ignore your configurations, causing your router or switch to repeatedly enter Setup Mode.

EXAM ALERT

Be sure to recognize that a configuration register of 0x2142 is a typical setting for performing password recovery.

REVIEW BREAK

To solidify the startup process, the following is a recap of the stages of the boot-up, any fall-back procedures, and the memory locations involved:

1. POST, located in ROM, tests hardware.

2. Bootstrap, located in ROM, looks at the boot field in the configuration register to locate IOS. 0x2100 boots to ROMmon located in ROM.

3. 0x2101-0x210F prompts bootstrap to parse `startup-config` in NVRAM for any `boot system` commands. If it finds any commands, it does what they say.

4. If no `boot system` commands are found, the first file in Flash is loaded. If no file is found in Flash, TFTP boots. If no IOS file is found from TFTP, the device goes to ROMmon in ROM.

5. After IOS is loaded, the configuration register is checked. If it is 0x2142, ignore `startup-config` in NVRAM. If it is 0x2102, load `startup-config` in NVRAM. If there is no `startup-config`, TFTP autoinstall. If no TFTP autoinstall configuration is found, enter Setup Mode.

Challenge

As you read in this chapter, be aware that many operations are occurring behind the scenes when you gain access to a Cisco device and turn it on. In this challenge, I want you to logically think through what is occurring at each stage of the boot-up process and identify the memory architectures that are involved given the following scenario:

Your night administrator planned to upgrade the IOS on your company's router last night. When you came in to work the next morning, you saw a written note from the night admin frantically explaining how he began the IOS upgrade, but he accidentally kicked out the power cord mid-upgrade and does not know what to do. Unfortunately, the IOS upgrade had to erase the IOS image file in Flash memory to make room for the new IOS. You do not have any TFTP servers on your network.

1. You must initially gain access to the device. Because the IOS cannot be loaded, what is the most logical way to gain an EXEC session?

2. When you turn on the device, what is the first thing your router will do and what memory is involved?

3. The default configuration register is configured, so where will the bootstrap look first to locate the IOS?

(continues)

(continued)

4. If you have not made any previous configurations telling the router how to boot, where will it look next?

5. Because the file isn't complete here, what is the first fallback failsafe?

6. Knowing that will fail, in what mode will you be and in what part of memory is that located?

7. What will the prompt look like?

Challenge Answer

To gain access to a non-functioning device, you will need to use some means of out-of-band management such as the console or the auxiliary port. When the device is powered on, the POST in ROM tests the hardware. Because the configuration register is 0x2102 (the default), the router searches for `boot system` commands in the `startup-config`. Because there are no configurations stating where to boot, the router looks into Flash. Unfortunately, the Flash memory does not have a complete IOS because the upgrade process was interrupted. With that being said, the router tries to locate an IOS file on a TFTP server. Because the scenario mentioned that there are no TFTP servers on the network, the router falls back to ROMmon in ROM, which displays a prompt similar to `rommon 1 >`.

Navigating the IOS

Objective:

▶ Manage Cisco IOS

By now, you have a new-found love and respect for your Cisco equipment after knowing all the work that occurs when you turn on your router or switch. What better way to prove that love and respect but by mastering the IOS that the Cisco devices have so painstakingly found and loaded for your administration and configuration pleasure? This section looks at the hierarchical levels of the IOS and what type of interactivity you can encounter at each level.

EXAM ALERT

You will be able to eliminate several distracting incorrect answers in the exam by recognizing the level of the IOS hierarchy the commands will be found.

User EXEC

At your organization, you may have Level 1 technicians who are not strong in Cisco fundamentals; thus, you want to ensure only that they have access to basic troubleshooting and statistics without worrying that they might change the configuration or cause some other network catastrophe. Because a multitude of administrators might need to gain access to these Cisco devices, it makes sense to ensure that the first level of IOS hierarchy they encounter is somewhat limited in the extent of what can be done. This is the nature of User EXEC.

In User EXEC, you are limited in the number and type of commands that are available to you. For instance, the majority of show commands are available at this level of the IOS hierarchy because they do not detrimentally affect the router or the switch to perform these commands. In addition, you can test IP connectivity to other devices with ping as well as remotely administer other devices or troubleshoot all the way up to Layer 7 with Telnet. The Cisco IOS prompt for User EXEC is signified by the greater than sign (>) following the hostname of the Cisco device. For example, a Cisco router and switch with their default hostnames would look like Router> and Switch>, respectively. Figure 7.3 displays the commands that you have available at User EXEC.

```
Router>?
Exec commands:
  access-enable      Create a temporary Access-List entry
  access-profile     Apply user-profile to interface
  call               Voice call
  clear              Reset functions
  connect            Open a terminal connection
  crypto             Encryption related commands.
  disable            Turn off privileged commands
  disconnect         Disconnect an existing network connection
  enable             Turn on privileged commands
  exit               Exit from the EXEC
  help               Description of the interactive help system
  lock               Lock the terminal
  login              Log in as a particular user
  logout             Exit from the EXEC
  modemui            Start a modem-like user interface
  mrinfo             Request neighbor and version information from a multicast
                     router
  mstat              Show statistics after multiple multicast traceroutes
  mtrace             Trace reverse multicast path from destination to source
  name-connection    Name an existing network connection
  pad                Open a X.29 PAD connection
  ping               Send echo messages
  ppp                Start IETF Point-to-Point Protocol (PPP)
  release            Release a resource
  renew              Renew a resource
  resume             Resume an active network connection
  rlogin             Open an rlogin connection
  set                Set system parameter (not config)
  show               Show running system information
  slip               Start Serial-line IP (SLIP)
  ssh                Open a secure shell client connection
  systat             Display information about terminal lines
  tclquit            Quit Tool Command Language shell
  telnet             Open a telnet connection
  terminal           Set terminal line parameters
  traceroute         Trace route to destination
  tunnel             Open a tunnel connection
  udptn              Open an udptn connection
  where              List active connections
  x28                Become an X.28 PAD
  x3                 Set X.3 parameters on PAD
```

FIGURE 7.3 User EXEC command display.

Privileged EXEC

Assuming you need to acquire more functionality from your Cisco devices beyond basic troubleshooting and statistical displays, you have to have another layer of the Cisco IOS hierarchy in which you have access to all commands. Happily named, Privileged EXEC is the next level of the IOS, in which you have the same commands as you do in User EXEC, as well as some commands that can alter the Cisco device's functionality.

For example, in Privileged EXEC, you can perform `debug` commands that can show you hundreds of real-time routing and switching functions and report them to the console. Because this can cause quite a processing strain on the device, these commands are reserved for only those who can access Privileged EXEC. Additionally, some `show` commands such as `show startup-config` and `show running-config` can be seen only by those who should be able (privileged) to see the configuration of the devices (including passwords). Some other new and dangerous commands available in Privileged EXEC include `delete`, `clear`, `erase`, `configure`, `copy`, and `reload` (reboots the device), to name a few.

To gain access to Privileged EXEC, type the command **enable** from User EXEC. After you press Enter, the prompt changes from > to #, signifying that you are now in Privileged EXEC mode. Because anybody can read this section and learn how to get to these commands, it makes sense to have some way for the IOS to prompt for a password to authorize those who truly should be granted access. The next chapter discusses how to apply these passwords to restrict who gains access from User EXEC to Privileged EXEC. To return back to User EXEC, the reverse command is `disable`.

Global Configuration

One of the commands that you can access through Privileged EXEC is `configure`. This means that we have to enter yet another level of the Cisco IOS to make any configuration changes to the Cisco device. By typing the **configure terminal** command, you are telling the Cisco IOS that you are going to configure the Cisco device via your terminal window. The new level you enter after you complete this command is called Global Configuration. You can recognize it by looking at the command prompt, which will reflect `Router(config)#` for routers and `Switch(config)#` for switches.

Figure 7.4 displays a partial output of just some of the commands that are available in Global Configuration. Note that the commands `delete`, `debug`, `clear`, `configure`, and `copy` do not show up in the list of commands. You have a different set of commands available to you at this level of the IOS versus Privileged and User EXEC. This means that you must exit Global Configuration to use these commands as well as `show`, `reload`, and other Privileged EXEC-specific commands.

Of equal note, after you enter a command in the IOS, it is immediately applied to `running-config` and applied to the device's operation. The configurations are not listed and then applied later like batch files or executed compiled programs. Configuration help is shown in Figure 7.4.

```
Router>enable
Router#configure terminal
Enter configuration commands, one per line.  End with CNTL/Z.
Router(config)#?
Configure commands:
  aaa                          Authentication, Authorization and Accounting.
  aal2-profile                 Configure AAL2 profile
  access-list                  Add an access list entry
  alias                        Create command alias
  appfw                        Configure the Application Firewall policy
  application                  Define application
  archive                      Archive the configuration
  arp                          Set a static ARP entry
  async-bootp                  Modify system bootp parameters
  backhaul-session-manager     Configure Backhaul Session Manager
  banner                       Define a login banner
  bba-group                    Configure BBA Group
  boot                         Modify system boot parameters
  bridge                       Bridge Group.
  buffers                      Adjust system buffer pool parameters
  busy-message                 Display message when connection to host fails
  call                         Configure Call parameters
  call-history-mib             Define call history mib parameters
  call-manager-fallback        SRST for Cisco Call Manager fallback. For Call
                               Manager Express configuration use the
                               'telephony-service' command
  carrier-id                   Name of the carrier associated with this trunk
                               group
  ccm-manager                  Call Manager
  cdp                          Global CDP configuration subcommands
  chat-script                  Define a modem chat script
  class-map                    Configure QoS Class Map
  clns                         Global CLNS configuration subcommands
  clock                        Configure time-of-day clock
  cns                          CNS agents
  config-register              Define the configuration register
  configuration                Configuration access
  connect                      cross-connect two interfaces
  control-plane                Configure control plane services
  crypto                       Encryption module
  default                      Set a command to its defaults
  default-value                Default character-bits values
  define                       interface range macro definition
  dial-control-mib             Define Dial Control Mib parameters
  dial-peer                    Dial Map (Peer) configuration commands
```

FIGURE 7.4   Partial Global
Configuration command display.

EXAM ALERT

Newer releases of Cisco IOS are making it possible to utilize some of these commands across the levels of the Cisco IOS hierarchies. However, for exam purposes, put on a pair of Cisco horse blinders to this new functionality and focus on the original levels and syntaxes described throughout this book.

As the name states, any configuration that is applied in this level applies globally to the Cisco router or switch. Here we can perform configuration tasks such as changing the hostname of the router or switch, creating a login banner, creating a password to prompt users trying to gain access to Privileged EXEC, and many others. It is also at this level of the Cisco IOS hierarchy that you can enter several different sub-configuration modes to apply specific configurations for things such as interfaces, routing protocols, and EXEC lines (which are discussed throughout this book).

Interface Configuration

Directly from Global Configuration, you can configure interface-specific commands that apply only to interfaces specified in the configuration. Now you can enable the interfaces, assign IP addresses, set speeds, and configure other interface commands. Once again, the commands that are available at this sub-configuration level of the IOS are not applicable at Global Configuration or Privileged EXEC and User EXEC.

To configure an interface, you must specify the interface you want to configure. If the device has fixed (non-modular) interfaces, you simply specify the type of interface followed by the interface number (and remember Cisco routers start their numbering schema with 0). For example, the 1600 series router has a fixed ethernet interface that cannot be removed from the router. To configure that interface, you type **interface Ethernet 0** from Global Configuration. Most devices today utilize the modular configuration in which you have to specify the module number as well as the interface number because these devices can change functionality depending on the type of module inserted into them. For example, to configure the second WAN serial interface on the first module on a 2800 series router, you would input **interface serial 0/1** where **0** is the module number (first module starts with 0) and **1** is the interface. The prompt in Interface Configuration Mode is displayed as `Router(config-if)#`, regardless of the interface type. This means you must keep track of what interface you are configuring because the prompt does not specify the type.

Line Configuration

Also accessed from Global Configuration, line configurations are specific to those EXEC lines through which a user can gain access to the Cisco device. Specifically, you can configure options such as logins and passwords for a user trying to gain User EXEC access to the console and auxiliary ports, as well as the 5 vty (virtual teletype) Telnet lines into a router or switch. From Global Configuration, you must utilize the keyword, `line`, followed by the EXEC line you want to configure. For example, to configure console-specific commands, you would type **line console 0** from Global Configuration. The prompt changes to `Router (config-line)#`, regardless of the line you are configuring.

Context-Sensitive Help

Even though the Cisco IOS is a command-line interface, it is not without its help features to help you through your navigation of the IOS. Specifically, to see what commands are available at any level of the IOS, you can use the help feature of the IOS, the question mark. By typing ? (no Enter keystroke necessary) at any level of the IOS, you get a listing of all the commands available and a brief description of the command, such as you saw in Figures 7.3 and 7.4.

Quite often, the list of available commands may extend beyond one terminal screen. This is apparent because the string —More— is displayed at the bottom of the list on the screen. To see the next page of listed commands, you can press the space bar and the command list scrolls another terminal screen's length. If you prefer to see the commands line by line, you can keep hitting the Enter key and it displays only the next command each time you press it. On the chance that you have found the command you were looking for in the list, you can hit any key (pause for inevitable "where's the any key?" joke) to get back to the command prompt.

In some instances, you may not recall the command that you are looking for, but you do remember the first letter of the command. Let's say, for example, the command is in Global Configuration and starts with the letter *l*. You could use the question mark and scroll through all the commands; however, the IOS enables you to see the commands starting with *l* if you type the letter, followed immediately by the question mark (no space in between), as demonstrated below. Similarly, if you remembered that the command started with log, you can type those characters, followed immediately by the question mark, to see the commands logging and login-string.

```
Router>enable
Router#configure terminal
Enter configuration commands, one per line.  End with CNTL/Z.
Router(config)#l?
l2tp-class  lane   li-view        line
logging     login  login-string
Router(config)#l
```

Keep in mind that many commands in the IOS require a string of keywords to comprehend what you are trying to achieve with the command. For instance, if I was searching for the command logging and hit the Enter key, the IOS would report back an error to the terminal screen that the command was incomplete because it does not understand where I want to send my logging information. If you are unsure of the commands available, once again, you use the question mark for command help. In this case, you must put a space after the first keyword followed by the question mark. The IOS then displays a list of commands that are valid after the keyword logging, as displayed here:

```
Router(config)#logging ?
  Hostname or A.B.C.D  IP address of the logging host
  buffered             Set buffered logging parameters
  buginf               Enable buginf logging for debugging
  cns-events           Set CNS Event logging level
  console              Set console logging parameters
  count                Count every log message and timestamp last occurrence
  exception            Limit size of exception flush output
  facility             Facility parameter for syslog messages
  filter               Specify logging filter
  history              Configure syslog history table
  host                 Set syslog server IP address and parameters
  monitor              Set terminal line (monitor) logging parameters
  on                   Enable logging to all enabled destinations
  origin-id            Add origin ID to syslog messages
  queue-limit          Set logger message queue size
  rate-limit           Set messages per second limit
  reload               Set reload logging level
  server-arp           Enable sending ARP requests for syslog servers when
                       first configured
  source-interface     Specify interface for source address in logging
                       transactions
  trap                 Set syslog server logging level
  userinfo             Enable logging of user info on privileged mode enabling

Router(config)#logging
```

> **EXAM ALERT**
>
> In the simulations on the Cisco exam, you can use ? for help when configuring or troubleshooting the Cisco device. If you get stuck in a simulation, utilize the help feature extensively because you do not get docked points for using this feature.

Abbreviations

To make things easy for administration, the Cisco IOS enables you to abbreviate commands as long as you type enough characters for the IOS to interpret the command that you want to input. For instance, the previous example involved trying to locate the command that started with *l* in Global Configuration. Because there were several commands that started with *l*, you would need to type in more characters to find the `logging` command. Specifically, you would need to type **logg**, which is just enough characters for the IOS to understand that you want to use the `logging` command. If you want the IOS to complete typing the command for you, you can hit the Tab key and it autocompletes the command when you provide enough characters.

> **EXAM ALERT**
>
> The simulations on the exam support some of the abbreviations; however, not all of them are supported. With that being said, it is a good idea to be able to type the entire command in case it is not supported for abbreviation. The Tab autocomplete, however, is not supported on the exam simulations.

> **EXAM ALERT**
>
> Some multiple-choice questions and answers may show you the completed command, whereas others may show you the abbreviated one. Do not discount a valid answer if the full command syntax is not used.

Shortcut Keys

To make terminal editing simpler and faster, Cisco has created several shortcut keystrokes that can speed up IOS navigation. The most useful of these shortcuts enables you to cycle through your command history to re-use or edit previously typed commands. You can use both the up and down arrow keys or Ctrl+N and Ctrl+P (if arrow keys are not supported at your terminal) to cycle through the last 10 commands in the history buffer relative to the level of the IOS you are currently located. Table 7.2 lists some other useful terminal editing keystrokes that will help you navigate within a command line.

TABLE 7.2   Cisco IOS Terminal Editing Keystrokes

Keystroke	Function
Ctrl+A	Move the cursor to the beginning of the command line.
Ctrl+E	Move the cursor to the end of the command line.
Ctrl+B	Move the cursor back one character.
Ctrl+F	Move the cursor forward one character.
Esc+B	Move the cursor back one word.
Esc+F	Move the cursor forward one word.

The terminal editing keys discussed so far are very useful for moving within a particular level of the IOS. However, you need to know how to navigate back from those different levels of the Cisco IOS. Namely, if you need to go back one level of the IOS, simply type the command `exit`. For instance, if you are in the Interface Configuration mode of the IOS and you need to go back to Global Configuration, just type **exit**, and your prompt display should change from `Router(config-if)#` to `Router(config)#`.

Suppose you are back in the interface configuration and you need to ping or traceroute to your neighbor or do a `show` command to verify that the interface is working. Recall that this variety of commands can be performed only in Privileged EXEC or User EXEC. To return to these levels of the IOS hierarchy, you can type **exit** until you are all the way back. You can also use the keystroke Ctrl+Z or the keyword `end`, which will automatically take you back to Privileged EXEC, regardless of how deep in the configuration levels you happen to be.

Common Syntax Errors

As mentioned before, the IOS reports back error messages if you have not provided the correct syntax for a command. The three syntax error messages that you may encounter are as follows:

▶ **Ambiguous Command**—This error is displayed when you have not typed enough characters for the IOS to distinguish which command you want to use. In other words, several commands start with those same characters, so you must type more letters of the command for the IOS to recognize your particular command.

▶ **Incomplete Command**—The IOS has recognized your keyword syntax with this error message; however, you need to add more keywords to tell the IOS what you want to do with this command.

▶ **Invalid Input**—Also known as the "fat finger" error, this console error message is displayed when you mistype a command. The IOS displays a caret mark (^) at the point up to which the IOS could understand your command.

Below is an example for each of these three error console messages. Also notice that this configuration snapshot now includes abbreviations to get into Privileged EXEC and Global Configuration.

```
Router>
Router>en
Router#conf t
Enter configuration commands, one per line.  End with CNTL/Z.
Router(config)#r
% Ambiguous command:   "r"
Router(config)#router
% Incomplete command.
Router(config)#routre rip
                   ^
% Invalid input detected at '^' marker.
```

STEP BY STEP

7.1 Navigating the IOS

1. Go into Privileged EXEC by typing **enable** or **en** (or any abbreviation you feel comfortable with).

2. Enter Global Configuration by typing **configure terminal** or **config t**.

3. Enter the Line Configuration mode for the console by typing **line console 0** or **line con 0**.

4. Look at the list of commands available by using **?**.

5. Press the space bar to cycle page by page or Enter to cycle line by line.

6. Return back to Global Configuration by typing **exit**.

7. Enter the interface configuration for serial 0/0 by typing **interface serial 0/0** or **int ser 0/0**.

8. Exit back to Privileged EXEC by typing **Ctrl+Z** or **end**.

Use the output below as a loose reference of what the output might look like:

```
! Step 1
Router>
Router>en
! Step 2
Router#conf t
Enter configuration commands, one per line.  End with CNTL/Z.o
! Step 3
Router(config)#line con 0
! Step 4
Router(config-line)#?
Line configuration commands:
  absolute-timeout          Set absolute timeout for line disconnection
  access-class              Filter connections based on an IP access list
```

```
  activation-character        Define the activation character
  autocommand                 Automatically execute an EXEC command
  autocommand-options         Autocommand options
  autohangup                  Automatically hangup when last connection closes
  autoselect                  Set line to autoselect
—More—
! Step 5
  buffer-length               Set DMA buffer length
***Output Removed for Brevity
! Step 6
Router(config-line)#exit
! Step 7
Router(config)#int ser 0/0
! Step 8
Router(config-if)#end
Router#
*Sep 26 23:40:41.019: %SYS-5-CONFIG_I: Configured from console by console
```

Chapter Summary

This chapter delved into the many intricacies surrounding the Cisco internetwork operating system. Specifically, you learned at least five ways to gain access to IOS. The two out-of-band methods are through the console and auxiliary interface. In-band methods such as Telnet, HTTP, HTTPS, and SSH require some level on configuration of the Cisco devices before you can remotely manage them.

To load the IOS, Cisco routers and switches have to complete a series of systematic stages. Initially, the device tests the hardware and loads the bootstrap code, both located in ROM. If the configuration register boot field has not been manipulated (values 0x1-0xF), then the boot-strap queries the `startup-config` in NVRAM for any `boot system` commands. If no commands are present, the first file in Flash memory is loaded into RAM. If the file in Flash is missing or corrupt, the Cisco router or switch broadcasts for help to any local TFTP servers. If that fallback fails, the router or switch returns back to ROM and loads ROMmon. After the IOS is loaded, the Cisco device can load the startup configuration in NVRAM (assuming you didn't change the configuration register to 0x2142 for password recovery). If the startup configuration is not present, the router or switch tries to autoinstall from a TFTP server. If that fails, the device enters the configuration dialog, Setup Mode.

If you were to cancel out of Setup Mode by answering "no" or typing `Ctrl+C`, you would give yourself the opportunity to conquer the mighty mountain of the Cisco IOS navigation hierar-chy because you would immediately enter into User EXEC mode. In User EXEC, you have limited functionality (the majority of `show` commands, `ping`, `traceroute`, `Telnet`, and so on) and would need to use the command `enable` to enter Privileged EXEC to gain access to all the commands at that particular level. From here, you can enter Global Configuration by typing **configure terminal** to configure parameters that apply to the entire device. Global Configuration can then be utilized as a jumping-off point to enter sub-configuration modes, such as for interfaces, EXEC lines, routing protocols, and many other sub-configuration modes.

At any point in IOS, you can see the commands available by using ? at the command prompt. If you were to get an ambiguous command error, Cisco IOS requires that you enter more char-acters to a keyword because multiple commands might share those beginning characters. You can easily discover the commands that start with certain character by immediately typing **?** after those letters. Incomplete Command errors signify that the command string required more keywords to know what to do with the command keyword. To see the commands avail-able after a specific keyword, you can also use the ? preceded by a space to see what commands are valid. Invalid input errors indicate that the command was mistyped somewhere. In these situations, you can cycle through the previous commands by using the up and down arrows or Ctrl+P and Ctrl+N. After you find the mistyped command, you can use other terminal editing keys to navigate the cursor to the point where the mistake was made. To exit configuration modes, you can type **exit** to go back a level at a time. To go directly to Privileged EXEC, type Ctrl+Z or **end**.

Key Terms

▶ Configuration register

▶ Boot field

▶ POST

▶ ROMmon

▶ Console port

▶ Auxiliary port

▶ SSH

▶ Bootstrap

▶ User EXEC

▶ Privileged EXEC

▶ Setup Mode

▶ `running-config`

▶ `startup-config`

▶ Interface configuration

▶ Line configuration

▶ Terminal editing keys

▶ In-band

▶ Out-of-band

Apply Your Knowledge

Exercises

7.1 Navigating a New Router

You have just received a new router that you will have to install at a customer's location in two days. To ensure you appear confident in your installation, you decide to take the router out for a test drive so you can be comfortable with the IOS navigation before arriving onsite.

This exercise assumes you have a router to utilize that is not in production.

NOTE

If you do not have an actual router, you can always follow along by using simulated software such as SemSim (www.semsim.com) or Boson's NetSim (www.boson.com). If your budget is tight, open up Notepad and type the commands as you would if you were in the router itself. Practicing these commands and understanding the level of IOS at which they should be typed are critical to your success in the ICND1 exam and as a CCENT technician.

Estimated Time: 15 minutes

1. Plug the router into the power outlet and connect your console cable between your PC's COM port and the console port on the router.

2. Open your terminal program and set the settings for 9600 baud, 8 data bits, no parity bits, 1 stop bit, and no flow control.

3. Power on the router and notice bootstrap and IOS decompression from Flash output similar to Figure 7.5.

```
System Bootstrap, Version 12.3(8r)T9, RELEASE SOFTWARE (fc1)
Technical Support: http://www.cisco.com/techsupport
Copyright (c) 2004 by cisco Systems, Inc.

Correcting the backup nv_flash
PLD version 0x10
GIO ASIC version 0x127
c1841 processor with 262144 Kbytes of main memory
Main memory is configured to 64 bit mode with parity disabled


Readonly ROMMON initialized
program load complete, entry point: 0x8000f000, size: 0xc100

Initializing ATA monitor library.......
program load complete, entry point: 0x8000f000, size: 0xc100

Initializing ATA monitor library.......

program load complete, entry point: 0x8000f000, size: 0x17d0954
Self decompressing the image :
################################################################################
################################################################################
################################################################################
############################### [OK]
```

FIGURE 7.5 IOS bootstrap and IOS decompression.

4. Because this is the first time the router has been turned on, a startup-config is not present in NVRAM, so you will inevitably go to Setup Mode. Exit Setup Mode by answering "no" to the question, Would you like to enter the initial configuration dialog? [yes/no].

5. In User EXEC, type **enable** to enter into Privileged EXEC.

6. Enter Global Configuration by typing **configure terminal**.

7. See what commands are available in this mode by using the question mark for help.

8. Type l and press Enter to see the ambiguous command error.

9. Type li to see the incomplete command error.

10. Type **line consoul 0**, purposely misspelling the word console to see the invalid command error.

11. Press the up arrow or Ctrl+P to cycle to the previous command.

12. Enter Ctrl+A to go to the beginning of the command.

13. Enter Esc+F to move the cursor forward one word.

14. Move the cursor forward, using Ctrl+F, until you are at a point where you can correct the spelling to *console.*

15. Exit back to Privileged EXEC by entering Ctrl+Z or type the command **end**.

16. Exit out of Privileged EXEC by typing **disable** or the keyword **exit**.

Review Questions

1. What is the effect of changing the configuration register?

2. Why would a Cisco administrator use boot system commands?

3. What are the memory components in a router and what purpose do they have in the booting process?

4. What cabling and terminal settings are required for out-of-band management?

5. What is the significance of having User EXEC mode in addition to Privileged EXEC mode?

Exam Questions

1. What type of cable would you connect to manage your Cisco device from the COM port of your PC?

   ○ **A.** Cross-over cable

   ○ **B.** Straight-through cable

   ○ **C.** Patch cable

   ○ **D.** Rollover cable

2. Which are two methods of exiting out of Setup Mode? (Choose two)

   ○ **A.** Ctrl+C

   ○ **B.** Ctrl+Z

   ○ **C.** Answer no

   ○ **D.** Type **end**

3. You have just been given a router that will not save its configuration. As you boot up the router, you confirm that despite saving the configurations several times, the router enters Setup Mode consistently. What might be a possible cause?

   ○ **A.** Flash memory is corrupt.

   ○ **B.** TFTP Server is down.

   ○ **C.** The configuration register is 0x2100.

   ○ **D.** The configuration register is 0x2142.

4. What and where are the commands that can alter the location for the bootstrap IOS process?

   ○ **A.** boot system command, NVRAM memory

   ○ **B.** boot enable command, NVRAM memory

   ○ **C.** boot strap command, Flash memory

   ○ **D.** boot system command, Flash memory

5. Assuming no boot commands, what is the default location of the IOS and what is the order of the two fallbacks?

   ○ **A.** NVRAM, TFTP then ROM

   ○ **B.** Flash, TFTP then ROM

   ○ **C.** ROM, Flash then TFTP

   ○ **D.** TFTP, Flash then ROM

6. Which of the following is considered a typical default configuration register?

   ○ **A.** 0x2100

   ○ **B.** 0x2142

   ○ **C.** 0x2101

   ○ **D.** 0x2102

7. Which of the following are in-band management EXEC methods? (Choose two)

   ○ **A.** SSH

   ○ **B.** FTP

   ○ **C.** Console

   ○ **D.** Telnet

   ○ **E.** Auxiliary

8. Which of the following valid commands assign an IP address to an interface from Interface Configuration mode?

○ **A.** `Router(config)#`**ip address 192.168.1.1 255.255.255.0**

○ **B.** `Router(config-if)#`**ip address 192.168.1.1 255.255.255.0**

○ **C.** `Router#`**ip address 192.168.1.1 255.255.255.0**

○ **D.** `Router>`**ip address 192.168.1.1 255.255.255.0**

○ **E.** `Router(config-line)#`**ip address 192.168.1.1 255.255.255.0**

9. If your network does not have a TFTP server and your router's configuration was erased, what will the prompt look like when you reboot?

○ **A.** `rommon 1 >`

○ **B.** `Router(boot)>`

○ **C.** `Would you like to enter the initial configuration dialog? [yes/no]:`

○ **D.** The router would not be able to boot.

10. Which two commands will return you to Privileged EXEC? (Choose two)

○ **A.** Ctrl+Z

○ **B.** `end`

○ **C.** `disable`

○ **D.** Ctrl+C

11. Which three components are located in ROM? (Choose three)

○ **A.** bootstrap

○ **B.** POST

○ **C.** `startup-config`

○ **D.** IOS file

○ **E.** ROMmon

○ **F.** `running-config`

Answers to Review Questions

1. By changing any of the values in the configuration register from its default value of 0x2102, you are altering how the router or switch operates during initialization. The last hexadecimal field in the configuration register is the boot field. This value determines whether the device boots to ROM and loads ROMmon (0x0). Values of 0x1-0xF indicate that the device parses the startup configuration in NVRAM for any `boot system` commands. If the third hexadecimal character in the configuration register is a 0x4, the device ignores the startup configuration in NVRAM and enters the Setup Mode dialog.

2. The `boot system` commands provide flexible means of specifying from where to load an IOS. This is especially useful if you require specifying a specific IOS file to load in Flash (if multiple files exist) or on a TFTP server.

3. ROM contains the POST program and the bootstrap code for the initial stages of the booting process. Flash memory stores the IOS files. The configuration register is stored in NVRAM along with the startup configuration that contains any `boot system` commands.

4. The console and AUX ports both use the rollover cable. The terminal settings should reflect the following parameters: 9600 baud, 8 data bits, no parity bits, 1 stop bit, and no flow control.

5. User EXEC is useful if you have to give access to technicians who need rights to basic verification commands. Privileged EXEC enables access to the remaining command modes, including those commands that can affect the router or switch's operations.

Answers to Exam Questions

1. **D.** The cable to connect your terminal to the Cisco device's console or auxiliary port is a rollover cable. Answers A, B, and C are cables that are used for ethernet networking.

2. **A, C.** To exit out of Setup Mode, you must answer "no" to the `Would you like to enter the initial configuration dialog? [yes/no]`: question, or enter Ctrl+C at any prompt. Ctrl+Z and the End key are shortcuts to exit back to Privileged EXEC.

3. **D.** When the third hexadecimal character in the configuration register is a 4, the `startup-config` is ignored. This is a useful utility if you are doing password recovery; however, it is important that you remember to change it back to 0x2102. A is incorrect because the configuration is not stored in Flash. B is not viable because the Cisco device looks for a config on the TFTP only if the `startup-config` is missing. C will force the router or switch into ROMMON mode, which means the configuration never gets loaded because the IOS needs to be loaded first.

4. **A.** The `boot system` commands located in the `startup-config` in NVRAM can manually force the router or switch to boot the IOS from somewhere other than its default locations.

5. **B.** When no `boot system` commands are used, the bootstrap loads the first file in Flash memory. If that file is missing or corrupt, it tries to load an IOS from a TFTP server first. If there is no network connectivity or TFTP server present, the device enters ROMmon in ROM.

6. **D.** A normal configuration register is 0x2102. A forces the router or switch into ROMmon. B ignores the `startup-config`. C would load the first file in Flash; however, it is not the default configuration register.

7. **A, D.** The three in-band management session methods are SSH, Telnet, and HTTP. Answers C and E are out-of-band; B is not a management session method.

8. **B.** Without even discussing the actual configuration of the command, the question stated that it must be in Interface Configuration mode, which means the command prompt will look like `Router(config-if)#` or `Switch(config-if)#`.

9. **C.** Without a TFTP for autoinstall and with the startup-config missing, the router or switch enters Setup mode, which prompts you with `Would you like to enter the initial config-uration dialog? [yes/no]`. Answer A is the ROMmon prompt and D is the prompt for RxBoot mode.

10. **A, B.** Ctrl+Z and End returns you to Privileged EXEC, no matter in which level of the configuration hierarchy you are. C returns you to User EXEC from Privileged EXEC mode. D is used to exit out of Setup Mode.

11. **A, B, E.** POST, bootstrap code, and ROMmon all reside in ROM. Startup-config is located in NVRAM, and running-config is located in RAM. The IOS file is typically located in Flash memory.

Suggested Readings and Resources

1. Boney, James. *Cisco IOS in a Nutshell.* O'Reilly Publishing, 2001.

2. "Using the Command-Line Interface," www.cisco.com.

3. "Rebooting" for an explanation of the booting process, www.cisco.com.

CHAPTER EIGHT

Foundation Cisco Configurations

Objectives

This chapter covers the following Cisco-specified objectives for the "Implement a small routed network" section of the 640-822 ICND1 exam:

▶ **Access and utilize the router CLI to set basic parameters**

▶ **Connect, configure, and verify operation status of a device interface**

▶ **Verify device configuration and network connectivity using ping, traceroute, telnet, SSH, or other utilities**

▶ **Manage IOS configuration files (including: save, edit, upgrade, restore)**

▶ **Manage Cisco IOS**

▶ **Implement password and physical security**

▶ **Verify network status and router operation using basic utilities (including: ping, traceroute, telnet, SSH, arp, ipconfig), SHOW & DEBUG commands**

▶ **Configure, verify, and troubleshoot DHCP and DNS operation on a router (including: CLI/SDM)**

▶ **Implement static and dynamic addressing services for hosts in a LAN environment**

Outline

Introduction   **242**

Global Configuration   **242**

Altering the Boot Sequence   242

Changing the Hostname   244

Creating a Login Banner   244

Assigning a Password for Privileged
EXEC Mode   245

Domain Name–Specific Commands   246

Enabling SSH   247

Line Configurations   **248**

Securing Console Access to User
EXEC   248

Securing Auxiliary Access to User
EXEC   250

Securing Telnet and SSH Access
to User EXEC   250

Router Interface Configurations   **253**

Assigning an IP Address   254

Enabling the Interface   255

LAN-Specific Commands   255

WAN-Specific Commands   256

Saving Configurations   **256**

**Using the show Command to Get
Information**   **258**

Verifying Your Configurations   259

Viewing Interface Statuses
and Statistics   260

show interfaces Command   261

show ip interface brief Command   263

show controller Command   263

IOS File Version show Commands   264

Troubleshooting Commands   **266**

**Backing Up and Restoring Configurations
and IOS Using TFTP**   **269**

Neighbor Discovery with CDP   **272**

**Using Telnet for Virtual Terminal
Access**   **276**

Terminal Monitor   277

IOS DHCP   **278**

Chapter Summary   **281**

Key Terms   282

Apply Your Knowledge   **284**

Exercises   284

Review Questions   285

Exam Questions   286

Answers to Review Questions   289

Answers to Exam Questions   290

Suggested Readings and Resources   291

Study Strategies

▶ Read the information presented in the chapter, paying special attention to tables, Notes, and Exam Alerts.

▶ As you are reading through each section, keep in mind on which level of Cisco IOS Software these commands exist.

▶ If possible, practice the syntax of every command discussed throughout this chapter (and book) with real or simulated Cisco equipment.

▶ Pay close attention to the functionality associated with these commands. It is tempting to focus too hard on the command syntax itself, which ultimately makes you lose focus on the reason you are learning about the command in the first place. The ICND1 exam tests you on both why you are typing the command and how to type it.

▶ Complete the Challenge Exercises throughout the chapter and the Exercises at the end of the chapter. The exercises will solidify the concepts that you have learned in the previous sections.

▶ Complete the Exam Questions at the end of the chapter. They are designed to simulate the type of questions you will be asked in the ICND1 exam.

Introduction

Now that you have a firm understanding how to navigate Cisco IOS Software, it is time to put that knowledge to the test by exposing yourself to the huge number of commands that are available for configuration and verification. This chapter is specifically arranged to ensure that you understand on which layer of Cisco IOS navigation hierarchy each command resides. With the chapter divided into these sections, you will learn to apply these commands correctly if presented with a Cisco configuration objective for the exam and the real world. Additionally, you should notice similarities and form an association between the syntax and functionality of the commands and the level of IOS to which they can be applied and utilized. Having this knowledge at your fingertips will prove invaluable when configuring simulations or eliminating distracting answers on the ICND1 exam.

Global Configuration

Objectives:

▶ Access and utilize the router CLI to set basic parameters

▶ Manage Cisco IOS

As mentioned in the Chapter 7, "Foundation Cisco IOS Operations," Global Configuration commands affect the entire router or switch's operations. Recall also that you enter Global Configuration by typing `configure terminal` from Privileged EXEC, which changes the prompt to `Router(config)#` or `Switch(config)#`. This section looks at the syntax and functions of some basic Global Configuration parameters that you can configure in a switch or a router.

> **NOTE**
>
> The majority of configuration command discussed throughout this entire book can be negated or removed if you type the keyword no, followed by the command again. The same syntax rules must apply when removing the command (you must type the command correctly and you must be in the correct level of the IOS hierarchy where the original command exists).

Altering the Boot Sequence

The previous chapter discussed two means of altering the default boot sequence of a router. Namely, you learned that by changing certain fields in the configuration register, you can force the Cisco device to perform actions such as booting from ROM and ignoring the startup configuration. In Global Configuration, the `config-register` command enables you to manipulate those fields and ultimately change the normal default operations of the router or switch.

For example, if you wanted to manipulate the configuration register to enter ROMmon on the next reboot, the Global Configuration command would look like this on a router:

```
Router(config)#config-register 0x2100
```

On the next boot, this router instructs the bootstrap to immediately boot into ROMMon in ROM. The prompt displays rommon 1 >, signifying that the manipulation was successful and you are indeed in the mini-IOS.

CAUTION

Don't Change Configuration Register Fields Unless Necessary In this book, we mention only a couple of the boot field values and the configuration field values. Do not randomly experiment with the configuration register to see the outcome. You could very well change a configuration parameter that will cause the router or switch to boot abnormally, change the console speed (leaving you guessing what speed you need to use to get terminal connectivity), or not boot at all.

If you accidentally change these settings, you can try to change the configuration register back by forcing the device to go directly to ROMmon mode on boot-up. From a console connection, turn on the device and send a break sequence (Ctrl+Break Key in HyperTerminal) from your terminal window in the first 60 seconds. You see the rommon 1 > prompt, indicating that you are in ROM Monitor. From here, enter the following command:

```
rommon 1 >confreg 0x2102
```

You should see a response similar to the following:

```
You must reset or power cycle for new config to take effect
rommon 2 >
```

At this point, you can recycle the power on the device or type the ROMmon-specific command, reset, to reboot the device because you have restored the default configuration register to ensure normal operations.

The second Global Configuration command to globally affect the startup sequence that was mentioned in the previous chapter is the boot system command. With this command, you can optionally instruct the bootstrap to boot from specific locations, and even tell it which file to load if there are multiple IOS files at that location. Two different examples of the boot system commands are as follows:

```
Router(config)#boot system tftp c2600-do3s-mz.120-5.T1 172.16.1.1
Router(config)#boot system flash c2600-do3s-mz.120-5.T1
```

The first command instructs the bootstrap to locate the IOS on the TFTP server located at 172.16.1.1. The second boot system command configures the bootstrap to specifically load the IOS file c2600-do3s-mz.120-5.T1 in the possible event that Flash has multiple IOS image files on it. In examples where you have multiple boot system commands in a sequence, such as the example just given, the bootstrap tests each command in successive order until it successfully locates and loads an IOS.

Changing the Hostname

Throughout this and the last chapter, you saw that the default prompt for a router starts with the hostname Router. You should change the hostname to uniquely identify the Cisco device in your internetwork. This is especially useful if you are using Telnet to remotely manage multiple devices and you need to identify to which device you are connected. The syntax for the command to change the hostname of the Cisco device is hostname, followed by the name you have chosen (up to 25 characters) as illustrated here:

```
Router(config)#hostname CCNA2811
CCNA2811(config)#
```

Notice that once we type the hostname command, the prompt immediately is changed to its new hostname (in this case, CCNA2811).

Creating a Login Banner

It is advisable to display a login banner as a means to provide notice of acceptable use or as a warning to anyone attempting to gain unauthorized access to your Cisco device. In Cisco terms, this is known as the message of the day. This message is displayed to any user attempting to gain an EXEC session on all terminal lines in the IOS. An example configuration for the message of the day is as follows:

```
CCNA2811(config)#banner motd # This is a private system and may be accessed only by
authorized users.  Unauthorized access is strictly prohibited and will be enforced to
the full extent of the law.#
```

Notice that the banner motd (message of the day) command example contains a # character before and after the message. This is known as a delimiting character and is used to inform the IOS where your banner begins and ends. This can be any character, so it makes sense to use a character that is not present in the banner itself. For instance, if the delimiting character were "v", the banner would be displayed as This is a pri.

EXAM ALERT

Remember that the command to configure a login banner is banner motd.

CAUTION

No Need for a Warm Welcome   Be extremely careful of the message that you choose in your login banner. A login banner can be useful if you need to seek legal action against an intruder to your Cisco device. On the flip side, however, the wrong login banner can work against you. For example, if your login contains the word "welcome" or similar inviting words, this can be used as grounds for defense for an unauthorized user to gain access because it can be considered as invitation to your device.

Assigning a Password for Privileged EXEC Mode

Objective:

▶ Implement password and physical security

Gaining access to Privileged EXEC essentially means you have access to all the functionality of the IOS, including those commands that can detrimentally affect the router or switch. With that being said, it makes sense to secure access to Privileged EXEC to ensure those who gain access are indeed skilled and authorized to do so. This is achieved in Global Configuration with the creation of an enable password, which prompts anyone attempting to access Privileged EXEC with a password that is known only by those who truly are privileged.

The command to assign a password to gain access to Privileged EXEC can be achieved with one of the following two commands:

```
CCNA2811(config)#enable password myenablepassword
CCNA2811(config)#enable secret mysecretpassword
```

TIP
Be careful not to accidentally put the additional keyword *password* after the enable secret command. Otherwise, your secret password would be "password," followed by your actual password. In addition, the commands are case sensitive, so make sure you don't accidentally put the wrong case in the command.

So what is the difference between the two commands? The enable secret password is secure because it utilizes a non-reversible one-way MD5 (Message Digest 5) cryptographic hash of the password so it cannot be deciphered by anybody who can see the configuration. On the other hand, the enable password command is in clear text and can be seen by anyone that gains access to that configuration. In practice, it is customary to utilize the enable secret command for the security that it provides over the enable password command. The following configuration demonstrates a secure enable password configuration, and the resulting prompt that occurs when you try to re-enter Privileged EXEC:

```
CCNA1841>enable
CCNA1841#configure terminal
Enter configuration commands, one per line.  End with CNTL/Z.
CCNA1841(config)#enable secret giforgot
CCNA1841(config)#end
CCNA1841#
*Aug 12 21:46:38.055: %SYS-5-CONFIG_I: Configured from console by console
CCNA1841#disable
CCNA1841>enable
Password:
```

EXAM ALERT

When the `enable password` command and the `enable secret password` command are used in the same configuration, the `enable secret` command overrides the `enable password` command. For example, using the preceding configuration examples, the password would be "mysecretpassword" to enter Privileged EXEC.

It is possible to encrypt the password used in the `enable password` command by using the following Global Configuration command:

```
CCNA2811(config)#service password-encryption
```

This command actually encrypts all clear text passwords in your configuration, including passwords you assign to the EXEC lines (discussed later). This is useful in case anyone happens to actually see your configuration because the password cannot be distinguished visually upon initial sight. Be advised, however, that the encryption used is a Cisco proprietary encryption, which is easily broken to reveal the actual password. When choosing between this method and the `enable secret` method for secure Privileged EXEC, use `enable secret` because its encryption is exponentially stronger.

EXAM ALERT

The `service password-encryption` command encrypts all clear text passwords in the configuration with a Cisco proprietary encryption.

Domain Name–Specific Commands

Objective:

▶ Configure, verify, and troubleshoot DHCP and DNS operation on a router (including: CLI/SDM)

Quite often, you have to test connectivity or connect to a multitude of devices from your router or switch. Unless you have all their IP addresses memorized or you have a trusty topology map with you wherever you go, you might find it difficult to accurately recall their IP address information. To assist you when such challenges arise, the Cisco IOS can statically or dynamically support domain name resolution on the Cisco device. This way, you can refer to the devices by a recognizable hostname versus an IP address.

The command to create a static entry in the IOS configuration file is `ip host`. For example, given the following command:

```
CCNA2811(config)#ip host corerouter 172.16.1.1
```

The IOS automatically forms a name-to-IP association in a host table so that every time you refer to *corerouter*, it translates that hostname to the IP of 172.16.1.1.

In instances where there are far too many devices to create individual static host entries, you might be better suited to have a DNS server keep the hostname-to-IP records. With that infrastructure in place, you can have your Cisco device use these servers for the name translation. The command to specify the DNS Server(s) (up to six) is the `ip name-server` command as shown here:

```
CCNA2811(config)#ip name-server 172.16.1.254 172.16.1.100 172.16.1.2
```

Given the previous `ip name-server` command, when referencing a device by its hostname, the router will query the DNS servers with the IP addresses of 172.16.1.254, 172.16.1.100, and 172.16.1.2 to resolve that hostname to an IP address.

Domain resolution is automatically enabled on your Cisco device. If you have not configured a DNS server, it tries to resolve hostnames by sending a broadcast out all its active interfaces. This can be irksome when you accidentally type a command in User or Privileged EXEC and the IOS attempts to resolve the command thinking that it is a hostname. To disable this feature, use the following command:

```
CCNA2811(config)#no ip domain lookup
```

One final domain-specific command is to assign your Cisco device to an IP domain. This command has several purposes in a Cisco networking environment; however for our purposes, it will be crucial in enabling SSH connectivity to our Cisco device as discussed in the next section. The command to assign a default domain name to a Cisco device is `ip domain-name`, as demonstrated here:

```
CCNA2811(config)#ip domain-name examprep.com
```

Enabling SSH

As mentioned in Chapter 7, SSH is a secure (and Cisco preferred) method of remote access to Cisco devices because the terminal connection which uses RSA public key cryptography for authentication and encryption of the data sent over the terminal connection. Because this terminal connection utilizes encryption, two prerequisites for configuring SSH is to have IPsec (DES or 3DES) IOS feature-set on the Cisco device and have an SSH-supported terminal client such as Putty and SecureCRT.

Assuming your Cisco device meets the prerequisites for SSH, the first step in enabling SSH connectivity to the Cisco IOS is to configure a hostname (other than its default) and assign the device to a domain as previously discussed. The only remaining step in the SSH process is to generate an RSA key for the encryption. The default key length is 512 bits, however, it is recommended to have a key of at least 1024 bits in length for additional security strength. The command to generate this key is `crypto key generate rsa` as demonstrated here:

```
CCNA2811(config)#crypto key generate rsa
The name for the keys will be: CCNA2811.examprep.com
```

```
Choose the size of the key modulus in the range of 360 to 2048 for your General Purpose
Keys. Choosing a key modulus greater than 512 may take a few minutes.

How many bits in the modulus [512]: 1024
Generating RSA keys ...
[OK]
7w1d: %SSH-5-ENABLED: SSH 1.5 has been enabled
```

Notice how the key generating process uses the hostname and domain name of the device when generating the key; therefore, those configuration steps must be performed first. Also notice that at the completion of the key generation, SSH is automatically enabled.

> **NOTE**
>
> Starting with Cisco IOS Software Release 12.3(4)T, Cisco IOS devices support SSH version 2. Version 2 is more flexible and addressed some active attack vulnerabilities from version 1.

One final element to the SSH configuration is to define a username and password for authentication. This username/password pair will be used when you configure your SSH client to connect to IOS. The command to define this username and password pair is username *username* password *password* in Global Configuration. For instance, if you want to use *SSHusername* as your username and *SSHpassword* as your password, the configuration would look like the following:

```
CCNA2811(config)#username SSHusername password SSHpassword
```

Line Configurations

This chapter previously discussed how to secure access to Privileged EXEC by using the `enable password` or `enable secret` command. However, this assumes that any administrators can still gain User EXEC to the Cisco device. The problem with this configuration is that you can send excessive pings or Telnet to another device from your router or switch in User EXEC. Because the ping and Telnet traffic are coming from your private router or switch, they might not be blocked by a security device such as a firewall. This section looks into how to secure access to the User EXEC by assigning a password on the EXEC lines into the Cisco device.

Securing Console Access to User EXEC

Objective:

▶ Implement password and physical security

Console access necessitates that an admin have physical access to the device itself. If your Cisco router or switch is physically accessible to non-authorized personnel (not highly recommended), you should take preventative measures to add another level of security by having the devices prompt anybody trying to get to User EXEC via the console port for a password. The following three commands ultimately achieve that goal:

```
CCNA2811(config)#line console 0
CCNA2811(config-line)#login
CCNA2811(config-line)#password myconsolepassword
```

The first command navigates the IOS to a sub-configuration mode for the console port. The second command instructs the IOS to prompt anybody connecting to this EXEC line for a login, using the password chosen in the third command.

TIP

It does not matter if you type the `password` command before the `login` command. The important factor is that both commands are configured.

To add yet another additional level of security comfort, it is also advisable to have the IOS close the console session after so much time of inactivity (no typing) in the session. After the EXEC session is closed, the admin has to enter the console password (assuming the above console configuration was in place) to get into User EXEC again. This is generally useful for those emergency bathroom breaks that arise after a couple cups of coffee or those unscheduled fire drills.

By default, the console session closes after 10 minutes of inactivity which, unfortunately, is plenty of time for someone to jump on to your terminal and change passwords and lock you out if you are not present. To change that setting, use the `exec-timeout` command followed by the number of minutes and seconds the IOS should wait to time out. For example, if you want the console to close after 1 minute and 30 seconds of inactivity, the command should reflect the following:

```
CCNA2811(config-line)#exec-timeout 1 30
```

EXAM ALERT

The `exec-timeout` command identifies how long the EXEC terminal session will remain active when no commands are being typed. The syntax specifies the minutes followed by the seconds.

TIP

The IOS sends all alerts and notification messages to the console port by default. Unfortunately, this sometimes interrupts the command you are typing. To make your Cisco device more polite and stop interrupting you, use the `logging synchronous` command. After it is configured, IOS still send a notification to the terminal session, but returns a new line to the user with the information already entered.

Securing Auxiliary Access to User EXEC

Objective:

▶ Implement password and physical security

If your organization has decided to allow remote terminal access to your Cisco device through an external modem or terminal server connected to the auxiliary port, you have added another means of getting to User EXEC that you must secure. The auxiliary port is slightly easier to connect than the console port because physical access is no longer a mandate. As long as you know the phone number to dial into the modem, you can gain access to a User EXEC session. This ease of access should be counterbalanced with security measures to ensure authorized users are connecting to this EXEC line.

Conveniently, the commands are practically identical to those used to secure a console connection. The only major difference is the navigation to the auxiliary port as opposed to the console:

```
CCNA2811(config)#line auxiliary 0
CCNA2811(config-line)#login
CCNA2811(config-line)#password myauxpassword
CCNA2811(config-line)#exec-timeout 1 30
```

Securing Telnet and SSH Access to User EXEC

Objectives:

▶ Implement password and physical security

▶ Verify device configuration and network connectivity using ping, traceroute, telnet, SSH, or other utilities

Telnet and SSH are by far the most insecure methods of establishing an EXEC session because any user with IP connectivity to the device can initiate a Telnet or SSH session to it. For this reason, the default state of these lines is to require that a vty password be set for anyone to achieve access to User EXEC. Otherwise, you will receive an error similar to the following:

```
Password required, but none set
```

In addition, if you do not have an enable password set on the device, you are not able to enter Privileged EXEC mode. The error you receive in this situation is the following:

```
% No password set
```

EXAM ALERT

Remember, by default a password must be set on the vty lines to give SSH and Telnet access to this device. An enable password must be set to access Privileged EXEC over a Telnet or SSH session.

Once again, the configuration is similar to those of the console and the auxiliary port; however, the navigation of the Telnet lines is slightly different than what you find with the rest. To assign a login password to all the vty lines into the device, you must specify the range of those vty lines in your navigation. For instance, most routers allow five Telnet or SSH sessions into them. To encompass all the vty lines, you have to identify them starting with the first line (remembering that numbering begins with 0), followed by the last (0-4 is a total of 5 lines), as shown here:

```
CCNA2811(config)#line vty 0 4
CCNA2811(config-line)#login
CCNA2811(config-line)#password mytelnetpassword
CCNA2811(config-line)#exec-timeout 1 30
```

The question usually begs, "What would happen if you configured only line vty 0 or you put a different password on each vty line?" To answer the first part of the question, if you configure only line vty 0, the router prompts the first user for a password. If another user tries to connect with that first Telnet session still running, he cannot log in to the router (remembering that the default state is that a password must be set as mentioned in the earlier Exam Tip).

On the other hand, if you assign different passwords to each of the vty lines, you can connect on all the lines; however, you have no means of choosing or knowing to which vty line you are connected. You would have to guess the password within three tries (IOS only allows three attempts).

EXAM ALERT

Be sure you are easily able to supply a configuration to any number of the EXEC lines depending on the scenario given.

Challenge

Securing access to your router or switch is an inevitable challenge that you will face on the exam as well as throughout your Cisco career. In this challenge, you apply the configurations you just learned to ensure that you also secure access from User EXEC to Privileged EXEC.

1. Through your console, connect an EXEC session and enter into Privileged EXEC, followed by Global Configuration.

2. Configure your console port to prompt for a login and use the password **captnstubing**.

3. Reduce the default inactivity console session timeout to 2 minutes and 10 seconds.

4. Configure your auxiliary port to prompt for a login and use the password **bartenderisaac**.

5. Reduce the default inactivity console session timeout to 3 minutes

(continues)

(continued)

6. Configure all five Telnet lines to prompt for a login and use the password **yeomangopher**.

7. Change the default hostname to **TheLoveRouter**.

8. Configure the default IP domain to be **comeaboard.com**.

9. Enable SSH by generating a 1024-bit RSA key.

10. Create a username **jmcoy** and password **cruisedirector** for SSH.

11. Secure Privileged EXEC by using a command that displays the password **theloveboat** in clear text.

12. Secure Privileged EXEC by using a command that performs the strongest encryption on the enable password, **something4every1**.

13. Which command will allow you to enter Privileged EXEC with them both configured?

14. Encrypt all the clear text passwords in the configuration using a Cisco proprietary encryption.

Your configuration should look like the following (with possible variation on the abbreviation of the commands):

```
! Step 1
Router>enable
Router#configure terminal
Enter configuration commands, one per line. End with CNTL/Z
! Step 2
Router(config)#line console 0
Router(config-line)#login
Router(config-line)#password captnstubing
! Step 3
Router(config-line)#exec-timeout 2 10
Router(config-line)#exit
! Step 4
Router(config)#line aux 0
Router(config-line)#login
Router(config-line)#password bartenderisaac
! Step 5
Router(config-line)#exec-timeout 3 0
Router(config-line)#exit
! Step 6
Router(config)#line vty 0 4
Router(config-line)#login
Router(config-line)#password yeomangopher
Router(config-line)#exit
! Step 7
```

```
Router(config)#hostname TheLoveRouter
! Step 8
TheLoveRouter(config)#ip domain-name comeaboard.com
! Step 9
TheLoveRouter(config)#crypto key generate rsa
The name for the keys will be: TheLoveRouter.comeaboard.com
Choose the size of the key modulus in the range of 360 to 2048 for your General Purpose
Keys. Choosing a key modulus greater than 512 may take a few minutes.
How many bits in the modulus [512]: 1024
Generating RSA keys ...
[OK]
7w1d: %SSH-5-ENABLED: SSH 1.5 has been enabled
! Step 10
TheLoveRouter(config)#username jmcoy password cruisedirector
! Step 11
TheLoveRouter(config)#enable password theloveboat
! Step 12
TheLoveRouter(config)#enable secret something4every1
! Step 14
TheLoveRouter(config)#service password-encryption
```

In this configuration, anyone connecting to the console port needs to enter the password *captnstubing* before gaining an EXEC session via the console port. After 2 minutes and 10 seconds of inactivity, the sessions close and users have to enter in the password again to return to User EXEC. Likewise, anyone accessing the router from the auxiliary port needs to enter the password *bartenderisaac* at the login prompt and has to re-enter that password after 3 minutes of inactivity. Up to five administrators can Telnet or SSH into this router, at which point they all have to enter the password *yeomangopher* at the login prompt. RSA was enabled by using the crypto key generate rsa command and specifying the key length as 1024. The key generated used our configured IP domain, comeaboard.com, and the default hostname of Router (since that was unchanged).

Because the enable password command and the enable secret command are used in this configuration, the password *something4every1* inevitably will be used to enter Privileged EXEC because the enable secret command overrides the enable password. The final command, service password-encryption, encrypts the enable, vty, aux, and console passwords so they are not visible to anyone who can see the configuration.

Router Interface Configurations

Objective:

▶ Connect, configure, and verify operation status of a device interface

Because a primary purpose of Cisco routers and switches is to transfer data between their interfaces, the configuration parameters that you apply to these interfaces dramatically affect how these devices operate in an internetwork. These interface configurations vary depending on the type of interface you are configuring and even which Layer 2 frame encapsulation you are utilizing for WAN interfaces. This section looks specifically at some of the basic configurations that you can apply to LAN and WAN interfaces on a router.

Assigning an IP Address

Recall from Chapter 1, "Standard Internetworking Models," that the basic functionality of a router is to forward packets from one network to another, using logical addressing. If you configure an IP address on an interface, that router systematically assumes that all packets that are destined for that IP address's network should be routed out that specific interface. For instance, if you assign the IP address of 192.168.1.1 with a subnet mask of 255.255.255.0 on a serial interface, the router automatically assumes when that interface is enabled that all packets destined for 192.168.1.x are to be sent out the WAN serial interface.

As you can see, assigning an IP address to an interface plays a pivotal role in a router's primary routing operation. The command to help fulfill that role on a given interface is `ip address`, followed by the assigned IP address for that interface and the subnet mask. For instance, if you wanted to assign the IP address of 192.168.1.1 with a subnet mask of 255.255.255.0 to the serial 0/0 interface of the 2600 modular router, the configuration would look like this:

```
Router(config)#interface serial 0/0
Router(config-if)#ip address 192.168.1.1 255.255.255.0
```

> **NOTE**
>
> Remember, if this was a router with a fixed interface (not modular), the command might look something like this:
> ```
> Router(config)#interface serial 0
> Router(config-if)#ip address 192.168.1.1 255.255.255.0
> ```

The first line in the configuration navigates you to the appropriate interface that you wish to configure. In this case, it is the first serial interface in the first module on the 2600 router (serial 0/0). The second command assigns the IP address of 192.168.1.1 to this interface. After this interface is enabled (discussed in next section), this router forwards any packets destined for 192.168.1.x 255.255.255.0 out its serial 0/0 interface.

> **NOTE**
>
> Because a router needs to forward packets between networks, you cannot configure two interfaces with IP addresses that are part of the same subnet. For example, you cannot configure serial 0 for 192.168.1.1 255.255.255.0 and interface ethernet 0 with an IP of 192.168.1.2 255.255.255.0. Because both IPs exist on the 192.168.1.0 network, the router cannot distinguish to which interface to send packets destined for 192.168.1.x. When a configuration error such as this is attempted, the router informs you that the IP network overlaps with another interface and does not let you assign the second IP address.

For documentation and reference, you can assign a description to this interface by using the description command on the interface:

```
Router(config-if)#description This is my first interface description.
```

Enabling the Interface

All router interfaces are in a disabled (shutdown) state by default. It is the duty of the configuring administrator to enable the interface by using the no shutdown command. If properly configured and connected to the network, the interface comes up and begins routing data in and out that interface. An example of administratively enabling the interface with the no shutdown command is as follows:

```
Router(config)#interface serial 0/0
Router(config-if)#no shutdown
```

TIP

If your interface is not connected to any other devices to communicate at Layer 2, you can use the no keepalives command on the interface to keep your interface active. A keepalive is a mechanism that the IOS uses to send messages to itself or to the other end to ensure a network interface is alive.

LAN-Specific Commands

Many of the LAN interfaces on a router have auto-sensing capabilities such as duplex and speed. For instance, a Fast Ethernet interface can run at speeds of 10mbps or 100mbps at half- or full-duplex. It is generally a good idea to manually assign an interface's duplex and speed in case your connected device does not support auto negotiation. The configuration to manually set the speed and duplex on an interface is fairly straightforward, as follows:

```
Router(config)#interface FastEthernet 0/0
Router(config-if)#speed 100
Router(config-if)#duplex full
```

WAN-Specific Commands

When configuring synchronous serial interfaces, you may discover that you have to configure some additional parameters to ensure proper functionality of your Wide Area Network (WAN) interfaces. For instance, when you have a serial cross-over cable between two routers' serial interfaces in a lab environment, the serial interface with the DCE cable attached to it has to provide timing for the network for data to be recognized on this link. The command to provide this synchronous timing on the network is `clock rate`, followed by the speed in bits per second.

Additionally, WAN serial interfaces automatically assume that the circuit connected to them is of T1 speed (1.54mbps). In instances where you have set a lower clock rate or you are connecting to a WAN service that is using sub-T1 speeds or virtual circuits (discussed later in Chapter 15, "Wide Area Network Connections"), it is imperative to redefine the bandwidth that is connected to the interface for accurate operation of routing decisions. You can achieve this redefinition by using the `bandwidth` command followed by the speed of the circuit in kilobits per second.

The following configuration demonstrates both of these commands in action for a router in a lab simulating a 64kbps circuit:

```
Router(config)#interface Serial 0/0
Router(config-if)#clock rate 64000
Router(config-if)#bandwidth 64
```

Saving Configurations

Objective:

▶ Manage IOS configuration files (including: save, edit, upgrade, restore)

If you are like me, you like living on the edge by configuring your devices during scheduled brown-outs in a room full of people with size 15 feet who are prone to accidentally kick the power cord out of your Cisco device. The problem with that lifestyle is that when the power returns to your router or switch, the hard work you put into your configuration is gone because all your configurations were made to the running configuration stored in volatile RAM. This is unfortunately true, unless of course, you save your configuration file into NVRAM and make that your startup configuration.

The versatile command that deserves all this credit for saving your hides is the `copy` command. With this command, you are telling the IOS to copy a file from one file system to another. Some options you have after the `copy` command are `running-config`, `startup-config`, `flash`, and `tftp`. The last two are discussed later in this chapter; the Global Configuration command to save the configuration in a switch or router IOS is as follows:

```
Router(config)#copy running-config startup-config
```

EXAM ALERT

Cisco advises that you do not need to save the configuration in a simulation. Despite my danger-seeking lifestyle, I highly recommend you err on the safe side by saving your configuration in case this policy changes in the future.

TIP

After performing the `copy running-config startup-config`, later IOSs ask you for the filename that you want to call the configuration file with [`startup-config`] in brackets. If you hit the Enter key, it saves it as the startup-config that will be loaded on next reboot. Saving it with a different filename saves the configuration, but that configuration will not be the one that is loaded.

EXAM ALERT

If you want to return your router or switch to its default configuration, you can use the Privileged EXEC command, `erase startup-config`, and reboot the device with the `reload` command. After the router or switch reboots, you should enter into Setup Mode because the configuration in NVRAM was erased.

STEP BY STEP

8.1 Configuring Router Interfaces

1. Go into Privileged EXEC by typing **enable**.

2. Enter Global Configuration by typing **configure terminal**.

3. Go into the Fast Ethernet interface 0/0 and configure the IP address of 172.16.1.1 /16 by typing **ip address 172.16.1.1 255.255.0.0**.

4. Enable the interface using the **no shutdown** command.

5. Type `exit` and go into the Serial interface 0/0 and configure the IP address of 192.168.1.1 /24 by typing **ip address 192.168.1.1 255.255.255.0**.

6. Enable the interface by using the `no shutdown` command.

7. Type **end** or press Ctrl+Z to go back to Privileged EXEC, and save the configuration by using **copy running-config startup-config**.

The result should look similar the following:

```
! Step 1
Router>enable
! Step 2
Router# configure terminal
```

```
Enter configuration commands, one per line. End with CNTL/Z
! Step 3
Router(config)# interface fastethernet 0/0
Router(config-if)# ip address 172.16.1.1 255.255.0.0
! Step 4
Router(config-if)# no shutdown
! Step 5
Router(config-if) #exit
Router(config)# interface serial 0/0
Router(config-if)# ip address 192.168.1.1 255.255.255.0
! Step 6
Router(config-if)# no shutdown
! Step 7
Router(config-if)# Router(config-if)#end
00:04:48: %SYS-5-CONFIG_I: Configured from console by console
Router# copy running-config startup-config
Destination filename [startup-config]?
```

Using the show Command to Get Information

Objective:

▶ Verify network status and router operation using basic utilities (including: ping, traceroute, telnet, SSH, arp, ipconfig), SHOW & DEBUG commands

As an administrator of Cisco routers and switches, it is inevitable that you will have to get information and statistics to verify the functionality of those devices and the networks that are connected to them. The crux of every command to view these statistics is the show keyword. This section explains what information you can gain from several of these show commands and tells you how to interpret outputs of those commands.

TIP

Some of the show commands will have quite a lot of extraneous output that may not be pertinent to what you are trying to discover. In some extreme cases, this can go on for pages and pages of output and you could spend quite a bit of time weeding through all the information. To assist you finding specific information, the Cisco IOS now gives you the ability to filter the output by adding a pipe symbol (|) followed by the keyword include, exclude, or begin and the expression you want to filter. Include will only show you outputs that include the expression that you define in the command. Exclude provides the exact opposite service in that it will show you all the output except for the expression you specify. Finally, begin will show you the full output beginning at the point the expression is found.

Verifying Your Configurations

Without a doubt, verifying your configurations is one of the most widely used show functions in the Cisco IOS. What better way to double-check or troubleshoot your configuration could there be besides seeing it displayed right in front of you? One caveat to these particular show commands, however, is that you must be in Privileged EXEC to see the configurations. This makes logical sense because you don't want anybody from User EXEC to see your passwords in the configurations.

To see the active configuration that is running in RAM (that is, running-config), simply type **show running-config**. Similarly, the command show startup-config displays the configuration that will be loaded after you reboot the router or switch. The following example shows the show running-config command, and the output of some of the router configurations discussed in this chapter, performed on an 1720 router with a fixed Fast Ethernet interface:

```
CCNA1720#show running-config
Building configuration...
Current configuration:
!
version 12.4
service timestamps debug uptime
service timestamps log uptime
service password-encryption
!
hostname CCNA1720
!
enable secret 5 $1$nLCr$gNidpLSZvMnm2wFW6ACLm0
enable password 7 14120A0A0107382A29
!
boot-start-marker
boot-end-marker
!
!
memory-size iomem 15
no aaa new-model
ip subnet-zero
ip host corerouter 172.16.1.1
ip name-server 172.16.1.254
!
!
ip cef
!
interface FastEthernet0
 ip address 172.16.1.1 255.255.0.0
 no ip directed-broadcast
 full-duplex
!
```

```
interface Serial0/0
 bandwidth 64
 ip address 192.168.1.1 255.255.255.0
 no ip directed-broadcast
 no fair-queue
!
ip classless
ip http server
!
banner motd ^C This is a private system and may be accessed only by authorized users.
 Unauthorized access is strictly prohibited and will be enforced to the full
 extent of the law.^C
!
line con 0
 exec-timeout 1 30
 password 7 045802150C2E
 login
line vty 0 4
 exec-timeout 1 30
 password 7 02050D480809
 login
!
End
```

NOTE

Notice that in the output of the show running-config command there are commands such as serv-ice timestamps debug uptime, ip subnet-zero, and so on that have not been discussed. These are all configurations that are created by default by the IOS, and may vary depending on the version of the IOS that is loaded. On that same note, some configurations do not even show up in the IOS configuration even though they are configured on the router or switch. For instance, both interfaces were administratively enabled in this configuration despite the lack of the command no shutdown being displayed on each interface configuration.

EXAM ALERT

One of your best resources on a simulation that has a troubleshooting scenario is the show running-config command. By looking at the configuration and recognizing incorrect or missing entries, you can determine what items must be fixed in a particular device to regain connectivity in the simulated network.

Viewing Interface Statuses and Statistics

Beyond a doubt, the next four show commands will serve as the most useful tools in determining interface functionality and the performance of the network connected to those interfaces. Some of the outputs for these interface-specific show commands display similar statistics;

nevertheless, each command serves a unique purpose depending on what facet of the interfaces you are trying to investigate.

show interfaces Command

The most detailed show command that displays statistics about the status of the interfaces and the network traffic for that interface is the show interfaces command. This command shows you statistics for all interfaces on the router or switch; however, if you wish to view information about only a single interface, you can specify that interface in the command (for example, show interfaces serial 0/0). The output that follows illustrates the show interface output for a Fast Ethernet interface:

```
Router#show interfaces FastEthernet 0/0
FastEthernet0/0 is up, line protocol is up
  Hardware is Gt96k FE, address is 001a.2f66.fa1a (bia 001a.2f66.fa1a)
  Internet address is 172.16.0.1/16
  MTU 1500 bytes, BW 100000 Kbit, DLY 100 usec,
     reliability 255/255, txload 1/255, rxload 1/255
  Encapsulation ARPA, loopback not set
  Keepalive not set
  Full-duplex, 100Mb/s, 100BaseTX/FX
  ARP type: ARPA, ARP Timeout 04:00:00
  Last input 00:00:10, output 00:00:10, output hang never
  Last clearing of "show interface" counters never
  Input queue: 0/75/0/0 (size/max/drops/flushes); Total output drops: 0
  Queueing strategy: fifo
  Output queue: 0/40 (size/max)
  5 minute input rate 0 bits/sec, 0 packets/sec
  5 minute output rate 0 bits/sec, 0 packets/sec
     322 packets input, 70336 bytes
     Received 322 broadcasts, 0 runts, 0 giants, 0 throttles
     0 input errors, 0 CRC, 0 frame, 0 overrun, 0 ignored
     0 watchdog
     0 input packets with dribble condition detected
     343 packets output, 72188 bytes, 0 underruns
     0 output errors, 0 collisions, 3 interface resets
     0 babbles, 0 late collision, 0 deferred
     0 lost carrier, 0 no carrier
     0 output buffer failures, 0 output buffers swapped out
```

A common statistic of most of the interface show commands is the actual status of the interface itself. This is identified in the first line of output of the show interfaces commands. The first part of the status identifies the Layer 1 information of the interface, followed by the Layer 2 line protocol status.

If you understand the interface statuses you are ultimately building a solid foundation to accurately troubleshoot any malfunctioning interface. For example, if your interface is in an "up/line protocol up" state, you have eliminated Layer 1 and Layer 2 malfunctions for that interface. From this point, you can determine whether the problem on the interface is perhaps a Layer 3 problem (IP addressing, routing, and so on). Table 8.1 lists the possible values of this command.

TABLE 8.1   Interface Status Values

Layer 1	Layer 2 (line protocol)	Possible Symptoms
Up	Up	None. Interface is functional.
Up	Down	Encapsulation mismatch, lack of clocking on serial interfaces, missing keepalives.
Down	Down	Cable is disconnected or attached to a shut down interface on the far-end device.
Administratively Down	Down	Local interface was not enabled with the no shutdown command.

EXAM ALERT

Be able to recognize the interface status meanings and determine the possible reasons for that status.

The rest of the output of the show interfaces command is also extremely useful for gaining information about the interface and the network. Of course, you won't be expected to know all the elements listed in this output; however, Table 8.2 displays some of the valuable common statistics descriptions.

TABLE 8.2   Show Interface Output Descriptions

Output	Description
Hardware is AmdFE, address is 0003.e32a.4080	The MAC address of the ethernet interface.
Internet address	Assigned IP address.
MTU 1500 bytes, BW 100000 Kbit, DLY 100 usec, reliability 255/255, txload 1/255, rxload 1/255	The Maximum Transmission Unit (frame size) for this interface, logical bandwidth (default or set with bandwidth command), cumulative delay, interface reliability, inbound and outbound load.
Encapsulation ARPA	Layer 2 frame encapsulation on interface.
Half-duplex, 100Mb/s, 100BaseTX/FX	Duplex and speed of interface.

TABLE 8.2 *continued*

Output	Description
`Received 0 broadcasts, 0 runts, 0 giants`	The number of broadcasts, runts (below minimum frame size), and giants (above maximum frame size).
`0 collisions`	The number of collisions that occurred on that segment.
`0 late collision`	Late collisions occur when your interface is set for half-duplex and you are connected to a full-duplex interface.

EXAM ALERT

You may be presented with the output of a `show interface` command with the intention of testing your knowledge of being able to identify problematic elements in the output. For instance, a high load value is evidence of a saturated link, a large number of late collisions is a duplex mismatch, excessive collisions might be indicative of being plugged into a hub, and so on.

show ip interface brief Command

If the goal of your `show` command is to get a condensed output of the interfaces' status and their IP addresses, the `show ip interface brief` command conveniently shows you a minimal display of these statistics as illustrated here:

```
Router#show ip interface brief
Interface              IP-Address       OK? Method Status                Protocol
FastEthernet0/0        192.168.100.154  YES DHCP   up                    up
FastEthernet0/1        unassigned       YES unset  administratively down down
Serial0/0              unassigned       YES unset  administratively down down
```

show controller Command

Although the output of the `show controller` command is unintelligible to everyone except for the Cisco TAC (Technical Assistance Center), one particularly useful extract from this output is in the `show controller serial` command. The needle in this haystack of statistics is the line of output that identifies whether a DTE or a DCE cable is attached to the serial interface. This is useful if you are connecting to your router remotely and you are not sure whether your router should be providing the clocking (if you are the DCE interface). The following excerpt example illustrates this useful output:

```
Router>show controller serial 0/1
Interface Serial0/1
Hardware is PowerQUICC MPC860
V.35 DCE cable, clockrate 64000
...output omitted...
```

IOS File Version show Commands

The following section discusses how to back up your IOS to a TFTP server or download a new version of the IOS to your router or switch. Tasks of this magnitude, however, cannot be performed unless you do some initial legwork. Namely, you must perform some essential steps such as identifying the amount of Flash memory, the IOS filename located in Flash, and the current IOS version that is running on the device.

Different Cisco IOS versions and feature sets will ultimately dictate the size of the IOS file and the amount of Flash and DRAM memory required to run the IOS. If you are planning to upgrade to a new IOS, you must make sure that you have enough memory (the more, the better) in your device. To see the amount of Flash you have and the current IOS file stored in Flash memory, utilize the `show flash` command as follows:

```
Router>show flash
System flash directory:
File  Length    Name/status
  1   5510192   c2600-is-mz.120-3.T3.bin
[5510256 bytes used, 2878352 available, 8388608 total]
8192K bytes of processor board System flash (Read/Write)
```

Typically, the filename of the IOS file in Flash correctly reflects the actual IOS version running currently on the device. However, an administrator can easily change the filename to his or her own purposes, or there could be multiple IOS files stored on the Flash and you are not sure which one is running currently. To ensure the correct version of IOS, use the widely practical `show version` command.

As the following output demonstrates, the `show version` command displays a plethora of information well beyond the version of IOS running. Table 8.3 explains some of the useful output of this multifaceted command.

```
Router#show version
Cisco IOS Software, 1841 Software (C1841-ADVIPSERVICESK9-M), Version 12.4(3g), RELEASE
SOFTWARE (fc2)
Technical Support: http://www.cisco.com/techsupport
Copyright (c) 1986-2006 by Cisco Systems, Inc.
Compiled Mon 06-Nov-06 01:23 by alnguyen

ROM: System Bootstrap, Version 12.3(8r)T9, RELEASE SOFTWARE (fc1)

CCNA1841 uptime is 8 hours, 35 minutes
System returned to ROM by power-on
System image file is "flash:c1841-advipservicesk9-mz.124-3g.bin"


This product contains cryptographic features and is subject to United
States and local country laws governing import, export, transfer and
use. Delivery of Cisco cryptographic products does not imply
third-party authority to import, export, distribute or use encryption.
```

Importers, exporters, distributors and users are responsible for
compliance with U.S. and local country laws. By using this product you
agree to comply with applicable laws and regulations. If you are unable
to comply with U.S. and local laws, return this product immediately.

A summary of U.S. laws governing Cisco cryptographic products may be found at:
http://www.cisco.com/wwl/export/crypto/tool/stqrg.html

If you require further assistance please contact us by sending email to
export@cisco.com.

Cisco 1841 (revision 6.0) with 236544K/25600K bytes of memory.
Processor board ID FTX1046W1X1
2 FastEthernet interfaces
1 Serial(sync/async) interface
2 Virtual Private Network (VPN) Modules
DRAM configuration is 64 bits wide with parity disabled.
191K bytes of NVRAM.
62720K bytes of ATA CompactFlash (Read/Write)

Configuration register is 0x2102

TABLE 8.3   Show Version Output Descriptions

Output	Description
Cisco IOS Software, 1841 Software (C1841-ADVIPSERVICESK9-M), Version 12.4(3g), RELEASE SOFTWARE (fc2)	The IOS feature set, version, and release.
ROM: System Bootstrap, Version 12.3(8r)T9, RELEASE SOFTWARE (fc1)	The version of the bootstrap code in ROM.
Router uptime is 8 hours, 35 minutes	The length of time the device has been running.
System returned to ROM by power-on	How the device was started.
System image file is "flash:c1841-advipservicesk9-mz.124-3g.bin"	The name of the IOS file that was loaded and the location of that file.
with 236544K/25600K bytes of memory	The amount of RAM in the system allocated to the devices processor, followed by memory allocated for packets. The total RAM is calculated by adding the two values together (236544K+25600K =49144K, or 48MB).
191K bytes of NVRAM	The amount of NVRAM for the startup-config.
62720K bytes of ATA CompactFlash (Read/Write)	Total amount of Flash memory.
Configuration register is 0x2102	The current configuration register.

REVIEW BREAK

Table 8.4 reviews the `show` commands discussed in this chapter, including their functions and whether they are in User EXEC or both User EXEC and Privileged EXEC.

TABLE 8.4   Show Command Review

Command	User EXEC/ Privileged EXEC	Output
`show running-config`	Privileged EXEC	Current configuration in RAM.
`show startup-config`	Privileged EXEC	Configuration in NVRAM to be loaded at next boot.
`show interfaces`	Both	Interface status, IP address, encapsulation, bandwidth, reliability, load, MTU, duplex, network statistics.
`show ip interface brief`	Both	IP address and status of interfaces.
`show controller serial`	Both	Microcode of interface, including whether DTE or DCE cable is attached.
`show flash`	Both	IOS filename and amount of used and available Flash memory.
`show version`	Both	IOS version, IOS filename, uptime, memory amounts, configuration register.

Troubleshooting Commands

Objectives:

▶ Verify network status and router operation using basic utilities (including: ping, traceroute, telnet, SSH, arp, ipconfig), SHOW & DEBUG commands

▶ Verify device configuration and network connectivity using ping, traceroute, telnet, SSH, or other utilities

Troubleshooting a Cisco device and the networks to which it is connected is an integral part of being a Cisco administrator. Most of your troubleshooting can be solved by verifying your configurations and the device's operations, using the `show` commands mentioned in the previous section. However, at times you may need to use additional commands to help identify and troubleshoot faults in the network.

Specifically, the `clear` command in Privileged EXEC resets statistical information that is being stored for the outputs of your `show` commands. For example, if you saw that the output of the `show interfaces serial 0/0` command and noticed excessive late collisions, how do you know whether those are recent statistics or collisions that occurred last week? Using the `clear counters` command resets those statistics so you can view up-to-date information from the `show interfaces` output.

One of the most widely utilized commands for troubleshooting is the `ping` command. `ping` uses ICMP echo and echo reply messages to verify connectivity to IP devices. To ping a specific device from User EXEC or Privileged EXEC, enter `ping` followed by the IP address or hostname of the device you are trying to verify, as follows:

```
Router#ping 192.168.1.1
Type escape sequence to abort.
Sending 5, 100-byte ICMP Echos to 192.168.1.1, timeout is 2 seconds:
.!!!!
Success rate is 80 percent (4/5)
```

Notice that the ping response contains a period (.) followed by four exclamation marks (!). An exclamation mark character is indicative of a successful receipt of a reply to the ping. The period character indicates that a timeout has occurred for that particular ICMP echo packet. In some instances, you may receive a `U` character, which signifies a Destination Unreachable ICMP message. These messages are indicative that a router along the packet's path to the destination did not know how to reach the destination network. When this occurs, the router sends a Destination Unreachable message back to the packet's source.

EXAM ALERT

ICMP Destination Unreachable messages are sent by a routing device when it does not know how to reach the destination network. The router sends this ICMP message back to the packet's source.

EXAM ALERT

Notice that in the output of the `ping` command, the first ping packet timed out. This actually is quite normal when pinging a device on a LAN because the router or switch might have to resolve the MAC address on the data link segment with an ARP request. Any successive pings shortly after should receive 100% of replies.

Similar to other operating systems, you can manipulate some of the options in a ping echo request, such as the datagram size and the timeout period in the Cisco IOS. To specify these options, you need to use an extended `ping` command. This command requires you to be in Privileged EXEC and is used by typing **ping** followed by the Enter key (no IP address). From there, you can change the default parameters such as the datagram sizes, timeout, and the number of packets sent, as shown in the following example:

```
Router#ping
Target IP address: 192.168.1.1
Repeat count [5]: 10
Datagram size [100]: 200
Timeout in seconds [2]: 5
Extended commands [n]: y
Source address or interface:
Type of service [0]:
Set DF bit in IP header? [no]:
Validate reply data? [no]:
Data pattern [0xABCD]:
Loose, Strict, Record, Timestamp, Verbose[none]:
Sweep range of sizes [n]:
Type escape sequence to abort 192.168.1.1, timeout is 5 seconds:
!!!!!!!!!!
Success rate is 100 percent (10/10)
```

EXAM ALERT

The extended ping must be entered in Privileged EXEC. The command is ping followed by the Enter key.

Another useful ICMP utility is the traceroute command. As the name states, traceroute sends ICMP messages and receives a reply from every routing device along the path to the destination. This is useful in situations where you suspect a router on the route to an unreachable network is failing. The command syntax for traceroute is similar to the ping command. In fact, you can also perform an extended traceroute by using the traceroute command in lieu of the ping keyword.

```
Router#trace 192.168.1.1
Tracing the route to 192.168.1.1
1 192.168.100.1 4 msec 0 msec 4 msec
2 10.1.1.3 4 msec 4 msec 0 msec
3 192.168.1.1 0 msec 0 msec 4 msec
```

EXAM ALERT

traceroute is an ICMP utility that tests the connectivity to a device by receiving responses from each routing device along the path to the destination. It is especially useful when you suspect a router on the route to an unreachable network is failing.

The final troubleshooting command (for now) is another exclusive Privileged EXEC command that should be used only when all other troubleshooting has failed. The debug command displays real-time information on such things as routing updates, packet forwarding, and interface keepalives, to name a few. The reason behind the cautionary tone of this explanation is because the debug command is very processor intensive and can generate a lot of information on your terminal screen. For this reason, it is highly recommended that you use these commands only in emergency situations or in a lab environment. If you must troubleshoot on a production router, be sure to issue the show processes command as follows:

```
RouterA#show processes
CPU utilization for five seconds: 0%/0%; one minute: 0%; five minutes: 0%
...Output Omitted...
```

The majority of the output will not make sense; however, the top of the output lists the CPU utilization up to the last 5 minutes. If any of these values exceeds 60%, do not use the debug commands. If you do, your router is likely to seize up from over-utilization.

> **EXAM ALERT**
>
> It is recommended to use the show processes command before using any debug commands to verify the router's current CPU utilization.

When you are finished troubleshooting, you can turn off debugging by putting a **no** in front of the command, or you can turn off all debugging by typing **no debug all** or **undebug all**. Specific debugging commands are discussed throughout the course of this book.

> **EXAM ALERT**
>
> If your device is seizing up from too much debug processing, turn it off by using the no debug all or undebug all commands.

> **TIP**
>
> To see accurate timestamps for your debug messages, it is highly recommended that you configure the clock to reflect the correct date and time by using the clock command in Privileged EXEC. In addition, to add a timestamp to the debug output, use the service timestamp command in Global Configuration.

Backing Up and Restoring Configurations and IOS Using TFTP

Objective:

▶ Manage IOS configuration files (including: save, edit, upgrade, restore)

Recall from the "Saving Configurations" section that you used the copy command to copy the running config in RAM to the startup config in NVRAM. By using this command, you are basically copying this configuration file from one filesystem component to another. Such is the case if you want to back up and restore configurations and IOSs to and from a TFTP server.

EXAM ALERT

The TFTP server is used to back up and restore configurations and IOS images.

A fair amount of setup and preparation is required to achieve this functionality, but the rewards of being able to back up and restore these files are well worth it. Specifically, the following preparations need to be in place for your switch or router to transfer these files to and from a TFTP server:

1. The TFTP server must have the TFTP service running. You can search the Internet for evaluation TFTP servers from companies such as SolarWinds and FutureSoft.

2. Your device must be cabled correctly. If you're using a switch, plug the TFTP server into the switch with a straight-through ethernet cable. If you're going directly between a router and the TFTP server, use a cross-over cable.

3. You must have IP connectivity to the server. In other words, your interface should be on the same subnet as the server.

4. There must be enough room on the TFTP server and your device's memory to store these files. If your Flash memory cannot store two files, the IOS erases the old file from Flash memory before copying the new one.

After all the preparations are in place, and you have verified connectivity between the TFTP server and your Cisco router or switch, you can use the `copy` command again to transfer files. Remember, the `copy` command instructs the IOS to copy from somewhere to somewhere. The available keywords, once again, are `startup-config`, `running-config`, `tftp`, and `flash`. When the `tftp` keyword is used, the IOS follows up with a few subsequent questions to help the IOS identify the IP address of the server, and the filenames of the source and destination files.

For example, to copy the IOS from a TFTP server to the Flash memory of the router, your command would look something like the following:

```
Router#copy tftp flash
Address or name of remote host []? 172.16.1.254
Source filename []? c2600-is-mz.120-3.T3.bin
Destination filename [c2800-is-mz.123-3.T3.bin]?
Copy 'c2800-is-mz.123-3.T3.bin' from Flash to server
as 'c2800-is-mz.123-3.T3.bin'? [yes/no]y
!!!!!!!!!!!!!!!!!!!!!!!!!!!!!!!!!!!!!!!!!!!!!!!!!!!!!!!!!!!!!!!!!!!!!!!!!!!!!!!!
...output omitted...
Upload to server done
Flash device copy took 00:01:24 [hh:mm:ss]
```

> **NOTE**
>
> Similar to utilities such as ping and traceroute, successful copying of files to and from a TFTP server is displayed with an exclamation mark (!).

Similarly, if you wanted to upgrade your IOS to a new version or you want to restore a previously backed up IOS from your TFTP server, the command would be copy tftp flash. Remember, if your flash memory does not have enough space for your current IOS file and the new one, the process erases your old IOS file to make room for the new one. If you accidentally lose power during the file transfer, you inevitably end up in ROMmon. At that point, you can download the IOS again from the TFTP server or copy the image over the console.

After the IOS image is loaded to your Flash memory, you have to reboot the device for that IOS to run (because your current IOS is still decompressed and running in RAM). To reboot a Cisco device, use the reload command from Privileged EXEC. Do not forget to save any configuration changes that you made with the copy running-config startup-config command before rebooting the device because the router or switch uses the contents of your startup configuration when it reinitializes. In many current IOS versions, the IOS reminds you that your configuration has modified and asks you whether you want to save it. Answering "**yes**" to this prompt saves your configuration to NVRAM:

```
Router#reload
System configuration has been modified. Save? [yes/no]: yes
Building configuration...
[OK]
Proceed with reload? [confirm]
04:31:02: %SYS-5-RELOAD: Reload requested
```

> **EXAM ALERT**
>
> The reload Privileged EXEC command reinitializes the router or switch. The content in the startup configuration is loaded on boot-up.

The copy command can also be used to back up and restore your configurations. For example, to back up your current configuration, you can type copy running-config flash. Alternatively, you can always save your configuration to a text file by capturing the text output of your terminal program and doing the show running-config command. If you want to paste the configuration back into the Cisco device, just go into Global Configuration and paste the text back into the terminal program window.

> **EXAM ALERT**
>
> The show running-config command does not show commands such as no shutdown. If you paste the configuration into a new configuration, the interfaces remain shut down unless you edit the text file and place the no shutdown command in the interface configurations or enter the commands in the configuration afterward.

Cisco Integrated File System

With DOS and UNIX command navigation in mind, the Cisco IOS has adopted a command structure that can be used regardless of what router platform you are on. These Integrated File System (IFS) commands use URL syntax to specify files in either the device's local memory or on network servers that you would like to see or copy. The commands such as show and copy are still the same; however, when specifying file locations, you use a URL to indicate the location and file name. This syntax also helps you perform commands like in our TFTP section without requiring the IOS to ask us questions because we are indicate all the information in the command line. For instance, in the previous section, we used the copy tftp flash command to download a new IOS to our router. This was followed by a subset of questions to identify the file names and IP address of the TFP server. With the IFS, we could do all that in one command such as the following:

```
Router# copy tftp://172.16.1.254/c2600-is-mz.120-3.T3.bin flash:c2600-is-mz.120-
3.T3.bin
```

Table 8.5 shows some of the keywords we recently learned and showing what they would be using the IFS.

TABLE 8.5   Integrated File System Keywords

Traditional Command Keyword	Integrated File System Keyword
flash	flash:*filename*
tftp	tftp://*tftp_IP*/*filename*
running-config	system:running-config
startup-config	nvram:starup-config

Neighbor Discovery with CDP

Imagine it is your first day at work and your boss wants you to create a topology map of the network, including model numbers, IPs, and IOS versions of all the Cisco equipment. Eager to impress the boss, you want to get this task done as soon as possible. The problem is that the equipment isn't allocated in the same building and your security badge won't allow you into other buildings. Thus, console access isn't possible and you don't know the IP addresses of the other devices to use SSH or Telnet into them. Instead of spending that free time looking in the want ads because you are afraid you are going to get fired, you can call upon a very useful protocol called Cisco Discovery Protocol (CDP) to gather information of directly connected Cisco neighbors.

As the name indicates, CDP is a Cisco proprietary protocol that operates at the Data Link layer. One unique feature about operating at Layer 2 is that CDP functions regardless of what Physical layer media you are using (UTP, fiber, and so on) and what Network layer routed protocols you are running (IP, IPX, AppleTalk, and so on). CDP is enabled on all Cisco devices by default, and is multicast every 60 seconds out of all functioning interfaces, enabling neighbor Cisco devices to collect information about each other. Although this is a multicast message, Cisco switches do not flood that out to all their neighbors as they do a normal multicast or broadcast.

EXAM ALERT

Remember the defining characteristics of CDP are that it is a proprietary Layer 2 protocol that can run regardless of the Layer 1 and Layer 3 configuration. It also is enabled by default and sent as a multicast to directly connected Cisco neighbors only.

The amount of information you can display ultimately depends on the command you use. For instance, the following example illustrates the output of the `show cdp neighbors` command:

```
CCNA2811>show cdp neighbors
Capability Codes: R - Router, T - Trans Bridge, B - Source Route Bridge
                  S - Switch, H - Host, I - IGMP, r - Repeater
Device ID        Local Intrfce     Holdtme     Capability   Platform   Port ID
Bldg1-3550       Fas 0             128         S I          WS-C3550-2 Fas 0/22
Engineering1801  Ser 0/1           134         R            1801       Ser 0/0
```

Table 8.6 explains the output depicted in the preceding example.

TABLE 8.6 `show cdp neighbors` Output Explanation

Output	Explanation
Device ID	Neighbor's configured hostname.
Local Intrfce	Local interface in which you received this information.
Holdtme	CDP hold-down timer to keep track of how long it has been since you received information from that neighbor and how many seconds to wait until you consider that neighbor dead.
Capability	The capabilities of the Cisco devices as explained in the legend at the top of the output.
Platform	The model number of the Cisco device.
Port ID	The interface in which the neighbor device sent out this CDP information.

By using the **show cdp neighbors detail** command or the **show cdp entry *** command, you can gain even more information about your neighbor Cisco devices. Specifically, you can see all the information from the **show cdp neighbors** output in addition to the Layer 3 information and the IOS version of your directly connected neighbors. Figure 8.1 illustrates the detailed output of these commands.

```
CCNA2621>show cdp neighbor detail
-------------------------
Device ID: Bldg1-3550
Entry address(es)
Platform: cisco WS-C3550-24,  Capabilities: Switch IGMP
Interface: FastEthernet0/0,  Port ID (outgoing port): FastEthernet0/22
Holdtime : 143 sec

Version :
Cisco Internetwork Operating System Software
IOS (tm) C3550 Software (C3550-I9Q3L2-M), Version 12.1(13)EA1a, RELEASE SOFTWARE (fc1)
Copyright (c) 1986-2003 by cisco Systems, Inc.
Compiled Tue 25-Mar-03 23:21 by yenanh

advertisement version: 2
Protocol Hello:  OUI=0x00000C, Protocol ID=0x0112; payload len=27, value=00000000FFFFFFFF010221FF00000000000000
0D65D04E00FF0000
VTP Management Domain: "ThirteenBlack"
Native VLAN: 1
Duplex: full

-------------------------
Device ID: Engineering1601
Entry address(es):
  IP address: 192.168.100.5
Platform: cisco 1601,  Capabilities: Router
Interface: Serial0/1,  Port ID (outgoing port): Serial0
Holdtime : 145 sec

Version :
Cisco Internetwork Operating System Software
IOS (tm) 1600 Software (C1600-NY-L), Version 12.0(6), RELEASE SOFTWARE (fc1)
Copyright (c) 1986-1999 by cisco Systems, Inc.
Compiled Wed 11-Aug-99 01:13 by phanguye
```

FIGURE 8.1 `show cdp neighbors detail` or `show cdp entry*` output.

Based upon this information, you can already begin to see the topology layout of these three devices, as illustrated in Figure 8.2.

Serial 0
IP: 192.168.100.5

Engineering 1601
1601 Router
IOS version 12.0(6)

Serial 0/1
IP: 192.168.100.6

Fast Ethernet 0/0
IP: 172.16.100.1

Fast Ethernet 0/22

Bldg1-3550
Catalyst 3550
IOS version 12.1(13)EA1a

FIGURE 8.2 Example topology derived from CDP output.

At this point, I am sure you are completely in awe of the wonders that CDP can bring to your administrative duties; however, there are times you may wish to disable CDP. As mentioned before, CDP is a Cisco proprietary protocol enabled by default on all Cisco devices. So what happens when you are not connected to a Cisco device? Although the bandwidth usage is minimal, it still serves no purpose to continue sending CDP advertisements to non-Cisco devices that cannot interpret this protocol. In addition, it is a good idea to disable CDP for security reasons because you can gain so much useful information that could prove fatal in the wrong hands.

You can disable CDP in one of two ways: globally on the Cisco device or on an interface-by-interface basis. To disable CDP for the entire device, you have to configure the `no cdp run` command in Global Configuration. Otherwise, you can specify on which interfaces to disable CDP advertisement by navigating to those specific interfaces and using the `no cdp enable` command in the interface configuration.

EXAM ALERT

Keep in mind for the exam that the two commands to disable CDP are `no cdp enable` and `no cdp run`.

Challenge

Imagine that the lead engineer has asked you to install a new router in the lab rack. You connect the serial interfaces together with a v.35 cross-over cable and install the router in the rack. Complete the following steps to get the two devices to communicate:

1. Through your console, connect an EXEC session.

2. The cross-over cable is not labeled. What command can you type to verify if your end is the DCE or the DTE connector?

3. To get the two routers to communicate with each other, you have to assign an IP address in the same subnet as the old router's serial interface. You know the lead engineer uses /30 subnets on his serial interfaces, but you need to figure out what IP address he used. What command can you type to find this information from your local router?

4. Enter the serial configuration.

5. The IP address he used was 192.168.40.41. Configure the only available IP address left in that subnet.

6. You have the DCE connection, so provide clocking for a 128K network.

7. Exit back to Privileged EXEC and save your configuration.

To see whether you have a DTE or DCE cable attached to your serial interface, you should type the `show controllers serial` command. Because the interface is already enabled, CDP information should be mulitcast between your routers. To see the neighbor's configured interface IP address, type **show cdp neighbors detail** or **show cdp entry ***.

The configuration should look like the following (with possible variation on the abbreviation of the commands):

```
Router>enable
Router#configuration terminal
Router(config)#interface s0/0
Router(config-if)#ip address 192.168.40.42 255.255.255.252
Router(config-if)#clock rate 128000
Router(config-if)#end
Router#copy runnig-config startup-config
```

Using Telnet for Virtual Terminal Access

Objective:

▶ Verify device configuration and network connectivity using ping, traceroute, telnet, SSH, or other utilities

Telnet is widely used as an in-band management protocol today for remotely administering Cisco devices. As long as you have IP connectivity to the Cisco device and have configured a password on the vty lines, you can remotely administer your Cisco switches and routers.

In User EXEC and Privilege EXEC of the IOS, it is possible to Telnet from your Cisco device to another device. By typing `telnet` followed by the IP address that you are trying to reach, you initiate a Telnet session from your local router or switch. In all actuality, you do not even need to use the `telnet` keyword. If you just type an IP address or a hostname (assuming name resolution), the IOS automatically assumes you are attempting to Telnet to that host.

For example, if you Telnet from the 28111 router to the remote 1801, the output would look similar to the following:

```
CCNA2811>telnet 192.168.100.5
Trying 192.168.100.5 ... Open
User Access Verification
Password:
Engineering1801>
```

At this point, you can configure the Engineering1801 router as if you were directly consoled into it. However, there may be a time where you need to jump back to your original router to incorporate additional configurations, verify connectivity, or Telnet into other devices. While connected to the remote device, you can suspend your Telnet session temporarily and return to the origin of the Telnet session (CCNA2811 in our example). The useful, but strangely awkward keystroke to suspend a Telnet session in **Ctrl+Shift+6** followed by hitting the **x** key. Keep in mind that this only suspends the Telnet session; the session is still connected and running in a background process.

EXAM ALERT
Know that the keystroke combination `Ctrl+Shift+6`, *x* suspends a Telnet session.

As shown in Figure 8.3, you can verify the Telnet sessions that have originated from the local device by using the `show sessions` command. This example initiates and suspends two separate Telnet sessions from the CCNA2811 router.

```
CCNA2621>telnet 192.168.100.5
Trying 192.168.100.5 ... Open

User Access Verification

Password:
Engineering1601>
CCNA2621>telnet 172.16.1.100
Trying 172.16.1.100 ... Open

User Access Verification

Password:
Bldg1-3550>
CCNA2621>show sessions
Conn Host          Address          Byte  Idle Conn Name
   1 192.168.100.5  192.168.100.5       0     0 192.168.100.5
*  2 172.16.1.100   172.16.1.100        0     0 172.16.1.100
```

FIGURE 8.3   Multiple Telnet session example.

Notice that each session connection is numbered and there is an asterisk next to connection 2. This is the last Telnet session that was suspended and it is the session that will be resumed if you hit the Enter key without typing a command. You can also choose which Telnet session to resume by typing **resume**, followed by the connection number.

Ctrl+Shift+6, x suspends the Telnet session, but how do you actually close the Telnet session when you are finished? The answer is twofold. You can close a Telnet session from the originating local device by typing the keyword **disconnect** followed by the connection number. From the device into which you are Telnetted, you can also type **exit** or **logout** from User EXEC or Privileged EXEC.

EXAM ALERT

Be familiar with the multiple ways you can resume and disconnect a Telnet session.

Terminal Monitor

By default, your Cisco devices send their notification messages such as debug outputs, interface alerts, and system error messages to the console port. This means that you cannot see these notifications over a Telnet session to another device by default.

To have these messages copied to the vty lines, you need to use the terminal monitor command in Privileged EXEC mode of the device to which you are telnetted. For instance, in the configuration shown, Router A Telnets into Router B and enters Privileged EXEC mode to type the terminal monitor command. debug outputs, notifications, and errors messages are then sent over the vty lines to be viewed by the remote terminal.

```
RouterA>telnet 10.1.1.1
Trying 10.1.1.1 ... Open
User Access Verification
Password:
RouterB>enable
Password:
Router#terminal monitor
```

> **EXAM ALERT**
>
> The `terminal monitor` command copied debug outputs and error messages to the vty terminal lines.

STEP BY STEP

8.2 Telnet Practice

1. Telnet into your neighbor router by typing **telnet**, followed by the IP address.

2. Suspend that Telnet session by using the **Ctrl+Shift+6**, **x** keystroke.

3. Verify that suspended Telnet session by typing **show sessions**.

4. Disconnect the Telnet session by typing **disconnect**, followed by the connection number (should be 1).

IOS DHCP

Objectives:

▶ Configure, verify, and troubleshoot DHCP and DNS operation on a router (including: CLI/SDM)

▶ Implement static and dynamic addressing services for hosts in a LAN environment

One of Cisco's many goals is to make their routers more versatile than simply just routing packets. Case in point, Cisco has incorporated security, switching, wireless, and/or voice in their line of Integrated Service Routers to provide multi-functionality out of a single device. In that same vein, the Cisco IOS has some convenient features that can provide services to small-to-medium size businesses minimizing the reliance on other devices and servers. One of those services that the Cisco router can provide is to act as DHCP server for a LAN to assign DHCP-enabled devices an IP address, address of the default gateway, domain name, and the DNS server address.

To start the configuration for this service, you have to configure your ethernet interface and make sure that it is up, administratively enabled, and an assigned an IP address as described in this chapter. This makes logical sense since this is the interface that is connected to the DHCP-enabled clients. The next step is to logically define the DHCP address pool using the `ip dhcp pool` *poolname* command. Once you enter this command, the router prompt will indicate that you have entered a DHCP sub-configuration mode that looks like the following:

```
CCNA2811(config)#ip dhcp pool examprep
CCNA2811(dhcp-config)#
```

EXAM ALERT

Make sure the interface is enabled and has an IP address assigned for DHCP to work properly.

Once in `dhcp-config`, you can specify the parameters that will be passed to the requesting clients. For instance, to define the IP network scope that the router will use when leasing IPs, you use the `network` command followed by the subnet (not single IP) and the subnet mask in decimal form:

```
CCNA2811(dhcp-config)#network 172.16.0.0 255.255.0.0
```

You can also use CIDR notation for the subnet mask as demonstrated here:

```
CCNA2811(dhcp-config)#network 172.16.0.0 /16
```

Now, when devices with DCHP enabled come online and send a DHCP request for an IP, the Cisco router will receive that information and respond with an IP from the 172.16.0.0 network. In addition it can also be configured to assign the default gateway (which is probably the router), the address of the DNS server, the domain name of the LAN, and specify the length of time the IP is leased by the client. The configurations for these parameters are as follows:

```
CCNA2811(dhcp-config)#default-router 172.16.100.1
CCNA2811(dhcp-config)#dns-server 172.16.100.50
CCNA2811(dhcp-config)#domain-name examprep.com
CCNA2811(dhcp-config)#lease 7 2 45
CCNA2811(dhcp-config)#exit
```

Given the preceding configuration, DHCP-enabled clients will be assigned to the examprep.com domain and have a default gateway of 172.16.100.1, use 172.16.100.50 as a DNS server to resolve domain names to IP, and DHCP lease of this information will last for 7 days, 2 hours, and 45 minutes.

Since we already statically assigned the IP address of 172.16.100.1 to our default gateway and 172.16.100.50 to our DNS server, we want to make sure the router does not assign these IP addresses to device or else it would cause an IP conflict in our network. To exclude an IP address or an IP address range, use the `ip dhcp excluded-address` *ip-address* in Global Configuration for a single IP or define a range of IPs using the same command but defining a start IP and end IP.

In our example, we want to exclude the IP's 172.16.100.1 and 172.16.100.50, so our configuration would look like:

```
CCNA2811(config)#ip dhcp excluded-address 172.16.100.1
CCNA2811(config)#ip dhcp excluded-address 172.16.100.50
```

If we used that 172.16.100.x range for other statically assigned devices, we could simply just exclude all IP addresses from 172.16.100.1 through 172.16.100.254 like this:

```
CCNA2811(config)#ip dhcp excluded-address 172.16.100.1 172.16.100.254
```

To verify what devices are assigned IP's from our router's address scope, use the show ip dhcp binding command:

```
CCNA2811#show ip dhcp binding
Bindings from all pools not associated with VRF:
IP address         Client-ID/          Lease expiration        Type
                   Hardware address/
                   User name
172.16.100.2       01e0.041f.a632.a2   Dec 27 2007 11:59 PM    Automatic
```

> **CAUTION**
>
> **DHCP Can Cause Router Amnesia**   When I say router amnesia, I am referring to the loss of memory that can occur when you enable DHCP, especially in larger networks. Since this service requires maintaining all the IP leases it administers, it is possible to consume all of your router's memory resources if your network is too large and you have a lengthy lease time. In other words, use this service sparingly if your network fits the small-to-medium sized mold. In addition, if you have not done so already, upgrade the router's memory to whatever level or whatever budget you can afford to help unburden some of the information it will need to retain when DHCP is enabled.

Some of you may be reading this DHCP functionality and realize that you do not need it because you already have a configured and fully functional DHCP server. The Cisco IOS also give you the option to configure your router's interfaces to be a DHCP client as well; allowing you to use your existing DHCP server and have it assign an IP address to your interface. The command to do this is similar to statically assigning an IP address to your interface, except you specify the keyword dhcp instead of an actual IP address:

```
CCNA2811(config)# interface FastEthernet 0/0
CCNA2811(config-if)# ip address dhcp
```

The address that is assigned to the router's interface cannot be seen by using the show running-config command since it is a temporary address. Instead, you can verify it by using the show dhcp lease command:

```
CCNA2811#show dhcp lease
Temp IP addr: 172.16.100.2 for peer on Interface: FastEthernet0
Temp  sub net mask: 255.255.0.0
   DHCP Lease server: 172.16.1.1, state: 3 Bound
   DHCP transaction id: 1967
   Lease: 16000 secs,  Renewal: 3000 secs,  Rebind: 16000 secs
Temp default-gateway addr: 172.16.1.1
   Next timer fires after: 00:00:32
   Retry count: 0   Client-ID: cisco-0019.e86a.6fc0-Vl1
   Hostname: CCNA2811
```

Chapter Summary

This chapter dealt with a plethora of commands and their respective syntaxes and outputs. In Global Configuration, you learned how to manipulate the startup process using either the `config-register` or `boot system` commands. Additionally, you saw how to use the `hostname` command to name your router or switch and how to create a message-of-the-day login banner with the `banner motd` command. To secure Privileged EXEC, you saw that the `enable password` command displays the password in clear text; however, the `enable secret` command encrypts the password using a one-way MD5 hash and overrides the `enable password` command if both are configured. For DNS-specific functions, you discovered that you can create static DNS entries with the `ip host` command or specify DNS servers using the `ip name-server` command.

In the line configuration for console, Telnet, and the aux port, you saw that you can configure a layer of security by having administrators enter a password to get into User EXEC. This was achieved by using the `login` and the `password` combo in the line configuration of each EXEC line. Additionally, you saw the utility of the `exec-timeout` command for changing the default timeout for an inactive EXEC session. Because these passwords are all in clear text, you can encrypt them in Global Configuration, using the `service password-encryption` command.

The configuration of interfaces entails assigning an IP address to a physical interface in a using the `ip address` command followed by the IP address and subnet mask or the keyword `dhcp` for dynamically assigned IP's by a DHCP server. One final imperative interface configuration step entails using the `no shutdown` command to administratively enable the interface.

You know from this chapter that the `copy` command can be used to meet several objectives such as saving the configuration, backing up and upgrading your IOS from a TFTP server, and backing up and restoring your configurations. You learned that the syntax of the `copy` command is copy from a source to a destination. The keywords you can use to identify the source and destination are `startup-config`, `running-config`, `tftp`, and `flash`.

To see your configurations, you now know that the `show running-config` command can show you the active configuration in RAM, and that `show startup-config` displays the configuration booted from NVRAM that you saved with the `copy running-config startup-config` command. For verification and viewing statistics of interfaces, you discovered that the `show interfaces` or the `show ip interface brief` command show you that the interface statues can be one of the following: up/line protocol up (active), up/line protocol down (Layer 2 down), down/line protocol down (Layer 1 down), administratively down/line protocol down (interface requires `no shutdown` command). What's more, the `show controller serial` command can show you whether the interface has the DTE or the DCE cable connected to it in a lab environment with a cross-over serial cable.

You can sleep better at night knowing now that your Cisco devices, by default, receive Layer 2 proprietary CDP multicast messages from directly connected Cisco devices that advertise the hostname, local and remote interfaces, capabilities, device model, and its hold-down time.

You saw these statistics by using the `show cdp neighbors` command; however, you also saw the IOS revision and the Layer 3 address of your neighbors by using the `show cdp neighbors detail` or `show cdp entry *` command. Disabling this useful utility was demonstrated with the `no cdp run` command in Global Configuration or `no cdp enable` in the interface configuration.

In this chapter, you also learned that you can Telnet into other devices from your Cisco router or switch. You suspended the Telnet session by using the **Ctrl+Shift+6, x** keystroke and verified that Telnet session by typing **show sessions**. Closing the Telnet session was achieved by typing **exit** or **logout** while in the active Telnet session, or **disconnect** followed by the connection number in the device where the Telnet originated.

Finally, we saw how Cisco routers have expanded their functionality beyond routing packets to include providing DHCP services for small-to-medium sized LANs. When DHCP-enabled clients send a DHCP request to the router, it responds with an IP address from its configured scope of IPs. In addition, the router can provide the address of the DNS server, default gateway, and the domain name of the LAN. To configure these parameters, you have to define the logical DHCP pool using the `ip dhcp pool pool_name` command, which will take you into a dhcp-config mode where you define the network and other parameters that will be passed to the clients.

Key Terms

- ▶ config-register *register*

- ▶ boot system *location filename*

- ▶ hostname *hostname*

- ▶ banner motd *delimiting_char banner delimiting_char*

- ▶ enable password *password*

- ▶ enable secret *password*

- ▶ service password-encryption

- ▶ ip host *hostname IP*

- ▶ ip name-server *dns_server_IP*

- ▶ ip domain-lookup

- ▶ login

- ▶ password *password*

- ▶ exec-timeout *minutes seconds*

- ▶ ip address *address subnet_mask*

- ▶ clock rate *speed(bps)*
- ▶ bandwidth *speed(kbps)*
- ▶ no shutdown
- ▶ copy *from* to
- ▶ erase startup-config
- ▶ show interfaces
- ▶ show ip interface brief
- ▶ show controller
- ▶ show flash
- ▶ show version
- ▶ show cdp neighbors
- ▶ show cdp neighbors detail
- ▶ cdp run
- ▶ cdp enable
- ▶ telnet *IP_address*
- ▶ Ctrl+Shift+6, x
- ▶ show sessions
- ▶ resume *conn#*
- ▶ disconnect *conn#*
- ▶ terminal monitor
- ▶ ping
- ▶ Destination Unreachable
- ▶ extended ping
- ▶ debug
- ▶ ip dhcp pool
- ▶ show ip dhcp bindings
- ▶ ip address dhcp
- ▶ show dhcp lease

Apply Your Knowledge

Exercises

8.1 Configuring a New Router

You are now onsite at the customer's location and it is time to prove your configuration skills by setting up their router with the following parameters. This exercise assumes you have a router that is not in production to utilize.

Estimated Time: 25 minutes

1. In Global Configuration, assign the hostname, CstmrARtr, create an appropriate login banner, and use the strongest encryption for access to Privileged EXEC with the password, giforgot.

2. In line configuration, secure Telnet and console access by using the password imnotsure.

3. For the LAN interface, assign the IP address of 172.16.31.17 /28 and enable the interface.

4. For the serial interface, assign the IP address of 192.168.1.17 /30 and enable the interface.

5. Verify the status of your interfaces by using the `show interfaces` and `show ip int brief`.

6. Verify your active configuration and save it to NVRAM.

That configuration should look similar to the following 2811 configuration:

```
Current configuration:
!
version 12.3
service timestamps debug uptime
service timestamps log uptime
no service password-encryption
!
hostname CstmrARtr
!
enable secret 5 $1$PHvQ$Gouu3MIDqY9G5d9hq9tr7/
!
boot-start-marker
boot-end-marker
!
memory-size iomem 15
no aaa new-model
ip subnet-zero
!
!
ip cef
!
```

```
!
interface FastEthernet0
 description /28 is 255.255.255.240 in decimal notation
 ip address 172.16.31.17 255.255.255.240
 no ip directed-broadcast
!
interface FastEthernet1
 no ip address
 no ip directed-broadcast
 shutdown
!
interface Serial0/0
 description /30 is 255.255.255.252 in decimal notation
 ip address 192.168.1.17 255.255.255.252
 no ip directed-broadcast
 no fair-queue
!
ip classless
!
banner motd ^C This is a private system and may be accessed only by authorized users.
? Unauthorized access is strictly prohibited and will be enforced to the full
? extent of the law.^C
!
line con 0
 exec-timeout 0 0
 password imnotsure
 login
 transport input none
line vty 0 4
 password imnotsure
 login
!
end
```

Review Questions

1. What is the purpose of configuring passwords on the line configurations?

2. What are the available keywords for the copy command?

3. How is CDP useful to a Cisco administrator?

4. What ICMP protocol commands can help you determine whether you have IP connectivity to a device?

5. What is the significance of x and y in the output of the show interfaces stats output: x/line protocol is y?

Exam Questions

1. You wish to assign the password Cisco to only the first Telnet line. What series of commands will achieve this?

   ○ **A.** `line vty 0 4, login, password Cisco`

   ○ **B.** `line vty 0, login, password cisco`

   ○ **C.** `line telnet 0, login, password Cisco`

   ○ **D.** `line vty 0, login, password Cisco`

2. You just issued the `show ip interface brief` command. You noticed that interface serial 0 is down/line protocol is up. What can be determined by this output?

   ○ **A.** Physical layer is up.

   ○ **B.** Data Link layer is down.

   ○ **C.** You cannot have a down/line protocol is up status.

   ○ **D.** The interface is active.

3. What are two commands that you can use to encrypt the password that allows you access into Privileged EXEC? (Choose two.)

   ○ **A.** `service password-encryption`

   ○ **B.** `enable secret_password`

   ○ **C.** `enable password password`

   ○ **D.** `encrypt enable password`

4. You copied and pasted a known working configuration from a text file into your new router via the terminal window; however, you do not have connectivity out all your interfaces. Why?

   ○ **A.** You have to use TFTP to copy a configuration.

   ○ **B.** The font in your text file was not Courier New.

   ○ **C.** You have to do a `no shutdown` on the interfaces.

   ○ **D.** The baud rate of your terminal program needs to be set to 38800.

5. What command shows you the configuration register?

   ○ **A.** `show version`

   ○ **B.** `show config-register`

   ○ **C.** `show interfaces`

   ○ **D.** `show flash`

6. You entered the following configuration in global config:

```
Router(config)#enable password cisco
Router(config)#enable secret giforgot
Router(config)#no enable secret giforgot
```

What will happen when you log out and try to re-enter Privileged EXEC?

- ○ **A.** There will be no password.
- ○ **B.** The password will be *cisco*.
- ○ **C.** The password will be *giforgot*.
- ○ **D.** Both passwords will work.

7. Which of the following commands does not close a Telnet session?

- ○ **A.** `exit`
- ○ **B.** `disconnect`
- ○ **C.** `Ctrl+Shift+6, x`
- ○ **D.** `logout`

8. Given the partial configuration output,

```
interface FastEthernet0
 description /28 is 255.255.255.240 in decimal notation
 ip address 172.16.31.17 255.255.255.240
 shutdown
```

Which of the following would you see when you issue the `show ip interface brief` command?

- ○ **A.** FastEthernet 0   172.16.31.17... up   up
- ○ **B.** FastEthernet 0   172.16.31.17... up   down
- ○ **C.** FastEthernet 0   172.16.31.17... down   up
- ○ **D.** FastEthernet 0   172.16.31.17... administratively down down

9. Given the following output, what can be determined about this interface? (Choose two.)

```
FastEthernet0/0 is up, line protocol is up
  Hardware is AmdFE, address is 0003.e32a.4080 (bia 0003.e32a.4080)
  Internet address is 172.16.1.1/16
  MTU 1500 bytes, BW 100000 Kbit, DLY 100 usec,
     reliablility 255/255, txload 235/255, rxload 235/255
  Encapsulation ARPA, loopback not set
  Keepalive set (10 sec)
  Half-duplex, 100Mb/s, 100BaseTX/FX
```

```
ARP type: ARPA, ARP Timeout 04:00:00
Last input never, output 00:00:10, output hang never
Last clearing of "show interface" counters never
Queueing strategy: fifo
Output queue 0/40, 0 drops; input queue 0/75, 0 drops
5 minute input rate 0 bits/sec, 0 packets/sec
5 minute output rate 0 bits/sec, 0 packets/sec
   0 packets input, 0 bytes
   Received 0 broadcasts, 0 runts, 0 giants, 0 throttles
   0 input errors, 0 CRC, 0 frame, 0 overrun, 0 ignored
   0 watchdog, 0 multicast
   0 input packets with dribble condition detected
   31 packets output, 2673 bytes, 0 underruns
   0 output errors, 0 collisions, 1 interface resets
   0 babbles, 156848 late collision, 0 deferred
   0 lost carrier, 0 no carrier
   0 output buffer failures, 0 output buffers swapped out
```

- ○ **A.** There is a duplex mismatch.
- ○ **B.** The administrator needs to do a no shutdown on this interface.
- ○ **C.** The bandwidth is incorrect.
- ○ **D.** This link is congested.

10. Given the following output, how can you reconnect to Telnet session 2? (Choose two.)

```
CCNA2811#show sessions
Conn   Host                 Address           Idle  Conn Name
1      131.108.100.152      131.108.100.152   0     131.108.100.152
*2     126.102.57.63        126.102.57.63     0     126.102.57.63
```

- ○ **A.** disconnect 2
- ○ **B.** Enter
- ○ **C.** Ctrl+Shift+6, *x*
- ○ **D.** resume 2
- ○ **E.** logout

11. Which of the following is not a necessary step in copying configuration and IOS files to and from your Cisco router and switch and a local TFTP server?

- ○ **A.** The TFTP server software must be running.
- ○ **B.** Your router should be directly connected with a straight-through cable.
- ○ **C.** Your interface must be on the same subnet as the TFTP server.
- ○ **D.** You should test whether you have IP connectivity by pinging the server from your router.

12. What command assigns the last IP address in the 10th subnet of the network 192.168.100.0/29? Zero subnets are allowed.

   ○ **A.** `ip address 192.168.100.80 255.255.255.240`

   ○ **B.** `ip address 192.168.100.79 255.255.255.248`

   ○ **C.** `ip address 192.168.100.70 255.255.255.240`

   ○ **D.** `ip address 192.168.100.73 255.255.255.248`

   ○ **E.** `ip address 192.168.100.78 255.255.255.248`

13. Given the following output,

```
Router>show flash
System flash directory:
File   Length   Name/status
  1    5510192  c2800-is-mz.123-3.T3.bin
[5510256 bytes used, 2878352 available, 8388608 total]
8192K bytes of processor board System flash (Read/Write)
```

What is the command used and what will be the outcome of upgrading to a 7KB IOS file from a TFTP server?

   ○ **A.** `copy tftp ios`, the current IOS file will be erased.

   ○ **B.** `copy flash tftp`, the current IOS will be unchanged.

   ○ **C.** `copy tftp flash`, the current IOS file will be erased.

   ○ **D.** `copy tftp flash`, the new IOS file is too large and it will go into ROMmom.

Answers to Review Questions

1. The password configurations on the terminal lines serve as a way to protect your router or switch from anyone gaining access to User EXEC.

2. The `copy` command tells the Cisco device to copy a file from somewhere to somewhere. The available keyword options for the `copy` command are `startup-config`, `running-config`, `tftp`, and `flash`.

3. CDP enables Cisco administrators to gain information from directly connected Cisco devices without requiring that they be connected with a terminal session. The `show cdp neighbors detail` or `show cdp entry *` command displays the Layer 3 address and the IOS version of the neighbors.

4. `ping` and `traceroute` use ICMP to test IP connectivity. `ping` tests if one device has connectivity to another device. `traceroute` displays the path the packets take to reach the destination. `traceroute` is useful for determining faulty routers along the path to the destination.

5. Given the `show interfaces` output x/line protocol is y, x represents the Physical layer status of the interface. y represents the Data Link layer status.

Answers to Exam Questions

1. **D**. To assign a login prompt and password for only the first vty line, you have to navigate to line vty 0. Answer A is incorrect because `line vty 0 4` is configuring all five vty lines. B has the correct navigation; however, the password is case sensitive. C is incorrect because the navigation to enter the Telnet lines is `line vty 0`.

2. **C**. The first part of the `show ip interface brief` command represents the status of the Physical layer, followed by the Data Link layer status. It is impossible to have this output because you cannot have Layer 2 without Layer 1 functionality. Answer A is incorrect because the Physical layer represented on the left side of the forward slash is down. B is also false because the Data Link layer represented on the right side of the forward slash is up. D is incorrect because an active interface is up/line protocol is up.

3. **A, B**. The `enable secret` command encrypts the password with a one-way MD5 hash. The `service password-encryption` encrypts the `enable password` command and all other clear text passwords. C is incorrect because the command does not encrypt the password. D is not a valid command.

4. **C**. The configuration was saved to Notepad through the use of the `show running-config` command and copied from the terminal window into the file. The problem that occurs is that the `no shutdown` command does not display in the configuration, which means when the configuration is pasted back into a new router, the interfaces are still administratively shut. A is incorrect because you do not require TFTP to copy configurations that are saved in a text file on your computer. B is false because the font is not essential. D is incorrect because the baud rate does not need to be changed.

5. **A**. `show version` displays the current configuration at the bottom of the command output. Answer B is incorrect because the command does not exist. Answers C and D are valid commands, but they will not display the configuration register.

6. **B**. If the `enable secret` and `enable password` command are in the same configuration, `enable secret` overrides `enable password`. However, the example removed the `enable secret` command, leaving only `enable password` left in the configuration. Thus, the password to get into Privileged EXEC is *cisco*. A is incorrect because the `enable password` command was not removed. C and D are incorrect because the `enable secret` password was removed from the configuration.

7. **C**. Ctrl+Shift+6, x suspends the Telnet session. Answers A, B, and D are incorrect because those commands will actually disconnect the Telnet session.

8. **D**. Because the interface configuration is configured in a shutdown state, the interface status should report the fast ethernet interface as administratively down/line protocol is down. Answers A, B, and C are incorrect because a shutdown interface does not have the Physical layer or the Data Link layer in an up state.

9. **A, D**. Because there is an excessive number of late collisions in the output, it is safe to assume that there is a duplex mismatch. Also, the link is 92% congested as indicated by the load statements (235/255). B is incorrect because the interface status is up/line protocol is up. C is incorrect because the bandwidth is accurate for a FastEthernet interface.

10. **B, D.** You can resume the suspended Telnet sessions in this device by hitting the Enter key or typing the keyword, `resume`. Answers A and E disconnect the Telnet session and C suspends it.

11. **B.** If connecting directly to a TFTP server from a router, you must use a cross-over cable. Answers A, C, and D are necessary steps to copy files to and from a TFTP server.

12. **E.** With a /29 or 255.255.255.248 subnet, the increment of these subnets is 8. Starting with 0, counting 10 networks gives you a Network/Subnet identifier of 192.168.100.72 (0,8,16,24,32,40,48,56,64,72). The last IP address in that subnet is 192.168.100.78. Answer A is a network ID and the wrong subnet mask. Answer B is the broadcast address for that subnet. Answer C is that last IP address in ninth subnet with the wrong subnet mask. D is the first valid IP address in that subnet.

13. **C.** The command to upload your IOS from a TFTP server is `copy tftp flash`. Given the `show flash` output, there is not enough space for another 7KB file, so the current IOS file will be erased during the copy process, after which the actual download of the new IOS will occur. Answer A is incorrect because the `ios` keyword does not exist. B is false because there is not enough room in Flash for both files, so the current IOS is will be erased.

Suggested Readings and Resources

1. Odom, Wendell. *CCENT/CCNA ICND1 Official Exam Certification Guide (CCENT Exam 640-822 and CCNA Exam 640-802)*, 2nd Edition, Cisco Press Publishing, 2007.

2. Boney, James. *Cisco IOS in a Nutshell*, O'Reilly Publishing, 2001.

3. "Configuration Fundamentals Command Reference," www.cisco.com.

CHAPTER NINE

Understanding the Cisco SDM

Objective

This chapter covers the following Cisco-specified objective for the "Implement an IP addressing scheme and IP services to meet network requirements for a small branch office" section of the 640-822 ICND1 exam:

▶ **Configure, verify, and troubleshoot DHCP and DNS operation on a router (including: CLI/SDM)**

Outline

Introduction	296	Monitoring	310
Getting Started	296	Chapter Summary	312
		Key Terms	312
Global Configurations	298		
Changing the Hostname, Banner, Domain Name, and Secret Password	299	Apply Your Knowledge	312
Router Access	303	Exercise	312
DNS	304	Review Questions	312
DHCP	305	Exam Questions	313
		Answers to Review Questions	315
Router Interface Configurations	308	Answers to Exam Questions	316
Assigning an IP Address	308	Suggested Readings and Resources	316
Enabling the Interface	309		
Saving and Verifying Your Configurations	310		

Study Strategies

▶ Practice using the SDM in a lab environment.

▶ Learn how to set up basic router operation on an SDM-capable device.

Introduction

The Cisco Security Device Manager (SDM) is a web-based tool that was developed by Cisco for its IOS software-based routers. The SDM tool gives users the option to configure and monitor a router without using CLI. Chapter 8, "Foundation Cisco Configurations," covers a large number of CLI commands. This chapter reviews how to use the SDM tool for router configuration, verification, and monitoring from a web browser.

Getting Started

Only certain router models with more current IOS versions support SDM. For a complete list of router models and supported IOS versions, check http://www.cisco.com. This chapter demonstrates the SDM using a Cisco 851W router. This model router comes from Cisco with a "Cisco Router and Security Device Manager" CD. Cisco SDM Express is also installed on the router flash. If you are uncertain whether SDM is installed on the router flash, you can open a web browser and enter http://*insert router IP address here* in the address field to see if the SDM page loads. Note that a prerequisite to using SDM is an IP-configured interface that is in an administratively up/up state. This means that you need to manually configure that interface with an IP address and subnet mask and perform a `no shut` command before SDM will work. While you are logged into the router manually, also add the command `ip https` to allow for browser connectivity. Finally, ensure that the router does not have an access list in place that blocks the incoming HTTPS connection. Other outside factors might also prevent SDM from loading properly, such as services or Java plugins on the connected computer.

Figure 9.1 shows the welcome page that loads when you open the Cisco Router and Security Device Manager CD.

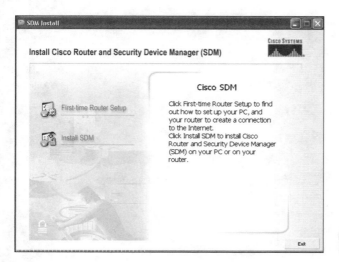

FIGURE 9.1 Install Cisco Router and Security Device Manager (SDM).

From this screen, you can choose First-time Router Setup or Install SDM. Figure 9.2 explains First-time Router Setup. If SDM is not already installed, you go through the step in First-time Router Setup and then choose Install SDM.

FIGURE 9.2   Install Cisco Router and Security Device Manager (SDM): First-time Router Setup.

If you click First-time Router Setup, you are routed to an HTML file with detailed connection instructions. There is also a drop-down box where you may select the router model for more specific model details, as shown in Figure 9.3. The drop-down box shows models 831, 836, and 837, but selecting this option also works for the 851 model router.

FIGURE 9.3   First-time Router Setup: Select your router.

After you have successfully connected to the SDM, a separate window opens, as shown in Figure 9.4.

FIGURE 9.4   Cisco Router and Security Device Manager (SDM): Home.

As you can see in Figure 9.4, the SDM home page has clickable buttons across the top labeled Home, Configure, Monitor, Refresh, Save, Search, and Help. Two sections display general router information. The top section, About Your Router, shows basic hardware and software details about the router. The bottom section, Configuration Overview, is broken into four subcategories: Interfaces and Connections, Firewall Policies, VPN, and Routing. As you make configuration changes to the router, the relevant fields are updated with the new information. Let's move on and make some configuration changes on the router.

Global Configurations

Objective:

▶ Configure, verify, and troubleshoot DHCP and DNS operation on a router (including: CLI/SDM)

To begin router configurations, click the Configure button at the top of the Home page. Figure 9.5 shows the main Configure page of the SDM. The Configure tab has a vertical sidebar with more clickable options that are called Tasks. They include Interfaces and

Connections, Firewall and ACL, VPN, Security Audit, Routing, NAT, Intrusion Prevention, Quality of Service, NAC, and Additional Tasks.

FIGURE 9.5   Configure Interfaces and Connections.

Changing the Hostname, Banner, Domain Name, and Secret Password

From the Configure page, click Additional Tasks in the left vertical sidebar. The Additional Tasks page opens, as shown in Figure 9.6. It has a list of additional tasks and a list of device properties. When expanded, Router Properties shows a few configurable items, including hostname, domain name, banner, and the enable secret password.

Double-click any of the item names to open a new window, as shown in Figure 9.7. Here you can change the router's hostname, domain name, banner, and secret password all in one window.

This window has two tabs. On the Device tab, click in each field and enter the desired Host (hostname), Domain (domain name), and Banner (message of the day). Figure 9.8 shows a sample configuration.

FIGURE 9.6 Configure, Additional Tasks.

FIGURE 9.7 The Device Properties window.

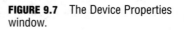

Device Properties

Device | Secret Password

Set the host name and Domain name for the device

Host: CCNAPrep

Domain: examprep.com   ex: cisco.com

Enter the text for Banner (Message of the Day)

This is a private system and may be accessed only by author

OK | Cancel | Help

FIGURE 9.8 Hostname, domain, and banner configuration.

Click the Secret Password tab, shown in Figure 9.9, and enter a new password twice. Note that the window represents your password with asterisks.

Device Properties

Device | **Secret Password**

Current Password: <none>

Enter New Password: ****************

Re-Enter New Password: ****************

OK | Cancel | Help

FIGURE 9.9 Secret password configuration.

After you have entered a new hostname, domain name, banner, and enable secret password, click OK at the bottom of the window. The SDM automatically sends the new configuration commands to the router, as shown in Figure 9.10. Click OK again to close that window and return to the Additional Tasks page.

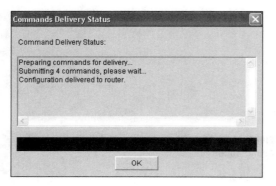

FIGURE 9.10   Commands Delivery Status window.

If you return to the Home page at this point, you see your router's new hostname in the top-right corner, as shown in Figure 9.11. You can also click the View Running Config button to see the current configuration of your router.

FIGURE 9.11   Home page with a new hostname.

Challenge

From the Cisco SDM, configure the following information on the router:

Host: CCNAPrep

Domain: examprep.com

Banner: This is a private system and may be accessed only by authorized users. Unauthorized access is strictly prohibited and will be enforced to the full extent of the law.

Secret Password: mysecretpassword

NOTE

After you click OK, the router prompts you to enter the new secret password information. Leave the user-name field blank, and enter your secret password to keep the SDM session connected.

Router Access

There is another way to configure username and password information using the SDM. On the Additional Tasks page, click Router Access to see what options can be configured using this tool, as shown in Figure 9.12.

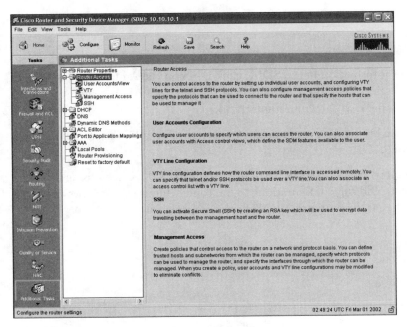

FIGURE 9.12 Configure, Additional Tasks, Router Access.

Click User Accounts/View. You see a line item with the secret password entry you created in the preceding section with a privilege level of 15 and a username of cisco. If the line item is highlighted, click the Edit option in the top right of the window. You now have the option to change the username, password, and privilege level of this account, as shown in Figure 9.13.

FIGURE 9.13   Edit a username.

DNS

To configure DNS server information in the SDM, click DNS on the Additional Tasks page. In the DNS Properties section, click the Edit button at the top right of the page. A separate DNS Properties window opens, as shown in Figure 9.14.

Click the Add button in the DNS properties window to open the Add a DNS server IP address window, shown in Figure 9.15.

In this window, you can input the DNS server IP address and click OK. Click OK again in the DNS properties window to add the configurations to the router. Figure 9.16 shows the DNS properties section with the newly configured DNS server information.

FIGURE 9.14 Configure, Additional Tasks, DNS.

FIGURE 9.15 Add a DNS server IP address window.

DHCP

From the Additional Tasks page, you can also add a DHCP pool to the router. Click DHCP to see the two options for DHCP configurations: DHCP Pools and DHCP Bindings (see Figure 9.17).

In the DHCP drop-down menu, click DHCP Pools, and then click the Add button at the top right of the page. A separate window called Add DHCP Pool opens, as shown in Figure 9.17. The DHCP Pool Name, DHCP Pool Network, Subnet mask, Starting IP, and Ending IP fields are mandatory. The Lease Length section is automatically filled in by the SDM, but you can change it to meet your individual requirements. The remaining fields are optional. Figure 9.18 shows the Add DHCP Pool with the fields filled in for a sample configuration.

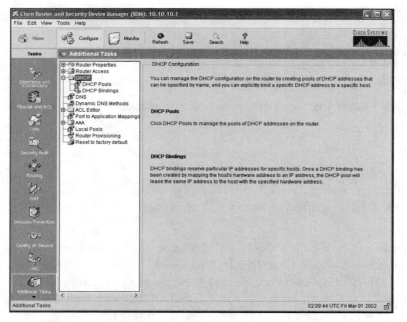

FIGURE 9.16 DNS properties with a new DNS server.

FIGURE 9.17 Configure, Additional Tasks, DHCP.

FIGURE 9.18 Add DHCP Pool window.

As soon as all of the parameters are filled in to your business specifications, click the OK button to configure the router. Figure 9.19 shows the DHCP Pools section with the newly configured DHCP pool properties.

FIGURE 9.19 DHCP Pools with a new DHCP pool configuration.

Router Interface Configurations

To configure router interfaces, you must be in the Configure tab of the SDM. On the left vertical sidebar, click Interfaces and Connections. This is the first option listed under Tasks. The two tabs on this page are Create Connection and Edit Interface/Connection. Click Edit Interface/Connections to see all of the interfaces that are set up on the router and their current status, as shown in Figure 9.20.

FIGURE 9.20   Configure, Interfaces and Connections, Edit Interface/Connection.

Assigning an IP Address

To assign an IP address to another interface, you can double-click the interface name to open another configuration window. On interfaces where an IP address assignment is applicable, this window includes tabs for Connection, Association, NAT, General, and QoS. The Connection tab shows the current IP address information (if any) of the interface, which you can change. Figure 9.21 shows the configuration window for interface Fast Ethernet 4. The router is configured with a static IP address of 10.10.10.1 and a subnet mask of 255.255.255.0.

FIGURE 9.21 Interface Feature Edit Dialog - FastEthernet4.

Enabling the Interface

If you look back at the top right of Figure 9.20, you see an option to Disable interface Fast Ethernet 4. If you click an interface where the status is currently Down, such as the high-lighted interface in Figure 9.22, you can Enable the interface from the SDM.

FIGURE 9.22 Configure, Interfaces and Connections, Edit Interface/Connection, Enable.

Saving and Verifying Your Configurations

After any router configuration changes, you *must* save the configuration by clicking the Save button. The SDM asks if you are sure about the save and then sends a `copy running-config startup-config` command to the router. As soon as the save is complete, the bottom of the SDM shows this message: "Running config copied successfully to Startup Config of your router." To verify your router configuration, return to the Home page of the SDM. Click the View Running Config button to open the Show Running Configuration window, as shown in Figure 9.23.

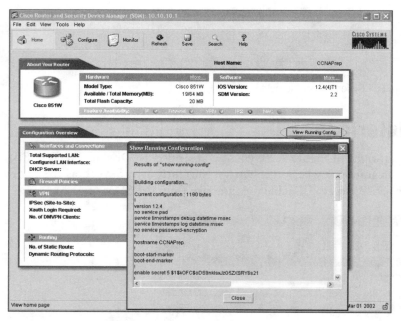

FIGURE 9.23   Show Running Configuration window.

Monitoring

Cisco SDM also offers device monitoring, which you can access by clicking the Monitor tab at the top of the page. The sidebar shows seven monitoring options (see Figure 9.24): Overview, Interface Status, Firewall Status, VPN Status, QoS Status, NAC Status, and Logging. As we discussed in Chapter 4, "General Network Security," logging is an important security feature on a network device. CPU, Memory, and Flash usage are shown in this view.

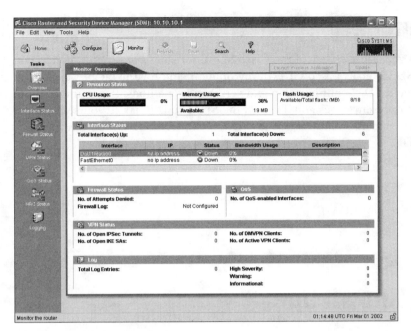

FIGURE 9.24 Monitor Overview page.

Chapter Summary

Now that you've seen a general overview of the Cisco SDM, for supported router models you can choose to use the SDM versus Cisco CLI. In my opinion, and for the CCNA exam, you should know both CLI and SDM configuration and verification methods. I encourage you to continue navigating the different pages and Tasks in the SDM to familiarize yourself with all available tools. If you are uncertain how to use an SDM Task, try the Help button for additional details and tutorials.

Key Terms

- ▶ Security Device Manager (SDM)
- ▶ Command-line interface (CLI)

Apply Your Knowledge

Exercise

9.1 SDM Configuration

The best way to learn SDM is to keep practicing the configurations on a test router. In this Exercise, configure the WAN interface on your router for the following IP address and subnet mask:

IP address: 192.168.1.1

Subnet mask: 255.255.255.0

Be sure to log back into the SDM with your new IP address!

Estimated Time: 5 minutes

Review Questions

1. What is the Cisco SDM?

2. What are the ten tasks listed in the vertical sidebar of the SDM?

3. What four properties can be configured in the Router Properties section of the SDM?

4. What options can be configured in the Router Access portion of the SDM?

5. What steps would you take to configure the WAN IP address on a router using SDM?

Exam Questions

For questions 1 through 5, refer to Figure 9.25.

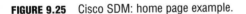

FIGURE 9.25 Cisco SDM: home page example.

1. What is the router's hostname?

   ○ **A.** Router

   ○ **B.** CCNA

   ○ **C.** CCNAPrep

   ○ **D.** CCNA851

2. From the home page of the Cisco SDM, what would you click to see the router's running configuration?

   ○ **A.** Configure

   ○ **B.** View Running Config

   ○ **C.** Monitor

   ○ **D.** Search

3. Which feature is not available on the router shown in Figure 9.25?

   ○ **A.** IP

   ○ **B.** Firewall

   ○ **C.** VPN

   ○ **D.** IPS

4. From the home page of the Cisco SDM, what would you click to configure the router's hostname?

   ○ **A.** Configure

   ○ **B.** View Running Config

   ○ **C.** Monitor

   ○ **D.** Search

5. To send a `copy running-config startup-config` command to the router with the SDM, which button would you click?

   ○ **A.** Configure

   ○ **B.** Monitor

   ○ **C.** Refresh

   ○ **D.** Save

6. How would you navigate the SDM to find and enable an interface?

   ○ **A.** Configure, Interfaces and Connections

   ○ **B.** Configure, Additional Tasks, Router Properties

   ○ **C.** Configure, Additional Tasks, Router Access

   ○ **D.** Configure, Interfaces and Connections, Edit Interface Connections

7. The Monitor screen on the SDM gives statistics for what three types of usage?

   ○ **A.** Memory

   ○ **B.** CPU

   ○ **C.** Disk Activity

   ○ **D.** Flash

8. Which of the following is configured from Router Properties?

   ○ **A.** IP Address

   ○ **B.** DHCP

   ○ **C.** SNMP

   ○ **D.** Secret Password

9. What privilege level is assigned to an account that is given a secret password?

    ○ **A.** 15

    ○ **B.** 10

    ○ **C.** 5

    ○ **D.** 0

10. User accounts can be added and edited in which section of the SDM?

    ○ **A.** Router Properties

    ○ **B.** Router Access

    ○ **C.** ACL Editor

    ○ **D.** DHCP

Answers to Review Questions

1. The Cisco Security Device Manager (SDM) is a web-based tool that Cisco developed for its IOS software-based routers. SDM allows users to configure and monitor a router without using CLI.

2. Interfaces and Connections
   Firewall and ACL
   VPN
   Security Audit
   Routing
   NAT
   Intrusion Prevention
   Quality of Service
   NAC
   Additional Tasks

3. Host Name
   Domain Name
   Banner (Message of the Day)
   Secret Password

4. User Accounts
   VTY Line Configuration
   SSH
   Management Access

5. From the Home page, select Configure, Interfaces and Connections, Edit Interface/Connection and then double-click the WAN interface. On the Connection tab, select static or dynamic IP address and enter the IP address and subnet mask.

Answers to Exam Questions

1. **C.** The hostname of the router shown is CCNAPrep.

2. **B.** To see the running configuration of your router, click View Running Config.

3. **D.** IPS has a red circle with an X next to it, indicating that it is unavailable on this router. Answers A, B, and C are incorrect because they have a green circle with a check mark, indicating that these are available features on the router.

4. **A.** To get to router configuration options, the best answer to this question is to click the Configure button. Answer B is incorrect because it shows the router's running configuration. Answers C and D are incorrect because they do not allow for device configuration.

5. **D.** With SDM, you click the Save button to send a `copy running-config startup-config` command to the router.

6. **D.** To find and enable an interface, you need to select Configure, Interfaces and Connections, Edit Interface Connections. Answer A is incorrect because it does not continue to the Edit Interface Connections tab. Answers B and C are incorrect because they refer to sections of the SDM that are used for general router properties or router access configurations.

7. **A, B, D.** The Monitor screen gives statistics on memory, CPU, and flash usage.

8. **D.** The secret password is configured in the Router Properties section of the SDM. Answer A is incorrect because the IP address is configured in the Interfaces and Connections section. Answers B and C are incorrect because they are not configured from Router Properties.

9. **A.** A secret password is given a privilege level of 15.

10. **B.** User accounts can be added and edited in the Router Access section of the SDM. Answer A is incorrect because it can only be used to add a secret password on the router. Answers C and D are also incorrect because they are not used to configure user accounts.

Suggested Readings and Resources

The following is recommended reading for general network security and related terminology:

1. "Cisco Router and Security Device Manager Q&A," http://www.cisco.com/en/US/products/sw/secursw/ps5318/products_qanda_item0900aecd800fd11b.shtml.

CHAPTER TEN

Introduction to Routing and Routing Protocols

Objectives

This chapter covers the following Cisco-specified objective for the "Describe the operation of data networks," and "Implement a small routed network" sections of the 640-822 ICND1 exam:

▶ **Determine the path between two hosts across a network**

▶ **Describe basic routing concepts (including: packet forwarding, router lookup process)**

▶ **Perform and verify routing configuration tasks for a static or default route given specific routing requirements**

▶ **Verify network status and router operation using basic utilities (including: ping, traceroute, telnet, SSH, arp, ipconfig), SHOW & DEBUG commands**

Outline

Introduction   320

The Default Gateway   320
  Verifying and Troubleshooting the Default
    Gateway   322

Routing Sources   323
  Administrative Distance   324

Static Routes   325
  Configuring Static Routes   326
  Floating Static Routes   327

Default Routes   328

Configuring Static and Default Routes
  with SDM   329

Verifying Static and Default Routes   330
  Dynamic Routing Protocols   331
  Routing Metrics   332
  Classful and Classless Routing Updates   333
  VLSM   336

Route Summarization   338
Interior and Exterior Gateway Routing
  Protocols   340
Distance Vector Routing Protocols   340
Link-State Routing Protocols   341
Advanced Distance Vector/Hybrid
  Routing Protocols   341

The Routing Table Revisited   342

Routing Redistribution   343

Chapter Summary   345
  Key Terms   346

Apply Your Knowledge   347
  Exercises   347
  Review Questions   348
  Exam Questions   348
  Answers to Review Questions   351
  Answers to Exam Questions   351
  Suggested Readings and Resources   353

Study Strategies

▶ Read the information presented in the chapter, paying special attention to tables, Notes, and Exam Alerts.

▶ Because routing is a method of passing IP packets along to Layer 3 forwarding devices, take the perspective of the routing devices as it receives the packet and try to determine the information required to send it on to the next forwarding device.

▶ Complete the Challenge and the Exercises at the end of the chapter. The exercises will solidify the concepts that you have learned in the previous sections.

▶ This chapter involves several mathematical challenges that are based on the subnetting foundations learned in Chapter 5, "Implementing IP Addressing." If necessary, review those concepts before tackling this chapter.

▶ Complete the Exam Questions at the end of the chapter. They are designed to simulate the types of questions you will be asked on the CCNA, ICND1, and ICND2 exams.

Introduction

So far, we have delved into many configurations of our routers that cover the administrative aspects of managing the device and providing basic connectivity. Don't forget, however, that the routers were originally designed and created to do one main function. To give you a hint, the function is in its name.

Recall that Layer 3 is responsible for determining the best path to a network, using logical addressing such as IP addresses. This chapter discusses the fundamentals of how Layer 3 devices such as routers and Layer 3 switches develop the routing logic to determine where to forward IP packets to reach a destination network.

The Default Gateway

Objective:

▶ Determine the path between two hosts across a network

To fully comprehend the routing of data, it helps to start where much of the data in a network originates: the computer. As application data is sent down the protocol stack, the source and destination IP addresses are added to the IP header. If the destination IP address is located on the same IP subnet as that on which the computer is, the computer adds the destination MAC address of that device at Layer 2 and sends it on the wire.

In instances where the destination IP address is on a remote network, it must send that traffic to a router on its segment that can forward the packet toward the destination network. Although you will forward traffic to this default gateway, the destination IP address remains unchanged. However, at Layer 2, the destination MAC address of the Ethernet frame reflects the default gateway's MAC address because this is the forwarding device on the local data link segment.

In the example illustrated in Figure 10.1, the PC sends traffic to the server on the remote 10.1.34.0 network. The source IP address and MAC address are those matching the PC. On the other hand, the Layer 3 destination IP address of the IP packet reflects the IP address of the server (10.1.34.101). Because the destination IP address does not exist on the PC's local subnet of 192.168.1.0, the PC encapsulates the router's Fast Ethernet 0/0 MAC at Layer 2 because that is the configured default gateway for this segment. The switch in this scenario is operating as only a Layer 2 switch. Thus, despite having an IP address for management, this is not the default gateway for this segment because it is only forwarding frames at Layer 2.

FIGURE 10.1   Default gateway example.

When the router receives the frame addressed to its interface MAC, it processes the Layer 3 information and consults its routing logic to determine whether it knows where to route the packet. Because the destination network is attached to the router, it knows to send the packet out its Fast Ethernet 0/1 interface. A new Ethernet frame using its Fast Ethernet 0/1 MAC address (1243 523F A26C) for the source MAC address and the server's MAC address (A345 764C F234) as the destination MAC are added to the original IP data as it is sent out to the destination segment.

Verifying and Troubleshooting the Default Gateway

Objectives:

▶ Verify network status and router operation using basic utilities (including: ping, traceroute, telnet, SSH, arp, ipconfig), SHOW & DEBUG commands

Suppose that in Figure 10.1 the traffic was a ping packet to test connectivity to the remote computer. If for some reason that ping failed, you would need to determine where the problem occurred. One method of testing the failure would be to make sure that you have connectivity to and from the originating PC and the default gateway.

The default gateway on a computer can be assigned manually in the operating system or dynamically from a DHCP server. To ensure that the local computer has its IP and default gateway configured correctly, you need to look at the local PC's configuration. This step differs depending on the operating system installed on the originating computer. Let's assume for this example that the computer is using Windows as its operating system. You would need to go to a command prompt and enter `ipconfig` to see how the computer's interface(s) are configured for IP. In Figure 10.2, you can see from the output on the computer that the computer has been dynamically assigned an IP address of 192.168.1.2 and a subnet mask of 255.255.255.0. Notice also that the default gateway is also configured correctly, pointing to the local router's Fast Ethernet 0/0 IP address of 192.168.1.1.

FIGURE 10.2 Windows computer gateway verification.

To seal the troubleshooting deal, notice that we went so far as to verify that the computer has a correct IP-to-MAC address binding for the default gateway by issuing the arp -a command from the command prompt to display the computer's ARP table. You can see from the output that the default gateway's IP address of 192.168.1.1 does correspond to its Fast Ethernet 0/0 MAC address. This ARP entry will continue to remain in the computer's volatile memory as long as it keeps getting used. If no packets are sent to this address for 5 minutes (default), the ARP entry is removed. If you want to manually clear your ARP table on your computer (useful in cases where you recently changed your default gateway), the command is `arp-d` followed by the IP address or a wildcard (*) to delete all ARP entries.

Seeing that the configuration of the originating PC is correct, next we should see if we have IP connectivity to the router's Fast Ethernet interfaces. Because this is a small network, we can simply ping those IP addresses. In larger networks with many routers in between, it might be administratively easier to do a traceroute (the `tracert` command in Windows) to discover at what point along the routed path the ICMP packet fails.

So what happens if we can ping the two interfaces? At this point, we know that a packet can traverse our network, reach the default gateway, and exit the router's remote network interface. The only culprit left is the remote PC. It is a pretty sure bet that the remote computer must have an interface problem or configuration error. Keep in mind that it too must return that packet to our network. Therefore, the remote computer must also have a default gateway configured so that it can return that packet to its remote network. Using the same steps as we used for the originating computer, we should be able to determine exactly what is causing this computer to not successfully return packets to our computer.

Routing Sources

Objective:

▶ Describe basic routing concepts (including: packet forwarding, router lookup process)

Routers are methodical, tactless devices in that they do not necessarily care about the individual IP addresses that exist on a subnet. Their sole obsession is to maintain their routing logic by keeping track of the networks that exist and which interfaces to use to send the traffic if an IP packet is destined for that network. By using routing devices to relay packets out of their interfaces to other forwarding devices or the destination network, the IP packet eventually reaches the destination.

At the heart of the routing logic for Layer 3 devices is the routing table. This table, located in volatile RAM, contains a mapping of all the best routes to networks that the router is aware of and the interfaces to exit to reach those networks. So how is the router aware of these networks? Generally, three routing sources can feed the routing table with this information:

▶ **Connected interfaces:** As soon as you assign an IP address to a working (up/line protocol up) interface, the router associates the entire subnet of the interface's IP address in the routing table.

▶ **Static routes:** These are manual entries that an administrator enters into the configuration to specify the destination network and the next hop (router along the destination path).

▶ **Routing protocols:** Protocols exchanged between routing devices to dynamically advertise networks.

Connected interfaces remain in the routing tables as long as the interface is active and has a valid IP address assigned to it. Static routes remain in the table as long as you do not remove the static route configuration and the next hop is valid (the interface to the next hop is up). Networks learned from dynamic routing protocols remain in the routing table as long as the next hop is valid and the routing devices do not stop hearing the network(s) being advertised from the neighbor routers.

Administrative Distance

Now that you are aware of the multiple sources of routing information, you must consider a feasible anomaly that could occur with your routing sources. Namely, if you have several sources of information such as connected interfaces, static routes, and multiple routing protocols, which one are you to trust when more than one source advertises the same network? For example, if a router learns about the 192.168.1.0/24 network from a routing protocol and a static route, how does the router decide which entry to place into its routing table?

The answer lies within a program logic in the IOS called the *administrative distance*. The administrative distances are values between 1 and 255 that are assigned to routing information sources. These values represent a level of trustworthiness of the information source, in which lower administrative distances are preferred over higher ones.

> **NOTE**
>
> The administrative distance applies only when multiple sources are advertising exactly the same subnet.

Table 10.1 lists the Cisco IOS default administrative distances for some of the routing sources.

TABLE 10.1   Default Administrative Distances

Routed Source	Default Distance
Connected	0
Static route	1
EIGRP (internal)	90
OSPF	110
RIPv1 and v2	120
EIGRP (external)	170

It should come as no shock that connected interfaces are the most trustworthy sources because they are connected directly to the local router. Static routes have a low administrative distance of 1 because the Cisco IOS assumes that you are competent administrators and any manual entry of a routable network is trusted over any dynamic routing protocols such as EIGRP, OSPF, and RIP.

Static Routes

Objective:

▶ Perform and verify routing configuration tasks for a static or default route given specific routing requirements

When you interconnect routers, as shown in Figure 10.3, they are aware of only their directly connected networks. Unless you configure a static route or use routing protocols, the routers will never know about their neighbors' other networks, because they are not connected. In other words, Router A is unaware of Router B's 172.17.0.0 network, and Router B is unaware of Router A's 172.16.0.0 network.

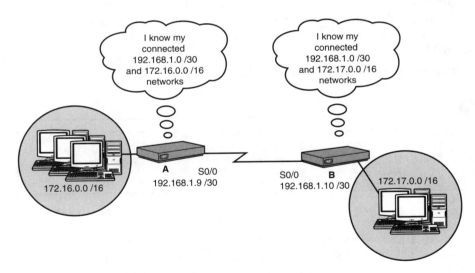

FIGURE 10.3   Static route exhibit.

So when do you use static routes as opposed to routing protocols? As mentioned before, static routes are manual configuration entries in which you tell the router how to get to destination networks that are not locally attached. This is useful in simple networks such as the one shown in Figure 10.3, in which there is a single link in or out of the networks, known as a *stub network*. Because there is only one link to get to the neighbor network, you don't need to worry about reacting dynamically if the path fails because there are no alternate paths to that network. Additionally, if you want to have complete control of your routing path decisions or you want to conserve bandwidth on your links (routing protocols consume bandwidth), static routes can provide you authoritative control without requiring any link bandwidth or resources because they require only a local configuration.

EXAM ALERT

Keep in mind that static routes are used when you have a stub network, want control of your routing decisions, or want to conserve bandwidth on links.

Configuring Static Routes

The general idea behind the static route is to tell the router how to get to a destination network that is not attached to it by going through another router's interface. It is similar to telling someone, "To go outside, go through that door." The syntax to configure a static route in global configuration mode is ip route followed by the destination network, destination subnet mask, and the next-hop IP address of the neighbor's interface. For example, to configure a route to the 10.0.0.0/8 network through the neighbor's serial interface of 192.168.2.5, the command would look like this:

```
Router(config)# ip route 10.0.0.0 255.0.0.0 192.168.2.5
```

NOTE

It is possible to specify the local interface instead of using a next-hop IP address on point-to-point links (a link with only two routers connected it on each side). On multi-access links such as Ethernet or Frame Relay, you should not use the interface because the local router does not know to which router to forward the information if multiple devices exist on the link.

In the stub network example shown in Figure 10.4, a static route to Router A and one to Router B were added, telling them about their neighbors' Ethernet networks. These entries are placed in their routing tables, specifying any packets that are destined for those respective networks must go to the IP of the neighbor's serial 0/0 interface. From that point, the packets are routed out Router A and Router B's Ethernet interface because those destination networks are directly connected to the router. This entry remains in the routing table as long as the next-hop address remains valid (the serial network does not go down) or the configuration is not removed.

FIGURE 10.4   Static route configuration example.

For several reasons such as security, processor resources, and routing path control, you can force the static route to remain in the routing table even if the next-hop interface goes down. This is easily achieved by adding the keyword permanent at the end of the ip route command.

Floating Static Routes

At the end of an ip route static route command, it is possible to add a parameter to assign this particular static route a higher administrative distance than the default administrative distance of 1. These entries, known as *floating static routes*, are not placed in the routing table if the subnet is being advertised by a routing source with a lower administrative distance. Floating static routes are useful when you have a standby redundant link to another network that will activate in the event of a primary link failure.

For example, consider the example configured in Figure 10.5. Because you have redundant point-to-point links, you can configure the primary static route as usual and include a floating static route to be used if the primary link fails. The 2 at the end of the second static route identifies that route as the floating static route. This entry does not show up in the routing table because the primary route advertises the same subnet with a lower administrative distance (if not specified, the default is 1). If one of the serial 0/0 interfaces on the primary link goes down, the next hop is no longer valid and is removed from the routing table. Because the floating static route has the next lowest administrative distance, that entry is put in the routing table and that link is used until the primary link returns.

FIGURE 10.5 Floating static route configuration example.

If an administrative distance is not specified, a Cisco router uses the default administrative distance for static routes (1). If an administrative distance is specified, it is being used as a floating static route if a redundant link fails.

Default Routes

Objective:

▶ Perform and verify routing configuration tasks for a static or default route given specific routing requirements

Static routes have proved their usefulness in situations where you want to add a network entry in a routing table when the network is reachable via a single path. This can turn into a daunting administrative task when there are a large number of networks in which you must configure static routes. This is especially true when you are connecting to your ISP because you do not want to configure a static route for every network on the Internet.

In these situations, you might be better served using something called a *default route*, as illustrated in Figure 10.6. This entry is a gateway of last resort for routers in that if a destination IP address does not have a network entry in the routing table, this route is used. The syntax for a default route is similar to a static route except that the destination and subnet mask are both 0.0.0.0:

```
Router(config)#ip route 0.0.0.0 0.0.0.0 192.168.1.10
```

FIGURE 10.6   Default route configuration example.

Again, you can specify the local interface as opposed to the next-hop IP address on a point-to-point link.

EXAM ALERT

Be sure to look closely at the wording in a question regarding a default route (gateway of last resort). When used in a router, the command is `ip route 0.0.0.0 0.0.0.0`; however, to configure a default route in a Layer 2 switch, it is `ip default-gateway` because Layer 2 switches do not have Layer 3 routing entries.

NOTE

In some situations a default route may appear dynamically in a routing table. Specifically, if you have configured your interface to dynamically be assigned an IP address and default gateway from a DHCP server using the `ip address dhcp` command, the router automatically places a default route in its routing table using the default gateway as the next hop.

Configuring Static and Default Routes with SDM

Using the Security Device Manager web-based configuration interface, you can easily configure static and default routes with just a few clicks of the mouse. Specifically, from the

Configure screen, select the Routing task to display routing configuration options. At the top of the screen shown in Figure 10.7 is a section dedicated to Static Routing. Here, when you click the Add button, a pop-up window displays the parameters that you can configure for static or default routes.

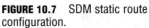

FIGURE 10.7 SDM static route configuration.

In the pop-up window, you specify the destination network and subnet mask, as you did for the IOS CLI command. The next hop defaults to a drop-down box that lists the interfaces, but you can select the IP Address option and specify the next-hop address. Also notice that there is a checkbox to make this route a default route, as well as a checkbox to make this a permanent static route entry. If you wanted to make this route a floating route, you could also put the distance metric for this route to an administrative distance value other than 1. After you click the OK button, the route is added to the running configuration of the IOS.

Verifying Static and Default Routes

The best way to verify a static or default route configuration is by checking that the route is evident in the routing table. The command to view the IP routing table is show ip route. If you want to see the routing entry for a specific network, you can append that subnet to the show ip route command (for example, show ip route 192.168.23.0). The following example displays the output of the show ip route command:

```
Router> show ip route
Codes: C - connected, S - static, I - IGRP, R - RIP, M - mobile, B - BGP
       D - EIGRP, EX - EIGRP external, O - OSPF, IA - OSPF inter area
       N1 - OSPF NSSA external type 1, N2 - OSPF NSSA external type 2
       E1 - OSPF external type 1, E2 - OSPF external type 2, E - EGP
```

```
        i - IS-IS, L1 - IS-IS level-1, L2 - IS-IS level-2, * - candidate default
        U - per-user static route, o - ODR, P - periodic downloaded static route
        T - traffic engineered route

Gateway of last resort is not set

S      172.17.0.0/16 [1/0] via 192.168.1.10
C      172.16.0.0/16 is directly connected, FastEthernet0/0
       192.168.1.0/30 is subnetted, 1 subnets
C         192.168.1.8 is directly connected, Serial0/0/0
S*     0.0.0.0/0 [1/0] via 192.168.1.10
```

Notice that the beginning of the output has a legend identifying the possible codes that can be listed in the routing table. In the table itself, you can see the two directly connected networks signified by the letter C. In addition, you can also see the static route to 172.17.0.0 and the static default route entries (indicated by the letter S), using 192.168.1.10 as the next hop. Also notice that the routing table identifies that the gateway of last resort (192.168.1.10) is set on this router because a default route was configured with the next hop to that address.

NOTE

You can clear out an entry in your routing table by using the clear command followed by the network or * for all networks in privileged EXEC mode. For example, to clear the 192.168.1.0 network from your routing table, you would enter the following:

Router# **clear ip route 192.168.1.0**

Dynamic Routing Protocols

When complex networks contain multiple interconnections, static routes are no longer a practical solution because they cannot adapt or react to changes in the topology. Not to mention, the configuration complexity can grow exponentially as you add more devices to the network.

EXAM ALERT

Do not confuse routing protocols with routed protocols on the exam. Routed protocols are protocols such as those in the IP protocol suite that are used to carry the data across our network. Routing protocols are exchanged between routing devices to determine the optimal path to route the routed protocols.

For example, given the network design in shown Figure 10.8, Router A knows only the three directly connected networks attached to the router. For IP packets to reach the 172.17.0.0 network via static routes, you would have to configure Router A to go through one of its neighbor routers, such as Router B. However, Router B also requires a static route to 172.17.0.0 because that network is not directly connected to it. Supposing that the router is using

Router F as its next hop, that router does not require a static route because it is directly connected. Unfortunately, our configuration undertaking does not stop there because we have to configure a static route in Router F and Router B back to the 172.16.0.0 network.

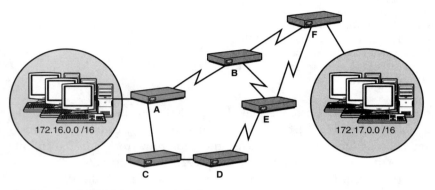

FIGURE 10.8   Complex internetwork design.

Granted, the configuration scenario shown in Figure 10.8 is not drastically difficult or strenuous, but imagine if the network contained 20 more routers. More importantly, consider what would happen if the link between A and B went down. Because the routes are statically configured in the routers, you must now go back and remove the static routes in Routers A and B and redirect the traffic by configuring static routes to go through Routers C, D, and E. Not to mention, you must remove and reconfigure static routes back to the 172.16.0.0 network in Routers F, E, D, and C.

To alleviate the administrative calamity you might have to encounter with static routes in complex networks, you can use dynamic routing protocols. If you configure routing protocols, the routers advertise their connected networks to the rest of the routers in the network, thus minimizing the amount of configuration required. In addition, routing protocols can detect and adapt to topology changes in the internetwork.

Routing Metrics

Because one of the core responsibilities of routing protocols is to build routing tables to determine optimal routing paths, you need to have some means of measuring which routes are preferred when there are multiple pathways to a destination. Routing protocols use some measure of metrics to identify which routes are optimal to reach a destination network. The lowest cumulative metric to a destination is the preferred path and the one that ultimately enters the routing table. Different routing protocols use one or several of the following metrics to calculate the best path:

▶ **Hop count:** The number of routing devices that the packet must travel to reach a destination network.

▶ **Bandwidth:** The cumulative bandwidth of the links to the destination in kilobits per second.

▶ **Delay:** The length of time (measured in microseconds) a packet takes from source to destination.

▶ **Reliability:** The consistency of the links and paths toward the destination based on error rates of the interfaces.

▶ **Load:** The cumulative amount of congestion or saturation of the links toward the destination.

▶ **MTU:** The maximum frame size that is allowed to traverse the links to the destination.

▶ **Cost:** An arbitrary number typically based on the bandwidth of the link.

Classful and Classless Routing Updates

As you will see in the following sections, routing protocols are categorized into several different classifications based on common characteristics and properties that they share. The first of these classifications revolves around the contents of routing updates that Layer 3 devices advertise to their neighbors. Specifically, if the routing updates do not contain the subnet mask along with their respective advertised networks, they are said to be *classful routing protocols*. Conversely, if the subnet mask is transmitted along with the network information, it is characterized as a *classless routing protocol*. This may seem like a trivial characteristic to define routing protocols, but as you will see, the results of the subnet mask being present or not in routing updates can affect the routing protocols you choose and how efficiently you can design your entire network.

With classful routing protocols, you assume that your network's design conforms to the class boundaries of IP subnets. In other words, major networks in your design use their default classful subnet masks as described in Chapter 5, "Implementing IP Addressing" (for example, Class A uses 255.0.0.0, Class B uses 255.255.0.0, and Class C uses 255.255.255.0). If you happen to subnet a major network into smaller subnets, classful routing protocols are disadvantageous, because they do not receive the revised subnet mask. For this reason, classful routing protocols process updates in one of two ways:

▶ If the network in the updates matches the same major classful network on the interface through which it was received, it uses the subnet mask of the interface and places it in the routing table.

▶ If the router advertises a network to a different major network out an interface that is not in the same major network, it automatically summarizes the network to its classful boundary.

For example, when Router B in Figure 10.9 sends an update to Router A using a classful routing protocol (RIPv1 in this example), it summarizes the 172.17.30.0/24 to a default Class B 172.17.0.0 network because it is going out the serial 0/0 interface, which does not contain a subnet in that major network. The 192.168.1.60 network, on the other hand, is in the same major network, so it does not automatically summarize that subnet. When Router A receives that update, it adds the 172.17.0.0 network to its routing table, specifying Router B's serial interface IP (192.168.1.10) as the next hop to reach that network. In addition, it adds the 192.168.1.60 network as well, using its interface mask because it is in that same major network.

FIGURE 10.9 Classful routing update scenario.

Now consider if the Ethernet segment of Router B's 192.168.1.60 network had a /29 subnet mask. The end result would still be the same as before in that Router B would advertise the 192.168.1.60 subnet and Router A would use its interface's subnet mask of /30. In these instances, classful routing protocols are not the optimal choice because Router A has a route to only a third of the 192.168.1.60 /29 subnet. For this reason, when you subnet a major network, you must be sure that you use the same subnet mask throughout your network design with classful routing protocols. This same subnet design is commonly referred to as a *Fixed-Length Subnet Mask (FLSM)* network design.

Classful routing protocols can also be problematic when major classful networks are subnetted and are haphazardly dispersed throughout the network, as illustrated in Figure 10.10.

When Routers A and C summarize their networks to Router B, Router B thinks that the 172.16.0.0 network is out both of its serial interfaces. This could easily result in traffic destined for 172.16.10.0 and 172.16.50.0 being load balanced out each interface, resulting in 50% packet loss because the packets are sent in a round robin fashion between both interfaces.

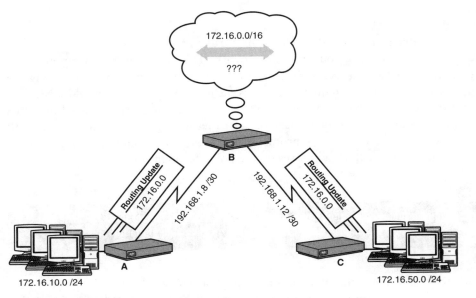

FIGURE 10.10 Discontiguous network example.

EXAM ALERT

Be sure to know that classful routing protocols support automatic summarization and must have a FLSM network design without any discontiguous networks.

Because classless routing protocols advertise the subnet masks in their routing updates, discontiguous networks are no longer an issue because routing devices are aware of the subnetted networks. In addition, the requirement of using the same subnet mask throughout the network ceases to apply because the routers do not automatically summarize the networks to a classful boundary. No longer inhibited by these constraints, you are free to use different subnet masks, known as *Variable-Length Subnet Masks (VLSMs)* in your network design. In addition, you now have full autonomy to manually summarize networks as you wish to help keep routing tables small to conserve resources. VLSM and route summarization are described in greater detail in the following sections.

> **EXAM ALERT**
>
> Be sure to know that classless routing protocols support discontiguous networks, VLSM, and route summarization.

VLSM

Using classless routing protocols affords you the luxury of having support for a VLSM network design. This is advantageous in your network planning because you can allot the appropriate number of IP addresses required for each link. Not to mention, by assigning the minimal number of IP addresses required for a given link, you conserve IP addresses. For example, you can use a /30 subnet mask for point-to-point links because you need only two available IP addresses and a /27 subnet mask on an Ethernet segment to accommodate 30 hosts. If you were using classless routing protocols, you would have to use a /27 for all links, which would inevitably waste 28 IP addresses on the point-to-point links.

> **EXAM ALERT**
>
> Remember that point-to-point links require only a /30 (255.255.255.252) subnet mask because you need only two usable IP addresses for the router's interfaces on each side of the link.

Throughout your certification and career, it is quite possible you will have to design your network given a usable subnet and host requirements for all your links. When tackling this designing task, be sure to adhere to the following guidelines:

1. If possible, start with the larger subnets first.

2. Write out the ranges that you have assigned to ensure that you do not accidentally overlap subnets.

3. Make sure your networks start on incremental boundaries (128, 64, 32, and so on).

> **EXAM ALERT**
>
> Be prepared to use VLSM to assign subnets to links given the subnettable network and host requirements.

Challenge

Given the design shown in Figure 10.11, determine how you can use VLSM to ensure that you are using the appropriate subnets given a design scenario. In this example, the zero subnets are available for use.

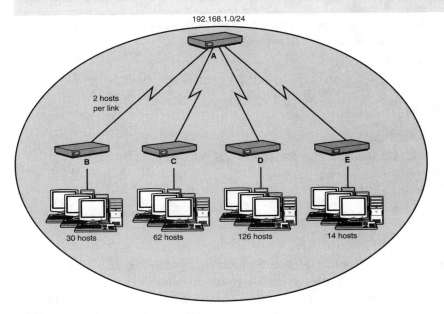

FIGURE 10.11 VLSM design scenario.

1. Remember to add 2 to each network to accommodate the network ID and broadcast address.

2. Calculate the network and subnet mask for Network D (the largest network).

3. Given the remaining IP addresses, calculate the network and subnet mask for Network C.

4. Given the remaining IP addresses, calculate the network and subnet mask for Network B.

5. Given the remaining IP addresses, calculate the network and subnet mask for Network E.

6. Given the remaining IP addresses, calculate the network and subnet mask for the four point-to-point links.

Challenge Answer

Network D needs to have a subnet that accommodates 128 addresses. A subnet mask of 255.255.255.128 or /25 provides enough hosts for that network. The next subnet for Network C begins at 192.168.1.128

(continues)

(continued)

(because you just took 128 IPs) and use a subnet mask of 255.255.255.192 or /26 to accommodate the 64 IP addresses. Network B is assigned the network of 192.168.1.192 with a subnet mask of 255.255.255.224 or /27 to give you 32 IPs. A subnet mask of 255.255.255.240 or /28 with a network ID of 192.168.1.224 is assigned to Network E for the 16 IPs required for that link. The four point-to-point links all use a 255.255.255.252 or /30 subnet mask using the last four networks: 192.168.1.240, 192.168.1.244, 192.168.1.248, 192.168.1.252. To summarize:

► **Network D:** 192.168.1.0 /25

► **Network C:** 192.168.1.128 /26

► **Network B:** 192.168.1.192 /27

► **Network E:** 192.168.1.224 /28

► **Point-to-point links:** 192.168.1.240 /30, 192.168.1.244 /30, 192.168.1.248 /30, and 192.168.1.252 /30.

Route Summarization

As already mentioned, classful routing protocols automatically summarize advertised networks to the classful subnet boundaries. Classless routing protocols, on the other hand, require you to manually control the networks being summarized to your neighbors in the router configuration. By aggregating a contiguous set of networks into an advertised summarized route, you keep the size of the routing tables to a minimum. Neighbors that receive the summarized route do not need to know about the individual subnets you create behind your router because they inevitably have to go through your router to get to them. The additional offshoot of this summarized picture is that your classless routing protocols do not need to notify those neighbors if one of those subnets goes down because they do not even have that subnet in their routing tables. Thus, you can isolate topology changes to be contained behind that summarizing router.

Because you are required to manually specify the networks you are to advertise, you must learn how to accurately summarize smaller subnets into one or several larger networks, or supernets. The rules for supernetting are similar to subnetting, except in this case, you are stealing bits from the network portion of an IP network to create a larger network. The rules for supernetting are as follows:

1. Be sure that the networks are contiguous (otherwise, you would be summarizing networks that you do not have behind the router).

2. Count the number of networks you want to summarize.

3. Determine an increment that is equal to or less than the number of networks.

4. Make sure your base networks start on incremental boundaries (128, 64, 32, and so on) for the number of networks you are summarizing.

5. Calculate the subnet mask by the number of bits you need to steal from the original subnet to equal that incremental value.

The beauty of supernetting is that the resultant network and subnet mask will designate many IP address networks in a single entry. The fact that you are stealing bits from the network portion of an IP address could quite easily violate the traditional barriers of classful addressing, known as *Classless Interdomain Routing* (CIDR).

For instance, it would not be uncommon to see a summary entry look like the following: 192.168.16.0 /20. This single entry used to be a Class C (/24), but four bits were stolen from the network portion to represent 16 networks ($2^4 = 16$). When you advertise this supernet to neighbors, they know that they must go through your router to get to networks 192.168.16.0 through 192.168.31.0 (16 total networks).

EXAM ALERT

Be prepared to determine the networks being advertised in a given supernet or determine the summary network, given the networks to be summarized.

Figure 10.12 illustrates a typical route summarization example in which Router B is summarizing all its subnetted networks to Router A as one supernetted network. Following the steps outlined previously, you can determine the aggregate network entry to advertise, as follows:

▶ The networks are all contiguous, so you can summarize them accurately.

▶ A total of 32 networks need to be summarized.

▶ 32 conveniently falls on an incremental boundary.

▶ Because the network is 192.168.64.0, 64 is an increment of 32 so we can use that as the base network for the summary route.

▶ You must steal 5 bits ($2^5 = 32$) from the /24 network, so /19 (24 − 5 = 19).

FIGURE 10.12 Supernetting route summarization example.

By creating the summary route 192.168.64.0 /19, Router A is required to maintain only that one entry in its routing table as opposed to the individual 32 subnets. If a topology change occurs in one of the subnets behind Router B, there is no need to advertise that change to Router A because it knows about only the summarized network.

> **NOTE**
>
> The number of summarized networks or the base network do not always conveniently fall on incremental boundaries. In those instances, it may take several summary network entries to encompass all the networks you want to summarize.

Interior and Exterior Gateway Routing Protocols

Routing protocols can fall under two major categories depending on the autonomy of the network on which the routing protocol exists. The identifying characteristic of the category to which the routing protocol belongs ultimately depends on whether the routing protocols exchanges updates within a network that is under your administrative control. When the network is under your control in your own administrative domain, it is known as an *autonomous system*. Routing protocols used to disseminate information to maintain routing tables and establish pathways inside an autonomous system are categorized as Interior Gateway Protocols (IGPs).

Conversely, the other category of routing protocols is designed to route in between these autonomous systems. For instance, Border Gateway Protocol (BGP) is a routing protocol that is used by ISPs for routing traffic over the Internet. Because the Internet comprises thousands of networks, each under different administrative control, you need to use an Exterior Gateway Protocol such as BGP to route in between these autonomous systems.

Distance Vector Routing Protocols

In addition to being an IGP/EGP or classful/classless, routing protocols can also fall into one of three classes. Again, the functionality and characteristics of the routing protocol dictate under which class it falls. The most long-standing of these classes is *distance vector routing protocols*.

Distance vector routing protocols concern themselves with the direction (vector) in which the destination lies and some means of measurement (metric) it takes to reach that destination. Distance vector routing protocols inform their directly connected neighbors of all the connected and learned networks they know about in their routing tables. In fact, they broadcast the contents of the entire routing table to their neighbors periodically, regardless of whether there is a change in the network topology. When the neighbors receive that routing information, they identify and add any new networks to their routing tables and update the metric before eventually passing it on to their neighbors. Because the routing table information is updated before it is sent on to neighbors, downstream routers do not learn that information first hand. For this reason, distance vector routing protocol update processing is often referred to as "routing by rumor." Distance vector routing protocols are discussed in greater detail in Chapter 11, "Distance Vector Routing Protocols."

Link-State Routing Protocols

As the name states, *link-state routing protocols* advertise the state of the links in the network. In fact, they advertise the states and metrics (cost) of all the links they know about for the entire topology to their neighbors, as opposed to just the best routes in your routing table. This detailed overview of the entire routing domain enables each router to calculate and make a decision on the best route from this first-hand information, rather than listen to what its neighbor believes is the best route. In fact, link-state routing protocols keep three tables: a neighbor table of all discovered neighbors, a topology table of all the possible routes to reachable networks learned, and a routing table that contains the best route based on the lowest metric calculated from the topology table.

At first, this may sound like a lot of information to be exchanged between routers; however, link-state routing protocols initially discover their neighbors when they first boot up and synchronize their topology tables. After the neighbor discovery and topology synchronization, they send only periodic hello messages to let their neighbors know they are still functioning. This is significantly different from distance vector routing protocols that periodically exchange the entire routing table, which can contain a large amount of information, depending on the size of the network.

In addition, link-state routing protocols react much faster when a topology change occurs in the network. In fact, these protocols were initially created in response to the slow convergence issues that you typically encounter with distance vector routing protocols. The downfall to these routing protocols is the resources they consume in the router. Namely, maintaining and processing three tables consume quite a bit of memory and processor power.

Advanced Distance Vector/Hybrid Routing Protocols

They say it usually takes three tries to get something absolutely right. The truth behind this saying is that you learn from the mistakes of the previous two attempts. Such is the case with advanced distance vector, often referred to as *hybrid* or *balanced hybrid* routing protocols. Because they take the best features and avoid the pitfalls of both distance vector and link-state routing protocols, hybrid routing protocols are a more proficient breed of routing protocols than their predecessors.

The Routing Table Revisited

Now that you have learned about the several types of routing sources, including static routes and dynamic routing protocols, it's time to revisit the routing table and solidify how network entries are added and used in routing decisions. To help illustrate this process, refer to the following show ip route output :

```
RouterA> show ip route
Codes: C - connected, S - static, I - IGRP, R - RIP, M - mobile, B - BGP
       D - EIGRP, EX - EIGRP external, O - OSPF, IA - OSPF inter area
       N1 - OSPF NSSA external type 1, N2 - OSPF NSSA external type 2
       E1 - OSPF external type 1, E2 - OSPF external type 2, E - EGP
       i - IS-IS, L1 - IS-IS level-1, L2 - IS-IS level-2, * - candidate default
       U - per-user static route, o - ODR, P - periodic downloaded static route
       T - traffic engineered route

Gateway of last resort is not set

R    172.17.0.0/16 [120/1] via 192.168.1.10, Serial0/0/0
C    172.16.0.0/16 is directly connected, FastEthernet0/0
     10.0.0.0/8 is variably subnetted, 4 subnets, 3 masks
D       10.2.0.0/16 [90/2297856] via 192.168.1.10, Serial0/0/0
D       10.3.0.0/16 [90/2297856] via 192.168.1.10, Serial0/0/0
R       10.0.0.0/8 [120/2] via 192.168.1.6, Serial0/0/1
D       10.1.0.0/16 [90/2297856] via 192.168.1.10, Serial0/0/0
D       10.4.0.0/16 [90/2297856] via 192.168.1.10, Serial0/0/0
O       10.4.0.1/32 [110/65] via 172.16.0.1, FastEthernet0/0
     192.168.1.0/30 is subnetted, 2 subnets
C       192.168.1.8 is directly connected, Serial 0/0/0
C       192.168.1.4 is directly connected, Serial 0/0/1
```

Notice that there are now several entries for directly connected networks, a static route, and several dynamic routing protocol entries from EIGRP, RIP, and OSPF. For each dynamic routing protocol, the network and subnet mask are being advertised by neighbor routers, followed by two numbers in brackets separated by a slash (/). The number to the left of the forward slash is the administrative distance of the routing protocol. The number to the right of the forward slash represents the metric that is being used by the routing protocol to determine the best path to the destination network. This information is immediately followed by the router from which it learned this information (thus, the next-hop address). The last item in the routing entry represents the interface packets must exit to reach those networks.

EXAM ALERT

You must be adept at deciphering the output of a routing table.

Assuming that several of the routing protocols advertised the same networks, how did these specific network entries come to be in the routing table? The obvious answer is that the interfaces, a static route, and multiple routing protocols were configured and the resultant table just appeared. However, to answer the question more specifically, each routing protocol determined which routes should be entered in the routing table based on the lowest metric to those destinations. In the chance that one or more routing sources is trying to place a network entry in the routing table for exactly the same subnet, the routing protocol with the lowest administrative distance is chosen because it is the most trustworthy.

After the routing table is built, packets are routed to their destinations by examination of the destination IP address in an IP packet and associating the network in the routing table with that IP address. If there isn't a match for the network lookup, the packet is forwarded to its default route. If the gateway of last resort is not set (as in this show ip route output), the packet is dropped, and an ICMP destination unreachable message is sent back to the source to indicate that the destination cannot be reached.

> **EXAM ALERT**
>
> Routing of packets is based on the destination IP address in a packet. If the router does not have an entry for the packet's associated network or does not have a default route, it sends an ICMP destination unreachable message back to the source.

In the show ip route output, several entries for the 10.0.0.0 network are listed in the routing table. Interestingly, there is a RIP entry for the 10.0.0.0 /8 network to go out serial 0/0/1 and four EIGRP-learned networks for 10.1.0.0 /16, 10.2.0.0 /16, 10.3.0.0 /16, and 10.4.0.0 /16, all destined for interface serial 0/0/0. Because the EIGRP networks are subnets of the major 10.0.0.0 network, which interface will the router use to route a packet destined, for example, for 10.1.0.3?

Cisco's routing logic answers this question by using a rule called the *longest match*. The longest match rule states that when a packet has multiple possible network entries to use, the more specific subnet is used over the less specific. In other words, the longer the number of bits in the subnet mask (thus the smaller subnet), the more chance it has of being the chosen network. In the routing table example, a packet destined for 10.1.0.3 would use the subnet with the longest prefix (subnet mask), which is the EIGRP route for 10.1.0.0/16 exiting interface Serial 0/0/0.

Routing Redistribution

You are likely to encounter in your Cisco travels certain situations in which you must run multiple routing protocols in your network. For instance, your company is in the process of merging with another company's network, and their routers are running a different routing protocol than yours. In addition, you may have to connect your Cisco router network to a non-Cisco routing infrastructure and you are using Cisco proprietary routing protocols.

In instances where you are running multiple routing protocols, it may be necessary to have networks advertised in one routing protocol injected into the other. Unfortunately, because routing protocols are so diverse in nature, they do not inherently interact or exchange information with each other when multiple routing protocols are running in the network. The transferal of network information from one routing protocol into another is a manual configuration called *redistribution*.

The redistribution configuration is typically done at one or a couple of routers that sit on the boundary between each routing protocol, as illustrated in Figure 10.13. These devices run both routing protocols and must be manually configured to inject the networks learned from one routing protocol into the next. Redistribution can occur in one of two fashions:

▶ **One-way redistribution:** Networks from an edge protocol are injected into a more robust core routing protocol, but not the other way around. This method is the safest way to perform redistribution.

▶ **Two-way redistribution:** Networks from each routing protocol are injected into the other. This is the least preferred method because it is possible that suboptimal routing or routing loops may occur because of the network design or the difference in convergence times when a topology change occurs. Figure 10.13 is an example of two-way redistribution.

FIGURE 10.13 Two-way redistribution example.

Chapter Summary

This chapter looked more closely at the operations involved in routing packets with Layer 3 devices such as routers and Layer 3 switches. You send packets from workstations on the local network to routing devices by configuring those devices with a default gateway IP address that matches the IP of your router. When the packet arrives at the router, it consults its routing table to determine whether the destination IP address in the IP packet has a match for the destination's network. If it does not have a matching entry, it looks to see whether the routing table has a default route. If no gateway of last resort is set, it drops the packet and sends an ICMP destination unreachable message back to the source. In instances where there are several matches for the destination network, it uses the entry that has the longest match.

The entries in the routing table can come from several routing sources. When the interface is operational and an IP address is assigned, they show up in the routing table as connected interfaces. Manual static route entries that were manually configured show up as an S. Routing protocols choose their best network paths by calculating the lowest metric for their respective routing protocols. If multiple routing sources advertise the same subnet, the source with the lowest administrative distance is placed in the routing table.

The routing protocols can fall into several categories, based on the characteristics that the protocols utilize. For instance, if a routing protocol does not advertise the subnet mask in its routing updates, it is a classful routing protocol. Classful routing protocols require the network design to have the same subnet mask in the design known as FLSM. In addition, these routing protocols cannot support discontiguous networks and automatically summarize network entries to the classful boundary when crossing interfaces in other major networks. When subnet masks include the routing advertisements, these updates are said to be classless. Classless routing protocols support VLSM network designs, discontiguous networks, and require manual summarization of networks.

If the routing protocol is designed to route inside an autonomous system, that routing protocol is an IGP. EGP routing protocols, on the other hand, are designed to route between autonomous systems.

Finally, routing protocols can belong to one of the following three classifications:

▶ **Distance vector:** The entire routing table is periodically sent to directly connected neighbors regardless of a topology change. These routing protocols manipulate the routing table updates before sending that information to their neighbors and are slow to converge when a topology change occurs.

▶ **Link-state:** All possible link states are stored in an independent topology table in which the best routes are calculated and put into the routing table. The topology table is initially synchronized with discovered neighbors followed by frequent hello messages. These routing protocols are faster to converge than distance vector routing protocols.

▶ **Hybrid:** By using the best characteristics from both link-state and routing protocols, these advanced routing protocols efficiently and quickly build their routing information and converge when topology changes occur.

Key Terms

- ▶ Default gateway
- ▶ Routing table
- ▶ Connected interface
- ▶ Hop
- ▶ Routing protocols
- ▶ Administrative distance
- ▶ Static routes
- ▶ Stub networks
- ▶ Floating routes
- ▶ Default route
- ▶ Classful routing protocols
- ▶ Classless routing protocols
- ▶ FLSM
- ▶ Discontiguous networks
- ▶ VLSM
- ▶ Route summarization
- ▶ Supernet
- ▶ CIDR
- ▶ Autonomous system
- ▶ IGP
- ▶ EGP
- ▶ Distance vector routing protocols
- ▶ Link-state routing protocols
- ▶ Advanced distance vector/hybrid routing protocols
- ▶ Longest match rule
- ▶ Redistribution

Apply Your Knowledge

Exercises

10.1 Create a Static and Default Route

This exercise tests your configuration skills in configuring a static and default route.

Estimated Time: 5 minutes

1. Enter privileged EXEC mode.

2. Enter global configuration mode.

3. Configure a static route for the 10.23.5.0/24 network using 192.168.64.2 as the next-hop address.

4. Configure a floating static route for the 10.23.5.0/24 network using 192.168.60.3.

5. Configure a default route to exit out of your serial interface.

10.2 Create a Summary Route

This exercise ensures that you can accurately supernet smaller subnets into one summary route.

Estimated Time: 5 minutes

Given the following networks, what is the summary route you can use to advertise these individual subnets to your neighbor router as an aggregate entry?

172.16.0.0 /16

172.17.0.0 /16

172.18.0.0 /16

172.19.0.0 /16

1. Count the number of networks you want to summarize.

2. Determine an increment that is equal to or less than the number of networks.

3. Make sure your base networks start on incremental boundaries (128, 64, 32, and so on) for the number of networks you are summarizing.

4. Calculate the subnet mask by the number of bits you need to steal from the original subnet to equal that incremental value.

Review Questions

1. What are the Layer 2 and Layer 3 characteristics of a packet destined for a network on a remote segment?

2. Why would you use a static route versus a routing protocol?

3. What are the characteristics of distance vector routing protocols?

4. What are the characteristics of link-state routing protocols?

5. What is the difference between classful and classless routing protocols?

Exam Questions

1. Given the following output, on which interface will a packet destined for 192.168.1.34 /24 be routed?

```
RouterA> show ip route
Codes: C - connected, S - static, I - IGRP, R - RIP, M - mobile, B - BGP
       D - EIGRP, EX - EIGRP external, O - OSPF, IA - OSPF inter area
       N1 - OSPF NSSA external type 1, N2 - OSPF NSSA external type 2
       E1 - OSPF external type 1, E2 - OSPF external type 2, E - EGP
       i - IS-IS, L1 - IS-IS level-1, L2 - IS-IS level-2, * - candidate default
       U - per-user static route, o - ODR, P - periodic downloaded static route
       T - traffic engineered route

Gateway of last resort is not set

C    10.0.0.0/8 is directly connected, Serial0/1
R    172.17.0.0/16 [120/1] via 192.168.1.10, Serial0/0
C    172.16.0.0/16 is directly connected, FastEthernet0/0
     192.168.1.0/30 is subnetted, 1 subnets
C       192.168.1.8 is directly connected, Serial0/0
```

   ○ **A.** Serial 0/1

   ○ **B.** Serial 0/0

   ○ **C.** Fast Ethernet 0/0

   ○ **D.** None of the above

2. Your network designer subnetted the major classful network of 192.168.2.0 into varying-sized subnets throughout your network. Which routing protocol category should not be your choice of routing protocol?

   ○ **A.** Classful

   ○ **B.** IGP

   ○ **C.** Link-state

   ○ **D.** ODR

3. Which of the following is not a characteristic of link-state routing protocols?

   ○ **A.** Fast convergence

   ○ **B.** Broadcasts routing table

   ○ **C.** Keeps track of neighbors in table

   ○ **D.** Knows all possible routes

4. Which of the following is not a subnet in the CIDR summary route 192.168.16.0 /21?

   ○ **A.** 192.168.16.0 /24

   ○ **B.** 192.168.20.0 /24

   ○ **C.** 192.168.24.0 /24

   ○ **D.** 192.168.23.0 /24

5. What is the consequence of using the following command?

   `Router(config)# ip route 0.0.0.0 0.0.0.0 192.168.10.2`

   ○ **A.** The entry will show up in the routing table signified with an R.

   ○ **B.** This entry is configured in a Layer 2 switch to send traffic to a Layer 3 routing device.

   ○ **C.** 192.168.10.2 is the IP address of the router that advertised this network in the routing protocol update.

   ○ **D.** If there is not an exact match in the routing table, packets will be sent to 192.168.10.2.

6. What is the consequence of using the following command? (Choose two)

   `Router(config)# ip route 192.168.20.4 255.255.255.0 10.1.1.1 3`

   ○ **A.** The 3 at the end of the command signifies that it is a floating static route.

   ○ **B.** The 3 at the end of the command signifies the hops to get to the destination.

   ○ **C.** The destination network is incorrect, so this command will not work.

   ○ **D.** The default administrative distance for this command is 120.

7. The network entry for 192.168.2.0 /24 is being advertised by RIP and OSPF. Which routing protocol displays the subnet in the routing table, and why?

   ○ **A.** OSPF because it has a lower metric

   ○ **B.** RIP because it is classful

   ○ **C.** OSPF because it has a lower administrative distance

   ○ **D.** RIP because it has a higher administrative distance

8. Which of the following is not a reason to use static routes?

○ **A.** To minimize configuration in complex networks.

○ **B.** To get finer control of routing decisions.

○ **C.** Destination networks are stubs.

○ **D.** To conserve bandwidth.

9. Given the following entries in a routing table, on which interface will a packet destined for 10.4.0.1 exit?

```
RouterA> show ip route
Codes: C - connected, S - static, I - IGRP, R - RIP, M - mobile, B - BGP
       D - EIGRP, EX - EIGRP external, O - OSPF, IA - OSPF inter area
       N1 - OSPF NSSA external type 1, N2 - OSPF NSSA external type 2
       E1 - OSPF external type 1, E2 - OSPF external type 2, E - EGP
       i - IS-IS, L1 - IS-IS level-1, L2 - IS-IS level-2, * - candidate default
       U - per-user static route, o - ODR, P - periodic downloaded static route
       T - traffic engineered route

Gateway of last resort is not set

C    172.16.0.0/16 is directly connected, FastEthernet0/0
     10.0.0.0/8 is variably subnetted, 4 subnets, 3 masks
I       10.0.0.0/8 [100/8976] via 172.17.0.2, FastEthernet0/1
D       10.1.0.0/16 [90/2297856] via 192.168.1.10, Serial0/1
D       10.4.0.0/16 [90/2297856] via 192.168.1.10, Serial0/1
O       10.4.0.0/30 [110/65] via 192.168.2.10, Serial0/0
```

○ **A.** Fast Ethernet 0/0

○ **B.** Serial 0/1

○ **C.** Serial 0/0

○ **D.** None of the above

10. Given the following entries in a routing table, which of the following are true? (Choose two)

```
RouterA> show ip route
...Output Omitted...

Gateway of last resort is 192.168.2.10 to network 0.0.0.0

C    172.16.0.0/16 is directly connected, FastEthernet0/0
     10.0.0.0/8 is variably subnetted, 4 subnets, 3 masks
I       10.0.0.0/8 [100/8976] via 172.17.0.2, FastEthernet0/1
D       10.1.0.0/16 [90/2297856] via 192.168.1.10, Serial0/1
D       10.4.0.0/16 [90/2297856] via 192.168.1.10, Serial0/1
S*      0.0.0.0/0 [1/0] via 192.168.2.10, Serial0/0
```

○ **A.** A packet destined for 192.168.100.2 will exit Serial 0/0.

○ **B.** The metric for network 10.4.0.0/16 is 90.

○ **C.** The metric for network 10.0.0.0/8 is 8976.

○ **D.** The routing protocol for network 10.1.0.0 has an administrative distance of 100.

Answers to Review Questions

1. When a packet is destined for a remote network, the Layer 3 source address is the workstation or device that is sending the traffic. The destination Layer 3 address is the IP address of the destination device. At Layer 2, the source address is the MAC address of the sending workstation or device. The destination Layer 2 address, however, is the MAC address of the default gateway. The default gateway is the routing device on the local segment that is responsible for forwarding packets from the local segment to remote networks.

2. Static routes are used primarily in stub networks or when the administrator wishes to have complete control over the routing decisions of their routing devices. Routing protocols are used in complex networks with multiple paths to a destination. Unlike static routes, routing protocols can dynamically react to topology changes in the internetwork.

3. Distance vector routing protocols periodically send routing table updates to their directly connected neighbors regardless of whether there is a change in the topology. These routine routing updates contain the contents of the entire routing table.

4. Link-state routing protocols initially discover their neighbors and retain that information in a neighbor table. Information about all possible routes is exchanged between these neighbors and stored in a router's topology table. After the initial exchange of information, link-state routers periodically send hello messages as opposed to full routing updates. With the knowledge of all possible routes in the topology, the routers calculate the best route to each destination and place them in the routing table.

5. Classful routing protocols do not contain the subnet mask in the routing updates. Networks using classful routing protocols require that a FLSM design does not support discontiguous networks. Classless routing protocols updates contain the subnet mask that enables the network design to support VLSM and discontiguous networks.

Answers to Exam Questions

1. **D.** A packet destined for 192.168.1.34 /24 would require a network entry for 192.168.1.0 in the routing table. Because there isn't an exact match for that network, the router sends it out the interface specified in a default route. This router does not have a default route configured, so the packet is dropped, and an ICMP destination unreachable is sent to the source. Answer A is incorrect because packets destined for the 10.0.0.0 /8 exit the serial 0/1 interface. Answer B is incorrect because packets destined for the 172.17.0.0 /16 exit the serial 0/0 interface. Answer C is incorrect because packets destined for the 172.16.0.0 /16 exit the Fast Ethernet 0/0 interface.

2. **A.** Because the network is designed with variable-length subnet masks, you should not use a classful routing protocol. B is incorrect because IGP routing protocols should be utilized inside your network. C is incorrect because link-state routing protocols support classless routing updates. D is incorrect because classless routing protocols support VLSM designs.

3. **B.** Link-state routing protocols do not broadcast their entire routing tables. They synchronize their topology table containing all possible routes with the neighbors they initially discover. Answers A, C, and D are all characteristics of link-state routing protocols.

4. **C.** Because the summary route stole three bits from the default Class C (/24), you are summarizing 2^3 or eight networks. 192.168.16.0 is in an increment of 8, so that is the base network. The range of networks that are summarized extend to network 192.168.23.0 for a total of 8 networks. Answers A, B, and D all fit in the range of networks that are summarized by the 192.168.16.0 /21 summary route.

5. **D.** The default route configured specifies that packets should be routed to the 192.168.10.2 next hop if there is not a specific match in the routing table. Answer A is incorrect because static route entries show up with the letter S in the routing table. Answer B is incorrect because by default this is a routing command that can be configured only in Layer 3 devices. IP default gateway is the command to configure a gateway of last resort for Layer 2 switches. Answer C is false because static routes are not advertised to other routers.

6. **A, C.** The 3 at the end of the static route command overrides the default administrative distance of 1 for a static route. This is probably being used to create a floating static route in a redundant network. The command, however, does not work because you have an inconsistent subnet mask with the destination network. The network ID should reflect 192.168.20.0 or the subnet mask should be 255.255.255.252. Answer B is incorrect because the 3 represents the administrative distance. Answer D is incorrect because static routes have a default administrative distance of 1.

7. **C.** OSPF has a lower administrative distance than RIP (110 vs. 120), so that entry shows up in the routing table because the lower administrative distance is preferred over higher ones. Answer A is incorrect because the metric of OSPF applies only if the OSPF routing protocol has multiple pathways to the 192.168.2.0 network. Answer B is false because classful or classless is not a factor in decisions between routing sources. Answer D is incorrect routing protocols with lower administrative distances are trusted over routing protocols with higher administrative distances.

8. **A.** Static routes require more configurations in a complex network because you have to configure a static route for each destination in every router. Answers B, C, and D are all valid reasons to use static routes.

9. **C.** Because the OSPF entry has the longest match for the 10.4.0.1 network, you use that route out Serial 0/0. The interfaces in answers A and B conceivably could be used; however, the longest match rule states that when a packet has multiple possible network entries to use, the more specific subnet is used over the less specific. Because the serial interface has the longest match (the most specific subnet), that is the interface the packet destined for 10.4.0.1 will use.

10. **A, C.** This routing table indicates that a default route is configured. Because there isn't a match for 192.168.100.2 in the routing table, it is sent out Serial 0/0 as specified in the default route. The numbers in the brackets represent the administrative distance followed by the metric. Thus, the

remaining correct statement is that the metric for the IGRP route for 10.0.0.0/8 is 8976. Answer B is false because the metric for the 10.4.0.0 /16 network is 2297856. Answer D is incorrect because the 10.1.0.0 /16 network is learned via EIGRP, which has an administrative distance of 90.

Suggested Readings and Resources

1. Alex Zinn. *IP Routing: Packet Forwarding and Intra-domain Routing Protocols*. Addison Wesley Professional, 2002.

2. Keith Kruepke, Paul Cernick, and Mark Degner. *Cisco IP Routing Handbook*. Hungry Minds, 2000.

3. "Routing Protocols," www.firewall.cx.

4. "IP Routing," technology support on www.cisco.com.

CHAPTER ELEVEN

Distance Vector Routing Protocols

Objectives

This chapter covers the following Cisco-specified objectives for the "Implement a small routed network" section of the 640-822 ICND1 exam:

▶ **Configure, verify, and troubleshoot RIPv2**

▶ **Verify network status and router operation using basic utilities (including: ping, traceroute, telnet, SSH, arp, ipconfig), SHOW & DEBUG commands**

Outline

Introduction   **358**

Distance Vector Operations   358

Routing Loops   360

Routing Loop Mitigation   **362**

Counting to Infinity   363

Split Horizon   363

Route Poison, Poison Reverse,
and Hold-Down Timers   364

Triggered Updates   366

Invalid/Dead Timers   367

RIP   **367**

RIP Characteristics   367

RIP Configuration   368

Passive Interfaces   371

RIPv2 Characteristics   371

RIPv2 Configuration   372

Configuring RIP with SDM   373

RIP Verification   374

Troubleshooting RIP   375

Chapter Summary   **379**

Key Terms   380

Apply Your Knowledge   **380**

Exercises   380

Review Questions   382

Exam Questions   382

Answers to Review Questions   384

Answers to Exam Questions   385

Suggested Readings and Resources   386

Study Strategies

▶ Read the information presented in the chapter, paying special attention to tables, Notes, and Exam Alerts.

▶ Keep in mind the characteristics of distance vector routing protocols and how those characteristics apply to RIP and RIPv2.

▶ Complete the Challenges and the Exercises at the end of the chapter. The exercises will solidify the concepts that you have learned in the previous sections.

▶ This chapter builds on the concepts discussed in Chapter 10, "Introduction to Routing and Routing Protocols." If you are not completely confident in your comfort with the fundamentals of routing protocols and their metrics, review Chapter 10 before proceeding with this chapter.

▶ Complete the Exam Questions at the end of the chapter. They are designed to simulate the types of questions you will be asked on the ICND1 exam.

Introduction

The preceding chapter looked at distance vector routing protocols from a sort of high-altitude overview. This chapter brings you closer so that you can see the specific protocols that belong to this routing protocol class and explore the unique characteristics and functionality they provide. You will also learn how to configure those routing protocols to meet your administrative needs and how to verify and troubleshoot their operation.

Distance Vector Operations

To recap, distance vector routing protocols are legacy routing protocols that help routing devices determine the networks that are present in a topology. Using a routing algorithm, known as the Bellman-Ford algorithm, distance vector routing protocols periodically broadcast routing updates consisting of the routing table to directly connected neighbors on adjacent data links, regardless of whether a change has occurred in the topology. When those devices receive that update, they compare it with their existing routing table information. If the distance vector metric for an entry in the routing update is greater (higher) than a current entry in the routing table, it is discarded. If the metric is equal or less, it is added to the routing table with an updated metric to include the path to the advertising neighbor. This entry eventually is passed to the next routing device where the process occurs over again.

> **NOTE**
>
> Many routing protocols, when the metrics on more than one route received by an update are equal, put both entries in the routing table and perform load balancing (transferring packets over both alternate paths).

Because these neighbors base their decisions on information that is not learned firsthand, distance vector routing protocol operations are often referred to as *routing by rumor*. In addition, each router in a distance vector routing topology has the same responsibility and function as the next router. In other words, distance vector routers contain flat relationships with each other.

> **EXAM ALERT**
>
> Distance vector routing protocols use the Bellman-Ford algorithm by broadcasting the entire routing table to directly connected neighbors regardless of whether a topology change occurs or not. The information in the update is added and recalculated before being sent to other neighbors.

Consider the example shown in Figure 11.1, which uses a classful distance vector routing protocol such as RIP version 1. Each router contains its directly connected networks in its routing table. Because the routing protocol is classful, the subnetted 192.168.1.0 network has a

Fixed-Length Subnet Mask (FLSM) design. In addition, the routing table entries contain the metric (hop count for this particular example) indicated by "0" because they are all connected. This is also followed by the interface that packets will exit to reach those networks. Without the use of static routes or routing protocols, the routers can never reach the networks that lie beyond their neighbor routers.

FIGURE 11.1 Distance vector routing initiation.

After you configure and enable a distance vector routing protocol, it advertises the networks in the routing table to its adjacent neighbors. For example, Router A broadcasts a routing update containing the 192.168.1.4 network as well as the 172.16.0.0 network to Router B. As soon as Router B receives that update, it compares the entries in its routing table with the information learned from Router A. Router B already knows about 192.168.1.4 as a directly connected network, so it disregards that entry because the directly connected network has a lower administrative distance than the routing protocol. Because the 172.16.0.0 network is new information, it adds that to its routing table with an updated metric of 1. The 172.16.0.0 network is one hop away through Router A. Similarly, when that entry is advertised to Routers C and D, the metric is updated again to 2 because it is two hops away (through Router B and then Router A).

Likewise, Routers A, C, and D receive an update from Router B containing two new networks that will be added to their routing table as two hops away. This process continues until each router has an accurate depiction of all the networks in the domain, as shown in Figure 11.2. In other words, the network will be converged. Despite having achieved full convergence, the routes will still advertise their routing table to their neighbors periodically, even if there isn't a change in the topology.

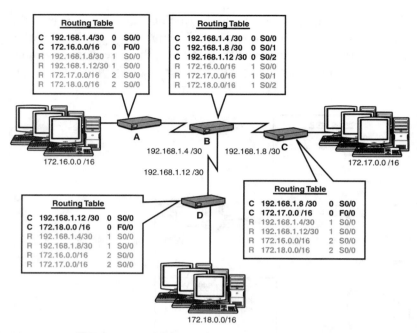

FIGURE 11.2 Distance vector routing converged scenario.

Routing Loops

One of the major concerns with routing protocols is the possible occurrence of a routing loop. Routing loops are hard to find these days because routing protocols have implemented many measures to mitigate them, but it is still important to examine the plausible historic events that necessitated the need for such measures. Additionally, there still is a slim possibility that these loops can occur regardless of the countermeasures in place.

To demonstrate a routing loop scenario, I will use the existing converged topology and introduce a link failure on Router A, as illustrated in Figure 11.3. Notice that the routing table in Router A changed to reflect only the remaining connected interface left since its serial link failed. Because the next hop to the protocol-learned networks is down, those entries are removed too. Likewise, Router B removes the connected interface as well as the network entry for 172.16.0.0 because that link and consequently the next hop to that network is down.

Imagine in this scenario that Router D sends its periodic update to Router B before Router B can advertise the topology change in its update. When Router B receives the update, it compares the information with its own routing table as distance vector routing protocols typically do. The new subnet information learned in the routing update is added to the routing table. In this unfortunate case, Router B learns (again) about the 172.16.0.0 and the 192.168.1.4

FIGURE 11.3 Link failure scenario.

networks and believes they can be reached through Router D (despite Router D originally having learned those routes via Router B). What's more, Router B adds its metric to get to Router D to reach the networks that don't even exist, as shown in Figure 11.4.

FIGURE 11.4 Incorrect update scenario.

Router B continues to update its neighbor routers periodically with the entries in its routing table. Unfortunately, the unreachable networks appear to be moving away because the hop count inevitably increases with each update from Router B and Router D for infinity. All the while, poor Router C also is fed false information about these networks from Router B and also has to keep adjusting its metrics as shown in Figure 11.5.

FIGURE 11.5   Routing loop.

With all three routers containing false information regarding those networks, any packets destined for the 172.16.0.0 and the 192.168.1.4 network are sent to Router D, who in turn, sends them right back to Router B, and so on. These packets will continue to bounce back and forth in the routing loop until the time to live field in the IP packets expire or the link becomes so saturated, traffic cannot flow between the two routers.

Routing Loop Mitigation

To avoid routing loops, distance vector routing protocols have implemented several countermeasures within the routing protocol operations. The following sections describe the preventative measures that have been put in place to mitigate routing loops. For obvious reasons, the majority of these is integrated within the routing protocol and cannot be disabled.

EXAM ALERT

Make sure you remember and comprehend the ways distance vector routing protocols mitigate routing loops.

Counting to Infinity

As demonstrated earlier, when routers are continuously passing updates to unreachable networks between each other, the metric continues to increase forever, which is known as *counting to infinity*. The easiest way to mitigate this routing protocol side effect is to incorporate a ceiling on the maximum hop count in the design of the routing protocol. Using this tactic, routers can determine a network to be unreachable after it reaches the maximum hop count allowed for that protocol. Table 11.1 lists the routing protocols and their maximum hop count values.

TABLE 11.1 Maximum Hop Counts

Protocol	Distance Vector/Link State/Hybrid	Maximum Hop Count
RIPv1	Distance vector	15
RIPv2	Distance vector	15
EIGRP	Hybrid	224
OSPF	Link state	Infinite

Notice that RIP version 1 and 2 both have a maximum hop count of 15, which drastically limits the size of the allowed RIP network. EIGRP, because it is has some distance vector routing protocol features, has a maximum hop count value of 224. OSPF is a link-state routing protocol that does not use or require a maximum hop count, so it can have an infinite number of hops.

EXAM ALERT

Be sure to remember the maximum hop counts for each protocol.

Split Horizon

Split horizon is similar to that old saying, "Don't ride out on the horse you rode in on." After hearing this little tidbit, if you were to turn around and say back to me that split horizon is similar to that old saying, "Don't ride out on the horse you rode in on," it would get redundant, confusing, and annoying pretty quickly. Such is the case with routing updates.

As you saw earlier, you can get into trouble when routers advertise networks back to the router from which they learned them. Split horizon fixes this dilemma by suppressing those networks in the routing updates being sent back to the source. In other words, split horizon does not advertise networks out the same interface as that from which it learned them.

Take the example shown in Figure 11.6. Because Router D learned about the 192.168.1.4, 192.168.1.8, 172.16.0.0, and 172.17.0.0 subnets from Router B, it does not advertise those networks back to Router B out Serial 0/0. In addition, because it heard Router B advertising the 192.168.1.12 network as well, it does not advertise that back out that interface either.

Thus, the only network that Router D will still advertise to Router B is the 172.18.0.0 network because that subnet was not learned via serial 0/0. Now when the link fails on Router A, Router B will not receive a misleading update about the 192.168.1.4 and the 172.16.0.0 networks because Router D and Router C do not advertise those networks back to Router B.

FIGURE 11.6   Split horizon updates.

NOTE

Contrary to what you might think, when a router advertises a network in a routing update to its neighbors, it adds the metric automatically, as shown in Figure 11.6.

EXAM ALERT

Be sure you understand the operations involved in split horizon.

Route Poison, Poison Reverse, and Hold-Down Timers

To avoid count-to-infinity routing loops, a maximum hop count is defined for a routing protocol so the metrics do not increment indefinitely in the event of a routing loop. With route poisoning, the router that recognizes the link failure poisons the affected networks by setting them to an infinite metric for that routing protocol. When that router sends this update to its neighbors, they are notified of the link failure and can update their routing table accordingly.

To illustrate the route poisoning concept, refer to Figure 11.7. Notice in this topology that a redundant route has been added between Router D and Router A. The resultant routing table for Router D now has a route to the 172.16.0.0 network through Router A because it is only one hop count as opposed to two hops through Router B. In addition, notice that Router D has equidistant hops to reach network 192.168.1.4. In this case, Router D keeps both routes in the routing table and load balances between both links for packets destined for that network. When the link fails between Router A and Router B, Router A and Router B set the affected networks to an infinite metric. In this example, because I am using RIP, the maximum hop count is 15, so 16 is an infinite metric.

FIGURE 11.7   Route poisoning.

When Routers C and D receive these updates from their neighbors, they can advertise the poisoned network out all their interfaces. With poison reverse, the routers override the split horizon rule and even send the update back to the source, which proves useful as an acknowledgment that those devices are aware of the topology change. At the same time, when Routers C and D receive the poisoned update, they put that network in a "possible down" state in their routing table, as illustrated in Figure 11.8. This is the work of the hold-down timer.

Hold-down timers are activated when a router receives a poisoned update from a neighbor indicating that a known network is now inaccessible. To ensure that the router does not hastily listen to alternate routes causing yet another routing loop, the router ignores updates with a poorer metric than the original until the hold-down timer expires. This gives the rest of the topology ample time to react to the link change. However, if an update is received with a *better* metric than the original route entry, the router discontinues the hold-down timer and uses that entry in its routing table.

FIGURE 11.8   Hold-down timers.

In Figure 11.8, when Routers A and B poison their route entries and pass them to Routers C and D, those poisoned networks are put in a possible down state and the hold-down timer is activated. In that time, Router B may receive updates from Router D about the 172.16.0.0 network because Router D has an alternate route. However, Router B must wait for the hold-down timer to expire before using the alternate path. For this reason, distance vector routing protocols are considered the slowest routing protocols to converge.

Triggered Updates

One way distance vector routing protocols speed up their convergence while helping avoid routing loops at the same time is something called *flash* or *triggered updates*. Because one of the contributing causes of routing loops is the lack of update information reaching all devices quickly enough, triggered updates enable the router to send the update immediately after a link fails, as opposed to waiting for its periodic update time.

Invalid/Dead Timers

In place of a link failure, what do you suppose would happen if Router A had some operational failures or you removed or changed the routing protocol configuration or networks? Other routers in the domain would not be aware of this change because it isn't a link failure that they can detect and react to. To ensure that these networks are not circulating indefinitely in a routing system, routing protocols have invalid, or dead, timers. If a router stops receiving updates from a router after a set amount of time, that router is considered to be dead and the networks that learned from that router are invalid. Likewise, if a particular network stops advertising with a routing protocol, that entry becomes invalid after the dead timer ages out. This timer is reset every time an update is received from a neighbor for each network in the routing table. When the timer expires, the router poisons the route and advertises that topology change to its neighbors.

> **TIP**
>
> You can clear out aged entries in the routing table quickly by using the `clear ip route` command followed by the network you want to remove, or use the wildcard, *, to remove all entries.

RIP

The first distance vector routing protocol that is discussed here is coincidentally one of the oldest routing protocols that is still used today. Circa 1988, Routing Information Protocol (RIP) for IP was defined in RFC 1058; however, its roots stem back to the 1970s at Xerox Corporation's Palo Alto Research Center. The following sections look at the characteristics and configurations involved with this resolute routing protocol.

RIP Characteristics

RIP is a fairly simple routing protocol in both characteristics and implementation. You already know that RIP uses hop count as its only metric, in which it can support up to 15 as a maximum. In instances where the metric is identical (for example, equal hop count) for a subnet, it load balances up to six equal paths (four by default). Like other distance vector routing protocols, RIP sends the contents of its routing table to its directly connected neighbors, regardless of whether there is a change in the topology. Particularly, RIP's update interval is every 30 seconds and its invalid timer is for 180 seconds. Thus, RIP (version 1) broadcasts its routing table every 30 seconds and considers a neighbor or a network to be dead after six missed updates.

Because RIP does not advertise subnet masks in its routing updates, it is also a classful routing protocol. Recall that this requires every subnet of a major network to have the same (fixed-length) subnet masks. In addition, RIP automatically summarizes subnetted networks to their default classful boundaries when sending the update over a different major network which, in turn, nullifies any support for a discontiguous network design.

> **EXAM ALERT**
>
> Although version 1 of RIP is considered outdated by the CCNA, ICND1, and ICND2 exams, it is important to know its characteristics and configuration because RIPv2 shares many characteristics and is similar in configuration.

RIP Configuration

The configuration for RIP is seamless as long as you remember these two simple rules:

▶ Advertise only your directly connected networks.

▶ Advertise only the classful network.

The first rule is imperative to keep in mind when configuring routing protocols. Remember that the point of the routing protocols is to advertise their known networks to each other so they can build their routing tables. With that being said, do not confuse the configuration of routing protocols with static routes. You do not specify a destination network with routing protocols as you would a static route. Instead, you specify local networks and let the routing protocols advertise them to each other.

Because RIP is a classful routing protocol and does not advertise subnet masks in its updates, the second rule is self-explanatory. Regardless of whether you subnetted major networks into smaller subnets, you have to specify only the subnet to its classful boundary. In other words, you specify the network portion of the IP address and use zeros for the host bits. To recap, the classful boundaries are listed in Table 11.2, in which N represents the network and H represents the host.

> **EXAM ALERT**
>
> It is imperative to know and practice the two rules for configuring RIP.

TABLE 11.2 Classful Network Boundaries

Class	First Octet	Network
A	1 to 126	N.H.H.H
B	128 to 191	N.N.H.H
C	192 to 223	N.N.N.H

To configure RIP and advertise the directly connected classful networks, you must enter the configuration mode for routing protocols, using the router keyword in global configuration mode followed by the routing protocol you want to configure. After you are in the routing protocol configuration mode (signified by the (config-router)# prompt), you specify the directly connected classful networks by using the network command. If you need to remove a specific network from being advertised, you need to enter the RIP routing process again and enter no followed by the keyword network and the network number you want to remove.

Using Figure 11.9 as an example, Routers A, C, and D each have two directly connected networks while Router B has three. To configure RIP to advertise the routing protocols, the configuration for Router A would look like the following:

```
RouterA(config)#router rip
RouterA(config-router)#network 172.16.0.0
RouterA(config-router)#network 192.168.1.0
```

FIGURE 11.9 RIP configuration scenario.

TIP

If you accidentally configure a network at the incorrect classful boundary, the IOS configuration automatically changes your configuration statement(s) to reflect the classful network.

EXAM ALERT

Be prepared to configure a routing protocol given a network topology. Even though there is IOS support to autocorrect your mistakes when entering the networks, as mentioned in the preceding Tip, do not rely on the exam to allow that as a correct answer.

Because Router A has the 172.16.0.0 network and the 192.168.1.4 network attached to it, the classful networks that are advertised are 172.16.0.0 because it is a Class B, and 192.168.1.0 because that network is a Class C. You do not need to include any other network statements because the routers will advertise each others' networks. After you define the networks with the `network` command, RIP begins to advertise and listen for updates on those interfaces that are contained in that classful network. For instance, if you did not configure the `network` `192.168.1.0` statement in Router A, you would never be able to send and receive updates on the serial interface, which would entail that Router B would never learn of the 172.16.0.0 network and Router A would never learn of the other networks in the topology.

EXAM ALERT

Keep in mind that the routing protocol does not listen to or learn from advertisements on an interface unless you include their respective networks in the routing protocol process with the `network` command.

Router B has three directly connected 192.168.1.x networks, so how many statements do you think you must configure for Router B to participate in RIP updates? Despite having three networks, you must advertise the classful networks in the RIP configuration; thus, you require only one statement for the 192.168.1.0 network that will, in essence, encompass all three subnets. Figure 11.10 shows the configurations for each router in this topology.

FIGURE 11.10 Completed RIP configuration scenario.

If you want to change the number of allowed equal paths to load balance with RIP, you can use the `maximum-paths` command in the routing process. For example, if you wanted to change the maximum paths to six equal paths, the configuration would look like the following:

```
RouterA(config)#router rip
RouterA(config-router)#maximum-paths 6
```

> **TIP**
>
> To disable load balancing over multiple equal paths, set the maximum paths to 1.

Passive Interfaces

Some of you may have looked at these configurations and noticed a strange flaw in our logic. Namely, we've established that when we configure each network to be advertised in the routers, updates begin being sent and received on the interfaces attached to those networks. But do we really need to be sending updates on LANs that do not connect to RIP routers? For instance, the Ethernet interface on Router A from Figure 11.10 that connects to the 172.16.0.0 network does not have a router on that LAN segment. In essence, we are wasting good bandwidth and processor cycles by broadcasting these RIP update every 60 seconds to a bunch of computers who do not need to receive them. To solve this dilemma for RIP and all other routing protocols, Cisco created a handy configuration option for routing protocols called *passive interface*.

With this additional configuration command, you specify an interface or interfaces to the routing protocol process that will no longer send routing updates. What is interesting, however, is that the interfaces will still receive and process updates on that interface. As a result, passive interfaces are useful not only for saving bandwidth, but also can be used to manipulate our routing policies by allowing us to determine whether or not we send routing updates to certain routers. The command to achieve this marvelous feat is `passive-interface` *interface* in the routing process configuration, such as shown here for RIP:

```
RouterA(config)#router rip
RouterA(config-router)#passive-interface fastethernet 0/0
```

With this command in place, updates are no longer sent out of Fast Ethernet 0/0. However, if for some reason an update was received on that interface, it would still process it and put it in its routing table.

RIPv2 Characteristics

In an attempt to keep up with modern needs from a routing protocol, RIP version 2 was created in 1994 to address many of the shortcomings of its predecessor. Many of the characteristics are similar to RIPv1; nonetheless, RIPv2 had some significant improvements:

▶ **Multicast updates:** Rather than broadcast its routing updates, RIPv2 uses a reserved multicast address of 224.0.0.9 to communicate with other RIPv2 neighbors. By using a multicast address, it does not waste the processing resources of non-RIP devices because only RIPv2 devices process messages to that address.

▶ **Classful or classless support:** RIPv2 is classful by default, but can be configured as a classless routing protocol, which allows for subnet masks to be sent in the routing updates. The implication of this enhancement entails that RIPv2 can support VLSM and discontiguous network designs.

▶ **Authenticated updates:** To ensure the origin of the routing update and protect from attackers spoofing routing updates, RIPv2 allows update authentication in which the passwords must match in all routers to validate the routing update.

EXAM ALERT

Be sure to remember the enhancements that RIPv2 holds over RIPv1.

RIPv2 Configuration

Objective:

▶ Configure, verify, and troubleshoot RIPv2

The configuration for RIPv2 is practically identical to RIPv1. In other words, you still must enter the RIP routing process with the `router rip` command and still must advertise the directly connected classful networks. To enable RIPv2, you have to enter the command `version 2` in the routing process:

```
RouterA(config)#router rip
RouterA(config-router)#version 2
RouterA(config-router)#network 172.16.0.0
RouterA(config-router)#network 192.168.1.0
```

By default, RIPv2 is classful. To configure this enhanced routing protocol to support classless routing updates, the only entry you need to configure is the `no auto-summary` command in the routing process:

```
RouterA(config)#router rip
RouterA(config-router)#no auto-summary
```

After you configure this command, the RIP version 2 updates being multicast to 224.0.0.9 are no longer be considered classful, because the subnet mask is advertised in the updates along with the network.

TIP

By default, RIP is configured to send version 1 and accept version 1 and 2 received updates. This means that routers that have not been changed to version 2 will still accept version 2 updates but will process them as version 1 (ignoring any subnet mask or authentication). Be sure to keep this in mind if you decide to revert your RIP configuration to version 1 by using the `version 1` command. This command instructs the router to receive only version 1 updates, which causes version 2 updates to be treated as an illegal version and be ignored. To revert to the default RIP configuration, a better command to use is `default version` in the RIP routing process.

EXAM ALERT

If a router is explicitly configured to run as version 1, RIP version 2 updates are considered an illegal version and are ignored.

Configuring RIP with SDM

RIP configurations using SDM are relatively similar and just as easy as configuring default and static routes. Select **Configuration, Routing**. Focus on the bottom of the screen for our dynamic routing protocols. When you click the **Edit** button, you see the pop-up window shown in Figure 11.11, in which you can specify your routing protocol parameters. You can enable RIP by checking the checkbox and specifying which version you want to run. Below that, you add the networks you want to advertise. Be sure that you specify each network that is directly attached to the router. This ensures that they are included in the routing updates and that the updates are sent and received on the interfaces associated with those networks. Finally, in the bottom of the window, you can check the checkboxes for the interfaces that you want to make into passive interfaces to save bandwidth or control which routers will have updates sent to them.

FIGURE 11.11 SDM RIP configuration.

RIP Verification

Objective:

▶ Verify network status and router operation using basic utilities (including: ping, traceroute, telnet, SSH, arp, ipconfig), SHOW & DEBUG commands

To verify RIP, you can use an assortment of show commands, each equally contributing to a wealth of information about the RIP routing protocol you configured. For instance, show running-config is an easy pick to show your configuration for RIP and the networks that you have configured. It is also a useful starting point if you are troubleshooting an existing implementation of RIP and you suspect missing or misconfigured network statements.

To ensure that RIP updates are being received from neighbors, show ip route proves the network configuration is functioning, because you will see RIP entries appear in the routing table:

```
RouterA#show ip route
Codes: C - connected, S - static, I - IGRP, R - RIP, M - mobile, B - BGP
       D - EIGRP, EX - EIGRP external, O - OSPF, IA - OSPF inter area
       N1 - OSPF NSSA external type 1, N2 - OSPF NSSA external type 2
       E1 - OSPF external type 1, E2 - OSPF external type 2, E - EGP
       i - IS-IS, L1 - IS-IS level-1, L2 - IS-IS level-2, * - candidate default
       U - per-user static route, o - ODR, P - periodic downloaded static route
       T - traffic engineered route

Gateway of last resort is not set

R    172.17.0.0/16 [120/2] via 192.168.1.6, Serial0/0/0
C    172.16.0.0/16 is directly connected, FastEthernet0/0
R    172.18.0.0/16 [120/2] via 192.168.1.6, Serial0/0/0
     192.168.1.0/30 is subnetted, 3 subnets
R       192.168.1.8 [120/1] via 192.168.1.6, Serial0/0/0
R       192.168.1.12 [120/1] via 192.168.1.6, Serial0/0/0
C       192.168.1.4 is directly connected, Serial0/0/0
```

The RIP entries are identified in the routing table with the letter R followed by the administrative distance and the hop count in brackets. The IP 192.168.1.6 is the next-hop address to reach those networks out of Serial 0/0/0.

Finally, to see detailed information about all the IP routing protocols configured on a routing device, use show ip protocols to see a plethora of information:

```
RouterA#show ip protocols
Routing Protocol is "rip"
  Sending updates every 30 seconds, next due in 24 seconds
  Invalid after 180 seconds, hold down 180, flushed after 240
  Outgoing update filter list for all interfaces is not set
  Incoming update filter list for all interfaces is not set
  Redistributing: rip
```

```
Default version control: send version 2, receive version 2
   Interface           Send  Recv  Triggered RIP     Key-chain
   FastEthernet0/0       2    2
   Serial0/0/0           2    2                       luckyrabbitsfoot
Automatic network summarization is in effect
Maximum path: 4
Routing for Networks:
   172.16.0.0
   192.168.1.0
Routing Information Sources:
   Gateway         Distance       Last Update
   192.168.1.6          120       00:00:11
Distance: (default is 120)
```

In this output, you can see the timers involved with the routing protocol, including the update interval of 30 seconds and the invalid and hold-down timers. The show ip protocols output also lists the interfaces participating in RIP and the version that they are configured to send and receive (in this case, version 2). On our serial 0/0/0 interface, you can also see that we have configured RIP authentication and that the key chain *luckyrabbitsfoot* is assigned to this interface. In addition, you can see which networks you are routing using RIP. This is useful for administrators who do not have access to privileged EXEC mode (and who therefore cannot use the show running-config command) to verify which networks are being advertised.

Troubleshooting RIP

Troubleshooting routing protocols always begins with verification of the routing configuration and status by using the show commands discussed in the last section. You can also test whether you have IP connectivity by pinging or you can test the route packets will take by using the traceroute command. However, if you need to get into the trenches, so to speak, and verify the updates as they are being sent and received, you need to use real-time troubleshooting tools entailing the debug command.

TIP

If you forget which debug processes you have running, you can issue the show debug command to list all the processes you are currently debugging.

To actively see real-time updates as they are being sent and received for RIP, use the privileged EXEC command debug ip rip, as demonstrated here:

```
RouterA#debug ip rip
RIP protocol debugging is on
RouterA#
*Aug  6 22:33:21.002: RIP: received packet with MD5 authentication
*Aug  6 22:33:21.002: RIP: received v2 update from 192.168.1.6 on Serial0/0/0
*Aug  6 22:33:21.002:        172.17.0.0/16 via 0.0.0.0 in 2 hops
```

```
*Aug  6 22:33:21.002:        172.18.0.0/16 via 0.0.0.0 in 2 hops
*Aug  6 22:33:21.006:        192.168.1.8/30 via 0.0.0.0 in 1 hops
*Aug  6 22:33:21.006:        192.168.1.12/30 via 0.0.0.0 in 1 hops
```

In this section of the debug output, the router receives an update from a neighbor with the IP address 192.168.1.6. This update is a version 2 update and has been authenticated using MD5. If any new subnets are learned from this update, they ultimately are placed in the routing table, using 192.168.1.6 as the next-hop address and Serial 0/0/0 as the exiting interface, because that is where this information was learned. Notice in this section that subnet masks are received in the update, solidifying the fact that you are running a classless routing protocol, RIPv2.

The next bit of output that follows is the local router sending its v2 multicast (224.0.0.9) update out its Fast Ethernet 0/0 interface. Most important, notice how the router increments the hop count by 1 before sending it to any neighbors on its LAN:

```
*Aug  6 22:33:23.598: RIP: sending v2 update to 224.0.0.9 via FastEthernet0/0
(172.16.0.1)
*Aug  6 22:33:23.598: RIP: build update entries
*Aug  6 22:33:23.598:    172.17.0.0/16 via 0.0.0.0, metric 3, tag 0
*Aug  6 22:33:23.598:    172.18.0.0/16 via 0.0.0.0, metric 3, tag 0
*Aug  6 22:33:23.598:    192.168.1.0/24 via 0.0.0.0, metric 1, tag 0
*Aug  6 22:33:23.598: RIP: ignored v2 packet from 172.16.0.1 (sourced from one of our
addresses)
```

Also, take note of the 192.168.1.0 entry that is being advertised out this Fast Ethernet 0/0 interface. Because the interface has an IP address of 172.16.0.1, which is not in the same major network, this router automatically summarized its subnetted entries to 192.168.1.0. Therefore, we can surmise by this debug output that we have not configured the no auto-summary on Router A. If this were the case, the entry would remain classless and look more like this:

```
*Aug  6 22:33:23.598:    192.168.1.4/30 via 0.0.0.0, metric 1, tag 0
```

The final output that follows is proof that split horizon is enabled and working on this router. This is evident because the router does not send any entries that it received on serial 0/0/0 from the first output explanation. Recall that split horizon keeps a router from advertising networks back out the interface from which it received that information. Because the 192.168.1.8, 192.168.1.12, 172.17.0.0, and 172.18.0.0 networks were received in the router's Serial 0/0/0 interface, they cannot be sent back out that interface.

```
*Aug  6 22:33:23.822: RIP: sending v2 update to 224.0.0.9 via Serial0/0/0 (192.168.1.5)
*Aug  6 22:33:23.822: RIP: build update entries
*Aug  6 22:33:23.822:    172.16.0.0/16 via 0.0.0.0, metric 1, tag 0
```

EXAM ALERT

Be sure you can decipher the output of a `debug ip rip` command.

Challenge

Given the following design in Figure 11.12, configure RIP on Router A to be able to communicate with the remainder of the preconfigured network.

172.16.100.0 /24   A 10.1.1.60 /30 B 192.168.1.8 /30 C   172.17.0.0 /16

FIGURE 11.12   RIP configuration challenge.

1. Remember to remove any existing static routes. Why?

2. Enter the configuration process for RIP.

3. Advertise Router A's networks.

   What will Router B do with the update from Router A?

   What will the networks look like when Router B sends them on to Router C?

4. Configure Router A to run RIP version 2.

5. Configure Router A to be classless.

   What will the update from Router A look like now?

Challenge Answer

You must first remove any static routes because they have a lower administrative distance than RIP. The configuration in steps 2 and 3 would look like the following:

```
RouterA(config)#router rip
RouterA(config-router)#network 172.16.0.0
RouterA(config-router)#network 10.0.0.0
```

Despite having subnetted the major networks in our topology, you must advertise the directly connected classful networks. When Router B receives that update, it adds the 172.16.0.0 entry into its routing table (because 10.1.1.60 is already directly connected) with a metric of 1 and uses Router A's serial interface as the next hop. The entry is not 172.16.100.0 because Router A auto-summarizes that network when exiting its WAN interface because that is on a different major network. When Router B sends that entry to Router C, it is sent as 172.16.0.0 with a metric (hop count of 2).

(continues)

(continued)

To configure Router A for RIPv2 and make it classless, you must add the following configurations:

```
RouterA(config)#router rip
RouterA(config-router)#version 2
RouterA(config-router)#no auto-summary
```

With this configuration, Router A does not automatically summarize the 172.16.100.0 network and it sends the subnet mask along to Router B. If B is running RIPv2 also, it keeps the network in its subnetted form of 172.16.100.0/24.

Chapter Summary

This chapter discussed the distance vector routing protocols, RIP and RIPv2. Both routing protocols are susceptible to routing loops and have several countermeasures in place to help mitigate these anomalies. For instance, both routing protocols have a maximum hop count to ensure that routing loops do not cause routers to increment the metric for infinity, and define a reasonable limit on the size of the network to which the routing protocol can scale. Split horizon contributes in the mitigation of routing loops by ensuring that routers do not advertise networks out the same interface as that on which those networks were learned. When a link fails, distance vector routing protocols poison the affected routes by setting them to an infinite metric and immediately shoot them out as a flash or triggered update. The split horizon rule is overridden in this instance to send a notice that the link is possibly down. The link remains in that state (unless it receives an update that has a better metric than the original network entry) until the hold-down timer expires. After the hold-down timer lapses, the router can use routes with less favorable metrics than the original.

Table 11.3 summarizes the characteristics of RIPv1 and RIPv2.

TABLE 11.3 RIP and RIPv2 Comparison

	RIPv1	RIPv2
Classful/classless	Classful	Both
Algorithm	Bellman-Ford	Bellman-Ford
Metric	Hops	Hops
Maximum hop count	15	15
Infinite metric	16	16
Update/invalid	30/180	30/180
Updates	Broadcast	Multicast (224.0.0.9)
Load balancing	Equal paths	Equal paths

To configure RIP, you must enter the routing process first with the router keyword in global configuration mode followed by the routing protocol. After you are in the routing process, you advertise the networks with the network command followed by the directly connected classful networks.

To enable RIPv2, you must add the command version 2 in the RIP routing configuration process. When you enable version 2, updates are no longer broadcast to neighbors, but rather are sent as multicasts to 224.0.0.9. In addition, because RIPv2 can be classless in addition to classful, you can disable automatic summarization of networks with the no auto-summary command. Additionally, RIPv2 supports update authentication.

To verify the routing process for RIP, you can use the `show ip route` command to view the IP routing table and examine whether networks have been learned from the routing protocol. In addition, `show ip protocols` displays the networks you are advertising in the local router, as well as the timers for each IP routing protocol.

When performing real-time troubleshooting, you can use the `debug ip rip` command. Be sure that you do not use these commands on a production router that is reporting high CPU utilization from the `show processes` output.

Key Terms

- ▶ Bellman-Ford algorithm
- ▶ Counting to infinity
- ▶ Route poison
- ▶ Poison reverse
- ▶ Hold-down timers
- ▶ Triggered updates
- ▶ RIP
- ▶ Passive interface
- ▶ RIPv2

Apply Your Knowledge

Exercises

11.1 Configure RIPv2 Router A

In this exercise and the next, you will configure RIP between two routers.

> **NOTE**
>
> This exercise assumes you have two nonproduction routers with a DCE to DTE serial cable or simulated software. If you do not have these on hand, write down what the configurations would look like.

Estimated Time: 20 minutes

1. Enter privileged EXEC mode on Router A.

2. Enter global configuration mode.

3. Configure and enable the Fast Ethernet interface on Router A to have an IP address of 192.168.1.1/24.

4. Configure and enable the serial interface on Router A to have an IP address of 10.1.1.1/30.

5. Configure the clock rate (if this is the DCE) for 64000 bits per second.

6. Enter the routing process for RIP.

7. Advertise the directly connected classful networks.

8. Enable version 2 of RIP.

9. Disable automatic summarization.

10. Exit to global configuration mode and create a key and key string for RIP authentication.

11.2 Configure RIPv2 Router B

Now that Router A is configured, you must configure its neighbor, Router B, to send and receive routing updates.

Estimated Time: 20 minutes

1. Enter privileged EXEC mode on Router B.

2. Enter global configuration mode.

3. Configure and enable the Fast Ethernet interface on Router B to have an IP address of 172.16.30.1/24.

4. Configure and enable the serial interface on Router B to have an IP address of 10.1.1.2/30.

5. Configure the clock rate (if this is the DCE) for 64000 bits per second.

6. Enter the routing process for RIP.

7. Advertise the directly connected classful networks.

8. Enable version 2 of RIP.

9. Disable automatic summarization.

10. Exit to global configuration and create a key and key string that matches Router A for RIP authentication.

11.3 Verify Routing

If configured correctly, you should be able to verify your RIP routing in this exercise.

Estimated Time: 10 minutes

1. In both Router A and Router B, do a `show ip protocols` to verify the networks that you are advertising.

2. Do a `show ip route` and verify that you have a RIP entry in your routing table from your neighbor.

3. If statements are missing, troubleshoot the routing process by using `debug ip rip`.

Review Questions

1. What are the mitigation methods distance vector routing protocols use to avoid routing loops?

2. What are the characteristics of RIP?

3. What additional features are present in RIPv2 that are not present in RIP?

4. What is the purpose of the `passive-interface` command?

5. What are the fundamental configuration steps for RIPv2?

Exam Questions

1. Given the following output, which of the following is a true statement?

```
CstmrARtr#show ip route
Codes: C - connected, S - static, I - IGRP, R - RIP, M - mobile, B - BGP
       D - EIGRP, EX - EIGRP external, O - OSPF, IA - OSPF inter area
       N1 - OSPF NSSA external type 1, N2 - OSPF NSSA external type 2
       E1 - OSPF external type 1, E2 - OSPF external type 2, E - EGP
       i - IS-IS, L1 - IS-IS level-1, L2 - IS-IS level-2, * - candidate default
       U - per-user static route, o - ODR

Gateway of last resort is not set

R    1.0.0.0/8 is possibly down, routing via 192.168.1.9, Serial0
C    172.17.0.0/16 is directly connected, Ethernet0
R    172.16.0.0/16 [120/1] via 172.17.0.2, 00:00:19, Ethernet0
     192.168.1.0/30 is subnetted, 1 subnets
C       192.168.1.8 is directly connected, Serial0
```

○ **A.** The 172.16.0.0 has an administrative distance of 1.

○ **B.** The 1.0.0.0 network is in a hold-down state.

○ **C.** The configuration for this router to advertise RIP should have a network 172.16.0.0 and a network 1.0.0.0 statement.

○ **D.** None of the above.

2. Given the following output, which of the following statements is false regarding the 0.0.0.0/0 network?

```
CstmrARtr#show ip route
Codes: C - connected, S - static, I - IGRP, R - RIP, M - mobile, B - BGP
       D - EIGRP, EX - EIGRP external, O - OSPF, IA - OSPF inter area
       N1 - OSPF NSSA external type 1, N2 - OSPF NSSA external type 2
       E1 - OSPF external type 1, E2 - OSPF external type 2, E - EGP
       i - IS-IS, L1 - IS-IS level-1, L2 - IS-IS level-2, * - candidate default
       U - per-user static route, o - ODR

Gateway of last resort is 192.168.1.9 to network 0.0.0.0

R     1.0.0.0/8 [120/1] via 192.168.1.9, 00:00:21, Serial0
C     172.17.0.0/16 is directly connected, Ethernet0
R     172.16.0.0/16 [120/1] via 172.17.0.2, 00:00:02, Ethernet0
      192.168.1.0/30 is subnetted, 1 subnets
C        192.168.1.8 is directly connected, Serial0
R*    0.0.0.0/0 [120/1] via 192.168.1.9, 00:00:21, Serial0
```

  ○ **A.** The 0.0.0.0 network was statically configured in this router.

  ○ **B.** The gateway of last resort is the 192.168.1.9 router.

  ○ **C.** The default route was advertised to the local router via RIP.

  ○ **D.** The default route was automatically redistributed in Router 192.168.1.9.

3. Based on the following output, which network may not show up in the routing table?

```
RouterA#debug ip rip
RIP protocol debugging is on
RouterA#
00:26:27: RIP: received v1 update from 192.168.1.6 on Serial0/0
00:26:27:       192.168.1.8 in 12 hops
00:26:27:       192.168.1.12 in 15 hops
00:26:27:       172.17.0.0 in 14 hops
00:26:27:       172.18.0.0 in 16 hops
```

  ○ **A.** 172.17.0.0

  ○ **B.** 192.168.1.8

  ○ **C.** 192.168.1.12

  ○ **D.** 172.18.0.0

4. Which two commands enable a distance vector routing protocol to be classless?

  ○ **A.** version 2

  ○ **B.** passive-interface

  ○ **C.** no auto-summary

  ○ **D.** router classless

5. Which of the following is not a mechanism to avoid routing loops?

- ○ **A.** Split horizon
- ○ **B.** Update authentication
- ○ **C.** Hold-down timers
- ○ **D.** Route poisoning

6. Which command should you implement before doing any `debug` commands?

- ○ **A.** `show running-config`
- ○ **B.** `show processes`
- ○ **C.** `undebug all`
- ○ **D.** `copy running-config startup-config`

7. Given the following output of a `debug ip rip`, which of the following is true?

```
00:57:27: RIP: received v2 update from 192.168.1.6 on Serial0/0
00:57:27:       192.168.1.8/30 via 0.0.0.0 in 1 hops
00:57:27:       192.168.1.12/30 via 0.0.0.0 in 1 hops
00:57:27:       172.17.0.0/16 via 0.0.0.0 in 1 hops
00:57:27:       172.18.0.0/16 via 0.0.0.0 in 1 hops
```

- ○ **A.** The routing updates are broadcast to their neighbors.
- ○ **B.** The router automatically summarizes these networks.
- ○ **C.** Networks 172.17.0.0 and 172.18.0.0 have an infinite metric.
- ○ **D.** The `no auto-summary` command is used in RIPv2.

8. Which characteristic does not go with its respective routing protocol?

- ○ **A.** Multicasts updates—RIP
- ○ **B.** 180 invalid timer—RIP
- ○ **C.** Classful—RIPv2
- ○ **D.** Classless—RIPv2

Answers to Review Questions

1. Because distance vector routing protocols are susceptible to routing loops, they have incorporated several countermeasures to help mitigate any routing loop anomalies. For instance, all distance vector routing protocols have a maximum hop count to avoid counting to infinity. In addition, split horizon prevents routers from advertising networks out the same interface in which they were learned. Upon learning about a failing network, routers poison the route by setting it to an infinite metric and send a triggered update to the router's neighbors. The router will not process new inferior information about the failed network until the hold-down timer expires to ensure that the failed network does not get accidentally reinstated.

2. RIP is a classful distance vector routing protocol that uses hop count as its metric (maximum of 15). RIP broadcasts the contents of the routing table to its directly connected neighbors every 30 seconds.

3. RIPv2 supports classless routing updates if the `no auto-summary` command is used. In addition, RIPv2 updates are sent as multicasts and can be authenticated using an MD5 password.

4. The `passive-interface` command indicates that the specified interface will not send routing updates; however, the interface can still receive and process updates. This is useful to control which routers are sent updates and to save wasted bandwidth and processing of broadcasts or multicasts on LAN segments.

5. To enable RIP, you must enter the routing process by using the keyword `router` followed by the routing protocol. When you are in the routing configuration process, you must advertise the directly connected classful networks attached to the router by using the `network` command followed by the classful network. To enable RIPv2, you have to add the command `version 2` in the routing configuration.

Answers to Exam Questions

1. **B.** Because the routing table update shows the 1.0.0.0/8 network as possibly down, it is currently in a hold-down state and waiting for the hold-down timer to expire before accepting a route with a higher metric. Answer A is incorrect because the AD is 120 and the hip count is 1. C is false because those network entries were learned via RIP, not advertised. D is incorrect, because B is correct.

2. **A.** Because the default route has an R statement next to it, it was redistributed automatically by the neighbor at 192.168.1.9. If it was statically configured, it would have an S indication next to the route. Answers B, C, and D are true because the 0.0.0.0 route was redistributed and advertised via RIP by the router with the IP address of 192.168.1.9.

3. **D.** Because the 172.18.0.0 has an infinite metric for RIP being advertised, it is most likely a poisoned route or a router that is not showing up in the routing table. Answers A, B, and C will show up in the routing table because their hop count is does not exceed the maximum hop count for RIP (15).

4. **A, C.** The only distance vector routing protocol that can be classless is RIPv2. The command to enable RIPv2 is `version 2`. To make it classless, you use the `no auto-summary` command. Answer B is incorrect because the `passive-interface` command is used to keep updates from being sent out that specific interface. Answer D is not a valid command.

5. **B.** Update authentication is not a mechanism to avoid routing loops. Split horizon, hold-down timers, and router poisoning are all mechanisms to avoid routing loops so answers A, C, and D are incorrect.

6. **B.** Before running any debug commands, you should check your router's current and past utilization with the show processes command. Answer A does not have any effect on the debug process. Answer C will turn off any debugging after the debugging process has been initiated. Answer D does not have any effect on the debugging process.

7. **D.** The update is indicative of a RIPv2 update that has been configured as classless with the no auto-summary command. This is true because the updates contain the subnet masks. Answer A is false because RIPv2 multicasts its updates to 224.0.0.9. B is false because the no auto-summary command disables automatic summarization. C is incorrect because an infinite metric for RIPv2 is 16.

8. **A.** RIPv2 sends its updates as multicasts, not version 1. Answer B is true because RIP has an invalid timer of 180 seconds. Answers C and D are also true because RIPv2 is classful by default but can be configured as classless.

Suggested Readings and Resources

1. Alex Zinn. *IP Routing: Packet Forwarding and Intra-domain Routing Protocols.* Addison Wesley Professional, 2002.

2. Keith Kruepke, Paul Cernick, and Mark Degner. *Cisco IP Routing Handbook.* Hungry Minds, 2000.

3. Anthony Bruno and Jacqueline Kim. *CCDA Exam Certification Guide.* Cisco Press, 2004.

4. "Routing Protocols," www.firewall.cx.

5. RIP and RIPv2 technology support on www.cisco.com.

CHAPTER TWELVE

Enabling Internet Connectivity with NAT

Objectives

This chapter covers the following Cisco-specific objectives for the "Implement an IP addressing scheme and IP services to meet network requirements for a small branch office" section of the 640-822 ICND1 exam:

► **Explain the basic uses and operation of NAT in a small network connecting to one ISP**

► **Enable NAT for a small network with a single ISP and connection using SDM and verify operation using CLI and ping**

Outline

Introduction   390

NAT Concepts   391

  Static NAT   392

  Dynamic NAT   393

  NAT Overload and Port Address
Translation   394

NAT Terminology   395

Configuring NAT Using Cisco SDM   397

  Configuring NAT Overload   397

    Advanced NAT Wizard   401

    Edit NAT Configuration   407

Verifying NAT Configuration   410

Troubleshooting NAT   413

Chapter Summary   415

  Key Terms   415

  Review Questions   416

Apply Your Knowledge   416

  Exam Questions   416

  Answers to Review Questions   419

  Answers to Exam Questions   419

  Suggested Reading and Resources   421

Study Strategies

▶ Read the information presented in the chapter, paying special attention to tables, Notes, and Exam Alerts.

▶ Focus on the Network Address Translation terminology. Understanding these terms is paramount to understanding the NAT configuration as a whole.

▶ When studying, focus on the static NAT configurations first, because these are the simplest. After you master this configuration, move on to NAT overload, followed by dynamic NAT.

Introduction

I can still remember the very first time I saw Network Address Translation (NAT) in action. "This is the most amazing thing I have ever seen," I said, with the same awestruck feeling as the first time you walk up and look over the Grand Canyon. Okay, perhaps it wasn't that fantastic, but at the same time, NAT is definitely at the top of my list of configurations I love to set up.

Despite it being one of the most widely implemented concepts in the world of network technology, NAT is one of the newer topics added to the CCNA exam. This is most likely because of its configuration complexity: It requires a thorough understanding of standard access lists to successfully deploy. However, Cisco is very wise in adding it to the entry-level exam, because nearly every network in the world uses NAT in some shape or form. Even home networks using Linksys, D-Link, and Netgear routers use NAT.

NAT was originally developed through a combination of Cisco engineers and the Internet Engineering Task Force (IETF) group in 1994 to overcome the quickly approaching IP address shortage. With the Internet popularity growing at a rate far faster than expected, the remaining public IP addresses would soon be depleted. At that time, TCP/IP version 6 (IPv6, which would have solved the IP address shortage) had been created in a draft status, but it would require a worldwide upgrade of network devices and operating system software to successfully deploy. Rather than upgrading all network-capable devices, the focus was placed on creating a gateway device that could enable multiple network devices to share a single IP address.

As this concept materialized, NAT was born. Theoretically, a router running NAT is capable of allowing more than 60,000 devices to share a single Internet-valid IP address. Practically speaking, the router resources (processor and memory) and WAN bandwidth are depleted long before that limit is reached. With thousands of devices capable of using a single public IP address, the life of TCP/IP version 4 (IPv4) has been extended years beyond what was thought possible.

NAT also acts as a natural security boundary by eliminating end-to-end traceability. If your router has only a single IP address that is connected to the Internet, the public IP address, which is assigned to the outside interface, does not belong to any one internal host. For example, imagine that your router's public IP address is 209.1.5.9, and all your internal hosts come from the subnet 192.168.1.0/24. Whenever one of the internal hosts accesses the Internet, it is seen as 209.1.5.9. However, if anyone from the Internet attempts to access 209.1.5.9, the address maps to no individual host, which makes the internal network invisible to the Internet.

NAT Concepts

Objectives:

▶ Explain the basic uses and operation of NAT in a small network connecting to one ISP

Although the introductory discussion of NAT covers the most popular uses of the technology, NAT can be used for much more. Before you go deeper into the specific uses, though, you must understand the foundation concepts.

As its core function, Network Address Translation does just that: translate addresses. It can take any IP address and make it look like another. This is why the creative geniuses behind TCP/IP defined three ranges of "private IP addresses" in RFC 1918. The following is a list of the three private address ranges:

▶ **Class A:** 10.0.0.0 to 10.255.255.255

▶ **Class B:** 172.16.0.0 to 172.31.255.255

▶ **Class C:** 192.168.0.0 to 192.168.255.255

TIP

You need to know the private IP address ranges.

You might notice that a private address range is defined for each class of address. This gives a company more flexibility to use different ranges based on the company size. As a general statement, most small companies use the 192.168.X.X range, most medium-sized companies use the 172.16.X.X to 172.31.X.X ranges, and most large companies use the 10.X.X.X ranges. Remember, this is just a general statement, not a solid rule.

It is commonly stated that these private addresses are nonroutable, but this is untrue. Thousands of companies around the world use these addresses and route them throughout their private networks just fine. This misunderstanding came about because all Internet service providers (ISPs) use access lists to block these addresses from entering or leaving their networks. It is accurate to say that these private addresses are not *Internet* routable, because if they were, there would be thousands of duplicate IP address conflicts every day.

As shown in Figure 12.1, networks connected to the Internet typically use these private IP addresses internally and then translate them when attempting to access the Internet. This enables you to have many duplicate addresses around the world without any conflicts, because they never communicate directly. This can cause problems with overlapping IP addresses when companies merge, but NAT can even be engineered to solve these problems.

With this foundation in place, you're ready to examine the styles of NAT.

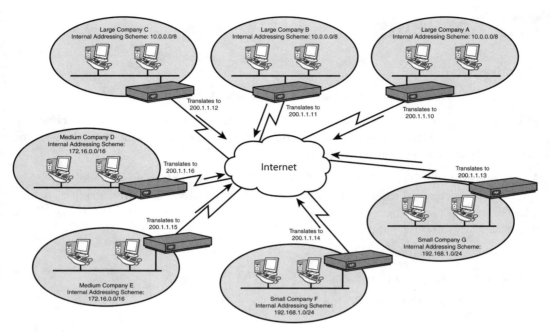

FIGURE 12.1 Network that uses a NAT configuration with private addressing.

Static NAT

Static NAT is the simplest form of NAT. It enables you to map one IP address to another in a one-to-one relationship. This is typically used to allow access to internal servers from the Internet that are using a private address space. In Figure 12.2, three servers are located on the internal network: a web server, an FTP server, and an email server. These three servers are assigned to a private IP address space (192.168.1.0/24) and would typically be inaccessible from the Internet. By using static NAT, you can map the private IP addresses to a public IP on a one-to-one basis, enabling these servers to be accessed from the Internet using the three public IP addresses shown in Figure 12.2.

This static NAT mapping goes both ways. When someone from the Internet accesses 200.1.1.1, it is translated to the internal address 192.168.1.1. Likewise, when the server 192.168.1.1 accesses the Internet, it is seen as 200.1.1.1. Although this form of NAT does not allow multiple internal hosts to share a single address, it does implement the security features of NAT by eliminating end-to-end traceability and enables servers that are sharing your private network to be accessed from the Internet.

Static NAT can also be configured to statically translate individual TCP or UDP ports. This awesome feature enables you to take a single IP address and translate one or many ports to

FIGURE 12.2 Static NAT address mappings.

either the same host or many different hosts. For example, you might have a router that has the external IP address 195.1.1.1. You can statically configure NAT so that when your router receives a request on 195.1.1.1, using TCP port 80 (HTTP), it redirects it to the internal address 192.168.1.50 on TCP port 80. However, when it receives a request on 195.1.1.1, using TCP port 21 (FTP), it redirects it to the internal address 192.168.1.100 on TCP port 21. In this way, NAT can act as a type of firewall (allowing only some ports through to specific hosts) and give you the flexibility of offering many services through the same IP address. Using static NAT with ports even makes it possible to redirect port numbers. For example, you might be using one of those scandalous DSL or cable Internet providers that block certain port numbers to keep you from running a web server from home. You can configure static NAT in such a way that when your router receives a request on TCP port 800 it redirects it to an internal IP address on TCP port 80.

Dynamic NAT

Static NAT is superb if you have a few hosts that need to be translated; however, if many hosts need to be translated, creating static entries for each one can be quite tedious. This is where dynamic NAT can help. Dynamic NAT enables you to define a pool of addresses to be translated along with a pool of addresses to which they are to be translated. The router then dynamically maps these IP addresses as the need arises. This is *not* the same thing as allowing multiple hosts to share the same IP address (known as NAT *overloading*). Dynamic NAT makes many one-to-one mappings without requiring you to configure them statically.

NAT Overload and Port Address Translation

Now we come to the form of NAT that made it famous. NAT overload, also known as Port Address Translation (PAT), enables a single IP address to support many internal clients. Whenever a host establishes communication with a server outside the NAT firewall, it tries to access a specific port number (known as the *destination port*). However, it also uses a source port number to allow for return traffic. Figure 12.3 shows how NAT overload also incorporates this source port number into the translation.

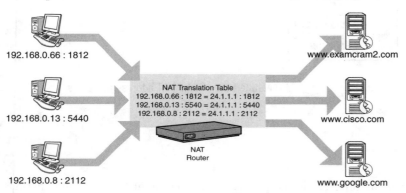

FIGURE 12.3   NAT overload uses port numbers to make translations unique.

The hosts communicating randomly generate the source ports. The NAT router then appends these to the public IP address to make the source *socket* (or IP address and port number combination) unique. When the Internet server replies to whatever request was made, it does so to the source IP and socket. When the NAT router receives the reply, it then can redirect it to the correct internal host by referring to its NAT translation table. Because hosts use random source ports, there is very little possibility that two hosts will choose the same source port number (one chance out of some 60,000). However, if two hosts do happen to choose the same port number, the NAT device causes one of the device sessions to reset and choose a different port number. By using unique port numbers, the router can originate thousands of requests from its single Internet IP address. This provides Internet access to the internal network clients while using just one Internet address.

To review, Table 12.1 shows the three forms of NAT and the styles of translation they perform.

TABLE 12.1   NAT Translation Forms and Types

NAT Configuration	Translation Type
Static NAT	One-to-one IP address translations
Dynamic NAT	Many-to-many IP address translations
NAT overload/PAT	Many-to-one IP address translations

NAT Terminology

Believe it or not, setting up NAT is not very difficult; it's learning the terminology used with NAT that can fry your brain. The first time you see these terms, it may make no sense to you, and that's just fine. It takes some time to soak in. Now, keep in mind that these are not "Cisco terms." Rather, they are an industry standard way of referring to the four different points in a NAT-based network. Before trying to understand four NAT address descriptions, you must understand the building blocks used to construct these terms:

▶ **Inside/outside:** These NAT descriptors refer to where a device is physically located. If a device is "inside," it is under your control; it is in your network. If a device is "outside," it is not under your control; it is outside your network.

▶ **Local/global:** These NAT descriptors refer to where an IP address is located *from the perspective of a NAT device*. The NAT device is a network device that has its address translated through a NAT router. It could be a PC, a server, an Xbox, or any other type of host that has a private address that is translated to a real address on the Internet. If the IP address is considered "local," it is seen as a device on the local subnet from the perspective of a NAT device (this may or may not be true). If the IP address is considered "global," it is seen as not on the local subnet from the perspective of a NAT device.

If that doesn't sound confusing, just wait until we start combining these terms for the four NAT address descriptions. Figure 12.4 shows a visual location of these address on the network.

▶ **Inside local addresses:** These addresses are the easiest to understand because they refer to everything inside your network. Remember the word *constructs* discussed just a moment ago: An address "inside" is physically located inside your network. From the perspective of the NAT device, it is "local," meaning it is seen on the internal network. If an inside local address were to communicate with another inside local address, that communication would be described as standard LAN connectivity. No routers would be needed.

▶ **Inside global addresses:** Now the terms begin to mix a little bit. Let's break this down into the individual pieces: First, the address is "inside," which means that it is physically located on your network; it is under your control. "Global" means that it is seen as an IP address not on the local subnet from the perspective of one of your NAT devices. Put all this together and you are left with the Internet valid IP address assigned to your router that is directly connected to the Internet. This is where a fundamental understanding of inside and outside can really help. If the address were an "outside global," it would not be under your control, meaning that it could be any of the millions of devices attached to the Internet.

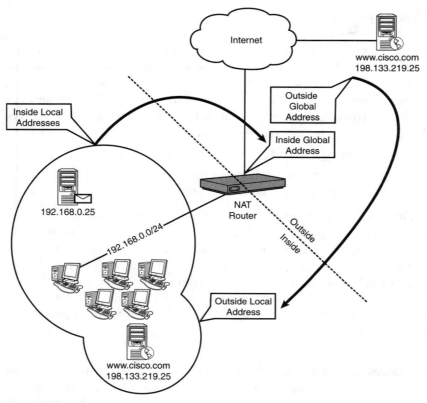

FIGURE 12.4 NAT terminology.

▶ **Outside global addresses:** Outside global addresses refer to devices that are physically "outside" your network—outside your control. These addresses are "global," meaning that the NAT devices on the inside of your network see these as nonlocal addresses. Put these two pieces together and you have a description of a standard Internet IP address.

▶ **Outside local addresses:** I saved the best for last. Outside local addresses confused me for quite some time until I fully understood the capabilities of NAT. First, let's look at the pieces: This address is physically "outside" your network, out of your control, out on the Internet. However, it appears to NAT devices as an IP address on the "local" subnet. What this describes is an Internet host translated as it comes through the NAT router *into* your local network. You can think of this as "reverse NAT," or just NAT in the other direction. As shown in Figure 12.4, when the cisco.com web server speaks to the internal hosts on the 192.168.0.0/24 network, they believe it to be co-located on the local subnet with them. They come to this conclusion because the NAT router translates the outside global address to something local (perhaps 192.168.0.1, the NAT gateway's address).

> **TIP**
>
> Understanding the four NAT address descriptors listed is useful not only for the ICND1, ICND2, and CCNA exams, but also for understanding any real-world NAT documentation.

Configuring NAT Using Cisco SDM

Objectives:

▶ Enable NAT for a small network with a single ISP and connection using SDM

Cisco gives you plenty of flexibility when setting up NAT on a Cisco router. Now, anytime you are reading technical documentation and come across the word "flexibility," your mind should naturally translate this to "complexity." Thankfully, Cisco hid many of the configuration details behind the beautiful SDM interface.

> **TIP**
>
> For the ICND1 exam, Cisco expects you to be able to configure NAT using the Cisco Security Device Manager (SDM) graphic interface. For the ICND2 and CCNA exams, Cisco expects you to be able to configure NAT using the command-line interface.

Configuring NAT Overload

NAT overload (also known as PAT) is required for just about any business that provides Internet access to its internal users. As discussed previously, this version of NAT allows you to share (overload) a single public IP address among many internal private IP addresses. Because of its common use, Cisco categorizes this as *Basic NAT* in the SDM interface. However, if you see the command-line equivalent to the Basic NAT overload configuration, you'll realize it's anything but "basic"! When we're done with the SDM, I'll show you the commands it generated as a "sneak peek" at the ICND2 exam.

To access the NAT configuration window in the SDM, click the **Configure** link and choose **NAT** from the Tasks sidebar. The window shown in Figure 12.5 appears.

To configure NAT overload, choose the **Basic NAT** radio button and click the **Launch the selected task** button. After the initial introductory screen, you're asked to select the outside and inside interfaces for NAT, as shown in Figure 12.6. The interface you select in the drop-down box should connect to your ISP. In this example, the Ethernet 1/0 interface connects to a local ISP. The range of IP addresses that you select using the checkbox represents internal IP address ranges. In this example, our internal network is represented by 172.30.2.0 to 172.30.2.255. If I were to translate the options shown in Figure 12.6 into a simple English

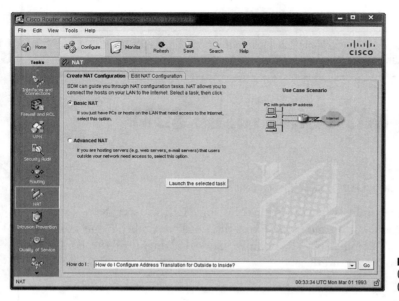

FIGURE 12.5 The NAT Configuration window in Cisco SDM.

FIGURE 12.6 Selecting the outside and inside interfaces for NAT.

statement, I would say, "Use NAT overload to translate any internal IP address starting with 172.30.2 to whatever IP address is assigned to the Ethernet 0/1 interface."

As soon as you click the Next button, you're done. Seriously! That's how simple Cisco makes the NAT overload configuration using the SDM GUI. The last thing you'll see is a summary screen verifying the options you've selected, as shown in Figure 12.7. When you click Finish,

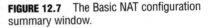

FIGURE 12.7 The Basic NAT configuration summary window.

SDM delivers the configuration commands to the router, and your network should be NAT-enabled.

I know you're thinking, "That was *way* too easy." Me too. Let's take a quick look at some select pieces of the running configuration just to make sure we really know what is happening behind the scenes:

```
NAT_ROUTER#show run
Building configuration...

Current configuration : 1160 bytes
!
interface FastEthernet0/0
 ip address 172.30.2.77 255.255.255.0
 ip nat inside
!
interface Ethernet1/0
 ip address 68.110.171.98 255.255.255.224
 ip nat outside
```

The first thing you'll notice is the `ip nat inside` and `ip nat outside` commands under the FastEthernet0/0 and Ethernet1/0 interfaces. The function of these commands is simple. They tell the router what interface connects to the outside world (your ISP) and what interface(s) connect to the inside world (your internal network). Keep in mind that you can have multiple inside interfaces without any difficulty. Having multiple outside interfaces can cause the router some confusion (which is why the Cisco SDM allows you to elect only a single outside interface). Let's move on a little further in the running configuration:

```
!
access-list 1 remark SDM_ACL Category=2
```

```
access-list 1 permit 172.30.2.0 0.0.0.255
!
ip nat inside source list 1 interface Ethernet1/0 overload
```

These commands are what I consider the "power commands" of NAT. Here's the idea: The first section represents an access list that allows the Cisco router to identify the internal network IP addresses (172.30.2.0/24 in this case). The access list is then utilized in the nat command below it. That one command is what puts this whole configuration in motion. The best way to understand that command is to imagine it as a conversation between you and the router. Trust me—the more you configure Cisco routers, the more conversations like this you will have:

> You: I want to do NAT (ip nat).
>
> Router: That's nice. Where would you like to NAT from?
>
> You: The inside of my network to the outside (inside).
>
> Router: Great! What interface would you like to use for the outside IP address?
>
> You: I'd like to use Ethernet1/0 (interface Ethernet1/0).
>
> Router: How would you like to use it?
>
> You: I'd like all internal IP addresses to share the single IP address on Ethernet 1/0 (overload).

That's the story! As the router puts these commands into action, all users in the 172.30.2.0/24 range are provided with Internet access.

Providing Internet access to the company through NAT overload is just one piece of the networking puzzle. Most companies have internal servers that need not only access *to* the Internet but access *from* the Internet. These are typically email servers, web servers, or FTP servers, to name just a few. Fortunately for your business, NAT provides a natural firewall between you and the Internet. Because private addresses are unreachable from the Internet, your internal network is protected from the outside world.

NOTE

Don't get a false sense of security by running NAT! Although NAT does protect your internal network from being reached directly from the Internet, it is not flawless network security. If one of the hosts on your internal network becomes infected with a virus or worm, it can initiate connections through the NAT gateway and allow return traffic (which could potentially be malicious) back into your network.

The problem with this natural firewall is that it also makes your internal servers unreachable from the Internet. To solve this, we can use static NAT mappings.

The SDM gives you a couple methods of setting up NAT mappings: configuring the mappings at the same time as NAT overload (using the **Advanced NAT** selection on the **Create**

NAT Configuration tab) or adding them individually from the Edit NAT Configuration tab. We'll talk about both methods here, starting with the Advanced NAT selection.

Advanced NAT Wizard

The Advanced NAT configuration wizard, shown in Figure 12.8, is most useful when you are setting up NAT overload and static NAT mappings at the same time. This section assumes that you did not work through the Basic NAT wizard previously (although the Advanced NAT wizard will still function if you previously completed the Basic NAT wizard).

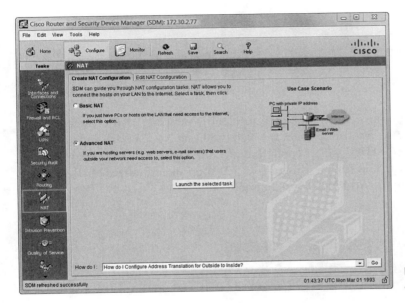

FIGURE 12.8 Beginning the Advanced NAT configuration.

To start the Advanced NAT wizard, simply select its radio button and click the **Launch the selected task** button. After you see the introductory page, the wizard asks you to identify the interface connected to your ISP, just as it did in the Basic NAT wizard. However, at this point you start to see something different: The wizard also asks if you are using any additional public IP addresses, as shown in Figure 12.9. Many organizations that run their own internal servers purchase additional, dedicated IP addresses for those servers. If your organization is using more IP addresses than what is assigned to the outside interface of your router, click the **Add** button and enter them one by one. If you do not have additional IP addresses, don't worry! We can do some really great stuff with the one IP address assigned to your router's outside interface (we'll talk about that in just a moment). In Figure 12.9, I have added the IP addresses 200.1.1.1 and 200.1.1.2 so that I can use them later in the configuration. We'll assume that our "virtual company" owns these two IP addresses.

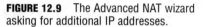

FIGURE 12.9 The Advanced NAT wizard asking for additional IP addresses.

After clicking the **Next** button, you're prompted to identify networks that connect to your internal network. In our case, we already went through the Basic NAT wizard and performed this step. Thankfully, Cisco SDM is smart enough to pick up on this and label the previously selected ranges as Designated, as shown in Figure 12.10. You can add ranges of IP addresses that are not listed by using the **Add Networks** button.

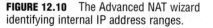

FIGURE 12.10 The Advanced NAT wizard identifying internal IP address ranges.

After clicking the **Next** button, we come to the window allowing us to configure our static NAT mappings. This is where the real action happens. We are initially given a blank window showing public-to-private IP address mappings. After you click the **Add** button, the Add Address Translation Rule window appears, as shown in Figure 12.11.

FIGURE 12.11 The Advanced NAT wizard's Add Address Translation Rule window.

From here, we can make our static NAT mappings. The simplest way to do this is to translate a single public IP address to a single private IP address. To accomplish this, you can type in the private IP address you would like to use and select the public IP address from the drop-down box, as shown in Figure 12.12.

FIGURE 12.12 Adding a static NAT mapping.

In Figure 12.12, I am planning on mapping the internal IP address 172.30.2.50 to the public IP address 200.1.1.1. However, before I do, I want you to notice the other option that is available: **IP address of Ethernet1/0**. If your organization has only a single IP address and that IP address is assigned to the router's outside interface, this selection allows you to use that IP address and map it to internal servers on your network. There are some restrictions when doing this, but we'll talk about those in just a moment. For now, I'll click the **OK** button, and the public-to-private mapping is made, as shown in Figure 12.13.

FIGURE 12.13 The first static NAT mapping is made.

I want to make a key statement at this point: Based on what I have just done, the *full* public IP address 200.1.1.1 is mapped to the private IP address 172.30.2.50. This means that if someone on the Internet accesses 200.1.1.1 on TCP port 80 (HTTP), that will forward into 172.30.2.50 on TCP port 80. Likewise, if someone on the Internet accesses 200.1.1.1 on TCP port 21 (FTP), that will forward into 172.30.2.50 on TCP port 21. It is a *full* mapping between the public address 200.1.1.1 and the private address 172.30.2.50. In contrast to a full mapping, I will configure a specific NAT port mapping.

Port mappings allow you to map individual ports on public IP addresses to individual ports on private IP addresses. This allows you to use each public IP address to its maximum potential. For example, my company might have an internal email server (which needs at least TCP port 25), an internal web server (needing at least TCP port 80), and an internal FTP server (needing at least TCP port 21). However, at this time my company has only a single public IP address of 200.1.1.2 (pretend that you never saw the other 200.1.1.1 IP address I just configured). I could use single-port mappings to map 200.1.1.2 TCP port 25 to the email server, 200.1.1.2 TCP port 80 to the web server, and 200.1.1.2 TCP port 21 to the FTP server! All with just one public IP address.

Here's how we can make it happen: Click the **Add** button to create a new NAT mapping. Just like before, enter the private IP address you'd like to map, and choose a public IP address from the drop-down menu. In this case, I'll use 172.30.2.10 as the internal email server and 200.1.1.2 as the public IP address (my final configuration window is shown in Figure 12.10). This time, we'll specify the service in the Additional Information section. Thankfully, Cisco SDM is so amazing that it already has a prebuilt mapping just for email servers! All I need to do is choose **E-mail server** from the Type of Server drop-down, as shown in Figure 12.14.

FIGURE 12.14 Mapping email services using port mappings.

The wizard also gives me the option to use an alternative port for receiving email. If my server is not using the standard TCP port 25 (SMTP) for receiving email, I can enter that here. Otherwise, I just need to click OK, and I'm good to go. The final mapping is displayed in the Advanced NAT wizard window, shown in Figure 12.15. Notice that port 25 is designated next to the public and private IP address. This is just a port mapping rather than a full IP address mapping.

NOTE

The Cisco router supports only individual NAT port mappings for the IP address assigned to the outside interface. You cannot fully map the outside interface IP address to an internal server because it is partially used for communication by the Cisco router.

We can now perform another two port mappings on the same 200.1.1.2 IP address, reusing it for the web and FTP servers. The Cisco SDM has built in **Web Server** selection under the Type of Server drop-down (just as it did for the email server previously). Rather than wasting space showing that configuration, let me show you something more interesting: the FTP server

FIGURE 12.15 A full IP NAT mapping and an individual port NAT mapping.

mapping. Again, I'll click the **Add** button to create a new mapping. I'll map the public IP address 200.1.1.2 to the internal FTP server address 172.30.2.11. This time, I'll choose **Other** under the Type of Server drop-down box (the Cisco SDM doesn't have a prebuilt FTP server mapping—yet). If you look at Figure 12.16, you'll notice that the SDM interface now gives us the opportunity to enter a value for the Original Port (received on the public IP address) and a value for the Translated Port (received on the private IP address). Most of the time, these values are the same, as shown in the Figure 12.16. Now, when 200.1.1.2 receives a request on TCP port 21, it translates it to 172.30.2.11 on TCP port 21.

FIGURE 12.16 Mapping specific NAT port numbers.

You could also perform port redirection by specifying a *different* port in either the Original Port or Translated Port fields. For example, if I entered 2100 in the Original Port field and kept 21 in the Translated Port field, the router would redirect (translate) requests received on 200.1.1.2 TCP port 2100 to 172.30.2.11 TCP port 21. You might be thinking, "Why on Earth would someone do this?!" There are plenty of reasons. Perhaps the network administrator did not want to use the well-known port number TCP 21 for the FTP server for security reasons. It could also be that port 21 on 200.1.1.2 was already used for another FTP server. Using TCP port 2100 would now allow you to run *two FTP servers off a single public IP address!* It doesn't get much better than that! Well, I suppose it could. Because 65,535 TCP ports are defined, we could theoretically run 65,535 FTP servers off a single IP address. Now we're talkin'!

> **NOTE**
>
> I (Jeremy) use this port redirection feature quite a bit for Microsoft's Remote Desktop Protocol (RDP). At my office, I have five servers running that I often need to access no matter where I am in the world. The RDP protocol allows me to access the desktop as if I were sitting directly at the server console. By default, RDP uses TCP port 3389. If I were to use only this port, it would require five public IP addresses to access each server. Instead, I set up the following port mappings:
>
> ► Public IP:3389 ▲ Primary Server:3389
>
> ► Public IP:3390 ▲ Email Server:3389
>
> ► Public IP:3391 ▲ CallManager Server:3389
>
> ► Public IP:3392 ▲ DNS Server:3389
>
> ► Public IP:3393 ▲ FTP Server:3389
>
> By doing this, I can use just a single IP address, yet access any server using RDP just by specifying a different port number.

Take a look at Figure 12.17 for a final view of all our NAT mappings, including the web server. After we click the **Next** button, we see a configuration summary screen showing all the mappings we've set up. Click **Finish** to end the Advanced NAT wizard and deliver the configuration to the router.

Edit NAT Configuration

Now we come to the second way to configure static NAT mappings using SDM: through the Edit NAT Configuration tab, shown in Figure 12.18.

This window is most useful if you have already set up Basic NAT (NAT overload) on the router and want to make changes to your NAT configuration in some way. Just by glancing around the configuration window shown in Figure 12.18, you can see quite a few options at your disposal:

► **Designate NAT Interfaces:** Opens a configuration window allowing you to allocate or reallocate which interfaces on your router connect to the inside or outside networks.

FIGURE 12.17 A combination of NAT rules.

FIGURE 12.18 The Edit NAT Configuration window.

▶ **Address Pool:** Allows you to create one or more pools of IP addresses that you can use for dynamic NAT (using NAT from one group of IP addresses to another; see the description earlier in this chapter).

▶ **Translation Timeouts:** Opens a configuration window that lets you set time limits for memory-resident idle NAT entries. For example, if someone opens a Telnet session through the NAT router and does not enter information, the router maintains the mapping in the NAT table for 86400 seconds by default. After this amount of time, the NAT entry is removed, and the Telnet session terminates.

▶ **Add:** Opens a window allowing you to add static or dynamic NAT mappings.

▶ **Edit:** Opens a window allowing you to edit the selected NAT mapping.

▶ **Delete:** Removes the selected NAT mapping.

You might also notice the **Clone selected Entry on Add** checkbox at the bottom of the window. If checked, this prepopulates the new NAT entry window (opened by clicking the **Add** button) with whatever entry you have selected. For example, let's say I wanted to create another static NAT mapping for our web server. I would like to map 200.1.1.2 TCP port 443 (HTTPS) to 172.30.2.12 port 443. Because I already have an entry mapping port 80 to this web server, I could check the **Clone selected Entry on Add** checkbox, select the current TCP port 80 mapping in the list, and click the **Add** button. The window shown in Figure 12.19 appears.

FIGURE 12.19 Adding a static NAT entry by cloning.

Nice! The **Static** radio button is already checked, the IP addresses have already been entered, and the correct interfaces are selected. All I have to do is change the Original Port and Translated Port fields to **443** and click **OK**. So easy a sea snail could do it! While we're here, let's talk about the configuration options in this window:

▶ **Static/Dynamic:** Choose the style of NAT you want to apply.

▶ **Direction:** This selector has caused plenty more confusion than it's worth. Your choices in the drop-down box are **From inside to outside** and **From outside to inside**.

The common misunderstanding is that this selector makes the translation a one-way street. The truth is that regardless of the direction you choose, the mapping is always two-way. For example, let's say I create a map by choosing **From inside to outside** and map the inside IP address 172.30.2.12 to the outside IP address 200.1.1.2. When the server 172.30.2.12 accesses the Internet, it is seen as 200.1.1.2. Likewise, if someone on the Internet accesses 200.1.1.2, he or she reaches the server at 172.30.2.12. It's a two-way translation. The good news is that you can always choose which direction makes more sense to you—outside-in or inside-out. This selector also gives you more flexibility when performing dynamic NAT.

▶ **Inside IP Address/Network Mask:** The inside address or pool of addresses you want to translate.

▶ **Outside Interface(s)/Type:** Allows you to enter the individual IP address or interface you want to translate. If the **Type** drop-down box has the IP address selected (shown in Figure 12.15), the IP address field can be modified. If the **Type** drop-down box has the interface selected, the Interface field can be modified.

▶ **Redirect Port/Original Port/Translated Port:** Allows you to choose the protocol and port numbers you want to translate.

After I click the **OK** button, the new static NAT translation is added. As I mentioned earlier, the **Edit NAT Configuration** tab is the best place to make changes to an existing NAT setup.

Verifying NAT Configuration

Objectives:

▶ Enable NAT for a small network with a single ISP and connection using SDM and verify operation using CLI and ping

To verify that everything is working, we need to return to our command-line interface. (The SDM can verify that packets are passing through interfaces but is unable to show us the detailed NAT information we need.) The first thing I want to do when I get to the command line is issue the show ip interface brief command (by far, my favorite command in all of Cisco) to get my bearings:

```
NAT_ROUTER#show ip interface brief
Interface              IP-Address      OK? Method Status                Protocol
FastEthernet0/0        172.30.2.77     YES NVRAM  up                    up
Ethernet1/0            68.110.171.98   YES NVRAM  up                    up
Serial1/0              unassigned      YES NVRAM  administratively down  down
Serial2/0              unassigned      YES NVRAM  administratively down  down
```

We can see our internal IP address (172.30.2.77) and our external IP address (68.110.171.98). Let's start by ensuring that we can reach the Internet *without* involving NAT by issuing a ping command directly from the router. I typically ping the world's best-known public DNS server at 4.2.2.2 anytime I want to test Internet connectivity:

```
NAT_ROUTER#ping 4.2.2.2

Type escape sequence to abort.
Sending 5, 100-byte ICMP Echos to 4.2.2.2, timeout is 2 seconds:
!!!!!
Success rate is 100 percent (5/5), round-trip min/avg/max = 20/23/28 ms
```

Beautiful. Now I'll configure an internal client to use this router as its default gateway and do some Internet surfing. I'll spare you the screen captures of me surfing the Internet—you'll just have to trust that I'm really surfing. Yep, there's my Apple homepage (I've recently become quite the Apple enthusiast). I'll also surf over to www.CiscoBlog.com to see if there's anything new. Okay, I'm done surfing. Now let's verify that NAT is occurring from the Cisco router's perspective. You can use two major commands to do so. Here's the first:

```
NAT_ROUTER#show ip nat statistics
Total active translations: 38 (5 static, 33 dynamic; 37 extended)
Outside interfaces:
  Ethernet1/0
Inside interfaces:
  FastEthernet0/0
Hits: 1211  Misses: 121
Expired translations: 88
Dynamic mappings:
—— Inside Source
[Id: 1] access-list 1 interface Ethernet1/0 refcount 33
```

The show ip nat statistics command verifies NAT from a more global perspective. The primary information you can gather is the outside and inside interface configuration and the number of hits and misses. The number of hits defines how many packets match an existing NAT mapping. For example, I went to www.CiscoBlog.com while I was surfing the Internet. The very first packet that went through the Cisco router was considered a "miss" because no existing NAT translation was created. So, the Cisco router created the NAT translation, passing the traffic from my internal client (172.30.2.177) to the www.CiscoBlog.com website. The website then received my connection, created a TCP socket, and streamed many packets back to my web browsing application. All those packets were considered "hits" by NAT because they matched an existing NAT translation.

The second command you can use to verify that NAT is working is the more popular of the two:

```
NAT_ROUTER#show ip nat translations
Pro Inside global      Inside local      Outside local      Outside global
——— 200.1.1.1          172.30.2.50       ———                ———
```

```
tcp 200.1.1.2:21        172.30.2.11:21      — — —              — — —
tcp 200.1.1.2:25        172.30.2.10:25      — — —              — — —
tcp 200.1.1.2:80        172.30.2.12:80      — — —              — — —
tcp 68.110.171.98:49221 172.30.2.177:49221 17.149.160.10:80   17.149.160.10:80
tcp 68.110.171.98:49222 172.30.2.177:49222 17.149.160.10:80   17.149.160.10:80
tcp 68.110.171.98:49223 172.30.2.177:49223 17.149.160.10:80   17.149.160.10:80
tcp 68.110.171.98:49224 172.30.2.177:49224 17.149.160.10:80   17.149.160.10:80
tcp 68.110.171.98:49225 172.30.2.177:49225 17.149.160.10:80   17.149.160.10:80
tcp 68.110.171.98:49226 172.30.2.177:49226 17.149.160.10:80   17.149.160.10:80
tcp 68.110.171.98:49238 172.30.2.177:49238 17.149.160.10:80   17.149.160.10:80
tcp 200.1.1.2:443       172.30.2.12:443     — — —              — — —
tcp 68.110.171.98:49236 172.30.2.177:49236 66.151.152.126:80  66.151.152.126:80
tcp 68.110.171.98:49237 172.30.2.177:49237 206.16.21.35:80    206.16.21.35:80
tcp 68.110.171.98:49242 172.30.2.177:49242 69.89.31.87:80     69.89.31.87:80
tcp 68.110.171.98:49244 172.30.2.177:49244 69.89.31.87:80     69.89.31.87:80
tcp 68.110.171.98:49245 172.30.2.177:49245 69.89.31.87:80     69.89.31.87:80
tcp 68.110.171.98:49243 172.30.2.177:49243 209.85.171.167:80  209.85.171.167:80
udp 68.110.171.98:49308 172.30.2.177:49308 4.2.2.2:53         4.2.2.2:53
udp 68.110.171.98:49309 172.30.2.177:49309 4.2.2.2:53         4.2.2.2:53
udp 68.110.171.98:49310 172.30.2.177:49310 4.2.2.2:53         4.2.2.2:53
udp 68.110.171.98:49311 172.30.2.177:49311 4.2.2.2:53         4.2.2.2:53
udp 68.110.171.98:49312 172.30.2.177:49312 4.2.2.2:53         4.2.2.2:53
udp 68.110.171.98:49313 172.30.2.177:49313 4.2.2.2:53         4.2.2.2:53
udp 68.110.171.98:49314 172.30.2.177:49314 4.2.2.2:53         4.2.2.2:53
udp 68.110.171.98:49315 172.30.2.177:49315 4.2.2.2:53         4.2.2.2:53
tcp 68.110.171.98:49227 172.30.2.177:49227 208.46.174.96:80   208.46.174.96:80
tcp 68.110.171.98:49228 172.30.2.177:49228 208.46.174.96:80   208.46.174.96:80
tcp 68.110.171.98:49229 172.30.2.177:49229 208.46.174.96:80   208.46.174.96:80
```

Wow—look at that! These are all the NAT translations my router is currently maintaining. This is how you can really tell if NAT is working. If you look at the first few translations, you'll be able to verify the static NAT mappings that we entered through the SDM just a few moments ago. The IP address in the Inside global column represents the address on the interface connecting to the Internet. The IP address in the Inside local column represents the internal IP address on your LAN. Do you see now why it's so important to know that terminology mentioned at the beginning of the chapter? If it's a little fuzzy, now would be a good time to flip back a few pages and review.

The static mappings have no data in the Outside local and Outside global columns because they are not currently in use (no one is accessing those IP addresses from the Internet at this time). If they were being accessed, we would see the IP address of the device accessing them in those two columns.

Now take a look farther down; you see a *bunch* of mappings on the inside global IP address 68.110.171.98 and the inside local IP address 172.30.2.177. The global IP address represents my ISP-assigned Internet address that I am using for NAT overload (all the internal clients share this one). The local IP address represents the internal client I was surfing the

Internet with. Next to each of those IP addresses is a colon, followed by a port number. These are the *source* UDP and TCP port numbers that my web surfing client uses to keep all its applications separate.

In the two rightmost columns (Outside local and Outside global), you see the public IP addresses that my web surfing client was accessing. I know what you might be thinking: "Why do you have *so many* entries in the NAT table? I thought you accessed just two websites!" You're right! I did access only two websites. However, my laptop had to do DNS lookups to access both the websites, and those websites were supported by many other servers. For example, the Apple website might have one server that supplies the raw HTML pages, another server that supplies all the graphics, another for flash content, and so on. For each of those servers, the client may have to do another DNS lookup (which is why you see so many requests to the 4.2.2.2 DNS server IP address), and the Cisco router has to maintain another NAT mapping to allow data through. On top of it all, this is just one laptop surfing the Internet! Imagine what this table would look like in a large corporate network. Good thing the show ip nat translation command supports plenty of filtering options!

Troubleshooting NAT

When you use the SDM to configure NAT, not too much can go wrong, but you can follow some general troubleshooting steps if things don't seem to be working correctly. To start, enter the following modified show running-config commands:

```
NAT_ROUTER#show running-config interface fastEthernet 0/0
Building configuration...

Current configuration : 111 bytes
!
interface FastEthernet0/0
 ip address 172.30.2.77 255.255.255.0
 ip nat inside
NAT_ROUTER#show running-config interface Ethernet 1/0
Building configuration...

Current configuration : 100 bytes
!
interface Ethernet1/0
 ip address 68.110.171.98 255.255.255.224
 ip nat outside
```

This filters the large running configuration to just the interfaces you'd like to see. What you want to verify is that the interface connecting to your internal network is configured as the ip nat inside interface and that the interface connecting to the ISP is configured as the ip nat outside interface.

If things look good there, do a ping from the router itself. This will test your Internet connectivity without the NAT process getting in the way. The problem could be a simple routing issue (such as missing a default route to your ISP). If things check out in the router-originated ping, try the ping from an internal client. Be sure you're pinging an IP address rather than a hostname (such as www.examcram.com). You don't want a DNS problem getting in the way. If the client can ping successfully, NAT is operational.

Last, but not least, is a command that has saved me plenty of troubleshooting time: `clear ip nat translations *`. This command wipes out the NAT table maintained on the router. Sometimes, when we are setting up a network, we end up with NAT entries in the table that don't belong there. It could just be from changing a client's IP address before NAT timeouts are reached, it could be that your public or private IP address changes, or it could just be that the router doesn't feel like NATing today. It's always worthwhile to try entering `clear ip nat translations *` from the privileged prompt before you get too deep in troubleshooting other issues. Don't worry; it shouldn't cause any connectivity problems for existing clients using the Internet. The router will just create a new NAT mapping the next packet that comes through. I have seen this command cause Instant Messenger clients to log out and log back in again, but people don't really use Instant Messenger clients for anything productive anyway, right?

Chapter Summary

You'd be hard-pressed to find any corporate network in the world providing Internet access without using NAT. Because of this, Cisco has added it as one of the core competencies of both a CCENT and CCNA certified individual.

The big-picture concept of NAT is fairly simple: converting one IP address to another. However, the technical details behind NAT are where the complexity lies. Most of the challenge with NAT is learning the terminology that describes the different addresses on a network. Inside local addresses are internal to a network. The inside global address represents the public Internet address assigned to your router. Outside global addresses represent all the hosts outside your network attached to the Internet with Internet IP addresses. Finally, outside local addresses represent hosts outside your network as they are seen by the internal NAT hosts.

A company planning to use NAT will deploy one of the three private address ranges on its internal network, which are prevented from routing to the Internet. It then uses one of the three forms of NAT—static NAT, dynamic NAT, or NAT overload—to translate these private ranges onto the Internet. Most networks use a combination of NAT overload and static NAT to accomplish most major network objectives.

Key Terms

- Network Address Translation (NAT)
- Port Address Translation (PAT)
- Static NAT
- Dynamic NAT
- NAT overload
- Private IP addresses
- Public IP addresses
- Inside local address
- Inside global address
- Outside local address
- Outside global address
- Port redirection

Review Questions

1. List the three private ranges of IP addresses typically used with NAT translations.

2. Three forms of NAT are used in networks today: static NAT, dynamic NAT, and NAT overload/PAT. What is the use of each of these forms of NAT?

3. You would like to see the current NAT translations passing through your router. What command would you enter?

4. You are troubleshooting NAT on your router. It appears as though some of the entries are mapped to incorrect IP addresses. How can you erase the current NAT translations and allow them to rebuild?

5. Your organization has an internal web server that it needs to make available to the Internet. What form of NAT will you use, and why?

Apply Your Knowledge

Exam Questions

1. You have an internal web server that has the IP address 172.16.5.9. You need to enable this server to be accessed on TCP port 80 from the Internet. What would be the best solution for this situation?

   ○ **A.** Static NAT

   ○ **B.** Dynamic NAT

   ○ **C.** NAT overload

   ○ **D.** Standard routing

2. Which of the following forms of NAT incorporates the source IP address (inside local) along with the source port number to make every translation unique?

   ○ **A.** Static NAT

   ○ **B.** Dynamic NAT

   ○ **C.** NAT overload

   ○ **D.** NAT port mapping

3. Which of the following is *not* a task you can perform from the Edit NAT Configuration tab of SDM?

   ○ **A.** Configure access lists for use with dynamic NAT.

   ○ **B.** Select inside and outside interfaces of the router.

   ○ **C.** Adjust NAT timeout values.

   ○ **D.** Configure NAT overload capabilities.

Refer to the following figure for Questions 4 and 5.

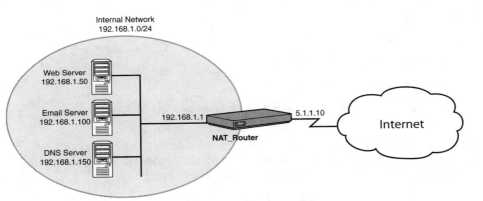

4. According to NAT terminology, the IP address 192.168.1.100 for the email server is considered an _____.

   ○ **A.** Inside local address

   ○ **B.** Inside global address

   ○ **C.** Outside local address

   ○ **D.** Outside global address

5. According to NAT terminology, the IP address 5.1.1.10 is considered an _____.

   ○ **A.** Inside local address

   ○ **B.** Inside global address

   ○ **C.** Outside local address

   ○ **D.** Outside global address

6. Which of the following represent a private IP address? (Choose two)

- ○ **A.** 192.168.5.205
- ○ **B.** 172.32.65.31
- ○ **C.** 10.168.5.205
- ○ **D.** 224.16.23.1

7. You are configuring a new router for NAT and would like to set up NAT overload and a single, static NAT mapping allowing access to an internal web server. What would be the most efficient way to accomplish this?

- ○ **A.** Basic NAT SDM wizard
- ○ **B.** Advanced NAT SDM wizard
- ○ **C.** Using the Edit NAT Configuration tab
- ○ **D.** Using the Basic NAT SDM wizard followed by the Edit NAT Configuration tab

8. You are using NAT overload on your company's Cisco router to provide Internet access to your internal network. The NAT process is overloading the IP address assigned to the router's outside interface. Which of the following statements are *not* true? (Choose two)

- ○ **A.** Multiple internal users cannot access the same website at the same time, because the website will see two requests coming from the same IP address.
- ○ **B.** Static NAT mappings can be added for the interface IP address, but only for specific ports.
- ○ **C.** Static NAT mappings can be added for the full interface IP address.
- ○ **D.** Cisco's NAT process will allow you to NAT not only to the interface IP address but also to other IP addresses not assigned to the interface.

9. You would like to see the active NAT translations that are happening on your router. Your primary interest is in the inside local IPs that are being translated. What command shows you this information?

- ○ **A.** `show ip nat statistics`
- ○ **B.** `show ip nat translations`
- ○ **C.** `show ip interface`
- ○ **D.** `show running-config`

10. You have just changed one of your internal computer's IP addresses, and it appears that it can no longer access the Internet. You have verified the correct subnet and gateway information. What commands should you perform on the router to ensure that cached information does not play a role in this failure? (Choose two)

   ○ **A.** `clear arp`

   ○ **B.** `clear ip route`

   ○ **C.** `clear ip nat translations*`

   ○ **D.** `clear startup-config`

Answers to Review Questions

1. The three private address ranges are as follows:

   Class A: 10.0.0.0 to 10.255.255.255

   Class B: 172.16.0.0 to 172.31.255.255

   Class C: 192.168.0.0 to 192.168.255.255

2. Static NAT is responsible for one-to-one translations. It is typically used to make private servers available on the Internet. Dynamic NAT is used to translate one pool of addresses to another. This is the least common form of NAT and is typically used to solve duplicate IP addresses when merging two networks. Last is NAT overload. This form of NAT is the most popular because it allows many internal hosts to share a common public IP address.

3. The correct command is `show ip nat translations` from privileged mode.

4. You can enter the command `clear ip nat translations *` to erase the current NAT table from memory. The table will naturally rebuild as users access the Internet.

5. Static NAT is most appropriate to make internal resources available to the outside world. This is because static NAT performs one-to-one translations allowing you to direct specific IP address requests to a public address to a privately addressed server.

Answers to Exam Questions

1. **A.** Static NAT provides the best solution when you need a 1:1 translation from a private address or port number to a public address or port number. Answer B is incorrect because dynamic NAT allows many hosts to be translated at the same time. Answer C is incorrect because NAT overload allows many internal hosts to share a single Internet IP address. Answer D is also incorrect. Standard routing does not work because private addresses are blocked from traversing the Internet.

2. **C.** NAT overload uses the source port number to send many unique requests out a single, public IP address. Answer A is incorrect because static NAT performs 1:1 translations from public to private

IP addresses. Answer B is incorrect because dynamic NAT performs many 1:1 translations without requiring manual entries. Answer D is incorrect because NAT port mapping is not a valid form of NAT.

3. **A.** You cannot create access lists for use with dynamic NAT from the Edit NAT Configuration tab. All other tasks can be performed from this window.

4. **A.** Inside local addresses encompass any address on your internal network that is translated to the outside network via NAT. Answer B is incorrect because the inside global addresses are the IPs assigned to the outside interface of your router. Answer C is incorrect because the outside local addresses are outside (Internet) addresses as they appear to a NAT device. Answer D is incorrect because the outside global addresses are standard Internet-attached devices.

5. **B.** The inside global addresses are the IPs assigned to the outside interface of your router. Answer A is incorrect because inside local addresses encompass any address on your internal network that is translated to the outside network via NAT. Answer C is incorrect because the outside local addresses are outside (Internet) addresses as they appear to a NAT device. Answer D is incorrect because the outside global addresses are standard Internet-attached devices.

6. **A, C.** The private address ranges are 10.x.x.x, 172.16.x.x to 172.31.x.x, and 192.168.x.x. Answers B and D fall outside these ranges.

7. **B.** The Advanced NAT wizard allows you to configure NAT overload and static NAT mappings at the same time in the same wizard. If you use the Basic NAT wizard (Answer A), you would have to follow it up with the Edit NAT Configuration tab, which is not the most efficient way to configure NAT. This makes both Answers A and D incorrect. Answer C is incorrect because using the Edit NAT Configuration tab would require you to manually set up NAT overload and the static NAT mapping individually, which is not the most efficient process.

8. **A, C.** When using NAT overload, multiple users *can* access the same website at the same time because the router uses unique source port numbers to distinguish each request. Also, when using NAT with the IP address assigned to the outside interface, you cannot create a static NAT mapping for the entire IP address, because this would make local router services unavailable. Both of the other statements are true.

9. **B.** The `show ip nat translations` command shows you all active translations currently in place on your router. It includes the inside local and global and the outside local and global addresses for each translation. Answer A is incorrect because the `show ip nat statistics` command tells you only how many translations are currently happening. Answer C is incorrect because the `show ip interface` command does not give you any NAT statistics. Answer D is incorrect because the `show running-config` command tells you only the NAT configurations you have set up.

10. **A, C.** The `clear arp` command ensures that the router does not have the incorrect MAC address mapped to the computer's IP address. The `clear ip nat translations *` command ensures that the cached NAT translations are not pointed to the wrong IP address. Answer B is incorrect. The `clear ip route` is not necessary because the routing table did not change and could cause downtime for your router. Answer D is incorrect because the `clear startup-config` does not remove any cached configuration.

Suggested Reading and Resources

1. Cisco TAC NAT Configuration Syntax, http://www.cisco.com/univercd/cc/td/doc/product/software/ios122/122cgcr/fipr_c/ipcprt1/1cfipadr.htm#wp1042290.

2. Chris Ward and Jeremy Cioara. *Exam Cram 2 CCNA Practice Questions*. Que Publishing, 2004.

3. How Network Address Translation Works, http://computer.howstuffworks.com/nat1.htm.

CHAPTER THIRTEEN

Foundation Switching Operations

Objectives

This chapter covers the following Cisco-specific objectives for the "Implement a small switched network" section of the 640-822 ICND1 exam:

▶ **Explain the operation of Cisco switches and basic switching concepts**

▶ **Perform, save, and verify initial switch configuration tasks including remote access management**

▶ **Verify network status and switch operation using basic utilities (including: ping, traceroute, telnet, SSH, arp, ipconfig), SHOW & DEBUG commands**

▶ **Identify, prescribe, and resolve common switched network media issues, configuration issues, auto negotiation, and switch hardware failures**

Outline

Introduction	**426**
Switching Functionality	426
Frame Transmission Methods	**427**
Store-and-Forward	428
Cut-Through	428
Fragment-Free	428
Half- and Full-Duplex Connections	**429**
Switching Design	**430**
Spanning Tree Protocol	**430**
Root Bridge	431
Root Ports	432
Designated Ports	434
Blocked Ports	435
Port State Transitions	**437**
Initial Switch Configurations	**438**
Assigning a Management IP Address to a Switch	439

Defining a Default Gateway	439
IP Assignment Using DHCP	440
Configuring Multiple Switch Interfaces	441
Verifying Spanning Tree Protocol	442
Troubleshooting Basic Switch Connectivity	**442**
Chapter Summary	**445**
Key Terms	445
Apply Your Knowledge	**446**
Exercises	446
Review Questions	448
Exam Questions	449
Answers to Review Questions	452
Answers to Exam Questions	452
Suggested Readings and Resources	454

Study Strategies

▶ Read the information presented in the chapter, paying special attention to tables, Notes, and Exam Alerts.

▶ One of the best practices when reading about switching functions is to visualize the information contained in the Ethernet frames and imagine how a switch uses that information to build its forwarding table and forward frames to other network segments.

▶ Complete the Challenge and the Exercises at the end of the chapter. They will solidify the concepts that you have learned in the previous sections.

▶ After you have read about and understood Spanning Tree Protocol, try to draw your own LAN design and determine the STP elections and port roles that will result from your design.

▶ Complete the Exam Questions at the end of the chapter. They are designed to simulate the types of questions you will be asked on the ICND1 exams.

Introduction

You have already learned in Chapter 3, "Data Link Networking Concepts," that you can use bridges and switches to segment a LAN into smaller collision domains. This chapter looks in close detail at the operations of bridges and switches. Specifically, you will investigate the transparent functionality that occurs when a switch is building and utilizing its frame forwarding logic, as well as the peculiar nature of Spanning Tree Protocol (STP) in redundant switched networks.

Switching Functionality

Objectives:

▶ Explain the operation of Cisco switches and basic switching concepts

Switches forward frames based on the Layer 2 Ethernet MAC addresses. These devices receive Ethernet frames transmitted from other devices and dynamically build a MAC address table based on the source MAC address inside those frames. This MAC address table is commonly referred to as a Content Addressable Memory (CAM) table.

These dynamic entries in the CAM table are not permanent, however. After the switch or bridge stops receiving frames from a certain MAC address (this varies, but it's typically five minutes), the entry is removed from the CAM table to save memory and processor resources. The exceptions to this are static MAC entries that have been manually configured on a port-by-port basis for security and control purposes.

When deciding to which port to forward the Ethernet frame, a switch consults this CAM table and forwards the Ethernet frame based on the destination MAC address of the Ethernet header. In instances where the destination MAC address is not in the table, it copies and forwards the frame out every port except the one at which it was received. This action is commonly known as flooding.

EXAM ALERT

It is important to remember that switches build their MAC address tables using the source address in an Ethernet frame header. In addition, they base their forwarding decisions on the destination MAC address in an Ethernet frame header.

Recall that switches segment LANs into collision domains; however, they still are in a single broadcast domain. Switches do not have entries for broadcast addresses (FFFF.FFFF.FFFF) or multicast addresses (0100.5E00.000-0100.5E7F.FFFF) in their CAM tables. As previously mentioned, when a bridge or a switch receives a frame with a destination MAC address not in its table, it floods that frame out every port.

For instance, consider the switched topology example illustrated in Figure 13.1. When Computers A, B, and C and Printer D originally sent an Ethernet frame, the switch recorded the source MAC address of that frame and the associated port in its CAM table. If Computer A sends an Ethernet frame destined for Printer D's MAC address of 1111.2222.3333, the switch forwards only that frame out to its Fast Ethernet 0/14 interface. If Computer A sends a broadcast with a destination of FFFF.FFFF.FFFF, that entry does not exist in the CAM table, so that frame is flooded out all interfaces except for Fast Ethernet 0/1.

0234.ABCD.EF56

1111.2222.3333

F0/1   F0/14

CAM TABLE

F0/1: 0234.ABCD.EF56
F0/12: 2342.DFA3.FF58
F0/12: 2342.DF25.6431
F0/14: 1111.2222.3333

F0/12

2342.DF25.6431

2342.DFA3.FF58

FIGURE 13.1 Switch address learning and forwarding.

Notice that Computers B and C are plugged into a hub. So what happens when Computer B sends an Ethernet frame to Computer C? The frame hits the Layer 1 hub, which regenerates the signal out all ports except the one it came in on (regardless of the MAC address because it is a Physical layer device). When the frame reaches the switch, the switch realizes that the source and destination MAC addresses reside on the same interface, so it does not send that frame on to any other ports. This process is also commonly known as *filtering*.

Frame Transmission Methods

Switches are often classified based on the method in which they process and forward frames in and out of their interfaces. This classification differs depending on the device's processing capabilities and manufacturer. The three transmission methods that a bridge or switch may use are discussed in the following sections.

Store-and-Forward

Properly named, the store-and-forward method of frame transmission involves the switch, which buffer (store temporarily in a small memory location) the entire Ethernet frame and perform a cyclic redundancy check (CRC) of that frame to make sure it is not a corrupted frame (damaged or abnormally changed in the frame's transmission). If the frame calculation detects a bad frame, it is dropped at that point. Thus, the frame is forwarded only if the CRC calculation results in a normal frame.

Because the entire frame is checked, store-and-forward switching is said to be latency (delay) varying. In other words, depending on the payload inside the frame, the switch takes varying processing times to buffer the entire frame and perform the CRC before sending it to its destination. Although this method sounds like a lengthy process, this is the most widely used method of switching in Cisco Catalyst switches because the hardware processors for the interfaces are so advanced and robust that the switch hardly works up a sweat.

Cut-Through

Cut-through transmissions are practically the antithesis of store-and-forward frame transmission. In fact, instead of processing the entire frame, cut-through switching entails the switch buffering just enough information to know where to forward the frame before sending it on to another segment. In other words, it looks only up to the destination MAC address in the Ethernet header and sends it on regardless of whether the frame contains errors.

This hot-potato method of frame transmission was once appealing for devices with low processing power. Because it has to inspect only the beginning of an Ethernet frame header, latency is not a factor with this method. The downside of cut-through switching, however, is that it still passes bad frames on to other segments because it does not perform CRC calculations of any kind.

Fragment-Free

In a true Goldilocks fashion, if cut-through is too hot and store-and-forward is too cold, fragment-free may be just right for you. Fragment-free is a hybrid of the two transmission methods because it buffers up to the first 64 bytes of a frame (all collisions occur within the first 64 bytes). This obviously is not as fast as cut-through; nevertheless, it ensures that many of the invalid frames in the LAN are not transmitted on to other segments. Figure 13.2 illustrates how much of an Ethernet frame is buffered and processed with each of the three transmission methods discussed.

FIGURE 13.2 Frame transmission comparison.

Half- and Full-Duplex Connections

Data communication on switch ports can occur in either half- or full-duplex transmissions. Half-duplex connections are unidirectional in that data can be sent in only one direction at a time. This is similar to two-way radios or walkie-talkies, in which only one person can speak at one time. With half-duplex communication in an Ethernet network, CSMA/CD (carrier sense multiple access with collision detection) is enabled, which results in 50 to 60% of the bandwidth on the link being available to be used.

Full duplex, on the other hand, is indicative of two-way communication in which devices can send and receive information at the same time. With these connections, CSMA/CD is automatically disabled, allowing for theoretically 100% of the bandwidth in both directions. In fact, it uses the two wires that typically are used for detecting collisions to simultaneously transmit and receive. Because CSMA/CD is disabled, that means the connection has to be in an environment where collisions cannot occur. In other words, it must be connected to a switch or directly connected with a cross-over cable.

EXAM ALERT

If you are connected to a hub, the connection must be half-duplex with CSMA/CD. When running full duplex, you must be directly connected to a switch.

NOTE

Because full duplex allows 100% in both directions, it is sometimes advertised at twice the speed. For instance, a 100Mbps interface might be marketed as achieving 200Mbps. Although it is advertised as 200Mbps, in reality, you are receiving 200Mbps of *throughput*.

Switching Design

You have already seen how switches operate when connected to end-user devices such as PCs, printers, and servers. However, when switches are connected to other switches to form a redundant network, a switching loop can occur. Figure 13.3 illustrates a scenario in which a switching loop can occur.

FIGURE 13.3 Redundant switch design.

In this design, redundant links interconnect the switches. Although it is a good idea to have redundancy in the network, the problem arises when a computer sends out a frame with a broadcast, multicast, or unknown unicast destination MAC address. Recall that any of these three transmissions causes a switch to copy and flood that frame out all ports except for the one on which it came in. So if Computer A sends a broadcast, Switch A floods that out to Switches B and D. Again, if this is a broadcast message, Switches B and D flood that frame out to Switch C. Staying true to its design, Switch C floods the frame back to Switches B and D, and so on. Broadcasts continuously circle the switched network until ultimately the amount of broadcast traffic consumes the switched network's bandwidth and all traffic ceases to flow. This unsettling scenario just described is called a *broadcast storm* and can be avoided completely by using a Layer 2 protocol sent among switches called the *Spanning Tree Protocol*.

Spanning Tree Protocol

Once a proprietary protocol from DEC, Spanning Tree Protocol (STP) was standardized and blessed by the IEEE specification, 802.1d. STP allows networks to maintain a level of redundancy while disabling the detrimental side effects that can occur such as broadcast storms. Enabled by default on most switches, STP forms noncircular (no looping) paths throughout the internetwork by performing an election and basing calculations on that election. These calculations dictate which ports should remain in a nonforwarding (known as blocking) state to eliminate redundant loops that can cause broadcast storms. STP also can react to changes in the switched network to ensure that the redundant links may be used in the event of a topology change such as a link going down. The following sections explain exactly how this remarkable protocol operates behind the scenes in a LAN.

EXAM ALERT

Remember that STP is standardized by the IEEE 802.1d specification and is used to prevent switching loops in a switched network.

Root Bridge

As previously mentioned, STP performs an election in the switched topology. The winner of this election serves as the base of all calculations and ultimately becomes the root to the spanning tree. Conveniently, this elected bridge or switch is called the *root bridge*. From the root bridge, noncircular branches extend throughout the switched network like those of a tree—a spanning tree.

NOTE

Don't let the term "root bridge" confuse you. When the 802.1d specification was drafted for STP, it was referred to as a "root bridge" because bridges were the prominent devices at the time. In modern times, it can just as easily be a switch.

So how does this election take place? You can rule out voting because each bridge or switch believes itself to be the root bridge at startup. The deciding factor on who becomes the root bridge is something referred to as the Bridge ID. The Bridge ID comprises two components:

▶ **Priority:** This is an arbitrary number from 0 to 61440, which can be administratively set in increments of 4096. The default value for priority is 32768, or 8000 in hex.

▶ **MAC address:** The 48-bit MAC address of the switch itself.

The device with the lowest Bridge ID becomes the root bridge. If a new switch or bridge is added with a lower Bridge ID to the switched network, a new election takes place, and that switch ultimately becomes the new root bridge for the switched network.

Consider the example shown in Figure 13.4. Notice that all switches have their default priority value of 32768 in their Bridge IDs. Thus, the lowest MAC address ultimately dictates who will win the election. Because Switch A has the lowest MAC address in the switched network, it will be the root bridge.

FIGURE 13.4 Root bridge election.

EXAM ALERT

Be prepared to be able to determine which switch is the root bridge, given a topology diagram of a switched LAN.

Because this election process occurs automatically with bridges and switches, it is highly advised that you change your priority in a robust and reliable switch in your internetwork as opposed to letting this election occur by chance. This is especially true because manufacturers choose the MAC address, and a lower MAC address could very well mean an old or low-end switch or bridge, which might not be the best choice for your root bridge. How to manually set the priority is discussed later in this chapter.

These Bridge IDs are advertised to each other through *Bridge Protocol Data Units (BPDUs)*. These messages are sent as multicasts every 2 seconds by the root bridge out its interfaces to other switches on adjoining segments who, in turn, forward them on to other connected switches. In addition, these messages also contain the Bridge ID of the root bridge in every update that is sent. As long as you are receiving BPDUs that contain a higher Bridge ID than your Bridge ID, you will remain the root bridge (because all devices assume they are the root at startup).

Root Ports

In addition to the local bridge ID and the root bridge ID, BPDUs contain information that helps switches perform calculations to decide which ports should be forwarding and which should be blocking to create a loop-free switched network. The key to this calculation lies within the cumulative cost back to the root bridge. Although it sounds as if these Cisco switches are keeping track of how much you paid for them, this is not what is meant when you use the term "cost." The cost is actually an inverse of the bandwidth for each link segment. Because it is the inverse, the lower the cumulative cost back to the root bridge, the faster the path is. Table 13.1 lists the standard costs used today in switches. It is possible to change these values administratively if you want to control which link becomes the best path to the root bridge.

TABLE 13.1   Port Cost Values

Interface	Cost
10Gbps	2
1Gbps	4
100Mbps	19
10Mbps	100

After the root bridge is determined, each nonroot switch or bridge forms an association back to the root bridge based on the lowest cumulative path cost back to the root. Whichever interface has the fastest route to the root bridge automatically becomes a forwarding port called the *root port*.

> **NOTE**
>
> The root port is determined for the entire switch. Thus, each switch should contain only one root port back to the root bridge.

The root bridge advertises a root path cost of 0 to Switches B and D. As the BPDU enters their interfaces, they add the cost value of that interface and advertise that to any adjacent switches on other segments. Every nonroot bridge determines its fastest path back to the root by looking at these BPDUs that it receives from other switches. For instance, Switch B knows that going out of the top segment back to the root has a cost of 4, and going through Switch C has a cost of 42. Because the top segment has the lowest cumulative cost, that becomes the root port for Switch B.

What would happen if there were a tie in the root path cost? For instance, Switch C has two equal-cost paths of 23 back to the root bridge through Switch B and Switch D. In the event of a tie, the following are calculated to determine the root port:

1. The port with a switch advertising the lowest Bridge ID.

2. If the same Bridge ID (parallel links to the same switch), the lowest port priority is used. The port priority is an arbitrary number assigned to an interface that can be administratively set to choose one link over another. The default value is 128.

3. If the same port priority, the ultimate tiebreaker is the lowest interface number—for example, Fast Ethernet 0/1 over Fast Ethernet 0/6, because the links are identical.

> **EXAM ALERT**
>
> In the event of equal path costs, the lowest Bridge ID is the first tiebreaker.

Figure 13.5 expans on the switched networking example to include the path costs.

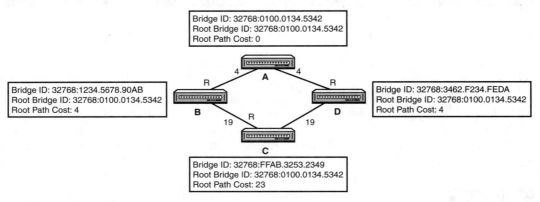

Bridge ID: 32768:0100.0134.5342
Root Bridge ID: 32768:0100.0134.5342
Root Path Cost: 0

Bridge ID: 32768:1234.5678.90AB
Root Bridge ID: 32768:0100.0134.5342
Root Path Cost: 4

Bridge ID: 32768:3462.F234.FEDA
Root Bridge ID: 32768:0100.0134.5342
Root Path Cost: 4

Bridge ID: 32768:FFAB.3253.2349
Root Bridge ID: 32768:0100.0134.5342
Root Path Cost: 23

FIGURE 13.5 Root port calculation.

Designated Ports

After every switch has determined its root port, the switches and bridges determine which port is to become the designated port for every segment that connects the two switches. As the name states, the designated port is the port on each interconnecting segment that is designated to forward traffic from that segment to another segment back to the root bridge. This too is determined through a calculation of the fastest way back to the root port. In the case of a tie, the same decision criteria applies to designated ports as root ports as described earlier.

In Figure 13.6, the designated ports have been calculated based on which switch is advertising the lowest cumulative cost back to the root on each segment. For instance, the BPDUs from

FIGURE 13.6 Designated port calculation.

Switch B to Switch C are advertising a root path cost of 19, whereas the BPDU being sent from Switch C to Switch B is advertising 38. Because Switch B has the lower root path cost, that is the designated port for that segment.

Blocked Ports

To this point, the discussion has focused on how to determine which ports will be forwarding traffic in a switched network. Yet to be addressed is the original point of STP, which is to remove any potential switching loops. To remove potential switching loops, switches and bridges keep any port that is not a root or designated port in a blocked state. Keep in mind that a blocked state is not disabled (shut down); the interface is just not participating in forwarding any data. Blocked interfaces still received BPDUs from other switches to react to any changes in the topology.

> **EXAM ALERT**
>
> Keep in mind for the exam that a blocked interface still receives BPDUs from other switches.

In Figure 13.7, notice that all the root ports have been elected, as well as the designated ports for each segment. Notice on the segment between Switch C and Switch D that a port connected to Switch C is not a root port or a designated port. This port blocks user data to ensure that a switching loop does not occur and expose the network to broadcast storms. This also means that any devices connected to Switch C sending Ethernet data to any device connected to Switch D will ultimately go through Switch B, and then Switch A, to finally arrive at Switch D.

FIGURE 13.7 Blocked port calculation.

Challenge

To ensure your understanding of STP, this challenge steps you through the scenario illustrated in Figure 13.8.

Bridge ID: 32768:0100.0134.5342
Root Bridge ID:
Root Path Cost:

Bridge ID: 32768:1234.5678.90AB
Root Bridge ID:
Root Path Cost:

Bridge ID: 4096:3462.F234.FEDA
Root Bridge ID:
Root Path Cost:

FIGURE 13.8   STP challenge scenario.

1. All switches believe themselves to be the root bridge at startup. After sending their BPDUs, which switch remains the root bridge, and why?

2. Every *nonroot* bridge determines its root ports. Which interfaces become root ports based on the election result?

3. Every segment must have a designated port to use to forward traffic onto other segments. Which interfaces on the three segments will be designated ports?

4. One port should remain that is not designated or a root port. In what state will this port be?

Challenge Answer

Figure 13.9 displays the end result of the STP election and calculation. Switch C becomes the root bridge in this design because the default priority was administratively changed in this design to 4096, giving Switch C the lowest Bridge ID. Because Switch A and Switch B are nonroot bridges, they must calculate their root ports based on the lowest cumulative cost back to the root bridge. For each segment, the switch with the lowest root path cost will be the designated port. Because Switch C's interface on the lower segment is not a root or designated port, that interface will be blocking.

Bridge ID: 32768:0100.0134.5342
Root Bridge ID: 4096:3462.F234.FEDA
Root Path Cost: 4

Bridge ID: 32768:1234.5678.90AB
Root Bridge ID: 4096:3462.F234.FEDA
Root Path Cost: 8

Bridge ID: 4096:3462.F234.FEDA
Root Bridge ID: 4096:3462.F234.FEDA
Root Path Cost: 0

FIGURE 13.9   STP challenge scenario answer.

Port State Transitions

You now know how STP removes switching loops in your switched LAN by electing a root bridge and calculating which ports should forward based on the lowest root path cost. However, as explained earlier, STP must be able to react to topology changes, such as a segment or switch going down, to ensure the redundant design is put to good use. When this type of change occurs, ports that were once in a blocking state could quite possibly transition to a forwarding state.

If devices were to immediately transition from a blocking state to a forwarding state, they could easily cause loops in the network because the topology change did not have a chance to propagate throughout the entire switched network. To remedy this dilemma, STP transitions into two intermediate states before moving to a forwarding role. In these transitionary states, the switch ensures that enough time has transpired to propagate the changes, and it undergoes a pre-forwarding routine to ensure that it will know where to forward the data when the interface is forwarding. Table 13.2 displays, in order, the possible STP states, their functions, and the time it takes to transition out of each state.

TABLE 13.2   STP Port States

State	Function	Transition Time
Disabled	Interface is administratively shut down or inoperative as a result of a security violation.	N/A
Blocking	Does not forward any user data. All ports start out in this state. Does not send, but still can receive BPDUs to react to topology changes.	0 to 20 seconds
Listening	Begins to transition to a forwarding state by listening and sending BPDUs. No user data sent.	15 seconds
Learning	Begins to build MAC addresses learned on the interface. No user data sent.	15 seconds
Forwarding	User data forwarded.	

It may initially take the switch 20 seconds to start the transition process to the listening stage because that is the default time limit that STP uses to consider a neighbor switch to be down. In other words, if a switch stops hearing 10 BPDUs (equal to 20 seconds) from an adjoining switch or bridge, it considers that device to be dead and must react to the new topology. This 20-second timer is known as the *max age timer*.

When a topology change occurs in the network, a nonroot switch sends a specific BPDU called a Topology Change Notification (TCN) out its root port back to the root bridge. This BPDU is one of the only times that a BPDU does not originate from the root bridge. As soon as the root bridge finally receives that notification, it broadcasts a special BPDU to all the switches in the network to start aging out old MAC entries in their CAM tables after about eight times faster (default is 300 seconds). At that point, the switches start rebuilding their CAM tables to reflect the new topology and forward frames accordingly.

The listening and learning states wait 15 seconds each by default, but can be administratively changed if you have a relatively small switched network. These 15-second intervals are commonly referred to as *forward delays* because they delay the transition to a forwarding state. It is important to consider that it could take up to 50 seconds for an interface to transition to a forwarding state when the topology changes. Consequently, no data is transferred in those 50 seconds—which in the networking world is about 10 phone calls of complaining end users.

EXAM ALERT

A STP topology change could take up to 50 seconds.

The max age and forward delay timers are based on a default network diameter of seven switches including the root bridge. Diameter (in switching terms) refers to the number of bridge or switches between any two hosts. If your network is, for instance, only a diameter of 2, you can decrease these timers because it doesn't take as long to propagate a change in the topology. Another benefit of STP is that these timers are ultimately dictated by the root bridge. Thus, to change the timers, you have to configure the change on only the root bridge, and it gets propagated to the other switches. This change could possibly backfire and cause switching loops in instances when you add more switches to the network and forget to change the timers. The next section discusses some safer alternatives to speed up the convergence time of STP when a topology change occurs.

Initial Switch Configurations

Objective:

▶ Perform and verify initial switch configuration tasks including remote access management

Catalyst switches, for the most part, are designed so that the default state of switch allows for basic Layer 2 functionality without requiring any configuration from the administrator. For example, the physical interfaces on the switch are already enabled, which means that you can plug a cable in the switch and the interface operates without requiring you to perform a `no shutdown` on that interface. Does that mean you don't have to learn about Catalyst switch commands? No such luck.

NOTE

Switch Ethernet interfaces are commonly referred to as *ports*.

The majority of the administrative configurations such as configuring hostnames, login banners, passwords, and Telnet/SSH access are identical to the configurations of the router IOS, as described in Chapter 7, "Foundation Cisco IOS Operations." These next sections look at a few commands and configurations that are specific to Catalyst switches.

Assigning a Management IP Address to a Switch

Cisco Layer 2 switches forward frames solely based on MAC addresses. On the other hand, Layer 3 switches and routers use IP addresses in their data forwarding decisions. So why assign an IP address to a Layer 2 switch?

Chapter 8, "Foundation Cisco Configurations," mentions that to remotely manage a device via SSH, Telnet, or HTTP, you need to have IP connectivity to the switch. Likewise, if you were to manage the switch using SNMP, you would also have to program your management server to use its IP address to gather statistics from the switch. All these management functions assume that an IP address is assigned to the device, which in the Catalyst switch's case does not have an IP address in its default configuration.

Unlike Cisco routers, Layer 2 switches do not assign IP addresses on all the physical interfaces. In fact, the interface to which you assign an IP address on a Layer 2 Catalyst switch is actually a virtual interface called VLAN 1. To assign an IP address to the entire switch, you use exactly the same syntax as a router's physical interface to configure the VLAN 1 interface:

```
Switch(config)#interface VLAN1
Switch(config-if)#ip address 172.16.1.100 255.255.0.0
Switch(config-if)#no shutdown
01:35:19: %LINK-3-UPDOWN: Interface Vlan1, changed state to up
```

Defining a Default Gateway

If you were to Telnet into the switch from the terminal on the far network, the Telnet traffic would traverse through the local router, across the WAN link, through the remote router, and finally to the switch. To return the Telnet traffic back to the terminal, the switch would have to send it to a routing device, because the terminal is on another network. To instruct the switch to send any traffic destined for another network to that router, you have to define a default gateway (also known as a gateway of last resort) as shown in Figure 13.10.

FIGURE 13.10 Remote management requirement for default gateway.

FastEthernet 0/0
IP:172.16.1.1/16

Vlan1
IP:172.16.1.100/16

The command to configure a default gateway is `ip default-gateway`, followed by the IP address of the router that is on the switch's segment in Global Configuration. Using the example in Figure 13.10, the configuration would look like the following:

```
Switch(config)#ip default-gateway 172.16.1.1
```

EXAM ALERT

The `ip default-gateway` switch command is used when a switch needs to send or return traffic to a remote network segment. The IP address specified after the `ip default-gateway` command is the router on the local segment that will route the traffic to the remote network.

IP Assignment Using DHCP

Similar to router interfaces, the IP assigned to the VLAN 1 interface and the default gateway can be dynamically assigned using a DHCP server. The configuration is also similar to DHCP-assigned router interfaces except that the configuration is applied to the logical VLAN 1 interface as opposed to a physical port on the switch:

```
Switch#configure terminal
Enter configuration commands, one per line. End with CNTL/Z.
Switch(config)#interface vlan 1
Switch(config-if)#ip address dhcp
Switch(config-if)#no shutdown
00:58:49: %LINK-3-UPDOWN: Interface Vlan1, changed state to up
Interface Vlan1 assigned DHCP address 172.16.1.100, mask 255.255.0.0
```

After the `ip address dhcp` command is applied, the switch sends a DHCPDISCOVER broadcast out on all switch ports assigned to VLAN1 (by default, all switch ports are assigned to VLAN1). If a configured DHCP server exists on those segments, it replies with the IP address for the VLAN 1 interface and default gateway for the switch. As such, there is no required configuration of an IP address or default gateway in the switch configuration. It must be said, however, that despite the fact that this does simplify some of the administration configuration or reconfiguration tasks that are necessary to manage a switch, it is not practical because you need to readily know the IP address of the switch to effectively manage it.

Verifying the IP address and default gateway assigned by the DHCP server cannot be achieved by showing the running or startup configuration. Instead, you can use output from the show dhcp lease command to verify the IP address and default gateway:

```
Switch#show dhcp lease
Temp IP addr: 172.16.1.100 for peer on Interface: Vlan1
Temp  sub net mask: 255.255.0.0
   DHCP Lease server: 172.16.1.1, state: 3 Bound
   DHCP transaction id: 1967
   Lease: 16000 secs,  Renewal: 3000 secs,  Rebind: 16000 secs
Temp default-gateway addr: 172.16.1.1
   Next timer fires after: 00:00:32
   Retry count: 0   Client-ID: cisco-0019.e86a.6fc0-Vl1
   Hostname: Switch
```

Configuring Multiple Switch Interfaces

By design, switches may have a plethora of interfaces that may require a similar configuration. For instance, if the first 20 ports of your switch need to be set to a speed of 100mbs and full duplex, you would be undertaking quite an administrative task of typing the same commands into each interface configuration for all 20 interfaces. To save time, the Catalyst switch's IOS contains a navigation and configuration command shortcut called interface range that enables you to define a range of switch ports and configure them simultaneously. The configuration can be condensed to something like this:

```
Switch(config)#interface range FastEthernet 0/1 - 20
Switch(config-if)#speed 100
Switch(config-if)#duplex full
```

TIP

Note that the syntax of the interface range command requires you to put a space between the starting and ending interfaces in the range separated by a hyphen.

NOTE

You can manually override the default autonegotiating speed and duplex settings for each interface as demonstrated.

Verifying Spanning Tree Protocol

Objective:

▶ Verify network status and switch operation using basic utilities (including: ping, traceroute, telnet, SSH, arp, ipconfig), SHOW & DEBUG commands

STP is enabled by default on all Cisco Catalyst switches. To verify spanning tree operation in your switch, you can issue the show spanning-tree command to see a display of the STP operations:

```
Switch>show spanning-tree

VLAN0001
  Spanning tree enabled protocol ieee
  Root ID    Priority    32769
             Address     000c.65d0.4e00
             This bridge is the root
             Hello Time   2 sec  Max Age 20 sec  Forward Delay 15 sec

  Bridge ID  Priority    32769  (priority 32768 sys-id-ext 1)
             Address     000d.65d0.4e00
             Hello Time   2 sec  Max Age 20 sec  Forward Delay 15 sec
             Aging Time 15
Interface        Role Sts Cost      Prio.Nbr Type
---------------- ---- --- --------- -------- --------------------
Fa0/1            Desg LIS 19        128.1    P2p
Fa0/23           Desg FWD 19        128.23   P2p
Fa0/24           Back BLK 19        128.24   P2p
```

Notice in this output that you can see the MAC address and the priority of the root bridge and the local switch (which happens to be the root bridge). In addition, you can see the timers used in 802.1d for port state transitions, including the max age and forward delay. Finally, this useful show command displays the interfaces that are active and participating in STP and their associated role and state in the spanning tree network.

Troubleshooting Basic Switch Connectivity

Objectives:

▶ Verify network status and switch operation using basic utilities (including: ping, traceroute, telnet, SSH, arp, ipconfig), SHOW & DEBUG commands

▶ Identify, prescribe, and resolve common switched network media issues, configuration issues, auto negotiation, and switch hardware failures

As always, when troubleshooting connectivity issues, use a layered approach and eliminate possibilities at each layer to home in on the possible cause of the problem. Over time, you will begin to develop a sixth sense about these problems and decrease the amount of effort it takes to accurately pinpoint a connectivity problem. In the meantime, let's look at some possible connectivity scenarios and walk through some possible deductions as to what might cause the problem.

In instances where you cannot gain console connectivity to the switch, you should ask the following questions:

1. Is the switch powered on and running? Although this seems like common sense, it is still valid to check to make sure the switch is powered on and successfully completed its bootup process. Catalyst switches all have LEDs (light-emitting diodes) on the switch face to signify that it is operating correctly. The system and status lights for the switch should both be a steady green if the device is powered on and operating normally.

2. Are your terminal connections correct? Verify that you have configured your terminal application correctly by setting the speed, flow control, and start and stop bits and ensure that you have the console (rollover) cable connected between your PC and the switch.

3. Did you or someone else change the console password? If you are gaining access to IOS but cannot log in, you may need to perform password recovery on the switch. Consult the switches' manual or look online at cisco.com for switch-specific steps to recover your password.

In instances where you cannot gain remote connectivity to the switch, you should ask the following questions:

1. Is the switch powered on and running? If possible, console into the switch or have someone check that the switch is powered on and successfully completed its bootup process.

2. Do you have IP connectivity to the switch? You can utilize troubleshooting commands from the switch such as `ping` to test connectivity between the switch and the management computer you are remotely connecting from. If your pings fail, verify that you have configured the default gateway for the switch and continue troubleshooting using the `traceroute` command to identify where along the forwarding data path the packets are failing.

3. Did you or someone else change the vty password or SSH login and password? If you are gaining access to IOS but cannot log in, you may need to reconfigure the SSH and Telnet passwords via the console to regain access to these remote management protocols.

In instances where the switch is not forwarding frames, you should ask yourself these questions:

1. Is the switch powered on and running? This would be fairly evident because all devices connected to the switch would be unable to communicate with each other. If possible, check that the switch is powered on and successfully completed its bootup process.

2. Does the switch have Layer 1 connectivity to the device(s)? The LEDs above the port may give you a quick indication if there is a problem with that port.

   To verify your cabling, ensure you are using a straight through Ethernet cable if connecting to a PC, router, or other end device. If connecting to another switch, you should have a cross-over Ethernet cable attached to those interfaces. What's more, you can also verify that the interfaces are not administratively shut down and are in an up/up state using the `show interfaces interface-id` command.

   Keep in mind that if you just connected the end device to the switch, it will take at least 30 seconds to transition to a forwarding state, as dictated by spanning tree protocol.

3. Does the output of the `show interfaces interface-id` command show you incorrect speed or duplex? An interface that does not become active or is constantly bouncing up and down may indicate duplex and/or speed mismatches from autonegotiation. This will be evident if the `show interfaces interface-id` output is displaying excessive collisions or the interface is in an up/down state. To remedy this problem, ensure that the switch and the end device are set for autonegotiation. To eliminate all doubt, manually set the speed and duplex parameters on the switch port(s) and the end device.

4. Does your switched internetwork intermittently stop forwarding frames? Recall that when new switches are added to a switched internetwork, it may take up to 50 seconds to have the switches converge to the new STP topology. If you are not adding switches to the network, verify that there isn't a faulty switch causing re-elections of the STP topology by using the `debug spanning-tree` command. This command shows real-time events of the spanning tree process and indicates whether a switch might have an interface that is going up and down causing re-elections in the STP topology.

Chapter Summary

This chapter has explored the mysteries behind Ethernet switching. Namely, it showed how switches build their MAC address table (also known as a CAM table), using the source MAC address of Ethernet frames, and forward, filter, or flood those frames based on the destination MAC. The method in which it forwards the frames differs from switch to switch. Specifically, the switch might use the latency varying store-and-forward transmission method, which buffers the entire frame and calculates the CRC before forwarding the frame. Cut-through switching looks at only the destination MAC address in an Ethernet frame, whereas fragment-free looks at up to the first 64 bytes, in which most collisions occur.

Switch connections can communicate in half duplex or full duplex, depending on the device to which they are connected. For instance, half-duplex connections are unidirectional and must be used when connecting to a hub because collisions must be detected. Full duplex can be used only when no possibility of collision exists, because it disables the collision detection circuitry to allow simultaneous bidirectional traffic. To ensure a collision-free environment for full-duplex connections, you must be directly connected to a switch.

When multiple switches are connected in a redundant design, STP (IEEE 802.1d) removes the possibility of switching loops, which can cause broadcast storms. It achieves this by electing a root bridge based on the lowest Bridge ID (priority + MAC) being advertised in BPDUs. After the root bridge is elected, every nonroot bridge forms an association to the root bridge by determining the port with the best path (lowest cumulative cost), which becomes the root port. For every segment, a designated port is also elected based on the fastest route back to the root bridge. In the event of a tie, the Bridge ID is used, followed by the lowest port priority, and finally the lowest port ID.

STP ports start in a blocking state, in which no data or BPDUs are being sent. If the port can forward frames, it transitions to a listening state for 15 seconds (forward delay), where it begins to exchange BPDUs. The learning stage follows for another 15 seconds to learn the MAC address on the interface and then finally transitions to a forwarding state.

Key Terms

- CAM table
- Store-and-forward
- Cut-through
- Fragment-free
- Half duplex
- Full duplex

- STP
- Root bridge
- BPDUs
- Bridge ID
- Root port
- Cost
- Designated port
- Blocking
- Listening
- Learning
- Forwarding
- Max-age timer
- Forward-delay timer
- `ip default-gateway` *gateway_IP*
- `interface range` *media port_range*

Apply Your Knowledge

Exercises

13.1 Basic Switch Configuration

This exercise reinforces the configurations involved in an initial setup of a Catalyst Switch. You may need to look back to Chapter 7 as a reference for some of the commands.

Estimated Time: 5 minutes

1. Power on your switch and enter user EXEC mode through the console.

2. In global configuration, assign the hostname, CstmrASwtch, create an appropriate login banner, and use the strongest encryption for access to privileged EXEC, using the password, giforgot.

3. Create a username of ccent with ssh4me as the password for SSH connectivity (requires cryptographic software image from Cisco.com).

4. In line configuration, specify Telnet and SSH as valid transport input protocols and to use the local username and password as the login on the first five vty lines.

5. Assign a management IP address of 172.16.31.30 /28.

6. Create the domain name of the switch to examcram.com.

7. Generate the RSA key for SSH.

8. Set the default gateway to be a hypothetical router address of 172.16.31.17 /28.

9. Using the `interface range` command, set the first three Fast Ethernet interfaces to be hardcoded as full duplex.

10. Verify your active configuration and save it to NVRAM.

The configuration should look similar to the following Catalyst 3550 configuration:

```
Current configuration : 1819 bytes
!
version 12.2
no service pad
service timestamps debug uptime
service timestamps log uptime
no service password-encryption
!
hostname CstmrASwtch
!
enable secret 5 $1$ueGU$jTruyGB16bJKo9AIa8kkO/
!
username ccent password ssh4me
ip subnet-zero
!
!
ip domain name examcram.com
ip ssh time-out 60
ip ssh authentication-retries 2
!
!
spanning-tree mode pvst
spanning-tree extend system-id
!
!
interface FastEthernet0/1
 no ip address
 duplex full
!
interface FastEthernet0/2
 no ip address
 duplex full
```

```
!
interface FastEthernet0/3
 no ip address
 duplex full
!
!!!Output omitted...
!
interface GigabitEthernet0/1
 no ip address
!
interface GigabitEthernet0/2
 no ip address
!
interface Vlan1
 ip address 172.16.31.30 255.255.255.240
!
ip default-gateway 172.16.31.17
ip classless
ip http server
!
!
banner motd ^C This is a private system and may be accessed only by authorized users.
Unauthorized access is strictly prohibited and will be enforced to the full
extent of the law.^C
!
line con 0
line vty 0 4
login local
 transport input telnet ssh
line vty 5 15
login
!
end
```

Review Questions

1. What do switches do when a frame with a new source and destination MAC address are received?

2. What is the purpose of Spanning Tree Protocol?

3. How is a root bridge elected?

4. How do you configure IP connectivity to a Layer 2 switch?

5. When is it appropriate to run a switch interface in half duplex versus full duplex?

Exam Questions

1. What two components make up a Bridge ID? (Choose two)

- ○ **A.** IP address
- ○ **B.** Port priority
- ○ **C.** MAC address
- ○ **D.** Bridge priority

2. Considering the following output:

```
Switch>show spanning-tree

VLAN0001
  Spanning tree enabled protocol ieee
  Root ID    Priority    32768
             Address     000c.418f.6542
             Cost        19
             Port        23 (FastEthernet0/23)
             Hello Time   2 sec  Max Age 20 sec  Forward Delay 15 sec

  Bridge ID  Priority    32769  (priority 32768 sys-id-ext 1)
             Address     000d.65d0.4e00
             Hello Time   2 sec  Max Age 20 sec  Forward Delay 15 sec
             Aging Time 300
Interface        Role Sts Cost     Prio.Nbr Type
- - - - - - - -  - -  - -. - - - -. - - - -  - - - - - - - - - - - - - - -
Fa0/23           Root FWD 19       128.23   P2p
```

which of the following is false?

- ○ **A.** This switch is the root bridge.
- ○ **B.** The forward delay times have been changed.
- ○ **C.** The max age timer has been changed.
- ○ **D.** The priority has been changed.

3. Given the following output:

```
Switch>show spanning-tree

VLAN0001
  Spanning tree enabled protocol ieee
  Root ID    Priority    32768
             Address     000c.418f.6542
             Cost        19
```

```
              Port        23 (FastEthernet0/23)
              Hello Time   2 sec  Max Age 20 sec  Forward Delay 15 sec
...Ouput Omitted...
```

what speed is the interface?

- ○ **A.** 10Mbps
- ○ **B.** 1Gbps
- ○ **C.** 10Gbps
- ○ **D.** 100Mbps

4. Which of the following can be determined from the following output?

```
Switch>show spanning-tree
...Output Omitted...
Interface        Role Sts Cost     Prio.Nbr Type
---------- -- -. ----. ---- ----------------

Fa0/5            Root LRN 19       128.5   P2p
```

- ○ **A.** This port has the slowest connection back to the root bridge.
- ○ **B.** The port priority has been administratively changed.
- ○ **C.** This interface is learning MAC addresses.
- ○ **D.** Data is being forwarded.

5. Based on Figure 13.11, which of the following STP roles will Switch A and Switch D have on their shared link? (Choose two)

FIGURE 13.11 STP topology exhibit.

- ○ **A.** Switch A will have a root port.
- ○ **B.** Switch D will have a designated port.

    ○ **C.** Switch D will have a blocking port.

    ○ **D.** Switch A will have a designated port.

6. Which frame transmission method is latency varying?

    ○ **A.** Store-and-forward

    ○ **B.** Cut-through

    ○ **C.** Fragment-free

    ○ **D.** All of the above

7. Why is the following output false?

```
Switch#show mac-address-table
          Mac Address Table
-----------------------------------

Vlan    Mac Address      Type       Ports
----    -----------      ----       -----
...Output Omitted...
  1     0300.3E9E.07E9   DYNAMIC    Fa0/3
  1     FFFF.FFFF.FFFF   DYNAMIC    Fa0/1
  1     0300.3E3E.531A   DYNAMIC    Fa0/3
```

    ○ **A.** There are no static MAC address entries.

    ○ **B.** There cannot be two MAC addresses learned on the same interface.

    ○ **C.** No multicast entries are shown.

    ○ **D.** A broadcast address should not be present in the CAM table.

8. What is the purpose of configuring a default gateway in a Catalyst switch?

    ○ **A.** To have the switch act as the default gateway for end devices connected to it.

    ○ **B.** To enforce all STP ports to a forwarding state so all switching traffic goes through the switch.

    ○ **C.** To enable Layer 3 routing in the switch.

    ○ **D.** To specify the IP address of the router that will forward requests made to the management IP address of the switch from devices on other subnets.

9. Which of the following are likely to occur when a switch with a higher Bridge ID is added to the switched topology? (Choose two)

    ○ **A.** A re-election will occur, and the new switch will become the root bridge.

    ○ **B.** The new switch will determine the fastest path back to the root bridge and make that its root port.

○ **C.** If the added switch creates a redundant path, at least one switch port in all of the interconnected switches will be in a blocking state.

○ **D.** The switch will immediately begin forwarding frames sent to it by end devices connected to it.

10. You just connected your interface to a hub. Which of the following must be true?

○ **A.** Your speed must be 10Mbps.

○ **B.** Your duplex must be full.

○ **C.** Your duplex must be half.

○ **D.** CSMA/CD must be disabled.

Answers to Review Questions

1. When a switch receives an Ethernet frame that contains an unknown source MAC address, it associates that MAC address with the receiving interface in the CAM table. When the switch receives an Ethernet frame with an unknown unicast destination MAC address, the switch floods that frame out every port except the one on which it was received.

2. Spanning Tree Protocol eliminates switching loops in environments when multiple switches are connected in a redundant design.

3. The root bridge is elected based on the switch that has the lowest advertised Bridge ID in the switches' BPDUs. The Bridge ID is composed of the priority plus the switch's MAC address. If another switch with a lower Bridge ID is added to the STP topology, a re-election occurs, and that switch becomes the new root bridge.

4. To gain IP connectivity to a Layer 2 switch, you must configure its management VLAN1 interface either manually with the `ip address` *ip-address mask* command or dynamically using the `ip address dhcp` command. If you are connecting to the device remotely from another network, the switch must also have a gateway of last resort configured statically using the `ip default-gateway` *ip-address* command or dynamically from a DHCP server.

5. When you connect to a hub, collision detection must be enabled; thus, you must run the interface as half duplex. Full-duplex interfaces have collision detection disabled and can be enabled only when the switch port is connected to another switch or an end device.

Answers to Exam Questions

1. **C, D.** The Bridge ID comprises the bridge priority plus the MAC address of the switch. Answer A is incorrect because Layer 2 switches do not use IP addresses for Bridge IDs. Answer B is incorrect because the port priority is used as a tiebreaker only when determining the root or designated ports.

2. **A.** The output displays the Root Bridge ID with a different MAC address than the local switch. So, this switch is not the root bridge. The timers and priority are all still their default values. B is incorrect because the forward delay timers are at their default value of 15 seconds. Answer C is incorrect because the max age timer is at its default value of 20 seconds. D is incorrect because the switch's priority is at its default value of 32768.

3. **D.** A port cost of 19 is 100Mbps. Answers A, B, and C are incorrect because 10Gbps has a port cost of 2, 1Gbps has a port cost of 4, and 10Mbps has a port cost of 100.

4. **C.** Because the interface is in the learning state, it is beginning to learn the MAC addresses on that interface. Answer A is incorrect because the port is the root port, indicating that it is the fastest back to the root bridge. Answer B is incorrect because the port priority has not changed from its default value of 128. Answer D is false because the port is in the learning state; it still is not able to forward traffic.

5. **C, D.** Switch A has the fastest way back to the root (itself) on that segment, so it will be designated. Because Switch D's interface is not a root or a designated port, it must be blocking. Answer A is incorrect because only nonroot switches and bridges have root ports. Answer B is incorrect because Answer D has the slowest path back to the root for that particular segment.

6. **A.** Only the store-and-forward are latency varying because they have to buffer frames of different sizes. Answers B, C, and D are incorrect because cut-through looks at only the destination MAC address, and fragment-free looks at the first 64 bytes, so their latency will not vary.

7. **D.** The source MAC address in an Ethernet frame should not be a broadcast (only destination addresses), so a switch should never have that entry in its CAM table. Answer A is insignificant because static entries are not mandatory. Answer B is incorrect because a switch can learn multiple MAC addresses on a single interface. Answer C is incorrect because multicast addresses should not be present in a CAM table by default.

8. **D.** The default gateway is the IP address of the Layer 3 routing device that is used when devices are issuing Telnet, SSH, HTTP, and SNMP requests to the switch. To respond to these requests, the switch must send the responses to the router who in turn will route them back to the end device. Answer A is false because the switch itself is not the Layer 3 gateway for other devices despite the fact that the Layer 2 frames are switched through it. The default gateway for end devices is still the router of the LAN. Answer B is incorrect because the default gateway is not related to STP. Answer C is incorrect because the `ip default-gateway` command does not enable Layer 3 routing in switches. The command to achieve Layer 3 routing is `ip routing` and is useful only if you have a Layer 3 switch.

9. **B, C.** Because this switch has a higher Bridge ID, it does not become the root bridge. It elects the fastest port back to the root bridge as its root port. If the added switch creates a redundant loop in the switched network, STP blocks one of the ports to avoid broadcast storms. Answer A is incorrect because the BridgeID must be lower than the current root bridge to force an election. Answer D is incorrect because the switch will still transition into the listening and learning states before forwarding frames.

10. **C.** When connecting to a hub, you have to be able to detect collisions; thus, you must be running half duplex. The speed doesn't matter, so Answer A is incorrect. Answers B and D are incorrect because setting the port to full duplex disables CSMA/CD.

Suggested Readings and Resources

1. David Barnes and Basir Sakandar. *Cisco LAN Switching Fundamentals*. Cisco Press, 2004.

2. Matthew J. Castelli. *LAN Switching First-Step*, Cisco Press, 2004.

3. "Spanning-Tree Protocol," www.cisco.com.

CHAPTER FOURTEEN

Implementing Switch Security

Objectives

This chapter covers the following Cisco-specific objectives for the "Implement a small switched network" section of the 640-822 ICND1 exam:

▶ **Implement and verify basic security for a switch (port security, deactivate ports)**

▶ **Verify network status and switch operation using basic utilities (including: ping, traceroute, telnet, SSH, arp, ipconfig), SHOW & DEBUG commands**

Outline

Introduction   **458**

Securing Physical Access to the Catalyst Switch   **458**

Securing Terminal Access to the Catalyst Switch   **458**

To Telnet or Not to Telnet   460

Additional IOS Security Practices   461

Layer 2 Security   **461**

Port Security   462

    Static MAC with Port Security   463

    Verifying Port Security   463

"See"DP   464

Chapter Summary   **466**

Key Terms   466

Apply Your Knowledge   **467**

Exercises   467

Review Questions   469

Exam Questions   469

Answers to Review Questions   471

Answers to Exam Questions   472

Suggested Readings and Resources   472

Study Strategies

▶ Part of being thorough in securing your switched network is to think like an attacker. With that in mind, try to consider ways in which your network is vulnerable and how you would go about gaining access if you were the attacker.

▶ Many of the topics discussed in this chapter can also be applied to securing your router. Keep that in mind when reading these topics as a refresher on how to secure your Cisco devices.

▶ Read the information presented in this chapter, paying special attention to tables, Notes, and Exam Alerts.

▶ Complete the Challenge and the Exercises at the end of the chapter. The exercises will solidify the concepts that you have learned in the previous sections.

▶ Complete the Exam Questions at the end of the chapter. They are designed to simulate the types of questions you will be asked on the ICND1 exam.

Introduction

Securing a network is an endless task. Every day there are new scripts and exploits, new vulnerabilities, and new methods to gain access to your network. Our job as Cisco administrators is to stay ahead of the game as much as possible and make it as difficult as possible to gain access.

As discussed in Chapter 4, "General Network Security," the basis of any good security implementation is a thorough security policy. Switched networks must be a pivotal piece of that security policy; however, they are typically the most overlooked. The fact that the LAN is tucked away inside your network provides a false sense of security, especially because some of your biggest threats might be the users attached to the switched network. This chapter examines how to secure access to the Cisco devices in your LAN as well as the traffic that flows through it.

Securing Physical Access to the Catalyst Switch

Similar to troubleshooting, our first layer of defense for securing the switched network should start at the Physical layer. Specifically, we need to secure access to the physical switch itself and the cables that are connected to it. It doesn't take a skilled attacker to physically destroy a switched network to which he or she has complete access.

With that being said, the first and probably most critical step of securing your network is to ensure that the switches themselves are secured in a cool room in which only you or those authorized have access. If users have physical access to the switches, they can easily console into the switch and perform a password-recovery exercise (easily found on the Internet) just by repowering the switch and holding down a button during power-up. Even unintentional attacks such as custodial staff unplugging your switches to run the vacuum can occur easily if not secured correctly. If you can, also make sure that the Ethernet cabling between the switches and end devices is not in plain sight and therefore can't be easily damaged. You don't want the last act by a fired employee to be taking down your entire network by ripping out your existing wiring.

Securing Terminal Access to the Catalyst Switch

After we have ensured that the switch is physically secured, the next layer of defense to implement is securing terminal access to the switch so that attackers cannot perform reconnaissance or manipulate configurations. Because there are several ways to gain access to the Cisco IOS, due diligence is required to ensure that all terminal connections are secured.

To start, the first logical terminal access to secure is the console and auxiliary port. Many might ask why, because we already physically secured the switch. To answer a question with a question, would you have an account at a bank that leaves your money out on a table because they have an alert security guard standing at the door? A layered defensive approach entails having security measures at each step of the way so that attackers will have many obstacles in their way in achieving their objective.

To secure access to the console and aux port, the simplest defense you can use is securing them with a password. Just as in router configurations, this is achieved in the line configuration using the `password` command. It is also a good idea to make sure that your passwords are strong passwords containing at least eight characters and that they have a combination of numbers, symbols, and lower and uppercase letters:

```
Switch(config)# line console 0
Switch(config-line)# login
Switch(config-line)# password EggsAmKr@m
Switch(config-line)# exit
Switch(config)# line auxiliary 0
Switch(config-line)# login
Switch(config-line)# password EggsAmPr3p
```

What's more, you can create a local username and password combination that is stored in the configuration. This username and password will be required to be entered when someone attaches to the console and gets an EXEC prompt. The only difference in the configuration is that you no longer need to specify a password in the line configuration, because you achieved that in defining the username and password combination, and you also must use the keyword `local` in the `login` command. This keyword tells the IOS to use the local username and password combination that can be found in the configuration:

```
Switch(config)# username jchambers password Sysco-Prez
Switch(config)# line console 0
Switch(config-line)# login local
Switch(config-line)# exit
Switch(config)# line auxiliary 0
Switch(config-line)# login local
```

Now, when someone attaches to the console or aux port, he or she is prompted for a username and password, such as the following:

```
Press RETURN to get started.
User Access Verification

Username:jchambers
Password:
Switch>
```

NOTE

If you configure the console and aux login to use the username and password using the `login local` command and a password configuration is present on the line as well, the IOS uses the username and password over the password line configuration.

TIP

You can use a special username and password command that encrypts the password similarly to the `enable secret` command. Conveniently enough, the command is `username` *username* `secret` *password*. This applies an MD5 hash of the password so that it cannot be easily acquired if the configuration is accessed.

To Telnet or Not to Telnet

Recall that although Telnet is a convenient way to gain EXEC access to the Cisco device, it also is extremely dangerous, because everything that is sent using Telnet is in clear text and can be intercepted by anyone eavesdropping on the session. With that being said, whenever possible, use SSH for remote terminal connectivity to the Cisco device. Recall that the configuration for enabling SSH on a Cisco device is as follows:

1. Change the default hostname of the Cisco device.

2. Configure a domain name with the `ip domain-name` command.

3. Generate the RSA key with at least a 1024-bit key with the `crypto key generate rsa` command.

4. Create a username and password.

A recommended third step in this process, however, is to limit the vty lines on the Cisco device to accept only SSH as an input protocol. In other words, this step entails disallowing Telnet into the vty lines. The command to limit the terminal input on the vty lines is `transport input SSH` on the vty line configuration:

```
Switch(config)# line vty 0 15
Switch(config-line)# transport input SSH
```

When you exclude the keyword `telnet` in the `transport input` command, only SSH is allowed as a terminal input protocol on all the vty lines.

Whether you are using SSH or are only left with using Telnet, make sure you have properly secured user EXEC access through the vty lines using the same methods as the aux and console. Specifically, configure a password on the vty lines or use the `login local` command to prompt for a username and password.

EXAM ALERT

By using the `transport input SSH` command, you limit SSH as the only transport protocol allowed on the vty lines

---

Additional IOS Security Practices

In addition to securing access to Cisco IOS, it is also a good idea to secure the contents of the configuration using some practical and simple configuration steps that we have discussed. This list is not exhaustive by any means, but it is a good beginning point:

▶ Encrypt your enable password to privileged EXEC using the `enable secret` command.

▶ Encrypt all other clear-text passwords in the configuration using `service password-encryption`.

▶ Create a login banner that warns against unauthorized access attempts to the EXEC prompt.

▶ Disable EXEC access on unused terminal access ports (such as aux ports) using the `no exec` command in the line configuration.

▶ Limit how long the terminal session stays idle to not exceed one minute with the `exec-timeout` command (`exec-timeout 1 0`).

Challenge

Now that you have a basic checklist of security do's and don'ts for physical security and connectivity to a switch, it is time to evaluate your existing switched network and consider if your switches are secured. If you do not have a switch network, imagine that you just received a switch, and think about what you should do to secure it. Then check yourself with the following questions:

1. Are the switch and its cables physically secured?
2. Are the console and auxiliary port secured?
3. If your switch has a supported IOS, are you running SSH for remote management?
4. If you do not have SSH, have you fully secured your vty lines for Telnet?
5. Are all passwords encrypted?

Layer 2 Security

Feeling satisfied with securing access to the physical switch and cables as well as access to the Catalyst switch IOS, our next step on our secure ladder is to get to the core of our switching functions and secure the possible vulnerabilities that occur at the Data Link layer.

The transparent functions that our switches perform, such as MAC address learning and forwarding, are taken for granted because they are just that: transparent. Consequently, these are the most overlooked aspects of switch security today, because we naturally assume that the default behavior of the switch's design is how it should be. Any thought of securing that behavior goes against the switch's basic operations. In the following sections, you will see that although the extra configuration steps might involve slightly more work, the end result is that you won't lose sleep wondering when the next attack might cause your cell phone to go off.

Port Security

Objectives:

▶ Implement and verify basic security for a switch (port security, deactivate ports)

Anybody who has physical access to the ports of your switches can easily attach another switch or hub to enable more devices to be on the switched network. If you want to limit the number of MAC addresses that can be dynamically learned on a switch port (for environments such as college campuses and hotels), you can enable the port security feature on your switch ports that are accessible to end users. With the `switchport port-security` commands, you can define the maximum number of MAC addresses to be learned on an access port. If this maximum number is exceeded, the switch port is put in an error-disabled state (by default) in which you have to reenable the interface by administratively shutting it down (with the `shutdown` command) and reenabling the port with the `no shutdown` command. Although this is a bit drastic, it is a surefire way to ensure that switch administrators know where the violation occurred and help identify the users who might be responsible.

To configure this port security functionality, you must enable this port security on each interface, followed by the maximum MAC count allowed on the interface (the default is 1). For example, if you wanted to restrict the number of MAC addresses allowed to 10, you would use the following configuration on the port:

```
Switch(config-if)# switchport port-security
Switch(config-if)# switchport port-security maximum 10
```

Furthermore, you can change the default action when a violation occurs on the secured port with the `switchport port-security violation` command:

```
Switch(config-if)# switchport port-security violation {protect | restrict | shutdown}
```

The default action is shutdown, which puts the port in the error-disabled state, as mentioned earlier. You can also choose to have the port increase a violation counter and alert an administrator using an SNMP trap with the `restrict` keyword. The `protect` keyword only allows traffic from the secure port; it drops packets from other MAC addresses until the number of MAC addresses drops below the maximum.

EXAM ALERT

The `switchport port-security maximum` command restricts how many MAC addresses can be learned on a switch interface. The `switchport port-security violation shutdown` command instructs the switch to disable the port when a violation occurs.

Static MAC with Port Security

The default state of Cisco Catalyst switches is to learn MAC addresses dynamically. For security purposes, you can assign static MAC addresses to an interface to ensure that a MAC address is recognized on only a specific interface. For instance, if you want to make sure that no one tries to connect to your switch and spoof (falsely assume the identity of) your server's MAC address of FA23.239B.2349, you could use the following port security command to statically assign that MAC address to the Fast Ethernet 0/2 interface:

```
Switch(config)# interface fastethernet 0/2
Switch(config-if)# switchport port-security
Switch(config-if)# switchport port-security mac-address FA23.239B.2349
```

This configuration leaves the maximum secure MAC address at its default of 1. If the switch receives another MAC address on Fast Ethernet 0/2, or the MAC address FA23.239B.2349 is seen entering a port other than Fast Ethernet 0/2, the port is disabled.

Port security also can save you some configuration by learning *sticky* secure MAC addresses. With the command `switchport port-security mac-address sticky`, the switch automatically configures the addresses already dynamically learned on the interface, as well as any new MAC addresses (up to the maximum) to be secure MAC addresses. These sticky addresses actually get added as sticky secure MAC configuration line entries in the running configuration. If you save the configuration and reboot the switch, those secure MAC addresses won't need to be relearned.

EXAM ALERT

Sticky addresses are secure MAC addresses that are dynamically learned on the interface.

Verifying Port Security

Objectives:

▶ Verify network status and switch operation using basic utilities (including: ping, traceroute, telnet, SSH, arp, ipconfig), SHOW & DEBUG commands

To verify the port security configuration parameters on the interface, as well as the number of security violations that have occurred on that interface, use the `show port-security interface` *interface* command:

```
Switch# show port-security interface fa0/2
Port Security                      : Enabled
```

```
Port Status                       : Secure-up
Violation Mode                    : Shutdown
Aging Time                        : 0 mins
Aging Type                        : Absolute
SecureStatic Address Aging        : Disabled
Maximum MAC Addresses             : 1
Total MAC Addresses               : 1
Configured MAC Addresses          : 1
Sticky MAC Addresses              : 0
Last Source Address               : fa23.239b.2349
Security Violation Count          : 0
```

Based on this output, you can see that port security is enabled and is not in a disabled state. The default actions for violations (shutdown) and maximum MAC addresses are configured on Fast Ethernet 0/2, with a configured MAC address of fa23.239b.2349.

To verify your configured port security addresses, use the show port-security address command:

```
Switch# show port-security address
          Secure Mac Address Table
------------------------------------------------------------------------
Vlan    Mac Address       Type              Ports   Remaining Age
                                                    (mins)

----    -----------       ----              -----   -------------
  1     fa23.239b.2349    SecureConfigured   Fa0/2    -
------------------------------------------------------------------------
Total Addresses in System (excluding one mac per port)    : 0
Max Addresses limit in System (excluding one mac per port) : 1024
```

Here you can see that your statically configured secure MAC address is configured on Fast Ethernet 0/2. Compare that output to a dynamically learned sticky MAC address, which shows the type as SecureDynamic as opposed to SecureConfigured:

```
Switch# show port-security address
          Secure Mac Address Table
------------------------------------------------------------------------
Vlan    Mac Address       Type              Ports   Remaining Age
                                                    (mins)

----    -----------       ----              -----   -------------
  1     fa23.239b.2349    SecureDynamic      Fa0/2    -
------------------------------------------------------------------------
Total Addresses in System (excluding one mac per port)    : 0
Max Addresses limit in System (excluding one mac per port) : 1024
```

"See"DP

This might sound like Cisco sacrilege, but you should consider disabling CDP on switch interfaces that do not need it, such as edge ports connected to end devices. If you consider the information someone can learn from CDP, you'll realize the major security liability it can be. From just a single CDP multicast, an attacker could learn the hostname, the local port on the switch that sent the CDP message, and the switch's IP address. With this information and strong motivation, it is only a matter of time before your switch and its networks are infiltrated.

Recall that to disable CDP on individual interfaces, you must configure `no cdp enable` on each interface. If you have no need for CDP, disable it globally on the switch with the `no cdp run` command.

Chapter Summary

Securing a switched network entails trying to protect all Layer 1 aspects of the switch, including access to the IOS itself. In addition, it is imperative to secure the switch's Layer 2 operations so that an attacker doesn't interrupt or damage the switched network.

Securing the Physical layer entails ensuring that the switch and its cables are in a secure environment where users cannot inflict damage on them. This step also gives added protection from users gaining console access to the switch to gain information to attack the network or attack or manipulate the switch itself. Leveraging the IOS's internal security measures such as logins and passwords for terminal access is also ideal in building a layered defense. When possible, it is also recommended that you use SSH instead of Telnet for remote access to the IOS, because the communications between the management computer and the switch are secured.

Data Link layer security involves securing individual ports using port security. Port security protects ports by defining a maximum number of MAC addresses that are allowed to be dynamically learned on an individual port. You can also manually specify the MAC address(es) that are allowed to be present in the source address of the Ethernet frame when entering that port. This can be a single static configured MAC address, or you can configure sticky learning, and the addresses will be dynamically added to the configuration. When a port security violation occurs, the default action is to disable the interface. When this occurs, you have to shut down the interface and administratively bring it back up. You can configure the switch port to just report the violation (restrict), or you can reject frames from nonsecure MAC addresses until the number of MAC addresses falls under the limit (protect).

In addition, CDP reveals potentially dangerous information in its multicasts; thus, it is recommended that you disable CDP globally or on interfaces that do not require it.

Key Terms

- ▶ Port security
- ▶ Error-disabled
- ▶ Restrict
- ▶ Protect
- ▶ Sticky secure MAC addresses

Apply Your Knowledge

Exercises

14.1 The Impregnable IOS

Now it is time to take the security features you learned about in this chapter and apply them to our switch. To start, we will walk through an exercise of securing access to the IOS and the passwords in the configuration.

Estimated Time: 15 minutes

1. Console into your switch.

2. Configure a username and password. If supported, make the password secured with an MD5 hash.

3. Change the default hostname, and configure a domain name for the switch.

4. Generate a 1024-bit RSA key.

5. Configure the console's login to prompt for the username and password.

6. Disable the auxiliary port from getting EXEC access.

7. Configure the login of the vty lines to prompt for a username and password.

8. Allow SSH only on the vty lines (remove Telnet).

9. Limit the timeout for EXEC sessions to 45 seconds.

10. Assign an MD5 hashed enable password.

11. Encrypt all clear-text passwords.

Your configuration should be similar to the following:

```
! Step 2
Switch(config)# username artvandelay secret Imp0rt3xp0rt
! Step 3
Switch(config)# ip domain-name examprep.com
Switch(config)# hostname Swtch2950
! Step 4
Swtch2950(config)# crypto key generate rsa
The name for the keys will be: Swtch2950.examprep.com
Choose the size of the key modulus in the range of 360 to 2048 for your General
Purpose Keys. Choosing a key modulus greater than 512 may take a few minutes.

How many bits in the modulus [512]: 1024
Generating RSA keys ...
[OK]
7w1d: %SSH-5-ENABLED: SSH 1.99 has been enabled
! Step 5
Swtch2950(config)# line console 0
```

```
Swtch2950(config-line)# login local
Swtch2950(config-line)# exit
! Step 6
Swtch2950(config)# line auxiliary 0
Swtch2950(config-line)# no exec
Swtch2950(config-line)# exit
! Step 7
Swtch2950(config)# line vty 0 15
Swtch2950(config-line)# login local
! Step 8
Swtch2950(config-line)# transport input ssh
! Step 9
Switch(config-line)# exec-timeout 0 45
Switch(config-line)# exit
! Step 10
Swtch2950(config)# enable secret MD5p@ssw0rd
! Step 11
Swtch2950(config)# service password-encryption
```

14.2 Layer 2 Security To-Do

With our switch secured, it is time to secure the switch's Layer 2 operations.

Estimated Time: 10 minutes

1. Enable port security on ports 1 through 5 using the `interface range` command.

2. Set the maximum number of dynamically learned MAC addresses to 10.

3. Change the default action of violations to disallow traffic from any newly learned MAC addresses over our maximum.

4. Configure the sixth interface to have only a single MAC address of 1234.5678.ABCD.

5. Configure the seventh interface to have secure MAC addresses sticky-learned.

6. Disable CDP globally.

Your configuration should be similar to the following:

```
! Step 1
Swtch2950(config)# interface range fastethernet 0/1-5
Swtch2950(config-if)# switchport port-security
! Step 2
Swtch2950(config-if)# switchport port-security maximum 10
! Step 3
Swtch2950(config-if)# switchport port-security violation protect
Swtch2950(config-if)# exit
! Step 4
Swtch2950(config)# interface fastethernet 0/6
Swtch2950(config-if)# switchport port-security mac-address 1234.5678.ABCD
Swtch2950(config-if)# exit
```

```
! Step 5
Swtch2950(config)# interface fastethernet 0/7
Swtch2950(config-if)# switchport port-security mac-address sticky
Swtch2950(config-if)# exit
! Step 6
Swtch2950(config)# no cdp run
```

Review Questions

1. What is the significance of securing physical access to a switch?

2. How can you harden (make secure) the Cisco IOS?

3. How can you ensure that only one specific end device is attached to a switch port?

4. Why could CDP be a potential security risk?

Exam Questions

1. Which of the following is not a violation action of port security?

○ **A.** Protect

○ **B.** Shut down

○ **C.** Notify

○ **D.** Restrict

2. Which of the following is not a recommended security implementation for securing the Catalyst switch?

○ **A.** SSH.

○ **B.** Disable the console port.

○ **C.** Configure the login and password for the vty lines.

○ **D.** Allow only specific management IP address(es) into the vty lines.

3. Which command produced the following output?

```
Switch# show port-security address
           Secure Mac Address Table
-------------------------------------------------------------------
Vlan    Mac Address       Type             Ports   Remaining Age
                                                       (mins)

----    -----------       ----             -----   -------------
  1     1234.5678.9ABF    SecureConfigured  Fa0/9      -
-------------------------------------------------------------------
Total Addresses in System (excluding one mac per port)    : 0
Max Addresses limit in System (excluding one mac per port) : 1024
```

○ **A.** Switch(config-if)# `switchport port-security sticky`

○ **B.** Switch(config-if)# `switchport port-security mac-address`
   `1234.5678.9abf`

○ **C.** Switch(config-if)# `switchport port-security mac-address`
   `sticky`

○ **D.** Switch(config-if)# `switchport port-security 1234.5678.9abf`

4. Given the following:

```
Switch# show port-security interface fa0/6
Port Security                      : Enabled
Port Status                        : Err-disabled
Violation Mode                     : Shutdown
Aging Time                         : 0 mins
Aging Type                         : Absolute
SecureStatic Address Aging         : Disabled
Maximum MAC Addresses              : 1
Total MAC Addresses                : 2
Configured MAC Addresses           : 0
Sticky MAC Addresses               : 0
Last Source Address                : fa53.c39b.af34
Security Violation Count           : 1
```

which of the following is a possible cause of the output?

○ **A.** Fast Ethernet 0/6 is receiving traffic and working correctly.

○ **B.** A static MAC address has been configured on Fast Ethernet 0/6.

○ **C.** Fast Ethernet 0/6 is learning sticky MAC addresses.

○ **D.** Fast Ethernet 0/6 is shut down because a violation has occurred.

5. Why is the following output false?

```
Switch# show port-security interface fa0/2
Port Security                      : Enabled
Port Status                        : Secure-up
Violation Mode                     : Shutdown
Aging Time                         : 0 mins
Aging Type                         : Absolute
SecureStatic Address Aging         : Disabled
Maximum MAC Addresses              : 10
Total MAC Addresses                : 50
Configured MAC Addresses           : 0
Sticky MAC Addresses               : 0
Last Source Address                : de26.287b.2490
Security Violation Count           : 0
```

◯ **A.** There are more MAC addresses than the maximum allowed and no violations.

◯ **B.** You cannot have the violation action be shutdown unless static secure MAC addresses are configured.

◯ **C.** Sticky addresses must be configured if there is more than one MAC address.

◯ **D.** The maximum MAC addresses cannot be changed from the default value of 1.

6. Which of the following is false regarding what happens when you use the `login local` command on line configurations?

◯ **A.** The switch uses the username and password configured from the global configuration.

◯ **B.** You are prompted for a login and password as long as you don't use the `password` command on the line configuration.

◯ **C.** This command can be configured on vty lines, the auxiliary port, and the console port.

◯ **D.** The password can be encrypted using the `username` *username* `secret` *password* command.

Answers to Review Questions

1. An attacker can maliciously cause physical damage to the switch and/or the cables connected to the switch and ultimately bring down your network. If the attacker wants to covertly attack the network or gain unauthorized access to other devices or networks, he or she can also gain console access to the switch and perform password recovery to reconfigure the switch or discover other devices. For these reasons, it is imperative to ensure that the physical equipment and cables are secured from unauthorized users.

2. The first step to hardening the Cisco IOS is to secure all points of terminal entry to the IOS. This entails assigning passwords (or usernames/password combinations) to the console, aux, and vty lines. Additionally, if any of these services are not being used, you should disable EXEC access. For remote access, you should use SSH over Telnet if possible and allow SSH only on the vty lines.

   After terminal access is secured, you should ensure that all passwords are encrypted in the configuration, disable CDP on interfaces that do not require it, and decrease the amount of time an EXEC session can remain idle.

3. To ensure that a single device is attached to a switch port, enable port security and allow only one MAC address as the maximum (the default). For additional security, manually or dynamically (using sticky learning) specify the device's MAC address.

4. CDP advertises pertinent information for discovery and troubleshooting. Information such as CDP-advertising ports, hostname, and IP addresses can be intercepted and used to attack the switch.

Answers to Exam Questions

1. **C.** Notify is not a valid action of port security. The three actions that can be configured are shut down, protect, and restrict.

2. **B.** Answer B is not a recommended security implementation because you will always require console access as a failsafe to gain access to Cisco devices. SSH, login/passwords for vty lines, and specifying management IP address(es) of management station(s) are all recommended security implementations.

3. **B.** Because the output indicates that the MAC address is SecureConfigured, it must have been manually configured using the `switchport port-security mac-address 1234.5678.9abf` command. Answers A and D are not valid command syntax for port security. Answer C is valid syntax, but the output for the MAC address would show up as SecureDynamic.

4. **D.** The port status of the output indicates that it is an error-disabled state, which means that a violation has occurred and that the default action (shutdown) has disabled the port. Because the maximum MAC addresses is configured as 1, and it has learned two MAC addresses, it is safe to say that this is the cause of the violation. Answer A is incorrect because the port is not in a Secure-Up (active) state. Answer B is incorrect because the count of configured MAC addresses is 0. Answer C is incorrect as well because the output indicates that the sticky MAC address count is also 0.

5. **A.** If the number of MAC addresses is exceeded, security violations should increase, and the configured action should take place (in this case, shutdown). Answer B is incorrect because you can have the violation be shutdown on dynamic, sticky-learned, or static MAC addresses. Answer C is incorrect because it is not required (although it might be more practical) to configure sticky addresses when there is more than one secure MAC address. Answer D is incorrect because the maximum MAC addresses can be configured to be more than 1.

6. **B.** You will still be prompted for a login and password, regardless of whether a password is configured. The switch uses the local username and password (which can be encrypted using the `username` *username* `secret` *password* command) and can be assigned to console, aux, and vty lines, so answers A, C, and D are incorrect.

Suggested Readings and Resources

1. Richard Froom, Balaji Sivasubramanian, and Erum Frahim. *Building Cisco Multilayer Switched Networks (BCMSN) (Authorized Self-Study Guide)*, 4th Edition. Cisco Press, 2007.

2. Wendell Odom. *CCNA ICND2 Official Exam Certification Guide (CCNA Exams 640-816 and 640-802)*, 2nd Edition. Cisco Press, 2007.

3. "Port Security," www.cisco.com.

CHAPTER FIFTEEN

Understanding Wireless Networking

Objectives

This chapter covers the following Cisco-specific objective for the "Explain and select the appropriate administrative tasks required for a WLAN" section of the 640-822 ICND1 exam:

▶ **Describe standards associated with wireless media (including: IEEE WI-FI Alliance, ITU/FCC)**

Outline

Introduction	**476**
The Business Case	**476**
The Players in the 802.11 Market	**477**
Entering the Radio Frequency World	**478**
Understanding Wireless Transmission	478
Unlicensed RF Bands	479
The Key to Successful Wireless: Channel Surfing	480
The 802.11 Standards Family	**483**
Party Like It's 1999: 802.11a and 802.11b	483

2003 Delivers: 802.11g	483
The Next Generation: 802.11n	484
Chapter Summary	**485**
Key Terms	485
Apply Your Knowledge	**486**
Exercise	486
Review Questions	486
Exam Questions	487
Answers to Review Questions	489
Answers to Exam Questions	489
Suggested Readings and Resources	490

Study Strategies

▶ Read the information presented in this chapter, paying special attention to tables, Notes, and Exam Alerts.

▶ Spend some time soaking up how Wireless Radio Frequency operates. This understanding is key to an optimized wireless network deployment.

▶ The ICND1 and CCNA exams focus only on the concepts behind wireless technology rather than the configuration. The Exam Alerts in this chapter and Chapter 16, "Wireless Security and Implementation Considerations," will guide you to specific areas of study.

Introduction

It was one of those moments I'll never forget. I (Jeremy) had just installed my brand-new D-Link 802.11b wireless access point in my home and slid the new PCMCIA wireless card into my laptop. I sat on the couch in another room, held my breath, and opened Internet Explorer. I was so excited to see my home page appear, I jumped up off the couch and yelled to my wife, "Sue! I'm on the Internet! Look!" I held my laptop high in the air to show that there were no wires attached. "Wow . . ." came the not-as-excited reply (she had become used to my ultra-geekdom by this point). I then proceeded to run around the house, laptop in hand, yelling, "I'm still on the Internet! I'm still on the Internet!" as I went in and out of each room. Amazing. Network connectivity without wires!

Fast-forward two years from that monumental moment. I am standing in an office talking to the VP of Sales for the organization. "What do you *mean* the wireless is down?" he says to me. "The wireless access point went bad. We have one on order. It should be here early next week," I reply. "So what am I supposed to do until then?" he counters. He follows my gaze to the Ethernet wall jack, about three feet from the desk. "You're going to have to plug in," I mutter as I pull an Ethernet cable from my bag. From the look of utter annoyance on his face, I might as well have told him that he'll have to walk five miles, uphill, in the snow before he will get his Internet access back.

What happened to the excited people running through companies screaming, "I have Internet!" with their laptops held high above their heads? Convenience happened—and the ultimate convenience at that: solid network connectivity without wires. Yes, 802.11 wireless networking has taken over the world faster than nearly any other network technology ever created. It is now rare to find even a small business without a wireless access point sitting on a shelf somewhere. It doesn't matter if users are sitting at home, at work, or at Starbucks; they've all come to expect that they will always be connected to the great network power of the sky.

The Business Case

The funny thing about wireless LANs (WLANs) is that the technology was just so cool that network administrators started deploying it and making up the business case as they went along. Wireless networks were a new way of looking at infrastructure, and within a few years of mainstream deployment, the applications that used this infrastructure began to emerge. One of the first changes businesses began to realize was the increased use of laptops within the organization rather than their stationary desktop counterparts. In 2005, laptops outsold desktops for the first time, accounting for 53% of all PC sales. That figure continued to increase in the following years as vendors began including embedded wireless network cards in the devices. Companies are now purchasing laptops for their employees for two reasons. Employees love laptops, because they get a "new computer" they can use at home, on vacation, and at the office. The companies love the laptop because the employee can now *work* while they are at home, on vacation, and at the office. Along with laptops, personal digital assistants (PDAs) began to support 802.11 wireless standards. These devices now allow employees to check email, voice mail, and the company intranet over a virtual private network (VPN), all while walking to a flight.

While a host of new wireless networking devices continue to emerge (including wireless VoIP phones), the most tangible benefit of wireless is found simply in not having wires. The IT cost of moving an employee from one cubicle to another ranges from $175 to $375, depending on the equipment present. When you realize that an average of 10 to 15% of staff moves every year, you can begin adding up the numbers for your organization. Likewise, eliminating cable runs in new or existing buildings can always provide traceable cost savings provided by wireless technology.

Finally, realize that wireless technology has moved to the point where even someone who knows nothing about networking can drive to a local electronics store and pick up a wireless access point requiring zero setup and configuration. Some users are so desperate to have wireless access at work that they bring in their own wireless network devices and build "mini-WLANs" in their cubicles, knowingly or unknowingly violating company policy. This can subject your organization to an enormous security risk that could have been minimized by using a centrally managed WLAN system.

The Players in the 802.11 Market

Objective:

▶ Describe standards associated with wireless media (including: IEEE WI-FI Alliance, ITU/FCC)

802.11 holds a host of standards that every vendor is scrambling to implement and every network admin is trying to keep straight. Three organizations play key roles in managing this wireless world:

▶ **International Telecommunication Union-Radiocommunication Sector (ITU-R):** Regulates the radio frequencies (RF) used for wireless transmission

▶ **Institute of Electrical and Electronic Engineers (IEEE):** Maintains the 802.11 wireless transmission standards

▶ **Wi-Fi Alliance:** Ensures certified interoperability between 802.11 wireless vendors

Entering the Radio Frequency World

Objective:

▶ Describe standards associated with wireless media (including: IEEE WI-FI Alliance, ITU/FCC)

Because of the simplicity associated with setting up 802.11 wireless networks in small office/home office (SOHO) environments, it can be easy to underestimate the task of deploying a wireless network on a corporate scale. Wireless access points (WAPs) use radio frequencies that are subject to interference and distortion. Likewise, when we move into the wireless network world, we take a step backward in our switch-based mind-set to the days of network hubs. Only one device attached to a wireless access point can send or receive at a time (half duplex). Understanding these facts is key to a successful WLAN deployment.

Understanding Wireless Transmission

Back in the day, the two competing LAN technologies were Ethernet and Token Ring. Many argued that Token Ring was the better technology because the users would never experience a collision of data on the network. This is because only one user could transmit data at a time due to the token-passing mechanism. Ethernet ended up winning the competition because its method of collision detection (CSMA/CD) allowed for higher transmission speeds.

When we move into the WLAN environment, we move our transmission methods to a collision avoidance (CSMA/CA) strategy because wireless devices have no collision detection mechanism. Likewise, because a wireless device that is sending data cannot receive data at the same time, WLAN devices run at half duplex as a rule. When you combine this limitation with signal degradation due to wireless range and interference, you'll find that wireless devices rarely run at the advertised speed (11Mbps for 802.11b, 54Mbps for 802.11b and 802.11a). Most of the time, the actual speed you are receiving is less than half of the maximum data rate!

Much of the wireless signal degradation is due to the nature of RF. Most of us are used to the land of Ethernet, where data signals travel cozily through a padded copper wire, free from most interference. Wireless RF signals are sent through the air using an antenna, and unfortunately, the air is an ugly place. The first challenge that the wireless signal faces is physical objects. Every object the signal must pass through can degrade the signal in some way. Reflective surfaces, such as metal or glass, cause RF waves to bounce off, shooting in a different direction. Uneven surfaces, such as a gravel road, piles of merchandise in a warehouse, a desk, or a cubicle can cause the signal to reflect and scatter in many directions. Finally, as wireless signals pass through physical objects, they are absorbed. This absorption rate differs depending on the type of material the signal passes through.

As if physical objects weren't enough, the wireless signal is also subject to interference. All 802.11 technology uses unlicensed wireless bands (discussed further in a moment). This means that they are not sanctioned by the United States Federal Communications Commission (FCC), and any wireless device can use them. In many ways, this is fantastic. Without unlicensed wireless bands, every new wireless network in the world would need approval from the FCC, along with all the licensing fees associated with the process! However, unlicensed RF bands also present the challenge of conflict. Cordless phones, Bluetooth, microwave ovens, and WLAN technology all share the same unlicensed RF band. Never before have network administrators faced the challenge of a Stouffer's Microwavable Macaroni Dish being responsible for a 1-minute network outage. It's a good thing this is reduced to 30 seconds in high-powered microwaves!

NOTE

The U.S. designates the FCC to manage the radio frequency bands. Other countries each have their own agency that manages radio frequencies. Often, these agencies mirror many of the rules that the FCC has specified. However, you may find differences as you move from country to country.

Unlicensed RF Bands

The FCC maintains three unlicensed RF bands called the Industrial, Scientific, and Medical (ISM) bands. Figure 15.1 shows where these RF bands fit in the entire wireless spectrum.

FIGURE 15.1 FCC unlicensed bands in view of the entire wireless spectrum.

The three specific bands are as follows:

▶ **900MHz band:** 902MHz to 928MHz

▶ **2.4GHz band:** 2.400GHz to 2.483GHz

▶ **5GHz band:** 5.150GHz to 5.3GHz and 5.725GHz to 5.825GHz

Keep in mind that these ranges of frequency are for the U.S. Other countries may support more frequencies, and others support fewer. Some countries may not allow unlicensed wireless transmission at all!

Every company that manufactures equipment that transmits wirelessly and that does not want to license frequencies from the FCC is forced to share these unlicensed bands. Combining different devices in the same area that are sharing the same frequencies results in interference. For our WLAN, that means impaired performance or potentially a completely unusable network, depending on the severity of the interference.

By far, more equipment uses the 2.4GHz band, making it more difficult to keep the airwaves free from interference. The more popular 802.11b, 802.11g, and 802.11n standards fit into this RF band. The 5GHz band is home to the 802.11a standard. On that note, let's also discuss some key facts about RF:

▶ **Fact #1:** The higher frequencies allow for higher data rates.

▶ **Fact #2:** The higher frequencies have shorter transmission distances (range).

▶ **Fact #3:** Shorter distances can be compensated for by using high-powered antennas.

▶ **Fact #4:** Every country has its own restrictions on how powerful your radio transmission can be for the unlicensed bands.

So, building a 500-foot-high tower on top of your company building powered by a small nuclear generator most likely is not an option for achieving campus-wide network coverage. The alternative solution requires you to purchase many small transmitters and strategically place them throughout your network.

The Key to Successful Wireless: Channel Surfing

Because government restrictions keep us from saturating our campus network with an ultra-powerful wireless signal, we are forced to deploy many transmitters (WAPs) that have a much smaller coverage radius. The problem with this solution is that these transmitters all use the same RF band. Because a good wireless design requires overlapping signals, we are stuck with a problem: the adjacent transmitters will interfere with each other.

Having a 10 to 15% overlap in signals, as shown in Figure 15.2, is a good design. With the right configuration, this overlap can allow clients to roam seamlessly between transmitters.

However, the client will experience heavy interference and performance degradation within the overlapping coverage areas.

Interference

FIGURE 15.2 The problem with overlapping wireless signals.

The solution? Wireless channels. Just because a wireless access point uses the 2.4GHz range of RF doesn't mean it consumes the entire range. The 2.4GHz RF band is divided into different channels, as shown in Figure 15.3.

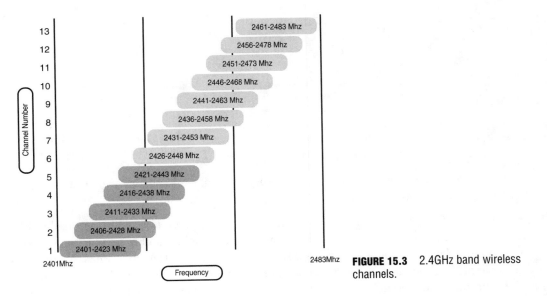

Channel Number

13	2461-2483 Mhz
12	2456-2478 Mhz
11	2451-2473 Mhz
10	2446-2468 Mhz
9	2441-2463 Mhz
8	2436-2458 Mhz
7	2431-2453 Mhz
6	2426-2448 Mhz
5	2421-2443 Mhz
4	2416-2438 Mhz
3	2411-2433 Mhz
2	2406-2428 Mhz
1	2401-2423 Mhz

2401Mhz

Frequency

2483Mhz

FIGURE 15.3 2.4GHz band wireless channels.

The 2.4GHz band supports up to 14 different channels (the FCC allows only channels 1 to 11 in the U.S.). Each channel consumes 22MHz of frequency bandwidth. When you walk through the setup wizard of a wireless access point, one of your options is a channel selector, typically populated with channels 1 to 11. Your goal is to put adjacent access points on separate channels. Be careful when doing this—it's not as simple as it looks! First, most of the wireless channels the FCC has sanctioned are overlapping. Figure 15.3 shows that Channel 1 (2401 to

2423MHz) overlaps with Channel 2 (2406 to 2428MHz), Channel 3 (2411 to 2433MHz), Channel 4 (2416 to 2438MHz), and Channel 5 (2421 to 2443MHz). Placing one access point on Channel 1 and an adjacent access point on Channel 3 would cause interference problems.

For this reason, it is commonly said that the 2.4GHz band supports only three channels: 1, 6, and 11. These three channels do not overlap with each other. With this in mind, we need to arrange our wireless access deployment into logical, nonoverlapping "cells," as shown in Figure 15.4.

FIGURE 15.4 Arranging 2.4GHz channels into logical, adjacent cells.

Looking at Figure 15.4 should make you realize that, indeed, deploying an organization-wide wireless network does take planning.

One of the big advantages that the 5GHz band has over the 2.4GHz band is the number of channels supported. Depending on your locale and the channels you choose, you could have up to 23 nonoverlapping channels in the 5GHz range! This makes it much more viable to find a clear channel without interference. Remember our Stouffer's Macaroni Dish microwave issue? Using different channels can be one solution to help alleviate some of the microwave interference.

EXAM ALERT

Understanding the concept of wireless RF channels is key—not only for proper network design, but also for the ICND1 and CCNA exams.

The 802.11 Standards Family

Now that you have a foundational understanding of RF signaling, we can move to the 802.11 standard. When many network administrators hear of 802.11 technology, their mind immediately equates this with the three or four popular wireless networking standards: 802.11a, 802.11b, 802.11g, and the prestandard (at the time of this writing) 802.11n. However, 802.11 describes much more than this when dealing with wireless networks. For example, 802.11e describes quality of service (QoS) standards for 802.11, and 802.11i is an enhanced wireless security standard, to name just a couple. In a way, 802.11 is similar to TCP/IP in that it depicts a suite of protocols and standards.

Of course, in this suite of standards, the most popular are the common 802.11a, 802.11b, 802.11g, and 802.11n. Let's look at the evolution of these standards.

Party Like It's 1999: 802.11a and 802.11b

In 1999, two competing standards were released: 802.11a and 802.11b. As with most brand-new standards, vendors did not really begin implementing and releasing equipment that used 802.11a or 802.11b until about 2002. The two standards offered the following features:

	802.11a	**802.11b**
RF Band	5GHz	2.4GHz
Bandwidth	54Mbps	11Mbps
Channels	Up to 23	3 (nonoverlapping)
Outdoor Range	Approximately 75 meters	Approximately 100 meters
Indoor Range	Approximately 25 meters	Approximately 45 meters

It's an interesting story how these two standards competed. 802.11a was clearly the better standard. It offered faster speeds (54Mbps versus 11Mbps), more channels (23 versus 3), and an overall cleaner RF band (nowhere near as many devices use the 5GHz band as the 2.4GHz band). Alas, the 802.11b standard won the competition (for now) just because it was more available. The silicon used to make the 802.11a chips was in short supply, and the industry was hungry for wireless, so it gobbled up 802.11b instead.

2003 Delivers: 802.11g

After the newness of the 802.11b standard wore off, users and administrators alike demanded more speed. The IEEE answered with the 802.11g standard. This standard borrowed much of the 802.11a technology and implemented it in the 2.4GHz RF band. One of the major hurdles that was overcome was to achieve backward compatibility with 802.11b, thus allowing

802.11g access points to also support 802.11b clients. For this reason, most access points are labeled as 802.11b/g. Let's pull the same stats on 802.11g as we did for 802.11a and 802.11b:

	802.11g
RF Band	2.4GHz
Bandwidth	54Mbps
Channels	3 (nonoverlapping)
Outdoor Range	Approximately 95 meters
Indoor Range	Approximately 40 meters

The Next Generation: 802.11n

At the time of this writing, 802.11n is currently in prestandard state, set to become a standard in September 2008. Therefore, I will write about the basics of what we currently think the 802.11n standard will become. 802.11n adds multiple input, multiple output (MIMO) technology to wireless cards and access points. Simply put, you now have multiple antennas that can send or receive between devices. This can bring about increased range and throughput. The irony of the situation is that even though the 802.11n standard is not yet complete, vendors are releasing prestandard devices, placing their bets on what they believe the standard will be. This is quite a risk, because it has yet to be decided which RF band 802.11n will use; it could use the 2.4GHz and/or 5GHz bands. Perhaps by the time you read this, the standard will have been decided. Here is what we currently know about 802.11n:

	802.11n
RF Band	2.4GHz and/or 5GHz
Bandwidth	248Mbps (with two receiving and two transmitting antennas, called "2 × 2")
Channels	Unknown
Outdoor Range	Approximately 160 meters
Indoor Range	Approximately 70 meters

NOTE

Many vendors are now supplying wireless network cards and wireless access points that support all three (802.11a/b/g) wireless standards. I would expect that the 802.11n standard will obtain similar support before long.

Chapter Summary

In less than a decade, 802.11 wireless technology has changed everything we thought a LAN environment to be. Many people believe that someday networks will become "a world without wires" as wireless technology becomes more developed and deployed. To successfully deploy a wireless network, it is essential to understand the basics of radio frequency (RF). The 802.11 wireless networking standards are designed to operate in the unlicensed bands of 2.4GHz (802.11b/g) and 5GHz (802.11a). These bands are subject to interference from a variety of devices, so care must be taken to choose the correct location, number of access points, and channels when deploying wireless networking devices. Many wireless spectrum analysis tools are available from the general market that can help with this process.

Because of interference and half-duplex operation, the actual throughput of a wireless device is typically half of the maximum specified by the standard. As new standards develop, the throughput and range of wireless technology will continue to increase.

Key Terms

- ▶ 802.11a, b, g, n
- ▶ Radio frequency (RF)
- ▶ ITU-R
- ▶ IEEE
- ▶ Wi-Fi Alliance
- ▶ 2.4GHz band
- ▶ 5GHz band
- ▶ Wireless channels
- ▶ CSMA/CA
- ▶ Multiple input, multiple output (MIMO)
- ▶ Wireless cells
- ▶ Wireless roaming

Apply Your Knowledge

Exercise

15.1 Designing a Wireless Network

Estimated Time: 15 minutes

This exercise helps you apply the knowledge of wireless design you have gained in this chapter. Figure 15.5 represents the design of a new office building you have acquired. Your organization would like to deploy 802.11g wireless that covers the entire building. It has seven Cisco wireless access points to use and would like to minimize the amount of wireless access available outside the building. Each access point provides 300 feet of unobstructed wireless coverage; however, each wall you pass through reduces this coverage by an average of 75 feet. The thicker walls surrounding the building reduce the coverage by 150 feet. Find the most effective location in which to place each wireless access point in the network. In addition, state what channel the wireless access point will use. The diagram scale is located at the bottom of Figure 15.5.

Scale ├────────────┤ = 100ft

FIGURE 15.5 Wireless network schematic.

Review Questions

1. Three agencies manage the standards and frequencies of wireless networks. List the names of these agencies and briefly describe their functions.

2. 802.11b/g is the more popular wireless standard worldwide. One of your fellow network administrators on staff states that 11 separate RF channels are available for use across your corporate network. Is this true? Should you use all 11 channels? Justify your response.

3. List the three RF spectrums that are considered unlicensed bands. Which wireless standards are associated with each?

4. Higher and lower frequencies on the RF spectrum provide different benefits. What are the benefits of higher frequencies (such as 2.4GHz and 5GHz) over lower frequencies?

5. List at least three business benefits of using wireless networking.

Exam Questions

1. What Cisco-founded organization ensures compatibility between all 802.11 wireless vendor equipment?

   ○ **A.** 802.11

   ○ **B.** IEEE

   ○ **C.** ITU-R

   ○ **D.** Wi-Fi Alliance

2. Which of the following wireless standards use the 2.4GHz RF band? (Choose two)

   ○ **A.** 802.11a

   ○ **B.** 802.11b

   ○ **C.** 802.11g

   ○ **D.** 802.11i

3. 802.11 wireless standards use which of the following transmission methods?

   ○ **A.** CSMA/CD, half duplex

   ○ **B.** CSMA/CD, full duplex

   ○ **C.** CSMA/CA, half duplex

   ○ **D.** CSMA/CA, full duplex

4. How many wireless channels are available in the U.S.A. for the 2.4GHz band without overlapping frequencies?

   ○ **A.** 1

   ○ **B.** 3

   ○ **C.** 11

   ○ **D.** 23

5. When wireless technology uses a higher frequency, what factors must you consider? (Choose two)

    ○ **A.** The higher frequency will allow for higher throughput.

    ○ **B.** The higher frequency will restrict throughput.

    ○ **C.** The higher frequency has more range.

    ○ **D.** The higher frequency has limited range.

6. You are the network administrator for Widgets, Inc., a worldwide distributing organization. You are planning on setting up a new wireless network for the organization. Which of the following are considerations for the new wireless network?

    ○ **A.** The geographic location of the office

    ○ **B.** The radio frequencies currently in use at the office locations

    ○ **C.** The radio channels currently in use at the office locations

    ○ **D.** The wireless cell configuration on the access point

7. To provide for successful client roaming, how should wireless cells be configured?

    ○ **A.** Wireless cells should use the same RF band and channel.

    ○ **B.** Wireless cells should use the same RF band but different channels.

    ○ **C.** Wireless cells should use different RF bands but the same channel.

    ○ **D.** Wireless cells should use different RF bands and channels.

8. Which of the following are advantages of 802.11a over 802.11b? (Choose two)

    ○ **A.** Increased throughput

    ○ **B.** Increased range

    ○ **C.** More channel diversity

    ○ **D.** Support for more clients

9. You are deploying a wireless network at a new office location. The office happens to be located next to an apartment complex with many existing wireless access points using all available channels in the RF band. Which agency would handle this situation?

    ○ **A.** ITU-R

    ○ **B.** IEEE

    ○ **C.** Wi-Fi Alliance

    ○ **D.** None of the above

10. What is the largest cost savings that organizations typically find with wireless technology?

○ **A.** Elimination of stationary equipment

○ **B.** Minimized office space due to roaming users

○ **C.** Access to new cost-savings applications

○ **D.** Cable installation and management cost

Answers to Review Questions

1. The agencies that govern wireless networks are as follows:

   The International Telecommunication Union-Radiocommunication Sector (ITU-R) regulates the radio frequencies used for wireless transmission.

   The Institute of Electrical and Electronic Engineers (IEEE) maintains the 802.11 wireless transmission standards.

   The Wi-Fi Alliance ensures certified interoperability between 802.11 wireless vendors.

2. The short answer to this question is that yes, 11 channels are available for use. However, it is not a good idea to use all 11 channels, because many of them overlap RF signals. In the U.S., you should use only channels 1, 6, and 11, because these channels have no overlap in RF signal.

3. The three unlicensed RF bands are as follows:

   900MHz: No mainstream wireless network technologies use this spectrum.

   2.4GHz: 802.11b and 802.11g use this spectrum.

   5GHz: 802.11a uses this spectrum.

4. Higher frequencies provide more bandwidth than the lower frequencies, but they also have a more limited range.

5. There are many reasons why a business may be interested in wireless networking. Here are four:

   Elimination of stationary equipment

   Minimized office space due to roaming users

   Access to new cost-savings applications

   Cable installation and management cost

Answers to Exam Questions

1. **D.** The Wi-Fi Alliance was founded by Cisco to ensure vendor interoperability on the 802.11 wireless standard. A vendor can obtain Wi-Fi certification, which assures customers that the equipment will interoperate with any other Wi-Fi certified device. Answer A is incorrect because 802.11 represents the wireless standard. Answer B is incorrect because the IEEE only manages

and approves the wireless standards. Answer C is incorrect because the ITU-R is focused on regulating the 802.11 RF bands.

2. **B, C.** 802.11b and 802.11g share the 2.4GHz band. This allows the newer 802.11g standard to be backward-compatible with 802.11b. 802.11a uses the 5GHz band, and 802.11i is a security standard that does not use a specific band.

3. **C.** 802.11 uses CSMA/CA (collision avoidance) with half-duplex transmission. Because of this, the maximum rate of transmission is rarely attained when communicating on an 802.11 wireless network.

4. **B.** In the U.S., only three nonoverlapping channels are available for the 2.4GHz band. Europe has four nonoverlapping channels, because access to other unlicensed RF bands is available. The moral of the story? If you're having trouble finding a free wireless channel in your area, move to Europe.

5. **A, D.** The benefit of using a higher frequency is the ability to obtain more bandwidth (throughput). The drawback is the limited range of the higher frequencies.

6. **A, B, C.** When deploying a new wireless network, you must take into account the geographic region, because government regulations dictate what unlicensed RF bands and channels are available for public use. Likewise, you must also see what wireless RF bands and channels are free (not in use) in your location to get a clean signal. Answer D is incorrect because wireless cells are not configured on access points; rather, they are a design concept.

7. **B.** To provide for client roaming, wireless cells should use the same RF band but different channels. This allows a client to move between wireless access points without interference caused by overlapping signals.

8. **A, C.** 802.11a has more bandwidth (54Mbps) compared to 802.11b (11Mbps) and more wireless channels available (up to 23). 802.11b does have more range than 802.11a because it uses the lower-frequency 2.4GHz band. Neither standard has any advantage as far as client support.

9. **D.** Although the ITU-R does manage the RF bands, it would not handle this specific situation. Both the 2.4GHz and 5GHz bands are considered unlicensed for a reason: no entity will manage them. The solution to the apartment situation would be to find out if the apartment wireless devices are transmitting at a higher-than-legal power or to change your company to the less-congested 5GHz band.

10. **D.** Although wireless provides many conveniences for businesses, the primary cost savings can be found in the elimination of cable installation and management.

Suggested Readings and Resources

1. Wikipedia 802.11 definitions, http://en.wikipedia.org/wiki/802.11.

2. How WiFi Works, http://computer.howstuffworks.com/wireless-network3.htm.

3. Chris Ward and Jeremy Cioara. *Exam Cram 2 CCNA Practice Questions*. Que Publishing, 2004.

4. Toby Velte and Anthony Velte. *Cisco 802.11 Wireless Networking Quick Reference*. Cisco Press, 2005.

CHAPTER SIXTEEN

Wireless Security and Implementation Considerations

Objectives

This chapter covers the following Cisco-specified objectives for the "Explain and select the appropriate administrative tasks required for a WLAN" section of the 640-822 ICND1 exam:

▶ **Identify and describe the purpose of the components in a small wireless network (including: SSID, BSS, ESS)**

▶ **Identify the basic parameters to configure on a wireless network to ensure that devices connect to the correct access point**

▶ **Compare and contrast wireless security features and capabilities of WPA security (including: open, WEP, WPA-1/2)**

▶ **Identify common issues with implementing wireless networks**

Outline

Introduction   **494**

Understanding the Threats   **494**

War Driving   494

Direct Hacking   495

Employee Ignorance   495

Deploying a Secure Wireless Network   **496**

Wireless Encryption   496

Wired Equivalent Privacy (WEP)   496

Wi-Fi Protected Access (WPA)   498

Wi-Fi Protected Access, Reloaded (WPA2 and 802.11i)   498

Wireless Authentication (802.1x)   499

Wireless Intrusion Prevention System (IPS)   500

Wireless Implementation Guidelines   **501**

Understanding Wireless Topologies   501

Understanding Wireless Data Rates   503

General Wireless Implementation Steps   506

Wireless Troubleshooting   506

Client Troubleshooting   507

Wireless Access Point Troubleshooting   507

Chapter Summary   **508**

Key Terms   508

Apply Your Knowledge   **509**

Review Questions   509

Exam Questions   509

Answers to Review Questions   512

Answers to Exam Questions   512

Suggested Readings and Resources   513

Study Strategies

▶ Read the information presented in the chapter, paying special attention to Notes.

▶ You will soon realize that Cisco does not directly cover any actual configuration of wireless equipment in the CCENT or CCNA exam certifications. This is because most wireless access points are fairly self-explanatory to configure. The certification exams expect you to understand the key concepts of wireless that apply universally to any vendor's equipment.

▶ There are some key differences between wireless security standards, such as encryption types and strength. Be sure to understand and recall these differences.

Introduction

Okay. I admit it. I (Jeremy) drove to a friend's house and arrived a bit early, so I decided to spend a few minutes in the car checking my email. I pulled my laptop out of the back and did a quick wireless scan of the neighborhood. Two SSIDs appeared: Linksys and Netgear, both without security. I joined the Linksys network and checked my online web mail. (I prefer to think of this as "borrowing" the Internet connection rather than "stealing" wireless.) That's when a bearded man with a tattered shirt and loaded shotgun came out the front door. Sorry; I just needed a dramatic twist.

Harmless enough, right? *Wrong!* Imagine a strange individual walking into your front office with a laptop and saying, "Would you mind if I plugged into that wall jack over there?" Yes, I would mind. That would undermine every written security standard we have in our organization. But that's exactly what happens when you fail to properly understand and implement the security standards available for wireless networks. Keep in mind that not all wireless security is created equal. Some security standards (such as WEP) may give you a false sense of security, because many network intruders eat WEP security keys for breakfast. This is why a good comprehension of wireless security is absolutely necessary, even for the novice network administrator.

Understanding the Threats

Introducing wireless networking into your organization opens the door to three new types of attacks on your network: war driving, direct hacking, and employee ignorance. Let me explain each of these in detail.

War Driving

You know you've entered a new realm of network security when "driving" becomes one of the intrusion efforts. This term actually originated from the days of old, when a similar method known as war dialing was in place. In the 1980s, most businesses connected offices through dialup connections, typically using modems. War dialing would consist of a hacker randomly dialing through the phone number range in his local area (for example, setting up his modem to dial numbers 100-0000 through 999-9999 in the U.S.). The dialing itself was not the hacking attempt; rather, it was a scan for phone numbers responding to modem signals.

War driving uses a similar concept. An intruder mounts an 802.11-compatible wireless antenna on his vehicle and drives through the city, identifying available wireless networks. When combined with a Global Positioning System (GPS) device, war-driving software (such as KisMet or KisMac) can be very accurate in pinpointing the available wireless networks on a map of the city. When the intruder returns home, he can analyze the available networks and plot his next steps of attack.

Keep in mind that war driving can discover wireless networks even if they are encrypted, authenticated, and/or using a "hidden" (nonbroadcast) SSID.

Direct Hacking

The direct hacking effort typically begins after the war-driving scan of the area is complete. The intruder then identifies what network(s) he wants to attack. The hacking effort can come in many forms:

▶ **Breaking into the WLAN:** As soon as the intruder has identified available wireless networks, he can try to break the encryption and/or authentication system. Although this can be accomplished (with much effort) from the attacker's home, it is usually attempted within range of the wireless signal. For example, the attacker can sit in the parking lot and attempt to break into the building's wireless network. If he is successful, he joins the wireless network and begins scanning the internal network of your organization to find available resources.

▶ **Decrypting data:** Because wireless network communication is transmitted into the air, anything that your users access from a wireless device has the potential to be captured by an intruder's wireless sniffer software. If this data is sent unencrypted, the intruder can simply reassemble the packets to regenerate the original file (such as a Microsoft Word document, an Adobe Acrobat PDF file, or even a VoIP conversation). If the data is encrypted, the intruder captures the data and returns home to attempt to break the encryption keys. If he is successful, he can reassemble the original files and steal corporate data.

▶ **Attempting a wireless DoS attack:** The final effort that can be accomplished by direct hacking methods is to unleash a denial of service (DoS) attack on the wireless network. If the intruder is successful, the wireless access point that he attacks is rendered inoperable to your company. This type of attack is not as common in a WLAN environment, because most companies have not yet moved critical network services to the wireless network. The hacker's efforts would be seen as more of a temporary inconvenience than a major network issue.

Employee Ignorance

Employee ignorance was the best term I could come up with for this category of security threat. Depending on the individual employee, I suppose you could substitute "insolence," "rebellion," or "stupidity" for the word "ignorance." Here's the concept: Your company policy dictates that you will not run wireless networking because of security threats. However, the "ignorant" employee has a laptop he really wants to use with wireless technology, which gives him the freedom to roam between areas while remaining connected to the network. The employee takes networking into his own hands and connects a low-end wireless access point to the network jack in his cubicle. With the click of a Cat 5 cable, your network security has been reduced to nothing, and a gaping hole into the network is now broadcast to the outside world. This same issue can occur even if your company provides a WLAN network and the user is just outside the range of the wireless signal. If appropriate detection measures are not taken, this massive hole in your network security can go undiscovered for months!

Deploying a Secure Wireless Network

Although volumes could be (and have been) written on wireless security, I would just like to discuss the 10,000-foot view of wireless security. This will give you an idea of the areas of focus when you are considering using wireless networking technology in your organization. As soon as you understand these areas, you can begin digging deeper into the technology to find the right fit for your wireless design.

> **TIP**
>
> The CCENT and CCNA certifications require only a foundational understanding of wireless security topics, which are discussed in this book.

Wireless security can be broken into three major categories: encryption, authentication, and detection.

Wireless Encryption

Objective:

▶ Compare and contrast wireless security features and capabilities of WPA security (including: open, WEP, WPA-1/2)

When you're ready for a technology roller coaster ride, begin studying the history of wireless encryption standards. I mentioned in the preceding chapter that wireless networking technology is so amazing that companies began using it long before the security standards were heavily tested and proven to withstand attacks. So, fasten your seat belt, and let's ride through the evolution of wireless encryption standards, starting where it all began: with WEP.

Wired Equivalent Privacy (WEP)

The WEP standard was the first measure of security released for wireless networking. This encryption method was based on the simple concept of using preshared keys (PSKs) to generate an encryption algorithm. Here's an overview of how the WEP encryption algorithm works: The WEP standard uses an encryption formula called RC4. This is essentially a mathematical formula that takes every piece of data you want to encrypt and scrambles it. The missing piece of this formula is the PSK, which you enter. This is visually demonstrated in Figure 16.1.

FIGURE 16.1 The mechanics of WEP encryption.

When the wireless access point receives data, it uses the reverse formula to decrypt the data. So, for WEP to work successfully, you must manually enter the PSK on both the wireless client and the wireless access point.

When WEP was originally released (in 1997), it used 64-bit encryption, which is considered weak by today's standards. You can compare 64-bit encryption to a math formula with 64 steps. Each step scrambles the original data more and more.

NOTE

The more bits you use for encryption, the more complex your encryption algorithm, and the more difficult it is to break. However, the more bits you use for encryption, the harder it is for your network device to communicate because of the processing power needed. This may result in slower network communication.

Unfortunately, within a few years of WEP's initial release, *major* security vulnerabilities were found. The wireless standards groups improved the strength of the WEP algorithm by releasing a 128-bit version in 2002, which some people refer to as WEP2. Although it makes the algorithm slightly more difficult to break, many flaws in the underlying design of WEP caused this security standard to crumble.

Wireless security was suffering in a huge way when WPA was released.

Wi-Fi Protected Access (WPA)

The wireless networking industry faced a major issue. A newer encryption algorithm was needed to combat the weaknesses of WEP, but the more complex encryption algorithms would require more-powerful 802.11-compatible wireless hardware to process the algorithm. By this point, the industry had already purchased millions of wireless access points and wireless cards, so simply saying, "Sorry! Go ahead and scrap all that equipment and buy new stuff." was not an option. In 2003, the Wi-Fi Alliance (a group of extremely smart people sponsored by many organizations) stepped forward and proposed WPA. WPA used a new encryption algorithm called Temporal Key Integrity Protocol (TKIP). TKIP ran on the same wireless hardware that was originally created, and it used a 128-bit encryption algorithm. It was engineered to dramatically increase the number of encryption keys that could be used and virtually eliminated the attacks that were successful on WEP keys. Although WPA was not flawless, it was a tremendous step forward from the original WEP standard.

Wi-Fi Protected Access, Reloaded (WPA2 and 802.11i)

WPA was never meant to solve the world's wireless security problems. Although it was *much* more secure than WEP, it did have the weakness of using the same old hardware that WEP used. Inherent in that hardware were a few security weaknesses that simply could not be overcome by changing the encryption formula. For that reason, the Wi-Fi Alliance quickly (in 2004) proposed an alternative standard casually called WPA2 and officially called 802.11i.

WPA2 uses a completely different encryption standard known as Advanced Encryption Standard (AES). This encryption standard was standardized by the U.S. government and has been extensively analyzed and tested. The WPA2 standard left behind the old hardware and required that users purchase new wireless hardware (both cards and access points).

To ease the transition, WPA2 hardware can run in backward-compatibility mode to support the original WPA and even WEP standards. This allows an organization to upgrade its wireless access points to the new hardware and still support the older WEP- and WPA-compliant clients. As the clients upgrade to newer wireless devices, WPA2 (and thus AES encryption) can be used.

Wireless Authentication (802.1x)

The wireless encryption we've discussed so far does indeed secure the data, but it has a couple of weaknesses. First, using a preshared key system means that you must go to every wireless device and accurately enter the PSK before the device can communicate on the network. Likewise, keeping the same PSK for an extended amount of time increases the chances of the encryption algorithm's being hacked, so it's a good idea to change the PSK on a regular basis. In a small network of 10 or so wireless devices, this may not be a big deal, but in a large network with hundreds or even thousands of wireless devices, this can be a full-time job. The second issue presented by a PSK system is the inability to remove access. For example, if you are using a PSK among your 50 laptop users on the network, and one of the users leaves the company, you must change the PSK for the 49 other wireless users to eliminate the security vulnerability from the former employee.

Simply relying on a shared PSK among all devices is not a secure or scalable solution for business. What was needed was a method of wireless authentication. This would allow you to have a system of granting or restricting access based on a variety of criteria, such as usernames and passwords or certificates. The industry responded with the ultimate authentication method, which we now know as 802.1x.

Usually when we think of network authentication, we think of accessing an operating system. For example, when you log into a Microsoft Windows domain, you must authenticate using a username and password to gain access to shared resources on the Windows-based servers. When you Telnet to a Cisco device, you must authenticate to gain access to manage the device using the Cisco IOS. 802.1x takes authentication to an entirely new level. Now, you must authenticate to gain access to the Layer 2 LAN network fabric. Now, to access the wireless access point and use the 802.11 network, you must authenticate. You can also apply 802.1x to LAN network switches. When a device plugs into an Ethernet port, it must authenticate before it gains access to that port and, thus, the network.

Think of the possibilities as soon as you begin using network authentication! When a user leaves the company, you can negate her user account on a Microsoft Windows server. This will cause her to lose the ability to log on to the Windows workstation and, at the same time, lose the ability to even plug into a switch port or attach to the wireless network! Talk about cutting off a user! Now, let me give you the basics of how this works.

802.1x designates three network devices that participate in network authentication: the supplicant, the authenticator, and the authentication server. Figure 16.2 shows the placement of these devices.

When the user wants to access the network, he must first send his authentication credentials (such as a username and password) to the authenticator, which forwards them to the authentication server. When the authentication server receives the credentials, it checks them against its database and then tell the authenticator whether the device has passed authentication. If the

Supplicant   Authenticator   Authentication
                                                    Server

FIGURE 16.2 Equipment participating in 802.1x authentication.

device fails authentication, its access to the network is terminated or severely limited, depending on how you (as the administrator) decide to restrict the device. If the device passes authentication, the supplicant and authentication server generate a dynamic encryption key known as the session key. This provides the same security as the PSK but does not require you to enter a PSK on the client or wireless access point.

I could say much more about network authentication, but, as I said at the beginning of this section, this is a 10,000-foot overview of the concepts. You now know what network authentication is all about and what it is used for. It's now up to you to continue past the CCNA in your Cisco studies to determine the best method to implement network authentication. Proceed into that world with a grave warning: Don't let the EAP monsters eat you alive! Don't worry; you'll know what I mean when you get there.

> **TIP**
>
> Keep in mind that WPA and WPA2 standards allow for static PSKs or dynamic keys when used with 802.1x. WEP allows only static PSKs.

Wireless Intrusion Prevention System (IPS)

By using wireless network authentication and encryption, we have addressed the concerns of war driving and network hackers. But what about those pesky users who plug unauthorized wireless access points into the network? For that we have wireless IPS. You can think of IPS as introducing a variety of detection lasers into your network. I think back to the 1996 movie *Mission Impossible* with Tom Cruise. In one scene, Cruise (well, Ethan Hunt, to be exact) must retrieve a chip from a secured computer room by twisting and contorting his body through a variety of lasers projected around the room. In the same sense, deploying wireless IPS for your network sets up a variety of "sensors" that detect when a policy has been violated. The minute a rogue access point shows up in the network, the system can alert you, pinpointing the location of the access point on a map of your campus. Amazing!

Network-wide IPS can detect a variety of additional suspicious movements around the network, in both the wired and wireless worlds. However, discussing the rest of those detections is part of the Cisco Certified Security Professional (CCSP) certification.

Wireless Implementation Guidelines

Objectives:

▶ Identify and describe the purpose of the components in a small wireless network (including: SSID, BSS, ESS)

▶ Identify the basic parameters to configure on a wireless network to ensure that devices connect to the correct access point

Now that you've read an overview of the wireless security considerations, let's talk about planning to implement wireless technology. There's much more to planning a wireless LAN deployment than putting a few wireless access points in place. You need to understand how the topology, distance, and placement of wireless access points can affect the efficiency of your wireless LAN.

Understanding Wireless Topologies

Webster's Dictionary defines "topology" as a branch of mathematics concerned with properties of geometric configurations (such as point sets) that are unaltered by elastic deformations (as stretching or twisting) that are homeomorphisms. The CCENT and CCNA exams stop short of requiring a full understanding of homeomorphism (or elastic deformation, for that matter). However, the exams do require you to have some knowledge of the placement of wireless access points in your corporate network. The first piece to understand is that anyone can deploy a wireless network in one of two forms: ad hoc or infrastructure.

Ad hoc wireless networks technically use an Independent Basic Service Set (IBSS) topology. This means that each wireless device independently manages the wireless network. This type of wireless network originates from and includes the wireless device, as shown in Figure 16.3.

This type of network can be created by users on-the-fly to share files or services with others. For example, someone on an airplane might want to share a folder of files with the person next to her. She can create an ad hoc wireless network and allow the other person to join and access the shared files over a network connection.

Ad hoc networks typically are very limited in range and security capabilities. You may want to consider restricting laptops in your corporation from starting ad hoc wireless networks, because they could be considered a potential security vulnerability.

Infrastructure wireless networks are a far more common topology. This involves using a dedicated piece of equipment (typically a wireless access point) to initiate and manage the wireless network. Wireless access points can be configured to use one of two infrastructure modes: Basic Service Set (BSS) or Extended Service Set (ESS). The BSS is the simplest form of wireless network. It includes a single wireless access point managing a group of clients, as shown in Figure 16.4.

FIGURE 16.3 Ad hoc wireless networking.

Channel 11

FIGURE 16.4 A single basic service set design.

An ESS is a wireless topology (note the word change from "network" to "topology") that includes two or more wireless access points providing extended wireless coverage across the network, as shown in Figure 16.5.

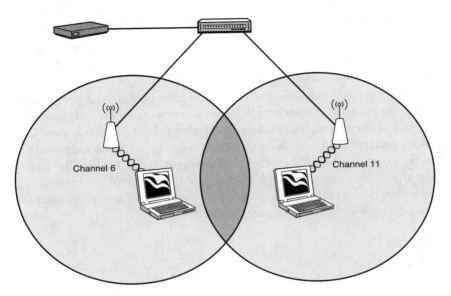

FIGURE 16.5   An extended service set design.

In Figure 16.5, notice that the wireless coverage overlaps. Wireless best practices state that you should have a 10 to 15% overlap in your wireless coverage. This allows you to implement seamless roaming, allowing a wireless client to move between access points with no service interruption. This is not as critical for data clients, such as laptops. Rather, real-time wireless clients such as 802.11-compatible cell phones, cordless VoIP phones, and some PDAs benefit from the overlapping coverage. Imagine dropping a phone call anytime you moved more than 300 feet in the network! More steps are involved in implementing seamless wireless roaming, but the 10 to 15% overlapping coverage is the starting point.

The second thing to notice in Figure 16.5 is that the channels are different on the two wireless access points. One of the wireless access points uses Channel 11, and the other uses Channel 6. This prevents the two wireless access points from interfering with each other. This channel concept is more fully discussed in Chapter 15, "Understanding Wireless Networking."

Understanding Wireless Data Rates

So you purchased a new 802.11g wireless access point and implemented it with clients running 802.11g cards. 54Mbps of pure wireless speed—right? Wrong! You may have purchased an access point capable of handling 54Mbps, but you will never reach that speed. *Never!* Repeated performance tests have revealed that actual data rates are about half of the theoretical data rate, on average. This means that your 802.11b access point typically averages about a 5Mbps actual data rate. 802.11g usually is in the 20Mbps range. You might be wondering why the standard says that you can handle 54Mbps when the actual throughput is much less. Well, there are many reasons.

Suppose you travel to the moon in an oxygen-free environment. You carry a single wireless access point and a single wireless card plugged into a single solar-powered laptop that does nothing but run the wireless card (no Bluetooth, no electrical interference). You sit with the wireless access point about 2 feet from the laptop and only send *or* receive data (never both). You *might* get close to the 54Mbps capability. But even that is stretching it. When you move from the world of cables into the world of wireless, you open yourself to an entirely different style of communication. One of the first considerations that you'll notice is the truth behind the range of the access point. Yes, in an obstruction-free environment, the 802.11b/g wireless signal can travel 300 feet. But couple that fact with the idea that higher data rates (11Mbps for 802.11b and 54Mbps for 802.11g) require stronger signals. You'll find that the data rates step down the farther you go from the access point. The following steps are defined for each standard:

▶ 802.11a and 802.11g:

  ▶ Step 1: 54Mbps

  ▶ Step 2: 48Mbps

  ▶ Step 3: 36Mbps

  ▶ Step 4: 24Mbps

  ▶ Step 5: 18Mbps

  ▶ Step 6: 12Mbps

  ▶ Step 7: 9Mbps

  ▶ Step 8: 6Mbps

▶ 802.11b:

  ▶ Step 1: 11Mbps

  ▶ Step 2: 5.5Mbps

  ▶ Step 3: 2Mbps

  ▶ Step 4: 1Mbps

So, when you picture wireless data rates coming from your wireless access point, think of them as a radial circle for each rate, with the rates continually decreasing the farther you go. This is represented in Figure 16.6.

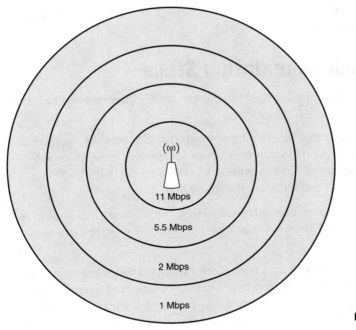

FIGURE 16.6   Wireless data rates.

You'll notice that no exact measurement is attached to each of the radial circles dictating speed around the wireless access point. That's because range is not the only criterion to consider when determining wireless data throughput. From Chapter 15, you'll remember that wireless shares the unlicensed FCC frequency bands with many other pieces of equipment. Bluetooth, other 802.11 wireless clients, cordless phones, and microwave ovens are just a few that can cause interference. Couple that with typical obstructions such as walls, cubicles, desks, and so on, and you have a wireless signal that varies from business environment to business environment. It is impossible to say just how far and "clean" the signal will be in your specific environment. Many companies make testing equipment that displays the signal strength and data rate to a laptop or PDA screen. This gives you a good idea of how wireless will fare in your environment.

NOTE

Because wireless technology uses a CSMA/CA mechanism, all clients adopt the speed of the slowest client on the access point. For example, if three wireless clients are attached to the wireless access point running at 24Mbps, and a wireless client some distance away attaches at 6Mbps, all clients will run at the lowest speed!

The saving grace of wireless data rates is the fact that most users will not notice. Most devices that use a wireless signal are used for lower-bandwidth communication. For example, a wireless VoIP phone consumes about 100Kbps of bandwidth. Laptops used in wireless environments typically surf the net or check email. Most devices that handle large data file transfers or other high-bandwidth communication typically are hardwired.

General Wireless Implementation Steps

With all those considerations floating around your mind, here are the general steps to implement wireless:

1. **Ensure hardwired operation:** Before adding any wireless to the network, connect a device (such as a laptop) to the same switch port where you plan to connect your wireless access point. Ensure that it operates as expected, verifying VLAN assignment, DHCP operation, and Internet connectivity (if applicable).

2. **Install the wireless access point in your tested switch port:** Some access points will connect using straight-through Ethernet cabling, and others may require a crossover cable.

3. **Configure a basic wireless network and test:** Keep this initial test extremely simple. Just implement a wireless SSID with no security. After it is configured, join the wireless network from a client, and test your connectivity. Ensure that the client obtains an IP address and can perform the same actions as when you use a hardwired connection.

4. **Add wireless security and test:** Implement the wireless security standard chosen for your network. It's usually best to begin with a preshared key system of security to keep it simple. After you have added the security, reconfigure the wireless client, and test again.

Working through these four steps, you have established a baseline for your wireless network. As you add more features or security standards on top of the existing foundation, you can return to a "last known good" configuration if something goes wrong.

Wireless Troubleshooting

Objective:

▶ Identify common issues with implementing wireless networks.

Wireless troubleshooting is far more complex than typical wired troubleshooting. Physical problems are much more elusive, because they deal primarily with interference rather than a simple cable break or failing switch port. For example, I recently deployed in a business a wireless network that worked great until 4 in the afternoon. As soon as we crossed the 4 p.m. barrier, all wireless connectivity was lost. After doing some spectrum analysis, we found that a nearby airport was using a device (we still aren't sure what it was) that completely flooded the 2.4GHz frequency range. The company decided to move to 802.11a (which was a fairly large network upgrade) to avoid this interference.

Likewise, wireless technology is fairly new to the industry. You may find that firmware for your access point has bugs and needs to be upgraded to a newer version to avoid persistent crashing (this happens far more often than you may realize). The following wireless troubleshooting checklist may be helpful as you attempt to diagnose the issue.

Client Troubleshooting

Most wireless issues are related to the client:

- **Verify that the wireless card is enabled:** Most new laptops have a button or switch that disables the wireless card to save battery life.

- **Move to a "known good" region of the building:** Do your testing in an area known to have a strong wireless signal. This may require using multiple wireless devices.

- **Verify that the client can identify the wireless network using the installed wireless utility:** If you are unable to identify wireless SSID(s) in your vicinity, the client's wireless card may be disabled, or the wireless access point may not be working.

- **Ensure that the wireless client has the correct wireless security information and supports your security standards:** You may need to re-enter the preshared key to ensure that you entered it correctly. Likewise, the wireless card may not support the wireless security on your network. Try connecting to an SSID that does not use security from the wireless device.

Wireless Access Point Troubleshooting

Most troubleshooting that deals with the wireless access point focuses on physical considerations:

- **Verify that the wireless access point is running the latest firmware version:** Nothing is worse than spending hours on a problem that is related to a bug in the wireless firmware.

- **Test the wireless reception radius at different times of the day:** Because of the varying degrees of interference that may occur over time, it is best to run multiple tests on your signal strength. You can do this simply and inexpensively by carrying around a laptop and observing the reception at differing locations.

- **Verify your wireless channel configuration:** If you have multiple wireless access points or are in an area where other access points may interfere, verify (using wireless software) the most saturated and unsaturated channels. For 802.11b/g, use channels 1, 6, or 11 in the U.S. For 802.11a, many more channels are available, and you should test for the cleanest frequency.

- **Consider the materials around and close to the access point:** Try to avoid installing the access point near metal objects, which reflect the signal. Realize that a concrete block wall will absorb much more signal than a drywall barrier.

Chapter Summary

All in all, deploying a wireless network is not for the fainthearted. Installing a wireless access point in the network essentially broadcasts and extends your network beyond the walls of your organization into treacherous territory. Wireless intruders can begin capturing data and breaking into the network without your ever knowing an attack is happening. This is why it is so critical to understand the security considerations before you attach wireless equipment in your environment.

When securing your wireless network, not all security standards are created equal. The initial WEP system of security offered only 64-bit encryption. It was easily broken because of the key strength as well as a number of flaws that plagued the initial WEP deployment. WEP2 increased the key strength to 128-bit encryption, but it still suffered many of the other weaknesses of WEP. WPA was released to address many of those weaknesses, but it was considered an interim solution while network users began migrating to new hardware. Modern networks employ WPA2 (aka 802.11i) to ensure up-to-date security standards in the world of wireless.

In addition to locking down the wireless network, many implementation considerations must be taken into account. Wireless is susceptible to RF interference. This adds many physical layers of troubleshooting that did not exist in the wired environment. Ensuring that your wireless cells include an acceptable amount of overlap and differing channels lays the foundation for ensuring adequate wireless coverage for your organization.

Key Terms

- 802.11a/b/g/n
- WEP 64-bit
- WEP 128-bit
- WPA
- WPA2 (802.11i)
- 802.1x
- Wireless Intrusion Prevention System (IPS)
- Basic Service Set (BSS)
- Extended Service Set (ESS)
- Radio Frequency (RF)
- 2.4GHz band
- 5GHz band

▶ Wireless channels

▶ Wireless cells

▶ Wireless roaming

▶ Wireless data rate

Apply Your Knowledge

Review Questions

1. List the three encryption standards you can currently use with wireless networking.

2. Describe the differences between WEP, WPA, and WPA2. What type of encryption does each use? What are their strengths and weaknesses?

3. List three potential vulnerabilities of a wireless network.

4. Because a wireless access point forces all clients to use the speed of the slowest client, how do you think you should ideally deploy your wireless access points?

5. What is the process for successfully installing a wireless access point?

Exam Questions

1. What is a rogue access point?

   ○ **A.** An unauthorized access point that has been placed on your LAN

   ○ **B.** An access point configured to broadcast the corporate SSID

   ○ **C.** An access point using WEP or WEP2 security

   ○ **D.** An access point that has been compromised by an intruder

2. When designing a wireless ESS system, how much cell overlap is recommended?

   ○ **A.** None. Cell overlap can cause interference.

   ○ **B.** 5 to 10%

   ○ **C.** 10 to 15%

   ○ **D.** 15 to 20%

3. What scenario would be an ideal case to implement WEP security?

   ○ **A.** You are running a small business network environment implementing the 802.11a wireless standard.

   ○ **B.** You would like to implement the 802.1x security standard using a Windows RADIUS server to authenticate users.

   ○ **C.** You would like to implement increased security instead of or in addition to the typical WPA or 802.11i standards.

   ○ **D.** You are required to implement wireless using older equipment that does not support WPA or WPA2.

4. You are sitting in a library and would like to share files with a coworker sitting across the table. To accomplish this, the coworker connects to a wireless SSID managed by your laptop. What type of network topology is this?

   ○ **A.** Unsecure

   ○ **B.** Ad hoc

   ○ **C.** Basic Service Set

   ○ **D.** Extended Service Set

5. You are using a Cisco 7921 wireless VoIP device. While speaking to your coworker on the phone, you are walking through multiple wireless cells. What type of network topology is this?

   ○ **A.** Unsecure

   ○ **B.** Ad hoc

   ○ **C.** Basic Service Set

   ○ **D.** Extended Service Set

6. Your organization uses a wireless security standard that requires people to authenticate to a back-end server with a valid active directory username and password before they are granted access to the wireless network. Upon successful authentication, the dynamic encryption keys are generated for use during the wireless session. What type of network security is in use?

   ○ **A.** WEP

   ○ **B.** WEP2

   ○ **C.** WPA

   ○ **D.** 802.11i

   ○ **E.** 802.1x (EAPOL)

7. Which of the following accurately describes the difference between WPA and WPA2?

   ○ **A.** WPA integrates with WEP encryption standards, whereas WPA2 is not backward-compatible.

   ○ **B.** WPA uses TKIP encryption, and WPA2 uses AES.

   ○ **C.** WPA uses preshared keys, and WPA2 allows for back-end user authentication.

   ○ **D.** WPA is used on 802.11a networks, whereas WPA2 is compatible with 802.11a/b/g networks.

8. You are troubleshooting a wireless laptop for a user in your organization. The wireless laptop cannot identify any available wireless SSIDs in the region. Your personal laptop can identify three SSIDs from the same location. The user has previously connected to the corporate network without issue. You have noticed increased interference from a neighboring company during different times of the day. What is the most likely cause of this issue?

   ○ **A.** The client wireless network card is disabled.

   ○ **B.** The RF interference has become too heavy for the client to view the available SSIDs.

   ○ **C.** The client wireless card is using the wrong frequency.

   ○ **D.** The signal is being absorbed before reaching the client laptop.

9. You suspect that one of your network users has violated the corporate security policy by plugging in a personal wireless access point in his cubicle. What Cisco security solution would allow you to detect this issue?

   ○ **A.** Cisco ACS Server

   ○ **B.** Cisco wireless IPS

   ○ **C.** Cisco wireless 802.1x

   ○ **D.** MAC address security

10. A network user has issued a trouble ticket stating that she is experiencing file transfers well below the 54Mbps speed that her wireless laptop claims to achieve. What are three valid reasons for this?

    ○ **A.** RF interference

    ○ **B.** CSMA/CA transmission method

    ○ **C.** Proximity to the access point

    ○ **D.** The duplex setting on the client's laptop

    ○ **E.** The client has not implemented 802.1x

Answers to Review Questions

1. The three encryption standards are WEP, WPA, and WPA2.

2. WEP uses the RC4 encryption algorithm. WPA uses the TKIP encryption method, which is more secure than WEP but not as secure as the WPA2 standard, which uses AES encryption. WEP does not have many strengths other than compatibility; all wireless devices can support the WEP standard. WPA has the strength of being interoperable with older WEP-compatible hardware, but it still has a few security weaknesses. WPA2 supports extremely strong encryption, but it is not backward-compatible with older wireless hardware.

3. Wireless networks are vulnerable to war driving, direct hacking, and employee ignorance.

4. Wireless access points should be deployed in a "tight configuration." This means that you should have many access points broadcasting smaller, more high-speed signals rather than a few access points broadcasting weaker signals that reach a larger radius.

5. First, ensure hardwire operation. Then, install the access point and test a basic network SSID with no security. Finally, add security and perform a final test.

Answers to Exam Questions

1. **A.** Rogue access points typically are brought in by internal corporate users with nonmalicious or malicious intent. Regardless of the intent, the rogue access point adds an enormous security liability to your network.

2. **C.** Wireless best practices recommend a 10 to 15% overlap of wireless cells. This allows for seamless roaming by wireless devices. Answer A is true only if the wireless access points are configured to use the same channel (frequency range). Because of this, you should never have adjacent access points using the same channel.

3. **D.** Both WEP (64-bit) and WEP2 (128-bit) encryption methods have been found to be insecure. The only time they should be used is in a network environment that uses older equipment and is unable to support the newer security standards.

4. **B.** Ad hoc networks are wireless networks generated from a participating device in the network, such as a laptop. These laptops can use many of the same security methods as BSS or ESS wireless topologies.

5. **D.** An Extended Service Set (ESS) wireless topology is the combination of two or more Basic Service Set (BSS) networks. This allows client roaming (between wireless cells) without service interruption.

6. **E.** 802.1x (less commonly known as Extensible Authentication Protocol over LAN [EAPOL]) adds a secure authentication system to a LAN environment. This technology can be used to secure both wired and wireless LAN connections. The other answers represent varying encryption standards.

7. **B.** WPA was released as an interim solution to improve the security of WEP. It uses an encryption method known as TKIP, which is more secure than WEP but not as secure as the WPA2 standard, which uses AES encryption.

8. **A.** The most likely cause of this issue is that the client wireless card is turned off. This happens frequently with laptops, because manufacturers commonly put a switch or button on the case of the laptop that easily turns the laptop on or off. The fact that it could not see any wireless networks while your personal laptop sat next to it reveals that wireless networks are reaching the location through the interference. The card cannot be the wrong frequency, because it previously connected to the corporate network without issue.

9. **B.** The Cisco wireless IPS system identifies rogue wireless access points added to the network. The 802.1x and the Cisco ACS Server are primarily responsible for user authentication and privileges. MAC address security can help disable a port with a rogue wireless access point, but it cannot detect the rogue's existence.

10. **A, B, C.** Wireless is susceptible to many types of RF interference. Likewise, the farther the client is from the access point, the lower her speed becomes. Finally, wireless uses a CSMA/CA transmission method, which causes the amount of bandwidth to diminish the more clients you add to the access point.

Suggested Readings and Resources

1. Wikipedia 802.11 definitions, http://en.wikipedia.org/wiki/802.11.

2. How WiFi Works, http://computer.howstuffworks.com/wireless-network3.htm.

3. Chris Ward and Jeremy Cioara. *CCNA Practice Questions*. Que Publishing, 2004.

4. Toby Velte and Anthony Velte. *Cisco 802.11 Wireless Networking Quick Reference*. Cisco Press, 2005.

CHAPTER SEVENTEEN

Wide Area Network Connections

Objectives

This chapter covers the following Cisco-specific objective for the "Implement and verify WAN links" section of the 640-822 ICND1 exam:

▶ **Describe different methods for connecting to a WAN**

▶ **Configure and verify a basic WAN serial connection**

Outline

Introduction   **518**

WAN Connection Types   **518**

Leased Lines   519

     In the Field   519

Circuit-Switched Networks   519

Packet-Switched Networks   520

Broadband   520

Virtual Private Networks (VPNs)   521

Metropolitan Ethernet
(Metro Ethernet)   521

The WAN Physical Layer   **522**

WAN Data Link Encapsulations   **523**

Serial Line Internet Protocol (SLIP)   523

Point-to-Point Protocol (PPP)   524

Cisco High-Level Data Link
Control (HDLC)   524

X.25 Link Access Procedure,
Balanced (LAPB)   524

Frame Relay   524

Asynchronous Transfer Mode (ATM)   524

PPP over Ethernet (PPPoE) and PPP
over ATM (PPPoA)   525

Cisco HDLC   **525**

PPP   **525**

Sub-Layer 1: ISO HDLC   527

Sub-Layer 2: Link Control
Protocol (LCP)   527

     Authentication   527

     Callback   529

     Compression   530

     Multilink   531

Sub-Layer 3: Network Control
Protocol   532

Configuring PPP   **532**

Authentication   532

Compression   534

Verifying PPP   **535**

Troubleshooting PPP   **537**

Chapter Summary   **539**

Key Terms   539

Apply Your Knowledge   **540**

Exercises   540

Review Questions   543

Exam Questions   544

Answers to Review Questions   546

Answers to Exam Questions   546

Suggested Reading and Resources   548

Study Strategies

▶ Read the information presented in the chapter, paying special attention to tables, Notes, and Exam Alerts.

▶ Although Wide Area Network configuration is important, many of the advanced configuration options discussed are reserved for the CCNP BCRAN exam. At the CCNA level, be sure to focus on understanding the concepts thoroughly.

▶ Because it is in widespread use, focus your energy on learning the ideas behind the PPP protocol. Be sure to pay special attention to the authentication concepts.

Introduction

In nearly all traditional Cisco texts, Wide Area Networks (WANs) are typically moved to the end of the book. This is amusing to me because WAN connectivity is usually listed in the top three functions of a router. WAN connections do just that: connect networks that have a wide area separating them. This type of connection requires you to work with one or more service providers that supply the logical connections between your locations.

The good news about WAN connections is this: These technologies only encompass only the Physical and Data Link layers of the OSI Model. Just like the concepts of ethernet and token ring, WAN links are just another method of transporting data between devices. So with only two layers worth of technology, WAN links should be fairly simple to learn, right? Well, that's the bad news: Because of the ever-increasing demands of the IT machine, WAN links have become increasingly complex to the point where they can be a specialization in themselves. Thankfully, the CCNA exam focuses primarily on two specific types of WAN connections:

▶ Leased Lines

▶ Frame Relay

EXAM ALERT

To prepare for the CCNA exam, you need to be very familiar with these WAN connections.

Although there are many more WAN connection types, these are currently the most popular. By studying these WAN connections you will learn the foundation concepts behind WAN connections in general, making it easier to learn any new WAN technologies as they emerge.

WAN Connection Types

Objective:

▶ Describe different methods for connecting to a WAN

The following three categories of WAN connections comprise most of the connections used by businesses around the world. As the name implies, each of the WAN connection categories contains multiple connection types. If you ever called a service provider and asked for a packet-switched connection, the next question would inevitably be, "What type?."

Leased Lines

This connection category is what most people are familiar with when they hear the term, "WAN connection." A leased line connection provides a dedicated, point-to-point link between two locations. The beauty of this connection type is that you have a virtual private road between your sites. You have complete control over the traffic on that road; nobody else can share the road with you. If you have a T1-speed connection (1.544Mbps) between your locations, that bandwidth is always dedicated to you, regardless of whether you use it or not. Therefore, leased lines are typically the most expensive connection types.

In the Field

The two factors that directly affect the cost of a leased line are:

▶ How far apart, geographically, the sites are located

▶ The amount of bandwidth required

Leased lines are the most appropriate when you need a fixed amount of bandwidth and complete control over all your traffic. Companies that are implementing Voice over IP (VoIP), which runs their telephone system over the data network, will usually vie for leased line connections. Because the telecommunications carrier (service provider) is dedicating the leased line bandwidth to you, they can provide a guaranteed level of service. This not only includes the uptime (reliability) of the line, but also delay requirements. The delay of the line is how long it takes a packet to get from the entry point to the end of the connection. Long delays can cause the quality of a VoIP call to degrade to the point of sounding like a bad cellular phone call. Because the service provider typically has end-to-end control over a leased line connection, they can guarantee a specific level of delay.

Circuit-Switched Networks

Anytime you hear the hum of a dial tone followed by the rhythmic beeping of digits, you are more than likely connected to a circuit-switched network. This type of connection establishes a dedicated channel (or circuit) for the duration of the transmission, and then tears down the channel when the transmission is complete. This is known as a *dial-on-demand connection*. The largest circuit-switched network in the world is the telephone system, which links together many different network segments to create an end-to-end circuit for each telephone call.

Circuit-switched networks can be called a "connection-oriented" network type. They are most useful when you have small amounts of data to reliably send at a time. Some circuit-switched networks charge on a per-use or per-minute basis (primarily ISDN), so the amount you pay for the connection is directly related to how much you use it. This type of connection would be ideal for a small office that uses local area network (LAN) connectivity during the day and then replicates all the updated data back to the main site in the evening. For example, you might have a sales office that creates a log of transactions that it sends back to the corporate headquarters at night.

Packet-Switched Networks

Packet-switched networks enable the service provider to create a large pool of bandwidth for their clients, rather than dedicate specific amounts of bandwidth to each client (as in leased lines). The client can then dictate what circuits they would like established through the service provider network between their sites (these are called *permanent virtual circuits*), providing an end-to-end connection. By using packet-switched networks to provide WAN connectivity, you can gain lower-cost WAN connections that can potentially provide more bandwidth to your locations.

When you sign up for a packet-switched network, the service provider gives you a guaranteed level of bandwidth. The higher your service guarantee, the more you pay for the connection on a monthly basis. The great aspect of a packet switched network is that you usually get more than you are guaranteed; depending on the type of contract you negotiate with the service provider, you could get much more bandwidth than you are guaranteed. However, you must realize that this bandwidth is just that: non-guaranteed. If you send extra traffic during a busy time of day, the service provider can drop the traffic and be well within the service contract. This also applies for delay guarantees. Because traffic sent through a packet-switched network may take different paths (depending on the service provider's infrastructure) to reach the destination, most service providers offer a very loose delay guarantee (if they decide to offer one at all).

Broadband

Broadband technology, in its base definition, is a system that enables you to send multiple signals over a wire at one time. The alternative technology, baseband, enables you to send only a single signal over the wire at a time. Broadband connections primarily encompass small office/home office (SOHO) WAN links that use cable modem or DSL technology to connect to the Internet. A cable service provider sends multiple signals over a cable coaxial line, enabling a home user to run many services, such as cable television, high-speed Internet, and telephone service, over a single line. Telephone providers are offering the same services through the copper phone line connections.

Medium and large businesses are just now beginning to consider cable and DSL connections as backup Internet connections for their main offices. Broadband technology is one of the newest WAN connection offerings to market, and has yet to prove its reliability on a long-term basis.

Virtual Private Networks (VPNs)

VPNs are not a specific type of WAN connection, but are often used to accomplish the same purpose as a WAN connection. Connections to the Internet have become widely available at an extremely low cost (when compared against the other types of WAN connectivity). Rather than purchasing dedicated circuits between locations, you can just purchase a standard Internet connection at each site. The quality of your Internet connection determines the quality of your WAN connectivity. After all sites have a connection to the Internet, you can then create tunnels through the Internet to each location, enabling the sites to connect through a full-mesh relationship (every site is directly connected, through the Internet, to every other site). These tunnels isolate the interoffice connectivity from the rest of the Internet traffic and secure the traffic through heavy encryption algorithms.

The VPN tunnels are created with the application of a heavy amount of encryption to the traffic sent between the locations. Because sending your company's private data across a public network, such as the Internet, could be perilous, you should scramble (encrypt) your data before sending it. Because the process of encrypting and de-encrypting data is extremely hard on a router processor, you may choose to offload this work to a router VPN card (a hardware add-on), a PIX firewall (Cisco's firewall platform), or a VPN concentrator (a specific device manages and maintains many VPN connections). Within this concept lie the advantages and disadvantages of using VPNs for your WAN connections. The major advantage is the cost: You can establish full connectivity between all your locations for a small fraction of what it would cost to purchase dedicated WAN links. You can also allow home users to connect into the office through a VPN connection to allow for telecommuting employees. The disadvantage is the delay incurred in applying the VPN encryption algorithms and the unreliable nature of the Internet. Although the Internet is the most redundant network in the world, because of the massive amount of traffic that crosses the Internet daily, the delay can be inconsistent.

Metropolitan Ethernet (Metro Ethernet)

Metro ethernet technology began to emerge early in the new millennium as a viable alternative to traditional WAN connections when connecting offices within a metropolitan area (primarily major cities). At the end of the century, .com-based businesses were booming. Many of these companies began laying complex fiber optic–based networks throughout many of the major metropolitan areas of the nation. When the world economy plummeted at the turn of the century, many of these .com companies went out of business, leaving huge amounts of unmanaged fiber cable under the city streets. This fiber was quickly acquired by local service providers and is slowly being leased to their customers.

Using this fiber to connect offices in the same general region allows for WAN links at speeds of 1000Mbps or greater, at a fraction of the cost of a standard T1 line. The WAN link can even terminate onto a standard Category 5E/6 UTP copper cable and plug directly into a switch using a fiber to copper converter at the customer premise. This enables the WAN connections to be managed completely through VLANs with no dedicated router hardware in place. The connections, which are already fast enough, become even faster.

Metro ethernet is beginning to stretch even between cities, as service providers are planting fiber-optic cable runs between major metropolitan areas. It shouldn't be too long before intra-nation WAN links are rated in terms of Gbps as a standard. Metro ethernet is becoming quite popular in government organizations that have many locations in the same general geographic region.

EXAM ALERT

For the CCNA exam, you should be familiar with the following network types:
► Leased Lines
► Packet Switched

The WAN Physical Layer

The physical connections for WANs are very diverse, primarily because of the diverse form factors that were created by CSU/DSU manufacturers. The Channel Service Unit/Data Service Unit (CSU/DSU) device is the box that connects and converts your WAN cabling to the service provider's WAN cabling. Although CSU/DSUs often have many lights, buttons, and LCD displays, they are typically nothing more than a glorified terminal adapter, converting between the service provider's cable and your local router connection. Figure 17.1 shows a typical physical layout for a WAN connection.

FIGURE 17.1 WAN physical connection points.

If a CSU/DSU is involved, you will be responsible for purchasing the cable that connects your router to the CSU/DSU unit.

Cisco routers primarily use serial interfaces when connecting to a WAN. The Cisco interfaces come in two types: DB-60 serial interfaces and Smart Serial interfaces. Typically, older routers use the DB-60 style interfaces, whereas newer routers use the Smart Serial interfaces. The DB-60 interface received its name because of the 60 pins in the interface. Smart Serial interfaces are much more space efficient, and can squeeze two interfaces into the same WAN Interface Card (WIC) that the DB-60 interface used.

These WIC interfaces can be installed into any of Cisco's mainline routers (1700 series, 2600/2800 series, 3600/3800 series).

After you have installed the interface, you must then purchase the cable that connects your router to the CSU/DSU. This cable converts from one of Cisco's two proprietary interface types (DB-60 or Smart Serial) to a standards-based CSU/DSU connector. Five primary standard connectors have been created for the CSU/DSU units: V.35, X.21, EIA/TIA-232, EIA/TIA-449, and EIA/TIA-530. The most common connector in North America is V.35.

Notice how these cables convert from the Cisco proprietary Smart Serial or V.35 connector to the industry standard V.35 connector, which would connect to the CSU/DSU device.

T1 interfaces use an RJ-48 connector. These interface types usually come with a built-in CSU/DSU, which eliminates the need to purchase an outside box and thereby eliminates another point of potential failure in your network. Upon initial inspection, the RJ-48 connector looks exactly like the RJ-45 connector used for ethernet technology, but don't be fooled! The RJ-48 connector is very different. First off, it is fastened to Shielded Twisted Pair cabling (STP) instead of the standard Unshielded Twisted Pair (UTP) of ethernet. This reduces line noise on these connections. This is important because WAN connectivity is much more susceptible to interference than LAN cabling. In addition, the voltage sent across these wires, the pin-out arrangement, and the line capacitance is different on the RJ-48 connection than RJ-45.

WAN Data Link Encapsulations

After you have the Physical layer plugged in, you must move up to the Data Link WAN encapsulation. Just as with the Physical layer, a variety of standards are available for the data link connections. However, the choice of the Data Link protocol is usually much simpler. As long as your WAN connection supports the Data Link encapsulation you use and you are using the same type of encapsulation on both ends of the connection, the WAN link will work. Sometimes, the type of WAN connection you are using forces you to choose one, specific Data Link encapsulation. For example, if you sign up with a service provider for a Frame Relay connection, you must use Frame Relay Data Link encapsulation. Likewise, if you sign up for an ATM connection, you must use ATM encapsulation. Other times, there may be some flexibility on the choice of protocol you can use. For example, if you sign up for a point-to-point T1 connection, you can use Cisco HDLC, SLIP, or PPP for your data link encapsulation. Here is a brief description of each of the encapsulation types.

Serial Line Internet Protocol (SLIP)

SLIP is a standards-based protocol for point-to-point serial connections that use only TCP/IP. This was primarily used for dial-up connections to the Internet back in the earlier days of the Internet. It has been widely replaced by PPP.

Point-to-Point Protocol (PPP)

This protocol has largely replaced SLIP connections for point-to-point WAN connections and dial-up networking. PPP was released as an improvement to SLIP and added support for non-TCP/IP protocols and encrypted authentication (among many other features). PPP is the most popular protocol for connecting point-to-point WAN connections.

Cisco High-Level Data Link Control (HDLC)

HDLC was originally designed as an open standard protocol, meaning all routers could support it. However, the open standard version of HDLC was pretty horrible. It did not support multiple network-layer protocols, which meant that you could support only one protocol (such as TCP/IP, IPX/SPX, or AppleTalk) over your WAN connection. In view of this shortcoming, Cisco modified the standard HDLC to support this missing feature. However, anytime a standard is modified, the protocol becomes proprietary. In this case, you can use HDLC only on Cisco routers to connect to other Cisco routers. HDLC is the default encapsulation on all serial interfaces on Cisco routers. Although HDLC does not have as many features as PPP, it does offer very low overhead, which makes your WAN connections very efficient.

X.25 Link Access Procedure, Balanced (LAPB)

This encapsulation is used on X.25-based networks, which is the predecessor to Frame Relay. Although X.25 is used rarely in well-developed countries, it has widespread use in countries not as technologically advanced.

Frame Relay

This encapsulation relates directly to the Frame Relay WAN connection, which is the faster successor to X.25. Frame Relay increased its speed capabilities by removing much of the error correction that is no longer needed on the more reliable circuits of today. Frame Relay has widespread use in nearly all well-developed areas.

Asynchronous Transfer Mode (ATM)

This technology is very similar to frame relay, but chops packets into very small pieces (53 bytes each) called *cells*. Because all the frames are exactly the same size, routers are able to process them much quicker. ATM also has the capability to run at very fast speeds because it adapts to run over fiber optic cabling.

PPP over Ethernet (PPPoE) and PPP over ATM (PPPoA)

These technologies have been implemented to allow service providers to harness the features of PPP on an ethernet or ATM connection. This technology is primarily used in DSL high-speed Internet deployments.

> **EXAM ALERT**
>
> The CCNA exam requires you to be familiar with the configuration of HDLC, PPP, and Frame Relay encapsulation types.

Cisco HDLC

As mentioned previously, HDLC in its truest form is an industry standard created by the International Organization for Standardization (ISO). These are the same folks who created the OSI Model (bless their hearts). Because the ISO version of HDLC lacked the support for multiple protocol use, Cisco modified it and caused HDLC on Cisco routers to become a proprietary protocol.

The beauty of HDLC is that it is very simple and works out of the box. Typically, if you are deploying a WAN connection with a Cisco router on each side of the link, it eliminates plenty of troubleshooting involved in trying to enable the connection with HDLC, even if you plan on using PPP in the long run. Because HDLC is so simple, there are no options to negotiate and you can rule it out of any troubleshooting you may encounter. If the link is not coming up, it is usually something on the service provider side of the business.

Because HDLC is enabled by default, you don't need to perform any additional configuration for the data link configuration of your serial interfaces. However, if the data link encapsulation was changed to something other than HDLC, you can re-enable HDLC by moving into interface configuration mode for the serial interface you want to use and type the command `encapsulation hdlc`.

PPP

Objective:

▶ Configure and verify a basic WAN serial connection

The PPP protocol has become the industry standard for connecting multi-vendor environments over WANs. Whenever people think about using an "industry standard" for anything, they usually think of the bland, saltine-cracker type of protocol. Surprisingly, PPP defies the norm and is one of the most feature-packed WAN protocols in existence. Although it functions at the Data Link layer of network connectivity, it comprises multiple sub-protocols that serve multiple functions. This provides you with a feature-rich connection, even when bringing up a WAN link between non-Cisco devices.

PPP can function over nearly any type of WAN connection that does not implement its own, specific mechanism for transporting data (such as frame relay and ATM). This means you can use PPP to connect if you are using an asynchronous (modem-like) connection or a synchronous (high-speed) point-to-point serial connection.

Although PPP fills a single layer on the OSI Model (the Data Link layer), it has multiple "sub-layers" that give it all its functionality. Each sub-layer adds specific functionality to the PPP protocol suite. Figure 17.2 depicts the three PPP sub-layers as they relate to the OSI model. Notice that all three of these sub-layers fit into the single Data Link layer.

Network Layer
Network Control Protocol (NCP)
Link Control Protocol (LCP)
ISO High-Level Data Link Control (HDLC)
Physical Layer

FIGURE 17.2   PPP sub-layers.

It is easy to get confused when expanding the already confusing OSI model into sub-layers for a specific protocol. This is just a logical view of the PPP protocol describing how it is able to include all the functions it advertises. The following sections look at each of these sub-layers, one at a time.

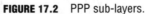

EXAM ALERT

You need to know the sub-layers of PPP and their functions for the CCNA exam because these directly relate to the features PPP provides.

Sub-Layer 1: ISO HDLC

Initially, seeing this layer in PPP seems quite odd. Wasn't HDLC a competing protocol to PPP? This sub-layer of PPP comprises the industry standard ISO HDLC. This sub-layer is responsible for allowing PPP to be supported by multiple devices. It gives the devices that run PPP common ground to stand on when they communicate with each other. As you will see in just a moment, the LCP layer above is responsible for negotiating all the features of HDLC. Because all devices that run HDLC may not support every single feature, the HDLC sub-layer enables the base PPP communication to continue, even if the platforms support different features.

Sub-Layer 2: Link Control Protocol (LCP)

You can think of the LCP sub-layer as the feature negotiation layer. All the features that PPP supports are negotiated by LCP. These features are:

▶ Authentication

▶ Callback

▶ Compression

▶ Multilink

EXAM ALERT

Be able to pick the features negotiated by LCP out of a line-up.

Authentication

The authentication features of PPP enable you to require a username and password for the connecting device to bring up the WAN connection. This is not a very important feature on leased line, point-to-point connections because the only way a hacker would be able to get a device connected to the WAN would be to render one of the on-site administrators unconscious and replace the on-site router with one of the hacker's own. The PPP authentication features are most useful for dial-up connections that could be reached by users connected to the Public Switched Telephone Network (PSTN).

For example, you may choose to connect a modem to your router through the AUX port to allow dial-up access, should all the LAN and WAN connectivity to the router fail. This modem would be assigned a phone number, accessible from any computer modem in the world. PPP authentication would require a username and password to be entered before the modem connection would bridge a successful connection.

There are two types of authentication supported by PPP: the Password Authentication Protocol (PAP) and the Challenge Handshake Authentication Protocol (CHAP).

PAP

This authentication protocol is one of the earliest authentication types to be released for WAN connectivity. If PAP is enabled for the connection, the call flow progresses as follows:

1. Client dials up to a router running PPP.

2. After the link (connection) is established, *the client* sends its username and password at the LCP (feature) layer.

3. The PPP router checks the username and password against its user database and allows or denies the client.

Although this list of three steps is a logical authentication process, it has a few flaws. First off, the client dictates the timing of sending the username and password; the server (router running PPP) receives the username and password whenever the client decides to send it. This causes the PAP mechanism to be susceptible to playback attacks. This is a type of attack where a hacker captures (sniff) packets from a conversation and then plays the packets back in an attempt to mirror the connection. Because the client is in complete control of the authentication attempt, the server accepts the played-back packets whenever the client decides to send them.

The authentication of PAP is also done in clear text, which makes it even more vulnerable to packet-sniffing intruders. Anyone who does have a way of monitoring the connection can capture the packets, break them open, and find the username and password used for authentication in clear text. Can you say, "network devastation"?

With all this being said, the only reason you would choose to use the PAP method for authentication is if you were using very old equipment that did not support the newer method of authentication, CHAP.

CHAP

CHAP is a much more secure procedure for connecting to a PPP-based system. The authentication process for CHAP goes like this:

1. Client dials up to a router running PPP.

2. The *router* sends a challenge message to the client.

3. The client responds with the *hash* of the password it is configured to use.

4. The router looks up the password hash against its database. If the hash matches, the client is allowed into the network.

5. After the client is authenticated, the router sends re-authentication messages at random intervals, requiring the client to send the password hash whenever prompted.

Doesn't that list already make you feel better than PAP? The first thing to notice is that the router (server) is in control of the authentication process. Rather than accepting the username and password whenever the client decides to send it, the router demands the username and password on its timeframe. If the client isn't ready to ante up with the credentials, the server immediately terminates the connection. This makes performing a playback attack much more difficult to accomplish.

Even if a hacker were to successfully execute a playback attack with CHAP, the random authentication interval ensures the hacker will not be connected for long. Executing the initial playback attack would require intricate timing for the hacker to be successful. The random authentication requests would be nearly impossible to keep up.

The clear text issues have also been solved by using a system known as *password hashing*. Without getting too deep into cryptography and security mechanisms, you must understand that this is not the same thing as encrypting a password and sending it across the network. Given the time, nearly any encryption algorithm can be broken if the data is captured. Using a hashed version of the password means that the client never actually sends the real password across the line. To accomplish this, the router (PPP server) and the PPP client must be configured to have the identical password. Before the client sends the password, it runs an irreversible mathematical algorithm on the password. The result of that algorithm is called the hash, which is sent to the server. The server runs the same algorithm on its password and compares the two hashes. If the answer is the same, the client successfully authenticates.

Now, you may be thinking the same thing I did when I first heard about this process, "Well, can't you just get the mathematical formula and reverse it to figure out what the password is from the hash? For example, if the formula is *(the password) 2 = the hash*, could you just take *the (hash÷2) = the password*?" Fair question, but just wait until you see the formula. The hashing method (formula) used is known as the MD5 hash. This formula has been *engineered* with the sole purpose of being irreversible. With that in mind, someone might capture the password hash and find out that it is 5,381,120,123,590. Now the trick is to reverse-engineer an irreversible formula to figure out how the algorithm came up with that answer. It would be much easier for hackers to render the IT staff unconscious at whatever site they were looking to compromise and steal the servers containing the data they needed.

Callback

Just as the name implies, the PPP callback functionality enables a dial-up server (or router) running PPP to use a predefined number to call the person back who initially dialed into the location. One of the major advantages of this function is the increased security: It requires the dial-up user to authenticate and then be present at the predefined phone number to be able to receive the return call. The other advantage is the toll consolidation. If you have long distance users dialing into the network, you leave your company at the mercy of the long distance carriers of your users. By using PPP callback, you can ensure that the company long distance charges are applied, which are typically much lower than normal carrier charges.

A PPP callback process goes through the following steps:

1. A user dials into a router using PPP and authenticates.

2. Upon a successful authentication, the router terminates the connection (typically without any notification) and dials the user back at the predefined number configured by the administrator.

3. Upon reconnect, the user authenticates a second time.

4. Upon a successful authentication, the user is granted network access.

Compression

When I first heard about compression on a WAN link, my mind flashed back to the days of the Stacker compression program of Microsoft DOS. This program slowed your computer down to a crawl to gain a few megabytes of storage space on a hard disk. Surprisingly, one of the two compression algorithms used on PPP WAN connections is named "Stacker"; however, the effects are much less devastating than they were with the old DOS program.

Using compression to make your WAN connection more efficient is not a new concept. These technologies have been around since the days of DOS. However, these technologies have become much more viable on today's networks because of the increase in CPU and memory resources on network equipment. The tradeoff when choosing to use compression is that you gain more WAN bandwidth by sacrificing your router's processor and memory resources. How much you sacrifice depends on the type of compression algorithm you use.

Stacker

The compression type analyzes the data that is being sent and replaces continuous streams of characters with codes. These codes are stored in a dictionary and looked up on the other end of the connection to rebuild the original data. The Stacker algorithm (which is actually called Lempel-Ziv) uses a "flat dictionary-style compression." This means that for every packet of data, it goes through the same process: Look up the character streams in the dictionary, replace the characters with codes, begin again. Therefore, it is very good for network connections that have constantly varying data types (such as SQL, HTTP, FTP, and so on) crossing them. It doesn't matter what the previous traffic was; the same compression algorithm is applied. The Stacker algorithm is notoriously heavy on CPU resources and has less effect on the router's memory resources.

Predictor

This compression algorithm received its name because it literally attempts to predict the next character stream that will be sent or received. It uses a similar dictionary lookup process as Stacker; however, it takes the most common characters looked up and builds a cached index file. Anytime some traffic needs to be sent or received, the index file is checked first. If the character stream (or codes) is not found in the index file, it then consults the full dictionary to find the necessary compression or decompression algorithm. Therefore, the Predictor algorithm works best on network connections that have fairly similar traffic patterns (that can be cached in the index file). For example, perhaps you have a WAN link back to a central office that houses an intranet server that users access to update the corporate e-commerce website. In this case, the traffic patterns would be very similar (HTTP/HTTPS) for most times of the day. The Predictor algorithm usually uses more memory resources and has less effect on the router's CPU than the Stacker algorithm (as long as the traffic patterns do not vary largely).

Microsoft Point-to-Point Compression

Microsoft has its own compression algorithm for PPP, aptly named the Microsoft Point-to-Point Compression (MPPC). This protocol offers slightly improved processor and bandwidth utilization for Microsoft Windows–based clients. Because other devices, such as Cisco routers, would need to support this compression algorithm for Microsoft Windows to use it, Microsoft released the algorithm as an RFC standard (RFC 2118). Under the licensing in this RFC, Microsoft permits other vendors to implement MPPC solely for the purpose of connecting to other MPCC clients. MPPC therefore is used only to allow Windows dial-up users to use compression.

Multilink

PPP multilink enables you to bundle multiple WAN connections into a single, logical connection. This could be as small as bundling two 33.6Kbps modems together to make a 67.2Kbps connection, or bundling four T1 lines together to give yourself a 6.176Mbps connection. The separate interfaces that are bundled together are no longer seen as individual interfaces, but rather join a larger "logical" multilink interface. You can assign this single interface its own IP address, configure authentication, or optimize the logical line with compression. It acts and feels like a real interface, even though it could potentially comprise many physical links.

There are two major benefits to using Multilink PPP (MLPPP). First off, the logical link becomes a single point of management. Rather than figuring out what the traffic utilization is on all the individual physical lines, you can focus your monitoring software (if you have some) on just a single interface. The second benefit to MLPPP is the fact that all physical links bundled in the logical group get *exact* load balancing. When I say "exact," I mean the down-to-the-exact-bit-level kind of exact. MLPPP chops all your packets (referred to as *fragmentation*) into exactly equal sizes before it sends them across the line. This leads to the one drawback of using MLPPP: slightly increased processor and memory utilization on your router.

Sub-Layer 3: Network Control Protocol

The final sub-layer of PPP is what gives it the functionality to allow multiple Network layer protocols to run across a single WAN link at any given time. I think of this layer as the PPP DUPLO® LEGO® block connector. Have you ever seen the DUPLO® blocks for small children? They all have that standard connector with which any other DUPLO® can connect so the child can put any two pieces together (which provides positive affirmation, I'm sure). In that same sense, the Network Control Protocol (NCP) sub-layer of PPP has open-source, network-layer connectors that anyone can plug into. For example, the TCP/IP protocol has a connector called IPCP (the CP stands for "control protocol") that enables TCP/IP to run across a PPP WAN link. IPX/SPX has a connector called IPXCP. With the open-source nature of this protocol, I could create a "Jeremy protocol" and then write a JeremyCP to allow it to run across a PPP WAN link. Cisco has written its own extension called CDPCP that enables the Cisco Discovery Protocol to run across a PPP WAN link, which enables the routers on each end of the connection to use CDP to see each other.

Configuring PPP

Objective:

▶ Configure and verify a basic WAN serial connection

The configuration of PPP without any options does not even deserve its own section. All you need to do is access the interface you would like to enable to run PPP and type the command `encapsulation ppp`. After you do that on both sides of the connection, you're finished. For example, if I wanted to configure PPP on the Serial 0 interface of a router, here is the process:

```
AccessServer#configure terminal
Enter configuration commands, one per line.  End with CNTL/Z.
AccessServer(config)#interface serial 0
AccessServer(config-if)#encapsulation ppp
```

After you begin turning on the options, the configuration can get a little more complex. This chapter discusses turning on PPP authentication and compression technology.

Authentication

The CCNA exam focuses on configuring PPP authentication between two Cisco routers rather than using authentication for dial-up users (this is covered in the Building Cisco Remote Access Networks CCNP course). Typically, when Cisco routers are performing authentication on a WAN link, the routers will be configured as two-way authentication. Two-way authentication means that both routers authenticate each other. Typically, when a dial-up user connects to a router, one-way authentication is performed (the user must authenticate to the Cisco router, not vice-versa).

To set up CHAP PPP authentication, you must do the following:

1. Turn on PPP encapsulation.

2. Configure the necessary hostname for the authenticating routers.

3. Create user accounts on each side of the connection.

4. Turn on CHAP PPP authentication.

At first, these steps may seem somewhat cryptic, but let me walk you through a configuration example and explain how all these pieces fit together. Refer to Figure 17.3 for a visual of this example configuration.

Serial0 – 10.2.2.1   Serial0 – 10.2.2.2

Hostname: Robin   Hostname: Pigeon

FIGURE 17.3 PPP authentication example.

This sample configuration enables two-way, CHAP PPP authentication between the Robin and Pigeon routers. For the sake of brevity, assume the router hostnames are already configured and PPP encapsulation has been enabled under the serial interfaces.

Before you begin, you need to understand the significance of the router hostname. By default, when a Cisco router attempts to authenticate with another router, it uses the router hostname as its PPP username to authenticate with the other side. In this example, the router with the hostname "Robin" crosses the PPP link and attempts to authenticate with the Pigeon router, using the username "Robin." The Pigeon router attempts to authenticate with the Robin router, using the username "Pigeon." You therefore need to create user accounts on each router that match the usernames the routers will use when authenticating. The following syntax accomplishes this:

```
Pigeon#configure terminal
Enter configuration commands, one per line.  End with CNTL/Z.
Pigeon(config)#username Robin password cisco

Robin#configure terminal
Enter configuration commands, one per line.  End with CNTL/Z.
Robin(config)#username Pigeon password cisco
```

Now, when the Robin router comes over to the Pigeon router and says "My username is Robin," the Pigeon router has a user database that identifies that username. Likewise, the

Pigeon router can now authenticate the Robin router. If you have any experience with Windows administration, this is an identical concept to creating user accounts for people to log on to their PCs.

CAUTION

The CHAP username and passwords are both case sensitive. If the hostname of your router begins with a capital letter, ensure you create the user account the same way.

When using CHAP authentication, you must use the same password for both user accounts. In this case, both the Pigeon and Robin router share the password "cisco." It must remain the same on both sides because CHAP never actually sends the password across the wire; it sends only the MD5 hash version of it. When the receiving side gets the hash, it runs the MD5 algorithm on its own password and compares the two hashes. If they match, authentication succeeds. The following is the complete configuration of both the Pigeon and Robin routers to enable CHAP PPP authentication:

```
Pigeon#configure terminal
Enter configuration commands, one per line.  End with CNTL/Z.
Pigeon(config)#username Robin password cisco
Pigeon(config)#interface serial 0
Pigeon(config-if)#encapsulation ppp
Pigeon(config-if)#ppp authentication chap

Robin#configure terminal
Enter configuration commands, one per line.  End with CNTL/Z.
Robin(config)#username Pigeon password cisco
Robin(config)#interface serial 0
Robin(config-if)#encapsulation ppp
Robin(config-if)#ppp authentication chap
```

EXAM ALERT

Be prepared to configure a PPP encapsulated, CHAP authenticated leased line connection in an exam environment. Be absolutely sure you understand that the passwords must be the same on both routers when configuring CHAP authentication.

Compression

Enabling PPP compression is a piece of cake. You just have to make sure that both sides of the connection enable it; if only one side of the connection enables it, the link fails. Using the

Pigeon and Robin scenario again, the following shows the steps you can take to enable compression:

```
Pigeon#configure terminal
Enter configuration commands, one per line.  End with CNTL/Z.
Pigeon(config)#interface serial 0
Pigeon(config-if)#compress  ?
  mppc       MPPC compression type
  predictor  predictor compression type
  stac       stac compression algorithm
  <cr>
```

That's it! Just use the compress command and type the mode of compression you would like to use, and let the bandwidth savings begin.

Verifying PPP

Objective:

▶ Configure and verify a basic WAN serial connection

To ensure your PPP connection came up successfully, you can always use the ol' faithful show ip interface brief command.

```
Pigeon#show ip interface brief
Interface        IP-Address     OK? Method Status      Protocol
FastEthernet0    10.1.1.2       YES NVRAM  up          up
Serial0          10.2.2.2       YES manual up          up
```

In this case, all is well with the Serial 0 PPP connection between the routers because the Protocol is stated as up. Remember, the Status column generally dictates the Physical layer connectivity, whereas the Protocol column focuses on the Data Link connectivity.

If you want to get a little more in depth with the PPP negotiation on the interface, issue the show interface <interface> command as follows:

```
Pigeon#show interface serial 0
Serial0 is up, line protocol is up
  Hardware is PowerQUICC Serial
  Internet address is 10.2.2.2/24
  MTU 1500 bytes, BW 1544 Kbit, DLY 20000 usec,
     reliability 255/255, txload 1/255, rxload 1/255
  Encapsulation PPP, loopback not set
  Keepalive set (10 sec)
  LCP Open
  Open: IPCP, CCP, CDPCP
  Last input 00:00:51, output 00:00:01, output hang never
```

```
Last clearing of "show interface" counters 05:07:30
Input queue: 0/75/0/0 (size/max/drops/flushes); Total output drops: 0
Queueing strategy: weighted fair
Output queue: 0/1000/64/0 (size/max total/threshold/drops)
   Conversations  0/1/256 (active/max active/max total)
   Reserved Conversations 0/0 (allocated/max allocated)
   Available Bandwidth 1158 kilobits/sec
5 minute input rate 0 bits/sec, 0 packets/sec
5 minute output rate 0 bits/sec, 0 packets/sec
   4127 packets input, 168000 bytes, 0 no buffer
   Received 0 broadcasts, 0 runts, 0 giants, 0 throttles
   84 input errors, 0 CRC, 84 frame, 0 overrun, 0 ignored, 0 abort
   8196 packets output, 404090 bytes, 0 underruns
   0 output errors, 0 collisions, 163 interface resets
   0 output buffer failures, 0 output buffers swapped out
   326 carrier transitions
   DCD=up  DSR=up  DTR=up  RTS=up  CTS=up
```

As you can see from the output above, the router has negotiated Link Control Protocol (LCP) options, which is indicated by the LCP Open state. If the LCP negotiations had failed (most likely because of an authentication problem), the LCP state would rotate between Listen, ACKSent, or TERMSent. This is the Cisco router trying to go through the negotiation of the LCP options. In the line below LCP Open, you can verify all the Network layer communication occurring across the PPP link. In this case, you can see IPCP (indicates the TCP/IP protocol), CCP (indicates compression is in effect—compressed control protocol [CCP]), and CDPCP (indicates the Cisco Discovery Protocol [CDP]). Technically, CDP is a Data Link protocol; however, Cisco adopted it to connect into the PPP options as a Layer 3 protocol.

EXAM ALERT

Be able to interpret the show interface command output as it relates to the PPP options.

Finally, if you would like to see how your PPP compression is working out, you can type the command show compress. This gives you the compression statistics for the line:

```
Pigeon#show compress
 Serial0
       Software compression enabled
       uncompressed bytes xmt/rcv 4215/4956
       compressed    bytes xmt/rcv 0/0
       1  min avg ratio xmt/rcv 0.223/4.621
       5  min avg ratio xmt/rcv 0.284/4.621
       10 min avg ratio xmt/rcv 0.270/1.372
       no bufs xmt 0 no bufs rcv 0
       resyncs 0
```

In this case, you have no compressed bytes because all the traffic sent over the PPP link was generated by the routers themselves (this traffic is exempt from compression).

Troubleshooting PPP

Objective:

▶ Configure and verify a basic WAN serial connection

Whenever you reach the troubleshooting section for any topic, you can be guaranteed some debug output. In this case, the debug commands for PPP are pretty darn useful: Most of the output is easy to understand. The most useful command that I have found to troubleshoot a PPP link is the debug ppp negotiation command. Check out this output:

```
Pigeon#debug ppp negotiation
1d02h: Se0 PPP: Using default call direction
1d02h: Se0 PPP: Treating connection as a dedicated line
1d02h: Se0 PPP: Phase is ESTABLISHING, Active Open [0 sess, 1 load]
1d02h: Se0 LCP: O CONFREQ [Closed] id 157 len 15
1d02h: Se0 LCP:    AuthProto CHAP (0x0305C22305)
1d02h: Se0 LCP:    MagicNumber 0x0709760C (0x05060709760C)
1d02h: Se0 LCP: I CONFREQ [REQsent] id 208 len 15
1d02h: Se0 LCP:    AuthProto CHAP (0x0305C22305)
1d02h: Se0 LCP:    MagicNumber 0x22D5B7B3 (0x050622D5B7B3)
1d02h: Se0 LCP: O CONFACK [REQsent] id 208 len 15
1d02h: Se0 LCP:    AuthProto CHAP (0x0305C22305)
1d02h: Se0 LCP:    MagicNumber 0x22D5B7B3 (0x050622D5B7B3)
1d02h: Se0 LCP: TIMEout: State ACKsent
1d02h: Se0 LCP: O CONFREQ [ACKsent] id 158 len 15
1d02h: Se0 LCP:    AuthProto CHAP (0x0305C22305)
1d02h: Se0 LCP:    MagicNumber 0x0709760C (0x05060709760C)
1d02h: Se0 LCP: I CONFACK [ACKsent] id 158 len 15
1d02h: Se0 LCP:    AuthProto CHAP (0x0305C22305)
1d02h: Se0 LCP:    MagicNumber 0x0709760C (0x05060709760C)
1d02h: Se0 LCP: State is Open
1d02h: Se0 PPP: Phase is AUTHENTICATING, by both [0 sess, 1 load]
1d02h: Se0 CHAP: O CHALLENGE id 156 len 27 from "Pigeon"
1d02h: Se0 CHAP: I CHALLENGE id 2 len 26 from "Robin"
1d02h: Se0 CHAP: O RESPONSE id 2 len 27 from "Pigeon"
1d02h: Se0 CHAP: I RESPONSE id 156 len 26 from "Robin"
1d02h: Se0 CHAP: O SUCCESS id 156 len 4
1d02h: Se0 CHAP: I SUCCESS id 2 len 4
1d02h: Se0 PPP: Phase is UP [0 sess, 1 load]
1d02h: Se0 IPCP: O CONFREQ [Closed] id 4 len 10
1d02h: Se0 IPCP:    Address 10.2.2.2 (0x03060A020202)
1d02h: Se0 CCP: O CONFREQ [Closed] id 4 len 6
1d02h: Se0 CCP:    Predictor1 (0x0102)
```

```
1d02h: Se0 CDPCP: O CONFREQ [Closed] id 4 len 4
1d02h: Se0 IPCP: I CONFREQ [REQsent] id 5 len 10
1d02h: Se0 IPCP:    Address 10.2.2.1 (0x03060A020201)
1d02h: Se0 IPCP: O CONFACK [REQsent] id 5 len 10
1d02h: Se0 IPCP:    Address 10.2.2.1 (0x03060A020201)
1d02h: Se0 CCP: I CONFREQ [REQsent] id 2 len 6
1d02h: Se0 CCP:    Predictor1 (0x0102)
1d02h: Se0 CCP: O CONFACK [REQsent] id 2 len 6
1d02h: Se0 CCP:    Predictor1 (0x0102)
1d02h: Se0 CDPCP: I CONFREQ [REQsent] id 5 len 4
1d02h: Se0 CDPCP: O CONFACK [REQsent] id 5 len 4
1d02h: Se0 IPCP: I CONFACK [ACKsent] id 4 len 10
1d02h: Se0 IPCP:    Address 10.2.2.2 (0x03060A020202)
1d02h: Se0 IPCP: State is Open
1d02h: Se0 CCP: I CONFACK [ACKsent] id 4 len 6
1d02h: Se0 CCP:    Predictor1 (0x0102)
1d02h: Se0 CCP: State is Open
1d02h: Se0 CDPCP: I CONFACK [ACKsent] id 4 len 4
1d02h: Se0 CDPCP: State is Open
1d02h: Se0 IPCP: Install route to 10.2.2.1
1d02h: %LINEPROTO-5-UPDOWN: Line protocol on Interface Serial0,
3changed state to up
```

Isn't that some great stuff?!? Okay, it does take a little bit of screening through all the output, but if you look about halfway through, you can see the exchange of the Robin and Pigeon hostnames. This shows the challenge/response action of the CHAP protocol. Thankfully, you can see a SUCCESS message to finish it off, showing the Pigeon and Robin routers have successfully authenticated each other. Near the bottom of the output, you see the CCP (compression negotiation) negotiate the Predictor algorithm between the two routers. Finally, at the end of the output, you see the link come up.

If your PPP connection is failing, this debug command will definitely show you the cause (as long as the failure is related to PPP). Another popular command is debug ppp authentication, which gives the same output, but slims it down to just the authentication information (because this is where many failures occur).

EXAM ALERT

Even though the debug output of the PPP connection and authentication may seem excessive, I would advise you to be able to examine it and diagnose a problem before taking the ICND1, ICND2, or CCNA exams.

Chapter Summary

Managing WAN connections is one of the primary functions of a router. WAN connections tie distant locations together into a common network infrastructure. Choosing a WAN connection has become more difficult in recent years because there are now many more WAN connection technologies at our disposal. However, the most popular WAN connection technologies boil down to three main categories: Leased Lines, Circuit Switched, and Packet Switched.

After you have chosen the Physical connection type you would like to use, you can then move up to the Data Link connectivity. For leased line connections, the two major protocols in use today are HDLC and PPP. On a Cisco router, HDLC has been modified to support multiple upper-layer protocols and has thus become proprietary. HDLC's major feature is the low amount of network overhead it causes on the WAN connection. Other than that, it is feature-less. PPP is the more popular data link protocol because it supports multi-vendor interoperability and a plethora of features.

Key Terms

- ▶ Leased lines
- ▶ Packet-switched networks
- ▶ Circuit-switched networks
- ▶ Broadband
- ▶ Virtual Private Networks (VPNs)
- ▶ Integrated Services Digital Network (ISDN)
- ▶ Metro ethernet
- ▶ X.25
- ▶ Frame Relay
- ▶ Asychronous Transfer Mode (ATM)
- ▶ High-level Data Link Control (HDLC)
- ▶ Point-to-Point Protocol (PPP)
- ▶ PPP over Ethernet (PPPoE)
- ▶ PPP over ATM (PPPoA)
- ▶ V.35
- ▶ X.21

- ▶ EIA/TIA-232, -449, and -530
- ▶ Link Control Protocol (LCP)
- ▶ Network Control Protocol (NCP)
- ▶ Password Authentication Protocol (PAP)
- ▶ Challenge Handshake Authentication Protocol (CHAP)
- ▶ Stacker compression
- ▶ Predictor compression
- ▶ Microsoft Point-to-Point Compression (MPPC)

Apply Your Knowledge

Exercises

15.1 Troubleshooting PPP Connections

One of the most common problems encountered when troubleshooting a PPP connection is authentication failures, which are due to the many parameters that must match for the link to successfully authenticate. In this exercise, you will incorrectly configure PPP authentication and walk through the steps necessary to troubleshoot the connection. Refer to Figure 17.4 for a visual of the connection.

FIGURE 17.4   PPP troubleshooting network diagram.

Estimated Time: 5-10 minutes

What you will do is configure the two routers for CHAP authentication across the PPP connection.
However, you will configure the username/password combination on one side of the connection as all
lowercase and watch the story unfold. First, get the PPP connection running:

```
Daniel#show ip interface brief
Interface          IP-Address      OK? Method Status      Protocol
FastEthernet0      10.1.1.2        YES NVRAM  up          up
Serial0            192.168.40.2    YES manual up          down
Daniel#configure terminal
Enter configuration commands, one per line.  End with CNTL/Z.
Daniel(config)#interface serial 0
Daniel(config-if)#encapsulation ppp
```

You now have the Daniel router configured for PPP; now configure the Ezekiel router on the other side.

```
Ezekiel#show ip interface brief
Interface   IP-Address     OK? Method Status                Protocol
Ethernet0   192.168.1.40   YES NVRAM  up                    up
Serial0     192.168.40.1   YES manual up                    down
Serial1     unassigned     YES NVRAM  administratively down  down
Ezekiel#configure terminal
Enter configuration commands, one per line.  End with CNTL/Z.
Ezekiel(config)#interface serial 0
Ezekiel(config-if)#encapsulation ppp
00:07:36: %LINEPROTO-5-UPDOWN: Line protocol on Interface Serial0,
3 changed state to up
1d14h: %LINEPROTO-5-UPDOWN: Line protocol on Interface Serial0,
3 changed state to up
Ezekiel(config-if)#^Z
1d14h: %SYS-5-CONFIG_I: Configured from console by console
Ezekiel#ping 192.168.40.2
Type escape sequence to abort.
Sending 5, 100-byte ICMP Echos to 192.168.40.2, timeout is 2 seconds:
!!!!!
Success rate is 100 percent (5/5), round-trip min/avg/max = 56/59/72 ms
```

It looks like the PPP link has been brought up successfully and you are now able to ping between the two routers. Now add the authentication piece to the picture:

```
Ezekiel#configure terminal
Enter configuration commands, one per line.  End with CNTL/Z.
Ezekiel(config)#username Daniel password examprep
Ezekiel(config)#interface serial 0
Ezekiel(config-if)#ppp authentication chap
00:11:11: %LINEPROTO-5-UPDOWN: Line protocol on Interface Serial0,
3 changed state to down
```

Notice that as soon as you turned on CHAP authentication for one side of the connection, the link went down. This is because one side of the connection is configured to require authentication while the other is not configured to support it. You can solve that problem and, at the same time, introduce the authentication configuration error.

```
Daniel#configure terminal
Enter configuration commands, one per line.  End with CNTL/Z.
Daniel(config-if)#exit
Daniel(config)#username Ezekiel password examcram
Daniel(config)#interface serial 0
Daniel(config-if)#ppp authentication chap
Daniel(config-if)#exit
Daniel(config)#exit
1d14h: %SYS-5-CONFIG_I: Configured from console by console
Daniel#show ip interface brief
Interface           IP-Address     OK? Method Status        Protocol
```

```
FastEthernet0      10.1.1.2        YES NVRAM  up            up
Serial0            192.168.40.2    YES manual up            down
```

Notice that the password examcram was used for the Ezekiel account rather than examprep. Because CHAP requires both passwords to be the same on both sides of the connection, the Serial0 link remains down. Now, if we did not know about this configuration error, the troubleshooting process would go something like this:

```
Daniel#show interface serial 0
Serial0 is up, line protocol is down
  Hardware is PowerQUICC Serial
  Internet address is 192.168.40.2/24
  MTU 1500 bytes, BW 1544 Kbit, DLY 20000 usec,
    reliability 255/255, txload 1/255, rxload 1/255
  Encapsulation PPP, loopback not set
  Keepalive set (10 sec)
  LCP Listen
  Closed: IPCP, CCP, CDPCP
  Last input 00:00:01, output 00:00:01, output hang never
  Last clearing of "show interface" counters 16:52:28
  Input queue: 0/75/0/0 (size/max/drops/flushes); Total output drops: 0
  Queueing strategy: weighted fair
<...output removed for brevity...>
```

Notice first that the line protocol is down, which indicates a Data Link failure. When you look down at the PPP negotiation (LCP), you can see that it is in the Listen state and the NCP protocol communication is Closed. This means the LCP layer of PPP has not successfully negotiated, and points you in the correct direction for troubleshooting. Now is a good time to perform a debug and see whether you can weed out what is going on.

```
Daniel#debug ppp negotiation
PPP protocol negotiation debugging is on
Daniel#
1d14h: Se0 LCP: TIMEout: State Listen
1d14h: Se0 LCP: O CONFREQ [Listen] id 51 len 15
1d14h: Se0 LCP:    AuthProto CHAP (0x0305C22305)
1d14h: Se0 LCP:    MagicNumber 0x098EF573 (0x0506098EF573)
1d14h: Se0 LCP: I CONFACK [REQsent] id 51 len 15
1d14h: Se0 LCP:    AuthProto CHAP (0x0305C22305)
1d14h: Se0 LCP:    MagicNumber 0x098EF573 (0x0506098EF573)
1d14h: Se0 LCP: I CONFREQ [ACKrcvd] id 131 len 15
1d14h: Se0 LCP:    AuthProto CHAP (0x0305C22305)
1d14h: Se0 LCP:    MagicNumber 0x002934B3 (0x0506002934B3)
1d14h: Se0 LCP: O CONFACK [ACKrcvd] id 131 len 15
1d14h: Se0 LCP:    AuthProto CHAP (0x0305C22305)
1d14h: Se0 LCP:    MagicNumber 0x002934B3 (0x0506002934B3)
Daniel#
1d14h: Se0 LCP: State is Open
1d14h: Se0 PPP: Phase is AUTHENTICATING, by both [0 sess, 1 load]
```

```
1d14h: Se0 CHAP: O CHALLENGE id 144 len 27 from "Daniel"
1d14h: Se0 CHAP: I CHALLENGE id 45 len 28 from "Ezekiel"
1d14h: Se0 CHAP: O RESPONSE id 45 len 27 from "Daniel"
1d14h: Se0 CHAP: I RESPONSE id 144 len 28 from "Ezekiel"
1d14h: Se0 CHAP: O FAILURE id 144 len 25 msg is "MD/DES compare failed"
1d14h: Se0 PPP: Phase is TERMINATING [0 sess, 1 load]
1d14h: Se0 LCP: O TERMREQ [Open] id 52 len 4
1d14h: Se0 CHAP: LCP not open, discarding packet
1d14h: Se0 LCP: I TERMREQ [TERMsent] id 132 len 4
1d14h: Se0 LCP: O TERMACK [TERMsent] id 132 len 4
Daniel#
1d14h: Se0 LCP: TIMEout: State TERMsent
1d14h: Se0 LCP: O TERMREQ [TERMsent] id 53 len 4
1d14h: Se0 LCP: I TERMACK [TERMsent] id 53 len 4
1d14h: Se0 LCP: State is Closed
1d14h: Se0 PPP: Phase is DOWN [0 sess, 1 load]
1d14h: Se0 PPP: Phase is ESTABLISHING, Passive Open [0 sess, 1 load]
```

You can watch in amazement as PPP goes from the Listen state into the REQ/ACK state (where it begins to negotiate the connection and authentication protocol). After the LCP state is Open, the full authentication phase begins. About halfway through the CHALLENGE/RESPONSE messages, you see the glaring FAILURE message that shows that the MD/DES compare failed. This means the password hashes are not the same for these routers. If you kept this debug turned on, it would continue to loop through the process again and again until you fixed the mismatched password. Turn off the debug and fix the password, and see what happens.

```
Daniel#u all
All possible debugging has been turned off
Daniel#configure terminal
Enter configuration commands, one per line.  End with CNTL/Z.
Daniel(config)#no username Ezekiel password examcram
Daniel(config)#username Ezekiel password examprep
Daniel(config)#
00:40:34: %LINEPROTO-5-UPDOWN: Line protocol on Interface Serial0,
3 changed state to up
1d14h: %LINEPROTO-5-UPDOWN: Line protocol on Interface Serial0,
3 changed state to up
```

Wow! Just like that, the link has come online. The configuration is now successful.

Review Questions

1. List the three categories of WAN connections.

2. You are installing a new serial WAN connection into your offices in Tucson, Arizona. The service has already terminated their end of the connection at the premises and provided you with a CSU/DSU device. What physical connections should you use on your Cisco router?

3. What four features are negotiated by PPP's LCP?

4. What is the function of PPP's Network Control Protocol?

5. PPP has the capability to use two different compression algorithms. What are they? What is the effect of these algorithms on your router? Why would you choose to use one algorithm over the other?

Exam Questions

1. Which of the following network types would encompass Frame Relay and X.25?

   ○ **A.** Leased lines

   ○ **B.** Circuit-switched networks

   ○ **C.** Packet-switched networks

   ○ **D.** Broadband

2. What type of serial transition cable should you use to connect your Cisco router to a CSU/DSU device that has a V.35 female connector?

   ○ **A.** V.35 male on the Cisco side to V.35 male on the CSU/DSU

   ○ **B.** DB-60 male on the Cisco side to V.35 male on the CSU/DSU

   ○ **C.** DB-60 male on the Cisco side to V.35 female on the CSU/DSU

   ○ **D.** V.35 male on the Cisco side to V.35 female on the CSU/DSU

3. What type of packet is used during the initial PPP link establishment process?

   ○ **A.** Authentication

   ○ **B.** LCP

   ○ **C.** NCP

   ○ **D.** HDLC

4. Which of the following describes the Password Authentication Protocol (PAP) used by PPP during the LCP process? (Choose two)

   ○ **A.** PAP exchanges passwords in clear text.

   ○ **B.** PAP uses a MD5 hashing function to send password information.

   ○ **C.** PAP enables the server to be in control of the authentication attempt.

   ○ **D.** PAP enables the client to be in control of the authentication attempt.

5. When is CHAP authentication performed?

   ○ **A.** On a certain time interval

   ○ **B.** When the user decides to send the username/password

   ○ **C.** When the link connection is established

   ○ **D.** When the link connection is established and on a periodic interval

6. What Cisco IOS configuration mode should you be in to enable PPP authentication?

   ○ **A.** Global configuration mode

   ○ **B.** Router configuration mode

   ○ **C.** Interface configuration mode

   ○ **D.** PPP LCP configuration mode

7. What type of WAN connection enables the company to purchase a simple Internet connection and tunnel their information through the network between their sites?

   ○ **A.** Leased-lines

   ○ **B.** Circuit-switched

   ○ **C.** Packet-switched

   ○ **D.** Virtual private network

8. What verification command can show you the current state of the PPP Link Control Protocol?

   ○ **A.** `show interface`

   ○ **B.** `show ip interface`

   ○ **C.** `show ppp interface`

   ○ **D.** `show wan interface`

9. Which of the following PPP sub-layers is responsible for Network layer protocol negotiation?

   ○ **A.** HDLC

   ○ **B.** CDP

   ○ **C.** LCP

   ○ **D.** NCP

10. Which of the following WAN connection categories would include dial-up modems?

    ○ **A.** Leased lines

    ○ **B.** Circuit-switched

    ○ **C.** Packet-switched

    ○ **D.** Metro ethernet

Answers to Review Questions

1. The three WAN connection categories are leased line, circuit switched, and packet switched.

2. When configuring the physical connectivity for a serial WAN connection, you need to purchase either a DB-60 or Smart Serial WIC card for your router. From there, you need to purchase a cable that converts from the DB-60 or Smart Serial card of your Cisco router to the industry standard adapter found on the CSU/DSU device that connects to the service provider.

3. The four features negotiated by the PPP Link Control Protocol (LCP) are compression, callback, multilink, and authentication.

4. The Network Control Protocol (NCP) enables the router to encapsulate multiple upper-layer protocols (such as IP, IPX, and Appletalk) over a PPP WAN connection.

5. The two PPP compression algorithms are Stacker and Predictor. The Stacker algorithm requires more processor resources and fewer memory resources. The Predictor algorithm uses more memory resources and fewer processor resources. Stacker is the best algorithm to use when there are varying traffic types crossing the PPP WAN connection. Predictor works best when you have similar traffic types using the PPP WAN connection.

Answers to Exam Questions

1. **C.** Frame Relay and X.25 fall under the packet-switched networks category. These networks establish connections through a service provider cloud using virtual circuits. Answer B is incorrect because circuit-switched networks include technologies such as modems and ISDN. Answer A is incorrect because leased lines use dedicated bandwidth between locations. Answer D is incorrect because broadband encompasses DSL and cable modem technology.

2. **B.** The Cisco side of the connection always uses either a DB-60 or Smart Serial connector (these are always male because the router has female ports). Because the CSU/DSU has a V.35 female connector, you should be using a V.35 male transition cable. All other answers are incorrect because they use either the wrong connector type or gender on the Cisco side.

3. **B.** The Link Control Protocol (LCP) is used to negotiate all options related to PPP during the link establishment phase. The Network Control Protocol (NCP) negotiates the upper-layer protocols only after the initial PPP link has been established. The HDLC layer of PPP is what allows for multi-vendor interoperability with the protocol. Answer A is incorrect because an authentication packet

falls under the LCP negotiations. Answer C is incorrect because NCP negotiates the upper-layer protocols. Answer D is incorrect because HDLC is used to give PPP an industry standard foundation when connecting to non-Cisco equipment.

4. **A, D.** PAP is the older of the two PPP authentication protocols. It has major security flaws, including the sending of passwords in clear text and allowing the client to choose when it sends the password. Answers B and C are incorrect because the MD5 hashing and server control is a function of the CHAP.

5. **D.** CHAP requires authentication both when the link is initially established and on a periodic basis thereafter. This is awesome because it combats playback attacks and packet sniffing (passwords are not sent). PAP requires authentication only when the link is initially established and when the client chooses to send the credentials, which is why answers B and C are incorrect. Answer A is incorrect because CHAP also sends authentication credentials when the link is initially established.

6. **C.** You enable PPP authentication from the interface configuration mode by typing the command `ppp authentication <chap/pap>`. All other answers are either irrelevant or non-existent (there is no PPP LCP configuration mode in the Cisco IOS).

7. **D.** VPNs enable companies to purchase simple Internet connections and tunnel their information through the networks between their sites. This information is heavily encrypted to ensure it is not compromised crossing the public network. This is far cheaper than any other type of WAN connection, but can suffer from the heavy encryption slowdown. Answers A, B, and C are incorrect because leased lines and circuit-switched and packet-switched networks require no tunneling or encryption capabilities.

8. **A.** The `show interface` command is used to verify the current state of the PPP LCP negotiations. This shows `Open`, `Listen`, `ACKSent`, or `TERMSent`, depending on the state of LCP at the time (you want LCP to show `Open`). The other `show` commands are either irrelevant or would produce invalid syntax.

9. **D.** NCP is used to negotiate the Network layer protocols. These negotiations are typically shown as in the syntax `<negotiated protocol>CP` in `show interface` output, such as IPCP (for the IP protocol), CDPCP (for the CDP protocol), or IPXCP (for the IPX protocol). Answer A is incorrect because HDLC is used at a lower layer of PPP to provide multi-vendor interoperability, and answer C is incorrect because LCP is used to negotiate PPP features. Answer B is incorrect because CDP has nothing to do with WAN links.

10. **B.** Circuit-switched connections encompass anything that has to dial a number to make a connection. These connections typically use the telephone company as a backbone. Answer C is incorrect as packet-switched networks include technologies such as X.25 and Frame Relay. Answer A is incorrect because leased lines do not dial because they are permanently established connections. Answer D is incorrect because metro ethernet is extremely high-speed connections running through a metropolitan area.

Suggested Reading and Resources

1. Cisco Introduction to WAN Technologies, http://www.cisco.com/univercd/cc/td/doc/cisintwk/ito_doc/introwan.htm.

2. Ward, Chris and Cioara, Jeremy. *Exam Cram 2 CCNA Practice Questions.* Que Publishing, 2004.

3. Quinn, Eric and Glauser, Fred. *BCRAN Exam Cram 2 (Exam 642-821).* Que Publishing, 2003.

Fast Facts

OSI Model in Review

Table FF.1 lists the seven layers of the OSI model and significant aspects of each layer.

TABLE FF.1   The OSI Model

OSI Layer	Important Functions
Application	Provides an interface between a host's communication software and any necessary external applications.
	Evaluates what resources are necessary and available resources for communication between two devices.
	Synchronizes client/server applications.
	Provides error control and data integrity between applications.
	Provides system-independent processes to a host.
Presentation	Presents data to the application layer.
	Acts as a data format translator.
	Handles the structuring of data and negotiating data transfer syntax to Layer 7.
	Processes involved include data encryption, decryption, compression, and decompression.
Session	Handles dialog control among devices.
	Determines the beginning, middle, and end of a session or conversation that occurs between applications (intermediary).
Transport	Manages end-to-end connections and data delivery between two hosts.
	Segments and reassembles data.
	Provides transparent data transfer by hiding details of the transmission from the upper layers.
Network	Determines best path for packet delivery across the network.
	Determines logical addressing, which can identify the destination of a packet or datagram.
	Uses data packets (IP, IPX) and route update packets (RIP, EIGRP, and so on).
	Uses routed protocols IP, IPX, and AppleTalk DDP.
	Devices include routers and Layer 3 switches.
Data Link	Ensures reliable data transfer from the Network layer to the Physical layer.
	Oversees physical or hardware addressing.
	Formats packets into a frame.

(continues)

TABLE FF.1 *Continued*

OSI Layer	Important Functions
	Provides error notification.
	Devices include bridges and Layer 2 switches.
Physical	Moves bits between nodes.
	Assists with the activation, maintenance, and deactivation of physical connectivity between devices.
	Devices include hubs and repeaters.

Application Protocols Supported by the Application Layer

TABLE FF.2 Application Layer Protocols

Application Protocols	Function
Telnet	A TCP/IP protocol that provides terminal emulation to a remote host by creating a virtual terminal. TeraTerm is one program that can be installed on a user computer to create Telnet sessions. This protocol requires authentication via a username and password.
Hypertext Transfer Protocol (HTTP)	Enables web browsing with the transmission of Hypertext Markup Language (HTML) documents on the Internet.
Secure Hypertext Transfer Protocol (HTTPS)	Enables secure web browsing. A secure connection is indicated when the URL begins with https:// or when there is a lock symbol at the lower-right corner of the web page that is being viewed.
File Transfer Protocol (FTP)	Allows a user to transfer files. Provides access to files and directories.
Trivial File Transfer Protocol (TFTP)	A bare-bones version of FTP that does not provide access to directories. With TFTP, you can simply send and receive files. Unlike FTP, TFTP is not secure and sends smaller blocks of data.
Domain Name System (DNS)	Resolves hostnames such as cisco.com into IP addresses.
Simple Mail Transfer Protocol (SMTP)	Sends electronic mail across the network.
Post Office Protocol 3 (POP3)	Receives electronic mail by accessing a network server.
Network File System (NFS)	Allows users with different operating systems (that is, NT and Unix workstations) to share files through a network. Remote files appear as though they reside on a local machine even though the local machine might be "diskless."

(continues)

TABLE FF.2 *Continued*

Application Protocols	Function
Network News Transfer Protocol (NNTP)	Offers access to Usenet newsgroup postings.
Simple Network Management Protocol (SNMP)	Monitors the network and manages configurations. Collects statistics to analyze network performance and ensure network security.
Network Time Protocol (NTP)	Synchronizes clocks on the Internet to provide accurate local time on the user system.
Dynamic Host Configuration Protocol (DHCP)	Works dynamically to provide an IP address, subnet mask, domain name, and a default gateway for routers. Works with DNS and WINS (used for NetBIOS addressing).

TABLE FF.3 **Control Information for Each Layer**

OSI Layer	Control Information Name
Application Presentation Session	Data
Transport	Segment
Network	Packet
Data Link	Frame
Physical	Bit

TABLE FF.4 **OSI Layers and Related TCP/IP Layers**

OSI Layer	TCP/IP Layer
Application Presentation Session	Application
Transport	Transport
Network	Internet
Data Link Physical	Network Access

TCP uses Positive Acknowledgment and Retransmission (PAR):

1. The source device begins a timer when a segment is sent and retransmits if the timer runs out before an acknowledgment is received.

2. The source device keeps track of segments that are sent and requires an acknowledgment for each segment.

3. The destination device acknowledges when a segment is received by sending a packet to the source that iterates the next sequence number it is looking for from the source.

TABLE FF.5   The TCP Segment Header Format

Source Port	Destination Port
Sequence Number	
Acknowledgment Number	
Miscellaneous Flags	Window (Flow Control)
Checksum	Urgent
Options	

TABLE FF.6   Applications Using TCP and Related Ports

Application	Port #(s)
FTP	20, 21
Telnet	23
SMTP	25
DNS (zone transfers)	53
HTTP	80
POP3	110
NNTP	119
HTTPS	443

TABLE FF.7   The UDP Header

Source Port	Destination Port
Length	Checksum

TABLE FF.8   Applications Using UDP and Related Ports

Application	Port #(s)
DHCP	67, 68
DNS (name resolution)	53
TFTP	69
NTP	123
SNMP	161

Network Domains

Two domains determine data transport reliability:

▶ **Broadcast domain:** A group of nodes that can receive each other's broadcast messages and are segmented by routers.

▶ **Collision domain:** A group of nodes that share the same media and are segmented by switches. A collision occurs if two nodes attempt a simultaneous transmission. Carrier Sense Multiple Access Collision Detection (CSMA/CD) sends a jam signal to notify the devices that there has been a collision. The devices then halt transmission for a random backoff time.

Cabling, Lines, and Services

▶ **Bandwidth:** The total amount of information that can traverse a communications medium measured in millions of bits per second. Bandwidth is helpful for network performance analysis. Also, availability is increasing but limited.

▶ **Crosstalk:** An electrical or magnetic field that is a result of one communications signal that can affect the signal in a nearby circuit.

  ▶ **Near-end crosstalk (NEXT):** Crosstalk measured at the transmitting end of a cable.

  ▶ **Far-end crosstalk (FEXT):** Crosstalk measured at the far end of the cable from where the transmission was sent.

Unshielded twisted-pair (UTP) cables are vulnerable to Electromagnetic Interference (EMI) and use an RJ-45 connector. Fiber-optic cables are not susceptible to EMI.

Use a straight-through cable to connect the following devices:

▶ Terminated directly into a dedicated hub or switch port

▶ From a PC to a switch or a hub

▶ From a router to a switch or a hub

Use a cross-over cable to connect the following devices:

▶ From switch to switch

▶ From router to router

▶ From PC to PC

▶ From a PC to a router

▶ From a hub to a hub

▶ From a hub to a switch

Spread Spectrum Wireless LANs allow for high-speed transmissions over short distances. Wireless Fidelity (Wi-Fi) is defined by IEEE 802.11.

TABLE FF.9 Summary of Ethernet 802.3 Characteristics

Standard	Speed	Media Type	Connector Used
10BASE-2	10Mbps	RG-58 coaxial	BNC
10BASE-5	10Mbps	RG-58 coaxial	BNC
10BASE-T	10Mbps	Category 3, 4, or 5 UTP or STP	RJ-45
10BASE-FL	10Mbps	Fiber-optic	SC or ST

TABLE FF.10 Comparison of Fast Ethernet 802.3u Characteristics

Standard	Speed	Media Type	Connector Used
100BASE-T4	100Mbps	Category 3, 4, or 5 UTP or STP	RJ-45
100BASE-TX	100Mbps	Category 5 UTP or STP	RJ-45
100BASE-FX	100Mbps	Fiber-optic	SC or ST

TABLE FF.11 Summary of Gigabit Ethernet 802.3ab Characteristics

Standard	Speed	Media Type	Connector Used
1000BASE-T or 1000BASE-TX	1000Mbps or 1Gbps	Category 5 UTP or higher	RJ-45

TABLE FF.12 Comparison of Gigabit Ethernet 802.3z Characteristics

Standard	Speed	Media Type	Connector Used
1000BASE-CX	1000Mbps or 1Gbps	Shielded copper wire	Nine-pin shielded connector
1000BASE-SX	1000Mbps or 1Gbps	MM fiber-optic	SC or ST
1000BASE-LX	1000Mbps or 1Gbps	MM or SM fiber-optic	SC or ST

MAC Addressing

A MAC address is hard-coded (burnt-in) on the network interface controller (NIC) of the Physical layer device attached to the network. Each MAC address must be unique and use the following format:

- ▶ Consists of 48 bits (or 6 bytes).

- ▶ Displayed by 12 hexadecimal digits (0 through 9, A through F).

- ▶ First six hexadecimal digits in the address are a vendor code or organizationally unique identifier (OUI) assigned to that NIC manufacturer.

- ▶ Last six hexadecimal digits are assigned by the NIC manufacturer and must be different from any other number assigned by that manufacturer.

Example of a MAC address: 00:00:07:A9:B2:EB

The OUI in this example is 00:00:07.

The broadcast address value is FFFF.FFFF.FFFF.

Framing and Duplex Types

802.3 frame information and parameters are as follows:

- ▶ The data-link header portion of the frame contains the Destination MAC address (6B), Source MAC address (6B), and Length (2B).

- ▶ The Logical Link Control portion of the frame contains Destination Service Access Point (DSAP), Source Service Access Point (SSAP), and Control information. All three are 1B long. The Service Access Point (SAP) identifies an upper-layer protocol such as IP (06) or IPX (E0).

- ▶ The Data and cyclical redundancy check (CRC) portion of the frame is also called the data-link trailer. The Data field can be anywhere from 43 to 1497B long. The frame check sequence (FCS) field is 4B long. FCS or CRC provides error detection.

Bridges and switches examine the source MAC address of each inbound frame to learn MAC addresses.

Switches are multiport bridges that use ASIC hardware chips for frame forwarding. Dedicated bandwidth enables the switch port to guarantee the speed assigned to that port. For example, 100Mbps port connections get 100Mbps transmission rates.

Hubs use half-duplex technology. Switches can be set up for full-duplex.

WAN Interfaces

WAN interfaces are used to provide a point of interconnection between Cisco routers and other network devices. Types of WAN interfaces include the following:

- Basic Rate Interface (BRI)

- Synchronous Serial

- Asynchronous Serial

- High-Speed Serial Interface (HSSI)

- T1 Controller Card

BRI is an Integrated Services Digital Network (ISDN) line that consists of two 64Kbps bearer (B) channels and one 16Kbps data (D) channel.

DCE equipment might consist of a:

- Modem

- Channel Service Unit/Data Service Unit (CSU/DSU)

- BRI NT-1

DTE equipment might consist of a:

- Router

- PC

- Server

Memory Types

Four memory components are used by Cisco devices. Those components include ROM, Flash, RAM, and NVRAM.

RAM contains the running IOS, with the exception of Run-From-Flash (RFF) routers. RAM also contains the running configuration or the active configuration that is used after a machine is booted.

IOS File Naming Conventions

Given the example filename c2600-ipbase-1.122-1.T.bin, from left to right, each portion of the filename represents the following:

- **c2600:** Hardware platform (Cisco 2600 router)
- **ipbase:** Feature set
- **1:** File format (compressed relocatable)
- **122:** IOS version number
- **l:** Maintenance release number
- **T:** Train identifier

Utilities Using ICMP

Internet Control Messaging Protocol (ICMP) is used by ping and traceroute utilities. Packet Internet Groper (ping) allows you to validate that an IP address exists and can accept requests.

- ping is an echo, and the response is an echo response.
- Routers send Destination Unreachable messages when they can't reach the destination network and they are forced to drop the packet. The router that drops the packet sends the ICMP DU message.

A traceroute traces the route or path taken from a client to a remote host. Traceroute also reports the IP addresses of the routers at each next hop on the way to the destination. This is especially useful when you suspect that a router on the route to an unreachable network is responsible for dropping the packet.

Network Security

Three classes of attack are commonly found in today's network environment:

- Access attacks
- Reconnaissance attacks
- Denial of service (DoS) attacks

Access Attacks

An access attack is just what it sounds like. It is an attempt to access another user account or network device through improper means. The four main types of access attacks are:

▶ Password attacks

▶ Trust exploitation

▶ Port redirection

▶ Man-in-the-middle

Reconnaissance Attacks

The four main subcategories or methods of gathering network data for a reconnaissance attack are:

▶ Packet sniffers

▶ Port scans

▶ Ping sweeps

▶ Information queries

Denial of Service (DoS) Attacks

DoS attacks are often implemented by a hacker as a means of denying a service that is normally available to a user or organization. The three main types of DoS attacks are:

▶ Distributed DoS

▶ TCP SYN

▶ Smurf

Mitigating Network Threats

The following actions can be taken to lessen the impact of an attack on a network:

▶ Authentication, Authorization, and Accounting (AAA)

▶ Cisco access lists (ACLs)

▶ Cisco IOS secure management features: SSH, SNMP, syslog, and NTP

▶ Encryption protocols: SSH, IPsec, and SSL

▶ Security appliances and applications: firewall, IPS, and IDS

IP Addressing

IPv4 addresses

▶ Consist of 32 bits.

▶ Are broken into four octets (8 bits each).

▶ Use dotted-decimal format; an example is 172.16.122.204.

▶ Minimum value (per octet) is 0, and the maximum value is 255.

▶ 0.0.0.0 is a network ID.

▶ 255.255.255.255 is a broadcast IP.

TABLE FF.13   IPv4 Address Classes

	First Octet	Second Octet	Third Octet	Fourth Octet
Class A	Network	Host	Host	Host
Class B	Network	Network	Host	Host
Class C	Network	Network	Network	Host

TCP/IP defines two additional address classes:

▶ **Class D:** Used for multicast addresses

▶ **Class E:** Used for research purposes

TABLE FF.14   Address Class Ranges

Class	First Octet Decimal Range
A	1 to 126
B	128 to 191
C	192 to 223
D	224 to 239
E	240 to 255

The 127.x.x.x address range is reserved for loopback addresses.

Default subnet masks:

- **Class A:** 255.0.0.0
- **Class B:** 255.255.0.0
- **Class C:** 255.255.255.0

Classless Addressing

Classless Interdomain Routing (CIDR) notation might also be used to identify the subnet mask. The CIDR notation for each network class can be determined by counting the 1s in binary or the number of bits that make up the network portion of the address.

The mask is written in slash notation as follows:

- **Class A:** /8
- **Class B:** /16
- **Class C:** /24

Private Ranges

IANA Private Address Space Allocations:

- Class A: 10.0.0.0 to 10.255.255.255
- Class B: 172.16.0.0 to 172.31.255.255
- Class C: 192.168.0.0 to 192.168.255.255

Subnetting

TABLE FF.15   Decimal to Binary Conversions

Class	First Octet Decimal Range
0	00000000
128	10000000
192	11000000
224	11100000

(continues)

TABLE FF.15 *Continued*

Class	First Octet Decimal Range
240	11110000
248	11111000
252	11111100
254	11111110
255	11111111

To calculate the hosts in a subnet, we can use the formula $2^H - 2$. The exponent H represents the number of host bits in a network.

To calculate the networks in a subnet, we can use the formula $2^N - 2$. The exponent N represents the number of subnet bits in a network.

The range of valid IP addresses in a subnet is the first IP address after the Network ID and the last IP address before the broadcast IP address.

The following represents IP subnetting:

IP address = 100.15.209.0

Subnet mask = 255.255.254.0

Network ID = 100.15.208.0

Broadcast IP = 100.15.209.255

Valid IP range = 100.15.208.1 to 100.15.209.254

IPv6

IPv6 is a workable IP version that was created in the event that the IP space from IPv4 is exhausted.

IPv6 address format summary:

▶ Defined by RFC 2373 and RFC 237.

▶ Consists of 128 bits with a 64-bit network prefix and a 64-bit local identifier.

▶ Represented by 32 hexadecimal digits broken into eight smaller groups of four.

▶ Uses CIDR notation (slash notation) to discern a subnet range, so you might see the same IP address subnetted and written out as
2001:0BD2:0200:08F1:0000:0000:0000:16AB/16.

The same IPv6 IP address can be written in all of the following ways:

2001:**0**BD2:**0**200:08F1:**0000:0000:0000**:16AB

2001:BD2:200:8F1:0:0:0:16AB

2001:BD2:200:8F1::16AB

Types of IPv6 Addresses

▸ **Link-local addresses:** Addresses that have the shortest reach of the IP address types. They can go only as far as the Layer 2 domain. These addresses are autogenerated with or without the use of a DHCP server. So, when an IPv6 node goes online, this address is assigned automatically.

▸ **Unique/site-local addresses:** Addresses that have a broader scope than link-local addresses. They can expand to the size of an organization and are used to describe the boundary of the organizational network. These are the private addresses for IPv6.

▸ **Global addresses:** Addresses that have the broadest scope of all. As the name indicates, these addresses are for global use—that is, for Internet communications.

▸ **Multicast:** Addresses that are extremely important because of their use for group communications and broadcast messaging.

Integrating IPv4 and IPv6

There are several ways to integrate IPv4 and IPv6 addressing. You can implement dual-stack, tunneling, or translation techniques to help IPv4 and IPv6 addresses exist on the network simultaneously.

Layer 3 Functions

Routers and Layer 3 switches perform the following functions:

▸ Do not forward broadcasts or multicasts by default.

▸ Make best-path decisions.

▸ Filter packets with access lists.

▸ Remove and add Layer 2 frames.

▸ Quality of service (QoS) rules for traffic types.

Routers decide which interface to forward a packet through by examining the network portion of each IP address.

IOS Terminal Access Methodologies

To gain access to an EXEC session to an IOS for configuration and administration, you can use the following methods:

► **Console:** Out-of-band CLI access via a rollover cable connected to the COM port of your terminal PC.

► **Auxiliary:** Out-of-band CLI access via rollover cable connected to external modem for remote access.

► **Telnet:** In-band CLI access to an active IP address on the device's vty lines using the Telnet protocol. Requires configuration.

► **SSH:** Secure encrypted in-band CLI access to an active IP address using the SSH protocol. Requires configuration.

► **HTTP/HTTPS:** In-band GUI access to an active IP address using the HTTP or HTTPS protocol. Requires configuration.

IOS Boot Processes

To solidify the startup process, the following is a recap of the stages of the bootup, any fallback procedures, and the memory locations involved:

1. POST located in ROM tests the hardware.

2. Bootstrap located in ROM looks at boot field in configuration register to locate IOS. 0x2100 boots to ROMmon located in ROM.

3. 0x2101-0x210F prompts the bootstrap to parse startup-config in NVRAM for any `boot system` commands. If there are any commands, do what they say.

4. If no `boot system` commands, load first file in Flash. If no file is in Flash, TFTP boot. If no IOS file found from TFTP, go to ROMmon mode.

5. After IOS is loaded, check configuration register. If 0x2142, ignore startup-config in NVRAM. If 0x2102, load startup-config in NVRAM. If no startup-config, TFTP autoinstall. If no TFTP autoinstall configuration found, enter Setup Mode.

IOS Navigation

TABLE FF.16   IOS Navigation Modes

Mode	Prompt	Description
User EXEC	Router>	Basic troubleshooting and verification
Privileged EXEC	Router#	All available commands including delete, clear, erase, configure, copy, and reload
Global Configuration	Router(config)#	Configurations that apply to the entire device
Line Configuration	Router(config-line)#	Configurations that apply to the terminal lines into a device
Interface Configuration	Router(config-if)#	Configurations that apply to interfaces
Subinterface Configuration	Router(config-subif)#	Configurations that apply to logical extensions of the physical interface
Router Configuration	Router(config-router)#	Configurations that apply to routing protocols

Context-Sensitive Help

The question mark shows all the available commands at that particular prompt. To see all the available commands that start with a letter or letter(s), type the letter(s) immediately followed by the question mark. To see the list of commands that follows a keyword, type the keyword followed by the question mark separated by a space. Commands can be abbreviated as long as there are enough characters to recognize what command you are entering.

Terminal Editing Keys

TABLE FF.17   Cisco IOS Terminal Editing Keystrokes

Keystroke	Function
Ctrl+A	Moves the cursor to the beginning of the command line.
Ctrl+E	Moves the cursor to the end of the command line.
Ctrl+B	Moves the cursor back one character.
Ctrl+F	Moves the cursor forward one character.
Esc+B	Moves cursor back one word.
Esc+F	Moves cursor forward one word.

Syntax Errors

▶ **Ambiguous command:** This error is displayed when you have not typed enough characters for the IOS to distinguish which command you want to use. In other words, several commands start with those same characters, so you must type more letters of the command for the IOS to recognize your particular command.

▶ **Incomplete command:** The IOS has recognized your keyword syntax with this error message; however, you need to add more keywords to tell the IOS what you want to do with this command.

▶ **Invalid input:** Also known as the "fat finger" error, this console error message is displayed when you mistype a command. The IOS displays a caret (^) up to the point where the IOS could understand your command.

Global Configuration Commands

Table FF.18   Global Configuration Commands

Command	Description
config-register *register*	Alters the configuration register.
boot system *location*	Specifies location to load IOS.
hostname *hostname*	Changes the name of the Cisco router or switch.
banner motd *char banner char*	Creates a message of the day login banner.
ip host *name ipaddress*	Configures a static mapping of a hostname to an IP address.
ip name-server *ip*	Specifies a DNS server IP address for dynamic name resolution.
ip domain-lookup	Enables automatic name resolution.
ip domain-name	Assigns a domain name to a Cisco device.

Securing the IOS

First and foremost, ensure that you physically secure access to your Cisco devices to ensure that there are no intentional or unintentional disruptions or access to the device itself.

To secure User EXEC to your console port:

```
Router(config)#line console 0
Router(config-line)#login
Router(config-line)#password password
```

To secure User EXEC to your aux port:

```
Router(config)#line aux 0
Router(config-line)#login
Router(config-line)#password password
```

To secure User EXEC to all five Telnet lines:

```
Router(config)#line vty 0 4
Router(config-line)#login
Router(config-line)#password password
```

To secure access to Privileged EXEC mode:

```
Router(config)#enable secret password
Router(config)#enable password password
```

The `enable secret` global configuration command encrypts the password using a MD5 hash. If the `enable secret` and the `enable password` commands are used at the same time, the `enable secret` password is used.

To encrypt the enable password and the line passwords, use the `service password-encryption` command.

SSH

To secure terminal access to the Cisco device, use SSH over Telnet. The steps to configure SSH are as follows:

1. Configure a hostname on the device other than the default hostname.

2. Configure a domain name for the Cisco device.

3. Generate an RSA key (at least a 1024-bit key is recommended) with the `crypto key generate` command.

4. Create a username/password combination with the `username username password password` command.

5. (Optional) Limit the vty lines to allow only SSH with the `transport input SSH` command.

Interface Configuration Commands

TABLE FF.19   Interface Configuration Commands

Command	Description
ip address *ip subnetmask*	Assigns an IP address to an interface.
no shutdown	Administratively enables an interface.
full-duplex	Changes the duplex setting to full duplex.
clock rate *speed*	Sets the timing speed of the network on a DCE interface in bps.
bandwidth *speed*	Sets the logical bandwidth setting for routing protocols in Kbps.
ip address dhcp	Dynamically assigns an IP address to an interface from a DHCP server.

Switch Commands

TABLE FF.20   Switch Configuration Commands

Command	Description
interface range *media range*	Configures several interfaces with the same parameters.
ip address *ipaddress*	Assigns an IP address to a VLAN interface.
ip default-gateway *ip*	Sets the gateway of last resort for a Layer 2 switch.
speed *speed*	Changes the speed of an autosensing link in Mbps.
duplex *duplex*	Sets the duplex of a switchport.

The Copy Command

The copy command is used to copy files from one location to another. For example, to save the current configuration, we copy the running-config in RAM to the startup-config in NVRAM using the copy running-config startup-config command.

The copy command is used to copy files between our device and a TFTP server. For instance, copy flash tftp backs up the IOS in flash to a TFTP server. copy flash tftp can be used to upgrade, downgrade, or restore an IOS back onto our device. Before copying to a TFTP server, the following preparation steps are in order:

1. The TFTP server must have the TFTP service running.

2. Your device must be cabled correctly. If a switch, plug the TFTP server into the switch with a straight-through Ethernet cable. If going directly between a router and the TFTP server, use a cross-over cable.

3. You must have IP connectivity to the server.

4. There must be enough room on the TFTP server and your device's memory to store these files.

The Show Command

TABLE F.21 General show Commands

Command	Mode	Output
show running-config	Privileged	Current active configuration in RAM.
show startup-config	Privileged	Configuration stored in NVRAM that will be loaded on reboot.
show interfaces	User and Privileged	Status of the interfaces as well as physical and logical address, encapsulation, bandwidth, reliability, load, MTU, duplex, broadcasts, collisions, and frame errors.
show ip interface brief	User and Privileged	Status of the interfaces and their logical addresses.
show controller	User and Privileged	Microcode of the interface including DCE/DTE cable connection.
show flash	User and Privileged	Filenames and sizes of IOS files stored in Flash memory.
show version	User and Privileged	IOS version, system uptime, amount of RAM, NVRAM, Flash memory, and configuration register.

Interface Status

Table FF.22 Interface Status Values

Layer 1	Layer 2 (Line Protocol)	Possible Symptoms
Up	Up	None. Interface is functional.
Up	Down	Encapsulation mismatch, lack of clocking on serial interfaces.
Down	Down	Cable is disconnected or attached to a shutdown interface on the far-end device.
Administratively Down	Down	Local interface was not enabled with the no shutdown command.

Cisco Discovery Protocol

Proprietary Cisco Layer 2 protocol that uses multicast to gather hardware and protocol information about directly connected devices.

Network layer protocol- and media-independent.

Enabled by default on all Cisco devices, but can be disabled globally:

```
Router(config)#no cdp run
```

or can be disabled on interface-by-interface basis:

```
Router(config-if)#no cdp enable
```

To learn the remote device's Layer 3 address and IOS version:

```
Router>show cdp neighbor detail
```

or

```
Router>show cdp entry *
```

Telnet

Telnet enables a virtual terminal connection to a remote device's IP address using the Application layer protocol, Telnet (TCP port 23 at Transport layer).

To Telnet from IOS, enter the keyword `telnet` followed by the IP address or hostname. If you only type an IP address or hostname in User EXEC or Privileged EXEC mode, IOS automatically assumes that you are Telnetting. To Telnet to a Cisco device, the vty passwords must be set, or you receive the "Password required, but none set" error. To access Privileged EXEC mode in a Telnet session, you must have enable password set, or you receive the "% No password set" error.

▶ To suspend the Telnet session, press Ctrl+Shift+6, x.

▶ To see a list of the active sessions in the originating router, use the `show sessions` command.

▶ To resume a suspended session, press the Enter key from User EXEC or Privileged EXEC mode, or enter `resume` followed by the session number.

▶ To close a Telnet session from the device we are Telnetted into, enter `exit` or `logout` from User EXEC or Privileged EXEC mode.

▶ To close a Telnet session from the originating device, enter `disconnect` followed by the session number.

▶ To see log messages in your Telnet session, use the Privileged EXEC command `terminal monitor` in the device that you are Telnetted into.

DHCP

Your Cisco device can act as a DHCP server and respond to DHCP requests on a segment. To configure the Cisco device as a DHCP server, you must first enable the interface that will receive the DHCP requests and assign an IP address to it. After the interface is enabled, you define the DHCP address pool with the `ip dhcp pool` *poolname* global configuration command. After you are in dhcp-config mode, you can define the DHCP address scope with `network` command followed by the IP subnet to be assigned. You can also define additional parameters such as the default gateway, DNS server, domain name, and length of the IP lease. To exclude IP addresses from being assigned (such as if you have statically assigned them to specific devices), use the `ip dhcp excluded-address` *ip-address* command to remove the IP(s) from the scope.

To verify the devices that have been assigned IP addresses from the DHCP address scope, use the `show dhcp bindings` command.

Switches

Switches have the following functions:

▶ Segment LANs into multiple collision domains.

▶ Learn MAC addresses by examining the source MAC address of each frame received and store them in a CAM table.

▶ Base their forwarding decisions based on the destination MAC address of an Ethernet frame.

▶ Flood broadcast, multicast, and unknown unicast frames out all ports except the one it was received.

A switch has three methods of forwarding frames:

▶ **Store-and-forward:** Latency varying transmission method that buffers the entire frame and calculates the CRC before forwarding the frame.

▶ **Cut-through:** Looks only at the destination MAC address in an Ethernet frame and forwards it.

▶ **Fragment-free:** Checks the first 64 bytes for frame fragments (due to collisions) before forwarding the fame.

Duplex Connections

▶ Half-duplex interfaces have one-way communications with suboptimal throughput because they operate in a collision domain in which CSMA/CD must be enabled. When connected to a hub, they must run half duplex.

▶ Full-duplex interfaces simultaneously send and receive, allowing higher throughput because CSMA/CD is disabled. Connections to other switches or devices can be full-duplex.

Port Security

This configuration limits the number of MAC addresses that can be dynamically learned on a switch port:

```
Switch(config-if)#switchport mode access
Switch(config-if)#switchport port-security
Switch(config-if)#switchport port-security maximum 1
Switch(config-if)#switchport port-security violation {protect ¦ restrict ¦ shutdown}
```

If a violation occurs, the default response of a Catalyst switch is to shut down the port. To have the port increase a violation counter and alert an administrator using SNMP, use the `restrict` keyword. The `protect` keyword only allows traffic from the secure port. It also drops packets from other MAC addresses until the number of MAC addresses drops below the maximum.

To secure an interface by statically assigning the permitted MAC address(es) attached to the port, use the `switchport port-security mac-address MAC_address` command on the interface. Alternatively, you can have the switch learn these addresses up to the maximum by using sticky-learned addresses with the command `switchport port-security mac-address sticky`.

Routing Characteristics

Packets originating from a nonrouting device destined for another network are sent to their default gateway (Layer 3 device on segment). The router consults its routing table to determine if the destination network can be reached. If not, the ICMP Destination Unreachable message is sent to the source. If so, packet is forwarded out interface associated with the destination network in routing table.

Routing Sources

▶ **Connected interfaces:** As soon as we assign an IP address to a working (up/line protocol up) interface, the router associates the entire subnet of the interface's IP address in the routing table.

▶ **Static routes:** These are manual entries that an administrator enters into the configuration that describes the destination network and the next hop (router along the destination path).

▶ **Routing protocols:** Protocols exchanged between routing devices to dynamically advertise networks.

When multiple routing sources are advertising the same IP subnet, the router uses the source with the lowest administrative distance.

TABLE FF.23 Default Administrative Distances

Routed Source	Default Distance
Connected	0
Static route	1
EIGRP (internal)	90
IGRP	100
OSPF	110
ISIS	115
RIPv1 and v2	120
EIGRP (external)	170

Static and Default Routes

Static routes are useful in stub networks in which we want to control the routing behavior by manually configuring destination networks into the routing table.

```
Router(config)#ip route 10.0.0.0 255.0.0.0 192.168.2.5
```

A floating static route can be configured when redundant connections exist and you want to use the redundant link if the primary fails. This is configured by adding a higher administrative distance at the end of a static route.

```
Router(config)#ip route 10.0.0.0 255.0.0.0 192.168.2.9 2
```

A default route is a gateway of last resort for a router when there isn't a specific match for an IP destination network in the routing table (such as packets destined for the Internet).

```
Router(config)#ip route 0.0.0.0 0.0.0.0 serial 0/0
```

With routing protocols, you can specify a default network, which is a network in the routing table that routing devices consider the gateway of last resort. Using their routing protocols, they determine the best path to the default network.

```
Router(config)#ip default-network 192.168.1.0
```

Dynamic Routing Protocols

In complex networks with multiple pathways to destinations, dynamic routing protocols enable routers to advertise their networks to each other and dynamically react to topology changes.

Routing protocols determine the best path based on the lowest metric.

Routing Metrics

Because one of the core responsibilities of routing protocols is to build routing tables to determine optimal routing paths, we need to have some means of measuring which routes are preferred when there are multiple pathways to a destination. Routing protocols use some measure of metrics to identify which routes are optimal to reach a destination network. The lowest cumulative metric to a destination is the preferred path and the one that ultimately enters the routing table. Different routing protocols use one or several of the following metrics to calculate the best path.

TABLE FF.24   Routing Metrics

Metric	Description
Hop count	The number of routing devices that the packet must travel to reach a destination network
Bandwidth	The cumulative bandwidth of the links to the destination in kilobits per second
Delay	The length of time (measured in microseconds) a packet takes from source to destination
Reliability	The consistency of the links and paths toward the destination based on error rates of the interfaces
Load	The cumulative amount of congestion or saturation of the links toward the destination
MTU	The maximum frame size that is allowed to traverse the links to the destination
Cost	An arbitrary number typically based on the bandwidth of the link

Interior and Exterior Gateway Routing Protocols

▶ **Interior gateway routing protocols:** IG routing protocols advertise networks and metrics within an autonomous system.

▶ **Exterior gateway routing protocols:** EG routing protocols advertise networks in between autonomous systems.

Classful and Classless Routing Updates

▶ **Classful routing:** The routing updates only contain the classful networks without any subnet mask. Summarization is automatically done when a router advertises a network out an interface that is not within the same major subnet. Classful routing protocols must have a FLSM design and do not operate correctly with discontiguous networks.

▶ **Classless routing:** The routing updates can contain subnetted networks since the subnet mask is advertised in the updates. Route summarization can be manually configured at any bit boundary. Classless routing protocols support VLSM designs and discontiguous networks.

Routing Protocol Classes

▶ **Distance vector:** The entire routing table is periodically sent to directly connected neighbors regardless of a topology change. These routing protocols manipulate the routing table updates before sending that information to their neighbors and are slow to converge when a topology change occurs.

▶ **Link state:** All possible link states are stored in an independent topology table in which the best routes are calculated and put into the routing table. The topology table is initially synchronized with discovered neighbors followed by frequent hello messages. These routing protocols are faster to converge than distance vector routing protocols.

▶ **Hybrid:** By using the best characteristics from link-state and routing protocols, these advanced routing protocols efficiently and quickly build their routing information and converge when topology changes occur.

Redistribution

Redistribution is the method of configuring routing protocols to advertise networks from other routing protocols:

▶ **One-way redistribution:** Networks from an edge protocol are injected into a more robust core routing protocol, but not the other way around. This method is the safest way to perform redistribution.

▶ **Two-way redistribution:** Networks from each routing protocol are injected into the other. This is the least preferred method because it is possible that suboptimal routing or routing loops might occur because of the network design or the difference in convergence times when a topology change occurs.

Distance Vector Routing Loop Mitigation

Distance vector routing protocols contain several measures to prevent routing loops:

▶ **Maximum hop counts:** To ensure that routing metrics do not increment until infinity in a routing loop, distance vector routing protocols have a maximum hop count.

TABLE FF.25   Maximum Hop Counts

Protocol	Distance Vector/Link State/Hybrid	Maximum Hop Count
RIPv1	Distance Vector	15
RIPv2	Distance Vector	15
EIGRP	Hybrid	224
OSPF	Link State	Infinite

▶ **Split horizon:** Subnets learned from neighbor routers should not be sent back out the same interface from which the original update came.

▶ **Route poisoning with poison reverse:** When a route to a subnet fails, the subnet is advertised with an infinite metric. Routers receiving the poisoned route override the split-horizon rule and send a poison reverse back to source.

▶ **Hold-down timers:** The amount of time a router ignores any information about an alternative route with a higher metric to a poisoned subnet.

▶ **Flash updates/triggered updates:** When a route fails, the router immediately shoots out an update as opposed to waiting for a normal update interval.

RIP and RIPv2

TABLE FF.26   RIP and RIPv2 Comparison

	RIPv1	RIPv2
Classful/classless	Classful	Both
Algorithm	Bellman-Ford	Bellman-Ford
Metric	Hops	Hops
Maximum hop count	15	15
Infinite metric	16	16
Hello/dead time	30/180	30/180
Updates	Broadcast	Multicast (224.0.0.9)
Update authentication	No	Yes
Load balancing	Equal paths	Equal paths

RIP Configuration

The configuration for RIP is seamless as long as you remember these two simple rules:

1. Only advertise your directly connected networks.

2. Only advertise the classful network.

```
Router(config)#router rip
Router(config-router)#network 192.168.7.0
Router(config-router)#network 172.17.0.0
```

RIPv2 Configuration

```
Router(config)#router rip
Router(config-router)#network 192.168.7.0
Router(config-router)#network 172.17.0.0
Router(config-router)#version 2
Router(config-router)#no auto-summary
```

Verifying and Troubleshooting RIP

TABLE FF.27   Verifying and Troubleshooting RIP Commands

Command	Output
show ip route	The routing table with RIP entries represented as "R"
show ip protocols	RIP timers, advertised networks
debug ip rip	Real-time display of RIP routing updates being sent and received

Before using any debug commands, verify the processor utilization using the show processes command.

Wireless Networking

Wireless networks have impacted our existing network environments profoundly over the last few years. Because this is the newest topic on the CCENT and CCNA exams, much of what you need to know is the foundations of wireless:

▶ Wireless networks exist by using FCC unmanaged/unregulated radio frequency (RF) signals. This allows corporations to implement wireless technology without FCC approval.

▶ The primary technologies that exist today are 802.11b, 802.11g, and 802.11a. 802.11b/g uses the 2.4GHz frequency range. 802.11a uses the 5GHz frequency range. The 2.4GHz band is much more saturated with consumer electronics (such as cordless phones and microwaves) than the 5GHz band. 802.11n is still in draft status at the time of this writing.

▶ Higher radio frequencies can handle more bandwidth but have less range than the lower radio frequencies.

▶ When implementing wireless technology in a larger building, adjacent wireless access points should use different channels to avoid interfering with each other.

▶ The primary channels used in the U.S. for 802.11b/g are channels 1, 6, and 11. These three channels do not have any overlapping frequencies with each other.

▶ The Wi-Fi Alliance is an organization whose aim is to create a cross-vendor certification of wireless equipment. Purchasing equipment certified by the Wi-Fi Alliance ensures that all the wireless networking gear you use will be compatible with each other.

Wireless Security and Implementation

Because wireless networking has become so prevalent in businesses, it is imperative that every network technician knows the foundations of wireless security. Table FF.28 describes the wireless encryption standards currently available.

TABLE FF.28   Wireless Encryption Standards

Security Standard	Encryption Strength	Key Distribution	Encryption Cipher
WEP	40-bit	Preshared keys	RC4
WEP2	104-bit	Preshared keys	RC4
WPA	128-bit	Preshared keys or 802.1x; TKIP allows dynamic key rotation	RC4
WPA2 (802.11i)	Varied strength; currently up to 256-bit	Preshared keys or 802.1x	AES

Wireless authentication adds an entirely new layer of security to your wireless network. Rather than simply requiring a preshared key (PSK) to gain access to the WLAN, users must authenticate using one of many EAP methods. Encryption keys are dynamically generated after a successful authentication.

Network authentication for LAN environments is called 802.1x (also known as EAP over LAN [EAPOL]).

When implementing wireless access points, you can use a Basic Service Set (BSS), which is a single access point. Or you can use an Extended Service Set (ESS), which is two or more BSSs that tie users to the same LAN. These typically have overlapping coverage areas.

The farther you move from a wireless access point, the more your speed decreases. 802.11a/b/g have the following steps:

802.11a and 802.11g:

▶ Step 1: 54Mbps

▶ Step 2: 48Mbps

▶ Step 3: 36Mbps

▶ Step 4: 24Mbps

▶ Step 5: 18Mbps

▶ Step 6: 12Mbps

▶ Step 7: 9Mbps

▶ Step 8: 6Mbps

802.11b:

▶ Step 1: 11Mbps

▶ Step 2: 5.5Mbps

▶ Step 3: 2Mbps

▶ Step 4: 1Mbps

Implementing a wireless network should typically be done in four steps:

Step 1. Ensure hardwired operation.

Step 2. Install the wireless access point in your tested switchport.

Step 3. Configure a basic wireless network, and test.

Step 4. Add wireless security, and test.

Network Address Translation (NAT)

NAT is in use on virtually every Internet-connected router in the world today. This technology acts as a security boundary and Internet address sharing system. The following facts are relevant to NAT.

NAT operates by typically translating private IP addresses to public Internet addresses. The following are the private address ranges as defined by RFC 1918:

▶ **Class A:** 10.X.X.X

▶ **Class B:** 172.16.X.X to 172.31.X.X

▶ **Class C:** 192.168.X.X

The three primary forms of NAT are as follows:

▶ **Static NAT** allows you to manually map one IP address to another in a one-to-one relationship.

▶ **Dynamic NAT** allows you to define a pool of addresses to be translated along with a pool of addresses they will be translated to.

▶ **NAT overload/PAT** allows a single Internet IP address to support many internal clients.

The standards bodies have developed many terms to describe the location of an IP address in the world of NAT:

▶ **Inside local addresses:** Refers to everything inside your network.

▶ **Inside global addresses:** The Internet valid IP address assigned to your router that is directly connected to the Internet.

▶ **Outside global addresses:** A standard Internet IP address accessible from any host connected to the Internet.

▶ **Outside local addresses:** How an Internet host is seen by the internal network as it is translated through the NAT router into your local network.

Wide-Area Networks

Wide-area network (WAN) connections tie together geographically distant locations, enabling them to communicate as if directly connected. The following facts are relevant to WANs.

WAN technologies only encompass the Physical and Data Link layers of the OSI model. The three major categories of WAN technology used to connect networks today are as follows:

▶ **Leased lines:** Provides a dedicated, point-to-point link between two locations.

▶ **Circuit-switched networks:** Establishes a dedicated channel (or circuit) for the duration of the transmission, and then tears down the channel when the transmission is complete.

▶ **Packet-switched networks:** Enables the service provider to create a large pool of bandwidth for its clients who establish connections through the shared bandwidth using virtual circuits.

Cisco routers connect to most WAN connections through their serial ports. The Cisco side of the connection uses either a DB-60 or Smart Serial port. The CSU/DSU that the Cisco router connects to will have one of five standard connectors: V.35, X.21, EIA/TIA-232, EIA/TIA-449, or EIA/TIA-530.

At the Data Link layer, Cisco routers primarily use one of two WAN encapsulations for leased line and circuit switched networks:

▶ **Point-to-Point Protocol (PPP):** The most popular, industry-standard, feature-packed protocol for connecting routers

▶ **Cisco High-level Data Link Control (HDLC):** A Cisco-proprietary, low-overhead protocol that makes your WAN connections very efficient between Cisco devices

HDLC is the default encapsulation on all Cisco serial interfaces. However, PPP is used to gain more features and industry standard capabilities when connecting over the WAN. It is made up of three sublayers:

▶ **ISO HDLC:** Responsible for enabling PPP to be supported by multiple devices.

▶ **Link Control Protocol (LCP):** Feature negotiation layer that performs the following functions:

  ▶ **Authentication:** Requires a username and password for the connecting device.

  ▶ **Callback:** Enables a dialup server (or router) running PPP to call back the person who initially dialed into the location using a predefined number.

  ▶ **Compression:** Makes WAN connections more efficient by minimizing the amount of data sent.

  ▶ **Multilink:** Bundles multiple WAN connections (or WAN channels in the case of ISDN) into a single, logical connection.

▶ **Network Control Protocol (NCP):** Gives PPP the functionality to enable multiple Network layer protocols to run across a single WAN link at any given time.

When configuring PPP authentication, you can choose between two authentication protocols:

▶ **Password Authentication Protocol (PAP):** Sends username and password once in clear-text format when authenticating.

▶ **Challenge Handshake Authentication Protocol (CHAP):** Sends a username and hashed password when demanded by the CHAP server.

When configuring PPP compression, you can choose between three compression types:

▶ **Stacker:** A flat compression algorithm that is notoriously heavy on CPU resources and has less effect on the router's memory resources. Useful for WAN links with many traffic patterns.

▶ **Predictor:** A dictionary-based compression algorithm that is notoriously heavy on memory resources and has less effect on the router's CPU resources. Useful for WAN links with similar traffic patterns.

▶ **Microsoft Point-to-Point Compression (MPPC):** Used for Microsoft Windows dial-up clients wanting to use compression.

To activate PPP encapsulation on an interface, use the following syntax:

```
Router(config)#interface serial 0
Router(config-if)#encapsulation ppp
```

When adding CHAP authentication to your configuration, you need to ensure that you create a user account that matches the hostname of the other side of the connection. In addition, the passwords must be the same on both sides. Here is a PPP CHAP authentication configuration between the Kirk and Spock routers:

```
Kirk(config)#username Spock password cisco
Kirk(config)#interface serial 0
Kirk(config-if)#encapsulation ppp
Kirk(config-if)#ppp authentication chap

Spock(config)#username Kirk password cisco
Spock(config)#interface serial 0
Spock(config-if)#encapsulation ppp
Spock(config-if)#ppp authentication chap
```

The show interface command is one of the most useful when verifying the PPP configuration. The connection is active when the LCP Open tag is seen, as shown here:

```
Router#show interface serial 0
Serial0 is up, line protocol is up
  Hardware is PowerQUICC Serial
  Internet address is 10.2.2.2/24
  MTU 1500 bytes, BW 1544 Kbit, DLY 20000 usec,
     reliability 255/255, txload 1/255, rxload 1/255
  Encapsulation PPP, loopback not set
  Keepalive set (10 sec)
  LCP Open
  Open: IPCP, CCP, CDPCP
```

When troubleshooting PPP authentication issues, use the debug ppp authentication command to observe the authentication process as it occurs.

Practice Exam

1. You are trying to enter a command in the IOS, and you receive the following console message: "Invalid input detected at ^." What should you do to correct this?

   - ○ **A.** Enter more characters for the IOS to understand the command.
   - ○ **B.** Enter more keywords so that the IOS understands what you want to do with the command.
   - ○ **C.** Check your typing syntax.
   - ○ **D.** Check your console connection.

2. Which of the following forms of NAT incorporates the source IP address (inside local) along with the source port number to make every translation unique?

   - ○ **A.** Static NAT
   - ○ **B.** Dynamic NAT
   - ○ **C.** NAT Overload
   - ○ **D.** NAT Port Mapping

3. What verification command can show you the current state of the PPP Link Control Protocol?

   - ○ **A.** `show interface`
   - ○ **B.** `show ip interface`
   - ○ **C.** `show ppp interface`
   - ○ **D.** `show wan interface`

4. Which of the following are Application layer protocols? (Choose the three best answers)

   - ○ **A.** Telnet
   - ○ **B.** JPEG
   - ○ **C.** HTTP
   - ○ **D.** FTP

5. Which of the following commands enable you to specify the datagram size in a ping to 10.1.1.1?

  ○ **A.** Router>ping -l

  ○ **B.** Router#ping

  ○ **C.** Router#ping 10.1.1.1

  ○ **D.** Router>ping 10.1.1.1

6. The NAT Overload feature on a Cisco router takes multiple inside local addresses and overloads a single _____ address.

  ○ **A.** Inside local

  ○ **B.** Inside global

  ○ **C.** Outside local

  ○ **D.** Outside global

7. Which Application layer protocol resolves hostnames or fully qualified domain names (FQDNs) such as www.cisco.com into IP addresses?

  ○ **A.** SMTP

  ○ **B.** NFS

  ○ **C.** NNTP

  ○ **D.** DNS

8. Which of the following configuration registers causes the IOS to boot from flash if no `boot system` commands are present?

  ○ **A.** 0x2100

  ○ **B.** 0x2106

  ○ **C.** 0x2140

  ○ **D.** 0x210P

9. When connecting a serial cable from the CSU/DSU to your Cisco router, what two standards are supported on the Cisco end of the connection? (Choose two)

  ○ **A.** EIA/TIA-449

  ○ **B.** Smart Serial

  ○ **C.** DB-60

  ○ **D.** RJ-45

10. Which layer of the OSI model handles dialog control among devices?

    ○ **A.** Application

    ○ **B.** Presentation

    ○ **C.** Session

    ○ **D.** Transport

11. Which of the following STP 802.11d port states actively learns MAC addresses? (Choose all that apply)

    ○ **A.** Blocking

    ○ **B.** Learning

    ○ **C.** Listening

    ○ **D.** Forwarding

12. Which of the following IP addresses represent public addresses? (Choose two)

    ○ **A.** 192.186.6.32

    ○ **B.** 172.31.20.55

    ○ **C.** 172.200.166.99

    ○ **D.** 10.255.255.5

    ○ **E.** 172.17.50.2

13. SNMP uses which port number?

    ○ **A.** 67

    ○ **B.** 68

    ○ **C.** 69

    ○ **D.** 161

14. Which of the following is a form of DoS attack? (Choose three)

    ○ **A.** TCP SYN

    ○ **B.** Smurf

    ○ **C.** DDoS

    ○ **D.** Trust exploitation

15. At the end of your Setup Mode dialog, you are asked whether you want to keep the configuration you created. This configuration will be present even if you reboot the device. Where is this configuration stored?

   ○ **A.** NVRAM

   ○ **B.** RAM

   ○ **C.** ROM

   ○ **D.** Flash

16. You are troubleshooting network connectivity issues between a client and a server. The server's IP address recently changed, and you would like to clear the client's ARP table. What command will accomplish this?

   ○ **A.** `arp -clear`

   ○ **B.** `arp -a`

   ○ **C.** `arp -c all`

   ○ **D.** `arp -d *`

17. _____ is an electrical or magnetic field that is a result of one communications signal that can affect the signal in a nearby circuit.

   ○ **A.** EMI

   ○ **B.** Attenuation

   ○ **C.** Crosstalk

   ○ **D.** Bandwidth

18. Which command allows only SSH through the vty lines?

   ○ **A.** Switch(config)#`ssh-service restrict`

   ○ **B.** Switch(config-line)#`password ssh-only`

   ○ **C.** Switch(config-line)#`transport input ssh`

   ○ **D.** Switch(config)#`line ssh 0 4`

19. A host is assigned the IP address 10.5.62.173/27. An application on the host attempts to contact a server with the IP address 10.5.62.158/27. What is the next step in the process of network communication?

    ○ **A.** The host sends an ARP message directly to the destination server to obtain its MAC address.

    ○ **B.** The host contacts the IP address of its default gateway to find the MAC address for the destination server.

    ○ **C.** The host sends an ARP broadcast to find the MAC address of its default gateway.

    ○ **D.** The host sends an ARP broadcast to find the MAC address of the destination server.

20. What type of UTP cable would you use to connect a switch to a PC?

    ○ **A.** Coaxial cable

    ○ **B.** Straight-through cable

    ○ **C.** Cross-over cable

    ○ **D.** Thin coax

21. Given the following output, which of the statements is false?

```
Routing Protocol is "rip"
  Sending updates every 30 seconds, next due in 2 seconds
  Invalid after 180 seconds, hold down 180, flushed after 240
  Outgoing update filter list for all interfaces is not set
  Incoming update filter list for all interfaces is not set
  Redistributing: rip
  Default version control: send version 2, receive version 2
    Interface        Send  Recv   Key-chain
    Ethernet0         2     2     examprep
    Serial0           2     2
  Routing for Networks:
    172.19.0.0
    10.2.0.0
  Routing Information Sources:
    Gateway          Distance       Last Update
  Distance:          80
```

    ○ **A.** The administrative distance has been changed.

    ○ **B.** This is version 2 of RIP.

    ○ **C.** Update authentication is configured.

   ○ **D.** The router configuration looks like the following:

```
Router(config)#router rip
Router(config-router)#version 2
Router(config-router)#network 10.2.0.0
Router(config-router)#network 172.19.0.0
```

22. What form of NAT allows you to translate one group of IP addresses to another in a 1:1 relationship with minimal configuration?

   ○ **A.** Port Address Translation

   ○ **B.** Static NAT

   ○ **C.** NAT Overload

   ○ **D.** Dynamic NAT

23. The Ethernet IEEE 802.3 specification defines which of the following LAN standards? (Choose the three best answers)

   ○ **A.** 10BASE-2

   ○ **B.** 10BASE-5

   ○ **C.** 10BASE-T

   ○ **D.** Wi-Fi

24. Which of the following networks are contained in the summarized CIDR route of 192.168.64.0 /19? (Choose all that apply)

   ○ **A.** 192.168.96.0 /24

   ○ **B.** 192.168.60.0 /24

   ○ **C.** 192.168.80.0 /24

   ○ **D.** 192.168.101.0 /24

25. Which of the following encapsulation types can be used on leased-line connections? (Choose two)

   ○ **A.** HDLC

   ○ **B.** Frame Relay

   ○ **C.** ISDN

   ○ **D.** PPP

26. Which devices are implemented at the Physical layer of the OSI model? (Choose the two best answers.)

     ○ **A.** Switch

     ○ **B.** Bridge

     ○ **C.** Hub

     ○ **D.** Repeater

27. Which of the following are 802.3 MAC sublayer Ethernet addresses? (Choose the three best answers)

     ○ **A.** IP address

     ○ **B.** Unicast address

     ○ **C.** Multicast address

     ○ **D.** Broadcast address

28. Which of the following would you typically configure as the default gateway for a PC?

     ○ **A.** The IP address of the local Layer 2 switch

     ○ **B.** The MAC address of the local Layer 2 switch

     ○ **C.** The IP address of the local router

     ○ **D.** The MAC address of the local router

29. Which of the following match the correct encryption algorithm with the wireless security standard? (Choose two)

     ○ **A.** WPA / TKIP

     ○ **B.** WPA2 / TKIP

     ○ **C.** WPA / AES

     ○ **D.** WPA2 / AES

30. Which Ethernet MAC 802.3 sublayer address type always starts with the hexadecimal characters 0100.5E?

     ○ **A.** Unicast address

     ○ **B.** Multicast address

     ○ **C.** Broadcast address

     ○ **D.** IP address

31. You no longer have IP connectivity to a remote router at a customer's site. From your location, what terminal option can you use to gain access to an EXEC session on the remote router?

- ○ **A.** Console port
- ○ **B.** Telnet
- ○ **C.** SSH
- ○ **D.** Auxiliary port

32. Which of the following commands would allow a network client to test connectivity to a destination device and verify the current delay for all routers traversed while making the connection?

- ○ **A.** ping
- ○ **B.** test
- ○ **C.** tracert
- ○ **D.** telnet
- ○ **E.** ssh -h -d

33. _____ occurs when a switch creates a dedicated path for sending and receiving transmissions with each connected host.

- ○ **A.** Microsegmentation
- ○ **B.** Half-duplex
- ○ **C.** Full-duplex
- ○ **D.** CSMA/CD

34. How does a switch forward frames when the destination MAC address is unknown?

- ○ **A.** It sends the frame out every port.
- ○ **B.** It drops the frame and sends an ICMP Destination Unreachable.
- ○ **C.** It sends an ARP request to find the MAC address and then sends the frame out the port that receives the response.
- ○ **D.** It floods the frame out every port except the one on which the original frame arrived.

35. How many wireless channels are available in the U.S. for the 2.4GHz band without overlapping frequencies for close-proximity wireless access points?

- ○ **A.** 1
- ○ **B.** 3
- ○ **C.** 11
- ○ **D.** 23

36. Which devices are implemented at the Data Link layer of the OSI model? (Choose the two best answers)

   ○ **A.** Hub

   ○ **B.** Repeater

   ○ **C.** Switch

   ○ **D.** Bridge

37. What range represents the first-octet value of a Class A address?

   ○ **A.** 0 to 126

   ○ **B.** 1 to 126

   ○ **C.** 128 to 191

   ○ **D.** 192 to 223

38. What Layer 2 protocol can identify information such as the IP address of Cisco devices connected to you?

   ○ **A.** ICMP

   ○ **B.** CDP

   ○ **C.** DNS

   ○ **D.** DHCP

39. You are using NAT Overload on your company's Cisco router to provide Internet access to your internal network. The NAT process is overloading the IP address assigned to the router's outside interface. Which of the following statements are *not* true? (Choose two)

   ○ **A.** Multiple internal users cannot access the same website at the same time, because the website sees two requests coming from the same IP address.

   ○ **B.** Static NAT mappings can be added for the interface IP address, but only for specific ports.

   ○ **C.** Static NAT mappings can be added for the full interface IP address.

   ○ **D.** Cisco's NAT process allows you to NAT not only to the interface IP address but also to other IP addresses not assigned to the interface.

40. You are the network administrator of ACME Corp. You have received a number of tickets from your San Diego office complaining about server connectivity issues. You verify the WAN interface connecting the corporate office to the San Diego office:

```
Router# show interfaces serial
Serial 0 is administratively down, line protocol is down
    Hardware is MCI Serial
    Internet address is 150.136.190.203, subnet mask is 255.255.255.0
    MTU 1500 bytes, BW 1544 Kbit, DLY 20000 usec, rely 255/255, load 1/255
    Encapsulation HDLC, loopback not set, keepalive set (10 sec)
    Last input 0:00:07, output 0:00:00, output hang never
    Output queue 0/40, 0 drops; input queue 0/75, 0 drops
    Five minute input rate 0 bits/sec, 0 packets/sec
    Five minute output rate 0 bits/sec, 0 packets/sec
        16263 packets input, 1347238 bytes, 0 no buffer
        Received 13983 broadcasts, 0 runts, 0 giants
        2 input errors, 0 CRC, 0 frame, 0 overrun, 0 ignored, 2 abort
1 carrier transitions
        22146 packets output, 2383680 bytes, 0 underruns
        0 output errors, 0 collisions, 2 interface resets, 0 restarts
```

The line protocol is down due to an HDLC encapsulation mismatch. HDLC is Cisco-proprietary and should be changed to PPP. The interface is experiencing input errors. The keepalive value is set too low. The interface is in a shutdown state. You are logged into a router and want to view the IP address of neighboring Cisco routers. What IOS command gives this information for the directly connected neighbors?

- ○ **A.** show ip clients
- ○ **B.** show cdp neighbor
- ○ **C.** show cdp neighbor detail
- ○ **D.** show ip links

41. What is the end result of the 192.168.2.0 network based on the following output?

```
RouterA# debug ip rip
RIP protocol debugging is on
RouterA#
00:26:27: RIP: received v1 update from 192.168.1.6 On Serial0/0
00:26:27:        192.168.2.0 in 12 hops
00:26:37: RIP: received v1 update from 192.168.1.12 on Serial0/1
00:26:37:        192.168.2.0 in 12 hops
```

- ○ **A.** The router forwards packets to 192.168.1.6 because it received that update first.
- ○ **B.** The router forwards packets to 192.168.1.12 because it received that update last.
- ○ **C.** The router ignores the updates because the maximum hop count is reached.
- ○ **D.** Both entries are put in the router, and it load-balances over both links.

42. Your organization uses a wireless security standard that requires users to authenticate to a back-end server with a valid active directory username and password before they are granted access to the wireless network. Upon successful authentication, the dynamic encryption keys are generated for use during the wireless session. What type of network security is in use?

    ○ **A.** WEP

    ○ **B.** WPA

    ○ **C.** 802.11i

    ○ **D.** 802.1x (EAPOL)

43. What is 00111000 10110011 01010111 11011010 converted into decimal format?

    ○ **A.** 56.179.87.217

    ○ **B.** 56.179.87.218

    ○ **C.** 56.179.87.219

    ○ **D.** 56.179.87.220

44. Which of the following security practices is incorrect?

    ○ **A.** Disable CDP on an interface with the `no cdp run` command.

    ○ **B.** Physically secure access to your devices.

    ○ **C.** Use SSH instead of Telnet.

    ○ **D.** Enable port security.

45. You are configuring your Cisco 2600XM router to connect across the WAN to a Cisco 3800 router. You would like to use the default WAN encapsulation. Will this work?

    ○ **A.** Yes. Cisco routers all support the same WAN encapsulation standards.

    ○ **B.** Yes. Newer Cisco routers support different WAN encapsulation standards, but they are backward-compatible with older WAN encapsulation types.

    ○ **C.** No. Newer Cisco routers use PPP as their WAN encapsulation types, and older Cisco routers use HDLC.

    ○ **D.** No. Newer Cisco routers use the industry-standard HDLC, and older Cisco routers use a proprietary version.

46. What is the broadcast IP of 212.84.5.66/26?

    ○ **A.** 212.84.5.125

    ○ **B.** 212.84.5.126

    ○ **C.** 212.84.5.127

    ○ **D.** 212.84.5.128

47. Which statement is true regarding the 10.1.100.0 network based on the following output?

```
CstmrARtr# show ip route
...output omitted...

Gateway of last resort is 192.168.1.9 to network 0.0.0.0

R    10.1.100.0 /24 [120/14] via 192.168.1.9, 00:00:11, Serial0
C    172.17.0.0/16 is directly connected, Ethernet0
R    172.16.0.0/16 [120/11] via 172.17.0.2, 00:00:02, Ethernet0
     192.168.1.0/30 is subnetted, 1 subnets
C       192.168.1.8 is directly connected, Serial0
```

- ○ **A.** The 10.1.100.0 network is 11 hops away.
- ○ **B.** RIPv2 is configured on this router.
- ○ **C.** Serial 0 has an IP address of 192.168.1.9.
- ○ **D.** The maximum hop count has been reached.

48. You suspect that one of your network users has violated the corporate security policy and plugged in a personal wireless access point in his cubicle. What Cisco security solution would allow you to detect and identify this issue?

- ○ **A.** Cisco ACS Server
- ○ **B.** Cisco Wireless IPS
- ○ **C.** Cisco Wireless 802.1x
- ○ **D.** MAC Address Security

49. What is the network ID of 212.84.5.66/26?

- ○ **A.** 212.84.5.0
- ○ **B.** 212.84.5.64
- ○ **C.** 212.84.5.128
- ○ **D.** 212.84.5.192

50. When pinging a device on a remote segment, which of the following are true of the packet as soon as it leaves the device that originated the packet? (Choose two)

- ○ **A.** The destination IP address is the default gateway.
- ○ **B.** The destination MAC address is the default gateway.
- ○ **C.** The destination IP address is the remote device's IP.
- ○ **D.** The destination MAC address is the local switch.

51. Which of the following are valid interface connections for serial WAN connections? (Choose three)

○ **A.** EIA/TIA-449

○ **B.** V.35

○ **C.** RJ-48

○ **D.** RJ-44

○ **E.** X.21

52. What does the c2600 portion of the Cisco IOS filename c2600-ipbase-1.122-1.T.bin represent?

○ **A.** Hardware platform

○ **B.** Feature set

○ **C.** Train identifier

○ **D.** IOS version

53. After telnetting from RouterA into RouterB, you realize that your debug outputs are not showing on the terminal screen in RouterB. How can you remedy this?

○ **A.** RouterA#`terminal monitor`

○ **B.** RouterA(config-line)#`terminal monitor`

○ **C.** RouterA#(config-line)#`terminal monitor`

○ **D.** RouterB#`terminal monitor`

54. While troubleshooting a serial connection, you issue the following command:

```
router# sh controllers serial 0/0
Interface Serial0/0
Hardware is PowerQUICC MPC850
DTE V.24 (RS-232) clocks stopped.
RX ring with 32 entries at 0x45560 : RLEN=5, Rxhead 0
00 pak=0x6044D78  ds=0x6044ED4 status=80 max_size=1524 pak_size=0
01 pak=0x60445F0  ds=0x604474C status=80 max_size=1524 pak_size=0
02 pak=0x6043E68  ds=0x6043FC4 status=80 max_size=1524 pak_size=0
03 pak=0x60436E0  ds=0x604383C status=80 max_size=1524 pak_size=0
04 pak=0x6042F58  ds=0x60430B4 status=80 max_size=1524 pak_size=0
```

What problem is indicated by the output, and what action will most likely solve it?

○ **A.** The serial interface is receiving PAK errors from the service provider. You must contact the service provider to resolve the issue.

○ **B.** A hardware failure has occurred. The serial interface should be replaced.

○ **C.** The router does not have a clock rate. It should be set on the opposite side.

○ **D.** The wrong end of the cable is connected. The serial cable should be reversed.

55. Which of the following bridge IDs will become the root bridge?

   ○ **A.** 1024FACE198476AB

   ○ **B.** 1024AB121704F52E

   ○ **C.** 102410241234FACE

   ○ **D.** 1024ABCD1234FACE

56. _____ allows an end device to receive power over a copper Ethernet cable.

   ○ **A.** Long-Reach Ethernet

   ○ **B.** Gigabit Ethernet

   ○ **C.** Fast Ethernet

   ○ **D.** Power over Ethernet

57. What command configures a default route in a Layer 2 switch?

   ○ **A.** `ip route 0.0.0.0 0.0.0.0 FastEthernet 0/0`

   ○ **B.** `ip default-gateway 172.16.1.1`

   ○ **C.** `ip default-network 192.168.1.0`

   ○ **D.** `default-route 172.16.1.1`

58. You are using a Cisco 7921 Wireless VoIP device. While speaking to your coworker on the phone, you are walking through multiple wireless cells. What type of network topology is this?

   ○ **A.** Multiservice

   ○ **B.** Roaming

   ○ **C.** Basic Service Set

   ○ **D.** Extended Service Set

59. You walk away from your terminal for five minutes to get some coffee. When you return, you notice that someone has made configuration changes to your router. Which three commands will keep this from happening in the future?

   ○ **A.** Router(config-line)#`line-timeout 1`

   ○ **B.** Router(config-line)#`login`

   ○ **C.** Router(config)#`password` *password*

   ○ **D.** Router(config)#`exec-timeout 1`

   ○ **E.** Router(config-line)#`password` *password*

   ○ **F.** Router(config-line)#`exec-timeout 1`

60. Which of the following is not a step in configuring SSH on your Cisco device?

- ○ **A.** Create an RSA key.
- ○ **B.** Configure a username and password.
- ○ **C.** Configure a domain name for your device.
- ○ **D.** Enable SSH on the vty lines.

61. You are configuring an office to use a Cisco router to connect to the Internet. The onsite network administrator would like to publish an internal email server, two internal web servers, and an internal FTP server to the Internet so that outside users can access them. What is necessary for this configuration?

- ○ **A.** You will need a public Internet IP address for each internal server. These addresses can be mapped using Static NAT features.
- ○ **B.** You will need a single public Internet IP address for this configuration and will use NAT Overload to share it between all four internal servers.
- ○ **C.** You will need a single public Internet IP address for this configuration and will use Static NAT to map specific ports to all four internal servers.
- ○ **D.** You will need two public Internet IP addresses to accommodate the internal web servers. The FTP and email server can be mapped to individual ports on either of the addresses.

62. Which of the following conditions could cause the port to transition to a disabled state? (Choose all that apply)

- ○ **A.** A BPDU is detected on a BPDU Guard-enabled port.
- ○ **B.** The port is not a root or designated port.
- ○ **C.** The switch connected to your port has a faster way back to the root.
- ○ **D.** A port security violation has occurred.

63. What is a typical reason why the first ICMP ping response times out?

- ○ **A.** The interface is in a sleep state.
- ○ **B.** The IP stack is not working correctly.
- ○ **C.** An ARP request and response must transpire first.
- ○ **D.** The local switch does not know the destination MAC address.

64. Given the following output, how can you close Telnet session 2? (Choose two)

```
CCNA2620# show sessions
Conn   Host                  Address            Idle    Conn Name
1      131.108.100.152       131.108.100.152    0       131.108.100.152
*2     126.102.57.63         126.102.57.63      0       126.102.57.63
```

○ **A.** Press the Enter key and enter `exit`.

○ **B.** Enter `disconnect 2`.

○ **C.** Press the Enter key and enter `disconnect 2`.

○ **D.** Enter `close 2`.

65. Which of the following is *not* part of configuring RIPv2 to be classless?

○ **A.** Advertise directly connected classful networks.

○ **B.** Specify the version of RIP as 2.

○ **C.** Specify the subnet mask in the `network` statement.

○ **D.** Enter the RIP routing process.

66. You connected your switch into a device at half duplex. What is a possible reason for not using full duplex?

○ **A.** It is a 10Mbps port.

○ **B.** You are connecting it to another switch.

○ **C.** You are using a straight-through cable.

○ **D.** You are connected to a hub.

67. Which of the following is not an additional feature of RIPv2 over RIPv1?

○ **A.** A full update followed by hellos

○ **B.** Update authentication

○ **C.** Multicast updates

○ **D.** Classless support

68. How many bits does an IPv6 address have?

○ **A.** 32

○ **B.** 64

○ **C.** 96

○ **D.** 128

69. Which of the following is an encryption protocol? (Choose three)

   ○ **A.** IPsec

   ○ **B.** SSL

   ○ **C.** NTP

   ○ **D.** SSH

70. Private addressing for IPv6 is represented by a _____ address.

   ○ **A.** Link-local

   ○ **B.** Global

   ○ **C.** Unique/site-local

   ○ **D.** Multicast

Answers to Practice Exam

Answers at a Glance

1. C	25. A, D	49. B
2. C	26. C, D	50. B, C
3. a	27. B, C, D	51. A, B, E
4. A, C, D	28. C	52. A
5. B	29. A, D	53. D
6. B	30. B	54. C
7. D	31. D	55. C
8. B	32. C	56. D
9. B, C	33. A	57. B
10. C	34. D	58. D
11. B, D	35. B	59. B, E, and F
12. A, C	36. C, D	60. D
13. D	37. B	61. D
14. A, B, C	38. B	62. A, D
15. A	39. A, C	63. C
16. D	40. C	64. A, B
17. C	41. D	65. C
18. C	42. D	66. D
19. C	43. B	67. A
20. B	44. A	68. D
21. D	45. A	69. A, B, D
22. D	46. C	70. C
23. A, B, C	47. B	
24. C	48. B	

Answers with Explanations

1. **C.** The "Invalid input detected at ^" terminal message indicates that the IOS understood the configuration command up to the caret marker. This type of message is typical when the command contains a typo. Answer A is the solution for an "Ambiguous Command" message. Answer B is the solution for an "Incomplete Command" message. Answer D is not viable because the terminal session is still connected.

2. **C.** NAT Overload uses the source port number to send many unique requests out a single public IP address. Answer A is incorrect because Static NAT performs 1:1 translations from public to private IP addresses. Answer B is incorrect because Dynamic NAT performs many 1:1 translations without requiring manual entries. Answer D is incorrect because NAT Port Mapping is not a valid form of NAT.

3. **A.** The `show interface` command is used to verify the current state of the PPP LCP negotiations. This shows Open, Listen, ACKSent, or TERMSent, depending on the state of LCP at the time (you want LCP to show Open). The other `show` commands are either irrelevant or would produce invalid syntax.

4. **A, C, D.** Telnet, HTTP, and FTP are all protocols supported by Layer 7, or the Application layer of the OSI model. Answer B is incorrect because JPEG is a Layer 6, or Presentation layer, supported protocol.

5. **B.** You must use an extended ping to specify the datagram size when pinging an IP address. To do an extended ping in the Cisco IOS, you must be in privileged EXEC mode, and the command is `ping` without specifying an IP address. Answer A is incorrect because that is a DOS command, not an IOS command. Answer C is incorrect because you do not specify the IP address after the `ping` keyword. Answer D is incorrect because you must be in privileged EXEC mode.

6. **B.** The inside global address is the public address on your router's external interface. The terminology may seem a little cryptic, but just remember for inside NAT (the style of NAT expected at the CCENT level), the inside/outside terms identify who controls the IP address (inside, you control; outside, someone else controls). The local/global terms identify a private or public address, respectively.

7. **D.** DNS resolves hostnames into IP addresses. Answer A is incorrect because SMTP sends email across the network. Answer B is incorrect because NFS allows users with different operating systems (that is, NT and UNIX workstations) to share files. Answer C is incorrect because NNTP offers access to Usenet newsgroup postings.

8. **B.** If the boot field in the configuration register is 2-F, the router or switch loads the IOS from flash when no `boot system` commands are present. Answers A and C will load into ROMmon because the boot field is 0. Answer D has a P in the boot field, which is not a valid hexadecimal character.

9. **B, C.** Cisco routers typically support DB-60, which is a 60-pin connection. Only one DB-60 interface is supported per WIC card. Because of this, Cisco developed the Smart Serial connector, which is much smaller and supports more condensed interfaces. Answer A is incorrect because EIA/TIA-449 connects to the CSU/DSU side of the connection. Answer D is incorrect because this is a LAN interface standard.

10. **C.** The Session layer of the OSI model handles dialog control among devices and determines the beginning, middle, and end of a session or conversation that occurs between applications (intermediary). The Application layer (Answer A) provides an interface between a host's communication software and any necessary external applications. The Presentation layer (Answer B) presents data to the Application layer. The Transport layer (Answer D) manages end-to-end connections and data delivery between two hosts.

11. **B, D.** During the learning and forwarding STP port states, the switch actively learns MAC addresses it receives on that interface. Answers A and C are incorrect because MAC addresses are not learned during the blocking and listening port states.

12. **A, C.** The only private addresses are from the ranges 10.0.0.0 to 10.255.255.255, 172.16.0.0 to 172.31.255.255, and 192.168.0.0 to 192.168.255.255. Because Answers A and C fall outside those ranges, they are considered public IP addresses.

13. **D.** SNMP uses port number 161. Answers A and B are incorrect because DHCP uses port numbers 67 and 68. Answer C is incorrect because TFTP uses port number 69.

14. **A, B, C.** TCP SYN, smurf, and DDoS are all types of DoS attacks. Answer D is incorrect because trust exploitation is a type of access attack.

15. **A.** When a configuration is saved, it is stored in NVRAM as the startup-config. Answer B is incorrect because the running-config is stored in RAM. Answer C is incorrect because POST and ROMmon are located in ROM. Answer D is incorrect because the compressed IOS file is stored in flash.

16. **D.** The client ARP table is often cleared during network changes. This can be accomplished using the syntax `arp -d *` from a command prompt. The `*` argument instructs the PC to clear all ARP entries rather than just a specific entry.

17. **C.** Crosstalk is an electrical or magnetic field that is a result of one communications signal that can affect the signal in a nearby circuit. Answer A is incorrect because EMI is the interference caused by electromagnetic signals. Answer B is incorrect because attenuation occurs over long distances as a signal loses strength. Answer D is incorrect because bandwidth is the total amount of information that can traverse a communications medium measured in millions of bits per second.

18. **C.** The `transport input ssh` command specifies that the vty lines will accept only the SSH-protocol. Answers A and D are incorrect because they are not valid commands. Answer B is a valid command, but it essentially assigns the password `ssh-only` to the vty lines. It is not specific to SSH.

19. **C.** A quick calculation of the subnet addresses defined in the question shows that the server belongs to the 10.5.62.128/27 subnet (addresses 10.5.62.128 to 10.5.62.159) and that the host belongs to the 10.5.62.160/27 subnet (addresses 10.5.62.160 to 10.5.62.191). Because of this, the host needs to contact its default gateway. To accomplish this, the host sends an ARP broadcast request to determine the MAC address of its default gateway.

20. **B.** When connecting a switch to a PC, you must use a straight-through UTP cable. Answer A is incorrect because coaxial cable typically is used for cable television. Answer C is incorrect because cross-over cables are used to connect like devices such as switches to other switches or PCs to

other PCs. Answer D is incorrect because thin coax (also known as thinnet) is used in older network topologies.

21. **D.** Answer D is the false answer because you must configure directly connected classful networks. Thus, 10.2.0.0 is incorrect because the classful network should be 10.0.0.0. Answer B is incorrect because, based on the output, the routing protocol configured is RIPv2 with update authentication. Answer A is incorrect because the administrative distance for RIPv2 is 120; however, the output shows the AD as 80. Answer C is incorrect because the output does show that update authentication is indeed configured.

22. **D.** Dynamic NAT allows you to configure multiple pools of IP addresses and translate between them. The router dynamically matches each IP address to one another as a request is made. Answer A is incorrect because Port Address Translation (PAT) is just another name for NAT Overload. Answer B is incorrect. Although Static NAT could perform this task, it would take quite a bit of configuration to manually map IP addresses in large pools. Answer C is incorrect because NAT Overload takes a group of IP addresses and translates them into a single (overloaded) IP address.

23. **A, B, C.** 10BASE-2, 10BASE-5, and 10BASE-T are all 10Mbps IEEE 802.3 ethernet standards. Answer D is incorrect because Wi-Fi is a wireless technology that is defined by IEEE 802.11.

24. **C.** The summary route for 192.168.64.0 /19 summarizes the networks from 192.168.64.0 /24 to 192.168.95.0 /24. Because 5 bits were stolen ($2^5 = 32$), 32 networks are being summarized. Answers A, B, and D are incorrect because they do not fall in the summary range.

25. **A, D.** HDLC and PPP are the only encapsulation types supported by Cisco on leased-line connections. Answer B is incorrect because Frame Relay is an encapsulation used on a Frame Relay packet-switched network. Answer C is incorrect because ISDN is a type of circuit-switched technology.

26. **C, D.** Hubs and repeaters are hardware devices used at the Physical layer of the OSI model to extend a network. Answers A and B are incorrect because switches and bridges are hardware devices used at the Data Link layer to segment a network.

27. **B, C, D.** Unicast, multicast, and broadcast addresses are Ethernet address types used at the 802.3 MAC sublayer. Answer A is incorrect because IP addresses are logical addresses used at the Network layer of the OSI model.

28. **C.** The default gateway is a routing device that is responsible for forwarding packets from one segment to another. When configuring the default gateway, you specify the IP address of the routing device. Answers A and B are incorrect because Layer 2 switches are not routing devices. Answer D is incorrect because you do not specify the MAC address when configuring the default gateway.

29. **A, D.** The WPA algorithm uses the TKIP algorithm to generate dynamic keys during a wireless session. This helped handle many of the security concerns of WEP. WPA2 (also known as 802.11i) uses the AES encryption algorithm, which is considered one of the best encryption standards available.

30. **B.** All multicast addresses start with 0100.5E. Answer A is incorrect because unicast addresses start with the OUI of the manufacturer NIC. Answer C is incorrect because broadcast addresses begin with FFFF.FF. Answer D is incorrect because IP addresses are not ethernet MAC sublayer addresses, and they use dotted-decimal format rather than hexadecimal format.

31. **D.** Modems typically are connected to the auxiliary port and are used as a "last-resort" method of accessing the remote router. Answers B and C are incorrect: Because you no longer have IP connectivity to the router, you cannot use SSH and Telnet. Answer A is incorrect because you cannot console into the router because it is in a remote location. The only viable solution left is to call into a modem that is connected through the Auxiliary port.

32. **C.** The traceroute (`tracert`) command can be compared to an enhanced ping. Rather than just testing connectivity to an end device, it tests connectivity to every device in the path, displaying the ping results (delay) for each device as it moves through the network to the destination.

33. **A.** Microsegmentation occurs when a switch creates a dedicated path for sending and receiving transmissions with each connected host. Answer B is incorrect because half duplex allows only one-way data transmissions. Answer C is incorrect because full duplex allows two-way data transmissions. Answer D is incorrect because CSMA/CD is an algorithm used for arbitration on an Ethernet network.

34. **D.** When a switch receives an unknown unicast, it learns the source MAC address and adds that to the CAM table. It also floods the frame out every port except the one it came in on. Answer A is incorrect because it does not send the frame out the port it came in on. Answer B is incorrect because it does not drop the frame. Answer C is incorrect because Layer 2 switches do not send ARP requests.

35. **B.** In the U.S., only three nonoverlapping channels are available for the 2.4GHz band. Europe has four nonoverlapping channels because access to other unlicensed RF bands is available. The moral of the story is that if you're having trouble finding a free wireless channel in your area, move to Europe.

36. **C, D.** Switches and bridges are hardware devices used at the Data Link layer to segment a network. Answers A and B are incorrect because hubs and repeaters are hardware devices used at the Physical layer of the OSI model to extend a network.

37. **B.** Class A addresses have a first octet value of 1 to 126. Class B addresses have a first octet value of 128 to 191. Class C addresses have a first octet value of 192 to 223.

38. **B.** CDP is a Layer 2 protocol that can be used to discover the Layer 3 addresses of directly attached Cisco devices. Answers A, C, and D are incorrect because these protocols do not provide the Layer 3 address of Cisco devices.

39. **A, C.** Multiple users can access the same website at the same time because unique source ports are used to differentiate between the connections. Also, when using NAT with the IP address assigned to the outside interface, you cannot create a static NAT mapping for the entire IP address, because this would make local router services unavailable. Answers B and D are true statements.

40. **C.** Entering show cdp neighbor from user or privileged mode uses the Cisco Discovery Protocol (CDP) to discover any directly connected Cisco device. By adding the detail variable for the command, the router displays the IP address information of the remote devices. This powerful command works at the Data Link layer of the OSI model and can discover directly connected devices even if no IP address is configured on the local or remote interface! Answers A and B are incorrect because they are not valid commands. Answer E is incorrect because it shows the IP routing table for the device rather than the neighboring router IP address information.

41. **D.** Because the update is coming from two different sources with the same metric, RIP load-balances over both equal paths. Answers A and B are incorrect because the order in which the updates were received is negligible. Answer C is incorrect because the maximum hop count for RIP is 15.

42. **D.** 802.1x (less commonly known as Extensible Authentication Protocol over LAN [EAPOL]) adds a secure authentication system to a LAN environment. This technology can be used to secure both wired and wireless LAN connections. The other answers represent varying encryption standards.

43. **B.** The first octet is 32+16+8=56. The second octet is 128+32+16+2+1=179. The third octet is 64+16+4+2+1=87. The last octet is 128+64+16+8+2=218. So the address in dotted-decimal format is 56.179.87.218. The last bit in the last octet is 0, which means that any address ending with an odd-numbered octet can be eliminated. All other answers have the wrong decimal conversion.

44. **A.** The command to disable CDP on an interface is `no cdp enable`. The `no cdp run` command is a global configuration command. Answers B, C, and D are all valid security practices.

45. **A.** Cisco routers (new and old) all use a Cisco-proprietary version of HDLC on their serial connections. Although an industry-standard HDLC exists, very few vendors support it. Answer B is incorrect because there are no "backward-compatible" WAN standards. Answers C and D are incorrect because newer Cisco routers still use the Cisco-proprietary HDLC as the default encapsulation.

46. **C.** The broadcast IP of 212.84.5.66/26 is 212.84.5.127. The next network ID after 212.84.5.64 is 212.84.5.128. To determine the broadcast IP, you subtract 1 from the next network ID, which in this case is 212.84.5.127. All other answers are incorrect because they are not the broadcast IP.

47. **B.** Because the 10.1.100.0/24 network is a RIP-learned subnetted network, it must have been learned via RIPv2, because RIPv2 can be classless. If the routing protocol were RIPv1, the network would be summarized to its classful boundary and would show up in the routing table as 10.0.0.0/8. Answer A is incorrect because the network is 14 hops away, as indicated by the [120/14]. Answer C is incorrect because Serial 0 has an IP address of 192.168.1.8, displayed as the connected interface entry. Answer D is wrong because the maximum hop count for RIP is 15.

48. **B.** The Cisco Wireless IPS system identifies rogue wireless access points added to the network. The 802.1x and the Cisco ACS Server are primarily responsible for user authentication and privileges. MAC address security can help disable a port with a rogue wireless access point, but it cannot detect the rogue's existence.

49. **B.** The Network ID of 212.84.5.66/26 is 212.84.5.64. The CIDR notation represents subnet mask 255.255.255.192. The binary equivalent of the subnet mask host field is 11000000. The binary equivalent of the 212.84.5.66 host field is 01000010. Using Boolean AND, the Network ID is 212.84.5.64. Answers A, C, and D are incorrect.

50. **B, C.** When pinging a remote device, the destination IP address is the IP address of the remote device. The MAC address, however, is the default gateway for that segment. Answer A is incorrect because the destination IP address is not the default gateway, because that is not the IP's destination. Answer D is incorrect because the default gateway is the destination address for the data-link segment.

51. A, B, E. The five primary standards that are used for serial interface connections (to the CSU/DSU) are V.35, X.21, EIA/TIA-232, EIA/TIA-449, and EIA/TIA-530. Answers C and D are incorrect because RJ-48 is the standard for a T1 connection, and RJ-44 is not a defined standard.

52. A. The c2600 portion of the IOS filename represents the hardware platform. In this case, it is a Cisco 2600 series router. Answer B is incorrect because the term ipbase refers to the IP Base feature set. Answer C is incorrect because the train identifier is T for Technical. Answer D is incorrect because the IOS version is represented by 122, or version 12.2.

53. D. The `terminal monitor` command copies and consoles messages to the Telnet sessions of an IOS router or switch. This command is done in privileged EXEC mode in the device you are Telnetted into. Answers A, B, and C are incorrect because they are either on the wrong router or in the wrong mode.

54. C. The key line in the output is "DTE V.24 (RS-232) clocks stopped." This indicates that the interface is connected but is not receiving a clock rate from the opposite site of the connection. When you see this single line of output, all other answers (A, B, and D) become irrelevant.

55. C. The lowest bridge ID becomes the root bridge. Because all devices have the same priority (1024), the lowest MAC address is the tie-breaker. Answers A, B, and D are incorrect because they have a higher Bridge ID than Answer C.

56. D. Power over Ethernet is a technology that allows an end device to receive power over a copper Ethernet cable. Answer A is incorrect because Long-Reach Ethernet (LRE) is an Ethernet specification developed by Cisco to provide broadband service over existing telephone-grade or Category 1, 2, or 3 wiring. Answers B and C are incorrect because Gigabit Ethernet and Fast Ethernet standards do not include the ability to supply power to an end device.

57. B. Because this is a Layer 2 switch, the gateway of last resort is configured by setting the default gateway. Answers A and C are incorrect because you cannot configure a default route or a default network in a Layer 2 switch. Answer D is not a valid command.

58. D. An Extended Service Set (ESS) wireless topology is the combination of two or more Basic Service Set (BSS) networks. This allows client roaming (between wireless cells) without service interruption.

59. B, E, and F. To secure your console connection when you walk away from the IOS terminal, you need to decrease the exec-timeout and set the login and password. These configurations must be performed in line configuration mode. All other answers are incorrect because they are performed in the wrong configuration mode.

60. D. Answers A, B, and C are true because you must configure a hostname and domain name for the device and generate an RSA key from that information. In addition, you must configure a username and password for the SSH to authenticate. As soon as the RSA key is generated, SSH is automatically enabled, so Answer D is false.

61. D. NAT can accomplish some pretty amazing feats, but sharing an IP address for two servers that use the same port number is not one of them. In this case, you need two public Internet addresses to allow both internal web servers to be accessed on TCP port 80. The other servers can use port 21 (FTP) and port 25 (SMTP) on either of the public Internet IP addresses. Answer A could be used to solve this problem, but it is not the best solution, because it would be more costly to deploy than Answer D. Answer B is incorrect because NAT Overload lets the servers share a single IP address only when accessing the Internet, not when the requests originate from the Internet. Answer C is incorrect because you could only map TCP port 80 on the single IP address to one of the internal web servers. The other could not be accessed from the Internet.

62. **A, D.** The port becomes disabled if a BPDU is detected on a BPDU Guard-enabled port, as well as if there is a port security violation. Answers B and C are incorrect because that would cause the port to be in a blocking state.

63. **C.** If the device that is being pinged is not in the local ARP cache, the pinging device must first do an ARP request for the device. Typically, the time it takes to resolve this causes the first ping to time out. Answer A is false because interfaces don't sleep. Answer B is incorrect because all pings would time out if the IP protocol stack were failing. Answer D is incorrect because the local switch will flood the frame and will not delay the ping to cause a timeout.

64. **A, B.** To disconnect the Telnet session, you can enter `disconnect` followed by the session number in the originating router. Or you can press the Enter key to resume the Telnet session and enter `exit` in the device you are Telnetted into to close the Telnet session. Answer C is incorrect because pressing Enter first resumes your session with the remote router and causes the `disconnect` command to fail. Answer D is incorrect because it is invalid syntax.

65. **C.** You do not specify a subnet mask when configuring RIPv2. Answers A, B, and D are incorrect because you do enter the RIP routing process and advertise directly connected classful networks and specify the version as 2.

66. **D.** When connecting to a hub, you must have the port running in half duplex, because CSMA/CD must be enabled. Answer A is incorrect because the speed is irrelevant. Answer B is incorrect because you can run full duplex when connecting to switches. Answer C is incorrect because it does not matter what cable is used.

67. **A.** RIPv2 has update authentication, multicasts updates to 224.0.0.9, and can support classless routing. Answer A is not a feature because it is still a distance vector routing protocol that sends continuous updates every 30 seconds instead of Hello messages, such as RIPv1.

68. **D.** IPv6 addresses have 128 bits. Answer A is the bit count for an IPv4 address. Answers B and C are incorrect because they are not valid IP address bit counts.

69. **A, B, D.** IPsec, SSL, and SSH are all encryption protocols. Answer C is incorrect because NTP (Network Time Protocol) synchronizes clocks on a network.

70. **C.** Unique/site-local addresses are the private address space for IPv6. Answer A is incorrect because link-local addresses represent the address automatically assigned to a device at Layer 2. Answer B is incorrect because a global address is a public IP address. Answer D is incorrect because a multicast address in IPv6 is the same as a broadcast IP address.

What's on the CD-ROM

The CD-ROM features an innovative practice test engine powered by MeasureUp™, giving you yet another effective tool to assess your readiness for the exam.

Multiple Test Modes

MeasureUp practice tests can be used in Study, Certification, or Custom Mode.

Study Mode

Tests administered in Study Mode allow you to request the correct answer(s) to and an explanation for each question during the test. These tests are not timed. You can modify the testing environment during the test by clicking the Options button.

You can also specify the objectives or missed questions you want to include in your test, the timer length, and other test properties. You can modify the testing environment during the test by clicking the Options button.

In Study Mode, you receive automatic feedback on all correct and incorrect answers. The detailed answer explanations are a superb learning tool in their own right.

Certification Mode

Tests administered in Certification Mode closely simulate the actual testing environment you will encounter when taking a licensure exam and are timed. These tests do not allow you to request the answer(s) and/or explanation to each question until after the exam.

Custom Mode

Custom Mode allows you to specify your preferred testing environment. Use this mode to specify the categories you want to include in your test, timer length, number of questions, and other test properties. You can modify the testing environment during the test by clicking the Options button.

Attention to Exam Objectives

MeasureUp practice tests are designed to appropriately balance the questions over each technical area covered by a specific exam. All concepts from the actual exam are covered thoroughly to ensure that you're prepared for the exam.

Installing the CD

The system requirements are as follows:

► Windows 95, 98, Me, NT 4, 2000, XP, or Vista

► 14MB of disk space for the testing engine

► An average of 2MB of disk space for each individual test

► Control Panel Regional Settings must be set to English (United States)

► PC only

To install the CD-ROM, follow these instructions:

1. Close all applications before beginning this installation.

2. Insert the CD into your CD-ROM drive. If the setup starts automatically, go to step 6. If the setup does not start automatically, continue with step 3.

3. Select **Start**, **Run**.

4. Click **Browse** to locate the MeasureUp CD. In the Browse dialog box, from the Look In drop-down list, select the CD-ROM drive.

5. In the Browse dialog box, double-click **Setup.exe**. In the Run dialog box, click **OK** to begin the installation.

6. On the Welcome screen, click **MeasureUp Practice Questions** to begin the installation.

7. Follow the Certification Prep Wizard by clicking **Next**.

8. To agree to the Software License Agreement, click **Yes**.

9. On the Choose Destination Location screen, click **Next** to install the software to C:\Program Files\Certification Preparation. If you cannot locate MeasureUp Practice Tests on the Start menu, see the next section.

10. On the Setup Type screen, select **Typical Setup**. Click **Next** to continue.

11. In the Select Program Folder screen, you can name the program folder where your tests will be located. To select the default, simply click **Next**, and the installation continues.

12. After the installation is complete, verify that **Yes, I Want to Restart My Computer Now** is selected. If you select **No, I Will Restart My Computer Later,** you cannot use the program until you restart your computer.

13. Click **Finish**.

14. After restarting your computer, choose **Start, Programs, Certification Preparation, Certification Preparation, MeasureUp Practice Tests**.

15. On the MeasureUp Welcome Screen, click **Create User Profile**.

16. In the User Profile dialog box, complete the mandatory fields, and click **Create Profile**.

17. Select the practice test you want to access, and click **Start Test**.

Creating a Shortcut to the MeasureUp Practice Tests

To create a shortcut to the MeasureUp Practice Tests, follow these steps:

1. Right-click your desktop.

2. From the shortcut menu, select **New, Shortcut**.

3. Browse to C:\Program Files\MeasureUp Practice Tests, and select the **MeasureUpCertification.exe** or **Localware.exe** file.

4. Click **OK**.

5. Click **Next**.

6. Rename the shortcut MeasureUp.

7. Click **Finish**.

After you complete step 7, use the MeasureUp shortcut on your desktop to access the MeasureUp products you ordered.

Technical Support

If you encounter problems with the MeasureUp test engine on the CD-ROM, please contact MeasureUp at 800-649-1687, or email support@measureup.com. Support hours of operation are 7:30 a.m. to 4:30 p.m. EST. In addition, you can find Frequently Asked Questions (FAQs) in the Support area at www.measureup.com. If you would like to purchase additional MeasureUp products, call (678) 356-5050 or 800-649-1687, or visit www.measureup.com.

Glossary

10BASE-T An IEEE 802.3 Ethernet standard that has a maximum segment length of 100m and has data transmission speed. 10BASE-T can use Category 3, 4, or 5 unshielded a 10Mbps twisted-pair (UTP) or shielded twisted-pair (STP) cables for connectivity.

802.11a An IEEE wireless networking standard released in 1999 that uses the 5GHz frequency range. 802.11a clients can theoretically transmit at a maximum speed of 54Mbps.

802.11b An IEEE wireless networking standard released in 1999 that uses the 2.4GHz frequency range. 802.11b clients can theoretically transmit at a maximum speed of 11Mbps.

802.11g An IEEE wireless networking standard released in 2003 that uses the 2.4GHz frequency range. 802.11g clients can theoretically transmit at a maximum speed of 54Mbps. This standard is backward-compatible with 802.11b clients.

802.11n A predraft standard for wireless networking that uses Multiple Input, Multiple Output (MIMO) signals to achieve higher throughput. Current predraft equipment uses the 2.4GHz frequency range.

802.1q An IEEE frame-tagging method over trunk ports that insert the 4-byte VLAN identifier inside the original Ethernet frame.

802.1x An authentication protocol geared toward LAN environments. 802.1x requires that users authenticate to the network before they are granted wired or wireless access.

A

AAA (Authentication, Authorization, and Accounting)   A group of three services that are used in conjunction with an authentication server and a software service such as Terminal Access Controller Access Control System (TACACS) or Remote Authentication Dial-in User Service (RADIUS) to provide a secure network connection with a record of user activities.

ABR (Area Border Router)   A router that sits between multiple areas in a hierarchical OSPF network. These routers are responsible for summarizing subnets to the rest of the OSPF autonomous system. Because they must maintain topology information from several areas, these routers are typically robust in resources.

access attack   A class of attack in which a hacker attempts to access another user account or network device through improper means.

access-class   The command used to apply an access list to vty ports.

access port   A switch port that has a single VLAN assigned to it. These are typically used for connectivity between end devices.

ACTIVE, INACTIVE, and DELETED PVC status   The three states of a Frame Relay PVC. Active means that the connection is good on both ends. Inactive means that the remote router is misconfigured. Deleted means that the local router is misconfigured.

adjacency   A term that describes the state after two OSPF neighbors have synchronized their topology databases.

administrative distance   An arbitrary value between 1 and 255 that is assigned to determine the trustworthiness of the routing sources.

advertised distance   The composite metric to a destination that is being advertised from our EIGRP neighbors.

AES (Advanced Encryption Standard)   The newest encryption algorithm. It is managed by the National Institute of Standards and Technology (NIST), a division of the U.S. government. It was designed to increase encryption strength beyond the DES and 3DES standards and yet be more efficient on the device's processor. As it stands today, AES offers 128-, 192-, and 256-bit encryption.

AH (Authentication Header)   One of the components that powers the IPsec security suite of protocols. AH defines capabilities for authentication and data-integrity algorithms but does not provide the capability for encryption.

Application layer   Layer 7 of the OSI model. Provides an interface between a host's communication software and any necessary external applications (that is, email, file transfers, and terminal emulation). This layer can also evaluate what resources are necessary to communicate between two devices and determine their availability.

area   A subdivision of an autonomous system composed of groups of contiguous networks and attached hosts. Used in link-state routing protocols to minimize routing update overhead and confine network instability.

ARP (Address Resolution Protocol)   A protocol that maps a known IP address to a MAC address by sending a broadcast ARP. When the destination IP address is on another subnet, the sender broadcasts ARP for the router's Ethernet port or default gateway, so the MAC address sent back is that of the router's Ethernet port.

ASP (AppleTalk Session Protocol)   A session layer protocol that manages client/server based communications, but is specific to AppleTalk client and server devices.

asynchronous   A serial interface that does not synchronize the clocks for the bit stream of the sending and receiving end of a serial link.

ATM (Asynchronous Transfer Mode)   A packet-switched connection type that reaches high speeds by dividing all packets into equal-sized cells of 53 bytes each.

attenuation   A term used to describe how a signal loses strength over long distances.

authentication   The process of requiring or prompting for credentials before a device can access the network.

autonomous system   A collection of routing devices under the same administrative control.

autonomous system number   An indicator in an IGRP and EIGRP configuration that identifies the autonomous system the routers are actively sending routing updates.

auxiliary port   An out-of-band management connection used to connect to an external modem with a rollover cable.

B

backbone area   Also known as the transit area, Area 0 is an area to which all other areas must connect.

BackboneFast   Cisco STP enhancement that skips the max-age timer when switches learn of a failure indirectly.

backbone router   Any router that is connected to Area 0.

Backward Explicit Congestion Notification (BECN)   A signaling method used by a Frame Relay service provider that attempts to drop the speed of a router sending excessive data.

balanced hybrid routing protocol   A class of routing protocol that uses the best characteristics from link-state and routing protocols. These advanced routing protocols efficiently and quickly build their routing information and converge when topology changes occur.

bandwidth   The total amount of information that can traverse a communications medium measured in millions of bits per second. Bandwidth is helpful for network performance analysis. Also, availability is increasing but limited.

bandwidth *speed*   An interface configuration command that assigns a logical speed to the interface for accurate routing metrics.

banner `motd` *delimiting_char* **banner** *delimiting_char*   A global configuration command to create a message-of-the-day login banner.

BDR (Backup Designated Router)   A routers that is elected in OSPF as a redundant device in case the Designated Router fails.

bearer channel (B channel)   Used as a building block for ISDN connections. Provides 64Kbps of bandwidth per channel.

Bellman-Ford Algorithm   A routing algorithm used by RIP and IGRP, which entails routing updates being received and updated before propagating the message to other routing devices.

binary   A computer language that is represented by a bit value of 0 or 1.

blocking   Ports that are not the root or the designated port in a STP election that are left in a blocking state. Data is not transmitted on these ports, but BPDUs can still be received.

Bluetooth   A wireless technology that uses a short-range wireless radio connection to allow various devices to interconnect. Such devices include cell phones, PCs, and personal digital assistants (PDAs). The only requirement to establish connectivity is a 10 meter range (approximately 33 feet) between communicating devices. When in range, Bluetooth uses an RF link in the 2.4GHz range that has a 720Kbps per channel capacity to transfer voice or data.

BOD (Bandwidth on Demand)   A Cisco extension to the PPP Multilink concept that allows more DDR connections to be brought up as bandwidth is needed and disconnected as bandwidth is not needed.

Boolean AND   A mathematical operation that can be used to identify the network ID and broadcast IP given an IP address and subnet mask.

boot field   The last hexadecimal character in a configuration register that specifies where to find an IOS.

bootstrap   Instructions loaded from ROM to activate the IOS loading code.

boot system *location filename*   A global configuration command that specifies locations and filenames to load the IOS.

BPDU (Bridge Protocol Data Unit)   A Layer 2 message sent in an STP environment to advertise bridge IDs, root bridge MAC addresses, and root path costs.

BPDU Guard   A Cisco enhancement to PortFast that prevents loops by moving an access port to a disabled state if a BPDU is received.

BRI (Basic Rate Interface)   An Integrated Services Digital Network (ISDN) line that consists of two 64Kbps bearer (B) channels and one 16Kbps data (D) channel. Voice, video, and data traffic can be carried over the B channels. Signals between telephone company switches use the D channel.

bridge   A hardware device at the Data Link layer that connects two segments in a single network or connects two networks. They simply forward data between those segments/networks without analyzing or redirecting the data.

bridge ID   A Spanning Tree Protocol switch identifier composed of a combination of bridge priority and MAC address.

broadband   A term used to describe high-speed Internet connections such as DSL or cable modems.

broadcast   An Ethernet LAN address in which a frame is sent to all devices in the same LAN. Broadcast addresses are always the same value—FFFF.FFFF.FFFF.

broadcast domain   A group of nodes that can receive each other's broadcast messages and are segmented by routers.

broadcast IP   The last IP address in a network. Every host bit for the broadcast IP address is turned on (or all 1s).

broadcast multiaccess (BMA) topology
Consists of multiple devices that access the same medium and can hear each others' broadcasts and multicast messages such as Ethernet networks.

broadcast subnet   The last subnet in a network, which has all 1s in the subnet field.

BSS (Basic Service Set)   Describes a network topology with an independent wireless access point managing a group of clients.

bus topology   A network topology that is set up so that the network nodes are connected via a single cable (also referred to as a trunk or a backbone). Electrical signals are sent from one end of the cable to the other.

C

CAM (Content-Addressable Memory) table   A table in RAM that stores MAC addresses in a switch.

CAS (Channel Associated Signaling)   A type of connection that incorporates signaling information with the data being sent. Also called Robbed Bit Signaling (RBS).

CCS (Common Channel Signaling)   A type of connection that separates signaling information from the data transmission. ISDN is a CCS-style technology.

CDP (Cisco Discovery Protocol)   A Layer 2 Cisco-proprietary protocol that advertises information to directly connected Cisco neighbors.

cdp enable   An interface configuration command to enable CDP on an interface (on by default).

cdp run   A global configuration command to enable CDP on a device (on by default).

CHAP (Challenge Handshake Authentication Protocol)   A strong authentication type used with PPP encapsulation. Passwords are hashed and sent multiple times over the course of a WAN connection.

CIR (Committed Information Rate)   The minimum speed guaranteed to a customer by a Frame Relay service provider.

Circuit Switched Network   A WAN connection type that encompasses dial-on-demand technologies such as modems and ISDN.

Cisco, ANSI, and Q933A LMI signaling   The three forms of Frame Relay LMI signaling. Cisco IOS 11.2 and later automatically detect the Frame Relay signaling type. Earlier versions of the IOS must be coded manually.

Cisco Frame Relay Encapsulation   A Cisco-proprietary Frame Relay encapsulation that can be used only when communicating through a Frame Relay service provider to other Cisco routers.

classful routing protocol   Routing updates contain only the classful networks, without any subnet mask. Summarization is automatically done when a router advertises a network out an interface that is not within the same major subnet. Classful routing protocols must have a FLSM design and do not operate correctly with discontiguous networks.

Classless Interdomain Routing (CIDR) A way to allocate and specify Internet addresses used in routing. Offers more flexibility than the original system of IP address classes.

classless routing protocol Routing updates can contain subnetted networks because the subnet mask is advertised in the updates. Route summarization can be manually configured at any bit boundary. Classless routing protocols support VLSM designs and discontiguous networks.

CLI (command-line interface) An interface that defines the method used to communicate with an operating system. In the case of Cisco, this is IOS.

client mode A VTP mode in which you cannot create, modify, or delete VLANs. Forwards advertisements received from the server but does not save VLAN configuration to the VLAN database.

clock rate *speed* An interface configuration command that specifies the clocking speed in bps.

collision domain A group of nodes that share the same media and are segmented by switches. A collision occurs if two nodes attempt a simultaneous transmission.

composite metric A metric used by IGRP and EIGRP composed of bandwidth plus delay by default. Can also support Reliability, Load, and MTU as well.

config-register *register* A global configuration command to alter the configuration register.

configuration register A 16-bit (four hexadecimal characters) value in NVRAM that specifies how the router or switch should operate during initialization.

connected interface As soon as we assign an IP address to a working (up/line protocol up) interface, the router associates the entire subnet of the interface's IP address in the routing table.

console port An out-of-band management connection used to connect to a PC with a rollover cable.

copy *from* to A privileged EXEC command that copies files from one location to another.

cost An arbitrary number typically based on the link's bandwidth.

count to infinity When routers are continuously passing updates to unreachable networks between each other in a routing loop, the metric continues to increase forever.

CPE (Customer Premises Equipment) Refers to equipment located on the customer premises, such as the router and typically the CSU/DSU.

crosstalk An electrical or magnetic field that is a result of one communications signal that can affect the signal in a nearby circuit.

CSMA/CD A process that sends a jam signal to notify the devices that there has been a collision. The devices then halt transmission for a random back-off time.

CSU/DSU (Channel Service Unit/Data Service Unit) A device that serves as an intermediary between the service provider and the WAN router. In most cases, the CSU/DSU provides clocking for the router.

Ctrl+Shift+6, x   A keystroke to suspend Telnet sessions and cancel lookups and pings.

cut-through   A frame transmission method that looks only at the destination MAC address in an Ethernet frame and forwards it.

D

data integrity   Using measures to ensure that data does not change in transmission. This typically is described as hashing data.

Data Link layer   Layer 2 of the OSI model. Ensures reliable data transfer from the Network layer to the Physical layer for transmission across the network.

data packet   A packet that transports data across the internetwork and is supported by IP and IPX protocols.

DCE (Data Circuit-Terminating Equipment)   Also called Data Communications Equipment. The term used to identify a device that connects the Data Terminal Equipment (DTE) to a service provider's communications line. Types of DCE are modems, CSU/DSUs, and BRI NT-1s.

DDR (Dial-on-Demand Routing)   A technology used to bring up network connections when needed and disconnect them after the need is satisfied. Typically used for ISDN connections.

DE (Discard Eligible)   Any traffic exceeding the CIR in a Frame Relay network is automatically marked by the service provider as Discard Eligible, which means that it could be dropped in case of network congestion.

default gateway   A gateway of last resort in switches and PCs. This default gateway is the IP address that hosts and switches send their traffic to when the destination is on another segment.

default route   A gateway of last resort for a router when there isn't a specific match for an IP destination network in the routing table (such as packets destined for the Internet).

demarc (demarcation)   The point at which the telco terminates its line to the customer.

DES (Data Encryption Standard)   One of the first electronic encryption algorithms to be used. It was originally developed by IBM to support a 56-bit key. By today's standards, DES is considered a relatively weak encryption.

designated port   On each STP segment, the switch with the lowest cumulative cost to the root has the designated port.

dialer interface   A logical interface that contains a configuration that can be applied to a physical interface when needed.

dialer list/dialer group   The syntax used to create a list of interesting traffic (dialer list) and apply that list to an interface (dialer group).

dialer map   Used to manually map a remote IP address to the phone number a router should dial to reach it.

dialer pool   A pool of physical interfaces that a logical, dialer interface can draw from when attempting to make a connection.

dialer profile   A newer form of DDR connection that allows you to define different configurations to be applied to an ISDN interface when certain destinations are dialed.

Diffie-Hellman Algorithm   An asymmetric (public and private key) algorithm that allows for secure exchange of encryption keys over a public network.

Digital Signal Level 1 (DS1)   Also called a T1, this line offers a 1.544Mbps data transmission speed. A single T1 consists of 24 digital signal level 0 (DS0) channels that are 64Kbps each and an additional 8Kbps that are reserved for management overhead.

Dijkstra SPF Algorithm   A routing algorithm used by OSPF and IS-IS that builds and calculates the shortest path to all known destinations.

discarding state   A Rapid Spanning Tree nonforwarding port state that entails a port that does not participate in the switched topology because BPDU updates are not actively being sent and MAC addresses are not being learned. Similar to 802.1d Spanning Tree Protocol's blocking state.

disconnect *conn#*   A user or privileged EXEC command to disconnect a suspended Telnet session.

discontiguous network   A major network separated by another major network that is automatically summarized, causing routing confusion.

distance vector routing protocol   A class of routing protocol in which the entire routing table is periodically sent to directly connected neighbors regardless of a topology change. These routing protocols manipulate the routing table updates before sending that information to their neighbors and are slow to converge when a topology change occurs.

distributed DoS attack   A type of DoS attack in which multiple systems are compromised to send a DoS attack to a specific target.

DLCI (Data Link Connection Identifier)   A data link address used by Frame Relay.

DNA SCP (Digital Network Architecture Session Control Protocol)   A proprietary Digital Equipment Corporation Networking (DECnet) Session layer protocol. Also referred to as a DECnet session.

DNS (Domain Name System)   An Application layer protocol that resolves hostnames and fully qualified domain names, such as www.cisco.com, into IP addresses.

DoS (denial of service) attack   A class of attack that is implemented to deny a service that is normally available to a user or organization.

DR (Designated Router)   Elected in OSPF to minimize routing update overhead that can occur in broadcast and nonbroadcast multiaccess topologies.

DTE (Data Terminal Equipment)   A device at the user end of a network that is connected to the service provider via the DCE device. Types of DTE are PCs, routers, and servers.

DTP (Dynamic Trunking Protocol)   A protocol used by Cisco to negotiate trunking.

DUAL (Diffusing Update Algorithm)   The algorithm used by EIGRP to determine the best loop-free path to a destination, as well as alternative paths in certain conditions.

dual-ring topology   A network topology that uses two rings for redundancy purposes. If a failure occurs on one ring, the other provides operability.

duplex   A device's communication mode. Can be either half duplex or full duplex, depending on the connection type.

Dynamic Host Configuration Protocol (DHCP)   An Application layer protocol that works dynamically to provide an IP address, subnet mask, domain name, and default gateway to network clients.

dynamic NAT Automatically performs NAT translations between two or more pools of addresses.

E

EGP (Exterior Gateway Protocol) A routing protocol that advertises networks between autonomous systems.

EIA/TIA-232, -449, and -530 Physical serial interface standards on CSU/DSU devices.

EIGRP (Enhanced Interior Gateway Routing Protocol) A Cisco-proprietary enhancement of IGRP to support classless routing, multiple routed protocols, a 32-bit composite metric, and the DUAL algorithm for fast convergence and loop-free routing.

EMI (electromagnetic interference) The interference caused by electromagnetic signals, which can decrease data integrity.

enable password *password* A global configuration command that sets a clear-text password for entering privileged EXEC mode.

enable secret *password* A global configuration command that sets an MD5 encrypted password for entering privileged EXEC mode.

Encapsulating Security Payload (ESP) One of the engines that can power the IPsec security suite of protocols. ESP defines capabilities for authentication, data integrity, and encryption algorithms.

encapsulation The process of adding a header or trailer to the Protocol Data Unit at each layer of the OSI model.

encryption The process of scrambling data, thus making it unreadable, before transmitting it over the network.

erase startup-config A privileged EXEC command that deletes the startup-config in NVRAM to return the router or switch to the original "out-of-box" configuration after reboot.

Error-Disabled A port security state in which a violation has occurred and the interface has been disabled.

ESS (Extended Service Set) A wireless topology that includes two or more wireless access points, providing extended wireless coverage across the network.

EtherChannel A Cisco link aggregation method that bundles multiple links between two switches into a single logical link.

Ethernet A LAN specification introduced in the 1970s when Xerox needed a networking system to connect PCs.

exec-timeout *minutes seconds* A line configuration command that specifies the length of terminal inactivity before closing the EXEC session.

extended access list A list of permit and deny statements capable of matching network traffic based on the protocol used, source IP address, source port number, destination IP address, and destination port number.

F

feasible distance The composite metric composed of the advertised distance to a destination plus the composite metric to reach that advertising router from the local router.

feasible successor route   A backup route in the EIGRP topology table that is enabled if the successor route fails. Determined if the advertised distance of the candidate feasible successor is less than the feasible distance of the successor route.

FECN (Forward Explicit Congestion Notification)   A signaling method used by a Frame Relay service provider. It attempts to drop the speed of a router sending excessive data by having a receiving router send traffic back to the sender tagged as a BECN message.

FEXT (Far-End Crosstalk)   The crosstalk measured at the far end of the cable from where the transmission was sent.

fiber   A cable that uses light rather than electrical signals to send data transmissions. These optical light signals travel a fiberglass core, and you might hear this technology referred to as fiber optics or optical cabling. Fiber is not susceptible to electromagnetic interference.

filter   A program or device that uses a defined set of criteria to break up data and signals.

flapping   A term used to describe a failing interface that is constantly going up and down.

flash   A type of system memory that is installed on either an electrically erasable, programmable, read-only memory (EEP-ROM), or Personal Computer Memory Card International Association (PCMCIA) card. Flash memory contains the Cisco Internetworking Operating System (IOS)

image. The router uses flash by default to locate the IOS when it is booted. Configuration files might also be stored on a flash card. Flash is also nonvolatile memory.

floating route   A route with a higher administrative distance that enters the routing table when the primary route fails.

flow control   A process that provides buffer controls that prevent packet flooding to the destination host. Buffers store bursts of data for processing when the transmission is complete.

FLSM (Fixed-Length Subnet Mask)   A design that assumes that subnet routes from different parts of their classful network all use the same subnet mask that they use. Any subnetted networks must contain the same subnet mask throughout the topology.

forward-delay timer   The time to transition from listening to learning and learning to forwarding. Each forward delay is 15 seconds.

forwarding   An STP port state in which the interface transmits and receives data.

fragment-free   A frame transmission method that checks the first 64 bytes for frame fragments (due to collisions) before forwarding the frame.

frame   A packet that is formatted by the Data Link layer of the OSI model for transmission to the Physical layer.

Frame Relay   One of the more popular packet-switched connection types that establishes site-to-site connections through a service provider network. Can attain speeds up to T3 and uses DLCI numbers as its Layer 2 addressing.

FTP (File Transfer Protocol)   An Application layer protocol that allows a user to transfer files and provides access to files and directories.

full duplex   Bidirectional transmissions enabling higher throughput because CSMA/CD is disabled. Connections to other switches or devices can be full-duplex.

full-mesh design   A costly, but fully redundant, packet-switched network design in which all routers are directly connected to all other routers through virtual circuits.

full-mesh topology   A network topology that is set up so that each device is directly connected to every other device on the network. This connection method has built-in redundancy. If one link goes down, the device transmits via another link.

G

GBIC (Gigabit Interface Converter)   An interface module that can be inserted into the Gigabit Ethernet slot on a switch to allow for different media connections to that port. The physical media can range from copper to single-mode fiber. A GBIC is also hot-swappable, so it can be installed without interrupting service to that switch.

global address   A type of IPv6 address with the broadest scope. These addresses are for global use—that is, for Internet communications.

H

half duplex   One-way communication transmission with suboptimal throughput

because it operates in a collision domain in which CSMA/CD must be enabled. When connected to a hub, half duplex must be run.

hashing   The process of running data through an algorithm that generates a result based on the actual data. This result is known as the hash. In most cases, this result is then sent with the data to the receiving device. The receiving device can then rerun the hash algorithm and compare the results to ensure that the data did not change in transmission.

HDLC (High-level Data Link Control)   A WAN encapsulation that can be used over leased lines and circuit-switched connections. Does not have many features, but uses minimal network overhead when communicating. Cisco's version of HDLC is proprietary.

hold-down timer   A routing loop mitigation process in which a router ignores any information about an alternative route with a higher metric to a poisoned subnet for an amount of time.

hop   A metric determined by the number of routers along the destination path.

host mask   255.255.255.255 or /32 subnet mask used on loopback interfaces to represent a single host.

hostname *hostname*   A global configuration command to name the router.

HSSI (High-Speed Serial Interface)   A high-speed interface that offers up to 52Mbps transmission rates to the WAN from a Cisco router. The higher speed capacity is relevant if the corporate backbone requires high-speed Internet access and VPN connectivity.

HTTP (Hypertext Transfer Protocol) An Application layer protocol that enables web browsing with the transmission of Hypertext Markup Language (HTML) documents on the Internet.

HTTPS (Secure Hypertext Transfer Protocol) An Application layer protocol that enables secure web browsing using SSL. A secure connection is indicated when the URL begins with https:// or when there is a lock symbol in the lower-right corner of the web page that is being viewed.

hub A multiple port repeater. A smaller hub consists of four or five ports and might be called a workgroup hub. When data is received, the hub then retransmits that data on all the other ports.

hub-and-spoke design One of the lowest-cost designs in a packet-switched network. All offices connect to a central office (the hub) through a single virtual circuit connection. If the hub router goes down, all connectivity through the packet-switched network is lost.

I–J–K

ICMP (Internet Control Messaging Protocol) A Network layer protocol that provides ping and traceroute utilities.

idle timer/fast idle timer Configuration parameters used with DDR connections to set the amount of time the connection should stay online without seeing interesting traffic.

IDS (Intrusion Detection System) A passive device that listens to traffic passing through a network to generate alerts and issue TCP resets if necessary.

IETF Frame Relay Encapsulation An industry-standard Frame Relay encapsulation that can be used when communicating with non-Cisco routers through a Frame Relay service provider.

IGP (Interior Gateway Protocol) A routing protocol that advertises networks and metrics within an autonomous system.

IGRP (Interior Gateway Routing Protocol) A Cisco-proprietary distance vector routing protocol that uses a composite metric to determine the optimal path.

in-band Management signals traversing over the same networking paths and interfaces as the data stream.

information query A type of query that is sent via the Internet to resolve hostnames from IP addresses or vice versa.

infrared A wireless technology that uses infrared beams to pass data across the network. A television remote uses infrared technology to send requests to the television set. Speeds can reach a maximum of 16Mpbs, and signals are used for short distance communications.

inside global address NAT terminology that describes the public address assigned to the NAT gateway.

inside local address NAT terminology that describes the private addresses behind the NAT gateway.

Integrated Services Digital Network (ISDN) A circuit-switched network that combines multiple B channels that can handle 64Kbps each with a single signaling (D) channel to form a WAN connection between two locations.

interesting traffic   Used when configuring DDR to tell the router what traffic is valuable enough to initiate a call using the DDR connection.

interface configuration   A configuration mode that sets parameters specific to the interface.

interface *range media port_range*
A switch global configuration command that navigates several switch ports that will ultimately share similar configuration parameters.

internetwork   The connection of more than one network. These networks are linked by hardware devices to function as a larger single network. An internetwork can also be called an internet.

inter-VLAN routing   Traffic routed from one VLAN to another by using an external router or a Layer 3 switch.

inverse ARP   A method that allows a Frame Relay router to automatically discover the remote routers by sending Inverse ARP messages to each local DLCI number it receives from the service provider.

inverse mask/wildcard mask   A complete reversal of the subnet mask that is used primarily when configuring OSPF and access list.

IOS   The software developed and maintained by Cisco to support a full array of system functions, applications (including Internet applications), and network hardware in a single software package.

IP (Internet Protocol)   A Network layer protocol that uses logical or virtual addressing to get a packet from a source to its destination. IP addresses are used by routers to make forwarding decisions.

ip access-group   A command used to apply an access list to an interface.

ip address *address subnet_mask*   An interface configuration command that assigns an IP address to an interface.

ip address dhcp   An interface configuration command that dynamically obtains an IP address for the interface.

ip default-gateway *gateway_IP*   A switch global configuration command that sets a default route/gateway of last resort for a Layer 2 switch.

ip dhcp pool   A global configuration command that defines a DHCP address pool.

ip domain-lookup   A global configuration command that enables dynamic name resolution lookups.

ip host *hostname IP*   A global configuration command to create a static map of an IP address to a hostname.

ip name-server *dns_server_IP*   A global configuration command that specifies up to six DNS servers for dynamic resolution.

IP Security (IPsec)   A protocol framework that provides many types of security for network communication. IPsec is commonly used in VPN connections.

IPS (Intrusion Prevention System)   An active device that is inline with the traffic path on a network. An IPS listens promiscuously to all incoming traffic to identify attacks, which the system can then block.

IPv4 (IP version 4)   A version of IP addressing that uses 32-bit addresses grouped into four octets. Each octet has a minimum value of 0 and a maximum value of 255. IPv4 addresses are presented in dotted decimal format.

IPv6 (IP version 6)   An IP address format that was created in the event that the IPv4 address space is exhausted. IPv6 addresses are 128 bits long and are represented by 32 hexadecimal digits broken into eight smaller groups of 4 bits, which are separated by colons.

ISL (interswitch link)   A Cisco frame-tagging method over trunk ports that encapsulates the original frame with a 26-byte header and a 4-byte CRC.

L

LACP (Link Aggregation Control Protocol) An IEEE standardized dynamic bundling protocol for negotiating EtherChannel bundles.

LAN (local-area network)   An internetwork that is limited to a local or small geographic area. An example of a LAN would be the individual computers or workstations that are connected on one floor of a building.

LCP (Link Control Protocol)   A sublayer protocol of PPP responsible for negotiating authentication, multilink, compression, and callback.

learning   An STP port state in which the interface begins to build MAC addresses learned on the interface.

leased line   Typically the most expensive WAN connection that constructs a dedicated, point-to-point connection between locations.

line configuration   A configuration mode that sets parameters specific to the terminal line.

link-local address   An IPv6 address type that can only go as far as the Layer 2 domain. These addresses are autogenerated when an IPv6 node goes online and are assigned automatically.

link-state routing protocol   A class of routing protocols in which all possible link states are stored in an independent topology table in which the best routes are calculated and put into the routing table. The topology table is initially synchronized with discovered neighbors followed by frequent hello messages. These routing protocols are faster to converge than distance vector routing protocols.

listening   An STP port state in which the interface begins to transition to a forwarding state by listening and sending BPDUs. No user data sent.

LLC (Logical Link Control)   A Data Link sublayer defined by IEEE 802.2.

LMI (Local Management Interface)   The signaling method used between a Frame Relay service provider and the customer premises equipment.

local access rate/line speed   The maximum physical speed a WAN connection is capable of reaching.

login   A line configuration command that enables prompting of a password on the terminal lines.

longest-match rule   In routing logic, dictates that when there are several subnetted entries for a destination network, the smallest and most specific subnet is chosen over others.

loopback interface   A virtual interface that does not go down unless the router is turned off. Used by OSPF to determine the Router ID.

LRE (Long-Reach Ethernet) An Ethernet specification developed by Cisco to provide broadband service over existing telephone-grade or Category 1, 2, or 3 wiring. Speeds vary between 5 to 15Mbps and can reach a maximum segment length of up to 5000m.

LSA (Link State Advertisement) Used by OSPF to send hello messages and update information on attached interfaces, metrics used, and other variables.

LSU (Link State Update) A specific type of LSA that entails new information being sent to neighbor routers after an adjacency has been formed with that neighbor.

M

MAC (Media Access Control) A Data Link sublayer defined by IEEE 802.3.

MAC address A hard-coded (burned-in) address on the network interface controller (NIC) of the Physical layer node attached to the network.

MAN (Metropolitan Area Network) An inter-network that is larger than a LAN but smaller than or equal in size to a WAN.

management VLAN VLAN 1 by default. The management VLAN contains the switch's management IP address and CDP and VTP advertisements.

man-in-the-middle attack A type of access attack that occurs when a hacker eavesdrops or listens for network traffic and intercepts a data transmission. As soon as the transmission is intercepted, the untrustworthy host can position itself between the two communicating hosts, interpret the data, and steal information from the packets sent.

max-age timer The maximum length of time a bridge port saves its configuration BPDU information. The value is 20 seconds by default.

MD5 (Message Digest 5) A hashing algorithm created in 1991 by Ronald Rivest, an MIT professor. Uses a 128-bit hash.

Metro Ethernet A new type of technology allowing for low-cost, high-speed fiber connections between offices within metropolitan areas.

microsegmentation The process in which a switch creates a dedicated path for sending and receiving transmissions with each connected host. Each host then has a separate collision domain and a dedicated bandwidth.

MIMO (Multiple Input, Multiple Output) An implementation of 802.11 wireless technology that uses multiple antennas at both the transmitter and receiver to improve the performance of the wireless connection.

MPPC (Microsoft Point-to-Point Compression) A PPP compression algorithm developed by Microsoft for Windows dial-up clients.

modem A device that converts a digital signal into an analog signal for transmission over a telephone line. The signal is converted back into a digital format when it reaches the device on the other end of that telephone line.

multicast An Ethernet LAN address in which a frame can be sent to a group of devices in the same LAN. IEEE Ethernet multicast addresses always begin with

0100.5E in hexadecimal format. The last three bytes can be any combination.

multimode A type of fiber cable that is generally used for shorter distances and is ideal for a campus-sized network.

multiplexing Combining multiple messages over a single channel.

N

named access list An access list identified by a name rather than a number. Can be standard or extended, and allows the deletion of individual access list lines.

NAT (Network Address Translation) A technique that translates a private IP address to a public IP address for outbound transmission to the Internet. NAT also translates a public IP address to a private IP address for inbound transmission on the internal network.

native VLAN VLAN 1 by default. Traffic originating from the native VLAN is not tagged over the trunk link.

NAT overload Allows multiple internal clients to share a single Internet IP address using port numbers to distinguish requests.

NAT pool NAT terminology that describes a pool of addresses that a router can use for NAT translations.

NBMA (nonbroadcast multiaccess) A WAN network design that allows multiple clients to attach, but not send broadcast messages to each other. Frame Relay is an example of an NBMA network.

NCP (Network Control Protocol) A sublayer protocol of PPP responsible for enabling multiple Network layer protocols to work over a PPP-encapsulated WAN connection.

neighbor table A table used by link-state and balanced hybrid routing protocols that maintains all neighbors discovered by receiving hello messages from other routers using the same routing protocol.

network ID Also called a network number or subnet ID, this address is the first IP address in a network. Every host bit for the network ID address is turned off (or all 0s).

network interface A network component that provides connectivity from an end-user PC or laptop to the public network. Depending on the interface, you might see up to three light-emitting diodes (LEDs) that help to determine status of the connection.

Network layer Layer 3 of the OSI model. Determines the best path for packet delivery across the network. Routed protocols such as IP are used to determine logical addressing that can identify the destination of a packet or datagram. The most common network device found at the Network layer is a router; however, Layer 3 switches might also be implemented.

NEXT (Near-End Crosstalk) The crosstalk measured at the transmitting end of a cable.

NFS (Network File System) (pertaining to a session layer) A Session layer protocol that accesses remote resources transparently and represents files and directories as if local to the user system.

NFS (Network File System) (pertaining to an application layer) An Application layer protocol that allows users with different operating systems (that is, NT and Unix workstations) to share files.

NNTP (Network News Transfer Protocol) An Application layer protocol that offers access to Usenet newsgroup postings.

nonbroadcast multiaccess topology Consists of multiple devices that access the same medium and cannot hear each other's broadcasts and multicast messages such as Frame Relay networks.

no shutdown An interface configuration command that administratively enables an interface.

NTP (Network Time Protocol) An Application layer protocol that synchronizes clocks on the Internet to provide accurate local time on the user system.

NVRAM (Nonvolatile Random-Access Memory) A type of system memory that stores the startup configuration. This configuration is loaded when the router is booted.

O

ODR (On-Demand Routing) An enhancement to CDP that enables a stub router to advertise the connected IP prefix.

OSI model A layered architecture model created by the International Organization for Standardization (ISO) to internetwork various vendor specific networks.

OSPF (Open Shortest Path First) An open-standard classless routing protocol that uses cost as a metric and uses areas to minimize routing overhead.

OSPF priority An arbitrary number configured on an OSPF interface to influence a DR and BDR election. Default is 1.

Out-of-band Management signals traversing a dedicated channel separate from the data stream.

outside global address NAT terminology that describes an Internet valid address accessible from any device connected to the Internet.

outside local address NAT terminology that describes an Internet valid address as it is seen from the internal network.

P

packet A unit of data that contains control information and might also be referred to as a datagram. Packets are used by the Network layer of the OSI model.

packet sniffer A software program or piece of hardware that captures, decodes, and analyzes traffic sent over a network.

packet-switched network A type of WAN connection that establishes connections using virtual circuits. ATM, Frame Relay, and X.25 fall under this category of connection.

PAgP (Port Aggregation Protocol) A proprietary dynamic bundling protocol for negotiating EtherChannel bundles.

PAP (Password Authentication Protocol) A weak authentication type used with PPP encapsulation. Usernames and passwords are transmitted a single time in clear-text format.

partial-mesh design A packet-switched network design that compromises between cost and redundancy by providing key locations with multiple virtual circuit connections.

partial-mesh topology   A network topology that has direct connectivity between some of the network devices, but not all of them, such as the full mesh topology.

passive interface   A routing process command that defines an interface that stops sending routing updates. The interface still can accept routing updates.

password attack   A type of access attack in which a hacker attempts to obtain a password for a device.

password *password*   A line configuration command that specifies the password to be prompted on a terminal line.

PAT (Port Address Translation)   A technique that translates a Transport protocol connection (TCP or UDP) from an outside network host/port to an internal network host/port.

PDU (Protocol Data Unit)   A unit that includes the message and the protocol/control information from the forwarding layer of the OSI model.

Physical layer   Layer 1 of the OSI model. Moves bits between nodes. Electrical, mechanical, procedural, and functional requirements are defined at the Physical layer to assist with the activation, maintenance, and deactivation of physical connectivity between devices.

ping (Packet Internet Groper)   An echo request sent by a device that uses ICMP at the Network layer to validate that an IP address exists and can accept requests. The response is called an echo response.

ping sweep   A tool that sends an echo request to numerous host IP addresses at the same time to see which host(s) respond(s) with an echo reply.

POE (Power over Ethernet)   A technology that allows an end device to receive power over a copper Ethernet cable. End devices that might use PoE include IP telephones, wireless access points, video cameras, and card scanners.

point-to-multipoint/multipoint subinterface   A subinterface that allows multiple DLCI numbers to be mapped to remote IP addresses under the same logical interface.

point-to-point subinterface   A subinterface typically used for Frame Relay that assigns a single DLCI number to a single subinterface and creates a point-to-point style connection through a packet-switched cloud.

point-to-point topology   A network topology in which two routing devices are separated by a segment.

poison reverse   A routing loop mitigation process in which a router receives a poisoned route and overrides the split horizon rule to send the subnet as "possibly down" back to the source.

POP3 (Post Office Protocol 3)   An Application layer protocol that receives email by accessing an Internet server.

PortFast   A Cisco STP enhancement that skips the listening and leaning port states for end-devices.

port redirection   NAT terminology that describes statically translating from one port to another.

port scan   A software program that surveys a host network for open ports.

port security A method to limit the number of MAC addresses that are dynamically learned on a switch port.

POST (power-on self test) A test performed by a ROM chip to initially test the hardware on bootup.

PPP (Point-to-Point Protocol) A WAN encapsulation type that provides many features and is supported by nearly all router vendors.

PPP multilink An industry-standard feature that allows multiple connections to be bundled into a single, logical connection between two network locations.

PPPoA (PPP over ATM) An encapsulation typically used by DSL service providers to gain the features of PPP over an ATM connection.

PPPoE (PPP over Ethernet) An encapsulation typically used by DSL service providers to gain the features of PPP over an Ethernet connection.

predictor compression A dictionary-based compression type that attempts to predict the traffic patterns that will be sent over a WAN connection. Is good for links that have very few types of traffic. Uses more memory resources than the sister compression type, Stacker.

Presentation layer Layer 6 of the OSI model. Presents data to the Application layer and acts as a data format translator.

PRI (Primary Rate Interface) A type of ISDN connection that uses 23 B channels and a single D channel. Provides bandwidth equivalent to a T1 line.

private IP address An address that is not routable over the Internet. These include

the 10.0.0.0/8 network, the 172.16.0.0 to 172.31.255.255/16 networks, and the 192.168.0.0 to 192.168.255.255/24 networks.

privileged EXEC The highest privileged command mode, which allows full access to all commands.

process ID A number between 1 and 65535 that represents a unique instance of an OSPF process. The process ID is locally significant (it does not have to match in all routers in the OSPF autonomous system).

protect A port security violation action in which frames from unsecure MAC addresses are dropped until the number of MAC addresses drops below the maximum.

proxy ARP (Proxy Address Resolution Protocol) A protocol that allows a router to respond to an ARP request that has been sent to a remote host. Some UNIX machines (especially Solaris) rely on Proxy ARP versus default gateways.

public IP address An address that is routable over the Internet.

PVC (Permanent Virtual Circuit) A permanently established virtual circuit through a service provider network.

PVST (Per-VLAN Spanning Tree) An instance of Spanning Tree Protocol runs for each active VLAN in a switched network.

Q

Q.921 The ISDN D channel protocol used at the Data Link layer.

Q.931 The ISDN D channel protocol used at the Network layer.

QoS (quality of service)   The method of prioritizing certain types of traffic when congestion affects performance.

R

RAM (Random-Access Memory)   A type of memory that is used for short-term storage of a machine's running IOS and running configuration. This is the only type of system memory that is not permanent.

RARP (Reverse Address Resolution Protocol)   A protocol that maps a known MAC address to an IP address.

reconnaissance attack   A class of passive attack in which a hacker surveys a network and collects data for a future attack.

redistribution   A method of configuring routing protocols to advertise networks from other routing protocols.

`reload`   A privileged EXEC command to perform a reboot of the router or switch.

remote-access VPN   A VPN connection type that allows telecommuting or mobile workers to connect to the corporate network from their PCs.

repeater   A device consisting of a transmitter and a receiver. When the repeater receives a signal, it amplifies the signal and then retransmits. This effectively enables the signal to travel over a greater distance.

restrict   A port security violation action in which a violation increases the violation counter and an SNMP alert is generated.

`resume conn#`   A user or privileged EXEC command resumes a suspended Telnet session.

RF (radio frequency)   A method of broadcasting that uses alternating current to produce radio waves. RF typically is used in 802.11 wireless networking.

ring topology   A network topology that is set up so that one device is directly connected to two other devices on the same network. When a device emits a data signal transmission, it is sent in a single direction to the next connected device. The transmission continues to pass along each device successively until it arrives back at the original transmitting device. This method creates a ring or a loop.

RIP (Routing Information Protocol)   A standard distance vector routing protocol that uses hop count as its only metric.

RIPv2 (RIP version 2)   An enhancement to RIP to support classless updates, router authentication, and multicast updates.

ROM (Read-Only Memory)   A type of system memory that contains the basic code for booting a device and maintaining power-on self test (POST), ROM Monitor (ROMmon), bootstrap, and RxBoot.

ROMmon (ROM Monitor)   A small codeset in ROM that allows you to perform elementary functions to manually get the router or switch back to a functioning state.

root bridge   The base of the STP topology calculations elected based on the lowest Bridge ID.

root port   A nonroot bridge port that has the lowest cumulative cost to a root bridge.

routed protocol   A protocol such as IP that can be routed using a router.

route poison   A routing loop mitigation process in which a router sets a failed subnet to an infinite metric and advertises it to its neighbor.

router ID   The IP address by which a device is known to an OSPF autonomous system. Determined by the highest active loopback IP address that is configured when the OSPF process starts. If your router does not have a loopback interface, it uses the highest physical interface IP address.

router-on-a-stick   An inter-VLAN routing method by trunking to an external router with subinterfaces.

route summarization   The process of advertising multiple network IDs into a single route.

route update packet   A packet that sends updates to neighbor routers about all networks connected to that internetwork and is supported by routing protocols such as RIP, EIGRP, and OSPF.

routing protocol   A protocol that exchanges network routes between routing devices to dynamically advertise networks. RIP, OSPF, and EIGRP are examples of routing protocols.

routing table   The routing logic stored in RAM, where packet forwarding decisions are made.

RPC (Remote Procedure Call)   A Session layer protocol that is the basis for client/server communications. Calls are created on the client and then carried out on the server.

RSTP (Rapid Spanning Tree Protocol)   IEEE 802.1w RSTP incorporates similar technologies as Cisco's PortFast, UplinkFast, and BackboneFast.

running-config   The active configuration running in RAM.

RxBoot   Also known as a mini-IOS, RxBoot is a limited IOS in ROM with enough functionality to load an IOS from a TFTP server.

S

SAN (Storage-Area Network)   A subnetwork or special-purpose network. Allows users on a larger network to connect various data storage devices with clusters of data servers.

SDM (Security Device Manager)   A web-based tool that was developed by Cisco for its IOS software-based routers. SDM gives users the option to configure and monitor a router without relying heavily on the CLI.

server mode   The default VTP mode that enables you to create, modify, and delete VLANS. These VLANs are advertised to other switches and saved in the VLAN database.

service password-encryption   A global configuration command that encrypts all passwords that are clear text in the configuration.

Session layer   Layer 5 of the OSI model. Handles dialog control among devices.

setup mode   An interactive dialog session to establish an initial configuration. Setup mode is automatically loaded when there is a missing startup-config in NVRAM.

SHA-1 (Secure Hash Algorithm 1)   A hashing algorithm published in 1995 by the NIST to increase the strength of the hash algorithm from the original MD5 standard. Uses a 160-bit hash.

show cdp neighbors A user or privileged EXEC command to display the device ID, local interface, holdtime, capability, platform, and port ID learned from CDP advertisements of directly connected neighbors.

show cdp neighbors detail A user or privileged EXEC command to display the output of the show cdp neighbors command in addition to the Cisco IOS version and the Layer 3 address of directly connected neighbors.

show controller A user or privileged EXEC command to display the interface microcode including whether a DTE or DCE cable connected to the interface.

show dhcp lease A user or privileged EXEC command to display the IP address assigned to the interface(s) configured by the ip address dhcp command.

show flash A user or privileged EXEC command to display the filenames and sizes of IOS files stored in flash memory.

show interfaces A user or privileged EXEC command to display the status of the interfaces as well as physical and logical address, encapsulation, bandwidth, reliability, load, MTU, duplex, broadcasts, collisions, and frame errors.

show ip dhcp bindings A user or privileged EXEC command to display the IP addresses dynamically assigned to devices from the DHCP-enabled router.

show ip interface brief A user or privileged EXEC command to display a summary of the interface statuses and logical addressing.

show sessions A user or privileged EXEC command to verify active Telnet sessions initiated from local device.

show version A user or privileged EXEC command to display the IOS version, system uptime, amount of RAM, NVRAM, flash memory, and configuration register.

SIA (Stuck In Active) timer Enabled when an EIGRP router goes into an active state in the event of a topology change. The SIA timer is the amount of time a neighbor EIGRP router has to respond to a query. The default is 180 seconds.

single-mode A type of fiber cable that is used to span longer distances than multi-mode fiber. Single-mode fiber also allows for a higher data rate and faster data transmission speeds.

site-to-site VPN A VPN configuration that directly replaces a private line connection by establishing a permanent or semipermanent connection between sites.

SMTP (Simple Mail Transfer Protocol) An Application layer protocol that sends email across the network.

smurf attack A type of DoS attack in which multiple broadcast ping requests are sent to a single target from a spoofed IP address.

SNMP (Simple Network Management Protocol) An Application layer protocol that monitors the network and manages configurations.

SPID (Service Provider Identifier) Sometimes required on ISDN lines upon dial-in for billing purposes.

split-horizon A distance vector routing protocol loop-prevention mechanism that prevents data from being sent back in the direction from which it was received.

SQL (Structured Query Language)   A Session layer protocol that functions as a query language that requests, updates, and manages databases.

SSH (Secure Shell)   A protocol that enables terminal encrypted connections to remote devices with an IP address.

SSL (Secure Socket Layer)   A protocol that provides a secure channel between two devices at the Application layer (Layer 7) of the OSI model.

SSL VPN   Also known as WebVPN. Allows users to connect to a VPN without requiring a client installation. Users access the VPN using a secure web page.

stacker compression   A flat compression type that uses the same compression algorithm for all traffic types. Is a good compression for links that have many types of traffic. Uses more processor resources than the sister compression type, Predictor.

standard access list   A list of permit and deny statements that can match network traffic based on the source IP address only.

star topology   A network topology that is the most commonly implemented network design. With this topology, there is a central device with separate connections to each end node. Each connection uses a separate cable. You might also hear this called a hub-and-spoke topology.

startup-config   A saved configuration stored in NVRAM that is loaded when the router or switch boots.

static Frame Relay map   A manual method of mapping a local DLCI number to the remote IP address it is capable of reaching over a Frame Relay cloud.

static NAT   Manually maps a NAT-translated address, typically between a public Internet address and a private internal address.

static route   A manual entry that an administrator enters into the configuration that describe the destination network and the next hop.

sticky secure MAC address   A MAC address dynamically learned using port security that the switch automatically configures to be secure MAC addresses.

store-and-forward   A latency-varying transmission method that buffers the entire frame and calculates the CRC before forwarding the frame.

STP (Spanning Tree Protocol)   A Layer 2 protocol that eliminates loops caused by redundant connections on a switched network.

STP (Shielded Twisted-pair) cable   A branch of twisted-pair cabling that uses an additional shield that provides an additional reduction of interference and attenuation.

stub network   A network with a single entry and exit point.

stub routing   An EIGRP routing feature that minimizes convergence in hub-and-spoke networks.

subinterface   A logical extension of a physical interface that is treated by the IOS as an actual interface.

subnet (subnetwork)   A smaller network created from a Class A, B, or C network.

subnet mask   A 32-bit address used by a network device to identify which part of an IP address is the subnet portion.

subnetting   The process of breaking a large network of IP addresses into smaller, more manageable address ranges.

successor route   The route in a topology table with the lowest feasible distance to a subnet. This route is also placed in the routing table.

supernet   A summarized route.

SVI (Switched Virtual Interface)   Created in a Layer 3 switch to perform inter-VLAN routing.

switch   A multiport bridge that uses an Application-Specific Integrated Circuit (ASIC) to forward frames at the Data Link layer. Each port of the switch has dedicated bandwidth.

Switched Virtual Circuit (SVC)   An on-demand virtual circuit through a service provider network.

switchport trunk allowed vlan   An interface configuration command that specifies which VLANs or VLAN ranges are permitted over a trunk link.

synchronization   A Rapid Spanning Tree Protocol process of blocking all nonedge point-to-point links before sending a proposal to ensure that a change in a switched topology gets accurately synchronized with all other local ports.

synchronous   A serial interface that synchronizes clocks for the bit stream of both the sending and receiving end of a serial link.

SYSLOG   A management feature that collects log messages from a Cisco device and sends them to a syslog server to keep a record of any network occurrences.

T

TCP (Transmission Control Protocol)   A reliable connection-oriented Transport layer protocol. TCP uses acknowledgments, sequencing, and flow control to ensure reliability.

TCP Established   A type of extended access list entry that can be added to allow return traffic, satisfying a client request.

TCP/IP (Transmission Control Protocol/Internet Protocol)   A suite of protocols developed by the Department of Defense to help develop internetworks.

TCP SYN attack   A type of DoS attack in which a SYN request is sent to a device with a spoofed IP address. The attacking system does not acknowledge the resulting SYN-ACK, which causes the session connection queues to fill up and stop taking new connection requests.

Telnet   A TCP/IP protocol that provides terminal emulation to a remote host by creating a virtual terminal.

telnet IP_address   A user or privileged EXEC command to initiate a virtual terminal session to a remote device.

terminal editing key   A shortcut key to navigate the cursor in lieu of the arrow keys.

TFTP (Trivial File Transfer Protocol)   An Application layer protocol that is a bare-bones version of FTP that does not provide access to directories. With TFTP, you can simply send and receive files.

token passing   A process in which a 3-byte token (or special bit pattern) is inserted in a frame and passed in a single direction from one node to another until it forms a complete loop. The node that has possession of the token is the only one that can send data at any given time on that LAN. Because only one node can send data at a time, collisions are avoided.

Token Ring   A LAN protocol that uses a token-passing media access technology in a physical ring or physical star topology, which creates a logical ring topology. Token Ring is defined by the IEEE 802.5 standard.

topology table   A table used by link-state and balanced hybrid routing protocols that maintains every possible route to any given subnet along with its associated metric.

traceroute   A Network layer tool that traces the route or path taken from a client to a remote host. Traceroute also reports the IP addresses of the routers at each next hop on the way to the destination.

transparent bridge   A bridge that goes unnoticed by the other devices on a network.

transparent mode   A VTP mode in which you can create, modify, and delete VLANs only on the local switch. Transparent switches do not participate in VTP but forward VTP advertisements received from servers. Also saves VLAN configuration in a VLAN database.

Transport layer   Layer 4 of the OSI model. Responsible for end-to-end connections and data delivery between two hosts. The capability to segment and reassemble data is a key function of this layer.

triggered update   A routing loop mitigation process in which a router immediately shoots out an update as opposed to waiting for the normal update interval.

Triple DES (3DES) algorithm   Produced to address the weaknesses of DES. This algorithm did not reinvent the wheel of encryption, so to speak. Instead, it ran the DES algorithm three times with different keys (thus the term 3DES). This significantly improved the strength of the original DES algorithm.

trunk   An interconnection between switches that multiplexes traffic from all VLANs to other switches.

trust exploitation   A type of access attack that occurs when a device or group of devices on a shared segment erroneously trust information that has been provided by an untrustworthy source.

U

UDP (User Datagram Protocol)   An unreliable connectionless Transport layer protocol. UDP headers contain only the source and destination ports, a length field, and a checksum.

unicast   An Ethernet LAN address that identifies the MAC address of an individual LAN or NIC card.

unique/site-local address   An IPv6 address type that can expand to the size of an organization and that is used to describe the boundary of the organizational network. This is the private addressing for IPv6.

UplinkFast A Cisco STP enhancement that skips the listening and learning port states on redundant trunk links to distribution layer switch.

user EXEC An initial command mode with limited commands to test connectivity and verify statistics.

UTP (Unshielded Twisted-Pair) cable A branch of twisted-pair cabling that uses four pairs of colored wire. UTP is vulnerable to EMI and uses an RJ-45 connector. There are five categories of UTP cable, labeled Category 1 to Category 5.

V

V.35 A physical serial interface standard on CSU/DSU devices.

variance A multiplier used in IGRP and EIGRP that enables these routing protocols to load balance over unequal paths.

virtual circuit A logical connection through a service provider network that makes the attached routers believe they are directly connected.

VLAN A Layer 2 method of segmenting broadcast domains. Each VLAN created in a switch represents a logical grouping of devices into their own broadcast domain.

VLSM (Variable-Length Subnet Mask) A design that allows you to allocate an IP subnet according to the needed number of hosts for that subnet. Requires classless routing.

VMPS (VLAN Membership Policy Server) A dynamic method of associating MAC addresses with VLANs.

voice VLAN Sometimes called auxiliary VLANs, voice VLANs create a separate broadcast domain on an access port to logically segment and administer VoIP traffic.

VPN (Virtual Private Network) A type of network connection that allows secure transmission of network data over the Internet between two or more locations.

VTP (VLAN Trunking Protocol) A Layer 2 Cisco-proprietary protocol that minimizes the administrative overhead involved in replicating VLAN configurations by having a VTP server advertise the VLAN configurations.

VTP domain A collection of switches participating in VTP advertisements.

VTP pruning Reduces unnecessary flooded traffic, such as broadcast, multicast, unknown, and flooded unicast packets to other switches by repressing flooded traffic to switches from inactive VLANs.

W

WAN (wide-area network) An internetwork that covers more than one geographical area.

WebVPN Also known as an SSL VPN. Allows users to connect to a VPN without requiring a client installation. Users access the VPN using a secure web page.

Wi-Fi Alliance A group of large companies that own and control the Wi-Fi Certified logo and ensure that 802.11 wireless equipment is cross-compatible.

wildcard mask Sometimes referred to as an inverse mask. Used to identify to the IOS how much of an IP address should be applied to a criterion in a configuration statement. A 0 means that the corresponding bit must match. A 1 means to ignore the corresponding bit value.

windowing   A process used by TCP in which windows are determined by the receiving system to limit the amount of data segments (bytes) that can be sent by the source device without an acknowledgment from the recipient. Window sizes vary and can change throughout the duration of a connection.

wireless cell   Defines a region of coverage by a wireless access point.

wireless channel   Defines distinct ranges of radio frequencies that are used for 802.11 transmission. Your goal in designing wireless networks is to ensure that wireless coverage from adjacent access points uses different channels so as not to interfere with each other.

wireless fidelity (Wi-Fi)   A wireless networking standard defined by IEEE 802.11. The 802.11 standard allows for transmission speeds of up to 1 to 2Mbps and uses a radio frequency of 2.4GHz.

wireless roaming   The ability of a wireless client to move between different wireless access points without losing network connectivity.

WPA (Wi-Fi Protected Access)   Offers a stronger encryption scheme than the original WEP standard without changing wireless hardware requirements. Implements Temporal Key Integrity Protocol (TKIP) and the Message Integrity Code (MIC).

WPA2 (Wi-Fi Protected Access 2)   Also known as 802.11i. Implements a stronger security system for wireless networks using the Advanced Encryption Standard (AES) encryption cipher.

X–Y–Z

X.21   A physical serial interface standard on CSU/DSU devices.

X.25   The predecessor packet-switched technology to Frame Relay. X.25 used excessive error checking, which slowed down the connection.

X Window   A Session layer protocol that communicates with remote UNIX machines and allows the user to operate the device as if it is attached locally.

zero subnet rule   The first subnet in a network that has all binary 0s in the subnet field.

Index

NUMBERS

3-layer hierarchical models, 33

10-Gigabit Ethernet (10GbE), 99

10BASE-FL Ethernet networks, 95

10BASE-T Ethernet networks, 95

10BASE2 Ethernet networks, 94

10BASE5 Ethernet networks, 94

100BASE-FX, 96

100BASE-T4, 96

100BASE-TX, 96

802.11 (wireless networks), 476-477

    802.11a, 65, 483

    802.11b, 65, 483

    802.11g, 65, 483-484

    802.11i (WPA2), wireless network security, 498

    802.11n, 484

    channel surfing, 481

    data transmission, 478-479

    IEEE, 477

    ITU-R, 477

    overlapping signals, 480-481

    RF bands, 479-480

    Wi-Fi Alliance, 477

802.1x (wireless authentication), 499-500

802.3. *See* Ethernet; IEEE 802.3

802.3u. *See* Fast Ethernet

1000BASE-T, 97

1000BASE-X, 98

A

AAA (Authentication, Authorization, Accounting), network security, 130, 133

access attacks, 559

man-in-the-middle attacks, 124

password attacks, 123

port redirection, 124

trust exploitation, 124

Access layer (hierarchical models), 34

ACK packet, 28

ACL (Access Control Lists), network security, 130, 133

ad hoc wireless networks, 501

administrative distances (IOS), 324

Advanced NAT wizard (NAT Configuration window), 401-407

ambiguous command syntax errors, 566

answers (practice exams), 602-609

AP (Access Points), wireless networks, 501, 507

Application layer

OSI model, 15-16, 550

protocols list, 551-552

TCP/IP model, 26-27

ARP (Address Resolution Protocol), 33, 144-145

asynchronous serial interfaces, 190

ATM (Asynchronous Transfer Mode), WAN, 524-525

attenuation, 58

authentication

802.1x (wireless authentication), 499-500

PPP, 527

callbacks, 529-530

CHAP, 528-529, 533-534

compression, 530

configuring, 532-534

MPPC, 531

MPPP, 531

PAP, 528

Predictor algorithm, 530

Stacker algorithm, 530

wireless networks, 578

autonomous systems, 340

auxiliary ports, 212

password configuration, 459-460

User EXEC access, securing, 250

B

backups, TFTP servers

routers

configurations, 269-271

IOS files, 270

switches

configurations, 269-271

IOS files, 270

bandwidth, 58, 554

bandwidth command, 256

banner motd (message of the day command), 244

banners

login, creating, 244

SDM, changing in, 299-301

baseband, WAN, 520

Basic NAT wizard (NAT Configuration window), 397-400

BGP (Border Gateway Protocols), 340

binary, 145

binary-to-decimal conversion, 146-147

converting to decimals, 561

decimal-to-binary conversion, 148-149, 157-158

blocked ports, 431, 435

Bluetooth technology, 66

Boolean AND, 154-155

boot processes, IOS, 564

boot system command, 243

bootstrap process, 215

BPDU (Bridge Protocol Data Units)

blocked ports, 435

designated ports, 434

root ports, 432-433

BRI (Basic Rate Interface), 189-190, 557

bridges, 101-103, 571

blocked ports, 435

Bridge ID, 431-433

designated ports, 434

diameters, 438

frame-forwarding, 428

MAC filtering, 104

primary tasks of, 102

root bridges, 431-433

broadband, WAN, 520

broadcast addresses, 89

broadcast IP, 152, 157

broadcast storms, 430

BSS (Basic Service Sets), WAP, 501

bus topologies, 54

C

cable

coaxial cable, 59-60

cross-over cable, 62

fiber-optic cable, 63-64, 554

rolled cable, 63

straight-through cable, 61-62

twisted-pair cable, 60-63, 554

call setups. *See* three-way handshakes

callbacks, PPP authentication, 529-530

CAM (Content Addressable Memory) tables, 426

catalyst switches, 458-461, 572

CD-ROM

installing, 612-613

test modes, 611

CDP (Cisco Discovery Protocol), 272

disabling, 275

Layer 2 security, 464

no cdp enable command, 275

no cdp run command, 275

show cdp neighbors command, 273

certification mode (CD-ROM), 611

channel surfing (wireless networks), 481

CHAP (Challenge Handshake Authentication Protocol), PPP, 528-529, 533-534, 581-582

CIDR (Classless Interdomain Routing), 155, 339, 561

circuit-switched networks, 519, 580

Cisco 3-layer hierarchical models. *See* hierarchical models

classful network boundaries, RIP, 369

Classful Routing, 333-334, 575

Classless Routing, 333-340, 575

clear ip nat translations * command, troubleshooting NAT, 414

clock rate command, router configuration, 256

coaxial cable, 59-60

collision domains, segmenting/creating, 100

compression, PPP authentication, 530-531, 534-535

config-register command, 242

configure command, 222. *See also* Global Configuration

configuring

default routers, SDM, 329-330

NAT overload via SDM

advanced configuration, 401-407

basic configuration, 397-400

editing configurations, 407-410

verifying configurations, 410-413

NAT via SDM, 397

PPP

authentication, 532-534

compression, 534-535

RIP, 368-370, 373, 577

RIPv2, 372

routers

assigning duplexes, 255

assigning IP addresses, 254

assigning speed to, 255

backing up IOS files via TFTP servers, 270

backing up via TFTP servers, 269-271

bandwidth command, 256

clock rate command, 256

enabling interfaces, 255

LAN-specific commands, 255

no keepalives command, 255

no shutdown command, 255

returning to default configurations, 257

saving configurations, 256

verifying configurations, 259-260

WAN-specific commands, 256

SDM

banners, 299-301

domain names, 299-301

global configurations, 298-307

hostnames, 299-301

router interface configuration, 308-310

secret passwords, 299-301

static routers, SDM, 329-330

switches

assigning IP addresses via DHCP, 440-441

assigning management IP addresses to, 439

backing up IOS files via TFTP servers, 270

backing up via TFTP servers, 269-271

defining default gateways, 439

multiple switch interfaces, 441

returning to default configurations, 257

Connection-Oriented Communication sessions, 28

console access, securing to USER EXEC, 248-249

console ports, 210-211

context-sensitive help, 565

copy command, 256, 272, 568

copy running-config flash command, 271

copy tftp flash command, 271

Core layer (hierarchical models), 35-36

counts to infinity, mitigating, 363

CPE (Customer Premise Equipment), 191

CRC (Cyclic Redundancy Checks), 428

cross-over cable, 62, 554

crosstalk, 59, 554

crypto key generate rsa command, 247-248

CSMA/CD (Carrier Sense Multiple Access Collision Detection), 94, 429

CSU/DSU (Channel Service Units/Data Service Units), 191-192, 522

Ctrl+Shift+6 keyboard shortcut, suspending Telnet sessions, 276-277

custom mode (CD-ROM), 611

cut-through method (frame forwarding), 428

D

Data Link layer, 100

bridges, 101-104

Ethernet

addressing, 87-90

framing, 91-92

FDDI protocols, 86-87

switches, 102-105

OSI model, 21-23, 550

Token Ring protocols, 84-85

Data Link WAN encapsulations, 523-525

data packets, Network layer (OSI model) routing, 170

data transmission, wireless networks, 478-479

DCE (Data Communications Equipment), 23, 190, 557

DDoS (Distributed Denial of Service) attacks, 127

dead/invalid timers, 367

debug command, 268-269, 375

debug ppp authentication command, 538, 582

debug spanning-tree command, 444

decimals

   binary-to-decimal conversion, 146-147

   decimal-to-binary conversion, 148-150, 157-158, 561

   decimal-to-hexadecimal conversion, 150-151

default gateways (routing), 320-321

default routes, 328, 573

   configuring via SDM, 329-330

   verifying, 330-331

delays (forward), 438

demarcation points, 191

description command, assigning descriptions to router interfaces, 255

designated ports, STP, 434

desktop layer (hierarchical models). *See* Access layer (hierarchical models)

Destination Unreachable messages, ICMP, 267

device monitoring, SDM, 310

DHCP (Dynamic Host Configuration Protocol), 571

   IOS

      ip dhcp excluded-address ip-address command, 279

      ip dhcp pool poolname command, 278

      show ip dhcp binding command, 280

   IP addresses, assigning to switches, 440-441

   router amnesia, 280

   SDM, configuring, 305-307

dial-on-demand connections (WAN), 519

discovery protocol, 570

distance vector routing loops, preventing, 576

distance vector routing protocols, 340-341, 358-359

distribution frames, 64

Distribution layer (hierarchical models), 35

DNS (Domain Name Servers)

   SDM, configuring, 304

   TCP/UDP support, 30

DoD (Department of Defense) model. *See* TCP/IP model

domains

   collision domains, segmenting/creating, 100

   names

      configuring resolution, 246-247

      changing in SDM, 299-301

DoS (Denial of Service) attacks, 559

   DDoS attacks, 127

   wireless networks, 495

DRAM (Dynamic Random Access Memory), 193. *See also* RAM

DS1 (Digital Signal level 1) services, 190

DTE (Data Terminal Equipment), 23, 191-192, 557

duplexes

   interfaces, 572

   logic, 105-106

   router assignments, 255

dynamic NAT (Network Address Translation), 393, 580

dynamic routing protocols, 331, 574

   distance vector routing protocols, 340-341

   hybrid protocols, 341

   interior/exterior gateway routing protocols, 340

   link-state routing protocols, 341

   routed protocols versus, 331

E

Edit NAT Configuration window (SDM), 407-410

EGP (Exterior Gateway Protocol), 574

EIA/TIA (Electronic Industries Association/Telecommunications Industry Association), 192

EMI (Electomagnetic Interference), 59

enable password command, 245, 253, 567

enable secret command, 245, 253, 461, 567

encapsulation, 24

encryption

  IPsec, 132-133

  SSH, 132-133

  SSL, 132-133

  wireless networks, 496-498, 578

erase startup-config command, 257

ESS (Extended Service Sets), wireless AP, 501

Ethernet, 87, 93

  10-Gigabit Ethernet (10GbE), 99

  10BASE-FL, 95

  10BASE-T, 95

  10BASE2, 94

  10BASE5, 94

  802.3 characteristics, 95

  802.3u standards, 97

  802.3z standards, 99

  addressing, 87-90

  Fast Ethernet, 96

  framing, 91-92

  Gigabit Ethernet

    1000BASE-T, 97

    1000BASE-X, 98

    GBIC, 189

    ports, 189

  LRE, 100

  Metro Ethernet, WAN, 521

  switch interfaces. *See* ports

exams (practice)

  answers, 602-609

  MeasureUp, 612-613

EXEC

  IOS access, gaining, 564

  ping command, 267

  Privileged EXEC, 221-222

    debug command, 268-269

    passwords, assigning to, 245

    ping command, 268

    securing, 567

    Telnet, virtual terminal access, 277

    terminal monitor command, 277-278

  sessions. *See* terminal options

  Telnet, virtual terminal access, 276-278

  User EXEC, 220

    auxiliary access, securing, 250

    console access, securing, 248-249

    securing, 566

    securing access to Telnet, 250-253

    SSH access, securing, 250-253

    virtual terminal access, 277

exec-timeout command, 249, 461

exterior/interior gateway routing protocols, 340

F

Fast Ethernet, 96

FDDI (Fiber Distributed Data Interface) protocol, 86-87

feature sets (IOS), 194

FEXT (Far-End Crosstalk), 59

fiber-optic cable, 63-64, 554

files, IOS naming conventions, 558

filtering MAC addresses, 427

firewalls, 132-133

Flash, 193

  copy running-config flash command, 271

  copy tftp flash command, 271

  show flash command, 264

flash updates (routing), 366

floating static routes, 327, 573

FLSM (Fixed Length Subnet Masks), 334

forward delays, 438

fragment-free method (frame forwarding), 428

fragmentation, MLPPP, 531

frame-forwarding, 426-428, 571

Frame Relays, WAN, 524

full-duplex connections, switches, 429

full-duplex modes, 105

G

gain, 67

gateways

    routing

        default gateways, 320-321

        interior/exterior gateway routing protocols, 340

    switches, defining default gateways, 439

GBIC (Gigabit Interface Converters), 189

Gigabit Ethernet

    10-Gigabit Ethernet (10GbE), 99

    1000BASE-T, 97

    1000BASE-X, 98

    GBIC, 189

    ports, 189

Global Configuration, 222-223

    banner motd (message of the day command), 244

    boot sequences, changing, 242-243

    boot system command, 243

    commands list, 566

    config-register command, 242

    crypto key generate rsa command, 247-248

    domain name resolution, configuring, 246-247

    enable password command, 245

    enable secret command, 245

    host names, changing, 244

    hostname command, 244

    interface configuration, 223

    ip dhcp excluded-address ip-address command, 279

    ip domain-name command, 247

    ip host command, 246

    ip name-server command, 247

    line configuration, 224

    login banners, creating, 244

    no cdp enable command, 275

    no cdp run command, 275

    Privileged EXEC mode, assigning passwords to, 245

    service password-encryption command, 246

    service timestamp command, 269

    SSH, enabling, 247-248

    SDM, 298

        banners, 299-301

        DHCP, 305-307

        DNS, 304

        domain names, 299-301

        hostnames, 299-301

        router access, 303

        secret passwords, 299-301

global IPv6 addresses, 563

global/local (NAT), 395

H

hacking wireless networks, 495

half-duplex connections, switches, 429

half-duplex modes, 105

hashing passwords, 529

HDLC (High-level Data Link Control), 524-525, 581

help, technical support, 614

hexadecimals, 150-151

hierarchical models, 33

hold-down timers, 366

hostname command, 244

hostnames, changing, 244, 299-301

hosts, calculating in subnets, 562

HSSI (High-Speed Serial Interface), 190

HTTP (Hypertext Transfer Protocol), 212

hubs, 67

hybrid routing protocols, 341

I

IANA (Internet Assigned Numbers Authority), 145, 156, 561

ICMP (Internet Control Messaging Protocol), 32-33, 144

    Destination Unreachable messages, 267

    ping command, 267

    traceroute command, 268

IDF (Intermediate Distribution Frames), 64

IDS (Intrusion Detection Systems), 133

IEEE (Institute of Electrical and Electronic Engineers), 477

IEEE 802.3. See Ethernet

IEEE 802.3ab. See Gigabit Ethernet

IEEE 802.3u. See Fast Ethernet

IEEE 802.3z. See Gigabit Ethernet

IFS (Integrated File System), 272

IGP (Interior Gateway Protocol), 340, 574

image files, naming (IOS), 195

incomplete command syntax errors, 566

information queries (reconnaissance attacks), 126

infrared technology, 65

inside global addresses (NAT), 395

inside local addresses (NAT), 395

inside/outside (NAT), 395

installing

    CD-ROM, 612-613

    SDM, 297

interface configuration (Global Configuration), 223, 568

interface range command, 441

interface status values (show commands), 569

interfaces. See networks, interfaces

interior/exterior gateway routing protocols, 340

Internet layer (TCP/IP model), 31-33

internetworks, 10

    LAN, 11

    layered architecture. See OSI (Open Systems Interconnection) model

    MAN, 12

    SAN, 13

    VAN, 14

    WAN, 12-13

invalid input syntax errors, 566

invalid/dead timers, 367

IOS (Internetworking Operating System), 193-195

    administrative distances, 324

    boot process, 564

    commands

        abbreviations, 226

        common syntax errors, 227-229

        listing, 224-225

        shortcut keys, 226-227

    configuration files, creatin static entries, 246-247

    context-sensitive help, 565

    DHCP

        ip dhcp excluded-address ip-address command, 279

        ip dhcp pool poolname command, 278

        show ip dhcp binding command, 280

    editing keystrokes, 565

    EXEC access, 564

    feature sets, 194

    file naming conventions, 558

Global Configuration. *See also* configure
command
    interface configuration, 223
    line configuration, 224
image files, naming, 195
loading, router/switches start-up, 215-218
navigation modes, 565
network security, 131-133
Privileged EXEC, 221-222, 567
routers, backing up via TFTP servers, 270
show flash command, 264
show version command, 264-265
SSH, 567
syntax errors, 566
trains, 194
Usec EXEC, 220, 566

IP (Internet Protocol) addresses, 31, 145
binary
    binary-to-decimal conversion, 146-147
    decimal-to-binary conversion, 148-149,
    157-158
Boolean AND, 154-155
broadcast IP, 152, 157
hexadecimals, 150-151
IPv4
    address classes, 151-153
    private (RFC 1918) addressing, 156
    subnet masks, 154-157, 163
    subnetting IP, 156-167
management addresses, assigning to switches, 439
NAT, 156, 391, 580
network ID, 152
routers
    assigning to, 254
    verifying assignment in, 280
SDM, assigning to, 308
subnet ID, 152

subnets, 562
switches, assigning to via DHCP, 440-441
ip address dhcp command, 440
ip default-gateway command, 440
**ip dhcp excluded-address ip-address command,
279, 571**
ip dhcp pool poolname command, 278, 571
ip domain-name command, 247
ip host command, 246
ip name-server command, 247
ip nat inside command, NAT overload configuration, 399
ip nat outside command, NAT overload configuration, 399
**IPS (Intrusion Prevention Systems), 132-133,
500**
IPsec (Internet Protocol Security), network security, 132-133
IPv4 (Internet Protocol version 4), 560-561. *See
also* CIDR
    address classes, 151-153
    IPv6 integration, 563
    private (RFC 1918) addressing, 156
    subnet masks, 154-157, 163
    subnetting IP, 156-158
        calculating hosts, 159-160
        calculating increments, 162-165
        calculating networks, 161-162
        determining range of valid IP, 165-167
        zero subnet rule, 162
IPv6 addresses, 562-563
**ISDN (Integrated Services Digital Network), BRI,
189-190**
**ISO HDLC (High-level Data Link Control), 527,
581**
**ITU-R (International Telecommunication Union-
Radiocommunication Sector), 477**

J - K - L

keyboard shortcuts, suspending Telnet sessions, 276-277

keystrokes, IOS editing, 565

LAN (Local Area Networks), 11
  interfaces, 188-189
  router configuration, 255
  WLAN
    hacking, 495
    Spread Spectrum Wireless LAN, 555

LAPB (X.25 Link Access Procedure, Balanced), WAN Data Link encapsulations, 524

Layer 1, 23. See also Physical layer

Layer 2 security, 21-23, 462-464. See also Data Link layer

Layer 3, 20. See also Network Layer (OSI model)

Layer 3 switches, 167, 170, 563-564

Layer 4, 18-19. See also Transport layer

Layer 5, 18. See also Session layer

Layer 6, 17. See also Presentation layer

Layer 7, 15-16. See also Application layer

layered architectures. See OSI model

LCP (Link Control Protocol)
  HDLC, 581
  PPP authentication, 527
    callbacks, 529-530
    CHAP, 528-529, 533-534
    compression, 530
    MPPC, 531
    MPPP, 531
    PAP, 528
    Predictor algorithm, 530
    Stacker algorithm, 530

leased line connections, WAN, 519, 580

Line Configuration, 224
  enable password command, 253
  enable secret command, 253
  exec-timeout command, 249
  logging synchronous command, 249
  service password-encryption command, 253
  User EXEC, securing
    auxiliary access, 250
    console access, 248-249
    SSH access, 250-253
    Telnet access, 250-253

link-local IPv6 addresses, 563

link-state routing protocol, 341

LLC (Logical Link Controls), 22-23

local/global (NAT), 395

logging synchronous command, 249

login banners, creating, 244

longest match rule, 343

loops (routing), 360-362
  counts to infinity, 363
  invalid/dead timers, 367
  route poisoning, 364-366
  split horizons, 363-364
  triggered updates, 366

lower layers (OSI model), 18

LRE (Long Reach Ethernet), 100

M

MAC (Media Access Control) addresses, 21-22.
See also Ethernet, addressing
  CAM tables, 426
  definition of, 556
  filtering, 427
  ports, limiting in, 462
  router assignments, 168
  static MAC addresses, switch port security, 463

MAC (Media Acces Control) filtering, bridges, 104

man-in-the-middle attacks, network security, 124

management IP addresses, assigning to switches, 439

MAN (Metropolitan Area Networks), 12

mapping NAT port numbers, 407

max age timers, 437

maximum hop counts, 576

MDF (Main Distribution Frames), 64

MeasureUp practice tests, 612-613

memory
    components, of, 193
    types of, 557

mesh topologies, 57

Metro Ethernet, WAN, 521

microsegmentation, 106

mitigating network attacks, 130-133, 559

MLPPP (Multilink Point-to-Point Protocol), PPP authentication, 531

modules (routers), 196-197

MPPC (Microsoft Point-to-Point Compression), PPP authentication, 531

multicast addresses, 89

multicast IPv6 addresses, 563

multilayer switches, 170

multimode (MM) fiber-optic cable, 64

N

NAT (Network Address Translation), 156, 579
    development of, 390
    dyannic NAT, 393, 580
    inside global addresses, 395
    inside local addresses, 395
    inside/outside, 395
    IP addresses, 580

local/global, 395

NAT overload, 394, 580
    configuring via SDM, 397-410
    mapping port numbers, 407
    show ip nat statistics command, 411
    show ip nat transition command, 413
    verifying configurations via SDM, 410-413

outside global addresses, 396

outside local addresses, 396

private IP addresses, 391

SDM, configuring via, 397

static NAT, 392, 580

troubleshooting, 413-414

NAT Configuration window (SDM)
    Advanced NAT wizard, 401-407
    Basic NAT wizard, 397-400

NAT overload, 394, 580
    port numbers, mapping, 407
    SDM, configuring via
        advanced configuration, 401-407
        basic configuration, 397-400
        editing configurations, 407-410
        verifying configurations, 410-413
    show ip nat statistics command, 411
    show ip nat transition command, 413

navigation modes (IOS), 565

NCP (Network Control Protocol), 532, 581

neighbor discovery, CDP, 272-275

network command, DHCP IOS, 279

Network Interface layer (TCP/IP model), 33

Network layer (OSI model), 20, 550
    ARP, 144
    functions of, 144
    ICMP, 144
    IP addresses, 145, 150
        binary-to-decimal conversion, 146-147
        Boolean AND, 154-155

broadcast IP, 152, 157

decimal-to-binary conversion, 148-149, 157-158

decimal-to-hexadecimal conversion, 150-151

IPv4 address classes, 151-153

IPv4 subnet masks, 154-157, 163

NAT, 156

network ID, 152

private (RFC 1918) addressing, 156

subnet ID, 152

subnetting IP, 156-167

Layer 3 switches, 167, 170

Proxy ARP, 145

RARP, 145

routers, 167-170

traceroutes, 144

networks

domains, determining data transport reliability, 554

ID, 152

interfaces, 67

security, 122

access attacks, 123-124, 559

DoS attacks, 127-129, 559

mitigating attacks, 130-133, 559

reconnaissance attacks, 125-126, 559

subnets, calculating in, 562

topologies

bus topologies, 54

mesh topologies, 57

ring topologies, 55-56

star topologies, 56-57

wireless networks, 501-503

wireless networks, 476

802.11a, 483

802.11b, 483

802.11g, 483-484

802.11n, 484

channel surfing, 481

data transmission, 478-479

IEEE, 477

ITU-R, 477

overlapping signals, 480-481

RF bands, 479-480

topologies, 501-503

Wi-Fi Alliance, 477

NEXT (Near-End Crosstalk), 59

nibbles, 151

no cdp enable command, 275, 465

no cdp run command, 275, 465

no command, 242

no debug all command, 269

no exec command, catalyst switch security, 461

no ip directed-broadcast command, 129-130

no keepalives command, 255

no shutdown command, 255, 271, 462

NTP (Network Time Protocol), network security, 132-133

NVRAM (Nonvolatile Random Access Memory), 193

O

OSI (Open Systems Interconnection) model, 14-15, 550-551

Application layer, 15-16

compared to TCP/IP models, 26

Data Link layer, 21, 23

layered communications, 23-24

list of layers, 24-25

lower layers, 18

Network layer, 20

Physical layer, 23

Presentation layer, 17

Session layer, 18, 550

Transport layer, 18-19

upper layers, 15

outside global addresses (NAT), 396

outside local addresses (NAT), 396

outside/inside (NAT), 395

overlapping signals (wireless networks), 480-481

P

packet sniffers, 125

packet-switched networks, 520, 581

PAP (Password Authentication Protocol), 528, 581

PAR (Positive Acknowledgement and Retransmission), 27

passive RIP interfaces, 371

password recovery (router/switch start-ups), 218

passwords

    attacks, network security, 123

    aux ports, 459-460

    enable password command, 245, 253

    enable secret command, 253

    hashing, 529

    Privileged EXEC mode, assigning to, 245

    recovery (router/switch start-ups), 218

    secret passwords, changing in SDM, 299-301

    service password-encryption command, 246, 253

    switch security, 459-460

PAT (Port Address Translation). See NAT overload

PDU (Protocol Data Units), 24

permanent virtual circuits, 520

Physical layer

    hubs, 67

    network interfaces, 67

    OSI Model, 23, 551

    repeaters, 66

    WAN, 522-523

physical security, switches, 458

ping command, 267, 558

    sweeps, 125

    switches, troubleshooting basic connectivity, 443

pinouts, 61

PoE (Power over Ethernet), 198

poison reverse, 365

ports, 439

    auxiliary ports, 212

        password configuration, 459-460

        User EXEC access, securing, 250

    blocked ports, 431, 435

    console ports, 210-211

    designated ports, 434

    Gigabit Ethernet ports, 189

    Layer 2 security, 462-464

    MAC addresses, limiting in, 462

    NAT port numbers, mapping, 407

    redirection, network security, 124

    root ports, 432-433

    scans, 126

    security, 572

    states, transitioning, 437-438

POST (Power-On Self-Tests), 214

PPP (Point-to-Point Protocol), 525

    CHAP, 581-582

    configuring

        authentication, 532-534

        compression, 534-535

    ISO HDLC, 527

    LCP, 527-534

    NCP, 532

    PAP, 581

    troubleshooting, 537-538

    verifying, 535-536

    WAN, 581

        Data Link encapsulations, 524

        troubleshooting authentication in, 582

PPPoA (PPP over ATM), WAN, 525

PPPoE (PPP over Ethernet), WAN, 525

practice exams

    answers, 602-609

    MeasureUp, 612-613

    questions, 585, 594, 598

Predictor algorithm, PPP authentication, 530

Presentation layer (OSI model), 17, 550

private addresses

    IANA, 561

    IP, NAT, 391

    RFC 1918, 156

Privileged EXEC, 221-222. *See also* configure command; User EXEC

    debug command, 268-269

    passwords, assigning to, 245

    ping command, 268

    securing, 567

    Telnet, virtual terminal access, 277

    terminal monitor command, 277-278

Proxy ARP (Address Resolution Protocol), 33, 145

Q - R

queries (information), reconnaissance attacks, 126

question mark (?), context-sensitive help, 565

RAM (Random Access Memory), 193

RARP (Reverse Address Resolution Protocol), 33, 145

rebooting cia reload command, 271

reconnaissance attacks, 559

    information queries, 126

    packet sniffers, 125

    ping sweeps, 125

    port scans, 126

redistribution (routing protocols), 343-344, 575

reload command, 271

repeaters, 66

RF bands, wireless networks, 479-480

RFC 1918 (private) addressing, 156

ring topologies, 55-56

RIP (Routing Information Protocol), 377

    characteristics of, 367

    configuring, 368-370, 373, 577

    passive interfaces, 371

    RIPv2 comparisons, 379, 576

    troubleshooting, 375-376, 577

    verifying, 374, 577

RIPv2 (Routing Information Protocol version 2)

    characteristics of, 371

    configuring, 372

    RIP comparisons, 379, 576

rolled cable, 63

ROM (Read-Only Memory), 193

ROMmon, router/switches start-up, 215

root bridges, 431-433

root ports, STP, 432-433

routers, 196-197

    amnesia via DHCP, 280

    boot sequences, changing, 242-243

    configuration

        backing up via TFTP servers, 269-271

        verifying, 259-260

    interface configuation

        assigning duplexes, 255

        assigning IP addresses, 254

        assigning speed to, 255

        bandwidth command, 256

        clock rate command, 256

        LAN-specific commands, 255

        no keepalives command, 255

        no shutdown command, 255

        returning to default configurations, 257

saving, 256

WAN-specific commands, 256

interface status/statistics, viewing

    show controller command, 263

    show interfaces command, 261-262

    show ip interface brief command, 263

IOS files, backing up via TFTP servers, 270

IP addresses, verifying assignment of, 280

Layer 3 functions, 563-564

Network layer (OSI model), 167-170

SDM, 296

    access configuration, 303, 308-310

    device monitoring, 310

    global configurations, 298-307

    installing, 297

show processes command, 269

smurf attacks, 129

start-up procedures

    bootstrap, 215

    configuration loading, 217

    IOS loading, 215-218

    password recovery, 218

    POST, 214

    practice challenge, 219-220

    ROMmon, 215

    setup mode, 217

routing

administrative distances, 324

Classful Routing, 575

classful routing protocols, 333-340, 575

default gateways, 320-321

default routes, 328-331, 573

dynamic routing protocols, 331, 574

metrics of, 332-333, 574

poisoning, mitigating, 364-366

redistributing, 343-344

RIP, 377

    characteristics of, 367

    configuring, 368-370

configuring via SDM, 373

passive interfaces, 371

RIPv2 comparisons, 379

troubleshooting, 375-376

verifying, 374

RIPv2

    characteristics of, 371

    configuring, 372

    RIP comparisons, 379

routing sources, 323-324

sources, 572-573

static routes, 325, 573

    configuring, 326, 329-330

    floating static routes, 327

    verifying, 330-331

summarization, VLSM, 338-340

update packets, Network layer (OSI model) routing, 170

routing by rumor, 358

routing loops, 360-362

counts to infinity, 363

invalid/dead timers, 367

route poisoning, 364-366

split horizons, 363-364

triggered updates, 366

routing protocols, 573

classes of, 575

distance vector routing loops, preventing, 576

distance vector routing protocols, 358-359

dynamic routing protocols

    hybrid protocols, 341

    interior/exterior gateway routing protocols, 340

    link-state routing protocols, 341

    routed protocols versus, 331

interior/exterior gateway protocols, 574

maximum hop counts, 576

redistribution, 575

routing tables, 342-343

S

SAN (Storage Area Networks), 13

SDM (Security Device Manager), 296

default routes, configuring, 329-330

device monitoring, 310

Edit NAT Configuration window, 407-410

global configurations, 298

banners, 299-301

DHCP, 305-307

DNS, 304

domain names, 299-301

hostnames, 299-301

router access, 303

secret passwords, 299-301

installing, 297

NAT Configuration window

Advanced NAT wizard, 401-407

Basic NAT wizard, 397-400

NAT overload configuration

advanced configuration, 401-407

basic configuration, 397-400

editing configurations, 407-410

verifying configurations, 410-413

RIP, configuring, 373

router interface configuration

enabling interfaces, 309

IP address assignments, 308

saving configuration, 310

verifying configurations, 310

static routes, configuring, 329-330

secret passwords, changing in SDM, 299-301

security (networks), 122

access attacks

man-in-the-middle attacks, 124

password attacks, 123

port redirection, 124

trust exploitation, 124

DoS attacks

DDoS attacks, 127

smurf attacks, 129

TCP SYN attacks, 128-129

mitigating attacks

AAA, 130, 133

ACL, 130, 133

encryption, 132-133

firewalls, 132-133

IDS, 133

IPS, 132-133

IPsec, 132-133

NTP, 132-133

SNMP, 131, 133

SSH, 131-133

SSL, 132-133

syslog, 131-133

reconnaissance attacks

information queries, 126

packet sniffers, 125

ping sweeps, 125

port scans, 126

service password-encryption command, 246, 253, 461, 567

service timestamp command, 269

Session layer (OSI model), 18, 550

setup mode (router/switch start-ups), 217

shortcuts (keyboard), suspending Telnet sessions, 276-277

shortcuts (MeasureUp practice tests), creating, 613

show cdp neighbors command, 273

show commands, 258

general commands list, 569

IFS, 272

interface status values, 569

list of, 266

router configurations, verifying, 259-260

show compress command, verifying PPP compression, 536

show controller command, viewing router interface status/statistics, 263

show controllers serial command, 275

show dhcp bindings command, 571

show dhcp lease command, 280, 441

show flash command, 264

show interface <interface> command, verifying PPP operation, 535-536

show interfaces command, viewing router interface status/statistics, 261-263

show interfaces interface-id command, 444

show ip dhcp binding command, 280

show ip interface brief command, viewing router interface status/statistics, 263

show ip nat statistics command verifying NAT overload configurations, 411

show ip nat transition command verifying NAT overload configurations, 413

show port-security address command, 464

show port-security interface command, 463

show processes command, 269

show running-config command, 259-260, 271, 280, 413

show sessions command, Telnet sessions, 276

show spanning-tree command, 442

show startup-config command, 259

show version command, 195, 264-265

single-mode (SM) fiber-optic cable, 64

site-local IPv6 addresses, 563

SLIP (Serial Line Internet Protocol), WAN Data Link encapsulations, 523

smurf attacks, 129

SNAP (Subnetwork Access Protocol), 93

SNMP (Simple Network Management Protocol), network security, 131-133

sources (routing tables), 323-324

speed, router assignments, 255

split horizons, mitigating, 363-364

Spread Spectrum Wireless LAN, 555

SSH (Secure Shell), 567
    catalyst switch security, 460
    enabling, 247-248
    EXEC sessions, 213
    network security, 131-133
    User EXEC access, securing, 250-253

SSL (Secure Socket Layer), network security, 132-133

Stacker algorithm, PPP authentication, 530

star topologies, 56-57

startup processes. See boot processes

static MAC addresses, switch port security, 463

static NAT (Network Address Translation), 392, 580

static routes, 325, 573
    configuring, 326, 329-330
    floating static routes, 327
    verifying, 330-331

store-and-forward method (frame forwarding), 428

STP (Spanning Tree Protocol)
    blocked ports, 435
    designated ports, 434
    port states, transitioning, 437-438
    root bridges, 430-433
    root ports, 432-433
    show spanning-tree command, 442
    troubleshooting, 444
    verifying, 442

STP cable, 60-61. See also twisted-pair cable

straight-through cable, 61-62, 554

stub networks, 325

study mode (CD-ROM), 611

subnet ID, 152

subnet masks, 163

CIDR notation, 155

FLSM, 334

IPv4, 154-155, 157

VLSM, 335-340

subnets, 562

subnetting IP (Internet Protocol), 156-158

calculating

hosts, 159-160

increments, 162-165

networks, 161-162

range of valid IP, determining, 165-167

zero subnet rule, 162

switches, 104-105, 197-198

basic connectivity, troubleshooting, 442-444

blocked ports, 435

boot sequence, changing, 242-243

catalyst switches, 572

securing physical access to, 458

securing terminal access to, 459-461

configuration

backing up via TFTP servers, 269-271

commands, 568

returning to default configurations, 257

default gateways, defining, 439

designated ports, 434

diameters, 438

filtering, 427

frame forwarding, 426-428, 571

full-duplex connections, 429

half-duplex connections, 429

interface range command, 441

IOS files, backing up via TFTP servers, 270

IP addresses, assigning via DHCP, 440-441

ip default-gateway command, 440

Layer 2 security, 462-465

Layer 3 switches, 167, 170

management IP addresses, assigning, 439

microsegmentation, 106

multilayer switches, 170

multiple switch interfaces, configuring, 441

physical security, 458

ports, 439, 462

primary tasks, 102

redundant design, 430

show dhcp lease command, 441

show interfaces interface-id command, 444

start-up procedures

bootstrap, 215

configuration loading, 217

IOS loading, 215-218

password recovery, 218

POST, 214

practice challenge, 219-220

ROMmon, 215

setup mode, 217

STP, 430-433

switchport port security mac-address sticky command, 463

switchport port-security command, 462

switchport port-security mac-address command, 572

switchport port-security maximum command, 463

switchport port-security violation shutdown command, 463

SYN packeet, 28

SYN-ACK packet, 28

synchronous serial interfaces, 190

syntax errors, 566

syslog, network security, 131-133

system requirements, CD-ROM installations, 612

T

T1 controller cards, 190

TCP (Transmission Control Protocol), 27-29

    applications that utilize, 553

    processes of, 552-553

    segment header formats, 553

    SYN attacks, 128-129

TCP/IP (Transmission Control Protocol/Internet Protocol) layer, 552

TCP/IP (Transmission Control Protocol/Internet Protocol) model

    Application layer, 26-27

    compared to OSI models, 26

    Internet layer, 31-33

    Network Interface layer, 33

    Transport layer, 27-30

technical support, 614

Telnet, 212, 570

    catalyst switch security, 460

    multiple session example, 277

    resuming sessions, 277

    showing sessions, 276

    suspending sessions, 276-277

    terminal monitor command, 277-278

    User EXEC access, securing, 250-253

    virtual terminal access, 276-278

terminal monitor command, 277-278

terminal options

    auxiliary ports, 212

    console ports, 210-211

    HTTP, 212

    SSH, 213

test modes (CD-ROM), 611

tests (practice)

    answers, 602-609

    MeasureUp, 612-613

TFTP servers

    routers

        configuration backups, 269-271

        IOS file backups, 270

    switches

        configuration backups, 269-271

        IOS file backups, 270

three-way handshakes, 28

throughput, definition of, 12

timers (max age), 437

timestamps, 269

Token Ring protocols, 84-85

topologies

    bus topologies, 54

    mesh topologies, 57

    ring topologies, 55-56

    star topologies, 56-57

    wireless networks, 501-503

traceroute command, 268

    RIP, 375

    switches, troubleshooting basic connectivity, 443

traceroutes, 144, 558

trains (IOS), 194

transmitting data, wireless networks, 478-479

Transport layer

    OSI model, 18-19, 550

    TCP/IP model, 27-30

triggered updates (routing), 366

troubleshooting

    debug command, 268-269

    NAT, 413-414

    ping command, 267

    PPP, 537-538

    RIP, 375-376, 577

    show processes command, 269

    STP, 444

    switches, basic connectivity, 442-444

traceroute command, 268

WAN, PPP authentication, 582

wireless networks, 506-507

trust exploitation, network security, 124

twisted-pair cable, 60-63

U

UDP (User Datagram Protocol), 29-30

applications that utilize, 553

headers, 553

undebug all command, 269

unicast addresses, definition of, 88

unique IPv6 addresses, 563

unshielded twister pair cables versus fiber-optic cable, 554

upper layers (OSI model), 15

User EXEC, 220. *See also* Priveleged EXEC

auxiliary access, securing, 250

console access, securing, 248-249

securing, 566

SSH access, securing, 250-253

Telnet

securing access to, 250-253

virtual terminal access, 277

UTP cable. *See also* twisted-pair cable

V

VAN (Virtual Area Networks), 14

verifying

NAT overload configurations via SDM, 410-413

port security, switch ports, 463-464

PPP operation

show compress command, 536

show interface <interface> command, 535-536

RIP, 374, 577

router configurations, 259-260

SDM router interface configurations, 310

STP, 442

virtual circuits (permanent), 520

virtual terminal access, Telnet, 276-278

VLAN workgroups, 34

VLSM (Variable-Length Subnet Masks), 335-340

VPN (Virtual Private Networks), WAN, 521

W

WAN (Wide Area Networks), 12-13

baseband connections, 520

broadband connections, 520

circuit-switched networks, 519

circuit-switched WAN, 580

Data Link encapsulations, 523-525

dial-on-demand connections, 519

HDLC, 581

interfaces

asynchronous serial interfaces, 190

BRI, 189-190

DCE, 190

definition of, 557

DTE, 191-192

HSSI, 190

synchronous serial interfaces, 190

T1 controller cards, 190

leased line connections, 519

leased line WAN, 580

Metro Ethernet connections, 521

packet-switched networks, 520

packet-switched WAN, 581

Physical layer, 522-523

PPP, 581-582

routers, 169, 256

VPN, 521

war driving, 494

WEP (Wired Equivalent Privacy), wireless networks, 496-497

Wi-Fi Alliance, 477

windowing, 28

wireless networks, 476, 577

802.11a, 483

802.11b, 483

802.11g, 483-484

802.11n, 484

802.1x (wireless authentication), 499-500

ad hoc networks, 501

AP

BSS, 501

ESS, 501

troubleshooting, 507

authentication, 578

channel surfing, 481

data rates, 503-505

data transmission, 478-479

encryption, 578

WEP, 496-497

WPA, 498

WPA2, 498

hacking, 495

IEEE, 477

implementing, 501, 506, 579

IPS, 500

ITU-R, 477

overlapping signals, 480-481

RF bands, 479-480

threats to

direct hacking, 495

employee ignorance, 495-496

war driving, 494

topologies, 501-503

troubleshooting, 506-507

Wi-Fi Alliance, 477

workgroup hubs, definition of, 67

workgroup layer (hierarchical models). *See* Distribution layer (hierarchical models)

workgroups, VLAN, 34

WPA (Wi-Fi Protected Access), wireless networks, 498

WPA2 (Wi-Fi Protected Access version 2), wireless networks, 498

X - Y - Z

X.25 link access procedure, balanced. *See* LAPB (X.25 Link Access Procedure, Balanced)

zero subnet rule, 162

LearnIT at InformIT

Go Beyond the Book